# IN SEARCH OF SOUTHEAST ASIA

# In Search of Southeast Asia

## A MODERN HISTORY

### REVISED EDITION

*David P. Chandler*
*William R. Roff*
*John R. W. Smail*
*David Joel Steinberg*
*Robert H. Taylor*
*Alexander Woodside*
*David K. Wyatt*

*Edited by David Joel Steinberg*

Allen & Unwin

First edition published by Praeger Publishers, Inc.
Printed in the United States of America

04   03   02                    10   9   8   7


**Library of Congress Cataloging-in-Publication Data**

In search of Southeast Asia.

   Bibliography: p.
   Includes index.
      1.   Asia, Southeastern—History.   I.   Chandler,
David P.   II.   Steinberg, David Joel.
DS525.I48   1987        959        87–19233
ISBN 0–8248–1110–0


University of Hawai'i Press books are printed on acid-free
paper and meet the guidelines for permanence and durability
of the Council on Library Resources.

# CONTENTS

# MAPS AND FIGURES

# PREFACE

On the small island of Mactan in the Philippines there is a monument erected by the Spanish in the nineteenth century to glorify God, Spain, and Ferdinand Magellan. In 1941, during the American era, a historical marker inscribed "Ferdinand Magellan's Death" was erected nearby. It stated: "On this spot Ferdinand Magellan died on April 27, 1521, wounded in an encounter with the soldiers of Lapulapu, chief of Mactan Island. One of Magellan's ships, the *Victoria*, under the command of Juan Sebastian Elcano, sailed from Cebu on May 1, 1521, and anchored at San Lucar de Barrameda on September 6, 1522, thus completing the first circumnavigation of the earth." Exactly a decade later, the by then independent Republic of the Philippines erected a second marker, entitled "Lapulapu." It read: "Here, on 27 April 1521, Lapulapu and his men repulsed the Spanish invaders, killing their leader, Ferdinand Magellan. Thus, Lapulapu became the first Filipino to have repelled European aggression."

This example illustrates vividly the historian's predicament. In the wake of such wide variation of interpretation of what at first appears as fact, the attempt of the historian to impose order on the past may seem a dubious undertaking. This book rests upon the assumption that in the interaction and expertise of collective authorship greater coherence can be found in the welter of human events. Starting in the fall of 1966, we began exchanging outlines and debating assumptions; in the summer of 1969, we gathered in Ann Arbor for a working seminar on modern Southeast Asian history. Together we rewrote the outline, divided our responsibilities, and criticized each other's work in the constant hope that we might produce a history that would examine the totality of modern Southeast Asia as well as its elements. There were handicaps, of course, including, for some of us, the inaccessibility of source material and, for all of us, limitations of time. None of us is an expert in Burmese history, and we probably have not been able to give that country the kind of treatment it deserves. We have come away from our joint effort convinced, however, that there is wisdom in studying Southeast Asia as a whole, not only because of the insights it offers for the comparative historian but also because, in the words of the motto of the Republic of Indonesia, there is unity in its diversity. The depth and perspective we have gained by viewing the region as a whole has enhanced our understanding of its parts. This said, it has to be conceded that there were of course some occasions on which, even after debate and recrimination, we had to agree to bicker.

The list of people we wish to thank is at least six times longer than would have been the case if only one of us had been involved. Our debts range across the world. We want to acknowledge our particular gratitude to Professors Gayl Ness and John Broomfield, of the Center for South and Southeast Asian Studies at the University of Michigan, for their support and enthusiasm at every stage of this project. Without Dr. David Pfanner, of the Ford Foundation, and Dr. William Bradley, of the Rockefeller Foundation, the book would not exist; we are deeply indebted to them personally and to the foundations they serve so ably. We also acknowledge with appreciation the financial support given to us by the National Endowment for the Humanities and by the Horace Rackham School at The University of Michigan. The maps have been prepared by Ronald Edgerton and the cartography was done by Karen Ewing. We all owe a debt to our students and would like especially to thank Stewart Gordon, Patricia Herbert, Theodore Grossman, and Norman Owen of the University of Michigan. Our sense of gratitude to Ronald Edgerton for his assistance, his accuracy, and his good cheer at every stage of this project is profound. Finally, we apologize to our five wives and eight children, who somehow endured while the summer, the autumn, and then the winter wore on.

Ann Arbor, Michigan
July 1970

# PREFACE TO THE SECOND EDITION

THERE is an excitement about doing something for the first time that often fades into habit or duty later. What made writing this book an exciting experience seventeen years ago, however, persisted when we convened to bring it up to date: the quality of the intellectual exchange, the liveliness of our arguments, the camaraderie, and the mutual respect. We still disagree on some of the things that divided us in 1969, but we share a commitment to the idea of the book and to its being available and up-to-date. For all its weaknesses, we believe it is a far better book than any one of us could write alone.

In undertaking a second edition, we agreed to recruit a Burma specialist and decided to reconvene, briefly, as a group. Robert Taylor was persuaded to join us; and a modest travel grant from the Joint Committee on Southeast Asia of the Social Science Research Council and the American Council of Learned Societies enabled us to assemble for a week in May 1986 in Ithaca. We collectively rewrote most of Part Five and all of the Bibliography; Taylor redid all the Burma portions of the book; and we revised portions of Chapters 1, 2, 5, and 8. On the basis of discussions in Ithaca, Chandler and Taylor did much of the work on Chapter 40, and Wyatt rewrote Chapter 32. We are grateful to the Joint Committee on Southeast Asia, and to those in Ithaca who helped in putting the pieces together—the Department of History of Cornell University, Steve Rogers of the Optical Scanner facility for the Humanities, Bruce Lockhart, and Chiranan Prasertkul. Damaris Kirchhofer of the University of Hawaii Press was instrumental in getting the first edition back into print, and this edition would not exist without her encouragement, patience, and advice.

Ithaca, New York
January 1987

# IN SEARCH OF SOUTHEAST ASIA

IN SEARCH OF SOUTHEAST ASIA

# Introduction

OVER the past two centuries, as a result of the human energies unleashed by the scientific, industrial, and nationalist revolutions, Southeast Asian societies have changed profoundly. This process of change, which continues unabated, can be dated from the middle of the eighteenth century, when Europeans in the region first had the power and inclination to impose on others their technical skills and new world view. The strong Western components of this process, however, have worked partially to obscure the nature of Southeast Asian history, because many historians have interested themselves primarily in external stimuli, to the detriment of the study of indigenous institutions. By thereby elevating foreigners beyond their position as actors on a common Southeast Asian stage, Southeast Asians have been reduced to roles as mere bit players, too weak to do more than reflect the brilliance of other civilizations. Southeast Asia faced similar challenges in earlier eras; indeed, it has perhaps interacted with a greater variety of external cultures for a longer period than has any other area of the world. From the vantage point of Southeast Asians, therefore, what is important in the history of the past two centuries is less the "modernization" or "westernization" others imposed on them than it is the process of acculturation through which their societies adjusted to their changing environment and circumstances.

Social change does not take place in the abstract. The evolution of values and the concomitant development of social institutions in a society are a complicated aggregate of individual human reactions and decisions. Change takes place in a community because people interact —sometimes consciously, sometimes not—with those around them. Occasionally, new ways are adopted because they seem attractive or promise some reward; at other times, people are forced to accept change as a result of coercion or more subtle forms of compulsion. The dissemination of ideas and the development of institutions are gradual processes, involving a few key people at first and then gradually spreading to the larger population. Since there is always a wide variety of attitudes, and since social patterns are always changing, one can never expect uniformity in whole societies. The designations "new" and "old," "traditional" and "modern," "alien" and "indigenous" can be no more than relative.

In the daily reality of living, people naturally adjust to their environment by making the best use they can of the ideas and institutions that envelop them. They rarely note the inconsistencies that seem so obvious to outsiders. To the devout Muslim from elsewhere, who defined Islamic "orthodoxy" by his own practice and custom, the Malay Muslim may have seemed lax. The Malay, however, commonly saw no problem in the way he expressed his faith or reconciled it with other social and cultural needs. Perspective, therefore, shapes perception. The Indian, Arab, or Chinese, who saw the culture of Southeast Asia as an extension of his own civilization, interpreted indigenous modifications as perversions of his own value system. Similarly, observers from the West, looking for what was familiar to them, have for many years seen Southeast Asia in ethnocentric terms. The task of the historian is made the more difficult by deeply ingrained value judgments and subconscious biases of this sort. This book strives to treat each society in Southeast Asia as a separate species and the region as a distinct genus.

There is natural and spontaneous change in all culture contact. In the process of transmission and translation, terms, values, and institutions are altered. Local context reshapes the contours of abstract concepts and specific structures. Whatever the meaning of a word or institution in its original environment, it changes as it takes its place with other forces in the new setting. The term "guided democracy," for example, can be understood only after one appreciates Sukarno and the Indonesian social matrix in the 1950s and 1960s, as well as the concept of democracy in the West. "Buddhist socialism," a term once used in Burma and Cambodia, is a similar example. From the Southeast Asian point of view, the origin of the concept is far less important than its meaning within the local environment. Similarly, it is often only marginally relevant whether a man's place of origin is Hong Kong, Calcutta, or Amsterdam, if he is acting in a Southeast Asian milieu. This does not deny his distinct identity or alien ways; it simply fits him properly into the indigenous scene. While a Singapore Chinese merchant might have had ties to a Canton business firm, and a French naval administrator in Vietnam was part of an imperial enterprise with headquarters in Paris, they must first be seen as participants in the history of Southeast Asia.

Acculturation is not a simple linear development; human interaction generates too many variables. The displacement of established tradition by new patterns of behavior is rarely easy. Accepted values are finely interwoven into the social fabric and usually have staunch defenders. The rate and character of change are determined by such things as the strength of existing institutions; the receptivity of the society to new ideas; the physical, intellectual, and moral power of the new concepts and of the people who transmit them; and the compatibility of the new values with the old. Some institutions seem to develop along a single line and then suddenly fragment; others appear to retrogress or to remain motionless. Some established values crumble upon the first encounter with competition; others continue to develop as if no challenge existed. Often the institutions and values that seem strongest prove to be the most vulnerable.

These observations concerning society and change supply one important dimension to Southeast Asian history. A second dimension stems from the physical and climatic environment. The relationship of land to people, the general ecological balance, and the margin of surplus have ordered many of the priorities by which Southeast Asians live their lives. Unlike China and India, most Southeast Asian societies were not troubled by overpopulation in the past. The history of China and India has been, in part, the constant struggle to establish social organisms that can maximize yields to minimize starvation. Except, perhaps, on the island of Java and in northern Vietnam, Southeast Asia has been spared this awesome constriction, at least until very recent times.

Southeast Asia may be defined as the area south of China and east of India. Known to the Chinese and Japanese as the South Seas (Nanyang or Nampō), the region has only recently been called Southeast Asia by most people. During World War II, the term was used to designate the theater of war commanded by Lord Louis Mountbatten, and it gained wide currency during the Vietnam War of the 1960s and 1970s. It includes the present political units of the Socialist Republic of the Union of Burma; the Kingdom of Thailand; the Lao People's Democratic Republic (Laos); the People's Republic of Kampuchea (Cambodia); the Socialist Republic of Vietnam; the Federation of Malaysia; the Sultanate of Brunei; and the Republics of Indonesia, Singapore, and the Philippines. While there are arguments for expanding the definition to include certain other territories for religious, ethnographic, linguistic, or topographical reasons—Taiwan, Hainan, or Sri Lanka, for example—or contracting it for similar reasons, the general consensus accepts current usage. As defined, Southeast Asia has a population of approximately one-third of a billion people living in a total land area of just over one and one-half million square miles (a little smaller than the Indian subcontinent). Slightly more than half of the territory is on the Asian mainland, and the rest is unevenly fragmented into the ten thousand islands that make up the archipelagos of Indonesia and the Philippines. More than half the population, however, lives on the islands.

A traveler who journeyed from one end of Southeast Asia to the other would note a similarity of flora and fauna, climate, and human cultivation. While the languages and architecture would change, one would be struck by the repeating patterns of wet-rice and slash-and-burn agriculture, found from Burma to Bali. Traveling on the mainland, east or west, one would move from delta to coastal mountain ridge to river valley and then across a series of river valleys and mountain ridges, until he finally reached the next delta on the other side. One would note that the mountain ridges frequently determined political boundaries and that the river valleys were fertile zones of civilization. Where water was plentiful one would find wet-rice farming; where it was scarce one would find fewer established communities and less intensive cultivation. Similar patterns would be evident through the island world. Moreover, wherever one went one would observe the importance of the monsoon in the seasonal lives of the people.

Southeast Asia lies within the tropical belt on either side of the equator. All too often the tropics are conceived of as exotic and endlessly fertile by those who live elsewhere. Visually they display a deceptive richness of vegetation. While there are areas of great soil fertility created by volcanic action, as in Java, and by alluvial deposits, as in the Mekong delta, the apparent fecundity of much of the area is caused by rapid photosynthesis rather than by soil chemistry. A precarious ecological balance exists within the region, especially in the tropical rain forests, where the forest cover derives its nourishment from the rapid decay of plant life and humus at its roots. The forest is, in effect, a hothouse where the cycle of nature accelerates sharply. The topsoil may be only a few inches deep, and yet the growing cycle can support itself with seeming ease, provided that equilibrium is maintained. If the virgin growth is cut or otherwise destroyed (as with defoliants in Vietnam), the rainfall is too much for the soil to absorb; the earth is quickly leached of its nutrients, becoming a useless savanna.

This ecological fragility has made much of Southeast Asia unfit for large concentrations of people. Only in the ecological niches of alluvial riverbank and volcanic loam have dense population centers formed. Heavy rainfall and resultant erosion have carried massive silt deposits down from the mountains and made fertile the banks of such rivers as the Mekong, Čhaophraya, Irrawaddy, and Red. A rather similar process has taken place along the shorter but steeper rivers on the islands. Where there was sufficient human need or incentive, generated by population pressure or profit motive, painstaking labor was employed to build extensive irrigation systems, but for most of the area the prospect this opened up of a double rice crop was not worth the effort. Many of the delta regions remained nonproductive until the nineteenth century, since the potential wealth of the soil was difficult to utilize without drainage and other technological skills. The Mekong delta, for example, was sparsely inhabited until the late eighteenth century, and the "rice bowls" of the Burmese and Thai deltas were barely cleared until the late nineteenth century, when a worldwide demand for rice produced boom conditions.

The ecology of Southeast Asia has played an important part in the area's history, especially by influencing the relationship between the concentrations of people who live in the fertile niches and those who dwell on the much less fertile periphery. Since the floodplains were ideal for wet rice, and since the hinterland was generally better suited for migrant slash-and-burn cultivation, very different cultural and social institutions emerged in these contrasting zones. Wet rice permits a density of population and a social wealth far greater than is possible in the less-favored regions. The major agrarian kingdoms in Burma, Thailand, Vietnam, Cambodia, and Java had authority that radiated outward from their capitals. The farther from the center one traveled, the less influence the center wielded. Prior to the nineteenth century, the wet-rice societies rarely established total control over the outlying areas. Whenever one state did attempt to impose dominance over an adjacent buffer zone, geopolitical tensions increased, because the balance of power was endangered. The upland people who were threatened were likely to appeal for support to one of the lowland societies, because highland groups often maintained ties with all their powerful neighbors. Mutual defense agreements were part of traditional tribute relationships. Only Cambodia among the major wet-rice societies lacked the luxury of buffer zones; its exposed position between Siam and Vietnam eventually led to its destruction as a major power.

The modern concept of national boundaries, as defined by the West, did not exist in Southeast Asia until the nineteenth century. One must not imagine the map of Southeast Asia in the eighteenth century as if it were a map of Europe in 1764, with Burma one pastel shade, Siam another, and Vietnam a third. Southeast Asians were not much concerned with the demarcation of frontiers. The inconclusive Vietnamese-Lao wars of the seventeenth century, for example, were resolved when the Lê emperor in Vietnam and the Lao king agreed that every inhabitant in the upper Mekong valley who lived in a house built on stilts owed allegiance to Laos, while those whose homes had earth floors owed allegiance to Vietnam. It is only quite recently that the rulers of the traditionally dominant societies have sought to establish a modern sense of allegiance to the notion of a nation-state identity, with its concomitant demand of loyalty from all citizens living within sharply defined national boundaries.

The technological power developed in the West was used to rework the ecological balance in Southeast Asia. Unhappy at the discomforts and dangers of tropical existence and unwilling to leave, the Westerners used their power to sanitize and soften nature. Conceptualizing this power as the white man's burden, they recognized an obligation, in Kipling's words, to "fill full the mouth of Famine and bid the sickness cease." Personal and humanitarian concerns fused with economic ambition. Drainage projects in the deltas of Burma, Siam, and Vietnam made humanitarians millionaires. In the Klang area of Selangor, the British first succeeded in eradicating the malarial *Anopheles* mosquito in an effort to reduce the mortality of rubber estate workers. Whatever the motivation, such manipulation of the environment produced radical change not only in the life cycle of the flora and fauna but also in human demography. The doctor or sanitary engineer was an important force for change within the human environment; modern transportation, new crops, and instant communications altered the world in which traditional Southeast Asia had existed.

The last two centuries have created a community of experience for the societies of Southeast Asia. Linguistic, religious, ethnic, and social isolation within each of the countries, if not always between them, has been lessened. As a result, each society has undertaken a search for a new and broader consensus—one that would harmonize established social institutions with changing conditions. Increasingly, as people participated in a range of new organizations and activities, they broadened their frame of reference from the village or the province to the nation. This new congruence of values has restructured allegiances, challenging primordial loyalties. Earlier distinctions of culture, society, and state have become blurred as nationalism has developed; the importance of genealogical and geographical origins has lessened, for some if not for all. The process of national development throughout Southeast Asia has involved both a reassertion and a reformulation of authority.

It is easy to mistake the processes of change for their end results, no less in the West than in Southeast Asia. The social and political and cultural changes that have transformed Southeast Asia over the past two centuries are embedded in processes that have no natural conclusion. If traditional polities have given way to the "modern" nation-state; if "traditional" authority has been reformulated in new terms; if the international capitalist economy has supplanted or refashioned old social and political relationships; and if the complications of global politics seem forever to have distorted the relationships between Southeast Asian states, this is by no means to imply that the processes of which these changes are a part have reached their ends. We can never reach a point where we can conclude that a society or state is now fully "modern," an economy completely "capitalist," or a legal system "just." Increasingly, contemporary Southeast Asians conduct a constant mental dialogue between their own past, as they perceive it, and the realities of their present, with a view to understanding their present and perfecting their future. In search of Southeast Asia's past, the historian hopes to contribute to the attainment of the same ends.

# PART ONE

# The Eighteenth-Century World

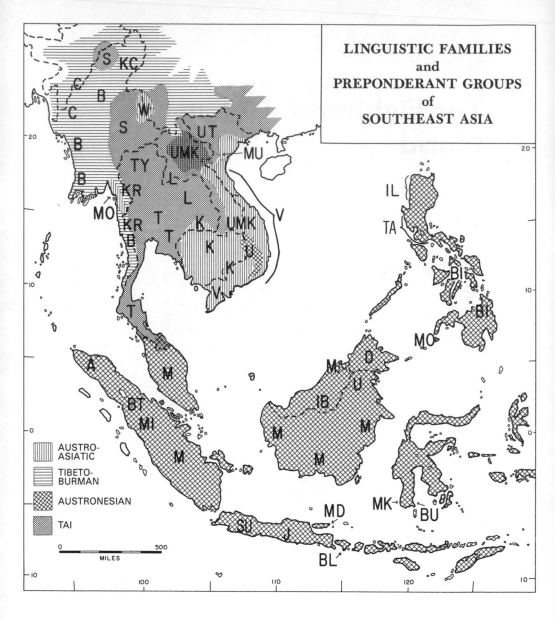

## LINGUISTIC FAMILIES and PREPONDERANT GROUPS of SOUTHEAST ASIA

AUSTRO-ASIATIC

TIBETO-BURMAN

AUSTRONESIAN

TAI

0 ————— 500
MILES

KEY

**Austro-Asiatic**
K — Khmer
MO — Mon
MU — Muong
UMK — Upland
Mon-Khmer
(Sedang,
Bahnar, Pear,
Hre)
V — Vietnamese
W — Wa

**Tibeto-Burman**
B — Burman
C — Chin
KC — Kachin
KR — Karen
(Red Karen,
White Karen)

**Austronesian**
A — Acehnese
BI — Bisayan
BL — Balinese
BT — Batak
BU — Buginese
D — Dayak
IB — Iban
IL — Ilocano
J — Javanese

M — Malay
MD — Madurese
MK — Makassarese
MI — Minangkabau
MO — Moro
SU — Sundanese
Ta — Tagalog
U — Upland Malay

**Tai**
L — Lao
S — Shan
TY — Tai Yuan
T — Thai
UT — Upland Tai
(White Tai,
Red Tai,
Black Tai,
Striped Tai)

# 1

# The Peasant World

IF, as certain sorts of science fiction suggest, humans had the power to retreat to eighteenth-century Southeast Asia, it is unlikely that they would find themselves in the palaces tourists visit today. More probably, they would happen instead upon a dusty road (a muddy one in the rainy season) and head toward a patch of green and gray on the close horizon —the nearest village. With emerald green ricefields on either side, they would pass occasional ox- or buffalo-drawn carts piled high with rice, old women taking fruit to market, or young men carrying a caged cock for fighting. A rise in the road would bring them into the shade of heavy trees arching over a huddle of bamboo and thatch houses. There they might stop at the communal well to quench their thirst and to wash off the dust and sun-glazed perspiration around their eyes. At various times of year, they would see whole families engaged in the pursuits of farmers everywhere—harvesting, or milling grain, or fishing; weaving, sewing, gossiping, courting, and cooking; fashioning implements of wood and bits of metal; celebrating birth or mourning death; tending the ill and educating the young.

The modern reader, like such travelers, might wish to hasten on to the city, where "real" history occurred. Although rural life in eighteenth-century Southeast Asia—or in the twentieth century, for that matter—has lacked its chroniclers, the activities of peasants then and now are still important. Visiting Europeans and keepers of court records hardly ever described the lives of peasants, as both took for granted their importance in the daily life and functioning of the state. More recent sources provide meager information to fill this vacuum; however, the combination of scattered historical references and a retrospective application of the insights of modern social science make it possible to sketch the broad outlines of Southeast Asian life two centuries ago.

Peasants are farmers, specifically those who live in societies controlled by elites in the capital cities and towns of premodern kingdoms —and also during the past century, in the rural areas of modernizing societies such as those of Southeast Asia. In the great agrarian kingdoms of eighteenth-century Southeast Asia—though not usually in the smaller trading states of much of island Southeast Asia—peasants constituted a good 90 percent of the population. Today, in the closing years of the twentieth century, though urban populations are growing enormously, peasants still constitute roughly a half of the population in the region.

Almost everywhere in Southeast Asia two centuries ago, these men and women adhered to the same world religions as the elites of their societies, though with a larger admixture of age-old animist beliefs and practices. Up to the twentieth century, at least, peasants were mostly illiterate in contrast to the literacy of the courts and the religious leaders of their societies.

## Wet-Rice Farmers

In mainland Southeast Asia, "peasant" and "wet-rice farmer" are virtually synonymous, but the situation in the islands is not so simple. In the Philippines the subjects of the Spanish state in the island of Luzon were mainly wet-rice peasants, but to the south in the Bisayan islands peasants grew mainly corn. In Indonesia, the subjects of Javanese, Balinese, Bugis, and Acehnese kings, among others, grew wet rice, but so did numerous other non-state ethnic groups throughout the vast archipelago.

Wherever there were relatively dense populations in Southeast Asia, they depended on complex agricultural techniques for the irrigated cultivation of rice. Peasants placed less importance upon land than on the muddy water of streams and rivers, which everywhere crossed the landscape, bringing with the floods of each rainy season rich nutrients washed down from the hills upstream. The rice paddies or *sawah* were basins to hold the seed and the water required for its growth. The prosperity of village and state thus required a sufficient supply of water for the irrigation of thousands of ricefields spread across the plains and valleys. Fields and their accompanying dikes were a capital investment for the peasant. In these fields, generations of peasants harnessed nature by setting their roots perhaps as much in water as in soil.

The varieties of rice, differing from place to place, were bred over centuries to survive and yield grain under particular climatic and soil conditions. In the Red River delta lands of northern Vietnam alone, there were at least 300 types of rice, each with its own properties, from which peasants chose to suit the local climate and the current year's rainfall. Even under considerable variation in growing conditions, peasants throughout the region could expect to harvest 20 to 25 bushels of grain per acre, so that even on very small holdings a family could sustain itself and meet its obligations. Where land holdings or yields were smaller, peasants grew two crops of rice a year, if weather or irrigation facilities permitted, as in northern Vietnam. Generally, however, peasants grew only a single crop of rice each year, which was usually sufficient to feed their families and cover taxes in grain where these were levied.

The agricultural cycle of wet-rice growing was consistent from place to place, although the timing varied with the onset and length of the year's monsoon rains. Wet-rice planting methods varied by region and according to the amount of rain dropped by the year's monsoon. In the eighteenth century, before the two-centuries' population boom in Southeast Asia, most wet-rice peasants probably broadcast rice seeds in the prepared soil of the rice paddy (field) at the approach of the rainy season. But some added an extra step in the sequence, first planting seed grain in small seedbeds and then transplanting the seedlings into the paddy—extra labor that produced larger crops, a procedure that became standard in most of Southeast Asia in the twentieth century. As the rice matured, peasants were kept busy maintaining their paddy dikes, and making sure that the water was at the right level for the rice as it grew, while the flow of river and stream water slowly diminished. When the grain heads were approaching ripeness, the peasants drained the paddies, for wet rice, with few exceptions, is harvested from dry ground like any other crop. The harvest was a time of festivity, with whole families in the fields working side-by-side and songs and jokes, which spilled with the rice across the threshing floor. During the dry months that followed, as the fields baked hard and dry, they were cleared of stubble. Then the farm tools were sharpened or repaired in preparation for the cycle ahead, while religious feasts and festivals, marriages and merrymaking filled the dusty, rainless days.

To grow and harvest their crops, peasants employed a few simple implements. Agricultural technology was least elaborate in regions where only one crop of rice was grown each year and where landholdings were comparatively large and most elaborate where the opposite conditions prevailed. Plows generally were of wood, sometimes tipped with an iron point, and wagons or sledges were often used to cart produce. Harvesting was much too important—economically, ritually, and supernaturally—to be undertaken with more than a single, hand-held blade. Throughout the region, draft animals were employed, especially in plowing and milling; the water buffalo was found everywhere, and oxen or bullocks were also used. Most peasant households had simple but practical threshing devices and many regions had stone milling equipment worked by human and animal power, though elsewhere women and children milled the day's rice in cupped wooden blocks with pounding poles. Wooden treadmills or waterwheels—and a host of other devices—raised muddy water to the fields from streams and ditches. In northern Vietnam, where the Red River had to be kept within its banks and double-cropping of rice was the rule, the dike system had attained a total length of some thousand miles by the nineteenth century. Most northern villages used canals and ditches to conduct water to their fields, and many dug ponds to hold water for use in the dry season. Over the centuries, Balinese peasants built a sophisticated network of irrigation channels, parts of which ran underground, to carry water down from the mountains to their paddies; peasant irrigation associations governing water rights and duties encompassed all villages along a given channel between steep ridges and were among the most important institutions in the uncommonly complex social order of Bali.

To supplement the basic diet of rice, peasants grew vegetables and fruit, raised chickens, ducks, and (except in Islamic areas) pigs, and fished not only in nearby streams but also in the flooded paddies. Poultry and fish were crucial to health, for they provided protein, which had either to be found or bought throughout the year. Normally through most of Southeast Asia, the peasant village was economically almost self-sufficient. Only items such as salt and cloth had to be purchased. The greater the need for such items, the more numerous were the outside trading contacts of the village and the more important the production of a marketable surplus of rice, secondary crops, or handicrafts. Only in a few areas such as the south central provinces of Vietnam, the cotton areas of central Burma, and the coastal regions of the Indonesian archipelago was a predominantly market economy a significant part of village life before the nineteenth century.

Through most of Southeast Asia, the lands peasants worked were not fully their own. Although kings claimed sovereign rights to the soil, communities joint proprietary rights, and villagers the right of actually using land, these claims did not approximate Western property ownership. For the most part, villagers themselves worked out how the resources available to them might best be distributed in order to serve the interests of individuals, families, and state. The patterns of rights to the use of land, strongly defended against external challenges, were well established in customary law and practice. In the Philippines, the Spaniards had transformed an older pattern of land-use rights into one of private ownership; they preempted for the crown all lands not specifically identified as belonging to an individual or village, thereby restricting the expansion of village lands to accommodate the needs of expanding populations. In Vietnam, strong pressures encouraged the accumulation of lands by officials and landlords, which by the eighteenth century had the effect of rendering many peasants landless. These developments, the harbingers of increasingly difficult economic circumstances, were deviations from an earlier general pattern in which peasants passed land on to their children—sons and daughters alike. The traditional mode of easing population pressure on agricultural land had been through the constant clearing and opening up of new areas, where these existed, by ambitious farmers or by deliberate government effort.

Southeast Asian rice-growing villages took a variety of physical forms. In some areas, like northeastern Thailand and lowland Laos, where settlement was dispersed, villages might be composed of a single, family-related group connected loosely to a larger political unit some miles away. Older villages on a densely settled plain might have larger populations of between sixty and one hundred families, either grouped in a single cluster or strung out on both banks of a canal. Around a central core, the groups within these villages were clearly and elaborately organized in terms of carefully differentiated social and functional roles. Still other villages were composed of a number of smaller units, the whole village being an aggregate—natural or artificial—of units that might have separate familial, economic, religious, or administrative identities. The basic unit of peasant life in the Philippines, for example, was the *pueblo,* which was composed of a number of *barrios,* while the Vietnamese village *(xa)* was made up of a number of hamlets. Between the household and the provincial capital there could be a wide range of potential social and administrative units. Southeast Asian villages varied considerably in size, organization, and appearance.

The variation in housing was similarly wide. Almost everywhere in Southeast Asia (except in Java, Bali, Lombok, and where Vietnamese or Chinese lived in large numbers), houses were built on piles or "stilts," raised some six feet or more off the ground. There was a considerable difference, however, between the communal dwellings of the Minangkabau of Sumatra, built to accommodate an extended matrilineal family, and the thatched bamboo hut of the Malay peasant. Fashioned of local materials, such as teak or bamboo, sometimes with stone pillar-bases, houses could be simple or elaborate. The chief architectural elements were a front porch, one or more interior rooms almost bare of furniture, enough windows for ventilation, and a steeply pitched roof to ward off the torrential downpour of the monsoons.

The few public buildings in villages might be the result either of common labor over a period of years or of the benefaction of a local notable or prosperous peasant. Only the larger village units would support major religious edifices—the parish churches of the Philippine *pueblos* or the village mosques of the Malay states or north-coast Java (which could not be established unless there were at least forty adult males in the community). The Vietnamese village often constructed its own bamboo palisade, and the Thai, Cambodian, or Burmese village its monastery. The talents of local craftsmen and of itinerant artisans were lavished on these structures; those that survive are a vivid reminder that by no means all the important art of Southeast Asia was concentrated in capitals.

## Peasant Fishermen

Throughout Southeast Asia, river, lake, and sea together provided a welcome and necessary addition to peasant diet. Fish, sometimes fresh but more often dried or otherwise cured, was the most frequent accompaniment to rice. The seas of Southeast Asia are rich in fish, and, though riverine communities often devoted a major portion of their energies to fishing, it was on the coastlines of the Malay Peninsula and

the Indonesian archipelago that the fishing village most clearly represented a distinct form of social and economic organization.

These villages, seldom prosperous even by peasant standards, tended
to be small and scattered. Set on white sands beneath waving palms and
casuarina trees, and situated near the outflow of a river or creek for
fresh water, the typical fishing village was the home of a dozen or so
families housed in rough bamboo dwellings along the beach. The
methods of fishing varied with locality, seas, and kind of fish, but line-
hooks, fish-stake traps, casting nets, shellfish pots, and boats and nets of
many sorts were used. Although most of the equipment was simply constructed from materials available within the village, it represented considerable capital outlay for the fishermen, more than could be raised by
single individuals or families. In addition, many fishing methods were
facilitated by cooperative labor—running the larger boats, for example,
or hauling dragnets. These two facts taken together—the need to mobilize resources and to share work—led to patterns of cooperation of a
kind peculiar to the fishing village economy. One might find in a village
several "rings" of fishermen working independently, each headed by an
individual directing operations. Sometimes the leader was chosen for
his larger share in equipping the venture, but more often, perhaps, he
earned his position by experience and technical skills thought to be
above the ordinary, by his presumed knowledge of the movements of
fish, and by his ability to propitiate spirits, thus ensuring a good catch.
Marketing also, in which shares taken out reflected a complex assessment of shares of time, capital outlay, and skill put in, was often a complicated joint enterprise.

### Village Artisans and Craftsmen

Larger peasant communities usually included among their members
artisans and craftsmen as well as religious practitioners, the devotees
and specialists required to deal with the uncertainties of the world.
These professionals were peasants who, having acquired special skills
by study or practice, often pursued the traditional sideline of their family. There were expert; in villages who were able to tell the farmer when
to sow or the young man whether he had chosen the right bride, or who,
like the Javanese or Malay *dalang,* could perform the shadow-play, a
mixture of social commentary, mysticism, and earthy humor. There
were mediums, sorcerers, astrologers, and medical practitioners. Other
villages had skilled artisans, village metalworkers, and carpenters, or
perhaps women especially noted for their weaving or plaiting, working
usually in the dry season when their fields did not require labor.

Some villages specialized in one craft or trade to the near-exclusion of
agriculture. Some produced salt by evaporation from shallow ponds of
seawater. Others produced pottery, paper, bricks, hats, umbrellas,
woven cloth, or jewelry. In a few places, as on Bali, such crafts were the

private property of hereditary caste groups, though family and village groupings, as in Vietnam and Thailand, were more common. Generally, because of the restricted availability of materials, one craft per village was the rule. In Vietnam, villages attempted to keep special industrial traditions and expertise to themselves by forbidding their women to marry outside the village or by refusing to teach skills to outsiders. Artisans, more susceptible than others to official exactions, were more heavily dependent upon marketing than were their neighbors. Their specialized functions were recognized by the government, hence they often were exempt from the seasonal labor and taxation required of other peasants. Nevertheless, they had to pay heavy taxes and to supply their products to the court at fixed prices—or none at all. Labor slavery of this kind probably inhibited the growth of industry by market restriction and price manipulation. Village handicrafts survived more because of the established demand for basic commodities than because of their inherent desirability or profitability as an economic enterprise.

## Slaves and Bondsmen

In the eighteenth century, slavery was practiced through most of Southeast Asia. There were hereditary, nonhereditary, temporary, and permanent slaves. Hereditary, nonredeemable slaves were usually descended from war captives, criminals, or traitors, or were the result of slave raids into the highlands. In the archipelago, both Christian and Muslim law forbade the enslavement of believers. Since, however, it allowed that of infidels, there were some Muslim slaves in the Philippines, Christian slaves from the Bisayas over wide areas of the archipelago, and animist slaves in almost all of the state societies of the islands, including the Dutch in Indonesia. In Burma, Cambodia, and peninsular Siam, there were monastery slaves who lived in villages as ordinary peasants and devoted the produce of their assigned lands to the upkeep of Buddhist monastic establishments. In Vietnam, those who entered slavery as punishment for crimes were often sent to military camps in frontier areas to open up new lands for cultivation. They could become peasant farmers on the land they worked when their sentences as labor slaves expired. Apart from ordinary slaves in Java, there were a number of slave outcaste communities serving the state in special functions like rope-twisting and maintaining harbor fire beacons. Usually they were outsiders by origin or had fallen by their actions from positions of respect. These people, few in number, were never extensively employed outside personal household service for the elite.

Debt bondage was much more common than outright slavery in the late eighteenth century, especially in Siam and Burma, and perhaps Malaya, where the rural economy had become increasingly monetized. A peasant in economic difficulty, needing cash for a wedding or to settle a gambling debt, might seek or have thrust upon him assistance from his neighbor or local chief, receiving either money or goods with a time limit for repayment. If he had not paid up at the end of this period he and his immediate dependents became debt-bondsmen until the debt was cleared. During this period, he might remain in his village rendering services or goods to his creditor by way of interest, or he might be taken into the creditor's household and provided with food, clothing, and protection in return for labor. He was paid nothing, hence repayment of his debt was hard. Many debt-bondsmen became obligated for life. The institution of debt-bondage was particularly well developed where manpower was in short supply. It offered obvious advantages to creditors, who were assured of cheap labor and of a force of men for use in war or in their bids for political power. The bondsman, however, might benefit as well. He remained in theory a free man, not a slave, and his social position was sometimes improved by his link with a member of the ruling class. Through the institution, in return for his surrender of freedom, he might gain protection, reasonably good living conditions close to a source of power, and exemption from the harsh labor and taxation imposed on his fellows. Although in some cases bondsmen and their families were ill-treated, escape to the hills was possible for those willing to give up the settled village life of the plain. Customary law generally provided detailed rules for the conduct of masters toward their slaves.

## Peasants outside the Village

For the most part, peasant men and women stayed at home. Everywhere in Southeast Asia, however, there were established outlets for the young, adventurous, and unconventional of the village community. In many cases, these outlets were respectable. The young Minangkabau who went roaming as a peddler for a few years on the trade routes of Sumatra and the Straits came home with riches and experience. Admired by the village, he could then claim a bride and settle down. Similar customs existed among most of the peoples of Sumatra, among the Lao, and elsewhere. Pious Muslims sought renowned Islamic scholars in their wanderings, and Buddhists took long pilgrimages. All these societies also embraced wandering troupes of actors and musicians. In addition, banditry was a frequent outlet throughout Southeast Asia for those displaced by warfare, in trouble, or unwilling to endure the restrictions of village life. Bandits—*jago* in Java, *tulisanes* in the Philippines, to mention only two of the best-known types—were organized in regular groups, with their own established customs and group culture, often headed by leaders renowned for their magical powers and bravado. Their depredations were sometimes later celebrated in folklore, but more often they were feared and hated.

Many other villagers regularly went away from home to perform compulsory labor service for the government—the corvée of the main-land states and Java, called *kerah* in the Malay states and *polo* in the Philippines. Generally speaking, it took two different forms: services rendered personally to local lords, and services owed impersonally to "the ruler." The latter form was probably best developed in the mainland states, where the *ahmudan* classes of Burma and the *phrai luang* classes of Siam were required to give three or four months each year to the service of the king. They might be gathered and sent off to dig canals or accompany a military expedition, leaving their families behind. They might be supervised for extended periods of time by men whom they had never seen. If health conditions were good, and often they were not, their annual labors might provide an opportunity for adventure, financial gain, and amorous exploits. The dangers, unpredictability, and possibilities of harsh treatment or living conditions, however, rendered this type of labor service something men usually tried to escape, preferring personal service in the establishments of officials. The personal service rendered by the *athi* classes of Burma and the *phrai som* of Siam, which was often spread more evenly throughout the year, was usually closer to home. It was frequently carried out under a local personage, who was given control over men as part of his remuneration of office. Performing their labor service in the households of local officials and rulers, and maintaining a relationship with a single master or family over several generations, these peasants had close personal ties to their patrons. The peasant could count on the support of his master or supervisor if he became involved in litigation, for example, and his master in return could expect the backing of his men in political moves. If this latter form of labor service was more heavily dependent on individual than on institutional arrangements and, thus, less secure over time than the formalized government labor service, it was more personalized and predictable for the people involved. It helped to integrate the village into larger political units.

In time of war, the role and importance of the peasant's labor changed radically. Few Southeast Asian states, dependent upon conscription to raise the troops they needed, had large professional armies. Vietnam maintained a particularly well-developed system of military conscription, which operated even in peacetime, with peasant conscripts serving four months each year and longer if campaigns demanded. While in Vietnam the service came under the impersonal supervision of a professional officer corps, elsewhere in Southeast Asia forces were usually raised through the normal channels of forced labor, with men going to battle as local or provincial units under their own chiefs and leaders; transporting their own food, equipment, and weapons; and sometimes even buying their own ammunition. The Spanish authorities in the Philippines, by stationing Pampangan troops from the island of Luzon in parts of the Bisayan islands, took advantage of animosities between linguistic groups. As elsewhere in the eighteenth century, wars could bring heavy casualties and great hardship to many people, while often campaigns or desultory warfare could take on the aspect of organized, large-scale brigandage, offering the young man opportunity for prizes and adventure, as well as for a rapid rise in social status after demonstrated skill on the battlefield.

## Social Structure

The immediate world of Southeast Asian peasants was peopled with their relations—their nuclear families and more distant relatives in the same village. Through most of the region, maternal relationships were as important as paternal ones. Though subject to stress from the patrilineal biases of Islam, Spanish Christianity, and the Confucian ethic, inheritance patterns indicate that bilaterality and the high position of women generally were cultural factors of enduring strength. As villages often contained only a small number of families, they were interlocked or joined to other villages primarily by marriage. Kinship ties provided individuals with sets of primary loyalties and defined their place in village society.

There were various forms of social interaction beyond the family. The patron-client relationship allowed for mutual understanding between superior and inferior in the social hierarchy. The client received protection and assistance in return for his support, service, and respect. In Siam, where the system was elaborately developed, these interactions occurred both within the formal structures of the bureaucracy, from the village upward, and outside formal administrative hierarchies through private relationships. By becoming a client of an official, a peasant could make more personal an often distant system of law and administration, perhaps obtaining the preferment that could secure his social advancement. Similar ends were served in a very different framework in the Philippines through a system of ritual kinship associated with Christian baptism; there, the ties of godparenthood linked individuals and families within and outside the village, both laterally and vertically in the social hierarchy.

## Values

Some of the strongest values of Southeast Asian societies are immediately apparent in their languages, which contain elaborate sets of pronouns used to express social distance and relationships among superiors and inferiors, intimates and strangers. The Javanese language still maintains almost distinct dialects for use in speaking to superiors, equals, and inferiors on the social scale. The same is true of Cambodian and Thai, where, in addressing officials, peasants referred to themselves with a self-abasing set of pronouns which emphasized their own low status. The maintenance of these hierarchical relationships was important to Southeast Asian societies. The ultimate in social disapproval was reserved for those thought guilty of shamelessness, presumption, ingratitude, or disrespect.

The life of the peasant was filled with risks. Infant mortality was high and life expectancy low. To meet the threat of the incalculable or unexpected, throughout Southeast Asia animism often provided peasants with explanations for crises in their daily lives. It was characterized by a belief in universal, local, and sometimes personalized spirits, which could interfere in human lives for good or ill and which controlled most events in human life. Called *phi* in Thailand, *nat* in Burma, and *nakta* ("ancestor people") in Cambodia, they were believed to be everywhere present and in need of propitiation. They might, like witches, be exorcised; their intentions might somehow be accessible by divination; and measures might be taken to ward off their evil effects or encourage their assistance.

The rituals associated with rice cultivation at every stage of the agricultural cycle were based on a recognition that the seed, the crop, and the land that bore it were inhabited by spirits or soul-substances that had to be exorcised, assuaged, or nurtured in order to secure the success of the harvest upon which life itself depended. In Malaya, the community, led by the village magician, celebrated the clearing of the ground before planting with rituals designed to insure the casting out of malign influences. Later, the tools used to break the ground and plant the seed were ceremonially prepared and cleansed to facilitate their work. The act of planting itself was a carefully prescribed enactment of conception, accompanied in its initiation by charms and prayer. After ripening, the crop was harvested with the tiny knife that, concealed in the hand, would not frighten to flight the beneficent soul of the rice now grown to maturity.

Tutelary and ancestral spirits abounded, often as village guardians. In Vietnam, the village tutelary deity received a seal of investiture from the imperial court. Representing the founder of a village or, for example, a general who had defeated Chinese invaders, the deity's tablet in the village communal house evoked village solidarity and participation in the community's past. Ancestor worship and hero veneration were highly developed only in Vietnam, where they constituted a regular part of everyday life. There, news of all important events was communicated to the souls of ancestors. The primary function of tutelary, ancestor, and associated observances was to emphasize, by the regular performance of rites, the stability, and identity of place and the immutability of family and hierarchical connections.

Though they often overlapped with the universalistic beliefs of the world religions—Buddhism, Christianity, and Islam—the animistic tra-

ditions were by no means superseded by them. The many elaborate
ceremonies, rites, and festivals of the year were major events in the lives
of rural communities.

## Laws

The religious life of the community enhanced as well as symbolized its
solidarity. Consent of all village members to the rule of local tradition,
particularly as expressed in customary law, was necessary for the successful functioning of communal life and for the ability of the village to
live in peace. Throughout the region, there were developed legal codes.
Some were the product of secular and ecclesiastical bureaucracies,
administered through courts of law or through the acts and decisions of
district chiefs and magistrates. For the peasant, formal litigation of this
sort, often carried out in inaccessible places, could involve high costs,
gifts for judges, and written documents which most litigants could not
read. In addition to these difficulties, the outcome could not be assured.
As most litigation was local and treated as if civil in character, it was in
the interests of peasant society to solve disputes within the village community rather than invoke outside authority.

Since villages were generally more stable than most courts or bureaucracies, Southeast Asians had well-tested rules for living together and
reliable means for resolving their differences. In the Malay and Indonesian world, this system of customary law was known as *adat*. In its original sense, *adat* simply means "custom," the right and proper conduct for
all the incidents of life from birth to inheritance. It was often local in
character, and minor individual variations were a matter of pride and
distinction to the communities concerned. Although codifications of *adat*
were sometimes recorded, one of the principal characteristics of the system was that, generally, it was not written down and consulted. Rather,
it resided in the memories of the older and more knowledgeable members of the community. Even though elaborate written codes were more
prominent in the mainland monarchies, there, too, law was primarily a
matter of local custom, a standard of equity and justice and a body of
local precedents against which most local disputes could be assessed and
settled within the community.

Life in the village was insular and armored against impingement
from outside. Close proximity for generations bred strong attachments
among its inhabitants—for the place where they had been born, for the
fields where they drew sustenance, for the ground where they buried
their dead. Rarely was the lure of town or city sufficient to pull villagers
away from their roots. The gulf between themselves and their distant
rulers was to the peasants greater than that between themselves and the
more palpable spirits who surrounded them in their daily lives.

# 2

## Non-State Peoples

FAR into the past, as today, Southeast Asia may well have been home for more different non-state ethnic groups than any other part of the world. Classifications differ, but around four hundred such peoples, speaking a multitude of languages, is a reasonable approximation—scattered through present-day Southeast Asia and spilling over into the wide region of what is now southwest China. In mainland Southeast Asia these peoples were mainly to be found on the great north-south mountain chains separating the river basins where the state societies were found, as well as the high plateaus of the interior. On the mainland, therefore, non-state groups are usually called the hill or upland peoples. By contrast, in island Southeast Asia (including the Malay Peninsula) such peoples were only marginally more likely to be found at higher altitudes than lower down, and an appreciable number of them lived at or near sea level. Though some of these groups lived at or near the coasts, they are conventionally called the people of the island interiors.

Whether on the mainland or in the islands, these hundreds of small peoples differed from those of dominant nearby state societies in many fundamental ways. There were a great many more such non-state societies, but in most cases they were a great deal smaller in population than the state societies. They did not have the very steep ladder of social rank all the way from slave to sacral king as in the state societies; most simply had village heads and elders, while some also had a superior social class of chiefs. Before about 1800, at least, few if any of these small peoples adhered to any of the world religions present in Southeast Asia, and few had any form of writing. Finally—with the exception of a few small groups of gatherer-hunters such as the Negritos of the Malay Peninsula or the Agta of northern Luzon, as well as a number of medium-size, non-state wet-rice growing groups, especially in Indonesia—the non-state peoples made their living by slash-and-burn (swidden) agriculture rather than the characteristic wet-rice paddies of the state societies of the area.

Slash and burn is one of the two main methods of agriculture that are ecologically practical in the Southeast Asian tropics over the long term; the other is wet rice. Tropical soils are generally very poor and if pressed too hard will turn into a reddish hardpan called laterite, which is good for nothing, or else will sustain only prairies of deep-rooted *Imperata* grass good only for hunting small game. The concentration of most of the year's rain in the two or three months of the monsoon generates exceptionally powerful forces of soil erosion.

Wet-rice paddies protect the soil with their shield of water in the rainy season and, while monsoon season erosion down the steps of the series of paddies is heavy, it is compensated for by eroding soil and nutrients coming in from paddies higher up. The strategy of slash and burn is nearly as effective but more complicated. The first step, beginning several months before the onset of the monsoon rains, is to fell the trees in the area chosen for the new season's fields and collect pruned branches and shrubbery to dry in the hot sun. Next comes the most critical moment in the whole cycle, upon which are focused the most urgent rituals of slash-and-burn societies: the day chosen to set fire to the litter in the fields. Firing too early before the monsoon arrives risks incomplete burning of the drying litter and loss of too much of the fertilizing ash; delaying the firing until the torrential rains have arrived means no firing at all, no ash, and disaster. A good burn followed by soaking rains leads to planting—beans of many sorts, squashes, banana trees, chili peppers, sweet potatoes, and other root crops, and the nearly universal main crop of dry-field rice—two to three dozen crops spread across the field and growing over the felled tree trunks in a miniature rain forest quite unlike the neat uniformity of a rice paddy or temperate zone row-planted field. After the planting comes weeding, maintaining fences against wild pigs, shooing birds away from the rice heads, and then harvest: the dry rice when it matures, the rest picked daily over months for meals.

The crops shooting up in the hot wet weather provide some protection against erosion, except on steep slopes, and the wood ash assures a good harvest the first year. Fields are replanted in the second year, and sometimes a third, but yield falls off noticeably and signs of gullying give a warning. After two years, usually, the farmers start new fields nearby, felling, burning, and planting among the logs as before. The old plot is left to the advancing forest. It takes something like twenty years in most of Southeast Asia for secondary forest to establish itself; meanwhile the swiddeners continue in two-year steps round an approximate circle centered on their village until—in the time it takes for a baby to grow to adulthood and marriage—they return to the original field, now ready to be cleared and burned again.

The swidden cycle powerfully influences the social life and values of those who follow its way. Because swidden villages require roughly ten times as much cultivatable land as they actually cultivate in any given year, population densities in swidden areas are much lower than those of perennial wet-rice areas. Because swiddeners are understandably unwilling to walk more than just so far from their villages to their fields, swidden villages are quite strictly limited in size to a few hundred people and are quite long distances from each other. Until new forces came to Southeast Asia in the nineteenth century, such small face-to-face village worlds, clearings in the wide forest, went with a fairly egalitarian community, no room for kings, little use for writing, and animistic religious beliefs centering on familiar local spirits of rice plant, spring, and ancestors.

The ethnographic map of Southeast Asia in the eighteenth century was as complex, as fragmented, and as particularized as the topography itself. In the upland mountains and plateaus of the mainland, most of the groups were related linguistically and ethnically to some of the peoples down below. Speaking languages akin to Burmese were such groups as the Karen and Kachin. There were numerous Tai peoples, related to the Siamese, Shan, and Lao, spreading from northeastern India to northern Vietnam and over into large areas of southwest China. Along the length of the mountains dividing Vietnam from Laos and Cambodia were many groups, some speaking Vietnamese and Tai languages and a wide variety of languages related to Khmer (Cambodian) or to the Austronesian languages. Linguistically the situation in island Southeast Asia was much simpler: almost without exception they spoke languages of the Austronesian family (also spoken in the Polynesian islands of the Pacific, as well as on the island of Madagascar off eastern Africa). Thus in the islands both state and non-state peoples spoke languages of the same family, though these languages were no more mutually understandable than Italian and French.

The non-state peoples shared many characteristics of social organization with the state peoples. Their villages were woven out of kinship and personal relationships into a strong and resilient fabric, which kept them cohesive in their relative isolation and facilitated their styles of agriculture and trade. Each group had its leaders, and most had specialists for the propitiation of the spirits, which were a profound part of everyday life. The complexities of non-state social organization tended to be a product of internal elaboration rather than external extension, as the dispersion of people over rough terrain made supravillage organization difficult. Although little is known about relationships among the non-state groups themselves, evidence would suggest that, though they were small and widely scattered they had a good many dealings with each other. Migration, intermarriage, barter trade relations, intergroup political structures, shared value and belief systems, and warfare all paint a picture of interacting social systems. Though they cannot be delineated clearly and should not be overstressed, the indications that exist about the relationships among and within at least the major groups should serve as a corrective to any general propensity to characterize individual groups as discrete, homogeneous, and isolated. Their isolation and political fragmentation were relative. Different Karen and Tai groups, for example, were sufficiently aware both of their own distinctiveness and of the general identity of their larger ethnic group to call themselves "White Tai" and "Striped Tai" or "Red Karen" and "White Karen," sharing as they did a common culture while remaining economically and politically distant in their own mountain valleys.

From the point of view of the non-state peoples, the much larger and more highly organized state societies were always problematical. Almost all the non-state peoples gladly traded local specialty products— bird's nests for the prized Chinese soup, various aromatic woods, spices, and the opium mainland groups grew themselves—for their more sophisticated state neighbors' weapons, pottery, salt, and other goods not easy for them to obtain or manufacture at home. For their own reasons they might seek the relative security of special political relations with a nearby state, though such connections often were made because some other state was threatening and were usually more stable with small states than with the larger kingdoms. With the smaller states, too, the non-state peoples often had long-term social and cultural links, complex and ambiguous, such as those between the Kachins and Shan states in the eastern and northern parts of present-day Burma.

But otherwise the non-state peoples mistrusted and feared their powerful neighbors. This was particularly true in mainland Southeast Asia. There the upland peoples, living in the mountain ranges separating the three large and still expanding states of Burma, Siam, and Vietnam, were regularly caught in the crossfire as royal armies marched through their lands, requisitioning rice, scouts, and soldiers and labor for carrying supplies. The numerous non-state societies of island Southeast Asia had much less to consider: the two large state societies in the region, Java and the Spanish Philippines, were more than a thousand miles apart and had relatively small non-state populations within their reach. The islands also differed in having more medium-size, wet-rice growing non-state peoples, such as the Minangkabau and Bataks on Sumatra and the Torajans on Sulawesi, than there were on the mainland.

Whether on mainland or islands, however, state societies—perhaps a hundred in all, large, medium, and small—rarely failed to exploit their non-state neighbors. They enforced tributary relations in which their counterparts accepted a subordinate political standing and paid tribute at intervals in valuable trade goods; they frequently raided the smaller societies for slaves to enlarge their own populations; they sent their armies across the others' lands when they wished; and, as civilized Buddhists, Christians, Confucians, Hindu-Buddhist Balinese, and Muslims, looked down on them as primitives.

At the same time, though, the relatively mighty had to be careful not to press their smaller neighbors too hard, lest the flow of valuable trade products be disrupted. In Cambodia, for example, the Pear people in the hilly southwest were exempted from taxation and labor service in exchange for an annual quota of cardamom, a spice much in demand for Chinese medicine. Beyond such merely practical considerations lay a deeper disposition of many of the state peoples to acknowledge a kind of spiritual priority in the greater antiquity of simple non-state peoples nearby. The Vietnamese, in recognizing the principal spiritual leaders of the Jarai as the kings of "Water Haven" and "Fire Haven," may only have been padding their list of tributaries. But the continued legitimacy of the kings of Luang Prabang was held to rest in part on a ritual connection with the Kha, a Mon-Khmer people in Laos whose very name (in Lao) meant "slave." Well into the twentieth century elite families in Bantam (West Java) prided themselves on their close ties with the Badui, a small swidden group in the interior, and regularly made pilgrimages to visit them. The ruling house of the state of Negri Sembilan in Malaya acknowledged that its claim to the soil of their state rested on marriage alliances with the women of a small people in the backwoods of their domain.

# 3

# Authority and Village Society

CONSIDERED individually, peasant villages and upland kin-groups were similar in many ways. Lowland villages, however, were integral parts of larger frameworks, linked to a supravillage world through local leadership, in which the key, though not the only, figure was a village headman.

The manner in which village headmen were chosen tended to reflect the power structure and values of the village as well as governmental concerns; when these were seriously opposed, the relationship between central authority and village was strained. The basic variables in the status and function of such headmen were the relative degree of social or economic division within the village, the degree to which external control was regarded as alien by the peasants, government attitudes toward villages and peasants, the administrative hierarchy through which control was exercised, and the demands that central authority placed on village society. A limited set of examples drawn from different parts of the region should suggest some of the different relationships in which the headman functioned.

In the customary Malay village, consisting of one or more groups of kinfolk linked by intermarriage, the position of primary authority fell to the headman *(penghulu),* who was usually a member of the principal or founding family and often had assumed the office by direct inheritance. Though from time to time a *penghulu* might have connections, with the district chief or other members of the aristocracy, he was more frequently from the peasant community to which he ministered and a farmer like his fellows. Though his appointment might in effect be hereditary, it was commonly vested in him by the explicit gift of the ruler of the state, whose sealed document of authority he might well bear. This imprimatur, and the suggestion (perhaps more often than the reality) of external sanction it carried, gave to the headman what little coercive authority he had. Apart from this, he relied for the most part on respect and on the mobilization of social disapproval. For this reason, it was usual to find that the *penghulu,* besides belonging to the traditionally most important family in the village, had somewhat more material wealth than his fellows and was perhaps acknowledged to have unusual force of personality, piety, or particular success in the techniques of agriculture and husbandry, in which all were in common engaged.

The Malay *penghulu* was responsible, along with other village notables —for it would be a mistake to see the office as a solitary autocracy—for keeping the peace in the village and surrendering serious malefactors to the district chief, for exercising a judicial function, for providing *kerah* labor and sometimes produce from the village, for the allocation of surplus land, and for functioning as the eyes, ears, and sometimes the right arm of his chief and overlord.

In sum, as the sixteenth-century Malacca Code provided, *penghulu* had to

> make themselves well acquainted with the following subjects, otherwise their functions are thrown away upon them: first the *Hukum Shera* [religious law]; second, the *Hukum Akl* [principles of natural justice]; third, the *Hukum Faal* [principles of right conduct]; and fourth, the *Hukum Adat* [custom, and customary law]. This done, they may be termed men.[1]

In the Philippines, an essentially Malay system of village organization was the basis upon which Spanish rule built its administration. The pre-Spanish chief, known as a *datu*, was retained in office and renamed *cabeza de barangay* (village headman). His allegiance to the colonial regime was co-opted by increasing his privileges and guaranteeing his status. Since each village had a number of key families, the elders *(principalia)* reshaped the Spanish system to accord with the high value placed on consensus. Although the headmanship was initially a hereditary position, it came in time to be rotated among the *principalia* who formed the village elite, from which the petty governor *(gobernadorcillo)* was selected. With the priest, the *gobernadorcillo* was of critical importance, since he was the fulcrum between the foreigners above him and the peasants below. He was usually the highest *indio* (indigenous) official in the Spanish bureaucracy, governing a *pueblo* composed of several *barrios* and at least five hundred adult tribute-tax–payers. Always deeply involved in the infighting among the *principalia*, this man also had clear administrative obligations to his superiors. He was expected to deliver tax revenues, goods, and labor for the *polo* tax and to serve the myriad other functions of government, and he was expected to remunerate himself for his efforts. As his ties were basically downward to the peasantry, his need to extract the required exactions, plus his own maintenance, put a constant strain on his relationship with the community.

By the middle of the eighteenth century, there was developing in Philippine rural society an economic elite increasingly interlocked with the *principalia*. This group, the *caciques*, derived wealth and power from landholding. Some inherited title to land, while others gained wealth through moneylending and foreclosure. Many of the latter emerged from the *mestizo* (mixed-blood) class. The impact of the *caciques* on the structure of the village was immense, as they came to play an increasingly important role in every aspect of village life.

Village headmen in central Burma, the *ywa thu-gyi* or *myei-taing,* generally came to office by hereditary succession through the male or sometimes the female line, or through marriage. Their succession appears to have reflected a social hierarchy in the village based on wealth and "right to rule," reinforced by continued possession of the office over generations. Their appointments were confirmed by the court only after their rights to succeed had been checked against written records and testimonials from their immediate superiors in the area in which they lived. Their responsibilities were heavy, for Burma's rural tax system was extremely complex and the administration of justice often tortuous. Although they lived in the village, they had a regular working relationship with the township headmen nearby. As these latter, too, received their positions by hereditary succession, patterns of personal and familial relations must have developed elaborately in the course of time; and indeed, the effectiveness of the village headman in representing the interests of his neighbors to higher authority must have depended on his ability to utilize these relations.

Most of the same considerations applied to the role and functions of headmen throughout the rest of the Buddhist world of mainland Southeast Asia. Through Lower Burma, Thailand, Laos, and Cambodia, however, headmen generally were informally elected from among the elder men in the village. Their age gave them an automatic high status, and their experience gave their judgments weight. Being the wise old men they were, however, they employed consultation and persuasion to perform the acts required of them by central authority and to settle disputes by conciliation and compromise. These were part of a style of leadership inculcated by folk tradition and encouraged by the values of village society, which put a high premium on avoiding conflict. The popular literature is full of tales about heroic provincial governors who in battle saved their towns and about brash country lads who by wit and winning ways won power and the governor's daughter, if not his wife. Village headmen were not such heroic characters; both government and village respected their critical mediating role, but this left them, as often as not, the bearers of ill tidings to both parties.

Village leadership in Vietnam shared some of the characteristics of the above systems. Vietnamese villages were governed by chiefs (*xa truong*), who were chosen by their fellows. But although the village notables may have chosen the village chiefs, the court had to approve them. They had to carry out the orders of the court and, of course, collect its taxes. They were also the servants, rather than the masters, of the village council of notables (*hoi dong hao muc*), which exercised the real leadership in the village. As a Vietnamese proverb put it, "The village association is a small court"—as opposed to the large court at the imperial capital. An elderly retired village chief who had become a notable after retiring from office enjoyed more prestige as a notable than he had enjoyed when village chief.

A basic reason why the notables were the true village ruling elite in Vietnam was that they did not perform specific tasks for the court in the way the village chief did. Their status was informal. While an active village chief served a specific three- or five-year unpaid term, the notables constituted a permanent body of members for life. The notables were a heterogeneous group, the composition of which varied from village to village. Wealth, old age, and academic attainment by themselves were not enough to legitimize authority, although they were cardinal qualifications. Illiterate landlords, for example, found it difficult to become notables. Among the notables, the man with the highest status who presided over their meetings might be the villager who had achieved in his lifetime the highest scholarly or bureaucratic grade or might simply be the oldest retired village chief.

Unlike their opposite numbers in Thailand and Burma, the village notables in Vietnam were not the clients of town-based officials. If they served the ends of the court, as they usually did, it was not because of patronage extended down to them, but rather because they were part of a theoretically open class system that encouraged their orientation toward the societywide bureaucracy. Many of them were the heads of literate families who dreamed of having their sons and grandsons pass the civil service examinations. In their eyes, the good reputation of the village depended upon its interaction with the court, at least to the extent that its communal self-esteem was directly related to the number of successful examination candidates it had produced over the centuries. The importance of this is that, while no traditional Southeast Asian court commanded mass communications media or mobilization systems or desired socioeconomic identity with the rural masses, the variety of styles of integration prevailing in societies as geographically close as Thailand and Vietnam was as crucial to the premodern history of the region as the uniform reliance upon rigid stratification and control over social mobility.

The Vietnamese case exemplifies the critical importance of consensus as both the source and the nature of village authority. The vital issues in village life were social and economic; they affected the relative status of each member of the community by easing and resolving conflict, by assigning labor and tax obligations, and by distributing the use of land. Customary law ultimately depended on village consensus and consent for its successful operation. In strongly hierarchical societies, the interests of individuals were given weight according to their social and economic status. The greater the variation in status, the more important it was for the village power structure to be representative.

# 4

## Provincial Powers

Ascending the social and administrative scale from the village toward the court or capital, it was in the provincial towns or district centers that one first encountered individuals acting in their everyday lives according to more broadly based loyalties. The Thai word for politics, *kanmüang,* means literally "the business of the province." Villages had to deal with the *müang* of the governor and his officials, rather than directly with the king. The provincial capital had direct connections with both ends of the administrative hierarchy. These strands met in the country towns where national and regional identities were shaped and made alive. Provincial and district towns, however, differed greatly from one part of Southeast Asia to another. Some were but larger villages, while others took on much of the appearance of a royal court.

There were at least three basic systems of bureaucratic administration. The first type was represented by the provincial administrations found in Burma, Siam, Cambodia, and Java, which were essentially based upon the control of manpower rather than the control of land. As far as the court was concerned, the primary function of the provincial administration in these places was to collect the taxes levied on the activities of the peasants and to mobilize the peasantry for labor service and warfare. Governors in the mainland states commonly were said to "eat" their provinces, and much of the time their rule may indeed have been as extractive as is suggested in popular literary tradition. Often, however, provincial administrators had to reciprocate with protection and services for what they obtained.

In such systems, provincial governors and district chiefs usually had two essential qualifications for office. First, because their fathers or other relatives had held the same posts before them, and because their uncles and cousins filled minor posts in the province, they had a network of family connections and a set of dependents or clients that, as patrons, they normally inherited. Their position within the local social hierarchy could not be ignored by the central government. Second, they had, by virtue of their social status, training for the tasks they came to assume. The sons of provincial and local officials were brought into public life at an early age, involved even as boys in the work of ruling. In Siam and Cambodia, they frequently served a period as pages at court and then returned home to begin climbing an administrative ladder that eventually would bring them to succeed their fathers. In Java, they went to the distant court less often, but they usually served in the households and retinues of their fathers and uncles, where they learned the family traditions and gained a knowledge of the working assumptions of political life. In all these societies, unlike Vietnam, academic training beyond a basic literacy was a minor qualification for office in comparison with practical experience, social grace, and the patterns of speech, dress, and manners that marked them as men of the ruling class. Even among such gentlemen, there was considerable scope for conflict, for primogeniture was not well established and polygamy was widespread among officials. Fraternal jealousies ran rampant, and competition for public office and inheritance was intense.

Thus, provincial government in Burma, Siam, and Cambodia was for the most part hereditary government by a provincial elite that had firm roots in the provinces. The nature of their rule stemmed principally from the manner in which they were integrated into the society of the province by kinship connections and informal patron-client relationships. Because of their connections upward, they must also be considered part of the state's bureaucracy. In most cases, there were regular contacts between, say, Burmese or Javanese provincial towns and the capital. Governors paid annual visits to the court to pledge their loyalty, deliver taxes, or attend state functions. A great many orders and reports flowed back and forth, and officials from the capital frequently were sent out to check tax or labor rolls or to invest new governors. The governor and his men were involved in transmitting the demands of the capital upon the villages, and they used its methods in doing so. By the eighteenth century, Siam had reached the point in administrative development where some provincial ruling families had won by marriage relations and political alliance a role in the politics of the capital, but, on the whole, such developments were exceptional. The provincial administrations in most of these countries remained rural; their importance came from their ability to control and mobilize the manpower of villages.

The provincial elite in Vietnam, in contrast to its Buddhist and Javanese counterparts, was characterized by the possession of land, leisure, and classical learning. A Vietnamese landlord who had not used his leisure to acquire scholarship could not normally be considered a member of the elite, since he had no hope of an official career and could not serve as an intermediary or "broker" between the court and the local community. The provincial bureaucracy itself, that is, the group of commissioned officials actively on duty in the provinces, was merely a specialized division of the more general provincial elite. It included provincial governors-general, governors, financial and judicial commissioners, prefects, and district magistrates who served in the provinces, prefectures, and districts of the country. Sub-bureaucratic clerks and underlings linked the district magistrate to the 30,000 or so villagers whom he governed. Poorly paid and poorly educated, their misdeeds could subvert the entire system unless they were strictly controlled. As Emperor Gia-long put it in 1811, "He who loves his ox first drives away its flies; he who loves his people first punishes the sub-bureaucrats. This is a well-established theory of government."[2]

While the provincial elite in Vietnam, in and out of bureaucratic office, enjoyed a security of economic position most of the time, the fortunes of its members could improve in times of dynastic weakness. Like their counterparts elsewhere in Southeast Asia, once they discerned through their bureaucratic connections that a dynasty was declining, they transferred the focus of their ambitions from the context of the court to their own families and native villages, determining to build up their position locally so as to survive the dynastic tempests they saw ahead. They attempted to accumulate more land and enjoyed a greater opportunity to do so, once the court's controls began to weaken. Trends at the end of a dynasty actually improved the opportunities of elite provincial families to check the downward social mobility of their sons. The dynastic cycle was a strange mixture of the increasing isolation and incompetence of hereditary emperors, who had not fought for their throne, and the conditional allegiance of provincial bureaucratic families to the throne, an allegiance dependent upon the capacity of the court to guarantee stability and to satisfy family ambitions for bureaucratic success. In the provinces, the downswing of the dynastic cycle meant the economic polarization of social classes. Independent producers, the middle level of the society, almost disappeared, while there was both a small movement toward the upper level of the society (landowners) and a very large movement of people toward the bottom level, that of the landless, who sold their labor to others. This landed character of provincial power contrasts sharply with the labor-oriented provincial elite of the countries to the west and south of Vietnam, though the rhythm of dynastic decline was essentially similar for both.

The third bureaucratic model of provincial administration was that of the Spanish in the Philippines. There, the top positions in the social and political order were filled by foreigners. Born either in the Iberian Peninsula *(peninsulares)* or in the empire (creoles), they rarely lived their whole lives in the Philippines. They came as bureaucrats, soldiers of fortune, and political appointees, and most considered the islands a hardship post. They clustered in the administration in Manila or served as the provincial governors *(alcaldes-mayores)*. This latter office offered great power and opportunity for the individual, especially because of the geographic fragmentation of the archipelago. Despite extensive legislation designed to keep the provincial governor from abusing his authority, he was rarely sympathetic to the native population. Moreover, the high turnover rate and specific prohibitions against marriage or other long-range ties in the region kept the institution an alien one. The usual provincial governor was far more involved with events in

Manila, Mexico City, or Madrid than he was with those in his province. As a result, he tended to be insensitive to local interests.

On the whole, and especially in Java and Vietnam, provincial authorities were securely integrated into the social and administrative hierarchy of the capital. By way of contrast, the nonbureaucratic systems in the Malay states of the peninsula, in western Indonesia, and in the Shan and Lao principalities tended rather to be localized systems of hierarchical order held together by tributary relations. In the Malay system, the key to political organization above the village was the district chief. Indeed, the ruler of a state was, in effect, a chief within his own royal district, his exercise of authority within the state as a whole deriving from his control over territorial chiefs scattered throughout his domain. These offices were essentially hereditary, though appointment and continued tenure depended at least theoretically on the pleasure of the ruler. Chiefs commonly held, under commission from the ruler, rights of control over a specified area of the state usually based on a stretch of the main river or one of its tributaries. These rights included the collection of taxation and tolls on riverine trade, the granting of concessions and monopolies, and the right to demand produce and labor from the inhabitants of the district. Because rivers were the principal means of transport and communication, district chiefs usually placed themselves advantageously at some strategic point on the main waterway of their territory, facilitating both tax collection and defense. Although the ruler's situation at the mouth of the principal river frequently gave him an economic advantage over the chiefs, they were virtually autonomous in their territories and jealous of their powers. The resultant tendencies toward strife and fission were counterbalanced only by a common recognition of the values and virtues of the institution of the sultanate as a validating mechanism for the whole system. It was to the advantage of the chiefs to maintain the sultanate, the symbol of state and source of legitimacy, as a basis for their position vis-à-vis each other, as a source of reward in dynastic maneuvering, and as the embodiment of the larger political entity, with its advantages for trade and defense. Thus, although the real power of a ruler might be little greater in political and economic terms than that of some of the senior chiefs, there was a general acceptance of his office, if not necessarily of his person, as formal head of state.

The chiefs in most of the Malay states, stretching from Aceh and Kedah to Sulu, were members of a hereditary ruling class and were ranked in complex orders of seniority, which served to define and determine relative position and influence. All rank and dignity was held to be served by unseen forces that punished insults to lawfully constituted authority. The concept of differential status and concern for its expression were of abiding interest to the traditional elite, with a correspondingly exclusive attitude toward those not privileged to belong to it. It was rare for a man to cross the barrier from the subject class, particularly in his own state, where his origins and background were known. Marriage outside one's own class also was exceptional, though marrying children into advantageously positioned families was a well-established means within the class of chiefs itself for indulging in the constant preoccupation with rank and influence. The main advantage of the rank of chief, apart from the value inherent in the prestige it bestowed, lay in the right it gave the holder and his kin to a share in the economic resources of the state. The basis and emblem of authority was manpower, so that much depended upon the ability of a chief to gather and retain a following, both from among his own kinsmen and from the peasantry. A typical chief's household consisted of dependent kin performing the necessary tasks of administering his lands and acting as secretaries or accountants and tax-gatherers or mercenaries and free volunteers, who provided a permanent, if often idle, armed force—the feared *budak-budak raja,* or raja's bully boys—and of debt-bondsmen and slaves.

In the Lao and Shan principalities of Burma, northern and northeastern Siam, and Laos, a similar system prevailed in which, more often than not, the "king" was a first among equals rather than a monarch set above his officials. The key political units, *müang,* were semi-autonomous, ruled by hereditary princely families. Their relations with their neighbors and distant suzerains generally consisted of sending annual gifts as symbols of submission, made substantial only in time of warfare, when the interests of all were served by joining together to repel invasion.

Through most of Southeast Asia in the eighteenth century, political and economic power were synonymous. Because property was usually subject to arbitrary confiscation by the ruler or his officials, and because manpower generally was more important than land, real wealth in most of the states lay in the right to the service and produce of others. Major exceptions were the landlords of Vietnam and the Philippines.

In Vietnam, landlordism was most extensive in the southern and south-central provinces, even though the population pressure was significantly lighter there than in the north. A consistent feature of rural Vietnam was the struggle between private landlordism and the ancient Vietnamese ideal of communal, village-owned property. Villages as communities owned public or communal lands that amounted generally to less than 20 percent of the land of the state and were meant to ensure that no peasant remained landless. Plots were assigned and reassigned regularly to members of the village by the notables, who usually kept the best ones for themselves. An undeniable trend was the growth of private estates carved out of these public lands, which in theory could be leased to private individuals only for publicly documented three-year terms.

Similar developments in the Philippines stemmed from different conditions and causes. There, the Catholic Church emerged as the greatest landlord, its holdings geographically concentrated and unevenly shared by the various religious orders. The Church, which had become an important source of credit to the colony through its charitable agencies, lent money with land as collateral, much as patrons elsewhere lent money on the collateral of labor. The problems of a landless peasantry were, unlike the case in Vietnam, new to the country. In the late eighteenth century, the orders began to give concessions to individuals to clear and improve its land. These men, called *inquilinos,* were allowed a certain number of years of tenure without rent and were thereafter charged rent-in-kind by the order. They, in turn, sublet their concessions to sharecroppers for about 50 percent of the yield. The peasant perennially went into debt, and the system was abused, as the sharecropper was forced to pay out more and more of his crop. The friars, who increasingly needed the rents from the estates to maintain their mission work, often failed to see the repressive quality of this institution and how their economic dealings compromised their authority.

Provincial and port towns, the headquarters of district chiefs, and upriver trading posts were modeled on the court or capital they served. A few carried forward the dignity and traditions of earlier days of independence, like Nakhǫn Si Thammarat in southern Siam, which had its own court and bureaucracy on the model of Ayudhya. Many more, however, had as great need for specialists and professionals as the capital, in order both to represent higher authority and to service its administrative functions.

A provincial government, such as that of Nakhǫn Si Thammarat, could be extremely complex. The titled officials there numbered 424, while the districts under its control contained 322 more, each man with specified rank, title, and responsibilities. For the most part, their functions were narrowly restricted to the administrative sphere, involving such duties as the control and supervision of conscripted labor; the collection of taxes, tolls, and duties; and the administration of courts of law. There were clerks, foremen of slaves, judges, policemen, customs and toll collectors, elephant trainers and keepers, translators for the port, accountants, and a host of others. There were Brahmans to consult with judges on points of law and physicians and astrologers to minister to the governor and his city. Some governors of that town had been noted in the past for their patronage of the arts, especially poetry and the dance-drama. With his officers, and surrounded by an elite of technical and professional experts, artistic talent, and religious devotion, the governor was more than an individual administering an area: He was the center around which the cultural life of a wide territory revolved.

In Java and Madura, the major provincial officials and local hereditary lords presided at courts *(dalem)* that were smaller replicas of the royal court in Central Java. The *dalem* was a large complex of buildings, often walled, containing the residence of the lord himself and his principal wife, separate apartments for his other wives, children and relatives, halls for official meetings and for *wayang kulit* (shadow drama) and dance performances, kitchens, stables, and numerous outbuildings for servants and grooms. The *dalem* was also, like the royal palace-city, the center of a universe, in this case, the region ruled by the provincial lord. Before it, to the north, stood the *alun-alun,* a grassy square with one or more great banyan trees at its center; on one side of the *alun-alun* stood the mosque; and around this complex spread the town, not usually very populous in this period but the place where virtually all nonpeasants in the region (apart from the rural *ulama*) were concentrated. The *dalem* was the political, in a sense magical, and cultural focus of the whole region; in the Sundanese areas of West Java and on Madura, moreover, it was the major institution through which Javanese culture spread out to the common folk in the outlying areas.

The actions of individual governors and chiefs did as much to determine the character of provincial rule as did any strength or weakness of administrative institutions. One could argue that inactive or inert or self-concerned administrations predominated in Southeast Asia in the eighteenth century. Certainly a considerable insensitivity to the problems of the peasantry existed where, as in Vietnam and the Philippines, problems of landlessness were building up; where labor was being abused, as in Burma and Siam; or where political strife dragged whole states into warfare, as in Cambodia and Java. A nineteenth-century Cambodian treatise on the interpretation of dreams stated that if one dreamed of a person without arms or legs, one was destined to become a governor. Such limbless creatures could do nothing else but eat, and in the eighteenth century there was no shortage of appetite or food.

# 5

## Religious Life and Leadership

In the course of its long history, Southeast Asia has known all the world religions, and since the seventeenth century three—Buddhism, Islam, and Christianity—have commanded the adherence of most of the region's population. All but Mahayana Buddhism are relative latecomers to the region. They share similar concerns for personal salvation and the religious life of individual communities, which distinguish them from the Brahmanical religion, distant and esoteric, so typical of the earliest kingdoms of Southeast Asia. The most important effect of the great religious changes of the thirteenth through the seventeenth centuries was the creation of religious systems and hierarchies that bridged the distance between the village and the court and encouraged the growth and dissemination of a culture that became vernacular and popular.

### Mahayana Buddhism

Mahayana Buddhism is the "northern school" of Buddhism, which spread historically from India to Nepal, Tibet, Mongolia, China, Korea, Japan, and northern Vietnam. Theravada Buddhism (sometimes called Hinayana) is the "southern school" or "southern family," which spread from India to Sri Lanka, Burma, Thailand, Cambodia, and Laos. To cite some of the differences between the two schools, Theravada Buddhism strictly follows the words of Gautama Buddha, whereas the Mahayana insists upon broader interpretations and is more eclectic. Theravada venerates only the Buddha himself as the founder of the religion and considers Mahayana, with its worship of *bodhisattva* (men, lay or ecclesiastical, who had become Buddhas-to-be but who compassionately helped others to reach Nirvana before entering it themselves) to be idolatrous. Theravadins practice religious devotion to save themselves, Mahayanists to save themselves and others. Mahayana tends to allow laymen and women a greater role in its religious community than does Theravada, which strictly separates monks from lay people. Theravada monks in such countries as Thailand and Burma wear saffron robes and accept alms for their food, while Mahayana monks in Vietnam wear brown robes and do not accept alms.

On the whole, Vietnamese patterns of cultural borrowing from

China dominated the evolution of Vietnamese Mahayana Buddhism. Because the Vietnamese were generally under the Chinese cultural sway, they were more likely to read Buddhist scriptures and religious tracts written in classical Chinese than those written in Indian languages. Buddhism in Vietnam, moreover, intermingled with Taoism and with popular refractions of Confucianism and existed as one element in a religious compound the Vietnamese themselves called "the three religions" *(tam giao)*. The Chinese and Vietnamese religious worlds overlapped so much in the eighteenth and nineteenth centuries that many southern Chinese priests could emigrate to Vietnam from Kwangtung and Fukien and develop large religious followings there. But Vietnamese Buddhism also had its "Southeast Asian" side.

Vietnamese Buddhists themselves like to stress that, in Chinese Buddhism, the two possible courses of action—"participation" in worldly affairs *(nhap the)* and hermitlike "abstention" from them *(xuat the)*— were usually kept rigorously separate from each other, as two mutually exclusive categories, rather than being dynamically combined. Vietnamese Buddhism, on the other hand, attempted, as the Emperor Minh Mang put it, "to reconcile the two aspects of participation in the world of men and abstention from the world of men, in order to create a special way of life for Buddhists: an emperor could be a monk and a monk could be the secular leader of his country."[3] Far more than his Chinese counterpart, the Vietnamese Buddhist believed that he possessed the theoretical license to engage in a life of both private "spiritual experimentation" and practical politics, basing the latter upon the former.

This synthesis of "participation" and "abstention," although an integral part of Vietnamese Buddhist political thought, remained an unattainable ideal in the eighteenth century, when institutional Buddhism was at an unprecedentedly low ebb. At that time, the Confucian court feared Buddhism not as a highly organized political rival but as an indirect ideological influence that could undermine the court's intricate bureaucratic order. The greatest writer of the period, Nguyen Du (1765–1820), under Buddhist influence, quite explicitly declared, in his poem "Chieu hon ca" ("Song Summoning Back the Souls of the Dead"), that in paradise "the superior and the lowly of this world are reseated in rank." In his poem, he also reminded the wandering souls of former court officials that "the more prosperous you were, the more hatred you accumulated. . . . Carrying such a weight of hatred, do you really think you should seek a way to reincarnate yourselves?"[4] The court embarked upon a policy of religious control, manipulating the recruitment of Buddhist monks and priests. To become a Buddhist ecclesiastic in Vietnam in the early nineteenth century, a peasant or scholar required an "ordination certificate" *(do diep)* from the court. Applicants for these ordination certificates had to travel to Hue itself, where they were given religious examinations. Furthermore, no Buddhist temple could be built in Vietnam at that time without the permission of the Nguyen court. The numbers of monks and acolytes at the larger temples were fixed by laity, and village chiefs who did not report surplus monks at local temples were punished. The court itself paid the salaries of the head monks at the major temples. It endowed important temples with their land and even gave them their names. It bestowed upon them teas, paper, incense, candles, and drugs, which it imported from China. At its command, Buddhist temples would celebrate a "land and water high mass" (in origin, a Chinese Buddhist ritual) for the souls of dead soldiers who had served the dynastic house. In addition to controlling the temples, the court sponsored and financed the construction of new ones, usually in the vicinity of Hue, where they were easier to supervise. Hue's emergence as a center of Vietnamese Buddhism dates from this period of court patronage and control.

Considered purely as an organized institution, Mahayana Buddhism occupied a much more modest place in Vietnamese society than Theravada Buddhism occupied in the Burmese, Siamese, or Cambodian societies. Needless to say, the heavily patronized Vietnamese Sangha became little more than a political instrument of the Nguyen emperors. By itself, it was poorly organized. There was no hierarchy of temples controlled by a central monkhood as well as by the court. There were no societywide Buddhist religious organizations to compete with the Confucian bureaucracy. The Vietnamese Sangha of the early-1800s was small compared to the Sangha of the Theravada states. The values of Confucian familism and filial piety (which required the procreation of sons to continue the family and its ancestor worship) made monasticism less popular in Vietnam than in neighboring societies. Widows and elderly women, on the other hand, commonly joined the important associations of temple nuns *(hoi chu ba)* in every village that possessed a temple. These women did good works, participated in temple worship at least on the first and fifteenth days of every lunar month, and paid rice dues to the temple in the same way that village men contributed dues to village communal feasts. Village religious life tended to be more stable—and more parochial—in the north than in the south. Pilgrimages to religious shrines in the agricultural off-season were a feature of Vietnamese rural society. But such pilgrimages were especially popular in the south, in regions like Ca Mau and Rach Gia, where there were few long-established temples to cater to worshippers or where the monks did not yet have sufficient prestige.

## Theravada Buddhism

Theravada Buddhism from Sri Lanka spread rapidly between the eleventh and the fifteenth centuries through the countries of mainland Southeast Asia from Burma to Cambodia and Laos. Every village had a monastery for its monks. A village was considered incomplete without one, though it might consist only of a small preaching hall *(vihara)*, an *uposatha* building for ordinations and rites, and a dormitory for the monks. Around these, other buildings and towerlike monuments (*cetiya*) containing relics of ancestors or exceptional men might in time be built, and a sacred tree, reminiscent of that under which the Buddha preached his first sermon, planted. The monastery was inhabited by a small group of celibate monks clad in saffron-orange or yellow robes who had taken vows of poverty, chastity, and devotion to a life of religious study and meditation. Their activities were governed by 227 specific disciplinary rules. Forbidden to touch money, and bound to accept alms for their food, they began each day with a walk through the village accepting the food offerings of willing householders. The monks returned to eat at their monastery, where food was prepared for them by students and pious hangers-on. Food obtained from the faithful was supplemented by garden produce and delicacies, never including meat, offered to the monastery by people eager to gain merit.

The Buddhist monkhood in village society provided all males time and opportunity to perfect their moral being, seek enlightenment, and to preach the *Dhamma,* the teachings of Buddhism, to the community. In a subsidiary fashion, the Sangha served as an outlet for the community's desire to perform meritorious deeds, particularly for women, who could best improve their moral state and hope for rebirth as men in their next incarnation by regularly offering food to the monks, attending preaching services, and offering a son to the monkhood for ordination. In day-to-day terms, the monkhood's most important function was to offer boys and young men a rudimentary education in reading and writing and the principles of their faith; for this reason, probably more than half the men of Siam, Burma, and Cambodia in the eighteenth century were functionally literate, at least able to read a simple piece of vernacular prose. To those who had the time or were unusually talented, monks offered advanced instruction not only in religious subjects but also in the arts and sciences of Indian civilization, from mathematics and astronomy to poetics and medicine. Such advanced instruction, however, was not often available. It was generally concentrated in the monasteries under royal or noble patronage in the towns, which could encompass large monastic populations, support paid government teachers, and provide incentives for the best trained, offering them official position or ecclesiastical advancement. At every level of society, however, the monastery was the repository of whatever the population (which, after all, provided the monks) admired and needed in the way of sciences and arts. In out-of-the-way monasteries, some of this learning was uncanonically connected with manipulating events, interpreting dreams, and setting astrological rules for conduct.

In village society, the institutions of monastery and monkhood provided a coherent model of religious action and belief, which transcended village concerns and tended to draw villages together by ties that were wider and deeper than those provided by language and agricultural custom. The abbot and monks of the village monastery belonged to a hierarchical ecclesiastical organization that extended, parallel with the civil hierarchy, all the way to the king. The organization was a channel for the transmission of information in both directions, up and down, and a vehicle of social advancement for those inside it. Monks frequently carried the complaints of their villages to higher authority, bypassing secular intermediaries, and the village abbot often was the most respected leader in the village, sometimes more effective in his leadership than the village headman, who deferred to him. Ambitious young men, who found the secular social avenues to their advancement tightly closed by law and custom, could, through ecclesiastical education and promotion, circumvent the restraints against social mobility and advance to positions of ecclesiastical authority. Moreover, if they found the monastic life too encumbering, they could leave it and be "reborn" into the secular world at a point higher than the one at which they had left it.

The Buddhist ecclesiastical hierarchy was for the most part organized territorially in each of the Buddhist countries, save that the forest-dwelling Araññika monks were organized separately. Each district and province had its own chief abbot, who was subject to the authority and discipline of his patriarch and the supreme patriarch *(sangharaja)* in the capital, whose decisions and injunctions were given force by civil authority. The Burmese Sangha had a long history of sectarian divisions, which weakened its cohesion and authority. The Siamese monkhood, by contrast, was carefully supervised by the crown, and, during some periods, prince-monks held high ecclesiastical offices. Royal patronage, steadily strengthened, had reached the point in Siam by the seventeenth century where the monarchy was fully supporting religious education through the sponsorship of royal monasteries, which became virtual universities for religious and secular studies. The teachers of noble and royal sons and preceptors of monarchs found it difficult to remain free of political entanglements, in spite of their discipline. Popular literature and chronicle accounts suggest that, on the whole, theirs was ultimately a strong moral influence. Monks could, and probably did, mobilize public opinion for or against kings and officials. They had so established their moral influence by the last half of the eighteenth century in Siam that no king could rule long without their approval.

Between the fourteenth century and the eighteenth, there were major intellectual and institutional developments in the Buddhist life of mainland Southeast Asia. On its arrival in the region, Buddhism had to contend not only with well-established animism in both village and court (the royal oaths of allegiance in all the courts included the threat of being punished by spirits if one broke the oath) but also with both court and folk Brahmanism in Cambodia and Siam. The Brahmanical tradition, unlike Buddhism, offered absolute and "scientific" certainty in its explanations and predictions of natural and human events. As long as

Buddhism was incapable of giving people certain answers when asked whether a military campaign should be undertaken or a marriage entered into, Brahmanism remained of primary importance in everyday life. With the gradual secularization of Indian science, the strengthening of Buddhist scholarship and popularization of sophisticated cosmological ideas, and eventually official and popular disapproval of Brahmanical rites and practices, the Brahmanical element in the religious life of much of the mainland weakened. The same developments worked more widely to reduce animism to an essentially residual category for the explanation of phenomena beyond moral and scientific reason. Hindu religious sites, such as the temple of Angkor Wat in Cambodia, and Brahmanical institutions, such as the concept of the *devaraja,* or god-king, fitted easily into Buddhist terminology and practice, producing no pangs of conscience or sense of contradiction. As if to mark the success of Buddhism's domestication in Southeast Asia, monks from Sri Lanka were visiting Siam and Burma in the eighteenth century to obtain valid ordinations and copies of religious texts then lacking in Sri Lanka, the original source of Southeast Asian Theravada Buddhism.

## Islam

The Muslim world of Southeast Asia stretched in a 3,000-mile crescent from the northern tip of Sumatra (where perhaps Islam had first arrived) to the islands of the southern Philippines. Whether or not it had come as an adjunct to trade (and the point continues to be disputed), Islam, in contradistinction to the landward Buddhism of the region, retained a close association with the coast, with the maritime pathways that threaded the archipelago, and with the port towns and riverine states—in short, with that complex of geographical and cultural factors known in Indonesian as the *pasisir.* Islam was organized in no church—despite the persistence of European observers in finding "popes and priests"—but nonetheless possessed institutions, structures, and patterns of communication that knitted its adherents together and joined them to the heartland of Islam in the Middle East. Chief among these, perhaps, was simply the movement of people. Itinerant Arabs, mainly traders but including teachers, had been a feature of the port societies of the archipelago for centuries. Some had formed settled communities, and individuals were often found in religious advisory capacities at the courts of local rulers or moving among the villages as teachers or simply "holy men." Youths traveled regularly to preachers of this sort, whether Arab or indigenous, forming around them communities of scholars known variously as *pondok* in peninsular Malaya, *langgar* in Sumatra, or *pesantren* in Java. Parts of the area—Kelantan and Patani, for example, or Demak in north coastal Java—were particularly known for these institutions, which attracted students from far and wide and acted as dissemination points for a zealous form of the faith. The *pondok,* too, were often centers for another of the institutions that linked Islam within and without, the Sufi *tarekat,* or orders of mysticism, which, sometimes to the disapproval of the rigorous, afforded a more emotional approach to God than other more restrained forms of worship. Ubiquitous in the region, the *tarekat* brotherhoods (of which the Shattariyah was in the eighteenth century perhaps the most prominent) were not highly organized and consisted mainly of individual *shaykh* who claimed common teachers, along with groups of village or *pondok* followers. Knowledge of belonging to the *tarekat* added to the sense of commonality given by Islam. Yet another form of movement within Southeast Asia was the pilgrimage to Mecca, the *haj,* which afforded both ideological renewal to the body of Islam and considerable status and prestige to returning practitioners.

Within Southeast Asian Islam, it is common to make a broad distinction between two basic patterns, one might almost say intensities, of the faith—that related most specifically to the *pasisir* areas already described, which included the Malay world and the eastern islands, and that found in Central Java. Doctrinally, the Javanese form of Islam was characterized by an idiosyncratic blend of indigenous, Hindu-Buddhist, and rather florid Sufi mysticism. In its more nativistic forms, it has been described by the term *abangan*—a term distinguished from the *santri* form held to characterize the *pasisir* regions. The *abangan* had absorbed Islam, along with elements of Hinduism, Buddhism, and animism, into a larger, Javanese, complex of belief, whereas the *santri,* taking their self-identification as Muslims more seriously, were more exacting in their observances of Islam. Organizationally, the ruling class in bureaucratic central Java relied for the administration of Islam upon what came to be an appointed hierarchy of officials, who functioned more or less as adjuncts of secular rule, staffing mosques, prayer houses, and religious courts—the "priesthood" of contemporary Dutch observers. Within central Java, the *santri* element was represented by the independent *ulama,* teachers and propagators of the faith at the village level, who based their knowledge of Islam on their esotericism as initiates in the *tarekat* and their espousal of an outwardly as well as inwardly Islamic mode of life. Standing aloof from, and at times fiercely critical of, Islamically imperfect secular governments, they formed a powerful focus for peasant discontent in times of trouble.

*Pasisir* Islam, exemplified particularly in the Malay states of the peninsula and Sumatra, possessed little or nothing in the way of structured Islamic authority. It is true that the sacral powers of the rulers of these states included responsibility for the defense and good governance of the faith, but in the realm of religion, as of political organization, these sparsely settled riverine states lacked either the resources or the stimulus for centralization of control. Though the theoretical responsibility of the traditional secular ruling class for the religious life of the people was never seriously questioned, it was seldom seriously tested either. From time to time, individual rulers and chiefs did, for pious or other motives, appoint religious officials of various sorts beyond those attached to their own mosques, but there was a marked absence of anything approaching hierarchical organization or systematic control. In these circumstances, religious authority tended to dwell in those members of village society who, by their piety and some pretense to learning and, perhaps, through having made the pilgrimage to Mecca, were accepted as fit to exercise it—as *imam* of mosques and religious teachers, or as *guru tarekat*. The rural *ulama* thus described did not constitute a separate social class. In the absence of anything more than an attenuated religious officialdom, the Malay states were without the tradition of institutionalized opposition between independent *ulama* and religious bureaucracy that marked Central Java.

The focus of village religious life was the mosque of general assembly, or the smaller *surau,* where the men congregated for prayers, met nightly during the fasting month (and at certain other times) to recite the Kuran, and held the religious exercises associated with the Sufi orders. For Malay youths, it was frequently also the sole place of education, where young boys learned by rote to recite the Kuran and were taught the basic tenets of their faith. If the intensity of religious life varied from place to place, it did so chiefly in response to particular individuals from within the village itself, who, through force of piety or esoteric knowledge, communicated their enthusiasm or ardor to others; there was neither hierarchy nor system to impose it from without.

Village mosques of assembly, as a rule, had only a small number of officers, chosen from among the villagers themselves. The principal functionary was the *imam,* who led public prayers, was responsible for running the mosque, celebrated marriages and recorded divorces, arbitrated (assisted by other elders) in disputes concerning religious law or practice, and was probably also the village teacher. Other officers were the *khatib,* who gave the prepared admonitory address (in Arabic) at the Friday prayer, and the *bilal,* who made the daily calls to prayer. Some of them may have been to Mecca, but most had derived what learning they had from attendance at a *pondok* for some years or simply within the village. This, and a small knowledge of the Arabic language, sufficed to ensure their recognition as *ulama,* a standing shared with those itinerant Malay, Indonesian, and Arab divines who, throughout the area, found respect and sometimes veneration for their saintly qualities (allied sometimes, it must be said, with commercial acumen) and necromantic skills. The authority wielded by traditional religious leadership of this kind, though persuasive within its terms of competence, was essentially derived from the peasant community itself, of which the *ulama* were a part, and was devoid of external sanction, except where the ruling class found an interest in enforcing it.

Nevertheless, there did exist a clear, if frequently inactive, association between the secular power and the religious life of the people. Indeed, to speak of the "secular" power in this context is inapt, for the relationship between ruler and ruled defied simple classification and certainly embraced the spiritual as well as the material well-being of the state as an entity. In many of the Malay states of the peninsula and East Sumatra, there were, from time to time, state *kathi* (magistrates), responsible to the ruler, who, at least in theory, had a general oversight of all mosques in the state. In Perak, and possibly elsewhere, there was an office corresponding to that of state *mufti,* or legal adviser, exercised in this instance by one of the eight major hereditary chiefs of the state, who, it was said, together with the heir presumptive to the throne, held religious jurisdiction over the subject class. Jurisdiction over the aristocracy was held by the heir apparent. The assimilation of religious authority to customary political authority suggested here was a common feature of the region, potential or realized, and was later to be of political importance.

What has been said so far tends to suggest that eighteenth-century Islam in Southeast Asia was a stable system at rest. It is important to emphasize, therefore, that quite apart from the inbuilt tensions to which attention has been drawn—between Javanist and Islamic elements in central Java, between religious bureaucracies and independent *ulama,* and between traditional secular leadership and the expression of religious authority—Islam was still at that time an expanding religion. In Borneo and Sumatra, for example, and even in Java, *pasisir* Islamic society formed a kind of fringe, within which were populations with indigenous religious systems that knew nothing of Islam or were resisting incorporation. The expansion of Islam was a process that was to accelerate and become far more complex in the years following.

## Christianity

Spain colonized the Philippines as an act of devotion. The proselytizing zeal to make the archipelago a "showcase of the faith" colored Spanish institutions with ecclesiastical concerns. To the Spanish monarchs, glory in this life and the next was to be found through mission work, and there could be theoretically no divergence of goals between the religious and temporal spheres. Priests and bureaucrats were dedicated to the service of crown and cross; the resultant congruence established an interpenetration of functions. The colony would not and could not have survived without the priests, and by the end of the Spanish era the country was described as a "friarocracy." The friars, who came originally to spread the faith, were the only Spaniards willing to live in the rural communities for their whole lives. They enforced Spanish law and molded peasant *(indio)* values. As the result of the early decision of the Synod of Manila in the 1580s, priests learned and then taught in the vernacular languages rather than in Spanish, so that, except for the urban centers, where a patois called *chabacano* was spoken, most Spaniards could not communicate with the *indios* except through the priests.

The actual relationship between Church and crown was very complex. By a series of papal bulls, the Spanish monarchs were given the right of exclusive patronage over the Spanish missionary effort. In return, the crown provided transportation, paid each priest's annual salary, and guaranteed support of the Church. The priest became a salaried government official, and the crown, through another concession, the *recurso de fuerza,* was able to intervene in ecclesiastical jurisdiction if its interests were jeopardized. These concessions, which were enlarged through legal interpretation by Spanish jurists, gave the crown two bureaucracies, one ecclesiastical and the other temporal. While this system remained effective during the first era of Spanish control, it became awkward as the interests of Rome and Madrid grew apart. By the mid-eighteenth century, there was no longer the congruence of interest that had once existed.

The tension between the crown and the Church was exacerbated by the struggle between the diocesan hierarchy and the religious orders. The Philippines had been converted initially by the friars (also known as regulars, from the Latin word for vows), who received from Pope Adrian VI the right to administer the sacraments and hold parishes free from supervision by the local bishops. Diocesan (often called secular) priests, in contradistinction to people in orders, were only to be given parishes that had not been assigned already, and, because the whole of the Philippines had been divided into spheres, there were few parishes left for diocesan priests. In theory, the friars were supposed to be shock troops, converting the heathen, transferring authority to the diocese, and then moving on to new areas. Moreover, the Council of Trent had attempted to curb the worldwide independence of the friars by ruling that a bishop had the right to episcopal visitation in any parish in his diocese. The bishops maintained that they must have the right to inspect and control all parish work and priests, whether regular or diocesan; the friars, in turn, argued that they had their own hierarchy, reaching up to the Pope.

What complicated the issue was the crown's dependence on the friars in running the colony. Since the friar was usually the only Spaniard in the hinterland, and since the crown discovered that only friars were willing to live and die in the *bundok,* the crown was unwilling to alienate the various religious orders. Each time the diocesan authorities in Manila attempted to impose the right of visitation, the friars would threaten to resign en masse. In 1750, after almost two centuries of trying, the diocesan authorities had only 142 parishes out of 569. More significantly, they were poor and small compared with those of the orders.

*Indio* priests were an obvious solution for diocesan officials unable to persuade Spanish diocesan clergy to endure the hardship of migration. Some Spanish temporal officials saw ecclesiastical advantages in using *indios* as a means of reducing the power of the orders. The friars savagely opposed such a move. For example, Fray Gaspar de San Augustin felt that the *indio* who went into the priesthood would do so "not because he has a call to a more perfect state in life, but because of the great and almost infinite advantages which accrue to him. . . . If the [*indio*] is insolent and insufferable with little or no excuse, what will he be when elevated to so high a station?"[5] Friar resistance effectively limited the number of *indio* priests to those trained by the orders to serve as assistants. Thus, they had only a smattering of education, enough to perform their subordinate jobs but not enough to make them learned in the faith.

The secular-religious controversy began as an administrative struggle within the Church. In time, however, it evolved into a racial tension between the friars, who remained almost exclusively Spanish, and the diocesan priests, who increasingly were non-Caucasian. The issue was to spark nineteenth-century Philippine nationalism. Since the clergy was an essential arm of the government, the struggle for *indio* parity transcended its ecclesiastical confines. While the Spanish crown and the Roman Catholic Church fell out of perfect union, they were so intertwined that they could not easily be separated.

The world religions which have so clearly dominated Southeast Asian religious life in recent centuries were not, of course, adopted word-for-word but were modified in many ways to accord with preexisting beliefs in the different areas where they took root. In the Philippines, Catholicism was adopted passionately but selectively by the lowland agriculturalists who came under Spanish rule in the sixteenth and seventeenth centuries. The earlier Hindu-Buddhist mysticism of Java and elsewhere in Indonesia made the adoption of mystical versions of Islam easier than the adoption of conventional legalistic versions of the faith. Brahmanical rites remained dominant at the courts of Siam and Cambodia long after the populations and rulers of these states had embraced Theravada Buddhism. The Mahayana Buddhism of northern Vietnam, when it reached the Mekong delta in the south, encountered and began to merge with the Theravada Buddhism of the Cambodian population there.

Equally important, the four dominant religions of recent centuries in Southeast Asia by no means exhaust the roster of religious beliefs which hold people's hearts. Animism—the complex of religious beliefs centering on innumerable spirits of departed relatives, economically important plants and animals, and features of the landscape—ordered the world in which most of the small communities of swidden cultivators lived. Shamans, individuals who had a natural facility for communicating with the spirits, put troubled families in touch with offended ancestors and prescribed the propitiatory offerings the former should make. They communicated with the souls of sickly children and prescribed cures, and presided over agricultural and other rituals. Many also practiced magic and sorcery.

But, if only numerically, animism was and is more important in the large populations of the great kingdoms in the area, where the world religions were implanted. Everywhere in Southeast Asia, in the minds of peasants and most members of the elites, Buddhism, Islam, and Christianity were fused with animism in a harmonious whole. Theravada monks in the lowland villages of Burma, Siam, and Cambodia, while maintaining the primacy of Buddhism, also provided essentially the same assistance as shamans did in the uplands. The twentieth-century Javanese *kebatinan* sects, each in their own ways, drew on Sufi mysticism along with the animism of the ancient Javanese spirit world. The Hindu-Buddhism of Bali is also suffused with an uncommonly elaborate animism.

# 6

# Traders and Markets

In the eighteenth century the village was, as it is today, the primary unit in the life of the people of Southeast Asia. Its links to larger units were administrative and cultural, through its own headmen and provincial governors or chiefs and monks or friars. In addition to these connections, however, and sometimes transcending them, were economic relationships that might extend a short distance to local markets, beyond them to a riverine or coastal port, to the capital, or even overseas. It is common to consider these economic relationships as flows of commodities or networks of trading connections; and on both these subjects recent research provides useful information. However, they also may be seen as the relationships of groups and individuals, given substance by the exchange of goods and services and providing grounds for actions of a political nature.

As an economic unit, the first concern of a village was for self-sufficiency through production of the grain on which its life depended. The minimum economic requirement was that it should produce sufficient rice to sustain itself. No village, however, lived on rice alone, and all required animal protein, vegetables, fruit, condiments, and salt to balance the daily diet. Most of these could be produced as secondary products but were not always available when needed, or efficiently produced, or—like salt—locally obtainable. Moreover, manufactured products, like iron and cloth, had to be found elsewhere. Thus, out of both convenience and necessity, peasants looked to local marketing and informal exchange to obtain the staple foodstuffs and other commodities they required for life.

In addition, by definition both fishing and craft villages were deficient in rice, as were many upland farming villages, while they all produced commodities the rice-farming villages desired. Fishing villages usually would work out informal exchanges of fish for rice with the rice-growing villages in their hinterland, carrying their fresh or dried fish and fish-paste upstream or along the coast to other villages or to regular or intermittent markets. Craft villages might market their basketry or pottery or cloth across the countryside in bullock-drawn carts or on long boats piled high on seasonal trading expeditions in the months following the rice harvest, when roads and tracks were passable and rice stocks high. In the market places of towns, at a periodic village market or annual fair, or informally along the route, a peasant might barter a chicken for good basketry, pottery, salt, or chili peppers. The meat of an old bullock or water buffalo might go toward the purchase of gold for a maiden's dowry or matron's vanity. Especially on the mainland, this was often a trade among women, who enjoyed the opportunity to gossip and arrange the marriages of their children. It was a vital and simple trade, little affected by government and international prices or wars and insecurity. No village could survive without it.

Tangential to this widespread trading was the commerce between the lowlands and highlands of the interior. It may have been best developed along the length of Vietnam, where highland woods, bamboo, and lacquer were traded for lowland fish sauce, dried fish, salt, and lime. Often the highlanders came for this trade to lowland rural markets, which were periodic, every three or five or fifteen days. The trade could become more complex when, for example, in central Vietnam the Hre people assumed the role of serving as commercial intermediaries between the Vietnamese and the more isolated Sedang and Bahnar peoples, though Vietnamese might still serve as peddlers—especially of salt —to the highland peoples.

Salt was the most important of the imports of inland villages, a commodity beyond the scope of purely local barter trade. With few exceptions, it was a coastal commodity, produced, as on the island of Madura off the east coast of Java, by evaporation from great salt pans constructed along the shore. It and other imported goods were distributed by traders of the coastal towns to the villages of the interior. On Java, the Javanese and Chinese merchants of the coast traded up the Solo and Brantas and other rivers, carrying salt, Chinese earthenware, textiles, and opium. There and elsewhere, peddlers and small traders set out from coastal ports with such goods for extended tours of inland towns and villages, bartering coastal products and imported goods for foodstuffs for the towns and goods suitable for export. On the whole, theirs was a difficult and often hazardous enterprise. They had to run a gamut of market and shop taxes; ferry, bridge, and road tolls; and, in the riverine states, the exactions of district chiefs or petty bureaucratic officers. Martaban in coastal Burma and Nakhǫn Si Thammarat in southern Siam, for example, were ringed with stations for the collection of transit dues on every road and waterway. Similarly, along the Solo River in Java, where such stations are recorded as early as the fourteenth century, tolls were heavy, increasing in the late eighteenth century to the point of constricting trade.

One important category of goods entered trade from producers with little or no compensation whatever. These were the goods accepted or required by some governments in lieu of, or as part of, taxes. Although a substantial proportion of this probably was rice, a large number of other products were involved. In Siam, they were collected on a number of different bases. Some were given over as a substitute for labor service, particularly when the crown desired the product and the producer lived in a remote area—for example guano (for the manufacture of gunpowder), ivory, sappan and other exotic woods, and swallows' nests (for Chinese soup). Others reached the royal warehouses as a proportion of a peasant's produce taken in tax, as on ricefields, orchards, or market gardens. In some areas, rice or other goods could be demanded of peasants at a fixed price set by government; this was the case in the Philippines, Dutch Java, and portions of Siam, although in such cases cash payment was involved. Elsewhere, goods were demanded as a substitute for taxes. The kings of Mataram in Java, for example, distributed their household requisitions among villages, one supplying the king's coconut oil, another his fish, others his rice, and still others the fodder for his horses. These were highly particularistic, personal, and direct economic relationships. All along their course upward through the administrative and social hierarchy, the commodities were subject to the exactions of intermediary officials, so that many groups and individuals were linked by their passage, each in some way dependent on the other.

Some of the above goods were deliberately produced for export and were usually collected through the same administrative and revenue devices but also—and, in the eighteenth century, increasingly—commercially, in a much less particularistic and personal fashion. By that date, commercial agriculture had begun in two locales. In West Java, commercial sugar production began in the seventeenth century when Chinese entrepreneurs "leased" the labor of villages from local authorities and made the peasants grow sugar cane. They built small processing mills to extract the sugar and exported most of the product through the Dutch East India Company (VOC). In Vietnam, sugar was produced for export in provinces like Quang Nam, where the Internal Affairs Office or imperial household treasury purchased it by an exploitative operation, euphemistically known as "harmonious buying," in order to control its export.

Just as specifically, commodities for export were the products of mining operations in the region, especially the tin of the Malay Peninsula and the gold of western Borneo. The most valuable article of trade in the peninsular Malay states was alluvial tin. Dutch records for the seventeenth century describe the large trading expeditions of the Sultan of Kedah, carrying tin across the Bay of Bengal to the Coromandel Coast; in the course of that and the following century the Dutch made a determined effort to monopolize, by means of treaties with local rulers, the export of tin from Kedah, Phuket, Perak, Selangor, and Sungei Ujong. This monopoly was extended in 1755 to the island of Bangka, off the southern coast of Sumatra, after tin had been discovered there early in the century. The peninsular ore was worked for the most part by Malays, though communities of Chinese miners were known before 1800. The industry was controlled by members of the ruling families of the Malay states, either by direct ownership of the mines or by levying tribute on production and export. Encouragement was given to the tin trade in the 1780s by a shortage of tin in China, and prices remained inflated until beyond the end of the century. The Chinese gold mining in western Borneo began around the middle of the century. On a large scale—tens of thousands of Chinese miners are alleged, even for the eighteenth century—this was commercial production by independent frontier groups organized into their own *kongsi,* or working communities, which paid some of their yield in tax to the coastal sultans. Similarly, Spanish attempts at mid-century to develop iron mining in the Philippines were contracted to an entrepreneur who imported Chinese labor for the task. Such developments cut two ways—toward an economic division of labor between indigenous peoples and the Chinese and toward monopolistic policies aimed at keeping mining activity under strict control, particularly where (as in Burma) precious metals and gems were involved.

Generally, then, agricultural and imported commodities and the products of local mines entered the market and trading systems of Southeast Asia either laterally through direct barter trade between producer and consumer or vertically through administrative institutions, and only rarely through monetized commercial transactions. Though the quantities of goods traded within the region must have been considerable, a large proportion of them was traded in the village or market town by peddlers and merchants traveling inland individually and by Malay and Bugis traders along the coasts, rivers, and streams. In the absence of written records, such trade, by nature small-scale and local, is virtually inaccessible to the economic historian. It is only where international trade tied into the local economy that more distinct patterns come into view; in this situation, state trading monopolies (like that of Ayudhya, based on the export marketing of commodities obtained through tribute and taxes) and large-scale Chinese and European seaborne commerce developed. These may be conveniently viewed in terms of geographically defined trading networks, which everywhere touched, but rarely overshadowed, local commerce.

There were, first of all, systems of local and long-distance highland and hinterland caravan and peddling trade. Well-established caravan routes crisscrossed the interior of the mainland, stretching from northern Burma and Siam into Vietnam and South China and carrying hill cotton, tobacco, silver, and forest produce by pack horse, oxen, mule, and elephant to periodic markets in return for horses, salt, and silk. Among those engaged in this trade were Chinese, Shans, and other Tai peoples. In Burma, the main center of such trade was Bhamo, where Chinese caravans brought warm clothing, silks, and copperware in return for cotton. To the east, there was a substantial overland trade between Vietnam and China, directed mainly by China's need to obtain the silver of Vietnamese mines in order to offset the bullion drain caused by the import of opium. These well-organized trading systems made a considerable profit for the Burmese and Vietnamese courts.

Southeast Asia's seaborne trade with China took place within an ancient framework of international relations usually referred to as the Chinese tributary system. China in theory regarded itself as the suzerain of all the states of Southeast Asia, receiving homage from each at specified intervals, at which time the "vassal" states presented their tribute of local products and in return received from the emperor Chinese goods of equal or greater value. The tributary system in practice was a regular system of legitimizing official trade and, at an early date, accommodated private trade on the side, first by Southeast Asian traders and later by Chinese merchants. By the time of the Ming dynasty (1368–1644), the private trade was predominantly Chinese and far outweighed in volume and value the official exchange of goods in tribute and gifts.

On the Southeast Asian side, a large proportion of the goods involved in trade was both bought and sold by royal trading monopolies. The Siamese and Cambodian kings, for example, who collected in their royal warehouses large amounts of goods in lieu of taxes or by monopolies of production and marketing, depended on external trade with China for much of their revenues. Roughly one-fourth of the revenues of the court at Ayudhya came from the profits of the royal monopolies. Malay sultans marketed some pepper and tin in this fashion, and, where the system was best developed, as in Siam, an elaborate bureaucracy was created to run this trade, collecting in the provinces goods most salable on the Chinese market, processing and storing them, and arranging for the wholesaling of goods imported through the same channels. In time, the system was extended to include the building and staffing of ships, often by Chinese immigrants who had settled down in the country to engage in the trade. The existence of such organizations was a source of some strength to the Siamese government, though it did create a vested interest in the China trade as such, as well as monopolistic practices not readily tolerated by European trading interests.

The South China Sea network was the most extensive and elaborate in the region. Strung from the major ports of the China coast, it extended in two directions: the "western" route to Vietnam, Siam, and Malaysia, and the "eastern" route to the Philippine and Indonesian islands. The Chinese court was hostile to the growth of this trade, since Chinese shipbuilders and shipowners were the potential creators and owners of independent and politically uncontrollable navies. Although the Chinese court frequently attempted to ban such trade, Chinese ports continued to develop. In 1741, for example, it was pointed out that the ban then under reconsideration by the court would result in unemployment for more than 500,000 people in South China alone.

The word "junk," an English derivation from the Malay approximation of the Amoy pronunciation of the Chinese word *ch'uan,* "ship," itself aptly symbolizes the multicultural nature of the South China Sea trade. In 1821, the overseas Chinese in Siam operated a fleet of some 136 junks, of which 82 operated in the trade with China and 34 sailed to Vietnam, Malaya, and Java. The ports of Vietnam traded primarily with the South China ports, sending about 100 ships north each year. A great many junks traded to Manila with merchandise for two annual galleons sent from the Philippines to Mexico. These junks were manned by Chinese crews, often resident in the foreign countries to which they regularly sailed and generally remunerated by permission to load the junks with small cargoes of their own for trading at their destination. They became thereby modest shareholders in the venture.

Extending the length and breadth of the South China Sea, this essentially Chinese trade was quite comprehensive. The major Chinese exports carried south were such luxury goods as silk and porcelain. Southeast Asian ports depended on such imports and on an export market for a wide range of local commodities, ranging from foodstuffs, such as rice, to luxury articles, Chinese-desired medicinals and aphrodisiacs, jungle produce, and such exotic products as birds' nests. The southern end of the route, including the Straits of Malacca, Borneo, and the southern Philippines in particular, was a difficult region for trade because of the multiplicity of petty ports and small cargoes, which were often carried by single traders on small ships, resulting in small-scale, complex trading systems. But by the eighteenth century the Chinese, through diversification and even third-party trade, had built up an extremely important trade in the region of the South China Sea, upon which the Siamese court and the Manila government, as well as many smaller ports (Sulu's exportation of pearls and Timor's trade in sandalwood, for example), depended for a high proportion of their revenues.

Within the South China Sea trading network traders other than Chinese were widely active. Malay, Sulu, and Bugis traders in their small *perahu* handled much local trade among the islands in the south; Vietnamese and Siamese junks occasionally extended existing Chinese trading patterns. Both the local and long-distance traders worked to integrate and expand this trading network. At three points on the fringes of the South China Sea—Manila, Batavia, and the Straits of Malacca—it was tied into other trading systems.

One of the reasons for the Spanish conquest of the Philippines was that Manila was a natural entrepôt for the China trade. The lure of the China market and the ease with which Chinese junks could bring goods to Manila made it a waystation between China and the New World. Indeed, so much silver and Chinese silk were transshipped that the merchants in Spain soon forced the Madrid government to impose strict limits on the value and volume of the annual Manila galleon. The galleon trade, which lasted about 250 years, was carefully controlled so that it yielded enough to keep Manila financially afloat but not so much that it crippled Spanish home industries. Space in the galleon was divided into shares, or *piezas,* of a fixed size, and the Spanish community of Manila lived on the income from the sale of space to shippers. The Church supplied most of the capital to buy the Chinese goods, outfit the galleon, and tide the community over, and it received 30 to 50 percent in interest when the galleon returned. When a galleon was lost or captured, the colony was virtually bankrupt. In 1743, for example, when the British admiral Anson captured the *Nuestra Señora de Covadonga,* he seized about 1.5 million pesos in silver.

The impact of the galleon trade on the Philippines was stultifying. Since the colony was heavily dependent, and since the galleon siphoned off most available capital, there was little interest in developing the country internally. By the mid-eighteenth century, the rigid mercantilist restrictions of this quasi-monopoly inhibited the development of trade patterns with other Southeast Asian states. The ease with which the colony could survive encouraged torpor and, for better or worse, kept the Spanish, except for the priests, isolated and uninvolved. The various restrictions also created endemic corruption, since the myriad restrictions were more honored in the breach than in the observance. The frequency of proscriptions against violating the rules indicates the universality of the abuse.

Most of the coastal and interisland trade in the Philippines—including that between Manila and the Muslim sultanates to the south—was handled by the Chinese or Chinese *mestizos.* The Chinese residing in the Philippines also had close ties with firms in China. These traders imported, through the South China Sea trading system, Chinese, Indian, and Southeast Asian goods destined for transshipment on the galleon and required in the colony itself. In turn, they exported the silver bullion through the same channels. Although the Spanish community was heavily dependent on the profits of the galleon, relatively few Spanish merchants and traders lived in Manila. Political connections with the Distribution Board—controlling available galleon space— proved a more effective way to make money than trading on an open market. Widows and Church charities had automatic rights to shares, which they sold annually to the few merchants. The number of traders participating in the galleon steadily contracted as the advantages of money and connection drove the small trader out of business. In the middle of the eighteenth century, there was neither a free enterprise system of entrepreneurs nor a great trading company; the Chinese did the work and shared the profits with the Spanish.

A second trading network centered on Batavia (Jakarta), the Asian headquarters of the Dutch East India Company (Vereenigte Oost-Indische Compagnie, VOC). The VOC (1602–1799) was a many-sided, far-flung enterprise—a trading company that was also a state. It was an ancestor of modern Indonesia as well as a pillar of the Dutch state in the seventeenth and eighteenth centuries; it was also the founder of modern South Africa, a major actor in the history of Sri Lanka, and the agent of an important movement in early-modern Japanese intellectual history. Its home office was in Amsterdam, where its directors, the so-called *Heeren Seventien,* the Gentlemen Seventeen, exercised a general supervision over its trade and political policy, ordered goods for the home market, sent off consignments of goods and reinforcements of officials and troops in the outgoing fleets, received and sold the cargoes of the returning fleets, and paid the stockholders' dividends. In time, however, its activities in the East, centered on the governor-general's castle in Batavia, came increasingly to have a life of its own. The governors-general were appointed by the Gentlemen Seventeen, a circumstance that gave the VOC a bureaucratic stability not shared by the kingdoms and powers it dealt with. But once in Batavia, half a year's sail from Amsterdam and with full autocratic powers over all company servants east of the Cape of Good Hope, they had virtual autonomy. Inevitably they and their subordinates—like the officials and private traders of the English East India Company and like the captain-general and priests of the Spanish Philippines—accommodated themselves to the real world in which they operated, with its own opportunities, dangers, and historical patterns.

In the first century of its existence, up to about 1700, the VOC grew into the classic trading-post empire, carrying on a busy trade along all the coasts of the Indian Ocean and China Sea from a network of bases at Capetown, in Arabia and Persia, along the Indian coasts, in Burma, Siam, and Vietnam, on Formosa, and at Nagasaki in Japan. From the beginning, however, its interest was focused, and its successes greatest, in the seas of the Indonesian archipelago. Obsessed, like all European merchants of the time, with the cloves and nutmeg that grew only in the Moluccan Islands at the eastern end of the archipelago, the Dutch concentrated their naval power on these small places. By the middle of the century, they had subjected their sultans, destroyed or enslaved their peasants, and secured a virtually complete monopoly of production and trade of the precious spices. This, in turn, unhinged what had been a historical axis of trade running along the Java Sea from the Moluccas to the north-coast port-states of Java, from there to the entrepôt of Malacca and onward to India—a trade that had brought Indian textiles to Java, Javanese rice to the Spice Islands and Malacca, and the spices to the outside world in general. The north-coast states of Java were conquered in the 1620s by the inland state of Mataram. The Javanese traders, who had dominated the trade over the whole route, were driven out of business by the VOC, which also captured Malacca in 1641. The company extended its naval dominance in the 1660s and 1670s, reducing the major Islamic trading powers, such as Makassar, Bantam, and Aceh, to vassalage and imposing a great variety of restrictive commercial treaties on them and on lesser trading states along the whole Java Sea route. It could not monopolize the major products of the rest of the area—pepper from Sumatra and Borneo, tin from the Malay peninsula

—for they were too widely distributed and their producers too numerous, strong, or agile, and so other traders, such as the Chinese and English, continued to do a large business. Nor was the company either inclined or able to monopolize the trade in the great variety of forest and sea products coming out of the islands along the Java Sea. Archipelago peoples, such as the Bugis and Malays, continued a lively trade in these departments. By the late seventeenth century, however, the VOC was the paramount naval power from Aceh to the Moluccas, dominating trade in these waters, carrying all the lucrative cloves and nutmeg, half or more of the tin and pepper, and much else besides.

From its height in the late seventeenth century, the VOC's naval and trading power along the Java Sea and Straits of Malacca declined steadily in the course of the eighteenth century. Two factors stand out among the causes of this long decline at sea. One is that, from the 1670s on, the company was increasingly drawn into the affairs of Java, so that by 1757, if not earlier, it was lord of the whole island with its several million inhabitants. This development was in the long run fatal for the VOC as constituted and for the interests of the Gentlemen Seventeen at home, but the governors-general and their subordinates found it both easier and more profitable for themselves than the wearisome business of naval patrol and trade through the archipelago. This tendency was reinforced by the continuing vigor of the maritime peoples and Chinese traders of the area and by the steady rise of British naval power and commercial activity throughout the century. By the mid-eighteenth century, this process was already far advanced. The VOC was well on the way to transforming itself into a territorial rather than a naval power, and the trading world of the Java Sea routes was reverting to the more open and pluralistic pattern it had had in the early seventeenth century and before.

Finally, there extended into Southeast Asia from the west a trading network linking the ports of the Indian subcontinent with others on the eastern shore of the Bay of Bengal, notably the Burma ports of the Irrawaddy delta, Siam's ports on the isthmus of the Malay Peninsula, and Malay ports dotted along the western coast of the peninsula and the opposite shore of Sumatra. In an exchange well established many centuries earlier, when the Malay port of Malacca was considered richer than London, the chief commodities were Indian cloth; rice and teak ships from Burma; the local products of western Indonesia and Malaysia, especially pepper and tin; and products, like spices, gathered in the region of the Straits of Malacca from farther afield. In this trade, a wide variety of peoples and states were involved in competition, including European traders and trading companies; Gujeratis, Muslims, and Chulias from India; occasional Persians and Arabs; and a few Armenians and Syrians in Burma.

Probably the most important single element in the Bay of Bengal trade was the English East India Company (EIC). Like the Dutch com-

pany, the EIC was a semigovernmental trading corporation directed
from Europe. Unlike the Dutch, however, the EIC had virtually no territorial possessions in Southeast Asia in the mid-eighteenth century—
the single exception being the out-of-the-way trading post at Benkulen
on Sumatra's west coast. The company's major trading ports in India,
however, and its slow-developing trade with China stimulated the Bay
of Bengal trade generally. And, although the EIC itself conducted little
trade with Southeast Asian ports, English private merchants—"country
traders"—were particularly active in the Bay of Bengal. As their activities grew in importance and as the company's trade with China
increased, the EIC was slowly drawn into a more active role in Southeast Asia.

Of the trading groups that conducted this international trade
throughout Southeast Asia, the most widespread and important was the
overseas Chinese. A common explanation for their commercial ascen-
dance argues that their extended family organizations and kinship networks provided them with greater capital resources than any that
Southeast Asian traders could muster; yet among Southeast Asians the
Vietnamese had a similar kinship system without being able to withstand the competition of overseas Chinese merchants any more successfully than their neighbors. The commercial supremacy of the Chinese
was really based upon a variety of other factors.

History itself favored the overseas Chinese merchants, since the vast
commercial world of the mainland Chinese empire from which they
came antedated the economies of Southeast Asia in development and
transcended them in size and sophistication. The fact that overseas Chinese merchants still maintained relationships, familial and cultural,
with the South China trading communities of their ancestors gave them
an unchallengeable position as middlemen between the markets of their
homeland and those of Southeast Asia. Southeast Asian political elites
found it convenient to permit outsiders to manage international trade.
Chinese merchants were mobile, freed of compulsory labor, and located
by government policy and their own preference in port areas. Southeast
Asian governments found it desirable to restrict the contacts of their
people with foreigners and strange ideas, thereby insulating them from
a commercial frame of reference as well.

In general, then, outsiders, whether Chinese, Arabs, Indians, or
Europeans, were most active and widespread as traders in Southeast
Asia in the eighteenth century. This is not, however, to argue that they
remained an indigestible lump in the stomachs of Southeast Asian
societies. The contrary is true; the Chinese, for example, seem to have
assimilated to Thai, Cambodian, and Javanese society more completely
in the eighteenth century than they were to do in the twentieth. The
skills of the Chinese community were important in economic life and
some came increasingly to be appropriated or exploited by courts and
governments that lacked them. In the Philippines, where Chinese *mesti-*

*zos* retained a separate identity more than their counterparts in Siam, they slipped into entrepreneurial and commercial roles when economic opportunities presented themselves.

Many of the same considerations apply to the Arabs living throughout most of the archipelago. Whether or not—as traders—they were responsible for the spread of Islam, they certainly served to perpetuate contacts between Islamic Southeast Asia and the heartland of the faith, and they had a religious and economic status that enabled them to enter society at a higher level than that of indigenous traders. This was true of many outsiders in Southeast Asia, who thereby were often much more socially and geographically mobile than most of the populations in which they worked. The effect of such developments was that economic, commercial, and professional organizations and accomplishments created parallel to Southeast Asian societies could, through the integration or assimilation of individuals or institutions connected with them, be appropriated to the use of the indigenous society.

Even on an economic level, the West was by no means the dominant actor on the Southeast Asian stage in the eighteenth century, except in the Philippines and small Dutch-ruled portions of the East Indies. The trade it conducted and generated had wide ramifications, but it was not exclusively a European trade. Indeed, it depended upon Asian traders, as did the galleon trade in the Philippines. If peasants in interior villages bought or bartered for Indian cloth brought to the region by Dutch or English traders, the trader operated in the same fashion as his Indian or Arab predecessor. Outside the Philippines and western Java, Asian traders were much more active than Europeans, and Arab or Malay or Vietnamese cultural and political influence was immeasurably more significant than Western influence. There was apparent by the mid-century, however, a thrust to European commercial and political expansion that was beginning to draw more European attention to the region and to create conditions more favorable to the introduction of European political power. As European ambitions extended to the world and as European industrial development created capital and demanded Southeast Asian raw materials, the earlier commercial pattern in Southeast Asia was challenged by new political complications. Not all the eighteenth-century states of Southeast Asia were equally prepared to meet this new phenomenon, a challenge as much cultural and technological as political and economic, which strained Buddhist monarchies and Muslim sultanates no less than the colonial outposts of Spain and the Netherlands.

# 7

## The Buddhist Kings

THE Theravada Buddhist monarchies of mainland Southeast Asia were products of a period of political upheaval and cultural change, which followed the collapse of earlier Indianized empires, as Theravada Buddhism spread through the area between the eleventh and the fifteenth centuries. The most prominent of these, extending from the border regions of southwest China to the neck of the Malay Peninsula, were the monarchies in Ava in central Burma, in Phnom Penh in Cambodia, and in Ayudhya, north of present-day Bangkok.

From these states emanated magical authority and physical power, which diminished as distance from the capital increased, until their hold was too weak to secure the allegiance of remote principalities or until they encountered the power of a neighboring kingdom. In the less-populated areas on their fringes were lesser Buddhist states, the Shan and Lao states of northeastern Burma, northern and northeastern Thailand, and Laos. The power and independence of this second group of states over time rose and fell in inverse relation to the strength of the monarchies in Ava and Ayudhya.

The institution of the monarchy played an important role in Theravada Southeast Asia by providing a system of social and political authority, which overlapped and transcended the values of Buddhism. Indian and Buddhist theories of kingship blended with indigenous political patterns and with such techniques as tributary diplomacy, which may have been derived from China, to produce an institution unique to Southeast Asia. Although the monarchies of Laos, to be sure, would be recognizable to a Burmese, there were sharp differences from country to country that reflected the historical experience of each.

Hindu-Buddhist traditions of kingship, introduced into Southeast Asia by the seventh century A.D., saw the monarch as a repository of *karma,* or merit, linking the kingdom to the cosmos and as possessing, both in his person and in his office, a relationship to the invisible world by which his body and his actions were made sacred. The king's advisers fixed the dates of the calendar that regulated the agricultural year. The monarch was also the patron of Buddhism and the arts. Indian and Buddhist literature offered to rulers and subjects models for kingly behavior like the hero of the *Ramayana,* an Indian epic, whose graceful and ordained victory over evil symbolized the ideal behavior of the monarch.

By portraying his subjects as "dust under the royal feet" or "slaves of the lord," court language and its accompanying etiquette kept the ruler at a distance from others. Physically concealed behind the walls of his palace, the Buddhist monarch often found his capacity to influence events outside his entourage limited; in many cases, the historical records, composed at court, exaggerate the king's effectiveness and importance. Inside the palace, his actions were regulated by Brahman advisers, and his opinions were formed from conversations with favorites. Constricted by a costume that, in Burma, weighed more than fifty pounds, acting on information that was always secondhand and frequently false, and stifled by protocol, astrology, and precedent, the Buddhist monarch of eighteenth-century Southeast Asia was frequently a prisoner of his situation. Since the population often viewed the monarch as godlike, an imminent Buddha, Buddhist monarchs occasionally proclaimed themselves gods. Twice in eighteenth-century Siam and Burma monarchs were deposed for proclaiming this delusion.

The palace crowned the kingdom; its construction repeated the symbolic design of the Hindu cosmos. The monarchy provided the ultimate coherence for societies organized socially, politically, and linguistically on hierarchic lines, justifying by its existence the wisdom and permanence of that kind of organization.

## Ava

The Kingdom of Ava was heir to the Empire of Pagān. Between the tenth and thirteenth centuries, the kings of Pagān had united the territory that forms the core of modern Burma in a single Buddhist state organized on common cultural concepts and administered through a loosely structured protobureaucratic system based upon the economic strength of the rice-producing irrigated Kyaukse valley. Later dynasties built upon this system. The critical administrative and political links on which the unity and security of Ava depended were of a patron-client nature, especially the relationships between the governors of the individual provinces *(myo)* and the king. Ava's permanent armies were based around the capital. The manpower and tax resources of the kingdom were apportioned by the king to various princes, officials, and members of the royal family called *myo-sa*, as they were said to "eat" *(sa)* the province that provided them with their incomes. Royalty residing in the capital delegated authority to their own local clients in the provinces in return for taxes and labor extracted from the local inhabitants.

The chief function of the government at Ava was to maintain order and support the Buddhist faith through coordinating manpower usage and collecting taxes. The state bureaucracy was centered on a ministerial council, the *Hlutdaw,* which exercised executive and judicial authority for the king. No act of state was valid unless sanctioned by and registered with the *Hlutdaw*. Each of the four chief ministers, or *wun-gyi,* had his own distinct but often overlapping sphere of operation. To assist them, the *wun-gyi* had large staffs of officers, including messengers, clerks, heralds, marshals, surveyors, and registrars of oaths, in addition to men responsible for public works. Control over state finances was reserved to the king through his privy council, the *byè-daik,* which was composed of four "inside ministers," *atwin-wun.* Palace affairs also were in their hands, and they often enjoyed status and sometimes authority greater than that of the *Hlutdaw.* Numerous other officers, however, operated more or less independently of both *Hlutdaw* and *byè-daik* and had their major contacts directly with the king in audience. This seems particularly true of the regiments of the regular army and the royal bodyguard, which provided the military might of the regime and the king's intelligence agents who checked on the activities of other officials.

In Burma, as elsewhere in Buddhist Southeast Asia, the rules governing succession to the throne were difficult to enforce because of the large number of aspirants. Royal polygamy made the development of a simpler tradition of primogeniture difficult. Because the *myo-sa* system created strong ties between princes and different elements of the capital bureaucracy and provincial towns, the political order was subject to fragmentation of power upon the death of a monarch. The authority of successor kings often was weakened by the rival schemes of their uncles and brothers. Competing sets of ministers in the *Hlutdaw* and *byè-daik* and military officers with their own sources of manpower, as well as a multitude of princes entering into direct relations with nobles and officers, made for fissiparous tendencies which militated against strong central control of the kingdom as court politics came to dominate the concern of monarchs often to the neglect of larger affairs of state.

From the collapse of the empire of Pagān in 1289 to the sixteenth century, the region now called Burma was divided among several contending political centers, each representing a variation of the Buddhist state form created at Pagān but expressing itself in a different language. The Mon speakers in the south, linguistically akin to the Cambodians or Khmer, centered on Pegu. The rulers of this state resisted incorporation into any greater state centered in the north until the middle of the sixteenth century. For three hundred years after the fall of Pagān, northern Burma was dominated by petty Tai-speaking princes from the contiguous Shan plateau who were never able to overcome local forces until Tabinshwehti, the Burmese ruler of Toungoo, conquered both the north and the south between 1539 and 1555.

The initial Toungoo dynasty's empire was not, however, particularly stable. Tabinshwehti and his immediate successors failed to create a sufficiently strong administrative system to keep in check separatist tendencies fueled by conflicting interests and rival symbols of identity. They eventually reestablished the central state in the north, at Ava, near the rice supplies of the Kyaukse region, which had been the economic heart of the Pagān empire. Despite its inland location, the Kingdom of Ava conducted considerable trade overseas across the Bay of Bengal as well as northward into China. The Restored Toungoo dynasty, which took control at the beginning of the seventeenth century and ruled for another 150 years, took advantage of this these trade resources in order to construct a more elaborate and effective administrative order. Recognizing that military might alone does not make a lasting political order, great efforts were extended in the direction of reform but by 1752 central dominance had given way to particularist forces and the Toungoo dynasty fell.

## Ayudhya

The Kingdom of Ayudhya was founded in 1351 as a petty Tai principality on the edge of the Cambodian empire centered at Angkor. Within a century, it had reduced its eastern rival to a shadow of its former self, while extending outward in all directions. The Ayudhyan monarchy borrowed heavily from Cambodian models in order to enhance the magical dignity and authority of the crown, to make of it a symbol capable of commanding at least the fear, if not the respect, of the culturally and racially mixed populations that fell under its control. Its administrative and political institutions resembled those of Burma in many respects.

Ayudhya was only fifty-five miles from the sea, connected to it by a stretch of the Čhaophraya River. It was a cosmopolitan city of many peoples and a wide variety of ideas. From its foundation, it was visited by merchants from China and the Middle East, and its distant contacts were maintained throughout its 400-year existence. The kings of Ayudhya thought of themselves partly in international terms. For example, King Naresuan in 1593 offered to assist the Chinese empire by attacking Japan, and King Narai in the 1680s was sufficiently attracted to European ideas and techniques to appoint a Greek adventurer, Constantine Phaulkon, as his prime minister (replacing the grandson of a Persian immigrant). The Thai sent tribute to the Chinese emperor, yet they never were so constrained by that relationship that they failed to see the opportunities of alternative arrangements.

As at Ava, the court of Ayudhya was the center of the cultural life of the kingdom. In addition to its specialized bureaucracy, the Thai court maintained a full compliment of artists, performers, and craftsmen, who filled the city with carvings, statues, monuments, and a succession of dramatic and musical performances. Talented poets and dancers, wherever found, were brought into the court or the households of high officials, who took pride in their writers-in-residence and dramatic troupes. Buddhism flourished under the patronage of the court; the hundreds of monasteries in and near the capital were major centers of secular as well as religious learning. The diffusion of the literary and

scholastic writings of the capital into the provincial towns and even villages suggests that, at least by the eighteenth century, the culture and
language of the kingdom were becoming increasingly uniform.

The Thai kingdom was run by a quasi-hereditary class of nobles
dominated increasingly by a small group of families. The functions of
government were concentrated in a single body of high officials, the six
*senabodi,* who were ministers of state. Although the administrative system laid down in the fifteenth century envisaged ministers each carrying out specialized tasks throughout the kingdom, four of the six ministers of the eighteenth century in effect ran omnibus ministries, carrying
out a full range of governmental functions in particular geographical
areas—the *kalahom* in the south and west, the *mahatthai* in the north and
east, the *phrakhlang* in the provinces at the head of the Gulf of Siam, and
the *krom müang* in the districts immediately surrounding the capital.
Each ministry collected taxes, administered law courts, constructed
public works, and attempted to maintain order, yet each retained some
vestige of its original functions—the professional army and mercenaries
remained under the *kalahom,* the *mahatthai* kept the elephant corps and
various specialized civil departments, the *phrakhlang* was still the treasurer of the court and conducted its foreign trade and foreign relations,
and the *krom müang* policed the capital. The ministries of lands *(krom na)*
and the palace *(wang)* were less favored ministries performing specialized functions.

Centralized administration was an accomplished fact in the kingdom of Ayudhya. This was undertaken among the provinces of the
Čhaophraya River valley in order to ensure the military security of the
kingdom. To withstand Burmese and Cambodian invasions, successive
kings had found it necessary to strengthen their control over nearby
provinces and to gain their resources of manpower. Farther afield, primarily in peninsular Siam but also in the southeastern provinces bordering Cambodia, the extension of central control over provincial
administration responded to the increasing importance of those areas in
international trade. For example, local ruling dynasties and families in
the provinces of the south—Nakhọn Si Thammarat, Phattalung, and
Songkhla—were replaced by governors sent from Ayudhya during the
seventeenth century, when the economic importance of that region
increased with a rise in international trade.

The court of Ayudhya was relatively stable in the seventeenth and
eighteenth centuries, primarily because of the relationship between the
king and his nobles. The Siamese practice of minimizing direct relations between the princes and the nobles undoubtedly reduced political
temperatures considerably. Succession contests usually concerned only
a small number of candidates and rarely resulted in the slaughter of the
losers, which at times was an element of Burmese succession. Political
conflicts in Siam tended to reflect the competition of major noble families for power more than royal preoccupations and infighting. The

nobles were the real element of continuity in the system, single families continuing for as many as seven generations with a member in a ministerial position. The nobles put and kept kings on the throne, and kings maintained the substance of royal power only by carefully manipulating public appointments so as to balance the noble families against each other or by bringing in others to compete with them. Royal rule was a delicate business for high stakes, not to be indulged in lightly by ambitious amateurs, and for the loser there was only the velvet sack into which he was put to be ceremonially beaten to death with sandalwood clubs.

From the sixteenth century on, the Siamese and Burmese courts were preoccupied with each other's affairs. They were bitter competitors and mortal enemies in a war that, with some silences, lasted over three centuries. Each king was jealous of his own prestige and mindful of the importance of repute in holding together an extensive empire. An event, act, or gesture at court that could be interpreted as a sign of weakness might lead to the defection of enough provinces and tributary vassals to bring about the downfall of the empire. The kings solicited vassals, promising them protection from other powers. In return, they demanded loyalty and assistance, as well as regular and substantial tokens of submission, such as the gold and silver ornamental trees regularly received in Ayudhya from the Malay sultanates of the peninsula and the northern and eastern Lao states. To the rulers of such second-level states, it was a complex world indeed. They had to measure carefully the strength of all their neighbors, taking the greatest care to avoid offending dangerous enemies and useful friends. It was not unusual to find in the Lao and Shan world of the north, on the Malay Peninsula, or in Cambodia what the Thai called a "two-headed bird" looking in two directions at once, paying tribute to both its neighbors.

## Phnom Penh

In the seventeenth and eighteenth centuries, Siamese and Vietnamese territorial expansion, to the east and south, respectively, had the effect of drastically reducing the area under Cambodian control. The pressure of its neighbors, principally by reducing sources of revenue, loosened the power of the Cambodian court. By the middle of the eighteenth century, the court was small, fractured, and institutionally brittle; its members and their clients were engrossed in the politics of personal and dynastic survival. In order to survive or to overthrow one another, royal or bureaucratic factions sought support wherever they could find it, especially from Ayudhya and Hue but also from regional leaders and minority groups. The prices paid to the neighboring states were large, in terms of territory, tribute, and the loss of freedom, and the size of the political debts incurred by each new monarch on his way to the throne frequently crippled his capacity to rule. As Cambodia's territory shrank along with the availability of manpower for warfare and production, so too did the range of options available to the court and to factions seeking to overthrow it. A "Vietnamese" or a "Siamese" monarch would assume the throne in Cambodia, surrounded by advisers helpfully provided by his patron state. Perhaps motivated by patriotism, and in any case without an alternative, the king's rivals would then seek help from the power not responsible for his accession.

The Cambodian court in the eighteenth century must be studied with this background firmly in mind. The court had little leisure in which to act out its traditional role. Cut off from access to the sea by Sino-Vietnamese adventurers who controlled the coast and by the Vietnamese who were migrating into the formerly Cambodian Mekong delta, the court was also isolated both from outside observers and from the benefits and hazards of extensive foreign trade.

The king's revenue, such as it was, came from a 10 percent tax levied on all rice production, as well as from a monopoly of both export and import trade and supervision of the production of (and internal trade in) products within the kingdom like lumber, dried fish, and hides. The king also received one-third of all legal fines (one-third went to the judge and the rest to the party winning the case). Royal expenditures were light, since goods and services commandeered by the palace were seldom paid for.

In the late seventeenth century, a Cambodian king married a Malay, took the name of Ibrahim, and embraced Islam. Assassinated by his nephew, he reappears in later Cambodian literature as the "king who left religion." In a less publicized case, a prince in the 1740s was secretly converted to Catholicism by a Bavarian missionary he had befriended. Either event would have been unthinkable at a more stable Buddhist court, and both indicate the kinds of looseness, or perhaps the tensions, that characterized the Cambodian court throughout this period,

Eighteenth-century Cambodian legal documents stress that deference was due to the monarch, but they indicate by many of the cases they recount that hierarchic restraints maintaining distance between the people and members of the royal family frequently broke down. One case relates that a monarch, out hunting in this period, strayed into a field and jostled a buffalo tender. Not recognizing the king, the tender addressed him angrily as "you." Relating the story later to his ministers, who accompanied the king on expeditions of this sort astride saddled oxen, the monarch boasted that it was proof of his great *karma,* or merit, that he had not killed the buffalo tender for his breach of courtesy. His ministers disagreed. What the story meant, they told him, was that the king had little business outside his palace, where etiquette was properly observed.

It should be stressed, however, that from the peasant's point of view the primary function of the Cambodian king was to enact, as in a dance, the moral victories appropriate to a monarch as reflected in classic and popular stories. Secondarily, the king was patron of the agricultural year. Each spring, as in Ayudhya and Ava, he plowed a ceremonial furrow on the palace grounds, initiating the agricultural cycle throughout the kingdom. In November, he held ceremonies to mark the end of the rainy season. His patronage of Buddhism and his enormous fund of *karma* were other aspects of the monarch's "image" for his people. In times of crisis, such as famine or invasion, villagers built models of his palace out of sand, attempting to gain for themselves the harmony with sky, earth, and under-earth that the king commanded.

## The Lao and Shan World

Compared to their neighbors, the mountain-valley states of the Buddhist Lao and Shan areas across the northern edge of mainland Southeast Asia were indeed petty principalities with small populations and limited wealth and power. They had personal links between one valley and the next and were much less affected by the state symbolism common to the more heavily Indianized world to the south. The Shans and Chiang Mai took pride in their more rigorous Buddhism and expressed disdain for the court Brahmanism of Ayudhya; however, their own symbolic "magic" was localized and politically less efficient.

The most common form of political and administrative organization in the northern states was based on a hierarchy of five princes or chiefs, the topmost being the ruler of the principality—its *chaomüang* or *sawbwa* or "Lord of Life." Each of the five had his own separate domain of districts or households providing him with taxes, products, and labor services, and each had his own separate administration to deal with them. This highly personal system worked well in small mountain valleys with limited populations, developing personal relationships into a framework that was as much a social as an administrative hierarchy.

Ava and Ayudhya followed different policies in dealing with the Shan and Lao states nearest them. Ava posted its own troops with officers to supervise the local rulers in the Shan states for more than 150 years. In this way they ensured control of the line of succession and helped to ensure that power was not consolidated against the court. Ayudhya, on the other hand, because it rightly feared Burmese ambitions in the area, was more defensive in its dealings with its northern neighbors. It encouraged the consolidation of the Lao states under their own leaders and for the most part confined its dealings with those states to diplomatic missions.

In the first half of the eighteenth century, both Ava and Ayudhya were too preoccupied with court politics and internal affairs to pay much attention to their vassal fringes. Ava faced serious raids from Manipur, on its northwest frontier, and then a Mon rebellion in the south. Confident that the Burmese were no longer a threat to their security, the kings of Ayudhya could afford to relax efforts to maintain good relations with

the Shan and Lao. The effects of the withdrawal of both these powers
were readily apparent. Chiang Mai rebelled against its Burmese governor in 1728 and soon entered into friendly relations with rebellious
Pegu. The ancient kingdom of Lan Sang in Laos disintegrated on the
death of King Suliyavongsa without heir in 1698 and split into three
small kingdoms, each ruled by distant claimants to the throne, in Luang
Prabang, Vientiane, and Champassak. Furthermore, even within the
orbits of these principalities, district and provincial towns resisted the
authority of their overlord, as the constant warfare of Lamphun, Lam-
pang, and Chiang Mai shows. Legitimacy was lacking, as was authority
that could transcend an individual claimant to a throne or one of a
group of towns. In a situation of great complexity, when the future and
intentions of Ava and Ayudhya were in doubt, no new order was possible until the great monarchies again could define and order the tributary systems that made sense of and to the Lao and Shan principalities.

# 8

## The Vietnamese Emperors

IF one dominant feature of the premodern history of mainland Southeast Asia was the cultural variety of its royal despotisms, the Vietnamese monarchy stood at the opposite end of the spectrum from the Ava and Ayudhya monarchs. The imported political theories which it attempted to apply in Southeast Asia had originated in China, not India.

The Vietnamese people today trace themselves back to a medley of about fifteen tribal groups, known as the Lac Viet, who inhabited northern Vietnam from the beginning of the bronze age. These tribes' leaders created a kingdom called Van-lang, which evidently ended in the third century B.C., but not before it had established the tradition of an independent agrarian polity in the Red River valley. The limited but significant Sinicization of the Vietnamese people began during the more than one thousand years of rule over northern Vietnam by the empire of China, from the second century B.C., to the tenth century A.D. In those ten centuries, the system of ethical and political doctrines we call Confucianism, based upon the teachings of the Chinese philosopher Confucius (551–479 B.C.), spread among upper-class Vietnamese scholars. Some Vietnamese students even represented the "protectorate of the pacified south," or "Annam" (as its medieval Chinese rulers condescendingly called Vietnam) in schools in the Chinese capital city itself.

Vietnam broke away from Chinese rule in the tenth century. By the eleventh century, the first major independent Vietnamese dynasty (the Ly dynasty, 1010–1225) had established what it regarded as its own "Great Viet" *(Dai Viet)* domain. This "Great Viet" kingdom had a capital city, Thang-long, where Hanoi is now; its own civil service examination system (A.D. 1075), increasingly based upon the Confucian classics; and its own national college for training Confucian scholars (A.D. 1076). The two major dynasties which followed the Ly (the Tran dynasty, 1225–1400, and the Lê dynasty, 1427–1788) strengthened the Ly tradition of building a Vietnamese kingdom upon Confucian principles, but with an extraordinary determination as they did so not to compromise Vietnamese independence. As one minor fourteenth-century Vietnamese ruler said, speaking for more important Vietnamese rulers ever since, "northern" (Chinese) and "southern" (Vietnamese) cus-

toms were different; blind imitativeness of China would "breed disorder."

Confucianism meant that the family and lineage were the foundation
of Vietnamese life and thought to a greater degree, in formal ideological
terms, than in any other Southeast Asian country. In theory, patrilineal
relatives could not marry each other. (But since there were intermar-
riages among the royal family during the Tran dynasty, we must not
exaggerate the maturity of Vietnamese Confucianism in the early medieval period.) Vietnamese worshipped their ancestors, with incense, rice
wine, betel, prayers, and obeisances, on the anniversaries of their
deaths and on other family occasions. The ancestral cult was designed
to keep the family united as an eternal corporation and to supply each
family with a gallery of paragons from the past whose memory might
improve the behavior of the living.

The political essence of the Confucian behavior Vietnamese rulers
wished their people to follow in the eighteenth century is revealed in
"The Forty-Seven Rules for Teaching and Changing" the people,
which the Lê court published in 1663 and reissued in 1760. The court
directed local officials to expound these rules to the "ignorant" men and
women of the villages. The rules asked family heads to regulate their
families by their own model comportment, which their children were
required to imitate, and to teach their children proper ethics "from
morning to night." Social order, therefore, was based upon persistent
ideological conditioning more than upon laws administered by the
state. Parents were the front line of defense of all political and educational authority. Pious children had to abstain even from publicly
uttering their parents' personal names, as a sign of respect. Not surprisingly, filial piety was the subject of the second "rule." It was the
supreme Confucian virtue, not merely one among others as elsewhere
in Southeast Asia. It required that children care for their parents when
they were old and make recurrent sacrifices to them after they died.
Rules three and nine also commanded younger brothers to respect older
brothers and not, even if they were wealthier than their older brothers,
presumptuously to claim equal status with them and thereby violate the
family age hierarchy. The point here was that informal relations among
brothers could be tense: in this property-conscious society there was no
formal doctrine of primogeniture. Rules four, eleven, twelve, and thirteen all anxiously dealt with the awkward position of wives in a patriar-
chal society in which brides not only married into their husbands' families, but owed their husbands' parents greater ritual obligations, when
they died, than they owed their own parents. The Lê monarchs
enjoined wives to obey their husbands, to become chaste and enduring
widows when their husbands died, and to cherish the children of their
husbands' concubines as if they were their own. Most such rules were
elaborations of the "three bonds" *(tam cuong)*: the loyalty of ministers to
their emperor, the obedience of children to their parents, the submission

of wives to their husbands. The "three bonds" were the social sacraments of late traditional Vietnam.

Significantly, the emperor's duties were hardly described in the forty-seven Lê government rules, for the optimistic fiction upon which the emperor's power rested was that he was already a morally perfect being who taught others. Heaven had commanded him to organize and instruct a harmonious political and social order which supposedly reflected an immanent cosmic plan. As a "Son of Heaven," the Vietnamese emperor was less august than an Indic god-king. If catastrophic storms or more human forms of disorder wrecked peasants' livelihoods, he faced the danger that ambitious men might clamorously suggest that he had lost his virtue, and with it the "mandate of Heaven." Even the most admired Vietnamese rulers, such as the founder of the Lê dynasty, believed that they had to install lowly officials known as censors, privileged complainers who were authorized to rebuke the ruler (and other officials) if the court's taxes became excessive or the court otherwise violated "ancient laws." Pretending to sagehood rather than divinity, the emperor tried to bring his government into as much visible conformity as he could with the ideals expressed in the Confucian classics, and in so doing preserve the indivisibility of the two processes of administration and moral indoctrination (*chinh giao*). As in other Southeast Asian political systems, stability was prized far more highly than liberty. Even the Tayson brothers, who gathered together the biggest peasant rebellion premodern Vietnam ever saw, announced originally that their purpose was to bring Vietnam from "disorder" to "order" by means of a "great peace" that would simulate the golden age of sagely rulers of a distant past.

In practice, the grandiose theory of monarchy Vietnam imported from China did not preclude strife or Vietnamese breaches and modifications of the theory's standards. The Lê emperors enjoyed real power for only about one century. After 1527, they were eclipsed by various lesser dynasties of regionally based rulers who in effect subdivided the Lê emperor's authority but could not permanently remove the Lê imperial house itself. In the eighteenth century, therefore, the Lê emperors continued to exist and to cling to an ossifying prestige, but Vietnam was really governed not by them but by the Trinh lords in the north and by the Nguyen lords in what is now central Vietnam. The Trinh and Nguyen lords (*chua*) created their own parallel courts and civil services. They fought a long, inconclusive struggle with each other for the absolute right to rule Vietnam. The failure of any one dynastic house to impose a politically satisfying unity upon Vietnam between 1528 and 1802 meant that the eighteenth century was haunted by a notable crisis of authority. Why was such fragmentation the fate of the Chinese imperial framework in Vietnam? There were possible structural reasons. Except in southern Vietnam from the end of the 1700s, Vietnam did not have a large landlord class, similar to the one in China, whose members' collective self-interest so strongly surpassed all local interests that they might have supported and financed a more continuously powerful imperial court. But there are also cultural factors, such as the resistance to overly lofty political pretensions which is embedded in everything from Vietnam's court literature to its village jokes. Anonymous poets had an endearingly Vietnamese tendency to deflate the mystique of even admired rulers, such as the greatest emperor the Lê dynasty produced, by depicting them in affectionately vulgar symbolism as rough-skinned but clever toads.

The Vietnamese emperor, and the Trinh and Nguyen lords, presided over a more bureaucratic government, in theory at least, than could be found elsewhere in Southeast Asia. It had functional specialization, as in the six government ministries (usually known as the Six Boards or *luc bo*) that divided among them such tasks, in the following order, as appointments of government officials; the collection of taxes and management of government finances; the administration of schools, examinations, and foreign relations, all regarded as "rituals"; the supervision of the armed forces; the administration of justice; and the construction of palaces, town walls, roads, and river dikes. This government also demoted officials who were found incompetent in periodic ratings tests. It forbade officials to serve in their home areas, on the grounds that they could not be objective administrators of localities in which they owned property. It operated on the basis of printed guidebooks and instructions, Vietnam having domesticated Chinese-style woodblock printing at least since the early fifteenth century. Above all, the government was composed of a peculiarly status-conscious group of scholar-officials whom Westerners have habitually called "mandarins." Not a hereditary nobility, scholar-officials were recruited through written examinations.

In the eighteenth century, examinations might occur at two levels: regional qualifying examinations, held every three years, and more important final examinations held at the courts of the Trinh or Nguyen lords. The Vietnamese students armed with writing brushes and paper who assembled in small tents for their examinations might have to pass multistage tests during which they were required to write classical Chinese poetry or answer "policy questions" related to historical statecraft. Under the Nguyen lords, after 1740, students who passed only the first stage received exemption from corvée for five years, but they could not receive government positions unless they passed all stages. The ultimate ambition of literate Vietnamese males was to become a member of the small, privileged elite of mandarins. (There were probably about 3,500 civil officials in northern Vietnam in the early 1700s.) Passing examinations was called the "big graduation"; marrying a wife was merely the "small graduation." In the villages, labor-exempt degree-holders formed "orthodox culture" *(tu van)* associations. Such associations held periodic sacrifices at small Confucian shrines and administered "studies fields" whose harvests paid for village teachers or for the education of poor village youths, although the cost of a mandarin's education remained prohibitively high for most peasants. After 1750, the cash-starved courts of the north sold access to the examinations and allowed rich students to hire professional scribes to write examinations for them. But even these abuses failed to weaken the villages' pride in having winners in the examinations. The lives and accomplishments of mandarins absorbed the Vietnamese imagination. Medieval poets symbolized scholar-officials variously as betel palms (which sheltered other people and were not easily uprooted); as watermelons (the redness of whose insides was believed to suggest loyalty); and as banyan trees (a worshipped presence in most villages, referring here to poorer scholars not in office who taught in village schools and commanded small associations of disciples). An individual eighteenth-century Vietnamese mandarin might see himself as reliving the honorable but melancholy life of Confucius, as did Nguyen Nghiem (1708–1775), the father of Vietnam's greatest poet.

Yet however much they may have borrowed from China, Vietnamese courts and their mandarins kept a Vietnamese soul. As one example, the greatest of all premodern Vietnamese law codes—the one in effect in the sixteenth, seventeenth, and eighteenth centuries—was influenced by Chinese law but treated women more generously than Chinese legal codes, in accord with the traditions of a Southeast Asian society whose women had on rare occasions been major politicians or writers. The Lê court's code allowed daughters to inherit family property almost equally with sons. It insisted that matrimonial property, instead of being incorporated into the husband's estate, be managed on a basis of equality between spouses. No such legal principles could be found in China.

Equally important, Confucianism, with its rich humanism and its love of booklearning, helped give Vietnam a history-addicted scholar class whose members were resolved to keep alive the terrible memories of past Chinese invasions of Vietnam, all of which had failed after the tenth century. The most noteworthy of these failed invasions had been Ming China's attempt to recreate the old "protectorate of Annam" by a military occupation of northern Vietnam, between 1407 and 1427. Lê Loi, the ultimate founder of the Lê dynasty, had led a Vietnamese resistance movement which heroically defeated this Chinese army and forced it to leave. And in the eighteenth century, the most formidable philosopher and historian living in Vietnam, Lê Quy Don (1726–1784), not only taught a self-consciously independent Vietnamese Confucianism, but also preached the evils of past Chinese imperialism. In one of his masterworks, a geographical history of central Vietnam written in 1776 and so vivid that it describes even the types of fishes swimming in the Perfume River at Hue, Lê Quy Don recalled unsparingly the miseries of Ming China's short rule over Vietnam: the corrupt Chinese officials, the abominable interference in the lives of the peasants, the stripped Vietnamese oyster beds, the hills raped for their gold, the looting of Vietnamese ivory and spices, the deceitful enticements and detentions of Vietnamese intellectuals, and the "unanimous" resentment of the Vietnamese people.

Ironically, by the second half of the eighteenth century, Vietnam itself had become an expansionist power, at the expense of neighboring peoples like the Lao and the Khmer whom Vietnamese courts regarded as being outside proper Confucian civilization. The long Vietnamese duel with the Indianized Cham people of central Vietnam had ended with the destruction of the Cham kingdom by 1697. The Chams became an ethnic underclass within the expanding Vietnamese kingdom. The Nguyen lords and their agents—including the leaders of Chinese refugees who had fled from China to what is now southern Vietnam between 1679 and 1708 as "Ming loyalists" who could not bear the fall of that dynasty in their Chinese homeland—now pushed even further south. By about 1760, they had absorbed from a troubled Cambodia the six Mekong delta provinces which the French were to know as Cochinchina. Vietnamese history textbooks today describe this southward advance as the "task of opening up empty lands."

But now Vietnamese rulers could no longer control the small landowning peasants and tenant farmers who composed the majority of Vietnam's own population. Their lives had sunk to dangerous levels of poverty, partly because of the conscription and taxes the Trinh and Nguyen lords had imposed on them in their long confrontation with each other. Among the many ambitious rebels who offered a political transformation, the most important were three brothers, known to us— from the name of their hamlet in south central Vietnam—as the Tayson brothers. They began a revolt in 1771. Preaching the equality of rich and poor, the Taysons redistributed the movable property (food and money) of hostile mandarins to the peasants and burned government tax registers. Spanish Franciscan missionaries who were eyewitnesses reported that the Vietnamese people greeted the Taysons as "virtuous and charitable thieves." They were also brilliant soldiers. Leading armies composed at various times of peasants, cattle dealers, petty clerks, Chams, Chinese, mountain Sedang, and even some scholars, the Taysons swept through the villages like a long overdue nemesis and smashed the old political system. With the Lê and Trinh dynastic houses in ruins, the most intelligent Tayson brother proclaimed himself Quang-trung emperor in December 1788. Quang-trung then proceeded to defeat the large army that the emperor of China, responding to all the turmoil, had sent into north Vietnam against him.

With this extraordinary man, about whose character the Vietnamese have hotly debated ever since, Vietnam's preeminent century of peasant unrest reached its climax and its end. Quang-trung's fertile and restless brain seems to have dreamed of inventing a new sort of Vietnamese kingdom. He ruled largely through military officers. But he revived archaic Chinese government titles, of the age when Confucius had lived, and his utopian advisers urged him to experiment with a more classically feudal government based upon enfeoffed relatives rather than bureaucrats, on the grounds that this was the way the ancient kings of China had most successfully resisted political chaos. Quang-trung also tried to compel all Vietnamese peasants to carry identity cards, with the slogan "the great trust of the empire" imprinted on them. This was evidently to be the prelude to mass mobilization for an invasion of southern China and the political reconstruction of the region under Tayson auspices. Surprising as this may sound, political boundaries which the twentieth century takes for granted were not accepted so unthinkingly in eighteenth-century Southeast Asia; and Vietnam could probably have matched the size of the Manchu armies that had conquered China the century before. Quang-trung, who actually allied himself with secret societies inside China, apparently dreamed of reestablishing the unity of a second century B.C. "Southern Viet" *(Nam Viet)* kingdom which had included Kwangtung and Kwang-si as well as northern Vietnam and which had tried to hold out against the permanent unification of what became the great Chinese empire. Just what would have become of this Vietnamese political and military explorer of near Napoleonic temperament if he had not died suddenly in 1792 we do not know. Quang-trung left behind him memories which excite some Vietnamese even now. But he failed to bequeath the Viet-namese people a solid new dynasty like the ones that had recently been created in Burma and Siam.

# 9

## The Malay Sultans

WHILE the eighteenth-century states of mainland Southeast Asia are recognizable today, those of island Southeast Asia (including the Malay Peninsula, which, brute geography aside, belongs for most historical purposes among the "islands") are not. The eighteenth-century Spanish colony of the Philippines, somewhat expanded, is the ancestor of the present Philippine Republic, but two hundred years ago there was no such thing as Malaysia or Indonesia. Instead, across this great arc of islands there was a bewildering variety of societies and political structures. To begin with, there were the innumerable small stateless societies of hunters and swidden cultivators found mostly in the interiors of the islands throughout the archipelago. Then, in the string of islands east of Java were two lively survivors from earlier historical eras: Bali, the last heir of the age of Hindu-Buddhist states in Southeast Asia, and Portuguese Timor, with its small Catholic *mestizo* community, as fiercely independent of Lisbon as it was exceptional among its Muslim and pagan neighbors. In addition, there were those rather anomalous powers, the Dutch and English East India companies, states of a sort but in any case armed merchants who exerted political influence along the seaways and in the ports of most of the archipelago. There were also two large and comparatively homogeneous societies, containing the only sizable concentrations of population in the islands: the Catholic Philippines, under Spanish rule, and Java, which in the mid-eighteenth century was largely controlled by the Dutch company.

Finally, and most characteristic of island Southeast Asia as a whole, were the Malayo-Muslim sultanates and chiefdoms of the coasts and rivers. The Muslim societies and states of the archipelago differed considerably among themselves. Java was a case apart, for its coastal sultanates had been overwhelmed in the seventeenth century. The relatively large wet-rice-cultivating populations of the Bugis and Makassarese in southwestern Celebes and of the Minangkabau heartlands in west-central Sumatra were also distinct in some respects. But even these two societies shared much of the common pattern of the Malayo-Muslim polities spread widely throughout the eastern archipelago—in Mindanao, the Sulu islands, the Moluccas, and some of the islands east of Bali—and concentrated more densely in the western archipelago along the coasts of the Malay Peninsula, Sumatra, Borneo, and on the small islands in the vicinity. The western archipelago, which for convenience may be called the Malay world, was the historical home of the Malayo-Muslim pattern, and in the mid-eighteenth century its numerous states still best exemplified that tradition.

Much of the Malay world was inhospitable to human settlement. Tropical, covered in dense rain forest, often mountainous, fringed by mangrove swamp, its soils leached by heat and torrential rain, the area offered little encouragement to extensive habitation. Only the rivers, with which the coastlines were deeply and frequently incised, made it possible, given available technology, to develop complex polities. Movement across the grain of the country was virtually impossible, and communications were therefore nonexistent except up into the headwaters of usually independent river systems or along the seaways of the coast.

These circumstances shaped the social, political, and economic structures that developed in the Malay world. They were rivermouth societies, for the most part, centered on port towns lying where the river debouched into the sea, placed so as to control what came down and to participate in what passed by. The political power, the "state" or *negeri,* at the mouth of the river, sought to establish sufficient authority over the peoples upriver and, in the interior, to ensure a flow of produce that could be taxed or sold. At the same time, it engaged in a complex power game with other rivermouth *negeri* in the area to take advantage of international trade and thus to increase or maintain its wealth. State boundaries tended to be vague and relatively unimportant, for what mattered was control of waterborne traffic, not land. The scale of political organization these activities either permitted or required was small in comparison to that of the great deltaic and agrarian states of the mainland and Central Java. Although from time to time concentrations of power were built up—systems of suzerainty, dependence, hegemony, alliance, and even commercial empire—they were vulnerable and impermanent. For the counters that bought them, made of political intrigue, dynastic maneuver, promise of immediate trading gain, periods of more efficient leadership, or military prowess, were available to all.

At the apex of the political structure of the *negeri* was the sultan, though this personal honorific from Islamic Turkey was less used in the eighteenth century than the ceremonial Malay *Yang di-Pertuan* (he who is made lord), often abbreviated to *Yam Tuan,* or the Indian-derived generic title for ruler, *raja.* The role of the *Yam Tuan* was first and foremost to express the symbolic unity of the state and to protect its order and integrity. In his person were embodied both *daulat,* the mystical reinforcement of personality conferred by kingship, and *kuasa,* supreme temporal authority. The aura of sanctity with which he was invested found outward expression in an elaborate apparatus of ceremonial practice and belief, which was of real importance, although sometimes it

represented no corresponding concentration of administrative strength
or power.

Surviving accounts of the installation of rulers make clear the sacral
and magical importance of the office. Succession was confined to members of a single royal lineage, usually male, with final confirmation by
the principal chiefs. A ruler's ascent to the throne was marked first by
ritual lustration, signifying exaltation from the ranks of his kinsmen and
the creation of a new and larger personality. He was then equipped with
the royal regalia, the emblems of office, ranging from symbolic
weapons, drums, and special dress to the state seal and ritual ornaments, all held to share in the supernatural qualities of kingship. A
senior official of the court mosque uttered the Kuranic text, "Lo! We
have set thee as a Viceroy upon the earth," to mark the ruler's position
as defender and arbiter of the Islamic faith. And finally, the assembled
chiefs performed before their *raja* a symbolic act of homage, repeated at
intervals throughout his reign at gatherings specially convened for the
purpose. The accepted norm of conduct toward the ruler was characterized by careful respect for proper forms of address and approach and by
the ideal of strict formal obedience to his commands.

In the Malay world of the eighteenth century, the life-style of a *raja* in
his riverine principality, though doubtless splendid in comparison with
that of his subjects, was modest when contrasted with that of his fellow
rulers in the great agrarian states of Southeast Asia. Though occasionally built of stone, his *istana,* or palace, was more probably a piled
wooden structure thatched with nipa palm *(attap)* and set in a bamboo-
fenced compound otherwise occupied by a motley collection of huts and
outbuildings for the members and servants of the royal household. The
compound, usually not more than two acres in extent, was, as a rule, set
near the riverbank commanding all movement on the principal artery of
communication; it was a scene of busy activity at the cooler hours of
morning and evening. The center of public life in the *istana* was the
*balai,* or audience hall (which might, on occasion, be a separate building), in which the business of the state was daily or at intervals conducted. Within stood the royal throne, draped in yellow hangings for
royalty. Before it was a shallow-stepped platform on which, to either
side, squatted the principal attendants of the ruler or, on occasion, the
carefully ranked chiefs.

Malay society was clearly graded. Its topmost rank, among whom the
ruler was naturally paramount, was the royal family itself—a numerous
group, especially by virtue of the practice of polygamy, which tended to
provide candidates for disputed succession and idle pretendership.
Below this came the nonroyal nobility or aristocracy, whose claim to
privilege lay in belonging to families with traditional rights to office or
position and to a share in the economic wealth of the state. It was from
his group, for the most part, that the "pillars of the state" were drawn,
though, as with the royal family, functioning positions were seldom as

numerous as candidates. Few of the Malay sultanates were equipped
with (or indeed required) anything resembling an elaborate bureaucracy, though titular offices based on the system in force in fifteenth-
century Malacca often remained. One result was that the ranking of
social class depended more frequently on noble descent or connection
than on actual administrative office. During periods of social conflict,
traditional but functionless nobles, away from the fountains of power,
might well, like dissident members of the royal family, afford source or
support for disaffection.

Nevertheless, there were ministers and administrators. One common
pattern had at the top level three or four principal officers of state (the
number often followed what had been Hindu cosmological theory): a
*temenggong* or *mentri* (first minister, as it were), *bendahara* (treasurer),
*laksamana* (commander-in-chief; literally, "admiral"), and a *hakim,* or
judge, who was probably also the chief religious dignitary. Below these,
though relative positions sometimes differed, might be a number of officers of trade, including a customs or port-dues official and a *shahbandar,*
whose task it was to act as liaison officer between the sultan and, in particular, foreign traders. These officials served in the *istana,* or at least in
the port town itself. In addition, there were usually district or territorial
chiefs who held, under commission from the ruler, rights of control over
a specified area of the *negeri:* a tributary or upper stretch of the main
river, or another river farther down the coast. District chiefs were
entitled to draw revenue from the area they commanded and were often
largely independent of the capital. They may be said, however, to have
shared in a general way in the management of the state, and their position often entitled them to consultation and participation when important matters of foreign or trade relations were being discussed.

Though a certain amount of the business taking place in the sultan's
*balai* might concern outlying parts of the *negeri,* interstate matters, trading policy, or other great affairs, much of it from day to day was certainly local or domestic in character, for the *Yam Tuan,* though first
among equals, was in an important sense merely a district chief. Much
of his time was devoted to administering his own parish, settling appeals
and petitions, arranging for renewal of licenses for monopolies or concessions concerning fishing or mining rights or the performance of
shadow plays and similar entertainments, receiving intelligence of crop
production, surrender of produce, taxation on river trade, or incipient
disaffection, and making a host of minor decisions in connection with
all of these. His revenues were commonly sufficient only to pay for the
administrative apparatus here described, to maintain an armed force of
some description, and to support the royal household and its customary
array of dependents.

The elements of weakness in this political system—vulnerable to sudden changes in prosperity or trading conditions or to attack—are fairly
clear. There was a permanent residue in the *negeri* of well-born persons

who considered themselves, for one reason or another, deprived of their due or at least of that which, with some effort, they and their following might obtain. Intriguing with people of this sort was a standard means, within interstate relations, of subverting one's neighbor. It was resorted to particularly, perhaps, by the European powers, which were by definition disqualified from the traditional dynastic power games. In addition, central financing (if indeed one can use this term), devoted largely to maintaining the royal household and some form of armed force, was seldom sufficiently secure to permit the accumulation of reserves adequate to withstand prolonged periods of stress. And the relative independence of districts led to inherent instability in the polity as a whole.

The European powers—the Portuguese in the sixteenth century, most strikingly the Dutch in the seventeenth century, and the English after the mid-eighteenth century—were able to exploit the vulnerabilities of the individual Malay polities and to disturb the system of which they formed a part. Recent historians have argued, plausibly, that European powers in the early centuries of their participation in the maritime trading networks of Southeast Asia, operating by means and on a scale no different from those of their Asian counterparts, did little either to alter the system radically or to affect the lives of the other participants. By the eighteenth century, as the effects of these intrusions accumulated, however, it becomes difficult to press this view with the same confidence, and the point has stimulated much discussion. The debate essentially has concerned whether the context—the actual structure and dynamics —was changed, or just the participants. As to the latter there is no doubt, as the Dutch East India Company, for example, substituted itself for Makassar in the eastern seas and replaced Aceh in relation to the pepper ports of Sumatra. Is it really the same play with a new actor taking some of the parts, just as the Indonesian *wayang kulit,* after the advent of Islam, acquired one or two new characters and a few alterations in emphasis? Or did the whole plot change, throwing the other actors into confusion, while everyone tried simultaneously to write his own script? A good case can be made for the second interpretation.

In particular, it can be argued that the European presence, increasingly superior in arms and relying especially on the exaction of commercial treaties from weaker powers, the compulsory stapling of trade in its own entrepôts, and the detachment of vassals and dependencies, contributed to the decay of the larger political units in the Malay world and to their fragmentation either into weaker states or into squabbling bands of marauders. The loss of commerce and revenue to the ruler and chiefs of a riverine Malay state produced a corresponding diminution or loss of political control—either inside the *negeri* or between it and its dependencies. In effect, in the eighteenth century the forces of instability represented by pretenders, rivals, opportunists, and knaves gained a freer rein for longer periods than had traditionally been the case. One result was the success of interlopers, adventurers, or usurpers, like Raja

Kechil in Siak, the Bugis in Selangor, or Sayyid Abdurrahman in Pontianak, who set themselves up inside the boundaries of previously established Malay realms of commercial empire. Another response was a great increase in what is often described as "piracy," which, like Clausewitz's definition of war as an extension of diplomacy, can be described as the continuation of trade by other means. It was the heyday of tough, lawless marauding communities, such as the Balanguingui and Ilanun of Mindanao and Sulu. Occasional marauding also became the recourse of many Malay chiefs, no longer fully able to sustain themselves and their followers in more settled ways.

How, then, did the Malay map of the western archipelago look toward the end of the eighteenth century? Aceh, at the northern tip of Sumatra, having reached the peak of its greatness in the early seventeenth century under Sultan Iskandar Muda, had since been on the decline. This appears to have been due in part to a succession of female sovereigns (a circumstance that gave free play to the energies of fissiparous territorial chiefs), but Dutch pressures exerted from their newly acquired base in Malacca (taken from the Portuguese in 1641) greatly assisted the process. The principal Dutch concern in the Straits of Malacca at the time was to control the trade of the peninsular Malay tin *negeri,* of which the most important, Perak, was a dependency of Aceh. The resulting decline of Aceh in this trade was accompanied by a loss of its control over the Minangkabau pepper ports of west-coast Sumatra, which found themselves forced to accept Dutch in exchange for Acehnese suzerainty. By the mid-eighteenth century, Acehnese power was largely confined to the northern half of Sumatra, and even there English private traders were evading Acehnese dues by dealing directly with its dependencies.

To the south, the Johore empire, which had fluctuated in fortune since inheriting the mantle and royal lineage of Malacca after the fall of that emporium to the Portuguese in 1511, was able to take advantage of the conflict between the Dutch and Aceh to strengthen its own position both in the peninsula and in east-coast Sumatra, where the *negeri* of Siak and Indragiri came under Johore authority in the mid-seventeenth century. Its situation, however, remained highly unstable. The next seventy years saw a series of complicated maneuvers for power and advantage, involving constantly changing alliances and feuds with the *negeri* of Jambi in South Sumatra, Bugis adventurers from the Celebes, the Dutch at Malacca, and the Minangkabau ruler, who had usurped the throne of Siak, and attended also by dynastic changes and power struggles around the throne of Johore itself. Together these events, which centered on the contest for control of the trade in Siak pepper and south Sumatran tin, brought the Johore sultanate to its knees. The principal advantage in the situation, however, was taken not by the Dutch but by bands of Bugis adventurers who were engaged in fashioning a new commercial empire based on a dual policy that combined indirect but effective control of some areas, as in Johore-Riau, and direct assumption of power in others, as in Selangor, on the west coast of the peninsula.

The Bugis, who had emerged from the Celebes in the late seventeenth century after the destruction of their Moluccan spice trade by Dutch monopolization, were an energetic maritime people known throughout the Malay world for their fierceness and courage. With some already established, first as marauders and then in more settled communities, in parts of Borneo, others were able, by intervention in Johore politics, to become in 1722 the virtual rulers at Riau, the Johore capital. From there, they proceeded to assert effective control over the tin states of Kedah and Perak and to create their own *negeri* in Selangor. These activities necessarily brought them into direct conflict with the Dutch in the peninsula and South Sumatra, in which the possessions of both contestants changed hands several times before the eventual Dutch occupation of Riau. This occurred not many years before the onset of the Napoleonic wars in Europe ended, for the time being, Dutch ascendancy in Southeast Asia.

Meanwhile, effective British interest in the area, born as much of strategic considerations related to the East India Company's China trade as of any desire to intervene largely in local trade or politics, increased first in Sulu and northern Borneo with the attempted establishment (1773) of a new entrepôt at Balambangan. When this venture failed, others were considered, culminating in the acquisition in 1786 of the island of Penang, ceded by the Sultan of Kedah in the hope (scarcely fulfilled) of gaining assistance against renewed Thai interest in controlling his own *negeri*. British participation at this point resulted in a further economic imbalance in the area, as both Kedah and Acehnese trade became diverted in part to the new settlement, with a consequent loss of revenue to their respective rulers. Dutch power collapsed in the wars of the French Revolution, but the British took over, at various times, all Dutch possessions in Southeast Asia. Though these were for the most part ultimately returned, it was clear that maritime Southeast Asian politics and trade had to accommodate yet another powerful European power in residence, for all the foreseeable future.

# 10

## The Javanese Kings

THE Javanese political tradition, like those of the Burmese, Thai, and
Khmer, goes back to the Hindu-Buddhist era in the first millennium
A.D., when the introduction of Indian political-religious ideas provided
a new and more capacious framework in which Southeast Asian political life could develop. From the eighth to the fourteenth centuries, a
series of kingdoms in Central and East Java expressed themselves in
terms very similar to those used by their contemporaries on the mainland. The kingdom was conceived as a representation on earth of the
cosmos, and the king therefore as an incarnation of Shiva, Vishnu, or
the Buddha, served by a priestly caste of literati and by ministers who
crouched reverently before him.

The political histories of Java and its mainland counterparts, however, took very different turns in the "religious revolutions" of the thirteenth century and after. The mainland monarchies adjusted easily to
Theravada Buddhism, which came out of an already familiar Indian
tradition, and the patterns of political life continued much as they had
before. On Java, by contrast, the last great Hindu-Buddhist state,
Majapahit, sagged abruptly around 1400, and for the next two centuries the political affairs of the island were dominated by a string of small
Islamic trading states stretched out along its north coast from Surabaya
to Bantam. In economic terms, this development reflected the new
importance of trade along the Java Sea between Malacca and the Spice
Islands, a trade dominated by Javanese merchants. In religion, the
north-coast Javanese—prince, merchant, and peasant—went over to
Islam along with the other trading peoples along the trade route. Politically, too, the Javanese of the north coast—the *pasisir*—turned to face
outward, and their string of sultanates joined the community of small
Islamic trading states spreading through the archipelago.

But whereas trade and Islam served to unite the scattered peoples of
the archipelago, they were divisive forces on Java, with its large agrarian base and its own strong cultural tradition. In this period, the outward-looking *pasisir* drew apart from the agrarian interior, where claimants to the grandeur of Majapahit lingered on into the early sixteenth
century and the Hindu-Buddhist tradition was as yet hardly challenged.
In the *pasisir* itself, the introduction of Islam inaugurated what was to be

an abiding tension in Javanese culture. The ambivalence fostered in this way is best illustrated by the myths that grew up around the careers of the half-historical Nine Wali, the reputed bringers of Islam to Java and founders of the *pasisir* states. Reduced to their fundamentals, the tales reveal one central preoccupation, an effort to reconcile Islam and Javanism. Thus, characteristically, the Nine Wali are credited with introducing not only Islam but also the *wayang kulit,* the shadow drama that is the epitome of pre-Islamic Javanese culture.

The balance of power between coast and interior shifted abruptly in the early seventeenth century, when a new dynasty, Mataram, with its center near present-day Yogyakarta, conquered all Java. But Mataram did not thereby simply obliterate the *pasisir* pattern. In a devastating series of campaigns, Sultan Agung (r. 1613–1645) restored the political unity of Java, destroyed forever the independent existence of the north-coast sultanates, and, with the help of the Dutch, condemned the once-flourishing Javanese merchant class to centuries of obscurity in the backwaters of Javanese life. But it was also in Agung's time that *pasisir* Islam rooted itself permanently in the Javanese interior. Agung himself was a pious Muslim who sought confirmation of his Islamic title of "sultan" in Mecca, consorted regularly with *ulama,* and established new courts using Islamic law.

But Agung characteristically bore the old Hindu-Javanese title for king, *susuhunan,* as well as the new Muslim title of sultan. He thus confirmed the religious tension already evident in *pasisir* belief and indeed presided over its extension to most of the Javanese population. His son, Amangkurat I (r. 1645–1677), moved back toward the Javanese pole of the synthesis, remaining *susuhunan* but dropping the title of sultan, abolishing his father's Islamic courts, and, on one occasion, slaughtering several thousand *ulama* whom he had collected at his court for the purpose. But the fine ambivalence of religious syncretism was now permanently entrenched, most strikingly symbolized, perhaps, in the Javanese calendar that Agung introduced in 1633, numbering its years according to the Hindu Shaka era (1 Shaka = A.D. 78) established from early times on Java, but nevertheless using the shorter Islamic lunar year in place of the Hindu solar one.

Leaving aside for a moment the role of the Dutch East India Company, the political structure of Java in Mataram times began—and, theoretically speaking, also ended—with the king. Since Mataram was an Islamic state, the king was no longer explicitly a god-king, as he had been earlier; he was, nonetheless, a sacral figure. One recognized a king by the *wahyu,* the divine light that descended upon him or shone from his eyes, and when the *wahyu* left him, one knew that his time as king was up. He was, to take the names of some of the Javanese kings, "He who holds the World on his Lap" (Hamengku Buwono) and the "Axis of the World" (Paku Buwono). As such, the king's function was to maintain the natural order in the kingdom, encompassing and reconciling perturbations if they occurred, so that the microcosmos would mirror the harmony of the cosmos. Thus, Sultan Agung's calendar of 1633 characteristically resolved the tension between the two different calendrical traditions, Hindu-Javanese and Islamic, by incorporating them in a new and harmonious unity. It goes without saying that there could, in theory at least, be no limits to the powers and rights of such a king.

The kingdom over which the Mataram king ruled had no boundaries. It was conceived of as a series of four concentric circles going outward from the capital into the indefinite distance. At the center was the *negara,* a Sanskrit word that, significantly, meant both "kingdom" and "capital," the palace-city from which the king sent forth the rays of his influence. The *kraton,* to give it its other, more familiar name, was moved three times before the division of the realm in 1755, being located in the area of modern Yogyakarta until the 1670s and after that near modern Surakarta (Solo). Wherever it was, the *kraton*—like its counterparts in the Theravada countries—was a vast complex of buildings and squares enclosed by walls and moats, its essentially sacral character shown by the fact that it was oriented to the points of the compass. Inside were the king, his queens and concubines, officials, royal dancers, the corps of female guards, and multitudes of servants. Outside the *negara* walls was the rest of the kingdom, the *negara* in the other sense of the word. The next circle was the *negara agung,* the core area, which in the seventeenth century consisted of the immediate Yogyakarta-Surakarta area and which grew considerably in the eighteenth century. Next came the *manca negara,* the outer provinces, which, at its greatest extent in the seventeenth century, occupied all the rest of Java but the western and eastern tips. Finally there was the *tanah sabrang,* the lands overseas, consisting of distant states, such as Palembang and Banjarmasin, which acknowledged Mataram suzerainty and sent tribute. In this respect, at least, Mataram's political theory and practice fitted very closely. The king's power, radiating outward from the *kraton,* was felt less and less strongly the farther it reached, until it faded out somewhere among the islands of the archipelago. The different concentric circles, too, were ruled on different principles.

In governing this kingdom, the Mataram kings generally did not use members of the royal family; their policy was to keep them at the court, as far as possible politically neutralized and content. In part of the *manca negara,* notably in some of the former distant states and in the Sundanese highlands of West Java, they incorporated hereditary local lords into the administration of the state. Otherwise they ruled through officials, men who, however independent they might be in practice, were, formally speaking, servants of the king. The operation, and even the formal structure, of this administration is not yet fully understood, but its general principles can be sketched. For practical purposes, it consisted of two main parts: officials who resided at court and constituted the central administration and officials who resided outside, particularly in the *manca negara.*

The structure of the central administration was particularly elaborate. It was encrusted with special offices and titles, many of them—such as the office of *patih,* the chief minister—going back to Majapahit times or earlier. It also had a pronounced sacral or magical character. There were, for example, four chief *wedana* under the *patih* (two of the left side, two of the right) and exactly twice as many lesser *wedana,* and the four plus the *patih* made a group of five found in state structures all over Indianized Southeast Asia, representing the center and the four compass points. The functions of these officials, in contrast to the structure, were imprecise; individuals' areas of responsibility and relative importance seem to have depended more on their personal relations with the king or their strength in court circles than on the particular offices they occupied. In Mataram, formal structure was as much political aesthetics as table of organization; a proper pattern was, after all, essential for the proper functioning of a microcosmos. Meanwhile, practical political business was conducted primarily in terms of personal relations.

The officials of the central administration did the king's own business in the populous *kraton* itself and the *negara agung* and acted on his behalf in his dealings with the more distant *manca negara.* The outside officials, on the other hand, were primarily concerned with the local worlds they governed. Even under strong kings like Sultan Agung and Amangkurat I, when the *kraton* watched them jealously and discipline was swift and harsh, they had a good deal of autonomy. Many ruled in what were natural geographical regions with an old history, and all had their own courts *(dalem),* sometimes very substantial, amounting to smaller *negara* within the larger one. Their territories varied widely in size, importance, and history, and the men therefore held different titles in the Mataram hierarchy of official ranks, but it is convenient to call them all *bupati* (regents), which was the general title later under the Dutch. In all these respects, they closely resembled the hereditary local lords alongside them in the *manca negara;* in time, too, their posts tended to become hereditary.

The tax system that supported this administration is better understood. "Tax system" may be misleading, because it suggests money taxes. Some taxes, notably port, river, and road tolls and a head tax on peasants, were normally levied in cash, but Mataram Java had very little cash in circulation and no currency system of its own (it used Spanish silver dollars and Chinese copper cash, among others). Most of the taxes, therefore, were taxes in kind (consumer products, such as food for the nonagricultural elite, and commercial products, such as pepper and rice), and taxes in labor (corvée duty, for building roads or a new *kraton* or *dalem,* personal service to king and officials, military duty).

The tax system reflected the concentric pattern of the realm very clearly. First, at the center, the king drew food and labor for himself and dependent members of his large court partly from royal lands sending their taxes directly to him and partly indirectly, as described below. Second, the rest of the royal family and the officials of the central administration were granted appanages by the king—that is, the right to collect for themselves a certain amount of produce or labor owed to the king as tax. Most appanages, other than tolls, were calculated in *cacah* (peasant family heads), and many lists have survived showing how many *cacah* in what region were assigned to various officials or princes. Most appanages were in the *negara agung*. Appanage-holders acquired what was due them by appointing a Javanese or sometimes Chinese *bekel* (bailiff, tax farmer), who did the actual collecting and sent them the proceeds after subtracting a share for himself. Third, officials or local lords in the *manca negara* collected their own taxes and brought a specified proportion of them to the *kraton* once a year when they came to attend the Garebeg Maulud (the celebration of the Prophet Muhammad's birthday) and pay homage. Inside their territories they granted appanages for the support of their own relatives and subordinate officials. Fourth and last, the vassals overseas had complete autonomy in taxation and simply sent tribute at longer and more irregular intervals.

The king and the local lords of the *manca negara* were hereditary, while officials were commoners and their sons were in theory no more likely to be appointed by the king than peasants' sons. In fact, however, there was a tendency for particular official posts, especially in the *manca negara*, to become hereditary in the family of the holder. In any case, even if they did not succeed their fathers in particular offices, the sons of officials almost invariably remained in the official class, the *priyayi*. Javanese society had a marked hierarchical character and pronounced class differences, most basically between the peasant (*wong cilik*, the little man) and the elite (*priyayi*, plus the few hereditary families above them).

The *priyayi* had a strong Java-wide cultural pattern, which they shared with the royal family and the hereditary local lords. *Priyayi* culture was very sensitive to status differences and expressed itself in an elaborate code of etiquette. Proper behavior, however, was more than a mere mark of social standing; it was an outward sign of inward refinement and spiritual accomplishment. A *priyayi* was *halus* (refined, able to control his emotions, attuned to God's will), and *wong cilik* were *kasar* (coarse, excitable, little more aware than the animals). Alongside this in *priyayi* culture was a strong knightly ethic: devotion to one's lord, a strong sense of honor, readiness to die in battle. In Mataram times, *priyayi* rode horses to battle, and there were weekly tournaments at the *kraton* and the various *dalem*. *Priyayi* culture found its fullest expression in the shadow drama, the *wayang kulit*, a vast storehouse of religious learning and moral teachings as well as high art and simple entertainment. Its stories, developed out of the Indian classics, the *Mahabharata* and the

*Ramayana,* inculcated the knightly ethic and *halus* behavior and offered
to the young *priyayi* an ample choice of character types on which to
model himself.

Two features stand out in a general view of Mataram Java. One is
that the Javanese economy was simple, laborious, and stiff. It rested
almost exclusively on the most elementary of bases, raw peasant labor.
It had very little currency for lubrication. Transport was rudimentary, a
few roads hardly better than paths, short rivers going every which way
and linked only by the Java Sea. In fact, only in a very limited sense
was there a Javanese economy at all. There were local economies, in the
thousands of villages and to some extent in the natural regions. Individual *priyayi* had what might be called private economies of their own,
each one taking care of his economic needs himself through his own
channels—his appanage, his *bekel,* his toll on the Solo River. All these
local and private economies were only very loosely and precariously
associated in a kingdomwide economy.

Laid over this congeries of local economies and societies was a political and cultural pattern wonderfully suited to the severe requirements
of making a Java-wide system. The king had very few economic means
of control; he could not stop *manca negara* officials' salaries, for example,
because there were none. He could use military force only when his officials came to the *kraton* bringing their peasant levies, for he had only a
few companies of his own. Java as a political entity rested on three
things: a common language and culture, a political myth that was universally accepted because it rested on and expressed common religious
beliefs, and the shared values of a Java-wide *priyayi* class. As the
Mataram dynasty rose under Sultan Agung in the early seventeenth
century and consolidated its power under Amangkurat I in the middle
of the century, these three factors overrode the patchwork of the island.
Mataram in that time was the strongest dynasty in Javanese history,
and Java was effectively a political whole.

The other side of dynastic glory is dynastic decline. What Sultan
Agung's armies and his *wahyu,* reverberating through the *priyayi* and
folk of Java, could build up could also be torn down by other armies and
other men's *wahyu* and by the intractability of the Javanese economic
landscape. In 1672, the volcano Merapi erupted, followed soon by a
comet and a great drought—signs that Amangkurat's *wahyu* was depart-
ing. Rebellion seethed and then burst out, driving him from the *kraton*
to death in exile. The legitimate heir soon was installed as Amangkurat
II, and the pieces on the political map were properly reassembled—one
pretender killed, another brought to homage at the court, Madurese
and Makassarese intruders sent home, and the Dutch rewarded for
their help with economic concessions and small pieces of the *manca
negara.* But it could not hold. Even the transfer of the *kraton* to a new and
auspicious site did not help. Mataram was falling apart, and Java had
entered on a time of troubles, which lasted three-quarters of a century

and ended with the realm dismembered and Batavia suzerain of the whole island.

The Dutch East India Company had established its overseas headquarters in Batavia in 1619, but for a long time Batavia remained on, but not really of, Java—a fort, a lively port town, and a few miles of lowlands on which Chinese grew vegetables and some sugar for export. The company's interests were in the spices of the Moluccas and the trade of all the archipelago. Batavia barely escaped obliteration at the hands of Sultan Agung in 1628 and 1629—from his point of view it was simply another *pasisir* state to be conquered in its turn. For half a century it worried about Mataram's might, sent missions bearing tribute, and bought its rice there.

In the early 1670s, when the rebellion against Amangkurat I inaugurated the dynastic decline of Mataram, the VOC was at the very peak of its success as a naval and trading power in the archipelago. It was not really interested in Java but was drawn into the developing vacuum of power by the need to protect its flank and by the possibility of certain economic advantages. The Dutch were not the only ones to be drawn into the affairs of Java in this way; during the next three-quarters of a century, not only Madurese and Makassarese but also Java Chinese and Balinese played major roles of their own in the wars that accompanied the disintegration of Mataram. All were participants in a Javanese historical process.

By 1757, a new political Java had emerged, one that remained undisturbed for half a century and, in its formal structure at least, largely unchanged until 1945. The kingdom of Mataram was divided among three houses, two senior ones (the Paku Buwono's of Surakarta and the Hamengku Buwono's of Yogyakarta) and a junior one (the Mangku Negara's of Surakarta). They ruled, with their territories and appanages all tangled up together, over the old *negara agung* and the inland parts of the *manca negara,* a long rectangle on the south central coast of Java. Along with the sultans of Bantam, these three houses were vassals of the VOC, still largely autonomous in their internal affairs but tied to Batavia through treaties, Dutch-appointed *patih,* and a certain habit of subordination. The rest of Java—a great bracket of lands enclosing the Mataram principalities—was VOC territory, ruled through *bupati,* bureaucratic nobles in their own lands, like their forebears, the *bupati* of Mataram's *manca negara.* Alien though it was, the VOC was now enacting a role in Javanese history. Its earlier naval dominion in the archipelago was decaying; it had gone ashore on Java and was now the successor to Mataram. The circles of the realm were reversed—coastal Batavia was now the center, the *bupati* now faced west and north, and Mataram princes were now outer vassals. But politically the underlying structure of Java had hardly changed. Socially, below a small conquering elite of Dutchmen, *priyayi* still lorded it over *wong cilik;* a multitude of local economies still sent tribute through political channels to a greedy but distant center. A Javanese document of the eighteenth century, indifferent to the company's outside connections but sensitive to the imperatives of Javanese history, could explain this. "Jang Kung" (Jan Coen, the governor-general who founded Batavia), it said, was the son of a wandering foreigner and a princess of West Java who was destined to bear kings. Through her, therefore, descended a legitimate dynasty of Java.

# 11

## The Spanish Governors

THE governor and captain-general of the Philippines appeared to be one of the most powerful rulers in Southeast Asia. From his position in the massive walled city of Manila, he was commander-in-chief, the king's own representative, and vice-patron of the Roman Catholic Church. As virtually all connection between the Philippines and Spain was via Mexico, the governor was insulated by time and space. Because all instructions and replacements had to await the galleon's arrival from Mexico, it could take close to a year before an order from the court reached Manila. If the governor chose to request clarification, he could avoid carrying out instructions he did not like. However, despite the pomp and his position at the head of the civil, military, and ecclesiastic bureaucracies, the governor's powers were but a fraction of what they seemed.

First, the governor's tenure was insecure and dependent entirely on the whim of the monarch. Since it was a patronage position for the king, he appointed his friends and supporters rather than men dedicated to the job. It was clearly understood, if rarely articulated, that the governor was to profit personally, provided he did not plunder too grossly. The whole system was predicated on presumed malfeasance; before an outgoing governor could depart for home, he had to undergo an official investigation, or *residencia*. Bribery was endemic to the system, and each outgoing official knew that he would have to use a certain percentage of his profit to buy his way out. Second, the administrative structure of the colony was such that the governor usually had to compete with his principal assistants in the Royal Council *(Audiencia)*. The bureaucracy was generally unresponsive and often openly hostile to the governor. Because petty officials also came to the Philippines to make their petty fortunes, few devoted much attention to the directives from Manila. The provincial governors, usually called *alcaldes-mayores,* established nearly autonomous fiefdoms, which were frequently on different islands or in remote areas. Third, the major Spanish concern in the colony was the galleon trade. Manila, the entrepôt, was a parasite, drawing what it needed from the interior but fundamentally uninterested in indigenous developments. The only viable link between the small urban community in Manila and the mass of peasants was the Church. The governor, therefore, was dependent upon the friars. Although he was the vice-patron of the Church, he could not command their allegiance automatically. He was in the anomalous position of requiring support from the clerics to rule the archipelago. The scope of his power seemed far more impressive in Madrid than in Manila; however, because he usually viewed his tenure as brief, his goal as staying alive in the tropics and returning home rich, and his legacy as perpetuating the system, he was rarely concerned over these restraints.

Most of these men were not ogres, however. They did not see any contradiction between personal ambition and official function. They were loyal to their monarch and devoted to propagating the faith. What is significant is that the office defined their actions and that even the so-called enlightened governors accepted the system without any hesitation. However, their strategy of perpetuating the system did not preclude change. One of the clichés of Philippine historiography is that the colony was inert from the early seventeenth century until the accession of the Bourbon king, Carlos III, in 1759 and the conquest of Manila by the British three years later. In reality, there was constant ferment below the seemingly placid surface. Indeed, many of the Philippine governors who seemed most interested in maintaining the status quo actually proved to be catalysts for change. The pressure of events forced them to make decisions with unforeseen ramifications. If we examine, for example, the problems of Governor Don Pedro Manuel de Arandía (1754–1759), we can see the process clearly.

At the minimum, military weakness could not be tolerated, since it jeopardized the colony. Consequently, Arandía, like many of his predecessors, attempted to reorganize the militia. He augmented the salaries of the troops to curtail venality, established the King's Regiment, and created four brigades of artillery and an artillery school. He reorganized the operations of the Cavite Arsenal. Arandía also attempted to reform the galleon trade, since this trade operation, which was the lifeline of the Spanish community, was riddled with corruption. He appointed a committee of distinguished citizens from Manila to oversee the apportioning and appraising of goods. When the committee itself was caught using its position for personal gain, he censured it sharply and began the process again. His efforts, conservative in conception, proved ineffective in application.

His equally conservative effort to break Chinese economic influence by expelling non-Christian Chinese, however, had radical consequences. Arandía did not foresee that his expulsion of the Chinese would have lasting impact on the development of the next two centuries of Philippine history; inadvertently, he opened the opportunity for the growth of the Chinese *mestizo* community, which up to then had been overshadowed by the Chinese themselves. Arandía specifically ordered the unconverted Chinese of Manila reconcentrated into a new ghetto (*parián*) and then repatriated. In his effort to lessen Chinese dominance of trade and commerce, he also ordered that the Christian Chinese who remained behind till the land rather than trade. He hoped to fill the domestic economic vacuum with a joint stock company of Spaniards. The company went out of business within a year and, through Chinese bribery and Spanish need, the Chinese slowly regained a part of their prior position. Arandía was not the first or the last governor to expel the Chinese; however, by making conversion the determinant in expulsion he reinforced the established Spanish policy of defining the alien on religious grounds and thereby stimulated the development of the Chinese *mestizo* continuity.

While marriages between Spaniards, usually creoles from the New World, and native women *(indias)* formed a small Spanish *mestizo* community, the great majority of the *mestizos* were children of Chinese-*india* marriages. The Chinese *mestizos* had distinct legal and political rights and an increasingly desirable social status. Their existence permitted the Spanish to harmonize economic interest, religious conviction, and political stability. The Spanish needed these people to keep Manila functioning; the Church welcomed them, since they were eligible for salvation and the sacraments. The Chinese, in turn, had an incentive to convert, in order to remain in the colony. Even if an individual had a wife in China, eventually returned there to die, and once home apostatized, he left behind *mestizo* children who were brought up entirely within the faith by their devout *india* mother. These children, integrated culturally into the community, moved freely, traded easily, and created their own subculture, which was not quite *indio* and not quite Chinese. The Chinese *mestizos* had their own section of Manila, Binondo, and became the most dynamic element in the society. In Arandía's time, they probably represented 5 percent of the total population, though they were a much larger proportion in the Manila area.

Arandía's efforts to reform the galleon trade and to break the power of the Chinese in Manila were prompted by his need to increase government revenue. The growing poverty of the colony not only inhibited the functioning of government but also severely restricted personal opportunities for Arandía himself and the whole Spanish community. The colony was dependent on the annual subsidy *(situado)* sent from Mexico, since it had no major revenue sources other than the galleon and taxes on the *indio*. Lacking the efficient bureaucracy needed to collect such taxes and unable to tax properly its one major revenue source, the galleon trade, it had to operate on a hand-to-mouth basis. This chronic poverty in the public sector would continue as long as the colony limped along on the restrictive practices of the mercantilist galleon. It was clear to Arandía, as it had been to his immediate predecessors, that either new trade routes had to be developed or some sort of internal development had to be effected. The efforts at developing iron mining were matched by increasing interest in agricultural products, especially pepper, cinnamon, indigo, and tobacco, in an effort to emulate VOC suc-

cesses in the islands to the south. A whole series of schemes advocated
reforms designed to turn the colony into a profitable operation.

The endemic warfare with the Muslim (Moro) sultanates in Mindanao and Sulu placed intolerable military expenses on the government,
inhibiting the development of the economy, since the Bisayan islands
and Mindanao were the regions in which the proposed developmental
schemes would take place. The Muslim raids of 1754, for example,
killed thousands, ravaged the coasts of Luzon and the Bisayas, subjected thousands more to slavery, and forced Arandía to devote prime
attention to this security menace. He did so by reorganizing the military, strengthening Spanish garrisons in Zamboanga and elsewhere,
shuffling his command, and, most importantly, attempting to establish
peace through diplomacy.

At the core of his Moro problem was the Sultan of Sulu, Muhammad
Alimuddin I (r. 1735–1773). Shortly after his accession, he had entered
into a peace treaty with the Spanish, which, among other things, offered
aid to either party if the other was attacked. This commitment by the
Spanish to Alimuddin achieved temporary peace, but it sucked the
Spanish into the internal affairs of the sultanate. Almost immediately,
Alimuddin called on Spanish forces to overcome an incipient rebellion.
Alimuddin, a remarkable man, interested in Christianity or in what he
could get from Christians, invited Jesuits to his capital city, Jolo. This
generated such opposition within the Islamic community that Alimuddin had to house the Jesuit priests within his palace. Before long, Alimuddin was forced out of power by his brother, Bantilan, who nominally ruled as regent but soon proclaimed himself Sultan Muhammad
Mu'izzudin. Alimuddin, now deposed, fled to Manila, where he again
asked the Spanish to restore him. In 1749, whether out of conviction or
for expediency, he was baptized over the skeptical opposition of the
archbishop as Don Fernando I, Rey Christiano de Jolo. While the
Spanish in Manila celebrated with four days of holiday, the response in
Sulu was all-out war. In 1750, the Spanish took Alimuddin to Zamboanga, where they prepared to force Bantilan to accept his brother
back. The Spanish discovered, however, that Alimuddin had been corresponding with various Moro chiefs and, claiming betrayal, brought
Alimuddin back to Manila as a prisoner and declared unceasing war.

When Arandía arrived, he attempted to negotiate an end to the
bloodshed. The Spanish lacked the power to defeat Bantilan, so
Arandía agreed to a peace conference in Jolo. It collapsed over the issue
of the release of Christians seized in Moro raids, since Bantilan claimed
that he no longer possessed the prisoners, who had been sold as slaves
throughout the Malay world. Arandía also attempted to operate
through Alimuddin, whom he paid a monthly stipend and treated royally. When, in 1755, Alimuddin asked to marry as a second wife a former concubine who had become a Christian, Arandía overruled the
archbishop's objections and had Alimuddin married in the governor's

palace. Arandía's efforts were cut short by his own death and by further complications caused by British and Dutch interest in Sulu and northern Borneo. What is significant is not Arandía's failure, since Spain never fully succeeded in "pacifying" the Moros or establishing suzerainty, but rather his efforts to grapple with a massive and rapidly changing situation whose ramifications influenced every aspect of Philippine life.

Arandía's efforts to solve the Moro problem put him in conflict with the Church. The political expediency of diplomacy prompted him to make decisions that seemed to violate Church concerns. By the time of his death, perhaps by poisoning, his relationship with the clerical hierarchy was antagonistic; there was no longer the automatic congruence of interest implicit in the established phrase, "in the service of both Majesties," cross and crown. The interpenetration of functions tied the temporal and ecclesiastical worlds into an alliance that neither side found satisfying. For example, as a result of Jesuit insensitivity to *indio* sensibilities on the island of Bohol in the Bisayas, the governors from 1744 to 1829 found themselves involved in trying to suppress the Dagohoy Rebellion. The ebb and flow of this war forced twenty governors to divert meager resources to support the Church in its demand to be restored on the island. Arandía's preoccupation with more pressing issues forced him to assign a low priority to the Dagohoy Rebellion; however, the friars on whom he relied saw his priorities as distorted. The governor and the friars needed each other, but the growing divergence of interest strained the structure.

While the governor's weakness was due in part to a general decline in Spanish power throughout the world, it was due even more to the constrictions under which he operated in the archipelago, for his theoretical power far exceeded his actual ability to govern. Isolation—geographic, linguistic, and racial—circumscribed his power to a limited community and a limited area. The unresponsiveness of his bureaucracy and the subtle strength of other forces in the society combined to modify his decisions.

The Spanish governor-general of the Philippines was not alone in finding the full exercise of his powers checked by other forces in the society. Like him, the rulers of Siam and Cambodia, for example, found the strength of provincial authorities sufficient to resist the full imposition of central control. Religious authorities throughout the region wielded a moral force that few rulers could ignore, and none could do wholly without the merchants, who rendered viable the taxation systems in which commodities frequently were as important as currency. The traditional autonomy of the village community everywhere was a counterbalance to the sometimes overambitious designs of the capitals. As long as social and economic change proceeded at a slow rate, the often delicate political systems that were a feature of the first half of the eighteenth century could survive without upheaval.

# PART TWO

# New Challenges to Old Authority

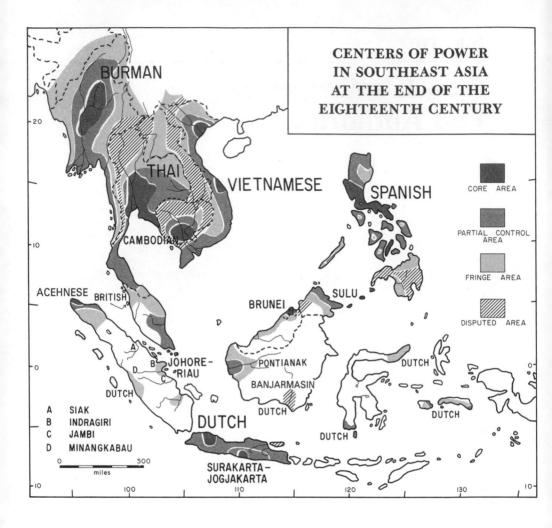

CENTERS OF POWER
IN SOUTHEAST ASIA
AT THE END OF THE
EIGHTEENTH CENTURY

CORE AREA

PARTIAL CONTROL AREA

FRINGE AREA

DISPUTED AREA

BURMAN

THAI

VIETNAMESE

SPANISH

CAMBODIAN

ACEHNESE  BRITISH

BRUNEI  SULU

JOHORE-RIAU

PONTIANAK

BANJARMASIN

DUTCH

DUTCH

DUTCH

DUTCH

DUTCH

DUTCH

A  SIAK
B  INDRAGIRI
C  JAMBI
D  MINANGKABAU

0        500
miles

SURAKARTA-
JOGJAKARTA

# Introduction

FOR purposes of analysis, the history of Southeast Asia for the century preceding 1870 can be broken into two periods. The first, extending to the early 1820s, was dominated by indigenous issues and themes. In those years, the role of the West was limited primarily to trade, which in most of the region was only a small percentage of the whole volume. Even in the Philippines, and in the other enclaves where the Europeans already governed directly, the West lacked the power it was to acquire subsequently. During that period, new groups of Southeast Asian leaders emerged to alter the power structure in virtually every society of the area. It was also an era of warfare, dynastic upheavals, population displacements, and intensifying struggles for both power and wealth among bureaucrats, merchants, landowners, and nobility. New states rose and others, like the Mon kingdom centered on Pegu and the principalities of Vientiane and Champassak in Laos, disappeared. Peasants were summoned to do the fighting, feed the winners, and finance the social changes from which they derived few benefits.

During the last half of the eighteenth century, three new dynasties came to power in the major mainland states. The first was the Konbaung dynasty in Burma (1752–1885). The wars the first kings of this dynasty fought against Siam broke the power of the Thai court at Ayudhya and set the stage for the appearance in 1782 of the Chakri dynasty, with its capital in Bangkok. Twenty years later, the Nguyen dynasty assumed power over Vietnam, placing its new capital at Hue. At first, the new dynasties were primarily concerned with legitimizing themselves, consolidating their administrative grip, and imposing their presence upon neighboring states. In Siam and Vietnam, and to a lesser extent in Burma, the first years were also marked by a far-reaching cultural and political renaissance caused partly by the energies released as newcomers gained power. Those events greatly influenced Southeast Asian history for this period and beyond; the last Nguyen emperor abdicated (to Ho Chi Minh) in 1945, and the Chakri dynasty, albeit limited by the constitutional reforms that followed the Revolution of 1932, still reigns today.

Unconcerned about events in Europe, Southeast Asian leaders were unprepared for the kind of commercial and political offensive the Europeans began to launch against the region after the Napoleonic wars.

British intrusion in Southeast Asia, partly at Dutch expense, reflected new commercial and maritime ambitions brought on by the industrial revolution. Southeast Asia's position on the sea routes between India and China, which had always been a feature of its economic and political history, resumed importance now. By a series of moves in the first quarter of the century, Britain sought to secure the eastern flank of its empire in India and to protect its routes to China. These included the establishment in 1819 of the city of Singapore, a war with Burma in 1824, and a commercial treaty with Siam in 1826. As the century wore on, Britain moved deeper into Burma and the Malay Peninsula. Industrialization in Europe also contributed to the development of export agriculture in the Philippines and in the Indonesian islands and to a new market for such export crops as sugar, coffee, and rice. As a result, new economic and social structures, as well as new landowning elites, appeared in Southeast Asia.

As the years shaded into those dominated by the West, many Southeast Asians sensed the rapidity of the process of change. At several points, leaders or their advisers sought either to deflect or to accommodate the West. Most notably in Siam, but also in Vietnam and Burma, internal reforms were enacted in an effort to stave off European control. Agricultural production, increasingly monetized, was shaped by world market conditions. However, as European influence began to spread after 1825, Southeast Asia became increasingly compartmentalized. By 1870, much of Southeast Asia's territory had passed formally into European hands, with the result that imperial interests began to inhibit interregional contact. Each colony became linked closely to the mother country. The area as a whole did not share, as it had previously and would in the future, a true community of experience. The middle fifty years of the nineteenth century saw a wide diversity in Southeast Asia's response to the West. Indeed, the themes of that period vary more sharply from country to country than they do in the high colonial era that followed; each must be traced carefully for an understanding of the tangled interaction of Western and Southeast Asian interests that developed in the period.

# 12

## Burma, 1752–1878

BY 1750, the Restored Toungoo dynasty and its predecessor had ruled Burma for three centuries. The forces that finally caused the collapse of this powerful empire were not much different from those that ended that of Pagān in the thirteenth century. With a succession of figurehead kings on the throne in the first half of the eighteenth century, the dynasty fell prey to divisive forces within and enemies abroad. Plundering parties of Manipuris raiding from northeastern India in the 1720s and 1730s undermined the credibility of Ava's military power. Rebels in the south in turn made a bid for power, only to be defeated by a counter-rebellion. Internal dissension, faltering royal leadership, and administrative weakness in the provinces around the capital further crippled the dynasty. Ava, the capital city, fell to the southern rebels in April 1752.

Alaungp'aya, deputy to the lord of Shwebo, a town a few days' march north of Ava, was a man of great personal force. Three times he repulsed progressively stronger forces sent by the conquerors of Ava to exact his allegiance. Word of his power spread and his troops and reputation swelled as he moved to the offensive. By the end of 1753, he camped under the walls of Ava; within a month, he took the former capital and cleared the center of the empire of opposing troops. Alaungp'aya shifted his headquarters from Shwebo to Ava, established a royal genealogy for himself, and founded Burma's last dynasty, the Konbaung (1752–1885).

Alaungp'aya revitalized the institutions of the old state and used them to defeat ethnic separatist forces in the south. His initial power came from his army, a force unparalleled in recent times, and grew as he developed a more complete array of hegemonic devices, including symbolic regalia and the means to manipulate ethnic identity. The momentum of his victories and the legends that swept around the new king provided him with an aura of supernatural power. By chain letters and sponsored ballads, he sowed fear among the populations ahead of his armies, thereby weakening the will of his opponents and creating massive defections. In promising release from slavery, he won over additional groups of men. During 1755, his armies moved as far south as Rangoon, and Pegu fell to his forces in May 1757.

Alaungp'aya's power was so great that in 1760 he sought to extend his influence by force to parts of the neighboring Siamese kingdom. The *casus belli* grew out of a local rebellion in Tavoy, in which the Siamese officials in neighboring Mergui and Tenasserim—then under the sway of Ayudhya—were thought to be involved. When the local authorities failed to accede to his demands, Alaungp'aya concluded that a display of force was necessary to maintain central authority in the south. The king had to make clear to potential dissidents that they could not hope for assistance from any rival monarch if challenging his authority. For reasons of prestige and honor, once begun, the war could not easily be abandoned, especially after Alaungp'aya's fatal wounding before the walls of Ayudhya in May 1760. In eight years, the king had created a state as extensive and powerful as any in Burma's history, and his successors and generals were fully conscious of the extent to which their survival depended upon the respect they commanded, both within and outside the kingdom.

For the next twenty years, Burma was at war. The failure of the 1760 campaign against Ayudhya was not soon repeated; subsequent campaigns were better planned and provisioned. Burma's armies gained a commanding strategic and political advantage by moving through the Shan and Lao states and the isthmus of the Malay Peninsula before launching a final assault; they took and sacked Ayudhya in April 1767. However, Alaungp'aya's second son, King Hsinbyushin (r. 1763–1776), soon found the core of the kingdom threatened from the northeast, where his army's activities in the Shan states had provoked a reaction from the Chinese governor of Yunnan, who launched four invasions of Burma between 1766 and 1769. The Burmese defenses held and the Chinese were forced to conclude a treaty at Kaungton late in 1769. Hsinbyushin, however, was displeased. He felt that the war had not been carried through to total victory, that his generals had assumed negotiating powers illegitimately, and that therefore his prestige had been damaged. Fearful of facing Hsinbyushin's wrath, his generals marched on Manipur to place a Burmese nominee on the throne. This victory against a minor state to the northwest was not enough salve for the monarch and the offending generals were sent into temporary exile in the Shan states.

Over the two decades following the death of Alaungp'aya, there was increasing political instability at court. Relations remained strained between the crown and its highest officers. Naungdawgyi had executed two generals on his accession to the throne in 1760, provoking an army rebellion. Neither he nor his successor, Hsinbyushin, ever felt completely secure. Hsinbyushin's treatment of the generals following the conclusion of the China wars was symptomatic of the nature of the court politics. Any challenge or slight to the king was interpreted as a threat to his power and the status which buttressed it and thus provoked ruthless and sometimes indiscriminate retaliation. Army units became enmeshed in political intrigues, and by the 1770s their performance in the field declined as commanders quarreled and morale sagged. As Siam recovered under Taksin and Burma's foothold in the Lao states was lost, the Konbaung empire was forced onto the defensive on the east, retaining of Alaungp'aya's conquests only the Tenasserim coast.

It was Bodawp'aya (r. 1782–1819), the fifth and last of Alaungp'aya's sons to reign, who managed to restore monarchical control. The early years of his reign were marked by large military campaigns providing evidence of his military prowess. His forces conquered the then independent kingdom of Arakan in 1784 and resumed warfare with Siam. Conquest soon abated, however, and Bodawp'aya turned instead to revitalizing the state's administrative system, especially its means of extracting revenue and manpower from civil society. His general revenue inquests of 1784 and 1803 were of critical importance. The country was canvassed, lands and rights assessed, tax and labor service obligations and exemptions scrutinized; the population was enumerated at just 2 million. The inquests revealed inconsistencies and injustices in the application of the norms of taxation which had to be corrected to ensure central control. The state also revoked many of the tax exemptions granted by earlier kings for religious communities; while these were not sufficiently large to sap the strength of the state, they did represent centers of power outside monarchical control.

Bodawp'aya's attack on the economic foundations of the Buddhist monkhood, as well as his intervention in clerical disputes to favor one sect at the expense of another, reflected one dimension of political conflict during his reign. Elements of the monkhood were hostile not only because of Bodawp'aya's economic reassessment and his partiality to some sects over others, but also because they objected to the king's religious excesses, such as his claim to be a *bodhisattva*. There were other divisions and conflicts. The interests of the *Hlutdaw* (supreme council of state), for the most part composed of elderly descendents of entrenched official families, clashed with those of the *atwin-wun*, the ministers of the royal household and civil servants with land grants often made at the expense of others. Advancement was frequently tied to kinship or geographic origin. The usual jealousies within the royal family and the jockeying for position and preferment among members of the official class meant many potential challenges to the throne. Thus, the king had to devote much of his time to balancing the forces at court if he was to remain on the throne. Information about events outside the court was often severely restricted because of the king's isolation as the exalted monarch and his dependence on his appointees.

Nevertheless, even though he was seventy-five at his death in 1819, Bodawp'aya retained a strong grip on public affairs to the end. His military campaigns continued, but never in so ambitious a fashion as in 1785. Apart from occasional forays into Siam and the quelling of rebellions, as in Arakan in 1797 and 1811, the king's imperial ambitions focused mainly on the small states on Burma's northwest frontier, especially Manipur and Assam. These petty principalities were open to outside interference from the economic and political power of the expanding British Indian empire. From 1804 onward, Burmese troops regularly campaigned in the region, often in support of potential vassals. The success of Konbaung armies in establishing hegemony over these states led to a resumed energy in the court and army to expand the empire further west, thus challenging the superior armed might of the British in India.

Many irritants in Anglo-Burmese relations developed during Bodawp'aya's reign as their interests and perceptions of a just order in the region were antithetical. Diplomatic contacts at the end of the eighteenth century were established, motivated on the British side primarily by Anglo-French rivalry, but after 1800 the principal issues of conflict were over differing concepts of sovereignty and territorial control. The frontier between Arakan and British Bengal was particularly sensitive as anti-Konbaung rebels often sought refuge in British territory. When Burmese troops pursued the rebels across the river Naaf, conflict was inevitable. The British viewed a demarcated border with sovereign control on their side as the only solution. Burma envisioned instead a zone of overlapping influences. Both sides knew their sovereignty to be violated by what they perceived to be the intransigence and ignorance of the other. The English East India Company, through its governor-general in Calcutta, convinced of its moral superiority, wanted to encourage local trade to provide capital for its operations in China. It was incensed at the treatment meted out to merchants in Rangoon by the king's officials who saw the merchants as a threat to their monopolistic powers. Furthermore, the British were disturbed by Burma's activity in Manipur and Assam, since this threatened the northeastern defensive alliances of the company. For their part, the Burmese officials could not understand British ideas of frontiers, extradition, and trade, which they viewed as eccentric deviations from the system of interstate relations which their state had long managed. Each side made misjudgments as to the strength and intentions of the other. The Burmese were insulted by the governor-general's insistence on carrying on relations with the court as though he himself were the equal of the king. Although Burma regularly sent missions to India, ostensibly for religious purposes, but also to seek allies and assess British strength, and although some at the court realized the risks in confrontation with the British, such assessments probably never reached the king in clearly stated terms. Diplomatic contact ceased in 1811, and as armed bands continued to operate in the region outside the control of either government, conditions on the Arakan frontier deteriorated and distrust mounted.

King Bagyidaw, who succeeded Bodawp'aya in 1819, saw no reason to change policies. Faced with revolts in Manipur and Assam and with the beginnings of British efforts to assist his enemies, he appointed General Bandula to be governor first of Assam and then of Arakan. In 1823,

Bandula's forces threatened the British protectorate of Cachar and occupied an island in the middle of the river Naaf. When his troops crossed the frontier, the British responded in force. A large seaborne expedition took Rangoon without a fight in May 1824. The British plan of making the Burmese submit by holding the delta region and merely threatening the capital failed, as the king's resistance stiffened. In 1825 the company's Indian troops began a slow advance north toward Ava. When they reached a point only one day's march from the capital, the Burmese acceded to terms that they found humiliating by the customary standards of Southeast Asian interstate relations. The Treaty of Yandabo, concluded in February 1826, required them to cede Arakan and the Tenasserim provinces to the East India Company, yield their position in Assam and Manipur, pay an indemnity equal to $5 million, and agree to the exchange of diplomatic representatives and the conclusion of a commercial treaty. What had begun as a minor irritant on the western frontiers had escalated and led to the loss of two peripheral territories and doubts about the king's abilities.

With the army beaten and scattered, the court impoverished, and the British in possession of Arakan and Tenasserim, Burma could do little to regain its lost position. Nonetheless, John Crawfurd, who came to Ava at the end of 1826 to negotiate the promised commercial treaty, found the court determined to yield no further concessions without compensatory gestures by the British. When Crawfurd refused to discuss political questions, the king conceded to him a vague and meaningless commercial treaty, and then only after he agreed to give them more time to raise money for the third and fourth installments of the indemnity required by the Yandabo treaty. Bagyidaw felt he had a strong case for the rectification of the borders between his and British territory. He was encouraged by accurate reports that the Tenasserim provinces were proving too expensive for the company to administer and that it was considering their retrocession. The king therefore sent a mission to Calcutta.

The mission, however, was unproductive, and it was not until the appointment of Major Henry Burney as British Resident in Ava in 1830 that meaningful negotiations between the two states were undertaken. Burney, who learned Burmese and made a sincere effort to understand the king's concerns, got on well with Bagyidaw. On examining court records, Burney became convinced that Burma's case for possession of the Kabaw valley east of Manipur was justified and persuaded his government to yield it, while he persuaded the Burmese to pay over the last sums due on the indemnity in February 1833. This brief period was the apex of reasonable British-Burmese relations in the nineteenth century, but in the following months the British government decided to retain possession of the Tenasserim provinces. When this decision became known in Ava, the prospects for reconciliation dimmed. The territorial concessions not only had weakened Burma physically and strategically vis-à-vis Siam but were also a blow to the prestige of the monarchy. Thus, over considerable opposition, Bagyidaw had been forced to pursue an outwardly conciliatory policy to regain the lost provinces. As the hopes for this policy's success evaporated, rivals for the throne began to emerge in the name of more effective policies.

From 1831 onward, Bagyidaw's uneasiness verged on paranoia, and by 1834 he was a recluse, while power devolved on his low-born queen and her brother. In 1837 Bagyidaw's own brother, the Tharrawaddy prince, seized the throne and had the queen, her brother, and Bagyidaw's only son executed. Bagyidaw himself, perhaps in deference to his great popularity, or in recognition of the fact that he had become indifferent to power, was allowed to live in seclusion near the palace.

In its origins, Tharrawaddy's rebellion apparently had little to do with external policy, being primarily an internal move against the queen and her brother in the absence of Bagyidaw, but it came to have a decisive effect upon Anglo-Burmese relations as well as on the politics of the court. Though Tharrawaddy did not denounce the Treaty of Yandabo, he refused to improve relations with the British and they continued to deteriorate. Nor would he accept the calls of many in the capital for renewed war against the British. Burney, who had tried to restrain the new king from massacring his opponents and had offered Bagyidaw asylum in British territory, soon was forced to retire from the capital. His successors found the atmosphere of Amarapura, Tharrawaddy's capital, and Rangoon so inhospitable that attempts to continue the residency were abandoned in January 1840, and Anglo-Burmese diplomatic contacts once more lapsed.

King Tharrawaddy's advisers were new men who had joined him in rebellion. When he took the throne, he had a number of Bagyidaw's family and ministers killed and replaced them with his friends and supporters. These latter men survived two subsequent palace revolutions, the accession of Pagan Min in 1846 and that of Mindon Min in 1852, and they provided a strong element of continuity through the next decades. Although Tharrawaddy's reign began with an overt gesture to revanchist sentiment, he and Pagan Min after him outwardly tolerated the status quo with England. The loss of territory was certainly unpleasant to Burma, but the king and his ministers were realistic about the obstacles that stood in the way of reconquest.

Without means of communication between the neighboring states, the possibility of renewed conflict was always present. In 1852 war broke out again as the British took action to protect their commercial interests, which the king's officials were trying to restrict. In 1850 a new *myo-wun*, Maung Ok, had been appointed in Rangoon. He followed his predecessors in applying heavy taxes and demanding other payments from the trading community in Rangoon by bringing indiscriminate criminal charges in order to bolster his income with court fees and bribes to avoid prosecution. Under Maung Ok, the level of complaints by the merchants to their government rose louder than ever. In November 1851, the Indian government sent a naval officer, Commodore Lambert, to Rangoon with three ships to investigate the cases of two British shipmasters who complained of having been imprisoned for murder by Maung Ok and of having been forced to pay nearly $5,000 for their release. Lambert ignored his instructions and single-handedly brought about war between the two states by seizing a ship that belonged to the king and taking it out of Rangoon. But the British Indian government had no real objection to a war with Burma at that time, partly, perhaps, because it saw advantages to be gained in Burma, but primarily because it was afraid of losing face. As Lord Dalhousie, Governor-General of India at the time expressed it, "We can't afford to be shown to the door anywhere in the East; there are too many doors to our residence there to admit of our submitting to that movement safely at any one of them."[6] By July 1852, a British expedition had captured the ports of Burma and begun a march on the capital.

Pagan Min had lost control of affairs, first to the Rangoon *myo-wun* and then to his rivals in the capital. Parts of the army and several ministers deserted him and threw their support to his younger brother, Mindon Min, who had opposed the war from the beginning and had withdrawn from the capital in December after a plot against him was uncovered. Mindon went to Shwebo to gather his forces and associate himself with the legend of Alaungp'aya; he then returned to take the capital and was crowned king in February 1853. Meanwhile, the British armies had taken Prome and advanced fifty miles beyond, so as to include a rich belt of teak forest within Lower Burma—a designation they invented after announcing its annexation. Mindon sent two Italian priests to meet with the British commanders in January, asking them to advance no further and await his negotiators. When the king's envoys reached the British camp in March, they attempted to persuade the British to give up their conquests in Lower Burma, but the victors refused. And so, as in 1826, the two sides were at an impasse—though now on a line much farther to the north. The British wished to have a treaty confirming their possession of Lower Burma and defining the conditions under which future relations would be conducted. Mindon refused to sign any such treaty, despite the almost unanimous urgings of his ministers. He is said to have reasoned that "it behooves me to be more cautious than anyone in an affair of this importance. I am responsible for the honor of the kingdom. If I were a Minister, or a Prince, perhaps I should give the same advice as they do."[7] He steadfastly refused to sign.

Early in 1853 hostilities ceased. Commercial and political relations remained as before or were arranged informally between Rangoon and Mandalay, where Mindon moved his capital in 1857. The vague nature of the frontier boundary drawn by British military commanders, which was neither recognized nor openly challenged by Mindon, the British-dominated riverine commerce between Upper and Lower Burma, and the relations of the two governments with the Shan and Karen rulers to the east, all constituted potent issues for continued conflict. There were those on both sides who thought that the second war had ended prematurely. On the British side were those increasingly attracted by the idea of trade northward with China and impatient with half conquest; and on the Burmese side were those who had expected that compliance with British demands would bring a British evacuation such as that which had followed the Treaty of Yandabo.

Mindon apparently came to the throne hoping to strengthen the power of the Burmese state sufficiently to maintain its independence and thus the longevity of the Konbaung dynasty. He attempted to do this in two ways. One was to strengthen popular support for the crown by reemphasizing the monarch's support for the institutions and ideals of the Theravada Buddhist faith. The other was by strengthening the administrative, military, and economic resources of the state. He thus hoped to demonstrate to the British that a third and final war with Burma would not be to their advantage. He was greatly helped by his four chief ministers of the *Hlutdaw,* three of whom had been *atwin-wun* under Tharrawaddy and Pagan. They brought him skills that were to serve him well, restraining him on several occasions when his patience wore thin.

The conditions under which the kingdom of Burma existed in 1853 made any program to revitalize and strengthen the state difficult. The king's domain was cut off from the rice-producing areas in the south on which it had come to depend, and many members of the royal family and nobility had lost the appanage districts there that had supported them. Though Mindon realized the need for new ways of ruling Burma, the reforms he undertook worked against the interests of other sections of the elite. But the changes introduced were easier to impose because of the defeat suffered in the 1852 war. The speed of the British victory underlined the gravity of the kingdom's situation, and the territorial losses had undermined the old revenue and administrative systems until they had become unworkable.

The monarch and his closest advisers realized that fundamental reforms had to be implemented quickly. The immediate pressure felt from the looming power of British India robbed them of the time to introduce administrative reform more gradually as the neighboring king of Siam was able to do. In 1861, Mindon moved to abolish the old *myo-sa* system by paying princes and officials regular salaries and stipends, thereby increasing their dependence on the capital and his control over them. He further increased his power by instituting an inspectorial system for provincial administration. To pay for this, he introduced a new income tax assessed on a household basis according to the relative prosperity of each; he abolished the *ahmudan* service class and required its members to pay taxes where they lived instead of to their personal master. By the 1870s, the new tax was providing some two-thirds of the royal revenues, while the remainder came from traditional sources, like the royal monopolies on teak, petroleum, and gems. To strengthen his revenues further without increasing the household tax, Mindon sought money from royal sponsorship of trade and commerce, through both the old monopolies and new state enterprises. He purchased and ran several river steamers. He constructed factories containing European machinery—manned sometimes by European technicians and managers—to process such agricultural products as lac, cutch, sugar, cotton, and silk. Mindon also went to some lengths to stimulate rice production. Although his measures had some success, they also had the effect of increasing awareness of how limited Burma's power had become by the second half of the century.

In a number of ways, Mindon tried to bring his kingdom into greater contact with the rest of the world. He sent some of his sons to study with an Anglican missionary, and he encouraged modern studies at his court. Short of compromising his principles, he did all he could to establish good relations with the British. He sent a mission to Calcutta in 1854, and he openly welcomed Arthur Phayre, who came to the capital in 1855 seeking a treaty to end the war. In 1862, Britain and Burma concluded a commercial agreement that eased the path of Upper Burma's exports into the newly created province of British Burma (combining Arakan, Pegu, and Tenasserim) and raised British hopes of trading overland with China. The treaty was further expanded in 1867. The agreements served the immediate interests of both parties: the king's desire to import arms and to establish a relationship with Britain in which some retrocession might be possible, and British hopes of entering China through its "back door." The primary issues in Anglo-Burmese relations, however, were ignored and the improvement in relations ended toward the end of the 1860s, when the British failed to keep their promise to allow Burma to import arms and when they fully integrated the province of British Burma into the Indian empire. The British then adopted a position of such arrogance that they were willing to forego diplomatic relations with the king rather than have their envoy remove his shoes for royal audience, as court etiquette demanded.

Internal changes at the court at about the same time also worked to hinder relations. Most of the ministers who had been prominent in the life of the court since the days of Tharrawaddy passed from the scene in the 1860s. The men who replaced them were not as skilled in managing state affairs. A palace coup attempt in 1866, during which two of Mindon's sons shot up a meeting of the *Hlutdaw*, killing the crown prince and several ministers, left the king unwilling to name a successor, a decision that led to ever greater intrigue in the court and, upon his death in 1878, the succession of a weak and junior prince. During the 1870s, Mindon's government conducted a rather more adventurous foreign policy than it had previously. Efforts to gain support from

France and Italy, however, seriously compromised the kingdom's position vis-à-vis the Indian government, which was unwilling to contemplate the prospect of third-power involvement in states on the frontiers of India. The fate of Burma was actually sealed by the First Anglo-Burmese War, which took two of Burma's provinces for India and involved the kingdom in conflicts that would not be resolved short of complete annexation, as was to occur in 1886.

# 13

## Siam, 1767–1868

In the century following the sack of Ayudhya by Burmese armies in 1767, the Siamese state, now centered on Bangkok, gained a coherence it had never known. While the old Kingdom of Ayudhya had been a political center of gravity, the strength of its pull lay in its armies, kings, and prestige. When these failed, its dominions fell apart. The reestablished kingdom, founded in 1782, was enabled to extend its power from the borders of China and Tonkin through to the Malay sultanates by its acquisition of a new strength in techniques, resources, and leadership, which it had previously lacked. After 1824, the Western threat and example played an important role in the development of the techniques, although Siam's ability to respond positively to the challenges was as much a product of internal development before that date as it was of the events that followed.

A new dynasty had established itself upon the throne of Ayudhya in 1688, in the aftermath of a court revolution provoked by French interference in Siamese affairs. Its early reigns were filled with strong personalities and almost constant court intrigues. Political conflict centered on the succession to the throne, and the absorption of the major noble families in court politics left provincial administration neglected. No king or noble felt sufficiently secure in his position to devote to nondynastic matters the attention they required. Consequently, the invasions by Alaungp'aya and his successors from 1759 onward caught the Kingdom of Ayudhya in a weak position internally and in regard to its vassals and client states.

The capture of Chiang Mai in 1762 gave the Burmese kings access to additional troops and supplies. It put the invading armies in a strategic position from which they could squeeze Ayudhya from the north. After a bitter siege of fourteen months, the ancient capital fell on April 7, 1767. Thousands were captured and led away to captivity in Burma, while many more died in battle or of sickness and starvation. The royal family and nobility were decimated, families were broken by death or captivity, and conventional morality could not easily withstand the pressures of hunger or the breakdown of social and administrative controls. The kingdom, so heavily dependent upon personal relationships and upon an ordered patron-client structure, came apart.

The Burmese armies, having plundered and destroyed the Siamese

capital and kingdom and having been forced to fight the Chinese on
their own northern borders, rapidly withdrew, leaving small garrisons
behind. At least five Siamese immediately moved to contest for the succession: the governors of Phitsanulok in the north and Nakhǫn Si
Thammarat in the south; a survivor of the royal family in the northeast;
a group of Buddhist monks near Uttaradit in the north; and the half-
Chinese former governor of Tak, named Sin, who had fled from
Ayudhya and had begun his campaign at Čhanthaburi in the southeast.
This last-named official—generally called Taksin—had the initial strategic advantages of easy water communications, a position nearer the
center of the old kingdom, and a personal following. Within months,
his shrewd generalship and force of personality won him a commanding
position in the area around the old capital. He defeated the remaining
Burmese forces on the western edge of the central plain and was
crowned king in December 1767. He constructed a new capital at
Thonburi, across the Čhaophraya River from present-day Bangkok. In
the next two years, while the Burmese were distracted by wars with
China, he defeated his rivals and built up his own administration.

As king, Taksin's lasting achievements were military. In subduing his
rivals and in pressing renewed campaigns against the Burmese, he
restored the configuration and influence of the Ayudhya kingdom in the
1770s. Campaigns in Cambodia had restored Siamese influence there
by 1779. In the north, Chiang Mai was captured in 1773, and a
Siamese-backed ruler, Čhao Kavila, was successfully established a few
years later. Major expeditions further east enforced Siamese hegemony
over the separate states of Laos in 1777–1779.

The king of Thonburi, however, was not successful as a politician.
He retired from the personal command of his armies in 1775 and stayed
in his palace, where he was increasingly attracted by the notion of his
own divinity. Like Alaungp'aya, he attempted to force the Buddhist
monkhood to accept him as a *bodhisattva,* thereby alienating them profoundly. His arbitrary and highhanded rule, undiminished in severity
after the Burmese threat receded, increased the opposition of the surviving nobility. Traders and those economically involved with them found
their former privileges revoked. Taksin gave his country firm leadership
and martial skills when it needed them most, but he spread the white
umbrella of kingship too narrowly to shade under it all the interests of
his court and kingdom. A revolt against the excesses of some of his officers broke out in Ayudhya in March 1782, quickly rallying all the opposition to the king until Thonburi was taken and the king surrendered.
Čhaophraya Mahakasatsük, the chief of Taksin's generals, who had
been campaigning in Cambodia at the time of the revolt, was named
king by the rebels and began his reign as King Rama I in April 1782.

This reign, which lasted until 1809, was critically important. Taksin
had reestablished the Siamese state, now centered at Thonburi/Bang-
kok, but he had failed to nourish the political institutions that could help

it prosper. In his policies and actions, Rama I set a new tone, establishing patterns of rule that went beyond a simple restoration of the *ancien régime* of Ayudhya. Most important, the relationship between the king and the elite was qualitatively changed. Rama I came to the throne without the rivals or opposition that had forced his predecessor to adopt a hard line, even though, like Taksin, he was himself in some sense a usurper. He was able to gain and to hold the confidence of the nobility by granting them representation in high office and by carefully consulting his officers in his decisions. He made clear his expectations for the performance of his officers, using his powers of appointment and dismissal early and well. He attempted to conciliate the royal survivors of his predecessors. He restored the orthodoxy and ecclesiastical hierarchy of the Buddhist monkhood and regularly asked its advice on moral issues. The reign of Buddhist morality gained substantially at the expense of older, non-Buddhist traditions. In general, his leadership was marked by open consultation and discussion, while the rule of principle reduced arbitrary authority and factionalism.

Something of the style of Rama I's reign is evident in his religious, legal, and literary work. Each new king was expected to extend his patronage to the Buddhist monkhood and to commission the copying of a new set of the Buddhist scriptures, the *Tipitaka*. A new king was also expected to confirm or deny the laws of his predecessor and to demonstrate his cultural legitimacy by poetic composition. Rama I went far beyond what was conventionally expected of a king. He called a council of the Buddhist monkhood in 1788 to undertake a thorough revision of the *Tipitaka* to restore accurate Pali texts. In 1805, he convened a legal commission to reorganize and edit the whole corpus of Siamese law and to bring it into conformity with contemporary standards of justice and equity. The king composed in flowing Siamese poetry perhaps the most monumental work in Siamese literature, the *Ramakian,* a version of the Indian *Ramayana* which runs to more than 3,000 pages of modern print. In proclamations and decrees reviving the ceremonial and official life of the court, the king took pains to explain himself and to justify his actions. Though all these works were, in a sense, traditional and orthodox in their orientation, the spirit and energy that moved them was new. They were suffused with self-consciousness, objectivity, and selectivity, and they took place within a more open framework of a new relationship between the king and his nobles.

Rama I's reign was marked by the extension of Bangkok's influence in the central portion of the Indochinese peninsula and by the reduction of Burmese military and political power. After a series of Burmese invasions in the south, west, and north between 1785 and 1797, the last major battles were fought in the extreme north in 1802–1805. At the conclusion of these, the Burmese were expelled from Chiang Saen, and Siamese contacts were established with the Lao and Shan states as far north as the Chinese frontier. In this warfare, the Siamese troops were joined on various occasions by levies from Chiang Mai, Nan, Luang Prabang, Vientiane, and Champassak, all of the Lao states in the north. In the south, particularly after the Burmese invaded the Malay Peninsula in 1785, the Siamese encountered considerable disaffection among the nearer Malay states. Strengthening their control over Nakhọn Si Thammarat and Songkhla, the Siamese then moved to bring Patani, Kedah, Kelantan, and Trengganu under closer supervision and surveillance. Generally, instability or divided loyalties anywhere on the periphery of the kingdom were viewed as a threat to Bangkok's security. The combination of forceful leadership, increasing domestic strength, and the distractions to which Burma and Vietnam were subject in the last two decades of the eighteenth century made possible a major revival and extension of Siamese power and influence.

Rama I's success culminated in the uncontested succession of his son to the throne as Rama II in 1809. The following years were sufficiently peaceful to permit the court to build upon the foundations laid down by Rama I. Rama II was even more a poet than his father had been, and though he withstood easily the small military challenges presented on his eastern and western frontiers, he was sometimes thought to be too lenient with his dependencies and client states. The major developments of his reign were political. Uncertain, perhaps, of his ministers and officials, he encouraged his brothers and other senior princes to take an active role in the administration, appointing some to act as superintendents over the affairs of various ministries. An important working relationship developed out of this policy between his eldest son, Prince Chetsadabodin, who was given superintendency over the ministry of foreign affairs and trade *(phrakhlang)*, and a high official of that ministry, Dit Bunnag, who was from a prominent noble family of the Ayudhya period and was closely related to the king's own mother. These two worked together to develop trade with China, to the profit of both official and personal accounts; both gained politically valuable new wealth as well as access to profitable foreign contacts. Through Dit, who later became minister—Chaophraya Phrakhlang—in 1822, Chinese planters introduced commercial sugar production around 1816. The crop soon became an important item of a new export trade with Western merchants, concentrated after 1819 in Singapore; in exchange, the Siamese were able to import, among other things, arms from American traders.

The British hoped to secure recognition of their possession of Penang; to restore the sultan of Kedah, who had been expelled from his state by Siamese troops in 1819, after surreptitious dealings with the Burmese; and to increase Siamese trade with Penang and Singapore. These hopes led the governor-general of India in 1822 to dispatch John Crawfurd as an envoy to the Siamese court. His mission was almost totally unsuccessful, as he could offer the Siamese no more than rational arguments for free trade in return for the substantial concessions he demanded. By the time a second mission, headed by Captain Henry Burney, reached Bangkok late in 1825, however, conditions there had changed.

Prince Čhetsadabodin, though the son of Rama II by a concubine, had succeeded to the throne as Rama III in 1824, primarily because of his maturity, his administrative experience, and his political backing. His younger half-brother, Prince Mongkut, born of a queen and barely twenty years of age, had recently entered the monkhood. Burney came seeking Siamese participation in the Anglo-Burmese War on the side of the East India Company, but he failed to obtain it. As soon as the news of the Treaty of Yandabo reached Bangkok, the Siamese reacted quickly to the presence and threat of a new neighbor on their western frontier by opening discussions with Burney. After protracted negotiations and maneuverings, the two sides reached agreement. In return for British recognition of the Siamese position in the Malay states, the Siamese conceded to British merchants changes in trading and duty procedures in Bangkok. The court agreed to take an immediate cut in its revenues in the long-run hope that it would make up in volume what it lost thereby. Čhaophraya Phrakhlang (Dit Bunnag) played a critical role in gaining acceptance of this arrangement, even though he personally and officially stood to lose most if the arrangement did not work out as planned. However, it succeeded. Siamese foreign trade increased dramatically, a new system of tax farming designed to circumvent the treaty was instituted, and the political threat of Britain abated for some decades. This success was the result of the strengths of the Bangkok monarchy—an open working relationship between the sovereign and his officials, a high institutional capacity for assessment of situations and solutions, and a quality of genuine receptiveness to the outside world through involvement in overseas trade.

For most of the reign of Rama III (1824–1851), the West only indirectly affected the economic and political life of the kingdom. This is not to say that the West was unimportant to the Thai in that period, but only to emphasize the fact that Siam's rulers, and probably the British as well, interpreted the 1826 treaty as an accommodation with which both sides could live and still be free to attend to more immediate matters. The seaborne trade through Bangkok increased, especially the export of sugar to Singapore, while the Phrakhlang and his supporters continued to strengthen their economic and political position. The new system of tax farming, under which the rights to collect internal taxes, transit dues, and commodity levies were awarded to private individuals (frequently Chinese immigrants), worked well. The combination of a new government determination to maintain its own labor supply by tattooing those considered liable for labor service and new economic developments, such as the rapid increase of bulk commodity exports, elicited quite different responses from some of the old nobility, whose wealth traditionally had stemmed from personal control of manpower and official position. Those who continued to think in terms of the old system effectively subverted the intent of the labor regulations by amassing large forces of debt-slaves for their personal service. By the 1850s, foreign observers estimated that half the population of the kingdom lived in a state of voluntary servitude, easygoing though it may have been. In contrast, the Bunnag family, some other elements of the nobility and royal family, and the Chinese immigrants based their wealth on new economic patterns of foreign and domestic trade, tax farming, and commercial agriculture. External developments like the world sugar markets and the heavy influx of Chinese immigrants newly available for wage labor, entrepreneurial services, and retail commerce made this latter response both easy and natural. It is not surprising that the Phrakhlang refused to leave his posts as minister of treasury, trade, and foreign affairs when he assumed concurrently the post of *kalahom* (minister of war and the southern provinces) in 1830; in his old ministry, he maintained a position from which he could keep up his trade and his contacts with the Chinese.

The British annexation of the Tenasserim provinces blocked the main route by which Burmese armies formerly had attacked the Siamese capital and reduced Siam's security risk on its western flank, at least so long as Anglo-Siamese relations were friendly. On the other hand, the conclusion of the Burney Treaty in 1826 encouraged the Lao ruler of Vientiane, Čhao Anu, to believe that his suzerain in Bangkok was weak and seriously threatened by the British. At the end of 1826, he launched a major attack on Siam across the Khorat Plateau and was within three days march of Bangkok before the Siamese could respond. Their counterattack, initially a small-scale punitive expedition, escalated for two years until it spread over most of the area of present-day Laos, from Champassak in the south to Xiang Khouang in the northeast, and it included troops from the northwestern Lao principalities of Nan and Chiang Mai. Faced with the difficulty of administering and defending the Lao areas east of the Mekong River against civil strife, dynastic quarrels, and Vietnamese ambitions, the Siamese decided to move tens of thousands of Lao from mountain valleys in eastern and southern Laos and to regroup them across the Mekong in the northeastern half of the Khorat Plateau. The small kingdom of Luang Prabang, isolated in the north and long friendly to Bangkok, was left alone, although Siamese interest and contacts there increased. These were the years when the Siamese first actively intervened in Laos on a permanent basis by encouraging and forcing the establishment of Lao provinces on the Khorat Plateau and by initiating their integration into the Siamese political order.

The Siamese armies, busy in the south and northeast in the 1830s, gained considerable field experience. Their officer corps, under the leadership of Čhaophraya Bodindecha (Sing Singhaseni), became more professional. They began to experiment with tactics and imported American weaponry. In the Cambodian crisis of the 1840s, the Siamese were in a much better position than they had been in earlier decades to compete against Vietnamese forces, which had benefited from French training and arms. The agreement with Vietnam of 1846 allowed the Siamese to maintain a resident at the Cambodian court. This capped the efforts of nearly two decades to adjust to the changes in the local balance of power in mainland Southeast Asia occasioned by Vietnamese expansionism and by the Treaty of Yandabo. The Siamese had dealt successfully with regional challenges to their authority in the Lao states, in Cambodia, and in the Malay states. Their military efforts had been followed by greatly increased use of royal commissioners, who frequently visited the tributary states, and by tightened administrative control over provinces where populations had been regrouped and defenses strengthened.

The influence of the West was quietly and selectively felt in Bangkok in this period. As late as 1850, there was seldom more than a handful of merchants and only a few missionaries present in the capital. However, a small group of important Siamese sought them out and learned from them. Prince Mongkut, passed over for the succession to the throne in 1824, began a personal quest for sustaining religious commitment and a satisfying intellectual system within the Buddhist monkhood. He rejected a life of meditation as well as what he felt was the laxity of traditional Buddhism, and, after an encounter with Mon monks, whose discipline was especially strict, he sought a return to what he felt was the rigor and universalism of canonical Buddhism. In 1828, he informally established a new Buddhist sect, the Dhammayut. With time to study and travel through the countryside, and later with ecclesiastical authority as the abbot of an important monastery, Mongkut soon began to extend his understanding of the world through the study of languages, science, and foreign ideas. He was not alone in these endeavors. Similarly engaged in such studies were Mongkut's full brother, Prince Chuthamani, several other important princes, and the eldest sons of the Phrakhlang (Dit Bunnag), among others. Some gained immediate practical advantages thereby: Prince Wongsathiratsanit studied medicine as the head of the royal physicians, Chuang Bunnag learned navigation and shipbuilding, to the profit of his father's trading efforts, and Prince Chuthamani studied military affairs by training and equipping a company of troops. Whatever the practical advantages or concrete knowledge gained, the significant legacy of these studies was simply the fact of close contact with the West and with each other on a regular basis over an extended period of time. These men, who closely followed the course of the "Opium War" in China and the activities of the Western powers in the region, were less likely to underestimate the West than their fathers or neighbors had been.

Envoys of the American and British governments came to Bangkok within a few months of each other in 1850–1851, demanding free trade and extraterritoriality. Neither was able to conclude a treaty with the

Siamese. They found the court divided and the progressives fearful of making concessions that might compromise their chances of manipulating the succession to the throne. Prince Mongkut and Chuang Bunnag appear to have been convinced that their country's future depended on a policy of generous accommodation with the West, which only those members of their generation who understood the West could accomplish successfully. They temporized, however, privately assuring the envoys that their demands would be met once Rama III and the older men around him had passed from the scene.

Quietly gathering support, partly through the use of their economic power and official position and partly through the manipulation of family relationships, the party of accommodation prepared for the end of the reign as Rama III fell ill in January 1851. The political climate became charged as Rama III attempted to elevate one of his own sons, whose supporters subtly attacked Prince Mongkut, the other most logical candidate for the throne. To prevent civil war, an extraordinary meeting of the highest dignitaries of the realm was held on March 15, when Chaophraya Phrakhlang made an impassioned plea on behalf of Mongkut—the "rightful heir," as he termed him—and declared that any who would challenge Mongkut's right would have to fight the Phrakhlang first. He carried the day; he had too much power for others to cross him, and the case he was pleading was clear. Accordingly, on March 25, Mongkut was approached by the Phrakhlang's officers and invited to ascend the throne. He agreed to do so. A guard was posted around Mongkut's monastery residence and remained there until early on April 3, when Rama III died, and Mongkut was escorted to the royal palace to be crowned. Mongkut insisted that his full brother, Prince Chuthamani, be elevated to rule jointly with him as his coequal and "second king," an arrangement that at least temporarily succeeded in neutralizing any potential rivalry from within the progressive party. Chuang Bunnag was appointed Chaophraya Si Suriyawong, minister of war and the southern provinces *(kalahom),* and chief among the king's ministers, while his younger brother, Kham Bunnag, became minister of treasury and foreign affairs. Their father and uncle, who together had run both those ministries for more than twenty years, were given honorific royal titles and, having reached old age, began to retire from public life.

Western demands soon were revived by Sir John Bowring, the British governor of Hong Kong and minister to China. By the time he arrived in Bangkok in March 1855, the Second Anglo-Burmese War had taken place. Mongkut's reading of the Singapore newspapers and his prior correspondence with Bowring had made clear what was expected of him. Mongkut and Suriyawong handled themselves skillfully with the British envoy. While Mongkut sat chatting with Bowring, offering him cigars and pouring wine, Suriyawong casually revealed his detailed acquaintance with European economic theory and the principles of good government. Bowring was thoroughly impressed. Though they exuded self-confidence and conviction, however, Mongkut and Suriyawong had political battles to fight at court and a thirty-day deadline, set by Bowring, against which to work. Extraterritoriality, the legal jurisdiction of consular officials over their own nationals, could be easily conceded, but Bowring's insistence on free trade at nominal duties and on the abolition of all Siamese government trading and commodity monopolies threatened the economic interests of many, at court and elsewhere. From Bowring's journal, it appears that Suriyawong's belief in the benefits of free trade—his conviction that the country could make up in trading volume what it lost on the duties paid by each ship and on each commodity—and his faith that alternative sources of income could be found to replace those lost by conforming to the treaty won the day against considerable opposition. The Bowring Treaty, signed in April 1855, served as the model for more than twenty such agreements signed between the Siamese government and foreign nations in subsequent years. Under its terms, the Siamese accepted extraterritoriality, the abolition of both royal and farmed-out commodity or trading monopolies and transit dues, and the establishment of *ad valorem* rates of 3 percent on imports and 5 percent on exports. Taxes on land held by British subjects were fixed at low rates, hindering the Siamese government from increasing the land taxes charged to its own citizens; earlier prohibitions on the export of rice were removed. The only concession to the Siamese was the stipulation that the import and sale of opium was to be a government monopoly. The Siamese gave away a great deal for the sake of security, without any way of knowing that they could withstand the sacrifices. They did so because they believed that they had to, because the threat of foreign intervention or war was real. They recognized this fact because they had followed so closely what had been happening in Burma and China.

To make the treaty work, Mongkut and his ministers had to undertake what Bowring recognized to be "a total revolution in all the financial machinery of the Government."[8] The old monopolies and tax farms were replaced with new excise monopolies farmed to Chinese—the opium, gambling, lottery, and alcohol monopolies—which provided the major share of government revenues well into the twentieth century. In addition, the economic possibilities of foreign trade were developed as rapidly as possible. The number of foreign ships visiting Bangkok soon increased more than tenfold, and Siam became one of the world's largest exporters of rice and teak. Government revenues recovered within one year and soon began a steady rise; the possible domestic political dangers to which Mongkut and Suriyawong had exposed themselves declined.

With greatly expanded foreign trade and contact, the tone of life in Bangkok rapidly changed. Harbor facilities, warehouses, and shops were constructed, and the king himself invested funds in new streets of shops. Following the traders came more missionaries, artisans, and professionals, and soon a few Westerners were formally employed by the Siamese as tutors, translators, police officers, labor officials and shipmasters. These numbered fourteen during Mongkut's reign. Their impact was echoed by the larger community of diplomats and missionaries, whose contacts with important Siamese officials were both regular and intense. Men like Mongkut and Suriyawong were aware that their country's fate in large measure depended on how much they learned from the West. They took pains to borrow and adapt Western ideas and techniques where their security was at stake, in the conduct of foreign relations, and in the organization and equipping of military forces. Foreigners were employed to represent the Siamese government abroad, later to be replaced by well-trained Siamese. Europeans were engaged to advise the foreign ministry, Suriyawong, and the king in Bangkok. The Siamese government hired drillmasters to train troops, and it imported new arms. A start was made in providing new government services required for the conduct of international trade or for the convenience of foreigners, for example, telegraphic and mail service and paved streets.

Although he had made these accommodations with the West—a supremely important commitment for his nation—Mongkut did not attempt to promulgate any fundamental reforms. The bureaucratic nobility remained essentially semihereditary and unsalaried, and its educational preparation and recruitment were virtually unchanged. No substantial revisions were made in Siamese law or in the system of slavery. Most of the military forces were untouched by reform, and the provincial administration remained both inefficient and resistant to central control. It is likely that Mongkut and Suriyawong felt that they had done enough and that the worst was over. They may have thought it foolish to proceed too rapidly with change, particularly since the pressure to reform, as voiced by the foreign consuls, was still not strong as late as 1870. As with most governments everywhere, reform for its own sake, or for practical purposes, was less a political issue at court in the 1860s than was political power, pure and simple. The nobility and royal family were divided on the issue of reform, its pace and extent, and on the issue of the relative balance between royal and bureaucratic noble power. These issues at times conflicted, pulling individuals in opposite directions. The climate of the political environment suggested caution; changes could not easily be introduced without upsetting the balance of power at court. However sincere Mongkut or Suriyawong were about reform, they believed that changes had to be introduced gradually and great care taken not to disturb established interests.

Two incidents occurred in the 1860s that might have caused the Siamese to reconsider both the nature of their relationship with the West and the relative urgency of domestic reform. First, the shelling of Trengganu by a British warship in 1862, after Suriyawong had been intriguing to extend Siamese control there and in Pahang, reminded the Siamese of the fragility of their relationship with Britain and of their own weakness in countering Western attacks upon the sovereignty of the kingdom. In 1863 came the first stage in the elimination of Siamese power and influence in Cambodia to the benefit of the French. King Mongkut was deeply distressed at the severance of a long-standing paternal relationship with the king of Cambodia, and he was frightened by the undisciplined behavior of the French naval authorities in Saigon. Mongkut's response to these events was idiosyncratic. Essentially optimistic and frequently naive in his dealings with Western nations, he seems to have hoped that his own charm, rationality, and good intentions would convince the West of Siam's right to survive as an independent nation. Neither incident was serious enough to force Mongkut to alter his basic policy, but both were harbingers of more difficult times ahead. The era of high imperialism had not yet reached Southeast Asia, and Mongkut was able to deal successfully with the West. One of these diplomatic efforts was to invite foreign consuls and the governor of the Straits Settlements to accompany him on a visit to the peninsular village of Wa Ko to witness a total eclipse of the sun in September 1868. There, he contracted the illness that caused his death five weeks later, at the age of sixty-five.

The ability of the kingdom to deal with the challenges thrust against it stemmed from a century of domestic developments. After the sacking of Ayudhya by the Burmese, the first kings of the Bangkok dynasty had reconstructed a kingdom that was alive to the dangers and opportunities around it. The smooth relationship between Rama I and his ministers led to the formation of durable interest groups at court, which lent flexibility to the workings of government and broadened the range of alternatives in the consideration of national economic and foreign policy. Economic innovation diversified the bases of wealth that could be brought to bear on the political process. The growing resident Chinese community rapidly proved a source of great strength, first in operating the tax-farming system of the third reign and then providing a rapidly expanding tax base, which kept the national treasury solvent at a critical period. Perhaps most important, though least tangible, was the self-confidence of a few Siamese leaders—their conviction that they could concede to the West without losing much—and their faith that they could persuade their countrymen to accept the sacrifices required of them. They felt strong enough to take economic and political risks for the sake of security. Each risk successfully accepted, from the treaty of 1826 to the treaty of 1855, strengthened the party of accommodation.

As a result of the long period of political and economic changes in Siam up to 1868, the political spectrum was expanded. New interests, ideas, associations, and commitments multiplied the alternatives in policies and political positions open to the court. The royal autocracy of the past became more difficult to sustain in the face of noble challenges to royal authority in defense of both established interests and radical change. The role of the monarchy, in the face of external demands, was to lead the nation to the acceptance of what was minimally necessary for its survival and to balance the personal and institutional interests at court in order to prevent conflict and paralysis. Mongkut trained his son Chulalongkorn to assume this delicate role, but his training was far from complete when the prince ascended the throne at the age of fifteen. The tests he would face were certainly no less severe than those his forebears, who provided him with a demanding example, had mastered.

# 14

## Cambodia, 1779–1863

CAMBODIAN history for the years preceding the establishment of the French protectorate in 1863 has often been inaccurately portrayed merely as a struggle for survival on the part of its governing class or as a footnote to the histories of Siam and Vietnam. Those years were marked by territorial losses, political disorder, and wars. They damaged Cambodia's stability, strained its institutions, and humiliated its people.

Dislocations and violence, moreover, had far-reaching economic effects. As the size of the kingdom diminished, so did its population and the revenues available to the court. As revenues fell, the court's eagerness to collect them increased. Pressure from the court for taxes and manpower alienated regional leaders, who frequently led their followers, or were pulled by them, into rebellion. Rebellious factions, in turn, were both a cause and a result of instability at the center. Disorder in Cambodia attracted the notice of the newly consolidated regimes in Bangkok and Hue, which offered assistance to one Cambodian faction or another for a price either disregarded or underestimated by the Cambodians at the time. The price was generally high, ranging from outright grants of territory or workers to the requirement that royal succession be determined by the protecting power. As the court slipped further into dependent status, the cycle continued. From Cambodia's point of view, the pattern of history in this period was a descending, narrowing spiral.

In the course of the eighteenth century, the Cambodian court lost control successively over the southwestern portion of the Mekong delta, a strip of coastline between Ha Tien and Kompong Som, and the northwestern provinces of Battambang and Angkor. In 1814, Siam annexed two small provinces on Cambodia's northern frontier and, at the time the French intervened, was preparing to administrator two more, northwest of the Cambodian capital. Although each of the losses occurred for different reasons, all four had the common effect of cutting Cambodia off from outsiders and from the benefits of trading directly with powers other than Vietnam and Siam. Significantly, when the court resumed the administration of the coastal strip in 1847, the Cambodian king, Ang Duong, quickly had a road built there and a port constructed from which Cambodian ships sailed to Singapore.

Dynastic turmoil was a constant feature of the Cambodian court.

During the first three-quarters of the eighteenth century, nine kings, five of whom reigned more than once, occupied the throne, often for only a few months. Disaffected members of the court fled into the no man's land of the Mekong delta or to the more formal protection offered them by the Siamese. In both places, these princes gathered troops, usually an ethnic hodge-podge under a mixed command, with which to regain power in Cambodia. In the late eighteenth century, Siamese ascendancy over the Cambodian court, backed by frequent Siamese invasions, reduced the turnover in the Cambodian royal house. Vietnam, racked at the time by civil war, was forced to accede temporarily. In 1779, a six-year-old prince, Ang Eng, was selected as king, while power remained in the hands of his pro-Siamese advisers. For the next eighty years, only three other monarchs, all direct descendants of Ang Eng, occupied the throne. Dynastic stability, however, was not accompanied until the 1840s by any real power on the part of the monarch.

In 1794, Ang Eng traveled to Bangkok to be crowned by Siamese officials, an unprecedented event in Cambodia's history. Shortly afterward, the Siamese court placed a pro-Siamese Cambodian official, Ben, in charge of a large tract of land in northwestern Cambodia containing the provinces of Battambang and Angkor. Those provinces soon severed their administrative connections with the Cambodian court and remained under loose Siamese administration, governed by Ben and his descendants, until they were restored to the French protectorate of Cambodia in 1907.

When Ang Eng died in 1796, the Siamese named no successor but continued to rule Cambodia through approved Cambodian officials. In 1805, Ang Eng's fifteen-year-old son, Ang Chan, was crowned in Bangkok. Upon returning to his capital, he quickly sought recognition from the recently constituted Nguyen dynasty in Vietnam. Emperor Gia-long, following Sino-Vietnamese diplomatic practice, replied by sending Ang Chan a Vietnamese seal of office and court costume for his entourage. Cambodia's quadrennial tribute to the Nguyen court was also set at this time. It consisted of the same kinds of forest products that Hue demanded in tribute of the intervening upland peoples. That the Vietnamese court saw as its duty the "civilizing" of Cambodia must have galled Ang Chan and his ministers, but, in the face of Vietnam's growing power and of the need to balance it against Siamese hegemony, they had no visible alternative.

Three of Ang Chan's brothers had remained at Bangkok in the custody of the Siamese court, and they accompanied a Siamese invasion of Cambodia in 1811, which cast Ang Chan aside for several months. In 1812, Ang Chan resumed the throne, aided by troops provided him by the eunuch overlord of southern Vietnam, Le Van Duyet. By 1816, his court had become a "two-headed bird," paying tribute to Bangkok as well as to Hue. The next fifteen years pass almost unnoticed in Cambodian sources. Their silence suggests the possibility that Siam and Vietnam, preoccupied elsewhere in any case, reached some sort of *modus vivendi* regarding Cambodia, perhaps legitimizing their separate spheres of influence. A British traveler, passing offshore in 1823, reported that the kingdom was divided into three parts—Siam and Vietnam each administered one, and the third, containing the court, remained independent.

Between 1829 and 1832, disorders in the provinces bordering Siam, in which the Cambodian court accused officials of being sympathetic to the Siamese, dismantled whatever diplomatic arrangements Vietnam and Siam may have made. In 1833, a Siamese army, accompanied again by Ang Chan's disaffected brothers, swept through the kingdom and into Vietnamese portions of the Mekong delta. The Vietnamese responded by invading Cambodia themselves, expelling the Siamese and reinstating Ang Chan, who died shortly afterward, in 1834. After his death, the Nguyen court renamed Cambodia Tran Tay, or "western commandery," and proceeded with plans to administer the kingdom directly, using Vietnamese officials.

Although Vietnamese motives for that decision remain obscure, they were probably related in some way to the recent death of Le Van Duyet. Perhaps no longer afraid that a Vietnamese advance into Cambodia would enlarge that overlord's extensive power vis-à-vis the court, the Vietnamese court felt the time ripe—and more convenient because of Ang Chan's death—to realize a long-standing ambition.

In Phnom Penh, in a move perhaps calculated to insult Cambodian institutions, the Vietnamese installed Ang Chan's teenage daughter as queen. The bewildered girl named her two sisters as vice-reine and heir presumptive, respectively, but real power fell to a group of Vietnamese bureaucrats who began to arrive in 1834 to remodel Cambodian society and administration. In contrast to the Siamese, who had been content in periods of overlordship to work through Cambodian institutions, which in any case resembled their own, Vietnamese concepts of government were too different and their contempt for Cambodia's administrative style too great for them to temper or delay what they viewed as an urgent civilizing mission. Vietnamese pressure against nearly every point of Cambodia's institutional structure soon produced revolts, at least one of which was ignited by Buddhist monks. The Cambodians particularly objected to the related imposition of cadastral records, census, and land taxes, although other features of Vietnamese administration, such as the recostuming of Cambodian officials and the renaming of the kingdom's provinces, must also have been offensive to the bureaucratic elite.

In 1841, after the Vietnamese had exiled the Cambodian queen to Hue and imprisoned one of Ang Chan's brothers there through a complicated ruse, revolts broke out among the Cambodians who were living in southern Vietnam. As a result, when the Vietnamese troops temporarily had to withdraw from Cambodia, the Siamese moved in, hoping to install Ang Chan's other brother, Ang Duong, on the throne. For the next three years, the chronicles state that no rice was planted and that the people lived on roots, while the Siamese and Vietnamese, aided by rival Cambodian factions, fought each other and devastated the land-scape. Peace negotiations calculated to save face for the exhausted armies lasted until 1846, when both sides agreed to withdraw from Cambodian territory and to accept Ang Duong as king. The treaty marked the resumption of Siamese influence at the Cambodian court. To seal the treaty, Ang Duong was crowned in his capital in 1848 by rep-resentatives sent there from both Siam and Vietnam.

Ironically, Ang Duong's divided fealty to Siam and Vietnam had the effect of liberating him to some extent from both. The chronicles and other reports give the impression that Ang Duong, who had remarkable administrative gifts, was unwilling to be anybody's puppet. Although he had spent most of his life in Siam, for example, one of his first actions on reaching the Cambodian throne was to forbid the use of Siamese administrative terminology, which had long been widespread. In 1853, moreover, he secretly communicated with the French court, transmit-ting a letter to Napoleon III in which he offered homage in exchange for friendship. The presents accompanying the letter were lost en route, and with them the French opportunity for intervention, since Ang Duong interpreted Napoleon's silence about the presents as indiffer-ence. In 1856, a French official named Montigny came to Cambodia to negotiate a full-scale commercial treaty, but Ang Duong backed away, partly because Montigny had discussed his plan already with the Siamese court, which had disapproved of it. Urged to accept France as an ally, Ang Duong said, "What do you want me to do? I have two mas-ters already, who always have an eye fixed on what l am doing. They are my neighbors, and France is far away."[9] The monarch would have welcomed informal French guarantees with which to strengthen his hand in relation to Siam and Vietnam, but the French in the late 1850s already had larger ideas in mind.

When Ang Duong died in 1860, he was succeeded by his eldest son, Norodom, then in his twenties. During the next five years, Norodom rode out a series of dynastic and religious rebellions, which broke out in northern Cambodia and on both sides of the Vietnamese frontier. Two rebel leaders claimed to be heirs to the throne; a third was Norodom's younger brother. Meanwhile, as the French consolidated their hold on the Mekong delta, where they had intervened in the late 1850s, they began to be interested in Cambodia, whose economic potential they considered enormous. Norodom, friendless and uneasy, welcomed the presents and attention given him by French naval officers who traveled upriver to his court from their headquarters in Saigon. In 1863, he signed an agreement with the French whereby he accepted their protec-tion as heirs to the suzerainty held by the Vietnamese, which the French asserted had lapsed with their intervention in Vietnam. Norodom neutralized this action by negotiating a secret protocol with Siam, pledging loyalty in order, perhaps, to be crowned king of Cambodia, for the Siamese retained his coronation regalia at Bangkok. Invited by his monastic sponsor, King Mongkut, to be crowned in the Siamese capital, Norodom set off in 1864, only to hear that the French flag had been hoisted above his capital while he was traveling to the coast. Hurrying back to his palace, Norodom apologized to the French, who hauled down their flag. It was the last time the French would do so for nearly 100 years, for French control was less than a year away.

# 15

## Vietnam, 1802–1867

In 1802, the Vietnamese state stood on the brink of a golden age unparalleled since that of the Hong Duc period of the late fifteenth century. From 1771 until 1802, the country had experienced a socially explosive peasant rebellion, led by the three Tayson brothers of Binh Dinh in south central Vietnam, which had destroyed the already moldering Lê dynasty (1427–1788) and then placed two Tayson emperors upon the Vietnamese throne. The first of these emperors, Quang-trung (r. 1788–1792), defeated a massive Chinese invasion of Vietnam aimed at restoring the Lê dynasty and bequeathed to his successors memories of his epic victories over Chinese armies, like the famous battle of Dong-da, near Hanoi, in 1789. By 1802, Tayson power had collapsed in turn, vanquished and superseded by the new Nguyen dynasty (1802–1945), which now ruled Vietnam from Hue. For the first time in history, a single Vietnamese court governed a united polity that stretched from the Kwangsi-Yunnan border all the way south to the Gulf of Siam. The predecessors of the Nguyen dynasty had never truly controlled both the Red River delta and the Mekong delta simultaneously.

The creation of the Nguyen dynasty in 1802 meant the dissolution of the bureaucracy that had supported the Taysons. Families that had been privileged under the Taysons now became outcasts under Gia-long (1802–1820), and families that had been outcasts under the Taysons became the newly privileged after 1802. One senior Tayson official was even publicly beaten to death before the Temple of Literature in Hanoi in 1803. Yet, although the scars of the eighteenth-century civil wars were slow to disappear, Gia-long's revival of the civil service examination system in 1807 permitted many families to ride above the political storms of the period and to maintain a continuity of influence and power. For example, Phan Huy Ich (1750–1822) served the Taysons, his son Phan Huy Chu (1782–1840) served the Nguyens, and their descendants are active in Vietnamese politics today. Vietnamese officials of the early 1800s came on the whole either from long-established scholar families, mostly in the north, that had survived the Tayson interregnum by such pursuits as teaching school, or from loyal officers in Gia-long's army and navy who had come mostly from the center and from the south. At first, the court rewarded them by giving them "allotment lands" *(khau phan dien)* on a hierarchical basis, the largest estates going to the highest officials. Since bureaucrats lacked private administrative power over their lands and could not subdivide them and give them to clients, and since any sufficiently talented scholar could enter the official class, this arrangement was not "feudal" in the medieval European sense. It soon gave way to a more centralized system of remuneration, which replaced the distribution of "allotment lands" with that of cash salaries. The Nguyen bureaucracy depended upon a communications system that was probably superior to any found in neighboring societies, thanks to the famous Mandarin Road *(quan lo)* with its regular relay stations, which ran from the north to the Mekong delta. Even in 1804, when the road was still being built, the officially specified rates of travel were thirteen days between Saigon and Hue and five days between Hanoi and Hue. Couriers were flogged if they were more than two days late.

In 1821–1822, a European visitor who had also lived in India, Java, and Siam wrote of Hue that its "style of neatness, magnitude, and perfection" made the achievements of other Asiatics look "like the works of children."[10] Yet the Nguyen golden age never really materialized. Two Vietnamese Marxist historians have counted 105 large and small peasant uprisings against the court in the period 1802–1820 alone, impressive evidence that the Hue bureaucracy, for all its relative efficiency compared to other Southeast Asian governments, had failed to create an adequate standard of living or security for its villagers. Compulsory labor service weighed heavily upon the peasants, who were conscripted to construct irrigation canals, city walls, roads, bridges, and above all the walls and new palaces at Hue. At higher levels of society, a minority of the intelligentsia indulged in satirical skepticism about the entire Vietnamese imperial system, which, from its court ceremonial to its Chinese-style Gia-long law code, was a calculated imitation of the more useful institutional features of the Ch'ing empire. A subversive woman writer like Ho Xuan Huong, for example, might employ such techniques as rhetorically transferring general discontents to the more visibly grotesque incarnations of Hue dynastic politics like the court eunuchs. The eunuchs were lowly inner officials whom Vietnamese emperors trusted because they lacked family connections to divert their loyalties, in much the same way that medieval European kings had confided in celibate clergymen. Delivering what amounted to a covert attack on the court itself, in one poem Ho Xuan Huong mockingly asked its eunuchs,

Why do the twelve midwives who cared for you hate each other? Where have they thrown away your youthful sexual passions? Damned be you if you should care about the twitterings of mice-like lovers, or about a bee-like male gallant caressing his adored one. . . . At least, a thousand years from now you will be more able to avoid the posthumous slander that you indulged in mulberry-grove intrigues.[11]

To be fair, this view—that the practical advantages of the imperial system were, like those inherent in the plight of its eunuchs, purely of a negative kind—was not a typical one in the early nineteenth century. Bureaucratic centralization in the Chinese manner was the weapon with which Emperor Minh-mang fought centrifugal trends, military and political, in the provinces. Vietnamese regionalism is sometimes over-emphasized by foreigners: The society's possession of a common family system, its common memory of folk tales and folk heroes, and its lack of any unconditional symbols of regional solidarity, like entirely separate languages, should be borne in mind. Yet under the first four Nguyen emperors southern Vietnam remained a frontier land, which participated only very poorly in the affairs of the empire. Of the 1,024,338 officially recorded male taxpayers in all of Vietnam in 1847, only 165,598 of them lived in the six southern provinces. The Hue court did not survey southern land-holding patterns until 1836. Then it discovered the existence of landlords, of poor people who lacked even enough land "in which to stick an awl," of squatters from one village who illegally occupied the lands of another, and of village chiefs unacquainted with methods of calculating acreages and marking land boundaries. Southerners found it easier to win positions of power in the government by remaining outside the civil service examination system, for example, by working through the army. Of the fifty-six doctoral degree-holders who won degrees at six Hue metropolitan and palace examinations in the period 1822–1840, only one was a southerner. "The people of the Gia Dinh area are very refined, but recently laziness and negligence have become the customs there," Minh-mang complained in 1832.[12] Poorer educational facilities and fewer resident families with long civil service traditions really accounted for much of the south's problem.

But it is an error to assume that, within the Confucian elitist context of "traditional" Vietnamese society, no technically advanced, culturally unifying forces were at work. A dynamic process like that of the vernacularization of the symbols and styles of politics—a process sometimes mistakenly considered to have occurred in Southeast Asian societies only after their collision with the "modern" West—manifested itself in Vietnam during the Tayson Rebellion and continued into the next century. The Tayson Quang-trung Emperor attempted, with limited success, to restrict the use of Chinese characters at his court in favor of the indigenous Vietnamese writing script, *nom,* which was employed to transcribe more effectively the language ordinarily spoken by the peasants. A special literary genre, which emerged during the 1771–1802 civil wars, the funeral oration *(van te),* which often began with the stock phrase "Alas!" *(than oi)* and was written in *nom,* was composed to praise illustrious soldiers who had died in battle. But although the funeral orations originated as relatively private literature, they soon metamorphosed into propaganda read before the public. In this way, the political controversies of the civil war were dramatically purveyed to wider audiences. A slight broadening of popular participation in elite culture was also heralded in the nineteenth century by the appearance of a court-sponsored work like the *Dai Nam Quoc Su Dien Ca (The National History of Imperial Vietnam in Explanatory Songs)* about 1865. The work popularized "great-tradition" history by converting it into colorful poetry, making it more real to Vietnamese outside the upper mandarin class.

For the intelligentsia, moreover, the definition of the moral universe in which they lived and the ways in which hardship had to be suffered in order to accumulate secret merit in this universe were expanded in a semirevolutionary way by the literary masterpiece of the early 1800s, Nguyen Du's 3,254-line poem, *"Doan truong tan thanh"* (roughly, "A new song about great heartbreak"), better known by the names of its three leading personages as the *Kim Van Kieu*. Although Du borrowed the story of this poem from a seventeenth-century Chinese novel dealing with the fortunes of a sixteenth-century Peking family (just as Shakespeare wrote about Romans and Italians), his poem's subject was actually the decadence of Vietnamese society as he personally had known it. The heroine of the poem, Kieu, displayed her filial piety by ignoring her own future happiness with her betrothed lover and selling herself into a life of prostitution in order to redeem her arrested father. At the end, however, her virtue triumphs over a maleficent destiny and earns her happiness. Vastly superior to its Chinese model, and indeed one of the great literary landmarks of Southeast Asia, the poem caused a stir because it depicted the weaknesses as well as the strengths of its admired characters, described decadence more realistically than symbolically, and unflinchingly gave its upper-class heroine a culturally and morally disapproved lower-class life as a bordello slave before returning her, at its conclusion, to the pinnacle of society by reunion with her mandarin lover. In a sense, it represented a vernacularization, or at least a permissive reorientation, of court conceptions of social mobility that hardly harmonized perfectly with conservative views of official morality. In Vietnam today, students write essays on the poem, newspapers use its characters as editorial paradigms, merchants sell wares like the "Kieu numbers game" *(lo to Kieu),* and soothsayers draw prophecies from it.

The world of the *Kim Van Kieu* was one in which predestination and the omnipresent evils of society were prominent causal factors but in which supernatural elements rarely received much emphasis. Proud of their rationality, the Vietnamese Confucian elite reacted with hostility to what they regarded as the irrational superstitions of the French Roman Catholic missionaries who were arriving increasingly in Vietnam around that time. Jesuit missionaries had been active in Vietnam as early as the seventeenth century. Some of them, like Alexandre de Rhodes (1591–1660), had attempted to convert the Vietnamese writing system from Chinese characters to European letters, a proposition that many mandarins considered subversive, since the wholesale adoption of romanized Vietnamese by the Vietnamese population would have temporarily severed Vietnamese society's connections with its Confucian texts and Buddhist sutras, both of which were written in classical Chinese and Chinese characters. During the civil wars of the late 1700s, the future Gia-long emperor had been aided in his successful campaign against the Taysons by a French bishop, Pigneau de Behaine (1741–1799). On the future emperor's behalf, Pigneau had journeyed to Paris in 1787 to negotiate a treaty with the court of Louis XVI—known as the Treaty of Versailles—in which France promised to commit frigates and soldiers to the anti-Tayson cause in return for commercial privileges in Vietnam and territorial concessions at Da Nang (Tourane) and Poulo Condore. The French Revolution made the treaty obsolete, but Pigneau appears to have converted to Christianity Gia-long's eldest son, Prince Canh, who had visited Paris with him. The prince's refusal to prostrate himself before the altar of his ancestors in 1792 provoked the future Gia-long into warning Pigneau that the conversion of too many of his officials to Christianity without some compensatory indulgence of Confucian forms would weaken the Vietnamese monarchy, since it would force the emperor to perform state ceremonies almost alone.

By the time the Nguyen dynasty was founded in 1802, both Pigneau and Prince Canh had died. But the sociopolitical repercussions of Vietnam's version of the Christian-Confucian "rites controversy" did not die with them. Independently of any arrangement with Paris, nearly four hundred French sailors and soldiers of fortune served Gia-long until 1820. Many of the citadel walls around Hue and assorted provincial towns in Vietnam were devised and constructed by French engineers at that time. Yet Gia-long's evanescent corps of French advisers failed to serve as a modernizing leaven in the Vietnamese body politic. From the beginning, they made themselves the spokesmen for French Catholic Christianity. Foreign ambitions of religious proselytization became fatally entangled in Vietnamese politics both at court and in the provinces. The most extreme example was the intimate association French missionaries achieved with Le Van Duyet, the semi-independent regional overlord of southern Vietnam, who hoped the missionaries could obtain Western guns for him. Since Duyet had also unsuccessfully attempted to block the accession to the Vietnamese throne of Minh-mang, Gia-long's fourth son by a concubine, who became emperor in 1820, Minh-mang not surprisingly considered the Catholic priests whom Duyet befriended at Saigon to be both the auxiliaries of his major political enemy in Vietnam and the fifth column of an aggressive foreign power. He issued his first decree outlawing the dissemination of Christianity as a heterodox creed in 1825, after a French warship had called at Da Nang and had landed a priest who soon began to preach the Gospel. Real persecution, with the execution of missionaries, began in the 1830s.

Despite the Nguyen court's ban upon proselytization and its execution of missionaries, Christianity continued to spread. Societywide inflation (*bach lang,* "blank coins," as the Vietnamese peasant called it), natural disasters, a long coastline that the court could not efficiently patrol, the temporary decline of Vietnamese Buddhism, and the absence of a resisting "gentry" class in the provinces numerically and qualitatively as strong as the one in China—all were possible explanations. In 1847, one year after the diocese of Vinh was founded, it claimed 68,000 Vietnamese Christians, more than half the 118,000 it was to claim after a quarter-century of colonialism, in 1909. Believing that Christianity was a "trick" by which Western nations planned to conquer Vietnam, Minh-mang created "canton teachers" among local scholars in Christianity-affected areas to lecture on Confucianism and circulated an imperial edict in 1839, about a year before his death, declaring that "those priests come from distant lands and are not members of our race. . . . Their followers' need of crosses greatly stems from what is not classical and is completely unadoptable."[13] He also sent an embassy to France to negotiate acceptable methods of controlling the religion with the French government (1840), but his envoys were not received.

On matters other than the religious question, ironically enough, the posture of the Vietnamese court toward Western civilization was hardly, as French missionary literature tried to pretend, one of static fanaticism. Minh-mang himself, more innovative and more technologically minded than any other Southeast Asian ruler of his era, was a scientific amateur who dabbled in experiments. For example, he personally manufactured a water wheel that would pump water through a conduit into his palace so that coolies would not have to carry it. He was an explicit admirer and user of Western products, like glass, cotton textiles, English gunpowder, and French brandy. By 1840, he had read the Old Testament in Chinese translation, informing his officials that he found it "absurd." In the late 1830s, like Mindon of Burma some twenty years later, he not only purchased several Western steamships but also built a factory at Hue in 1839 to construct steamships independently. That enterprise was a failure, however, essentially because the Vietnamese court attempted to copy the extrinsic features of the steamship without mastering the internal principles of the steam engine. As of 1839, the Vietnamese elite, led by Minh-mang, exhibited a naive optimism that Western technology could be privately appropriated by Vietnamese artisans without their having to cross any cultural barriers. The existence of Western machines was recognized empirically before the existence of a Western scientific culture was acknowledged philosophically.

During the Thieu-tri reign (1841–1847), French gunboats visited Vietnam on behalf of imprisoned Catholic missionaries, a move inspired by the success of British imperialism in South China. This was only a prelude to more systematic violence on both sides. Between 1848 and 1860, it has been estimated, some twenty-five European priests, 300 Vietnamese priests, and as many as 30,000 Vietnamese Catholics were killed in Vietnam. The response of the French navy was to attack and seize Saigon and the three southeastern provinces around it (Gia Dinh, Dinh Tuong, and Bien Hoa) in 1859–1862. The Treaty of Saigon of 1862 between France and the Vietnamese court, which ratified this conquest, in effect created the French colony known as "Cochinchina." The French military occupation in 1867 of three more southern provinces—Vinh Long, An Giang, and Ha Tien—completed the territory of colonial Cochinchina. It was accompanied by the dramatic suicide of Phan Thanh Gian (1796–1867), the southern bureaucrat who had been leader of the "peace party" favoring negotiations with the French rather than military resistance at the now faction-torn Vietnamese court. In addition to their conquest of southern Vietnam, which had been fought more effectively by local leaders than by the Nguyen emperor, the French forced the court to concede them freedom to disseminate Christianity in Vietnam and to promise them that it would no longer obstruct the conversion of Vietnamese.

The territorial diminution of the Vietnamese state in the 1860s may well have been less significant than the schisms in Vietnamese society that preceded it and developed along with it. Quite unprecedented was the specter of religious conflict, which was induced in part from the outside and which changed the nature of traditional intervillage disputes in Vietnam so drastically that they were no longer resolvable in terms of the existing values of the society. Christian villages like Duong Son in Thua Thien province in central Vietnam were constantly at war with their non-Christian neighbors. New religious differences coincided with old patterns of neighborhood separateness: The wide-range sociocultural system of Western Christianity, which was global in scale, impinged upon the unaltered narrow-range sociocultural system of Vietnamese villagers. Furthermore, the increase in scale of the system of cultural relationships of the Christian Vietnamese peasant was not balanced by a corresponding increase in the scale of his social relationships outside his village in Vietnamese society. For example, not only did the Christian peasant cut his hair, but his conceptions of time and of history became partly Westernized. He counted the years from the birthday of Christ, rather than clinging to the less ambitious, cyclical Vietnamese method of counting time by the reigns of individual emperors. His sense of historical time thus became related to Western history rather than to traditional Vietnamese political ideology. Yet his social parochialism as a Vietnamese villager remained undiminished. What had emerged was the formidable problem of the interaction of competing large-scale cultural systems with small-scale village politics, which lacked traditions of physical and social mobility and of "shared respect" in relations with strangers.

French intervention in Vietnam amounted, at least at first, to the opportunistic military exploitation of Vietnamese resistance to Catholic religious evangelism. The Vietnamese traditional order could not tolerate such evangelism, because Vietnamese institutions were based not upon the modern Western concept of the separation of church and state but upon the concept of the state as the political expression of the elite Confucian ideology. Catholicism, if it made inroads among the elite, would obviously qualify the nature of elite ideology. As Gia-long had implied to Pigneau in 1792, the nature of the state, which expressed elite ideology, would then have to change as well.

The traditional Vietnamese political system was not well organized to allow the indefinite peaceful competition and expression of many different and antithetical points of view, especially when such points of view were suggested by an aggressive alien culture. Conflict was regulated less by specific institutions than by the reflex of personal deference to superiors like one's father, one's emperor, or one's senior in the bureaucracy. The method, which was merely a political abstraction of the familial ethic, was simply not strong enough to withstand the merciless, unprecedented pressures of the 1860s.

The long reign of the Tu-duc emperor, from 1847 to 1883, has been neglected by scholars. One conventional picture of Tu-duc himself is that he was a reformer at heart, a prisoner of his Confucian bureacracy. Whether or not this picture is correct, the internal history of his reign was stormy. Because there were few legitimate channels of fundamental dissent at Hue, apart from obliquely worded memorials to the throne, an emergency that threatened the system could generate extraordinarily explosive conflicts and opposing interests within the Vietnamese elite— conflicts that were all the more explosive because they were normally repressed by the mechanism of filial piety, loyalty to the throne, and ritualistic self-deprecation. Typically, the position of Tu-duc himself was threatened during those years by both pro-Catholic and anti-Catholic rebellions against his authority.

As the Vietnamese imperial family had grown larger in the nineteenth century, it had begun to lose cohesion and to develop factions. The process accelerated under Tu-duc. While his predecessors had confronted insurrections only in the provinces, Tu-duc had also constantly to guard against a *coup d'état* within his own court and household, a new feature in the history of the dynasty. The first attempt to overthrow him was made in 1851–1853 by his half-brother, Prince Hong Bao, who had hoped to succeed Thieu-tri in 1847. Scheming to take the throne by force, Hong Bao formed a party of supporters at Hue, linked together by a blood oath, which attracted the allegiance and help of virtually every Vietnamese Christian in the area. Hong Bao apparently promised Vietnamese Catholics freedom and even privileges if he succeeded in displacing Tu-duc. He was arrested and imprisoned for life in 1853.

In 1864–1865 the throne was shaken by another attempted coup, this time with anti-Catholic overtones. After the signing of the 1862 treaty, which ceded the three southern provinces to France, the Confucian elite turned its wrath against all Vietnamese Christians and Tu-duc himself. Scholars at the regional examination sites of Thua Thien, Nghe An, Hanoi, and Nam Dinh demonstrated against the treaty, and had to be suppressed by soldiers. The Vietnamese elite feared "traitors" within its own ranks; an edict of the early 1850s had significantly given court officials who were secret Christians one month to recant, provincial officials three months, and ordinary people six months. Because the 1862 treaty gave Frenchmen the right to spread Christianity in Vietnam, it precipitated a religious war between Vietnamese Christians and non-Christians. And in 1864, an imperial prince named Hong Tap formed a party at the court whose purpose was to recruit an irregular army to kill Christians and assassinate certain bureaucrats. Members of the party included a prince consort, a grandson of Minh-mang, a district magistrate, and some twenty others, some of whom were the sons of high provincial officials. But this party's plot to gain control of the Hue citadel fizzled.

There was a more positive side to the spread of Catholicism among a stubborn small minority of Tu-duc's officials. While some crypto-Catholic officials in Hue, alienated from the emperor and unable to express dissent legitimately in Vietnam's traditional monistic political culture, were willing to participate in plots like the Hong Bao conspiracy, some Vietnamese Catholic scholars did blend their Catholicism with loyalty to Tu-duc. Beginning to function as constructive middlemen between Western civilization and the Vietnamese court, such Catholic loyalists favored far more changes in the status quo than the usual bureaucrat. For one thing, they knew more about the West. Furthermore, being Catholic, they could not increase their own power in the bureaucracy, at the expense of Confucian conservatives, without some changes in the system. But they were not pro-French, and they sought to preserve the monarchy. This small group of loyal Catholic middlemen within the elite could not have existed under Minh-mang. The disorder of the 1860s gave them their opportunity.

Their most famous member, and perhaps the most unusual official in nineteenth-century Vietnam, was Nguyen Truong To (1827–1871). To had received a traditional education and wrote superb classical Chinese. On the other hand, he had become acquainted at an early age with a French missionary priest, Gauthier, who taught him French and took him back to Italy and France in the 1850s. In Europe, To visited factories and was received in audience with Pope Pius IX, who made him a present of a hundred Western books. Back in Vietnam, as a provincial official, between 1863 and 1871, To sent a stream of memorandums to Tu-duc in which he proposed, in effect, that the emperor lead an institutional revolution in Vietnam. The revolution To proposed might have strengthened the monarchy but would have transformed the bureaucracy.

Among other things, To suggested that the court reduce the number of provinces, prefectures, and districts in Vietnam in order to reduce the number of officials who were performing useless tasks. The stipends of the officials who remained could then be increased as a measure against bribery and graft. Furthermore, To believed that the administrative and judicial powers within the bureaucracy should be explicitly separated, in conformity with the "separation of powers" doctrine of Western democratic theory. (To's endeavor to create a more specialized judicial administration was an attack on the Confucian ideal of the "generalist" bureaucrat, whose omnicompetence was a function of his supposedly superior morality.) To wanted to create military schools, directed by foreign specialists, which would train officers and produce a modern Vietnamese army. As a means of supporting his program of internal reorganization, To demanded a more equitable taxation system, based upon a new population census and land survey, which would increase the taxation of landlords, tax luxury goods, and increase the taxation of imported merchandise, so that the prices of imports would rise and the consumption of indigenous goods would be encouraged. He also hoped that cooperatives could be organized to expand Vietnamese commerce.

In addition to wishing to dismantle Vietnam's unspecialized Confucian bureaucracy, To attempted to revolutionize the social stratification that had produced it, ending the traditional dichotomy between the literate rulers and the illiterate ruled. He wanted the use of Chinese characters in Vietnam abolished and replaced by romanized Vietnamese that every peasant could quickly be taught to read. He hoped that romanized Vietnamese newspapers could be founded and distributed among the masses. (This proposal—the creation of newspapers to educate the masses—was also made to Tu-duc by another Catholic spokesman, Huynh Tinh Cua [1834–1907], a southerner who served as an interpreter to the French and eventually became Vietnam's pioneer journalist.) If the civil service examinations survived, To maintained, their survival should be conditional upon their testing knowledge of specialized subjects, such as law, science, and agriculture. In foreign affairs, the Hue court should emulate the example of Siam, not China, and send ambassadors abroad in order to understand international relations better.

This visionary blueprint of institutional revolution, created by a Catholic who believed passionately in the survival of his society but not of its traditional elite ideology, transcended the Tu-duc court's capacities for carrying it out. Its assault upon vested interests was total. Confucian scholars and bureaucrats, landlords, and the foreign merchants who would have been more heavily taxed would all have been its victims. Vietnamese legend has it that when To died in 1871, it was of acute melancholia at seeing his country drifting toward disaster and being unable to prevent it. What is significant, however, is that, as early as the 1860s, the outer fringes of the Vietnamese elite had produced a reformer many of whose recommendations were already more ambitions than any of the feeble modernizing policies the French colonialists would pursue in Vietnam between the 1880s and 1954. The French colonial regime, in a sense, was out of date before it was created.

A number of minor reforms were carried out at the Tu-duc court in the 1860s. In 1864, for example, the court launched a program of French-language training, inviting a Vietnamese Catholic priest, Nguyen Hoang, to come to Hue to teach students and to translate Western books. But French pressure was most insistent in Vietnam at the one point the Confucian bureaucracy could not concede without agreeing to its own extinction: the French right to transform Vietnam into an ideologically differentiated society, in which Catholicism could compete ideologically and institutionally with the bureaucracy. Since the Vietnamese tradition had not produced a political framework that could accept and accommodate the conflict that would have resulted—the very syncretism of the traditional "three religions," Buddhism, Taoism, and Confucianism, had minimized the need to devise European-style means of regulating the coexistence of different religions—many Vietnamese construed what the French called "religious freedom" as the beginning of political, ethical, and social paralysis.

# 16

## The Malay Peninsula to 1874

FOR the maritime Malay *negeri* of the peninsula, the last quarter of the eighteenth century was a tumultuous and confused period of changing alliances and fortunes. The century as a whole is sometimes called the Bugis century because of the political ascendancy achieved by those fierce and warlike traders from Makassar, who had established themselves as the paramount power in Malay waters as far back as 1722, when Daing Parani secured effective control over the Malaccan successor state, Johore. From the Johore capital on the island of Pulau Penyengat in the Riau Archipelago, where Parani's brother became "underking" to a puppet Malay sultan, the Bugis extended their control over the tin *negeri* of Kedah and Perak, against the rival ambitions of the Minangkabau ruler of Siak in eastern Sumatra, and, in 1742, a Bugis was installed as first sultan of the new *negeri* of Selangor, carved out of the western coast of the peninsula.

Malays and Dutch alike were disconcerted at the rise of Bugis power, which undermined established political relationships and threatened the tin trade, and a number of alliances were made at mid-century in an attempt to control a common foe. The Bugis responded by attacking Dutch Malacca in 1756, an enterprise in which they suffered defeat mainly as a result of Malay aid to their enemy. Bugis fortunes were at a low ebb for a time, but by the 1760s they had recovered, owing to the military prowess of the great warrior of the time, Raja Haji, under whose influence Johore-Bugis authority was reimposed on the principal Malay *negeri* flanking the Straits of Malacca, including Jambi and Indragiri on Sumatra and Kedah and Perak on the peninsula. Riau, the Johore capital, with a population allegedly of more than 90,000 (50,000 Malays, 40,000 Bugis, and a mixture of others), prospered, and, by the late 1770s, with Raja Haji as underking, its harbor was regularly frequented by hundreds of Bugis, Javanese, Siamese, and Chinese vessels, trading in fine goods and staples ranging from European chintz, Siantan silk-weave, and Javanese batik to the best shellac and top quality Siam rice. The best and most vivid Malay-language history of the time (the *Tuhfat al-Nafis,* written by a grandson of Raja Haji) adds that Riau was also a great religious and cultural center and a stopping place for itinerant Arabs from the Hejaz.

Riau's greatness did not last for long undisturbed, for in 1782 the

Dutch and the Bugis again fell out, and after an unsuccessful siege of Malacca (during which Raja Haji lost his life), the Dutch in 1784 expelled the Bugis from both Selangor and Riau. At Riau, they extracted from the Malay Sultan Mahmud a treaty permitting the establishment of a Dutch garrison and resident on Pulau Penyengat, but this arrangement had scarcely become effective when Ilanun sea raiders from Borneo, summoned by Sultan Mahmud, expelled the Dutch in turn—though Mahmud and the Malays also left, fearing Dutch revenge. The Bugis remained for the moment in Selangor (which they had regained) and in their possessions in Borneo.

In the meantime, in 1786, the British had established themselves at Penang by means of an agreement with the Sultan of Kedah; the agreement rapidly proved unsatisfactory to the latter, who was under strong pressure from an aggressive Siam. The two rival European powers— the Dutch to the south of the Straits, the English to the north—now became the target of an unstable Malay coalition, led by the homeless Sultan Mahmud of Johore-Riau, which set out to drive the aliens from the Malay world. The coalition was ineffectual, and the hope vain, though the Dutch were to be effectively removed from the scene for a time as a result of war in Europe. Ironically, however, the attack by revolutionary and expansionist France on the Netherlands in 1794 led to a temporary cessation of the rivalry between Britain and monarchist (though not revolutionary) Holland. William of Orange, having fled to London, instructed all Dutch governors and commanders overseas not to oppose the entry of British troops into Dutch possessions, to forestall the French. In return, the British undertook to make restitution of all colonies placed under their protection when peace in Europe was restored and the Dutch state reconstituted. So began the uneasy alliance between the two great European maritime powers with interests in Southeast Asia, which was to result, before the next century was out, in the extinction or subjugation of virtually all indigenous political authority throughout the Malay world.

Already the empire of Johore had all but disappeared as a political force, for, even after the restoration of Sultan Mahmud to Riau-Lingga by the English in 1795, persistent argument and feuding between Malays and Bugis concerning the succession to Riau itself and to the mainland dependencies of Johore proper and Pahang were tearing it apart. Sultan Mahmud's death in 1812 merely intensified the conflict, and a new era of British and Dutch cooperation commenced, with the Malay powers in disarray in the south and under attack from Siam in the north. The outcome could scarcely be in doubt.

Not all the Dutch possessions in Southeast Asia had obeyed Prince William's injunction, but in the course of the fifteen years following 1795, most fell to the British by one means or another, though some for only brief periods of time. From being an Indian power interested primarily, where Southeast Asia was concerned, in the free passage of trade through the Malacca Straits and beyond to China, the East India Company suddenly found itself the possessor not merely of a proposed naval station on Penang island but of numerous other territorial dominions and responsibilities. Nor were some of the company's servants at all reluctant to assume these responsibilities and, indeed, to extend them. Chief among the visionaries and expansionists, perhaps, was Stamford Raffles. When Java, which he coveted for England, was being given back to the Dutch in 1816 by a company anxious to return to a situation in which it was concerned not with territorial governance but with the through trade to the Far East, he urged upon his superiors the acquisition of the small fishermen's island of Singapore at the foot of the Malay Peninsula. What Raffles sought, aside from his desire to continue to thwart the Dutch, was a base from which to carry on "communication with the native princes; for a general knowledge of what is going on at sea, and on the shore, throughout the archipelago; for the resort of the independent trade, and the trade with our allies; for the protection of our commerce and all our interests; and more especially for an entrepôt for our merchandise."[14] These arguments were of much the same force and nature as had characterized maneuvers for commercial power in the archipelago throughout the eighteenth century; indeed, one can as easily imagine their use by "native prince" as by English trader or company servant. When Singapore was acquired by Thomas Stamford Raffles for the East India Company in 1819, the tactics employed were based on a time-honored means of subverting one's neighbor—the exploitation of disputed succession and the playing off of one claimant to territory against another. In this case, the Dutch, who had returned to Riau and were in effective control of the claimant to Singapore island, and who in addition feared the establishment of a rival entrepôt in the area, were annoyed. A long diplomatic wrangle followed. But Singapore survived as a British base, establishing one particularly important departure from the patterns of the past—it was set up as a "free port," living not by taxation upon trade but on trading activity itself. Its free status was to turn the island within a few decades into the most flourishing exchange port Southeast Asia had ever seen, the center of a vigorous and politically demanding mercantile community.

During the first few years of Singapore's existence, the British sought to reduce systematically the potentialities for disturbance, and hence for expensive political or military involvement, in the area in which they were then interested. They wanted both to reach an understanding with the Netherlands in the archipelago consonant with a foreign policy of supporting the Dutch in Europe as part of the balance of power against France and, in the interests of untroubled continuance of the trade between India and China, to secure peace in the environs of Singapore and, more especially, Penang, where Siam-Kedah tensions were proving disruptive. Underlying all this was a firm determination not to become involved in any major way in the internal affairs of the Malay *negeri* of the peninsula or to engage in any form of territorial aggrandizement.

The attempts to reach understandings with the Dutch and the Siamese were, on the whole, successful, though less so for a time in the latter case. By the Anglo-Dutch Treaty of 1824, a final settlement of the confused position following the Napoleonic wars was reached, and guidelines were laid down for the future. Under the treaty, Singapore was retained and Malacca turned over to the British in exchange for the surrender of their settlement at Benkulen in western Sumatra and for a recognition that Dutch interests were paramount in Sumatra and in the islands south of Singapore. In return for British willingness to abstain from all political interference in Sumatra, the Dutch gave a similar promise to stay out of the Malay Peninsula, a division of interests that, in the changed conditions of fifty years later, was to lead to the final separation of the political destinies of those two parts of the Malay world, breaking centuries-old patterns of interdependence as well as conflict.

Two years after the conclusion of the Anglo-Dutch Treaty, Henry Burney, a British envoy to the Siamese court, was successful in 1826 in concluding another treaty, which, while limited, did offer some real satisfaction to British interests in the Malay area. Under it, the Siamese agreed to accept the southern boundary of Kedah (whose sultan, in exile in Penang, the British undertook to restrain) as the farthest extent of direct Siamese control on the west coast and to recognize effective Perak and Selangor independence, putting an end to the harassments that had marked the preceding decade. Despite some years of uncertainty concerning the implementation and effectiveness of the 1824 and 1826 treaties, the result by mid-century was to establish the East India Company as the paramount power in the Malay Peninsula. The interests of the company, and relative peace in the neighborhood of its settlements, had been secured, though they were based on new notions of international law deriving from Western practice that were not fully accepted by all the participants and on political considerations that did not take sufficient account of the changing nature of trade or of the interests of traders.

In the years following its establishment, Singapore rapidly achieved paramountcy in the maritime commerce of Southeast Asia, a position earned partly by its strategic location but most importantly, perhaps, by its jealously protected free-port status. Before long it overhauled Penang in importance (also a free port, but less well situated for trade), and in 1826 it became the governmental center for what were known henceforth as the Straits Settlements of Singapore, Penang, and Malacca. Demographically, Singapore grew from a fishing village to a flourishing port town, which, by the time of the census taken in 1840, had a total population of more than 35,000. Variegated though this population was—and mid-nineteenth-century accounts of Singapore seldom fail to describe the concourse of Tamils, Arabs, Javanese, Bugis,

Minangkabau, Trengganu and Kelantan Malays, Bengalis, and countless others who thronged the streets and markets—by far the largest part, at least 50 percent, was Chinese.

Though the first Chinese immigrants to Singapore were from the neighboring settlement of Malacca, they came increasingly from South China itself after the arrival of the first junk from Amoy in February 1821. One observer listed the Chinese as engaged in 110 separate occupations. They were concentrated primarily in trade and merchandising of all kinds, in agriculture (from vegetable gardening for Singapore's growing population to pepper and gambier cultivation on the north side of the island), and in laboring of every description. The Chinese brought with them distinctive forms of social organization, which continued to characterize their life in Nanyang, the southern seas. None has occasioned more comment (and often misunderstanding) than the *hui*, or "secret society," which, in its various manifestations, formed the principal means of social solidarity among the Chinese and the means whereby recruitment to the community, absorption of newcomers, maintenance of discipline, and the organization of new economic enterprise could be undertaken.

With the access of settled trading conditions on the periphery of the Malay Peninsula, sheltered under British power and free trade practice, and with the expansion of population and trade that resulted, Straits Settlements merchants and financiers grew increasingly interested in the Malay *negeri* of the interior as a field of investment, while the rulers and chiefs of the *negeri* began in turn to look to the Settlements as a source of both money and manpower. Already in the 1830s, the ruler of Johore, long independent of the old polity at Riau, had encouraged Chinese agriculturalists to plant pepper and gambier in the interior of the state, and there were few major rivers on which Chinese shopkeepers and peddlers were not to be found in increasing numbers.

The real economic prize, however, was tin, or the opportunity, to mine it in the tin rich west coast *negeri*. European and Chinese merchants in Malacca, the natural outlet for Negri Sembilan (and later Selangor) tin, appear to have been the first to engage in large-scale investment in the mines, followed before long by Penang interests operating in Perak. Though loans were sometimes made to Malay chiefs, who used the money to make speculative advances to Chinese miners, the more usual pattern in the long run was for Chinese traders in the Settlements to make advances directly to Chinese miners and mine managers in the fields, while the Malay chiefs tapped the resulting production by drawing tribute and certain taxes. As a result of this process of expansion, which was accompanied by Chinese innovation in the actual techniques of mining, production greatly increased, and in the 1850s and 1860s there was a "tin rush" marked by large-scale Chinese immigration into the west coast states. As one example, Larut, in northwestern Perak, which had few Chinese residents in 1848, when tin was first found there, had an estimated population in 1872 of between 20,000 and 25,000.

Changes of this magnitude placed severe stress on the Malay political system. The traditional balance of power within the *negeri*—both between ruler and chiefs and among the territorial chiefs themselves— was based on relatively small differences in wealth. Access to greatly increased revenues, such as were open to those chiefs fortunate enough to be in control of the richer tin-bearing areas, introduced into the system radical elements of imbalance and desperate rivalries over the possession of the important fields. Rivalries among Malay chiefs were paralleled by those among different groups of Chinese miners, the latter usually organized by competing secret societies, which in turn were backed with men, money, and arms by wealthy Chinese merchants in the Straits Settlements. The interaction of these factors, complicated by Malay succession disputes and by piracy bred of the breakdown of traditional patterns of trade and the increasing climate of lawlessness, led to a situation on the west coast of the peninsula that, by the late 1860s, seemed to many observers in the Straits (most of whom, it must be said, had never set foot on the peninsula) to be degenerating into anarchy.

Already hard hit by a general trade recession east of Singapore, the Straits merchants, unable to pursue sustained economic exploitation of the western states (or to develop markets there for the increasing flow of cheap industrial goods from Europe), and irritated by what they felt to be the unduly restrictive operation by the Dutch of the tariff provisions of the 1824 treaty, began to press the Straits Settlements government to intervene. They were encouraged to do this by two independent developments: the gradual extension of Dutch authority up the east coast of Sumatra after 1850, and the transfer of authority over the Settlements from the English East India Company to the India Office and then, as a Crown Colony (after the Indian Mutiny), to the more amenable—or so the merchants hoped—Colonial Office in 1867.

Following upon the 1824 treaty with Britain, the Dutch, weakened economically in Europe by the Napoleonic wars and by continued disturbance on its borders, were largely preoccupied in Asia with the development of Java. By the 1840s, however, with the success of the system of forced cultivation known as the Culture System there, energies were released for further insinuation into what were Java-centrically known as the Outer Islands, in order to bring those areas within the scope and control of the Dutch tariff system. By 1865, the Dutch had extended their presence in Sumatra to the southern boundaries of Aceh and were beginning to threaten the independence of that state as well, using the suppression-of-piracy provisions of the 1824 treaty as a pretext.

Throughout the period, the English East India Company, and then the Indian government, had remained adamantly opposed to involvement in the internal affairs of the Malay *negeri* of the peninsula. Despite official policies, however, actual commitments in the area had tended to grow, though certainly not fast enough to satisfy the Straits merchants. Governors on the spot were prone to take action first and to explain it later. In this way, for example, Malacca found itself embarked on a "war" in 1831 with the tiny neighboring state of Naning over disputed tax collection. And in the early 1860s, in the course of the Pahang civil war, Governor Cavenagh took decisive action in Pahang and Treng-ganu to forestall Siamese intervention. At all times, the officials in Singapore and Penang found themselves under pressure from commercial interests to safeguard British subjects, British trade, or British protected persons in the peninsular states. Partly to relieve pressures of that sort and assuage mercantile anxieties over the downturn in trade and partly from motives that had nothing to do with Southeast Asia, the British government in 1871 concluded another treaty, by which, in return for a promise of equal treatment for British traders in Sumatra, the Dutch were given freedom to extend their sovereignty over the whole of that island. The treaty was Aceh's death warrant as an independent polity, although execution had to await the conclusion of a thirty-year war of resistance. Though these imperial maneuvers may have improved, for the moment, the position of British commerce, they did little to lessen the demands for similar aggressive action in the Malay states. Three years later, in 1874, in an about-face of policy that has been discussed by historians ever since, the Colonial Office gave approval to limited intervention in the confused affairs of Perak. The British forward movement had begun and, as an appropriately realistic Malay proverb acknowledged, "Once the needle is in, the thread is sure to follow."

# 17

# The Archipelago, 1750–1870

FOR the fifteenth through the seventeenth century, the great formative age in the history of island Southeast Asia, it is possible to deal with the history of the area as a whole—from Aceh and Kedah to Luzon and the Moluccas—in terms of certain great common themes. In that age, trade, stimulated by intense demand for cloves, nutmeg, and pepper, flourished and widened; along the trade routes, Islam spread throughout the islands, and Catholicism came to the northern Philippines; everywhere new port states arose and the Europeans made their entrance in force. These broad movements introduced or deepened certain commonalities of experience through much of island Southeast Asia—the Malay language as a lingua franca, the widespread fraternity of Islam, the general importance of trade as the economic base of politics, and European naval paramountcy.

By the mid-eighteenth century, if not earlier, these general movements had spent their force. The spread of Malay had halted, not to resume until the twentieth century. Islam was no longer a revolutionary force, and Catholicism, too, in its area in the northern Philippines, was then simply the established religion. Cloves, nutmeg, and pepper were no longer the prizes of world commerce; the economically important products—coffee, sugar, tobacco, and tin—were, or came to be, concentrated in the three centers of Java, the northern Philippines, and the Straits. The rest of island Southeast Asia was economically marginal.

It was also politically marginal. The Spanish had settled down in the northern Philippines, playing no part, aside from perennial disputes with their immediate Muslim neighbors, in the broader politics of the archipelago. The Islamic port states of north-coast Java had been reabsorbed into the agrarian life of Java, and so, in their own way, had the Dutch. Between the mid-eighteenth and late nineteenth century, the Dutch were mainly occupied with exploiting the economic possibilities that political control of Java's large population offered, having neither the capacity nor the inclination for the far-flung naval and commercial dominion they had exercised in the seventeenth century. A third major center was beginning to take shape in just this period, as the English East India Company moved in to establish bases in the Straits Settlements and to exert its influence over the affairs of the Malay Peninsula. But, though the British Navy dominated the seas, and Singapore the commerce, of the archipelago, the British had no desire for territorial rule in those years.

Economically and politically peripheral, the peoples of the rest of the archipelago felt the commercial pull of Singapore. They were harried by British antipiracy raids in the 1840s and after and by a series of Dutch military expeditions to Sumatra, Borneo, Celebes, and Bali between the 1820s and the 1860s. But it was not until after 1870 that they were caught up again in historical movements as broad and powerful as those before 1700: the advance of imperial rule, of Christian missionaries and Reform Islam, and of new export industries. During those 140 years or more, there was still room for the many societies spread out across the wide island world to pursue their own many histories and for a crowd of different actors and movements to flourish and collide. The novels and short stories of Joseph Conrad give an appealing picture of the vigorous and still autonomous life of the coastal Malayo-Muslim peoples of the western archipelago as late as the 1880s, when he served there as a seaman. Elsewhere in the archipelago during those years, still other varied local histories were being enacted.

Among those unrecorded by Conrad were various new communities of Chinese miners like those moving into the gold fields of western Borneo near the modern Indonesian city of Pontianak. There, the Sultan of Sambas, the leading local *negeri* of the time, brought in Chinese miners in the middle of the eighteenth century. They soon organized themselves into the typical Chinese frontier institution of the *kongsi*—at once secret society, mine management, and government—and negotiated new terms with the sultan, allowing him some share of the gold and assuring themselves complete self-government in their mining districts. The mines prospered, more kinsmen arrived, new and rival *kongsi* were founded. By the early nineteenth century, there were some 20,000 or 30,000 Chinese flourishing in an area where previously there had been only forest, some coastal Malays, and a few Dayak swidden cultivators. The affairs of their society took a drastic turn at mid-century, when a series of Dutch expeditions overwhelmed its resistance, while at the same time the gold began to run out. But Dutch rule was for a long time merely nominal, and the miners turned readily to subsistence farming, continuing into modern times as the largest element in the population of western Borneo.

While the Chinese mining community was taking shape in the lower basin of the Kapuas River, another development was taking place far upstream. There, small numbers of Iban Dayaks began to cross the watershed into the headwaters of the Lupar River in present-day Sarawak in search of new swidden areas. By the early nineteenth century, they had come into contact with Malay and Arab coastal chiefs subordinate to the Sultanate of Brunei. The warlike Iban soon joined the coastal chiefs and, under their leadership, took up the profitable and exciting business of local short-range marauding—hence the later name for the Iban, Sea Dayak. In 1839, an English adventurer named James Brooke arrived on the coast and, finding it to his liking, entered vigorously into its politics. It was typical of the situation in the archipelago at the time that the domain he set about building was from the beginning a purely personal and dynastic one, like that of many a Bugis or Arab wanderer in the period. Recognized in 1842 by the Sultan of Brunei as chief of the small Sarawak River district, he took his place in the Malay political system of the coast, styling himself *raja*—the most successful, it turned out, of the many white rajas in the archipelago in the nineteenth century. In his early years he obtained help from the British Navy in fighting Iban marauders, but thereafter he and his successors were largely on their own. His nephew and successor, Charles Brooke, who had served his apprenticeship among the Iban on the Lupar River, found the crucial formula. He managed to detach the Iban from their association with coastal Malay chiefs and to attach them to his own person instead. Thereafter, the Iban went to war on land under Raja Charles, helping him to extend his rule, while at the same time they continued the dynamic of Iban expansion begun a century earlier and spread over most of what was becoming the Brooke *negeri* of Sarawak.

It would be too simple to call the Iban pirates, though that is what contemporary Europeans called them, and they certainly seized innocent *perahu* on the high seas. Marauding was a recognized means of political advancement as well as a form of economic activity throughout the archipelago. It played an important role in the affairs of the Sultanate of Sulu, which Europeans considered the most notorious pirate and slave-raiding state of the time, and is therefore worth examining carefully in that context. Sulu, founded in the fifteenth century, reached the peak of its importance and prosperity in the eighteenth and early nineteenth centuries. As much as anything, its rise then was due to strong demand in China for luxury goods, such as birds' nests for soup, obtainable in the Sulu Sea area. Merchant shipping of the South China coast thronged the harbor of Jolo, the Sulu capital, and from there a net of trade routes reached out all over the northeast part of the archipelago.

Unlike the situation that developed in nineteenth-century Malay tin states, the Chinese came only as merchants; it was Sulus and their allies who procured the luxuries and sold them to the Chinese. Sulu society was like that of other Malayo-Muslim *negeri:* a pyramid of personal relations in which, at each level, a man's status and wealth depended on the number of followers he could successfully control and support. Below the Sultan was a class of *datu,* corresponding to Malay chiefs—independent-minded aristocrats who heeded the sultan only when he was a strong leader and who were constantly competing among themselves for greater prestige. Their followings consisted of freemen—who could themselves hope to become *datu* if they were successful in trade and raid —and of slaves. It is important to note that "slavery" in Sulu, as generally in the archipelago, was primarily a method for incorporating more people into the organized community. Slaves were sometimes sold as chattels, but they were usually enrolled in a *datu*'s following, alongside freemen. Their children could expect to become free.

It was ambitious Sulu *datu,* then, who acquired the birds' nests, pearls, and other specialties sold to the Chinese merchants in Jolo. As river chiefs on the north Borneo coast, they mobilized their followers to dive for pearls or to exact tribute in birds' nests from non-Muslim peoples in the interior. In exactly the same spirit, other Sulu *datu* (or leaders of the related groups called Ilanun, Balanguingui, or Bajau) went out marauding. They sought tribute, slaves to sell or add to their followings, and even ordinary trade. It was a harsh system—perhaps especially for the *indios* of the Bisayan Islands to the north—but not unusually so by the standards of the time. One should not be too hasty in accusing its contemporary European critics of hypocrisy, for they knew little about the workings of Sulu society, and they mistook the Malayo-Muslim version of slavery for their own older and far more brutal one. Still, it is evident that the British and Spanish gunboats that ravaged Sulu villages in the antipiracy campaigns of the mid-nineteenth century practiced the same merciless aggression as the Sulus in their raids on the Bisayas or Borneo.

Although the general religious pattern of the archipelago remained stable until the latter part of the nineteenth century, there were important exceptions in particular areas. During the expansion by the Balinese in the first half of the eighteenth century, at which time they played an important role in the East Hook of Java, they also took control of the western half of the neighboring island of Lombok, and Balinese Hindu-Buddhism came to root itself permanently there. In the early nineteenth century, the Minahassans of the northern arm of the Celebes, loosely associated politically with the Dutch company since the seventeenth century, converted to Protestantism, laying the foundations for a longstanding special relation with the Dutch in the colonial army and civil service. The most intense and complicated religious movement of the period, however, was that of the Padri among the Minangkabau of West Sumatra. The Minangkabau, mainly wet-rice farmers, constituted one of the larger ethnic groups in the archipelago. They had accepted Islam in the seventeenth century on their own cultural terms. Around 1800, however, a number of *haji,* returning from Mecca under the influence of Wahhabite fundamentalism, called for a return to Islamic purity and for abandonment of such forbidden practices as gambling at cockfights, drinking, and smoking. This Padri Movement, growing steadily in the first two decades of the nineteenth century, stimulated a reaction by the established leaders of Minangkabau society, the *adat* chiefs. There had already been fighting when the Dutch returned to the coast at the end of the Napoleonic wars determined to reestablish their suzerain powers of the seventeenth century. They soon made common cause with the *adat* chiefs—not only those in the coastal lowlands, to which Dutch claims had hitherto been confined, but also those in the interior highlands—who were seeking allies against the Padri and were willing to accept Dutch suzerainty in exchange. The ensuing skirmishes in the early 1820s had two aspects. From the Minangkabau point of view, they were a continuation of the internal struggle, with the Dutch now helping the *adat* party, while, to the Dutch, they represented an effort to enforce newly acquired claims to authority in the interior against the resistance of the Padris. In the 1830s, however, when a series of large Dutch expeditions and heavily fought campaigns made clear to all that the Dutch were aiming at full control of Minangkabau, the colonial issue increasingly overshadowed the original religious one. Some *adat* chiefs ceased to support the Dutch, and others turned against them, though it helped little; the rule throughout the nineteenth century was that, whenever the paramount powers were willing to pay the price, they could have their way. By 1840, the Dutch had added Minangkabau to the still small list of areas outside Java that they directly and closely administered. In the 1840s, they were able to inaugurate a compulsory coffee cultivation system there modeled on their practice in Java. The religious tension within Minangkabau society died down, to revive again at the turn of the century with the rise of Reform Islam.

# 18

## Java, 1757–1875

IN the 1670s, the Mataram dynasty had begun to fall apart, and, in the course of the civil wars of the next three quarters of a century, its place in the political life of Java was gradually taken over by the Dutch East India Company (VOC). The process reached a more or less stable conclusion with the partition of Mataram under VOC auspices in 1755–1757. Between that time, when the Dutch may be said to have attained full political control of the island, and the late nineteenth century, when the history of Java merged into that of the new Netherlands Indies, falls the last era in which Javan history is intelligible by itself and must be treated separately.[15] It was a period in which Dutch and Javans came to terms and created a common society. Dutch-Javan institutions, born in the confusion of the civil wars, became entrenched during the last years of the VOC. Although challenged from the outside in the decades of disturbance between 1808 and 1830, they resumed their development until increasing pressures brought many, but not all, of the old formulas to bankruptcy by the end of the century.

Though the VOC gained an increasing say in the political affairs of Java from the late seventeenth century, its military control was always precarious and its purposes unclear. In the seventeenth century, the Dutch on Java had been diligent servants of a great merchant company, and in the nineteenth century they gradually became civil servants of a colonial state. In the eighteenth century, however, they were essentially an alien war band, extracting what they could from conquered territories by the most expedient means. Culturally remote in their polyglot enclaves on the coast, seldom venturing into the interior except on military expeditions, generally uninterested in governance, and no longer even very dutiful servants of the company, they were nevertheless masters of Java. In this situation, the Dutch and local elites in different parts of Java found it necessary to come to terms with each other. Company rule, therefore, even where it brought changes, expressed itself in essentially Javan terms.

Dutch rule on Java was not imposed all at once but grew historically and hence was full of oddments and local variations. Everywhere but in Batavia itself, however, it rested on a variety of special arrangements with local elites. Batavia and its surrounding area of a few hundred square miles, with its polyglot population of Chinese, Chinese *mestizos,*

Eurasians, Dutch from Holland, Bugis and German soldiers, Balinese, Makassarese, and Indians, was ruled directly by Dutch officials. Here, too, in the eighteenth century were an increasing number of permanent appanages ("Private Lands," the Dutch called them, describing a modified Javan institution in their own terms) whose Dutch, Chinese *mestizo*, and Eurasian owners in effect ruled their own peasant subjects. Beyond Batavia, the Dutch ruled the areas ceded to them by Mataram—most of West Java, the north coast of Central and East Java, and the whole of the East Hook—through "regents," local lords whose credentials usually dated from Mataram times. Relations between the VOC and its lesser vassals, Bantam, Ceribon, and Madura, were marked by special features. Ceribon was an old ally; Bantam, formerly a trading rival, delivered large quantities of pepper at low fixed prices; the Madurese were military allies. Finally, the VOC treated its still very large and dangerous vassals, the principalities of Surakarta and Yogyakarta, very cautiously, maintaining the forms of independence, exercising control discreetly through Dutch-appointed *patih,* and demanding less tribute than from their other vassals.

Certain effects of Dutch rule were felt everywhere in Java. The company recognized and supported the local authority of regents and vassals because it was both unwilling and unable to govern millions of Javans without their aid, because it hoped thereby to gain their political support or appease their hostility in an always dangerous military situation, and because it wanted their help in exploiting the island. By recognizing the authority of these *priyayi* rulers, they necessarily accepted the Javan system—charismatic rule, patron-client relations, appanage, and the rest—within which they continued to operate. In this way, Dutch power maintained Javan institutions. Dutch rule, however, also changed the practice of Javan government in important ways. When Dutch officials on the north coast took bribes on a large scale from *priyayi* wanting appointments, new forces entered the political system. The VOC, too, was a politically stable and militarily powerful overlord, and its support greatly strengthened the position of *priyayi* in their dealings with the peasants beneath them, a change with important long-term consequences.

Other effects of company rule were more typical of the areas on which it made the heaviest economic demands, notably the interior of West Java and the north coast areas ceded to it by Mataram and over which it had greater control. The company's economic arrangements, like its political ones, were extempore and varied widely: It levied tribute in rice in one regency, in teak or indigo in the next, and only in coffee in another. There was a clear contrast, however, in the systems of exploitation in the two main areas of West Java and the north coast.

In Priangan, the hilly interior of West Java inhabited by Sundanese, the Dutch concentrated their efforts on coffee to the exclusion of all else. They introduced the coffee bush from Arabia around 1700, found that it flourished there, and experimented for a time with easy payments and more or less free peasant cultivation before settling down to a more profitable system in the 1720s. The company required its subordinates, the Priangan regents, to deliver specified annual quotas of coffee, which the regents in turn levied from their subjects as a tax in kind. In return (as well as paying the regents a small price for the coffee), the VOC levied no other taxes in Priangan, which left the regents free to continue their own traditional taxes in labor and rice. Under this "Priangan System," coffee became by far the most valuable export from Java and remained so until the 1860s. The Sundanese regents, rescued from insignificance in what had been a poor hinterland, became great lords. The Dutch commissioners for native affairs, occupants of an obscure old Batavian post who gradually took charge of all Priangan coffee, made fortunes lending money to the regents. The peasants, put to harsh work, built a new economy for Priangan and—in times of complete peace and increasing wet-rice production—had more children.

The economic arrangements arising in the older regencies of the northern coast, most of them under the governor of the north coast, were very different. The area produced little in the way of export products—mainly sugar and indigo—but it was more accessible to Dutch and Chinese, more heavily populated, and relatively advanced economically. A great variety of devices were developed to extract produce and cash from the peasants for the benefit of the company's overseas trade and its establishment on Java, and for the profit of Chinese merchants, of regents, and of the company's servants—especially the governors, who made even larger fortunes than the commissioners in Priangan. The Dutch coastal towns built houses and ships from the wood of the area and ate its tribute rice. The company farmed road and river tolls and market taxes to Chinese and also "leased" many villages to Chinese, who used the labor rights thus acquired to grow sugar and other crops. *Priyayi* normally paid bribes to Dutch officials to gain office, gave them "presents" on various occasions, and began themselves to lease out villages. All profited except the peasants and the company as an institution. But the long-term effect of such apparently sweeping changes was obscured or negated by the characteristic inclination of all concerned to operate in terms of traditional Javanese institutions. The Dutch ruled, but daily government remained in the hands of *priyayi;* production was increasingly commercial, but it continued to be organized in the older forms of tribute or appanage.

Politically and economically, the Javan and Dutch elites were closely entwined, but culturally they were estranged. The Dutch themselves were hardly touched by Javanese culture in this period—less so, indeed, than their more consciously superior successors in the nineteenth century. In the eighteenth century, they had not yet penetrated deeply into the interior of the island, and only a handful were stationed there. Living in towns on the north coast, they accommodated (when they did) to the cosmopolitan life long established in the ports of the archipelago, took Balinese or Makassarese slaves as concubines, and fathered Eurasians who spoke Portuguese or Malay, rarely Dutch or Javanese.

The same was true on the other side. Dutch culture in this period and through most of the nineteenth century held no interest for the peoples of Java. Javanese *priyayi* and Dutch captains communicated in Malay, nourished suspicions about each other's religions, and misunderstood each other's political beliefs. The cultural gulf mattered little to the conquering Dutch, and perhaps it mattered little to the Javanese *priyayi*, too —we know too little of Javanese cultural history to be certain. It seems likely, however, that they were sorely disturbed about the alien ways of their new lords, for the ideal of harmony so basic to Javanese culture was thereby threatened. The earlier intrusion of Islam had posed a similar threat, eliciting an intense effort at reconciliation and synthesis. But the new disharmony was more intractable. Hence the poignancy in a passage like the following from an eighteenth-century chronicle describing the decision of Paku Buwono II in 1743 to move the *kraton* of Mataram from Kartasura:

> The appearance of the Honored Lord did not differ from that which was usual when the times were still prosperous, but in his heart were darkening clouds as he continuously brooded over the destruction of the capital. . . . If one thought about it the pain grew greater, as one felt it the sadder one became that Kartasura was destroyed. The Patih was addressed, "Listen, Adipati, it is my heart's desire which cannot be resisted to move the capital. . . ."[16]

The feeling that the times were out of joint was one of the factors that influenced the remarkable flowering of *priyayi* culture in the eighteenth and early nineteenth centuries. A large new court literature grew up in this period, the art of *batik* achieved its classical form and colors (indigo blue and rust brown), the repertoire of the *wayang kulit* was enlarged and its music refined and developed, and a new dance drama, *wayang orang*, grew out of the *wayang kulit* tradition. Most characteristically, perhaps, the Javanese language was polished into an instrument of superb social precision, so that Javanese came to speak what were almost different dialects, according to whether they were addressing social superiors, equals, or inferiors. Through all the branches in which the cultural movement expressed itself ran a dominant tendency toward refinement and stylization. One effect, therefore, was to define ever more sensitively and completely the gulf between *priyayi* and peasant. A second was to make available an ever more capacious and perfect cultural world as a refuge from the disharmony in the political world of the time.

A very different kind of cultural change was going on in Priangan in the same period. Priangan had been a sparsely populated, swidden-cultivating region when it first received Islam from the Javanese port states in the sixteenth century and then came under Mataram rule in the early seventeenth century. In Mataram times, the *dalem* (courts) of the Sundanese regents were centers from which Javanese culture began to spread and around which Sundanese swidden cultivators began to settle and to grow wet rice like the Javanese. Dutch rule and the Dutch-run coffee system brought no corresponding influence of Dutch culture. Instead the "Priangan System," by elevating the prestige of the Java-nized regents and by stimulating economic activity and population growth, promoted the older trend. Javanese cultural influences, in increasingly well-rooted Sundanese variants, spread steadily through Priangan. The Sundanese did not become Javanese—they continued to speak their own language, for example—but by 1900 the process was complete; they belonged in all that was important to the general Javanese tradition.

The VOC, in whose name Dutch activity on Java was carried for-ward, was of course a much wider enterprise. The complex relationship between the hybrid Dutch-Javan society and the parent Dutch company is demonstrated by the growth and consolidation of the former in the second half of the eighteenth century, while the VOC as a worldwide trading company was falling apart. The causes and symptoms of the decline were a matter of Dutch, not Javan, history. It is enough to say that stiffening joints of oligarchic rule in Holland, the rising naval and industrial strength of England, rapidly mounting deficits, and universal corruption brought about the abolition of the VOC and the assumption of its debts, assets, and possessions by the Dutch state on the last day of the eighteenth century.

That event had no immediate effect on Java; the VOC system contin-ued unchanged for almost a decade more. But new forces had risen in Europe, their roots in the Enlightenment, the wars of the French Revo-lution, and the Industrial Revolution. After 1808, those forces were brought to bear in a rapid succession of assaults on what was by now the *ancien régime* of VOC Java. First, in 1808, came the new governor-gen-eral, Herman Daendels, Dutch by birth, a Napoleonic marshal by career and inclination; then, between 1811 and 1816, English conquest and rule under Lieutenant Governor-General Stamford Raffles, an Adam Smith liberal of great charm and energy; then, after 1816, restored Dutch rule for a decade and a half under a commissioner-gen-eral and two governors-general of varying but still non-"Javan" per-suasions. Thrusting noisily through the revolving door, these successive regimes rewrote the rules of government every five years and created a tangle of conflicting legislation—much of it merely on paper—as testi-mony to their reforming zeal.

Daendels and his successors came out from Europe determined to govern rather than simply to control Java; they challenged the whole system of arrangements by which company servants and Javans had accommodated to each other for more than a century. Between 1808 and 1830, the company's great vassals, the principalities of Central Java, lost most of their territory to direct Dutch rule, while the Sultanate of Bantam was abolished and its whole territory annexed. In exactly the same spirit, the great Dutch satrapies of the governors of the north coast and the commissioners for native affairs were broken up. In their place a uniform administrative hierarchy of residencies (headed by European residents), regencies, and districts (with Javan regents and district heads) was applied to most of the island. As the logic of the bureaucratic system required, the successive regimes strove to transform the regents from what amounted to petty vassals, ruling their own territories in essentially traditional ways, into ordinary civil servants. At various times, they were denied hereditary succession, were paid salaries instead of permitted customary land and tax rights, and were largely removed from the judicial system. Finally, Raffles introduced, and his immediate successors continued, a general cash land tax intended to shift the government's basic economic role from a "system of tribute" (with the government itself collecting and selling agricultural products) to a more modern "system of taxation" (in which it would collect taxes and provide general services, leaving production and commerce to private citizens).

Coming after the simple greed and comfortable collaboration of late VOC times, all this purpose and policy was impressive. The new regimes did in fact make many changes; but the process was slower than enthusiasts like Daendels and Raffles wished. In part, this was due to difficulties peculiar to the period: short-lived regimes, chronic war conditions, and constant pressure from home governments to make Java pay. For example, Daendels, who wanted to abolish corvée, levied an unprecedented quantity of corvée labor to build a great post road for the defense of the island. In a period when more and more of the island was coming under direct rule and Batavia was developing a more uniform administrative control, financial difficulties obliged Daendels, and Raffles in particular, to sell off great stretches of coastal West and East Java as "Private Lands," which was a step in just the opposite direction. During the whole period, for the same financial reasons, the new policies were simply not applied to Priangan; the urgently wanted coffee flowed out and the Priangan System, an archetypal arrangement of the *ancien régime,* continued undisturbed.

There were more fundamental obstacles, however. The institutions of Dutch-Javan society, developed over a century or more, were deeply rooted. Javan peasants, on the basis of past experience and current conditions, saw little advantage in growing export crops themselves, as Raffles had expected and as his system required. The majesty of a regent and the high status of *priyayi* in general, enlarged by the experience of VOC times, could not be abolished by administrative fiat. Most Europeans on Java were equally at home in the old institutions. Thus, when they took to producing commercial crops in the Central Java principalities in this period, they found it natural to buy rights to peasant labor from appanage-holders at the courts, as Chinese had leased villages previously.

The Java War, a great rebellion that ravaged the Javanese lands between 1825 and 1830, was the final crisis, which brought the confusion and experiments of the transitional years to an end. Out of it emerged the Culture System, introduced by a new governor-general, Johannes van den Bosch, in 1830. Like his predecessors since 1808, van den Bosch set out to govern, not simply to control, Java. He kept the land tax (though in an ancillary role), and he continued the development of a regular bureaucratic administration centering in a corps of European officials. Unlike his predecessors, however, van den Bosch determined to govern with the grain of local custom, and the key provisions of his Culture System harked back to VOC practice. Under the Culture System, Javan peasants were required to deliver specified quantities of export produce—or the land and labor necessary to produce them, which amounted to the same thing—as their principal obligation to the government. The government no longer exported the products itself, as under the VOC; that was done by the semiofficial NHM (Nederlandsche Handelsmaatschappij, Netherlands Trading Company). But dividing the VOC's old functions between the government and the NHM did not alter the essential fact that van den Bosch had returned to the "system of tribute." The government of Java was once again to be a machine for collecting export goods to ship home. In the same spirit, he formally recognized the traditional patterns of hereditary succession and rights over land and labor for the regents and, by thus restoring their prestige, aimed at the old practice of ruling in the Javan manner, through the personal authority of the *priyayi*.

The Culture System lasted for three or four decades as the basic regime of Java and during that period achieved just what van den Bosch had hoped for. It produced an enormous surplus in goods, which revived Dutch shipping, made Amsterdam again a great entrepôt for tropical products, and paid off Holland's public debt. Absolute peace returned to Java, the *priyayi* were content, and the people acquired a new reputation as "the most docile folk on earth." In 1861, an admiring Englishman, called (unbelievably) J. B. Money, summed it up in a book entitled *Java, or How to Manage a Colony.*

That is how the period looks from the point of view of a purely colonial history. The importance of the Culture System from the point of view of Javan history, however, was that it entrenched a peculiarly intimate association between the modern and the traditional, between metropolitan Dutch and Javan elements, which persisted long after the system as such was given up. A typical example of the symbiosis, and one with profound implications, was the way the sugar industry developed. Though there had been substantial sugar exports from the seventeenth century, the industry in its modern form was very much a child of the Culture System. Sugar cane has the same major requirements—a great deal of water and labor—as wet rice. Under the Culture System, the government required peasant villages in many wet-rice areas to devote sections of their land on a rotating basis to cane cultivation. At the same time, it gave out contracts to private Dutch individuals to process the cane, lending them funds for the expensive milling machinery, and requiring them to deliver the sugar to the NHM for shipment on government account. As this pattern spread and took root, the various parties involved became more and more deeply enmeshed in each other's affairs. The Dutch mill owner *cum* sugar contractor owned no sugar land and had virtually no full-time labor; he borrowed them temporarily, and very cheaply, from surrounding villages by orders from Dutch residents and Javanese regents. The latter, in their turn, were paid "cultivation percentages" based on production in their areas. Peasants continued to grow rice (more intensively, since part of their land was under cane) but they also cultivated the cane and, in the harvest season, worked in the mills for small wages. Their corvée obligations continued. They still served in the retinues and kitchens of *priyayi* officials, and they also built, by mid-century, the best road system in Asia to meet the needs of the sugar mills and other export industries.

At mid-century, Dutch liberals began a long and bitter campaign against the Culture System, and in the years around 1870 they succeeded in eliminating some of the most characteristic features of the system—cultivation percentages, compulsory use of land and labor for export crops, and sugar contracts. It is customary to speak of the fall of the Culture System in 1870 and to label the last thirty years of the century the Liberal Period. The distinction, however, is much sharper within the internal affairs of the small Dutch minority than it is for the general social history of Java. In sugar areas, for example, villages became in theory free to withhold land and labor from the mills. In practice, they had little or no choice. Dutch and Javanese officials, working through village headmen enrolled as agents of the system, made sure that the flow of sugar continued. Village and mill stayed closely tied while government irrigation projects opened new land to the sugar/rice combination, and the system spread rapidly in boom conditions.

In this way, more and more Javanese peasants were absorbed in a system that allowed (or required) them to carry on inside the shell of a familiar cultural and psychological universe, while they participated in what was emerging as one of the world's largest and most modern agricultural industries. Similarly, although liberal policies reduced the prerogatives of the *priyayi*—their claims to corvée services for example—and Dutch officials steadily took over more of the actual work of government, peasants still abased themselves before *priyayi,* and the Dutch honored the feudal compact in its essentials. The *priyayi* ideal carried on in an increasingly modern bureaucratic Java. There is the same quality of paradox about all the social life of Java in the later nineteenth century—the Javans embedded, by Dutch design and by their own preference, in familiar but eroding institutions, while at the same time carried swiftly on the currents of change.

The same interlocking of what was Javan and what was Dutch—and in this case Chinese, too—can be seen in the cultural life of Java in the nineteenth century. As the Dutch moved inward from their eighteenth-century coastal enclaves, they came to terms in many ways with Javan, especially Javanese, culture. Dutch officials and planters, isolated amid a large and culturally vigorous population, kept Javan mistresses and adopted a mixed *Indisch* (Indies) culture. Dutch officials kept retinues and used the *payung* (the sunshade of high-rank, carried by an attendant); all took to the *rijsttafel* (the Dutch term for the Javan meal of rice with many side dishes) and to Javan clothing when off duty; the more important or richer of them maintained large open establishments much like regents' *dalem*. Eurasians were even more thoroughly immersed in *Indisch* culture, and substantial numbers merged into the Javan community in the course of the nineteenth century.

The economic expansion of the nineteenth century drew increasing numbers of Chinese, mostly Hokkiens, to Java. In that period they became middlemen for the whole island, farming various taxes for the Dutch and trading in all sorts of imports and exports. The government treated them in the same spirit as it did Javans, recognizing them as a separate community with their own customs and leaders *(kapitans)*, but it interfered less in their internal affairs, while at the same time requiring them to live in Chinese quarters in the towns and restricting their movement with a system of travel passes. This did not prevent the Chinese from responding strongly to Javan cultural influence, if only because most of them before 1900 came as single men and therefore married Javans. Some became fully Javan—some regent families in East Java in particular were largely Chinese in origin. But the great majority adopted a mixed Javan-Hokkien cultural pattern called *peranakan,* which had its roots in the eighteenth century and earlier but was consolidated and stabilized in the nineteenth.

*Priyayi,* for their part, adopted some items of Dutch material culture, such as chairs, and in some respects took up the *Indisch* style, but mainly they nurtured their own great tradition, watching Dutch, Eurasians, and Chinese shifting culturally in their direction. In part this was due to Dutch policy, which aimed at keeping Javans as they were, culturally and otherwise. Until late in the nineteenth century, the government discouraged its officials from using Dutch in dealing with *priyayi,* preferring Malay, and made little or no provision for Dutch-language or any Western-type education for them, or for anyone else. But their own high culture had a deeper significance for the *priyayi* in the nineteenth century; it was a cloak they wrapped tighter about themselves as the winds of modernity blew more harshly. Not until early in the twentieth century did more than a handful have the courage or the desperation to cast it off.

# 19

## The Philippines, 1762–1872

THE most important phenomenon in Philippine history from 1762 to 1872 was the emergence of an elite whose membership transcended earlier social groupings and whose prime identification was with the archipelago itself. This elite, composed primarily of Chinese *mestizos* but also including Spaniards born in the islands, Spanish *mestizos,* and *indios,* shaped Philippine nationalism. Known as the *ilustrados,* or enlightened ones, these men gained education and self-awareness because of the radical economic, social, and political changes in the life of the colony. During the period, the Philippines was integrated into the world community to a greater extent than in previous centuries, partly because Spain was helpless to control developments and partly because the shifting focus of economic power transformed the archipelago into a major producer of certain export crops.

Philippine isolation was shattered by the British occupation of Manila in 1762. The attack, which came because Spain had allied itself with France against England, found the colony unprepared and ignorant of the alliance. Although Manila quickly fell, a member of the *Audiencia,* Don Simón de Anda, escaped to the interior, repudiated the surrender, and organized an effective resistance which limited British power in the Manila Bay area. Although the British restored the whole archipelago to Spanish control two years later, powerful social forces had been unleashed in the islands. The Chinese, misjudging English intentions and still smarting under the expulsion order of Governor Arandía, openly supported England, thus incurring increased Spanish hostility. The collapse of central Spanish authority also prompted a spate of *indio* uprisings of varying intensity in Pangasinan, Laguna, Cavite, Tondo, Iloilo, Zamboanga, Samar, Cebu, Panay, and Ilocos. Of these, the Ilocano revolt led by Diego Silang was the most serious. The uprising, which grew out of local grievances, prompted Diego Silang to ally himself with the English, since he felt that the English would not molest or disturb the *indios* but would instead treat them with regard and consideration.

When the Spanish government regained control of Manila, the colony was bankrupt. The British had captured the outbound galleon, *Santísima Trinidad,* in 1762 and seized about 3 million pesos. The inbound galleon, *Filipino,* did finance Anda's war resistance, but thereafter this vital lifeline stopped. The British had sacked Manila, seized the ships in the harbor, and departed with whatever bullion they could find. Moreover, by 1764 the seemingly limitless wealth of the Spanish empire had been spent, and rehabilitation could not be financed by the mother country. Entry into the China market by other European traders forced the Spanish to pay much more for Chinese goods than they had in the past. Bringing back the galleon was not enough; to restore authority, the Spanish needed a means of making the archipelago self-supporting.

The postwar governors, most importantly José de Basco y Vargas (1778–1787), attempted to apply new ideas to reform the system. The most famous of a whole series of reform plans was written by Francisco Leandro de Viana in 1765. Among its recommendations were direct communications with Spain via the Cape of Good Hope; the establishment of a trading company with permission to develop trade between Cadiz, Manila, and Canton; the encouragement of Spanish immigration; the creation of plantations; and the reform of the army, bureaucracy, and tax structure. Such ideas were profoundly disturbing to the conservative elements in the colony. As Governor Basco noted in 1780, "the first task must be to level the massive mountain of prejudice that stands in the way of the enlightened purposes of the central government."[17]

In 1781, Basco established an agricultural society to promote production by granting prizes, printing texts on techniques of cultivation, and publicizing the study of agronomy. He imported mulberry trees, for example, to grow silk in Bicol. In the private sector, a remarkably atypical entrepreneur named Francisco Salgado started to develop copper at Masbate, iron at Santa Inés, cacao, indigo, canvas weaving, and, most persistently, cinnamon. Among the many efforts, the only "success" was the establishment of a tobacco monopoly in 1781. The monopoly freed the Manila government from dependence on the galleon trade and the Mexican subsidy. In a pattern new to the Philippines, the government rigidly controlled crop volume, price, and market sale. By establishing forced delivery in the tobacco areas of northern Luzon, it created many of the hardships already familiar in the Moluccas. While the imposition of this system led to revolts in the tobacco region, it proved to be immediately profitable, and within a few years the insular treasury was able to remit money back to Spain.

The effort to develop export crops required a restructuring of the patterns of trade. It was here that the Bourbon reformers encountered the most intense opposition, since the galleon merchants clearly perceived the threat to their way of life. A Spanish man-of-war, the first ship to sail directly from Spain to Manila in 1765 in order to trade, was ignored by the galleon merchants, even though it was trading for the king's own account. The galleon merchants were a small and powerful group. Organized as a guild *(consulado)*, they tried to use their collective power to stifle change. However, the need for revenue and the new opportunities for profit were too great. Private traders, including some non-Spaniards, entered the trade with California, for example, bringing back sea-otter pelts for sale in China. Although this trade violated the monopolistic regulations governing all Spanish trade with the Americas, the galleon merchants could not stop it. They were also unable, in 1785, to block the establishment of the Royal Philippine Company. Designed to promote a worldwide Spanish trading network, the company was granted broad powers by the Spanish monarchy. It was permitted to sail around the world in either direction and was enjoined to stimulate Philippine economic development by investing 4 percent of its profits in economic development schemes in the archipelago. By 1790, more than forty voyages had been made; the company was investing in Philippine indigo, pepper, sugar, and cotton crops; and Manila had been opened legally to foreign ships if they carried Asian rather than European goods. But, despite its name, the company derived most of its profits from inherited Latin American routes. As a result, even before the chaos caused by the French Revolution, the company directors wanted to drop Manila as an enforced port of call, preferring instead direct access to China.

A campaign by the successive Bourbon governments against the friars paralleled their efforts in the economic sphere. As men of the Enlightenment, the Bourbon rulers were anticlerical; as social reformers, they wanted to challenge friar dominance in the archipelago. Governor Simón de Anda, for example, in a memorandum to the king, maintained that the friars should not meddle in worldly affairs and that they should sell their estates, even though they were just owners, since such business was inconsistent with their ministry. Anda argued that many of the estates, if not all of them, had been usurped from the *indios*. Indicting the friars on numerous counts, he urged the king to limit their power by episcopal visitation, to establish native seminaries for diocesan clergy to replace them, and to expel them from the colony if they failed to heed the king's command. In 1767, the Spanish king expelled the Jesuits from the entire Spanish empire. Under threat of the same treatment, the Dominicans in Manila reluctantly agreed to accept visitation by the king's confidant, Archbishop Basilio Sancho de Santa Justa.

The specific technique used in the antifriar campaign was the appointment of diocesan priests to parishes formerly held by friars. Centuries before, the Pope had granted the Spanish kings extraordinary powers as royal patrons of the Church in the Spanish empire. The governor, as vice-patron and representative of the king, had the right to appoint. Working in close harmony with the archbishop, who was seeking to strengthen diocesan authority at the expense of the friars, the governor selected diocesan priests for those parishes formerly held by the Jesuits and others that had been left vacant by death. Since there were fewer than ten Caucasian diocesan priests in the whole archipelago, *indio* and *mestizo* clerics had to be promoted. Their educational level was low, since the friars had never made any effort to train a native clergy. The conservative community in Manila, already deeply resentful of the movement, was delighted when some diocesan priests proved unable to bear their new burdens. The issue became a racial one, with the native priest held up to derision by the Spanish community. A joke of the time was that there were no longer any men to row the ferry boats in Manila because the archbishop had ordained them all. Although the Bourbon governors optimistically predicted that friar influence would yield gradually to the spread of enlightened ideas, the effect was to polarize the society and to force the friars into an even more reactionary position.

The friars started to regain their position as early as 1776, when they obtained from Madrid a temporary suspension of the replacement procedure. Under the wartime conditions of 1803, they successfully won the governor's support in their fight to retain three parishes, including an important one near Manila. In 1826, Ferdinand VII returned most Philippine parishes to friar control. The *indio* priests, now fully aware of Spanish clerical attitudes, were demoted to curates. Pro-friar advocates argued that the moral fiber of the colony had deteriorated primarily because of the *indio* and *mestizo* priests. They maintained that it was the friars who gave the Spanish their moral ascendancy.

The restoration of the clerical *status quo ante* was not matched in the economic sphere. The Royal Philippine Company, although maintaining the fiction of its interest in the islands, had more or less abandoned its effort by 1789. Only sixteen direct voyages were made to Manila between 1785 and 1820; the company was caught up in the worldwide disruption of trade caused by war. Although its charter was reissued in 1803, by 1819 the company showed a heavy loss. The hopes of its planners were never achieved. Moreover, the collapse of Spanish rule in Latin America ended the galleon age. In 1820, the Mexican revolutionary Agustín Iturbide seized the 2 million pesos realized that year from the sale of Manila goods. That *coup de grace* bankrupted the Manila *consulado;* by 1825 the total trade with the new world was less than 2 percent of the 1810 level. The demise of the galleon also ended the *situado.* Perhaps some 400 million pesos had flowed from the silver mines at Potosí to Manila during the galleon's long life. The termination of the flow caused not only economic dislocation but also Philippine dependency on Spain. The galleon had been a constant channel of communication and personnel and had kept the Spanish empire racially catholic as well as Catholic religiously.

The period from 1820 to 1825 was a watershed in Philippine history. The key issue, creole equality, was related to the existent economic dislocation, political uncertainty, and social change. During those years, many *peninsulares* arrived in Manila. These Iberian Spanish, recently expelled from Latin America, looked down on creoles. The *peninsulares,* including the friars, distrusted not only the creoles and *mestizos* born in Latin America but also those native to the islands. As empire loyalists, they saw as their duty the protection of the Philippines for Spain. However, since the Philippine bureaucracy was traditionally staffed by creoles and *mestizos,* the tension rapidly polarized the upper echelons of society. Pushed from power, the locally born creoles *(Filipinos)* saw the region as rightfully theirs and viewed the *peninsulares* as alien rulers. The frictions exploded in a revolt within the King's Own Regiment. Led by a Mexican *mestizo* captain named Andrés Novales, the revolt involved eight hundred troops. Although it was quickly suppressed, it seemed to confirm the worst fears of the *peninsulares,* who failed to realize that they themselves were the cause of the rebellion. Twenty-three of the ringleaders were executed, and many liberals were exiled, even though they were not implicated directly. The tightening of caste within the Spanish empire stratified Philippine society, forcing the creoles to identify themselves with their place of birth rather than with ancestry. Philippine nationalism emerged eventually from the process.

Restoration of the economic system, however, was the most immediate need, but the Spanish lacked the capital, the entrepreneurial skill, and the inclination to take charge of development. Mercantilist exclusion gave way to free trade and foreign commercial domination. By 1879, the Philippines had become "an Anglo-Chinese colony flying the Spanish flag." It developed an agricultural export economy, its cultivation occurring on small holdings. The only large estates were those owned by the friars, and they were rarely run as plantations. The key to development came with the arrival of the non-Spanish merchants who hooked the Philippines into the world community. These entrepreneurs, often tied to the great banking and trading companies of America, Europe, and China, did business in dollars or pounds rather than in pesos. Functioning initially as commission merchants who would advance the money for a future crop of sugar, copra, coffee, or hemp, they evolved into sophisticated merchant banking and insurance concerns with agents throughout the archipelago.

The Philippine sugar industry is a good example. Although sugar had been exported in the eighteenth century, old-fashioned processing curtailed production. In 1856, the island of Negros produced 280 tons of sugar. In 1857, Nicholas Loney, an Englishman working for Ker and Company, moved from Manila to Iloilo and opened the island of Negros to industry by offering Western machinery for which the planters could pay out of profits. Within a few years, there were thirteen modern mills on the island; by 1864, they produced 7,000 tons of sugar. Loney, noting that "most extensive tracts of fertile soil easily cleared, and well situated for shipments of produce, [were] to be had at Negros," observed that the *mestizos* were drawn to Negros by "the promising future of sugar planting interest."[18]

The development of an export economy is clearly reflected in the trade statistics. In 1825, the volume of trade was nearly 3 million pesos; fifty years later, it was fifteen times as large. Moreover, since Spain bought its sugar and tobacco more cheaply from Puerto Rico and Cuba, Philippine goods moved directly onto the world market. The Philippines was not integrated into the Spanish economy. The key exports of sugar, abaca, tobacco, and coffee, representing more than 90 percent of the total volume, had to find outlets throughout the world. The Spanish were forced, therefore, to open Manila and other cities as ports, if the colony was to survive. Moreover, to maintain a balance of trade, foreign goods had to be allowed into the islands. Except for wine, olive oil, and a few Spanish luxury items, the English dominated the import market with textiles, machinery, and other finished goods. These economic developments had lasting consequences for rice production. Prior to 1850, the islands had consistently exported rice, primarily to China; however, as the distance traveled by exports and imports increased, rice land was shifted to sugar or other crops and after 1870 the islands began to import rice. Since the Philippines, unlike Java, had a relatively sparse population and little irrigation development, the process of "agricultural involution" (as Clifford Geertz has termed it) rarely took place. The worldwide conditions, however, were important in explaining why the population increased greatly and the economy drifted away from self-sufficiency.

The economic changes had a profound effect on Philippine society. Within the Spanish community, the impact was divisive. The loss of economic control created a sense of malaise and frustration. Political tensions between liberal and conservative in peninsular Spain, which were evident from the 1812 constitution through the Carlist wars to the end of the century, broke the Philippine Spanish into two camps. The problem was exacerbated by the Spanish policy of deporting political prisoners of all persuasions to the islands. Moreover, since the liberals in Spain retained their strong opposition to the Church throughout the century, the friars in the Philippines became the rallying force for all conservatives in the archipelago. After they had been banned from Spain itself, many friars moved to Manila, where the atmosphere was more congenial. Technological improvements, which made it easier to reach Manila and to live comfortably there, also increased the willingness of lay Spaniards to emigrate with their wives. Madrid governments, which came and went with dazzling speed, bestowed patronage so lavishly that the Spanish bureaucracy in Manila, decreasing in effectiveness, doubled or tripled in size. Very few Spaniards ever left the comforts of Manila for agriculture. Thus, government service was the chief means of employment, corruption the fastest road to wealth. The weight and avarice of the bureaucracy, characterized by the institutionalized disregard for the commonweal that plagues the country even now, paralyzed governmental function.

The loss of the empire in Latin America was a trauma from which the

Spanish never fully recovered. Since they also were helpless to control the economic changes of the nineteenth century, they grew increasingly defensive. The specter of rebellion and bureaucratic inertia prevented them from undertaking the reforms the colony needed. Suspicious of everything, they alienated even the creoles, who were, of course, also Caucasian. The hostility from the Novales rebellion simmered during the entire century. In 1837, the Philippines was permanently banned from representation in the Spanish parliament (Cortes) in Madrid. In the islands, legislation was passed to mark by dress and privilege the different classes within society. Thus, for example, only Spaniards were permitted to wear ties; *indios* and *mestizos* were forced to wear their shirts loose, without any neck ornaments. The current national dress, the *barong Tagalog*, evolved from the proscription. Stratification was the device the Spanish used with the hope of keeping people in their place. Since economic developments unleashed new social pressures, their hope turned out to be naive.

If the Spanish retreated from change, the Chinese advanced toward it. The eighteenth-century Spanish desire to prohibit Chinese immigration eroded under nineteenth-century economic exigencies. In 1839, the Chinese were given "complete liberty to choose the occupation that best suits them." Subsequently, they were permitted to live anywhere in the archipelago, developing a symbiotic relationship with the foreign traders wherein they supplied raw materials and distributed imported goods. Operating through the *cabecilla* system of a central manager and rural agents—many of whom were related to each other—the Chinese created the bridge between the *indio* producer and the foreign export community. The Chinese population, which had been stable at 4,000 to 5,000 from the 1750s to the 1840s, reached about 18,000 in 1867; by 1876, it was about 30,000, mostly males. The opening of Hong Kong in 1842 and the unrest caused by the Taiping Rebellion of 1850–1864 were powerful inducements for immigration, but the opportunities in the Philippines itself provided the prime force.

The Chinese migrated partly in order to enter local trade. From 1754 to 1844, the Spanish had permitted the Spanish governors to dominate local trade, even though technically the Law of the Indies prohibited this. The provincial governor was allowed to pay a fine in advance, *indulto de comercio,* in order to make his fortune. This privilege, badly abused, so greatly restricted the flow of export goods that the central government felt compelled to abolish it in 1844. Although the Spanish officials had hoped that Spaniards would move into business, it was the Chinese who soon controlled retail trade by combining low overhead, hard work, and patronage with a developed credit network. Intense competition among the Chinese led to trading efficiency, permitting the colony to prosper. After 1857, when some economic restrictions were removed, the Chinese bid successfully for the right to collect taxes.

The repercussions of the Chinese penetration affected the Chinese *mestizo* community, which had profited from the anti-Chinese legislation of the earlier period and was threatened by the changing situation. Without access to credit and unable to operate on tight profit margins, the *mestizo* community shrewdly shifted its economic base into land and export crops, migrating to the Negros sugar lands, for example. *Mestizos* also played a major role in developing indigo for export. Most importantly, Chinese *mestizos* moved increasingly into rice production. The development of export crops, the conversion of land from rice to sugar, and the increasing shortage of the grain staple drove the price of rice upward and made rice production a profitable business. *Mestizos* acquired land in two ways. Some became lessees *(inquilinos)* on friar estates; they would open new land and would develop and sublet it to *indio* farmers for a percentage, usually high, of the crop yield. This system, in which the *mestizo* became the intermediary between the peasant and the friar landlord, was known as *kasamahan*. It became widespread in those areas around Manila where the Church had holdings and where the demand for new land was high. The second method was moneylending. Spanish law limited the *indio*'s debt to twenty-five pesos. To circumvent that statute, the *mestizo* would buy the land, granting the *indio* an option to repurchase later. Known as the *pactos de retro,* this system usually meant that the moneylender gained ownership. The farmers thus became tenants of the *mestizo* moneylenders, and the process became so prevalent that Father Zúñiga warned, "If no remedy is found, within a short time the lords of the entire Archipelago will be the Chinese mestizos."[19]

Despite the *mestizos'* successful economic response, the upsurge of Chinese immigrants posed a direct challenge to them. The new Chinese carried with them a sense of cultural superiority; they saw the Filipinized *mestizos* as cultural apostates. This attitude hurt the *mestizos,* who, despite their distinct legal status, lacked secure cultural roots. Adrift, although powerful, they tried to fuse with the creoles and Spanish *mestizos,* who were themselves, as we have seen, in the process of losing their Iberian identity. Thus, both groups searched for an identity together, and together the *mestizos* changed the term *Filipino* from its previously narrow meaning of a Spaniard born in the Philippines into a more national concept. The Chinese *mestizos* developed a set of values that was their own blend of *indio,* Spanish, and Chinese ideas. Most *mestizos* responded to the challenge of Chinese immigration by practicing Catholicism more devoutly, by adopting Spanish mores and style, and by becoming anti-Chinese. Moreover, lacking the standards of ethnic origin or family ancestry, the *mestizo* community stressed wealth as the arbiter of social status. Wealth was judged by land ownership; it became an empirical standard against which individuals could define social standing. Thus, Chinese immigration forced economic accommodation, setting in motion a process of "social Filipinization" with profound consequences for the future.

The impact of the above changes on the *indio* community was also profound. Since the Chinese *mestizo,* through his wealth and power, was close to the *indio* community, he transmitted to it values like the concern for wealth as a social arbiter, the appeal of ostentation as proof of status, and the new meaning of the term Filipino. By the mid-nineteenth century, the term *indio* was becoming a pejorative. Some of the *caciques* and *principalia,* especially those near Manila, had participated in the era of rapid economic development, interacting with both creoles and *mestizos.* The increasingly interdependent character of society opened new networks of communication. There were dislocations inherent in the process, but a growing congruence of loyalty was developing among sectors of society that had previously been legally distinct and socially distant.

The emergence of a sense of identity can be observed in the changing character of institutional life, especially in education. One Spaniard, noting that the "work-hand . . . [and] the goatherd do not read social contracts," warned in 1843 that the colleges in Manila should be closed, "because in a colony, liberal and rebellious are synonymous terms"; however, the number of people eligible for advanced education constantly grew.[20] Whereas previously the educational system had been limited to creoles, Spanish *mestizos,* and a few children of *indio principalia,* it was now broadened to include all groups. The process was greatly hastened when the Jesuits, readmitted into the archipelago in 1859, established Ateneo de Manila, a school that accepted *indios,* mestizos, and creoles without distinction. Enrollment at the University of Santo Tomas increased dramatically, and some of its "Royal and Pontifical" character was localized. A new and critically important elite social group emerged from these schools, an *ilustrado* class, which stood at the apex of the new Filipino community, cutting across all prior social and economic boundaries. Because it could speak articulately for the emerging Filipino community, it gained high prestige as an indigenous intelligentsia.

Many of the new *ilustrados* hoped to become priests but found that the hostility of the Spanish friars barred their advance. Clerical equality was the earliest major issue of Philippine nationalism. Conservative Spaniards were convinced that nothing would promote Philippine emancipation faster than the ordination of native priests. At the end of the century, a Spanish critic would note that the native priest was "a caricature of the priest, a caricature of the *indio,* a caricature of the Spaniard, a caricature of the *mestizo,* a caricature of everybody. He is a patchwork of many things and is nothing. I put it badly; he is something, after all; more than something . . . he is an enemy of Spain."[21]

The combination of racism and fear eventually contributed to the realization of the Spanish anxiety. The uprising of Apolinario de la Cruz in 1841 began because Cruz, a devout provincial Catholic, discovered that he could not enter a monastic order. Cruz then established a native religious brotherhood, the *Cofradía de San José,* which spread rapidly in the area near his home. His efforts to gain recognition for this order were rejected by the Spanish, and eventually, Cruz and his followers found themselves under attack. When the government attempted to suppress the movement, Cruz was able initially to defeat Spanish troops, killing the governor of Tayabas. The Spanish subsequently defeated the *Cofradía,* killed Cruz, and hung bits of his body throughout the *Cofradía* region. Thereafter, the Spanish responded by increased repression and hostility to Filipino clerical nationalism. They rounded up ranking Manila *mestizos* on suspicion of secretly assisting Cruz. In 1849, seven key parishes in Cavite were transferred back from diocesan to friar control. In 1859, with the return of the Jesuits to their eighteenth-century mission stations in Mindanao, the displaced Recollect friars were given all the remaining diocesan parishes in Cavite. By 1871, Filipinos staffed only 181 out of 792 parishes.

The decline of diocesan parishes coincided with the growing self-awareness of the intelligentsia. As a result of the Jesuit restoration, Father Pedro Pelaez, a Spanish creole who had risen within the diocesan ranks, led the fight against friar dominance. After he was killed in an earthquake in 1863, his place was taken by a *mestizo* named José Burgos, who wrote a manifesto in 1864 calling for clerical equity. Burgos, as synodal examiner of the archdiocese, wanted newly arrived Spanish priests to learn the local language before receiving parish assignments. The arguments of clerical *ilustrados* like Burgos received unexpected support when, in 1868, Spain swung back into the liberal camp. In 1870, the new archbishop of Manila petitioned the king that "propriety and equity" required support of the Filipino priests. When, as a result of an earthquake, the remains of Simón de Anda had to be moved, a massive crowd turned out to laud this friend of the native clergy. The benign reforms of Governor de la Torre encouraged a growing confidence that was shattered with the conservative restoration in Madrid—and with the appointment of a new governor, whose policy was to govern "with a cross in one hand and a sword in the other," to repeal de la Torre's liberalizing reforms, and to restore the friars to preeminence. In 1872, a mutiny against local grievances by the garrison at the Cavite Arsenal afforded the new governor, Rafael Izquierdo, an opportunity to arrest, try, and execute the leading advocates of Filipino religious nationalism, including Father José Burgos, Father Jacinto Zamora, and Father Mariano Gómez.

The archbishop refused to excommunicate the three priests, despite the pressure of the governor, because he believed they were being executed for their liberal views. His view is corroborated by the numerous arrests and deportations of many lay *ilustrados.* The repression led many others to flee to Europe or Hong Kong. It made martyrs of the three priests. Forty thousand came to witness the execution. Crowds heard Burgos cry out, "But what crime have I committed? Is it possible that I am to die in this way? My God, is there no longer justice in the land?"[22]

Izquierdo, by his ruthless and heavy-handed action, had created a symbol for the evolving Filipino intelligentsia. The greatest of the *ilustrados*, José Rizal, a fifth-generation Chinese *mestizo*, dedicated his novel, *El Filibusterismo*, to the memory of the three executed priests. The Philippine nationalist movement, the first in Southeast Asia, can be dated from their martyrdom in 1872.

# PART THREE

# Frameworks for Nations

# Introduction

THE most obvious feature of Southeast Asian history in the period between 1870 and 1940 was conquest, and subsequent political dominance, by the West. During the three or four decades after 1870 the Western powers rapidly completed their seizure of the area, subjugating the remaining kingdoms and peoples and leaving only Siam independent, though within the British sphere of influence. From conquest emerged strong colonial states which remained in full power—yielding only where they chose to, as in the Philippines—through the early decades of the twentieth century and up to 1940. It is not without reason that this three-quarters of a century is often called the high colonial age.

But if colonial rule spread swiftly and planted itself solidly, it departed even more swiftly in the 1940s and 1950s. It went through these remarkable ups and downs because it was part of a much larger historical process, the scientific and industrial revolution, which has transformed the whole world, including the West itself, in modern times. In the light of that revolution, direct Western rule in Southeast Asia may be seen as a short-lived frontier institution in a worldwide process of political change.

The colonial powers did not simply seize control of preexisting states. Cutting across established lines of political association or amalgamating previously separate societies, they created new political frameworks. On these they imposed modern bureaucratic systems and, over the decades, enlarged and perfected the apparatus necessary for such systems: government departments of all sorts, railroads, modern fiscal and tax systems. In this they acted as agents of a universal process, laying the foundations for modern nations just as others were doing in Europe, Japan, and elsewhere. The same process occurred in independent Siam under the management of a domestic elite.

While these grids were being extended over the Southeast Asian landscape, imposing on it a new kind of order, economic change was altering the substance of Southeast Asian life. Export industries, involving millions of people, rose rapidly after 1870; by 1940, most parts of the area had export-dominated economies. Population, steadily rising over the first three quarters of the nineteenth century, almost tripled between 1870 and 1940. The rise was accompanied by large migrations into and within the area. The money economy, centering on modern institutions in the burgeoning cities, spread widely through the countryside. These changes, too, were consequences of the scientific and industrial revolution, as Southeast Asia was caught up in the world economic revolution and took its place in the emerging world economy.

# 20

# The Making of New States

THE twentieth-century historian, who lives in a political world made up of "nations" neatly interlocking in a global jigsaw, must carefully wipe the windows of the mind in order to see the political map of Southeast Asia in 1870 as it was for contemporaries. That map was made up on different principles; it comprised an indefinite number of political centers, imposing or petty, whose influence receded through circles of more or less autonomous provinces and vassals until it reached and overlapped with other circles of influence. Six such centers were large old states rooted in the political traditions of fairly sizable and homogeneous populations: the Theravada kingdoms of Mandalay and Bangkok, the Confucian and Catholic states at Hue and Manila, and the grafted Franco-Cambodian and Dutch-Javan polities centering on Phnom Penh and Batavia. Three were novel colonial creations: the Commissionership of British Burma, the Colony of Cochinchina, and the Straits Settlements Colony. Beyond were two broad zones of petty centers: the belt of Shan-Lao principalities of the interior mainland and the predominantly Malayo-Muslim world stretching from Sumatra to Mindanao and from the Malay peninsula to the Moluccas. Scattered around and among all these, finally, were innumerable small non-state societies.

The political map of Southeast Asia had always been organized on these principles, but it was not to remain so much longer. The rather abrupt appearance of the newly fashioned colonies centered at Rangoon, Saigon, and Singapore foreshadowed the coming change throughout the area. In the next four decades, the map of Southeast Asia was redrawn to conform with the emerging world political order, a reorganization that had two closely related aspects.

One was a process of conquest and incorporation, as the numerous political centers of the old order were marshaled into six new units. Three of the larger old centers were conquered—Mandalay by the British, Hue by the French, and Manila by the Americans—and the peoples involved (Burmese, Vietnamese, and Filipinos) then became the cores of the modern colonies of British Burma, French Indochina, and the Philippines. The Shan-Lao and Malayo-Muslim zones were divided up among the powers, usually under forms of indirect rule. The mainland zone was partitioned among the British, Siamese, and French, becoming what are today the Burmese Shan States, north and northeast

Thailand, and Laos; the greater part of the island zone was incorporated into the Netherlands Indies, while the Malay Peninsula and
northwest Borneo came into British hands, and the easternmost islands
became what is now the southern Philippines. Cambodia was joined to
Vietnam and Laos in French Indochina, and the multitude of small
non-state societies fell into one or another of the larger units, often by a
combination of political and missionary activity. By about 1910, the
process was complete. Essentially all of Southeast Asia was incorporated into the six new states, defined now not by the power of centers
radiating outward through successive circles of receding influence but
by demarcated boundaries around their outer edges.

Implicit in this change in the scope of political power was a restructuring of the basis of political legitimacy. Most of the authority of the
traditional centers, both small and large, was derived from religion and
was based on the sacral qualities of the rulers' persons, regalia, and palaces. On the other hand, the rulers' power to govern, in the practical
sense, rested more on the control of military force than on routine
administrative machinery. Even Hue, Manila, and Batavia, the least
"traditional" centers in this respect, had their Son of Heaven and the
overseas deputy of His Most Christian Majesty; Philippine villages
were governed by friars, and Dutch officials went about under the
*payung* (ceremonial sunshades) of erstwhile Javanese god-kings. The
basis of rule changed rapidly between 1870 and 1910. The prestige of
the colonial governors of Burma, Indochina, and Malaya came from
their efficient military establishments and civil service, not from a
sacred majesty; the Americans did away with friar rule; the Dutch gave
up their *payung* and invented new secular ceremonies. One of the earliest acts of Chulalongkorn as king of Siam was to order his officials not
to prostrate themselves before his godly person. He was not thereby
abdicating power; like the colonial rulers in neighboring lands, which
he visited in his youth, he was setting forth toward a much more comprehensive kind of authority.

Everywhere, especially among the folk, the sacral royal traditions
lived on, for, deeply embedded in the traditional arts and languages,
they described the nature and meaning of political power as people
knew it to be. But everywhere, too, actual political authority came to be
exercised on secular bureaucratic principles. Modern administrative
networks spread out over the new political units; alongside them arose a
great variety of specialist services to serve new functions. The nature, as
well as the geography, of government had entered on a profound transformation.

## The Shan and Lao Principalities

In 1870, the whole mountainous zone of Shan and Lao principalities
stretching from the upper Irrawaddy to the Black River in northern

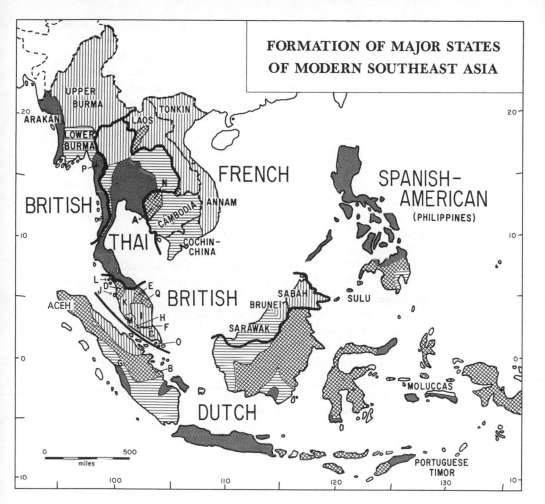

# FORMATION OF MAJOR STATES OF MODERN SOUTHEAST ASIA

UPPER BURMA

ARAKAN

TONKIN

LAOS

LOWER BURMA

P

BRITISH

N

THAI

CAMBODIA

ANNAM

COCHIN-CHINA

FRENCH

SPANISH-AMERICAN (PHILIPPINES)

L D E Q

J K

M I

ACEH

H

F

C

O

BRITISH

SABAH

BRUNEI

SULU

SARAWAK

B

G

DUTCH

MOLUCCAS

PORTUGUESE TIMOR

0          500
miles

0        100              110              120              130

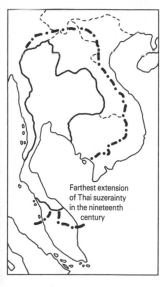

Farthest extension of Thai suzerainty in the nineteenth century

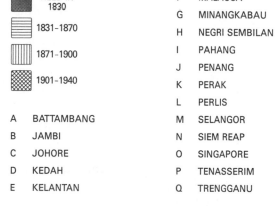

| | | |
|---|---|---|
| ■ HELD IN 1830 | F | MALACCA |
| ▤ 1831–1870 | G | MINANGKABAU |
| ▥ 1871–1900 | H | NEGRI SEMBILAN |
| ▦ 1901–1940 | I | PAHANG |
| | J | PENANG |
| | K | PERAK |
| | L | PERLIS |
| A BATTAMBANG | M | SELANGOR |
| B JAMBI | N | SIEM REAP |
| C JOHORE | O | SINGAPORE |
| D KEDAH | P | TENASSERIM |
| E KELANTAN | Q | TRENGGANU |

Vietnam and from Yunnan to the foothills north of the Čhaophraya River Plain remained much as it had been for a long time, a sparsely populated and independent world of its own in the interior behind the larger monarchies and peoples of mainland Southeast Asia. It played an oddly important role, however, in the European imperialism of the mid-nineteenth century. While the main European challenge was to the major monarchies near or on the coast—as events at Rangoon, Bang-kok, Da Nang, and Saigon in the 1850s demonstrated—European interest at the time focused (in large measure ignorantly) beyond the coastal areas and upon the Shan and Lao regions in the interior. The granting of trading rights to Western powers in the treaty-ports of China following the Opium War (1842) failed to generate the volume of trade that Europe and America had expected, and so the myth of a rich and populous inner China, inaccessible from the China coast, captured the imaginations of French and British commercial interests. Their immediate target was the province of Yunnan, which they hoped to reach by water or rail from Upper Burma, or up the Salween River, up the Mekong from Cambodia, or up the Red River from Hanoi. The traditional suzerainty of the Burmese, Siamese, and Vietnamese mon-archies over the principalities along those routes was misunderstood and denied. Particularly where such principalities were the tributaries of two or more larger states, there existed openings for conflict.

To the west, the non-Buddhist Karen states on the southern fringe of the Shan plateau became one scene of strife following the Second Anglo-Burmese War. Situated in the undefined border region between British Lower Burma and Mindon's kingdom, the two chief states were East-ern and Western Karen-ni, which by 1868 were divided between British and Burmese influence. In 1875, the British declared a protectorate over Western Karen-ni, while Eastern Karen-ni remained in closer rela-tions with Mandalay. Mindon's diplomatic defeat by the British over the creation of the protectorate was the immediate cause of the unwill-ingness of either side to give way in the famous "footwear" controversy.

The more than two dozen Buddhist Shan states were, with a few exceptions, tributaries of the Burmese kings. However, they became the objects of numerous expeditions sent from Lower Burma from the 1820s onward as they came to be of economic and strategic importance to the British. The Burmese court responded with renewed efforts to recover their allegiance. British, Burmese, and sometimes Chinese and Siamese interference tended to encourage local autonomy and civil strife. From mid-century onward, many states like Hsenwi in the extreme north were embroiled in political troubles as they resisted Bur-mese efforts to restore pro-Burmese rulers. With independent revenues from the increasing hill trade and with access to modern weapons, such states lay beyond the effective power of the Burmese court of the time. The principality of Kengtung, farther east, was the object of pressure from many directions. It suffered three Siamese invasions between 1849 and 1854, repulsing them with Burmese and Shan aid, though at the cost of increased Burmese influence. King Thibaw, in particular, attempted to tighten Burmese control over Kengtung but succeeded only in provoking a rebellion in 1881–1882. It soon spread to neighboring principalities, and it ultimately developed into the "Limbin Confederacy" of 1885, an alliance of Shan rulers under the Burmese Limbin prince, who came up from British Burma shortly before the outbreak of the Third Anglo-Burmese War. Its purpose was to end the warfare between the Shan states in order to enable them to withstand Burmese pressure and, perhaps, British designs.

The Kingdom of Lan Na at Chiang Mai, in what is now north Thailand, had been brought under the loose suzerainty of Bangkok in 1777, after forty years of almost constant warfare. Once the Burmese had been expelled from the area in 1804, the state was left more or less alone while it regrouped its depleted population in defensible towns and mounted occasional raids into the Shan states to capture manpower. After mid-century, as a result of new European interest in Chiang Mai's teak forests, disputed forest leases, and what British Burma viewed as unacceptable restraints on its trade in the region, the Bangkok monarchy became alarmed at the possibility that the rulers in Chiang Mai might bring on a collision between themselves and the British. Bangkok therefore put its own candidate on the throne of Chiang Mai in 1870 and, five years later, appointed the first Siamese resident commissioner there to guard its interests and to prevent further conflict with the British.

Similar unrest occurred in the Lao states to the east. Bangkok's suppression of the Anu Rebellion of 1826–1827 and the massive resettlement of the population of the middle Mekong valley on the Khorat plateau had left as independent Lao powers only the Kingdom of Luang Prabang and a few minor principalities to the east and north that were tributary to it. From 1872 onward, the whole northern region was threatened by bands of Chinese (known as Hǫ) from Yunnan who roamed the whole region, burning and plundering every settlement in their path, and reaching even to Vientiane in that year. Unable to cope with the intrusions himself, the king of Luang Prabang appealed to his suzerain in Bangkok. Through the 1870s and 1880s, the Siamese government sent repeated military expeditions northward. Coming only for short campaigns and moving too slowly to keep up with the Hǫ, they achieved little. In 1887, indeed, the Hǫ sacked Luang Prabang itself. The king managed to escape, with the aid of the French vice-consul, Auguste Pavie, but his faith in his Siamese suzerain was severely shaken, and French hopes for an easy annexation were encouraged.

On the whole, the influence and control of the Burmese and Siamese monarchies in the Shan and Lao region were no stronger in 1885 than they had been a century earlier. Although they attempted to strengthen their position, essentially they did so within a traditional framework of suzerainty and vassalage. Among the Shans, Burmese attempts to increase control by greater use of the suzerain's powers only provoked rebellion, which encouraged or facilitated the later extension of British power. Though similar Siamese efforts were more subtle (as in Chiang Mai) or forceful (as in Luang Prabang), the Bangkok monarchy could achieve no lasting change with the old methods. The outcome here, as elsewhere, was a new map of mainland Southeast Asia, drawn between 1885 and 1909 by French and British fiat and new Siamese initiative.

## The Province of Burma

The administrative and economic systems of British Burma developed in the shadow of British Indian practices and were justified in the name of nineteenth-century liberalism. The ultimately radical political consequences of the introduction of a capitalist economic system and the rule of British Indian law were unforeseen when first applied to the Tenasserim provinces and Arakan after the First Anglo-Burmese War in 1826 and not yet felt when the area of British rule was enlarged by the acquisition of the provinces of Lower Burma during the second war (1852–1853). Each region was initially a "division" of the Government of India, headed by a commissioner, but in 1862 the three were amalgamated under a chief commissioner in Rangoon. The Indian government, in its efforts to unify and centralize India, paid little attention to the many ways in which Burma differed from India. British colonial administration in Burma, for example, was founded upon Indian patterns of village leadership and land rights. The traditional relationships among village, township, and circle headmen in Burma were largely ignored, and an Indian system of direct administration was imposed. Efficiency and economic development, involving especially the export of rice and teak, were the watchwords of the government, as it steadily extended its uniform and alien administrative system over the countryside.

British economic interests, which were centered in Rangoon after its capture in 1852, soon gave impetus to the extension of British rule over the kingdom of Mandalay. Shipping and financial firms involved in foreign trade, along with such extractive industries as teak, had an interest in expanding their area of operations northward along the Irrawaddy River, as well as dreams of going farther afield into China. Through the Rangoon Chamber of Commerce, and similar organizations in Britain, they exerted constant pressure on the Rangoon, Calcutta, and London governments for more commercial concessions from King Mindon; and when Mindon and his successor failed to abolish all their own royal trading monopolies, they lobbied for the annexation of the remainder of the kingdom.

Anglo-Burmese relations deteriorated rapidly in the 1870s, as Mindon lost faith in the good will of the British and as they in turn increasingly lost patience with him. In 1872, desperate for recognition of the independent status of his kingdom, Mindon sent envoys to Europe. They were allowed an audience with Queen Victoria only when accompanied by the secretary of state for India, thus implying the status of an Indian vassal state, not a sovereign equal. They then tentatively sought recognition from the French and Italian governments but gained only commercial treaties. Mindon was boxed in by increasing British hostility and suspicion of his dealings with other European powers and by the reluctance or inability of France and Italy to assist his landlocked kingdom, which was most easily accessible through British Rangoon.

The accession of King Thibaw in 1878 played into the hands of those British demanding annexation. After the abortive palace coup of 1866, in which the previous heir to the throne had been killed, Mindon feared to name his successor. In an atmosphere of uncertainty, foreign danger, and intrigue, court politics intensified as factions prepared for the struggle over the succession. The situation was used by a faction led by a discarded queen of Mindon's, Hsinpyumashin, and a minister of the *Hlutdaw,* the Taingda Mingyi. They persuaded the ministers to choose the minor prince Thibaw by encouraging them to think they could control him. Once he was crowned, many other rivals for the throne were killed, and then the old dowager and her daughter Supayalat, Thibaw's junior queen, took effective control of state policies.

The British government in Rangoon expressed righteous indignation at the bloody succession struggle and recognized at the same time an opportunity to increase pressure on the Burmese kingdom. It dispatched troops to Mandalay forthwith on the pretext that the British representative there needed protection; the following year the representative was withdrawn as a sign of the government's moral disapproval. When Thibaw sent an envoy to the British governor-general in Calcutta to appeal for the resumption of friendly relations and to discuss a new treaty, his presence was completely ignored. But war in Afghanistan temporarily reduced British willingness to go any further in Burma. Thibaw tried, amid a difficult political situation and perhaps at the instigation of the most outward-looking minister, the Kinwun Mingyi, to conciliate British opinion and to seek an accommodation through negotiations in 1882. Thibaw's envoys claimed for Burma the right as a sovereign state to send ambassadors to the queen in London and when the claim was denied, asked at least to have a treaty drawn up in the name of the two sovereigns. In return, Thibaw offered to receive British representatives at his court with their shoes on. The British would not yield, offering only a royal treaty of friendship and a separate commercial treaty with the Indian government. Burma, denied equality, withdrew its envoys and in 1883 Thibaw's government embarked upon a policy to find a counterbalancing alliance by dispatching envoys to Europe to seek full recognition and aid from the French government.

The ensuing Anglo-French tension was the result not so much of

French intentions, as the British liked to think, but of the Burmese effort to play balance-of-power politics. However, the British view was made more credible by France's occupation of northern and central Vietnam. Nonetheless, the French refused to back Burma; the king's mission to Paris succeeded in gaining no more than revival of the toothless commercial treaty of 1873; in particular, the French refused in 1884 to sign a declaration that they would come to Burma's assistance if it were threatened by a third power. Early in 1885, when the Kinwun Mingyi earnestly sought some assurance of French support, all that Premier Jules Ferry would concede was a letter promising arms shipments overland from Tonkin—*if* "this is judged compatible with our interests." Individual Frenchmen went somewhat further, agitating for railroad and banking concessions, and almost gained the ruby monopoly from Thibaw. In particular, the French consul in Mandalay, M. Haas, took part, with approval from Paris, in Burmese litigation concerning the British Bombay–Burma Trading Corporation, in the hopes that the French might succeed to its teak interests in Burma.

In August 1885, just as the Ferry letter of January became known to the British, the Bombay–Burma Trading Corporation was assessed a fine of £73,333 by the *Hlutdaw,* having been found guilty of underpaying royalties due on teak logs extracted from forests in Mandalay's territory north of Toungoo. The events that followed sprang from the issues raised by these coinciding developments, from the treatment Mandalay was giving British commercial interests, and from the heightened Anglo-French rivalry following the conquest of Tonkin. Successive Liberal governments in London had been unmoved by the economic arguments for annexation put forward by British commercial interests in Rangoon, especially when British Indian armies were occupied elsewhere. But in late 1885 the armies were idle, a Conservative government more open than the Liberals to expansion was in power, and both economic and political fears of France urged them on. Thibaw was presented with a three-part ultimatum: that the teak case be put to the arbitration of the British chief commissioner of Rangoon; that a British resident be installed in Mandalay with a guard and allowed direct access to the king without having to remove his shoes; and ultimately and most humiliatingly that all Burma's foreign relations be put under the control of the Indian government.

The French tried to ease the crisis by offering a demarcation of British and French spheres of influence, but the British would have none of it. The Kinwun Mingyi urged a conciliatory reply to the ultimatum but was overruled by the Taingda Mingyi and Queen Supayalat, who did not take it seriously. Instead, an unyielding reply was returned. When the twenty-day ultimatum expired in mid-November, British forces promptly headed north, occupying Mandalay in a fortnight. The annexation of Upper Burma was announced on January 1, 1886, bringing to an end the Konbaung dynasty and Burma's independence.

The Third Anglo-Burmese War really began only after it had "ended." Although the king's army dissolved without central leadership, resistance broke out in the king's former domains and soon expanded into British Lower Burma as well. With the deportation of the king and the dissolution of the *Hlutdaw*, royal government collapsed, but authority was not automatically transferred to the British. Former military commanders, monks fearing the threat to Buddhism from foreign rule, and princely pretenders were joined by Shan *sawbwa* in opposing the imposition of British control. Their lack of coordination made their suppression easier, but it still remained a formidable task. More than 40,000 troops and Indian police were in the field by February 1887, while a Christian Karen militia was raised to help quell the rising in the south. The "Pacification of Burma," to use the title of the most complete contemporary account of the subject, was a good deal bloodier than the murder of Thibaw's relatives, as British troops burned down villages and carried out mass executions of people they termed rebels. Resistance gradually subsided while columns of troops sent into the frontier areas gained pledges of loyalty from traditional rulers. By about 1895, British military power succeeded in establishing effective control over the whole of Burma, which was defined by new frontiers, bringing to an end sixty years of tension and conflict.

## The Kingdom of Siam

The strongest pressures of Western imperialism reached Siam a decade or two later than Burma and Vietnam, giving the Siamese extra time. The kingdom needed the extra time, most immediately to resolve critical problems of domestic politics. King Chulalongkorn (r. 1868–1910) was fifteen when he succeeded to the throne, and for five years he was powerless in the hands of his regent, Čhaophraya Si Suriyawong (Chuang Bunnag). The young man traveled abroad—to the Netherlands Indies, Singapore, Burma, and India—and he gathered about him a large group of young men, many of whom had received a Western education. When he became king in his own right in 1873, he embarked with their support on a series of fundamental reforms, announcing the abolition of slavery, changing the judicial and financial systems, and establishing a council of state and privy council to advise him. The changes provoked a strong reaction. The "second king," Wichaichan, who had been named heir presumptive in 1868 by Suriyawong in the expectation that Chulalongkorn would soon die of illness, was alarmed at the forceful moves by the king and his supporters. Fearful of his own fate, he fled to the British consulate early in 1875. The British and French consuls, each moving beyond his government's instructions, attempted to make the incident an occasion for strengthening their influence in the kingdom, and for a time its survival seemed threatened. But they were thwarted by their home governments, who refused to act, while the king rallied his support. Chulalongkorn, it would appear, survived the crisis only by making promises; in the next ten years, many of the earlier reforms were rescinded, and no new ones were launched.

Only in the mid-1880s, as the ministers of his father's generation began to pass from public life, could King Chulalongkorn resume his reform program. Because most families of the old nobility were slow to send their children to modern schools, the king's own brothers (he had twenty-seven) were easily the best-educated men of their generation. One by one, they were put in charge first of departments and then of ministries. In 1885, following the urgings of some of the more impatient of his brothers and supporters, the king began the reorganization of the government into ministries structured on functional lines. The new system was inaugurated in March 1888, with the young ministers-designate, all brothers of the king, attending cabinet meetings before their ministries were formally proclaimed. Over the next four years, departments were rearranged, new ones were created, and men were prepared and trained for the new cabinet government, which finally went into operation in April 1892.

Among the most important of the changes accompanying the reorganization was an expansion and extension of the capital's controls over the provinces and distant dependencies. Patterning their system somewhat on the model of the British in India and Burma, the Siamese grouped their provinces into *monthon* (circles), controlled by commissioners who in many cases were also brothers of the king. Commissionerships were established at Luang Prabang, Chiang Mai, Phuket, and Battambang in the 1870s, and then at Nongkhai, Champassak, Nakhǫn Ratchasima (Khorat), and Ubon in the 1880s. The commissioners' powers and activities, however, became substantial only around 1890, when they began forcing the pace of reform, building local military units, and regularizing financial and judicial administration.

In most of the areas concerned, the new system marked the beginning of an important development, as the authority of Bangkok, like that of the colonial powers in the same period, spread outward, absorbing former vassals and consolidating its administrative control. But in Luang Prabang and Champassak it was too late, as the thrust of French imperial ambitions against Siam increased rapidly through the 1880s. The French chose to regard Siamese efforts at improving their control over outlying dependencies and at quelling the disturbances caused by the Hǫ in Laos as a new imperialism, which challenged the suzerain rights of Vietnam over the Lao principalities east of the Mekong. They manufactured claims to territory and posted agents there, provoking incidents that were blown up into a *casus belli*. They sent columns of troops into the regions of the lower and middle Mekong, where they met stiff Siamese resistance. In the tense days that followed in July 1893, the

Siamese shore batteries at Paknam fired on two French gunboats forcing their way up the Čhaophraya River to Bangkok. The Siamese, lacking sufficient force to roll back the French naval blockade then imposed, or to resist the military forces then in preparation on the Lao frontier, had no choice but to accept a French ultimatum demanding the surrender of all Lao territories east of the Mekong and the payment of a large indemnity.

Siam's survival through the period was to a considerable degree a product of Anglo-French rivalry. Each was anxious not to border the other or to allow the other a disproportionate advantage. Bangkok played upon the rivalry and made Siam a fulcrum for balancing the powers. The most that the French and English could agree on was to guarantee the independence of the Čhaophraya River valley in 1896. This left in doubt the fate of Siamese rule on the Malay Peninsula, in the southeastern provinces bordering Cambodia, and in the whole of what is now northeast Thailand. Bangkok was able to retain most of the above territory only through a combination of good luck, timely modernization, and diplomatic skill.

Through the king's personal diplomacy with the monarchs and governments of Europe, and through the workaday consular and embassy contacts that were Prince Devawongse's responsibility as foreign minister for forty years, Siam cultivated a reputation abroad for responsibility and for willingness to accommodate Western demands and to reform along Western lines. The image was in part sustained by the prominence of foreign advisers in the Siamese government, with Englishmen in the Ministry of Finance, Frenchmen in the Ministry of Justice, Danes in the provincial police, and Germans in the Railways Department. They made an impressive display and contributed much useful technological advice, but it was the basic policies of the ministries for which they worked that were decisive for the future of the country. This was particularly true in the case of the Ministry of the Interior under Prince Damrong Rajanubhab, which extended an increasingly modern administration over the provinces remaining in the kingdom. Prince Damrong enlarged the system of "circles" and high commissioners after all the provinces were handed over to his ministry in 1894, creating a system of provincial administration that made good use of limited numbers of modern-trained officials to administer vast areas through only eighteen *monthon* capitals. The powers and prerogatives of the princely and governors' families in the provinces rapidly eroded as they were displaced by men from the capital or as their forest leases were bought out by the central government. This was not accomplished without resistance. In 1902, three separate rebellions broke out—in the north, in the northeast, and in Patani in the south; suppressing them with its modernized army, the central government clearly demonstrated the new techniques and strength at its disposal.

Siam survived the crisis of 1893, but the Western powers still threatened its territorial integrity from without while encroaching on its sovereignty inside. Unresolved claims and undrawn boundaries preserved the possibility of further inroads on its territory. The treaties of the 1850s restricted many of its basic taxing powers, and an oppressive system of extraterritoriality placed not only Europeans but thousands of Chinese, Lao, Cambodians, Shans, and Burmese with French and British registration certificates outside Siamese legal jurisdiction. The difficulties with France were resolved in a series of treaties, which, by 1907, gave Siam its current eastern border at the expense of territorial cessions in Laos and Cambodia in return for an end to further claims and to French abuses of extraterritoriality in the kingdom. The British price for similar concessions was equally high; it was finally paid in 1909, when the Siamese ceded four of their Malay dependencies in the south —Kedah, Perlis, Kelantan, and Trengganu—to the British. The basic principle of extraterritoriality and the treaty restrictions on taxation remained in effect for some time. But the agreements after 1900 eased the pressure on Siam's sovereignty and, above all, secured the territorial boundaries of an internationally recognized state. When the Entente Cordiale brought Anglo-French rivalry to an end in 1904, and when World War I broke out, Siam's fears of Western imperialism rapidly diminished.

It was in the same quarter-century after 1885 that the real transformation of the internal structure of the kingdom began with the creation of a nation knit together by administrative control and countrywide institutions within defined boundaries. A system of modern government schools spread throughout the country between 1898 and 1910, as enrollments jumped from 5,000 to 84,000 pupils. The drafting of modern legal codes, the creation of modern military services and financial and tax administration, and the ending of compulsory labor service were all accomplished within a limited time. Ultimately, the chief obstacle in the way of reform and modernization was not conservative opposition, which died out in the decade after 1885 as the necessity of change became clear, but rather the extremely limited educated leadership available to carry it out. When this leadership, composed for the most part of young men trained abroad, came to prominence at the very end of Chulalongkorn's reign, the success of the reform program was assured, though it was far from completed.

## French Indochina

Of all the political creations that the age of imperialism brought to Southeast Asia, none was more artificial than French Indochina. Loyalty to the concept of a greater Indochina never germinated among the inhabitants of that multisocietal colony, although the concept clearly had its uses for Vietnamese nationalists with traditionalist designs upon Cambodia and Laos. French rule meant different things to and evoked different responses from the Vietnamese, Cambodian, and Lao peoples, whom its ambitious framework briefly covered.

The structure of French Indochina was complex. Of its five separate administrative regions, southern Vietnam (Cochinchina), under the ultimate authority of the colonial and naval ministries in Paris, was the only colony in the narrow constitutional sense. Central Vietnam (Annam), northern Vietnam (Tonkin), Cambodia, and Laos were technically protectorates under the ultimate authority of the French Foreign Ministry. After 1887, however, all five regions were brought under the sway of a single governor-general, with headquarters in Hanoi. Five regional heads served under the governor-general: the governor of Cochinchina and the *résidents supérieurs* of Annam, Tonkin, Cambodia, and Laos. There was a general budget for the whole of Indochina and also local budgets for the five regions. By a decree of 1899, the proceeds of indirect taxes (customs, taxes on opium, alcohol, salt, etc.) were reserved for the general Indochinese government, while the revenues from direct taxes (land and poll taxes) were assigned to the regional and local administrations.

Paul Doumer, governor-general from 1897 to 1902, was the outstanding architect of colonial institutions for Indochina. He centralized and presided over the specialized services of the colony—customs, the postal and telegraph service, forestry, and commerce—and also introduced the common general budget. During the Doumer regime, the Indochina Geographical Service was created, as well as the famous French School of the Far East (*École Française d'Extrême-Orient*) at Hanoi, a combination of language school, scientific establishment, and administrative service dedicated to the preservation of historical monuments. The governor-general was advised but not controlled by a government council (known as the *Conseil Supérieur de l'Indochine* from 1887 to 1911, and as the *Conseil de Gouvernement* after 1911), which considered in secret the general budget and tax assessments. It consisted of about twenty high French officials and five "indigenous high functionaries," Vietnamese, Cambodian, and Lao members chosen each year by the governor-general himself. Like the immense Doumer Bridge at Hanoi, such centralization improved communications, administrative and otherwise. But it could not impose anything more than a make-believe unity upon three quite different societies, one of which, Vietnam, was soon in revolutionary ferment.

*Vietnam.* The first stage of Vietnam's loss of sovereignty to the French had come in 1858–1867, when the French had absorbed southern Vietnam and converted it into the Cochinchina colony. The second stage was the period 1873–1885, when the French established a preponderant military presence in the north, blundered into war with China, and successfully made protectorates of northern and central Vietnam. In 1873, Admiral Dupré, the governor of Cochinchina, sent a military expedition to the north under Francis Garnier—both to bring the north within the sphere of French colonial commerce in Saigon and to acquire such a well-defined hegemony over the Vietnamese court itself that no British or German counterinfluences could ever be established there. Styling himself "the grand mandarin Garnier," he seized the Hanoi citadel briefly but was killed by a counterattack of Vietnamese soldiers and Chinese "Black Flags" (Chinese veterans of the Taiping Rebellion who, like the Họ in Laos, had streamed across the Vietnamese frontier as organized brigands). Nine years later, another French expedition, led by Henri Rivière, arrived in the north. The Hue court, exploiting its status as a vassal, requested Chinese intervention to save northern Vietnam from French occupation. Rivière was killed, the French rejected Peking's demand that they evacuate the north, and the Sino-French war over Vietnam that ensued (June 1884–April 1885) resulted in the defeat of China and the loss of all independence for Vietnam. That humiliating chapter in the age of imperialism is not forgotten today in either Peking or Hanoi.

One judgment that can be made about the French colonial administration of Vietnam is that Vietnamese society was much more fragmented and the differences in customs, thought, and ways of life among its three regions more acute in 1954 than they had been in 1885. The unprecedented division of Vietnam into three formally separate administrative areas—"Cochinchina," "Tonkin," and "Annam" (the last meaning "pacified south," a T'ang Chinese colonialist term for Vietnam which the French revived)—has been noted. In the long run, the cultural impact of the French was to be strongest in the south, where they ruled directly. It was to be weakest in the center, owing both to the survival of the traditional court at Hue and to the relative absence of French entrepreneurs and capital investment in central Vietnam. But administrative fragmentation was also the practice at the subregional level. Precolonial Vietnam was divided into thirty-one provinces. Under the French, the number of provinces virtually doubled to sixty: twenty-one in the south, sixteen in the center, and twenty-three in the north. This was precisely the opposite of what Vietnamese reformers like Nguyen Truong To had proposed in the 1860s—the reduction of provincial government in the interests of efficiency and better salaries. The creation in 1888 of special French extraterritorial sectors within the three cities of Hanoi, Haiphong, and Da Nang, which the French chose to govern directly, was another example of the multiplication of local administrative barriers.

French colonial policy in Vietnam moved between the two extremes of "assimilation," which meant the cultural and institutional Gallicization of Vietnam, and "association," which implied the maintenance of traditional Vietnamese institutions as legitimizing props for French rule. The history of the colonial government at Saigon in the early

1860s demonstrated the difficulties of either course of action. At first, all higher Vietnamese mandarins were removed from power and replaced by French officers. No Vietnamese was to occupy an administrative position higher than that of canton chief. Since the French did not have enough personnel of their own to make the scheme work, it lasted only until the end of 1862, when the mandarins were returned to their posts. But because many of the Vietnamese provincial officials were anti-French, this policy also had to be jettisoned. In the third, and compromise, formula, the most important agents of the new Saigon colonial regime were the officials known as inspectors of indigenous affairs. The inspectors (of whom there were about thirty in 1868, one to every 70,000 southern Vietnamese) were officers, surgeons, or engineers of the French Navy. But in order to win promotion they had to pass tests in which they demonstrated a rudimentary knowledge of Vietnamese, of the Vietnamese law code, of Chinese characters, and even of Cambodian and Thai.

In central and northern Vietnam, the colonial government expanded its authority after 1885, not so much by installing a new administrative system of its own as by the piecemeal confiscation of traditional Vietnamese authority. The legal bases of French rule, treaties concluded between France and the Vietnamese court in 1874, 1883, and 1884, had left the Vietnamese emperor at Hue a small but unmistakable residue of power. In 1897–1898 Doumer, the governor-general, appropriated that power. In 1897, he forced the Emperor Thanh-tai to issue an edict transferring all the powers of the court's highest representative in the north (the *kinh luoc*) to a French official. To tighten French control in central Vietnam, Doumer forced Thanh-tai to permit the French *résident supérieur* at Hue to preside over meetings of the Vietnamese court's Privy Council. This meant that the ministers of the court now became the ministers of the *résident supérieur*, not of the emperor. In addition, the *résident supérieur* for central Vietnam was given the right to approve the drafts of all imperial edicts before the Vietnamese emperor could sign them with his vermilion brush. Although the Six Boards of the traditional bureaucracy continued to exist in Hue, a French official was installed at each one. He had to agree to every decision of his respective board before the decision could be sent to the *résident supérieur* for final approval. Finally, the French appropriated the power to administer the finances of central Vietnam, denying the Vietnamese court the independent revenues the 1884 treaty had allowed it.

The form that the French consolidation of power took in the late 1890s potently influenced the course of modern Vietnamese political development. By quietly confiscating the political power of the Vietnamese court, the French destroyed the prestige of the only remaining symbol of Vietnamese unity, the monarchy, without creating any significant non-Confucian institutions to replace it. It could be said that they

ruled central and northern Vietnam more through the exploitation of
traditional institutions, which thus became useless to later Vietnamese
patriots, than through the creation of exemplary new institutions.

Local government in central and northern Vietnam under the French
was a diarchy. Day-to-day government in the thirty-nine provinces of
Annam and Tonkin was handled by two parallel but separate administrations, one French, one Vietnamese. Each province had a French
province chief who governed Europeans, foreign Asians, and those few
Vietnamese in his province who had become French citizens. Each
province also had a Vietnamese hierarchy—governor-general, governors, financial and judicial commissioners, prefects, and district magistrates—responsible for the governing of the Vietnamese. The Confucian examination system was not abolished in the center and the north
until 1919, so that down to the 1930s most Vietnamese provincial officials in these two regions possessed anachronistic examination-system
backgrounds. Perceptive anti-French scholars like Tran Te Xuong
(1870–1907), a degree winner of 1894, could observe that "out of ten
students, nine have stopped going to school. The girls who sell books by
profession close their eyes in slumber."[23] But to all appearances, the
classic provincial mandarinate continued long after 1885.

In the full-fledged colony of Cochinchina, such an indigenous administration by Vietnamese officials according to Vietnamese rules did not
exist. All Vietnamese were ruled by French officials according to
French laws. In the south, for example, it was the French province chief
who was responsible for ensuring that the land registers of each village
were kept up to date, whereas in the center and north it was the Vietnamese district magistrate. But colonial rule was more uniform over all
three regions than appearances might suggest. In the north, the French
*résident supérieur* headed both the French and Vietnamese provincial
administrations. In the center, the French *résident supérieur,* through his
control of the imperial Privy Council and Six Boards, was able to control all appointments in the mandarinate down to district magistrate.
Thus, even where Vietnamese continued to play a role on the political
stage, they were mimes acting out a French scenario.

*Cambodia.* In June 1864, following ancient custom, Norodom
crowned himself king of Cambodia. He received his crown from a
French naval officer sent up from Saigon and his regalia from a Siamese
official, for Cambodia was still a "two-headed bird." Siam's influence at
court, however, ceased after the treaty of 1867, by which France recognized Siam's claim to the ex-Cambodian provinces of Battambang and
Siem Reap, while Siam accepted the French protectorate over Cambodia.

Over the next twenty years, French efforts there consisted largely of
ineffectual attempts to curb Norodom's powers and to tidy his fiscal
procedures, with a view to siphoning off some of his revenue to pay

French administrative costs. Norodom balked at the reforms, and in 1884, when he refused to allow the French to administer Cambodian customs fees, France presented him with an eleven-point ultimatum, disguised as a convention, which permanently limited his powers. The document abolished slavery, permitted the alienation of land, extended the French resident's powers, and stated that Norodom was to agree to "such administrative, judicial, financial, and commercial reforms as the French Republic might, in the future, consider useful."[24]

While Norodom objected most to the reduction of his fiscal independence, the provisions relating to land and slavery cut across the interests of the provincial elite, heretofore unaffected by the French presence. In early 1885, the provincial elite precipitated a rebellion against the French. Hostilities lasted until the end of 1886, when the French agreed to postpone application of the controversial portions of the convention.

Norodom's role in the rebellion is obscure, but the part played by his younger brother, Sisowath, in helping the French to put it down was well known. Before and after the events of 1884–1886, the French made no secret of the fact that they preferred Sisowath to Norodom, and a French resident in the 1890s tried unsuccessfully to have Norodom declared insane with the aim of accelerating Sisowath's accession. After Norodom died in 1904, Sisowath was placed on the throne. He was too frightened of his brother, even in death, to officiate at his cremation. Shortly after his own coronation, in 1906, Sisowath left on a state visit to France, where the Parisians were "delighted with his blandness and courtesy."[25]

During their first forty years in Cambodia, which coincided with Norodom's reign, the French destroyed a few Cambodian institutions, renovated some, and froze others into place. The traditions of provincial autonomy, debt bondage, and dynastic warfare, for example, were slowly eroded, while the machinery of tax collection, royal monopolies, and palace administration was rebuilt to meet French needs. On the other hand, the Buddhist Sangha, the local judicial system, village education, and the nonadministrative aspects of kingship, to name only four, were allowed to function undisturbed. Paradoxically, as the French reduced the powers of the king, the stability their presence brought to his realm had the effect of gradually increasing his prestige. The annual allowance granted Norodom by the French from local taxes, for example, probably exceeded the revenues of any other nineteenth-century Cambodian king. Although Norodom was, in effect, a hostage of the French, they made no effort to diminish the ceremonial and religious aspects of the monarchy, which were the ones that linked Norodom directly with his people. By reducing the king's freedom of action, the French increased the effectiveness of the Cambodian monarchy as an ongoing institution.

In 1907, when Siam returned the provinces of Battambang and Siem Reap to the French protectorate of Cambodia, the kingdom had filled out to its present size. Minor frontier adjustments were made until the 1930s, always by the French without consulting the wishes of the Cambodian monarch or his government, whose functions had shrunk to those connected with ceremonies and provincial administration.

*Laos.* The political entity called Laos, confined for the first time in its history almost entirely to the eastern bank of the Mekong River, united for the first time since 1693, and with three of its four principalities ruled (without princes) by the French, formed a new state in Southeast Asia, largely by virtue of the lines the French had arbitrarily drawn around it.

Until the end of World War II, Laos was governed under rather casual *ad hoc* arrangements. In the north, the protected principality of Luang Prabang, where a single monarch, Sisavangvong, reigned from 1905 until his death in 1959, was under indirect French rule. The three other Lao principalities—Xieng Khouang, Vientiane, and Champassak—were administered more directly. Both forms of governance were in the hands of a French *résident* in Vientiane.

French rule in Laos, such as it was, was lightened by the cooperation of traditional leaders, the mildness of French economic involvement, the country's isolation, and the compliance of the Lao population. French novels about Laos alternate between rapture and glassiness, without suggesting that administrative matters occupied much of a typical Frenchman's day. Financially, the administration ran at a deficit, balanced by profits from operations in Cambodia and the components of Vietnam. By 1943, fewer than 30,000 of its population—estimated very roughly at a million—inhabited provincial towns, including the capital, and two-thirds of those were immigrants from Vietnam. As in Cambodia, the French arrived just in time to remove the Lao from Siamese protection. By drawing lines on the map, freezing the Luang Prabang dynasty in place, and securing the fondness of key figures in the Lao regional elite, the French bought time, for the Lao and for themselves, in which to proceed slowly on what they viewed as their civilizing mission there and elsewhere in Indochina.

## Island Southeast Asia

Between 1870 and 1910, the dominant political processes of incorporation and internal reorganization were much the same in the islands as on the mainland of Southeast Asia. But the results showed up more strikingly on the map, for in 1870 much of the geographical expanse of the archipelago had not yet been painted in any imperial color. It consisted of a whole world of small societies and *negeri,* predominantly Malayo-Muslim, still intact, and carrying on their own separate histories. The zone resembled that of the Shan and Lao principalities of the interior mainland in its political fragmentation and autonomy, but it stretched over a far wider area, its population was substantially larger, and, as events showed, it had greater economic potential. Perched around the rim of this vast no man's, or many men's, land were the stronger states of the archipelago: Dutch Java, with the largest population in Southeast Asia, the Catholic Philippines, and the naval and commercial power represented by the British Straits Settlements.

Just as the larger mainland states had always possessed spheres of political influence in the Shan and Lao world, so the British and Dutch had long been paramount naval powers among the islands, and they, together with the Spanish, maintained their spheres of influence there. These spheres had been growing more distinct in the half-century before 1870. The small societies and *negeri* within each sphere—vassals, allies, and victims—were often rather severely cramped by the attentions of the paramount powers. Nevertheless, as on the mainland, these were still spheres of influence—an influence only as strong as the most recent punitive expedition or the latest grateful pretender helped to a throne.

Around 1870—somewhat earlier in the case of the Spanish—the imperial powers began to press more heavily on the lesser *negeri* and peoples around them. Within a few decades they had divided up the whole island world and imposed effective administrative control on all but a few areas inside the new boundaries. It is a measure of the political creativity of those accomplishments that all three major nations of island Southeast Asia today have names of European rather than local origin. The changes after 1870 were least significant for the Philippines; it had acquired its Spanish name and its Catholic core in Luzon and the Bisayas in the sixteenth century, adding only a modest-sized Muslim region in the south in the late nineteenth century. The British-controlled area, finally sewn together formally as Malaysia in 1963, was a new creation of the high colonial period, a sector carved more or less arbitrarily out of the Malayo-Muslim world itself. Around the massive old core of Java, finally, the Dutch built up a 3,000-mile arc of island possessions into a new Netherlands Indies, which became Indonesia—much the largest, most heavily populated, and culturally diverse of the new states of twentieth-century Southeast Asia.

*The Netherlands East Indies.* The political system centering on Dutch Batavia in 1870 may be viewed, in a thoroughly Southeast Asian way, as a series of circles of influence. At the century was Batavia itself, where the governor-general controlled a small but relatively efficient bureaucratic apparatus, a small but relatively well-trained and effectively led Royal Netherlands Indies Army of about 35,000, and an even smaller naval force. The core of Batavia's domain comprised Java (with Madura), whose population of more than 17 million people was governed in the first instance by an elite administrative corps of not much more than a hundred Dutch officials. Alongside and below them was a somewhat larger class of *priyayi* officials headed by some eighty quasi-hereditary regents. The next circle, outside Java, embraced a number of areas under direct Dutch administration, notably Ambon and several other islands in the Moluccas acquired in the great age of the spice trade in the seventeenth century, the tin-rich island of Bangka off South Sumatra, and the Minangkabau heartlands in West Sumatra, conquered in the 1830s and yielding a modest profit from forced coffee cultivation. Finally, Batavia exercised a general suzerainty over most of the small *negeri* and societies on the broad sweep of islands from Sumatra to New Guinea, a suzerainty that required frequent and costly raids to maintain and that went little deeper than acceptance of Dutch overlordship by still-sovereign local polities.

As its familiar local name—*Kumpeni,* from the old Dutch East India Company—suggests, this wide and loose political system was as much a Southeast Asian state as a Netherlands domain overseas. The *Kumpeni* was founded on Dutch power, but Dutch power working mainly through the institutions of those subject to its influence, and thus through Javan *priyayi* and archipelago sultans and chiefs. Its internal organization reflected two and a half centuries of association between the Dutch and the peoples of Java and the archipelago under conditions in which the Dutch enjoyed few real advantages, apart from more efficient political organization and novel forms of economic and military power, over the overwhelmingly larger local populations.

After about 1870, however, the cumulative effects of the scientific and industrial revolution began to overturn the ancient parity between Dutch organization and Malaysian numbers. The *Kumpeni* began to change internally and at the same time to extend its area of direct rule, much as Bangkok was doing in the same years under Chulalongkorn. The new forces at work in the areas outside Java during the last decades of the nineteenth century are well illustrated by events in three adjacent areas of North Sumatra that around 1870 were in or just beyond the outermost circle of *Kumpeni* influence. Among the Toba Bataks, a sizable wet-rice-growing people in the interior not far north of Minangkabau, the decisive development was the arrival of German missionaries of the Rhenish Mission in the 1860s. The Tobas, animists on a largely Muslim Sumatra, responded promptly to the prospects opened by this encounter. By 1900, a large proportion had adopted Christianity, channeling through it a new dynamism that was to give them a disproportionately important role in twentieth-century Indonesia. Drawn along in the wake of this folk movement, Batavia found it fairly easy to extend systematic administration over the whole Toba area by the 1890s.

In the coastal area centering on modern Medan, to the north of the Tobas, the prime agent of change was the development, after 1863, of Dutch tobacco plantations. The petty sultanates of the area owed a shadowy allegiance to the Sultan of Siak, farther down the coast, and he in turn had nominally ceded all his domains to Batavia in 1858—political formulas quite typical of the *Kumpeni* period. But the success and rapid expansion of the plantations brought in immigrant Chinese, Javanese, and Dutch to overwhelm the original inhabitants, and by 1900 their sultans were stuffed (with emoluments) and mounted on display in what was now a thoroughly Dutch-administered East Coast Residency of Sumatra.

Batavia's most important late-nineteenth-century attempt at direct military expansion outside Java, in the large, independent Sultanate of Aceh on the northern end of Sumatra, was for a long time spectacularly, unsuccessful. The effort began in 1873 as little more than a conventional *Kumpeni* raid, stimulated by fear of British competition and intended simply to enforce subservience on an unruly "native state." It proved tolerably easy to occupy the capital and for a time to envassal the sultan, but, as in Upper Burma and northern Vietnam after 1885, the move only opened the way for lesser chiefs and the folk to begin a widespread guerrilla resistance. Indeed, for the next quarter of a century, it was often the Dutch forces that were resisting and the Acehnese who seemed on the point of winning. The Aceh War—it was "the Dutch War" for the Acehnese, of course—nearly bankrupted Batavia and tied up much of its small army, and in this way it prevented any rapid expansion of Batavia's authority elsewhere in the archipelago in the period.

Outside Java, change was not general or uniform in the last decades of the nineteenth century but instead was confined to particular areas, such as North Sumatra. Much of the outer circle of *Kumpeni* influence remained essentially as it had been in 1870 or even in the seventeenth century. Meanwhile, on Java, the move to break down the old Javanese/Dutch patrimonial system, begun prematurely in the time of Daendels and Raffles and then reversed in the early years of van den Bosch's Culture System, resumed in earnest. In a setting of booming export industries (lowland sugar, now in private hands, and upland tea, coffee, and cinchona plantations), of railroad building (150 miles in 1873, 1,200 in 1900), of newspapers, the telegraph, and modern banks, the comfortable old patrimonial association between the *priyayi* and the Dutch began to lose its meaning. In the world into which Achmad Djajadiningrat was born in 1877, the Regency of Serang, in Bantam, was conceived of as a *negeri;* as a boy, he served as a page in the court of his uncle, the regent, and was trained in the old ethics of the Javan *priyayi.* By 1901, he had been ushered through a Dutch-language education and was himself installed as one of the first of a modern class of regents, no longer lords of *negeri,* except perhaps to their peasant subjects, but members of an elite, Java-wide corps of Javan officials. Djajadiningrat was ahead of his time, but in the 1860s regents and Dutch officials lost their "cultivation percentages;" in 1874, the parallel European and native administrative services were reorganized and rationalized; and in 1882 regents were deprived of their rights to levy peasant labor for personal services. Dutch residents and other officials maintained their outward signs of patrimonial status for a time, but they increasingly plunged into paperwork and developed new specialist services, such as those for irrigation and forestry. The old-style regents and *priyayi* increasingly became decorative fixtures, while Dutch officials carried on an ever more modern administration.

A new wave of change began on Java after the turn of the century, in the first triumphant years of the "Ethical Policy." Among other things, the period saw the beginning of Dutch-language education for all *priyayi* and the penetration of modern administrative innovations to the village level. Several of the factors that contributed to the changes on Java also facilitated a new imperial movement in the islands beyond, where Dutch advances of the late nineteenth century, blocked by the Aceh War, were quickly brought to conclusion. The Ethical Policy, a Dutch version of the "white man's burden," provided a convincing rationale for reorganizing and not merely presiding over the political affairs of the archipelago. The acute budgetary pinch beginning in the mid-1870s was eased by new taxes at the end of the century; government revenue doubled between 1899 and 1912. Other factors were peculiar to the situation outside Java. The KPM (Koninklijk Paketvaart Maatschappij, or Royal Steamship Company) began operations in 1891 in order to break the virtual British monopoly of steam shipping and to lessen the tendency of archipelago trade to flow through Singapore rather than Batavia. As a semiofficial line, it provided mail service and troopships for the government, operating at a loss, if necessary, in marginal areas. Its growing net of routes and services drew together the Dutch-controlled islands as never before.

The Aceh War, too, was finally ended. After 1896, Dutch forces had shifted to a new strategy of ceaseless attack and patrol, and, by 1902, the Acehnese were at last fairly well subdued, in practice if not in spirit. The effects were many. The financial drain was finally ended, and troops were released for service elsewhere. Aceh produced, in the person of the army commander who had developed and applied the new policy, a classic example of an imperial governor-general, J. B. van Heutz (1904–1909). The *marechaussee*, the lightly armed, highly mobile special force so decisive in harrying the resistance in Aceh, proved a powerful tool for achieving the same results elsewhere in the islands.

By a series of quick thrusts, the remaining *negeri* and societies of Batavia's old outer sphere were brought under effective administrative control. When van Heutz retired in 1909, more than two hundred such states and chiefdoms had signed the Short Declaration introduced in 1898, which specified simply that they acknowledged Dutch rule and undertook to obey all Dutch orders concerning their lands. In those same years, the Dutch tariff law of 1873, originally applied only to Java and directly administered areas outside, was rapidly extended over most of the archipelago. Dutch currency steadily supplanted the great variety of coins customary in the different island areas and built up yet another uniformity, as did the ever-spreading services of the KPM. Thus, by 1910, in the "outer islands" as well as on Java, the *Kumpeni* was dead. In its place had arisen a new, comprehensive, and increasingly uniform Netherlands East Indies.

*British Malaya.* In January 1874, following an arranged appeal to the British by Raja Abdullah, one of the unsuccessful claimants to the disputed throne of the west-coast Malay *negeri* of Perak, three small groups of men met on the island of Pangkor, off the Perak coast. One of the groups was Malay, consisting principally of a number of the more important chiefs in the state, including Abdullah, but not the *de facto* sultan, Ismail, nor the remaining possible contender. The second group was Chinese, principally the leaders of the two rival secret societies that had been fighting over the tin fields of the Larut district of Perak. The third was British, led by the newly appointed governor of the Straits Settlements, Sir Andrew Clarke. Clarke had arrived in Singapore only a few weeks earlier, with instructions from the Colonial Office to inquire into and report on the current disturbances in the west-coast *negeri* and, in particular, to say whether or not he considered it advisable to appoint a British officer to reside in any of the states. In his brief acquaintance with the Straits, Clarke had come easily to share the view of the mercantile community there, which wanted intervention. Not one to waste time making recommendations to London, he arranged the Pangkor meeting to accomplish three things: to settle once and for all the disputed Perak succession, preferably in favor of Abdullah; to end the fighting among the Chinese miners; and to install a British officer with sufficient powers to bring order to the *negeri* in the interests of economic exploitation of its resources by aliens.

Within a week, these ends had been achieved, and the assembled Malay chiefs signed before the governor what became known as the Pangkor Engagement, a document providing that Raja Abdullah be recognized as sultan by the signatories; that the Perak court receive a British officer to be styled Resident, "whose advice must be asked and acted upon on all questions other than those touching Malay Religion and Custom"; and that the collection and control of all revenues and the general administration of the state be regulated under the advice of the Resident.

Certain of the fictions embodied in the document, and in the circumstances in which it was signed, were later to provide a continuing theoretical justification for the arrogation by the British of all effective power and authority not merely in Perak but in most of the remaining *negeri* of the peninsula. The "inability of the Malays to govern themselves," a cardinal clause in the arguments put forward to warrant the initial acts of intervention (though it was increasingly difficult to sustain for later episodes), was happily testified to by Abdullah's letter to Clarke— inspired by Clarke and drafted by a Singapore lawyer in touch with

Abdullah—which asked for "advice and assistance" in the running of the state. For Abdullah, who certainly assented to the letter even if he did not write it, the request was probably a ritual one, part of the traditional pattern of seeking help from stronger powers in the course of a contest for succession. Yet even if it were to be taken seriously, the best advice, in view of the admitted problems of exercising effective central authority in a Malay *negeri* in circumstances of disparate district wealth and mass immigration of warring Chinese miners, might well have been, "Get rid of the Chinese." But getting rid of the Chinese was the last thing the British had in mind. On the contrary, the key to any understanding of the agreement reached at Pangkor between the two principal groups—British officials and a section of the Malay ruling class—is supplied by the silent presence of the third, the Chinese miners and merchants. Thus emerged the creation myth of the British presence: that intervention was undertaken in the interests of the Malays themselves, which interests, it was said, would naturally remain paramount.

If that was the first and largest fiction during the creation of what became known as "British Malaya," a series of smaller enabling fictions followed. In Perak, and later in Selangor, Negri Sembilan, and Pahang, the fiction of the Resident's "advice" failed to obscure the reality that it was the Resident and his English bureaucracy who ruled, the sultan and his chiefs who advised and, occasionally, assisted. When federation of the four states was pushed through in 1895, in the interests not of the Malays but of British administrative convenience, the sultans were assured that in signing the new agreement they would not "in the slightest degree . . . be curtailing the right of self-government which they at present enjoy." A cynic might observe, of course, that these words described the situation exactly. Later still, in 1909, when a Federal Council was created as a suprastate legislative body, largely at the instance of the burgeoning European rubber interests and in order to curb the authority of the resident-general of the Federated States, the argument was that the council would restore to the sultans some of the authority they had lost at federation. But they sat merely as ordinary members, listening to proceedings conducted in a language they did not understand.

The Malay ruling class in the Federated States accepted the steady extension of British control over their affairs after 1874 for a variety of reasons. In the first place, in the early stages of intervention, those who rebelled were put down by force, as in Perak in 1875 and Pahang in the early 1890s. In the atmosphere of acceptance so engendered, it made sense to settle for what one could get—a political pension commensurate with previous income from tax and toll, subordinate office in the administration as a "superintendent of *penghulus*," or a seat in the early state councils, the appointive legislative assemblies of the separate states and advisory bodies to the Residents. For a sultan, acceptance of British rule entailed a reasonable income from the civil list, new and more elaborate palaces and other proud appurtenances, and, perhaps most important of all, the sort of respect and recognition for his position as head of state that would render *de facto* within Malay society itself the authority that had in the past so often been merely *de jure*. What the protectorate system protected most of all was the shape and structure of the traditional society, from the top down.

All this resembled what was going on in Kengtung, Banjarmasin, and dozens of other sparsely populated areas of Southeast Asia in this period. What set it off and gave it a fateful significance was the development in west-coast Malaya of a distinct new society, created by Chinese and British entrepreneurship, alongside the traditional Malay one. The two decades before the 1901 census saw an increase in the combined population of Perak and Selangor alone from about 130,000 to nearly 600,000, the larger part of it representing alien, predominantly Chinese, immigration. Though the process resembled patterns of development prior to 1874, which had, in fact, contributed to British intervention, the magnitude of the resulting demographic change marked it as an innovation in kind rather than degree. Immigration grew with the booming export economy; the value of exports, mainly tin, from the protected states rose from less than half a million Straits dollars in 1875 to more than 60 million in 1900. This in turn required and stimulated the building of railroads, roads, and other communications, which penetrated the western side of the peninsula and tied it together in ways impossible before. Finally, the establishment of a single European administrative service for the Malay States and the Straits Settlements as a whole produced an overlying uniformity in such diverse matters as public education, land legislation, and fiscal organization. Most of the changes had little to do with either peasant or prince, though it is true that the Malays reaped incidental benefits both from the Pax Britannica and from the rise in the general level of prosperity.

Between 1909 and 1914, British control over the remainder of the Malay *negeri* of the peninsula (save the territories to the north, still administered as provinces of Siam) was completed by the acquisition of Kedah, Perlis, Kelantan, and Trengganu in the north and Johore in the south. All of them in due course accepted "advisers" on the pattern of the residents of the Federated States, but with slightly reduced powers, which (reflecting the strength of the ruling elites in Kedah and Johore, and the unattractiveness of Kelantan and Trengganu to the export economy) left Malay participation in the governance of the state somewhat more intact. These states became known collectively as the Unfederated States, for they resisted all blandishments to join the federation. In an important sense, however, the peninsula of Malaya, "British Malaya," formed a unity after 1914, bounded by British political control.

*British Borneo*. About the same time that the British were extending control in the peninsula, there was a similar forward movement in northern Borneo, a movement not wholly British but ultimately under

British auspices. Already in the 1840s the leading coastal state of the area, Brunei, had granted the district of Sarawak to "Raja" James Brooke, an English adventurer, in return for assistance in putting down a Dayak revolt against overbearing Brunei Malays. During the next thirty years, Brooke absorbed other pieces of Brunei territory, moving northward up the coast, and he sought in vain to get formal British protectorate status for his domain. His nephew, Charles Brooke, who succeeded him in 1868, was at first no more successful in the latter quest. Eager to improve Sarawak's trading prospects and to continue the extension of its dominion at the expense of Brunei, Brooke tried to persuade the British to countenance his own absorption of the sultanate. Irritated at his attempts at territorial aggrandizement, the British Foreign Office refused to concur, continuing to insist on Brunei's integrity.

Meanwhile, the Sultan of Sulu, plagued by increasingly heavy intrusions by Spanish and other Europeans and by falling profits from the Borneo parts of his loose naval and trading domain, was open to persuasion, as the Sultan of Brunei had been earlier in dealing with James Brooke. In 1865, he entered into the first of a series of engagements by which he leased, sold, ceded, or otherwise transferred his claims to the northern part of Borneo to Western entrepreneurs. The precise form of the transactions has been a matter of international dispute in recent years, but the sultan's overriding interest throughout was the promise of annual payments for what was by now, for him, a lost cause. His Western counterparts—Americans, an Austro-Hungarian consul, and Englishmen—followed one another in untidy succession, but eventually, in 1881, the situation stabilized. The British government granted a royal charter to a newly created North Borneo Company for the exploitation of the part of northern Borneo now known as Sabah under certain conditions, including the supervision of its foreign relations by Britain.

The grant of the charter made it difficult for the British government to continue to oppose further acquisition of territory by Sarawak, but the growing rivalry between Brooke and the company for the rest of Brunei's territories threatened to extinguish the sultanate, and in 1888 Whitehall finally extended formal British protection to all three states. Though some erosion of Brunei on both the north and the south continued, it finally came to an end in 1906, when the sultan accepted a British resident, on the pattern of those already established in the peninsular states.

From that time forward, though all three territories in Borneo were administered separately, they were linked in some degree at the top by the governor of the Straits Settlements, who functioned as high commissioner for Borneo as well as the Malay states. Supervision of administration in Borneo was, however, considerably less than in the peninsula, and Sabah and Sarawak in particular developed along somewhat different lines. The governor of North Borneo ruled unhampered by all but a small advisory council consisting of five officials, a European planter, and a Chinese (later, a wholly appointed legislative council). In Sarawak, Brooke, who prided himself on his enlightened principles of government, did in fact do something to draw the peoples of the state into consultation by means of the Council Negri (most of whose Sarawak members, however, were Malays, very much a minority community in the state), and the General Council, which, held less frequently, was attended by upriver Dayak leaders as well. Both states were characterized by the kind of paternalism that does not hasten to see its children grow up.

*The Philippines.* Developments in the Philippines in the same decades were in some ways atypical. By 1870, Luzon and the Bisayas had already been ruled as a Spanish colony for three centuries, but Spain was in eclipse in Europe, and the economy in the Philippines was dominated by the British and Chinese. The islands were attractive to the rising imperial powers—Germany, Japan, and the United States. Moreover, Philippine society at the time was undergoing rapid change of a sort unknown elsewhere in Southeast Asia until the early twentieth century, which meant that Spanish rule was threatened internally by the prospect of a nationalist revolution. At the close of the century, both dangers materialized. In 1896, a revolution broke out, and two years later the United States went to war with Spain, defeating the Spanish forces at Manila and compelling Spain to surrender the Philippines for the price of $20 million.

In other respects, however, developments in the Philippines did resemble those elsewhere in Southeast Asia. Internal reorganization after 1870 proceeded much as in Java, the other old and locally ingrown European domain. The fiscal structure of the colony was reorganized with the abolition of the tobacco monopoly in 1881 and with a general tax reform in 1884. In 1886, there was an attempt at modernization of provincial administration with the appointment of provincial comptrollers and with the rearrangement of provincial governorships. The Spanish penal, civil, and commercial codes were extended to cover all inhabitants in the colony; the Becerra Law of 1889 established town councils *(ayuntamientos)* similar to those in Spain itself; and, in 1893, the Maura Law modernized municipal organization. In general, then, the quasi-feudal patterns of an earlier age were modified as the Spanish attempted the shift from a loose, indirect rule to a centralized, nonecclesiastical, direct rule.

Spanish expansion southward from Luzon and the Bisayas paralleled attempts at internal reorganization. Manila had long claimed Mindanao and the Sulu Islands as part of its domain, but, apart from the northern shore of Mindanao and an outpost at Zamboanga, it had never been able to validate its claim against the Muslim sultanates and peoples there. In the mid-nineteenth century, spurred on by the fear that those areas would fall to other European powers and buttressed by superior technology in the form of the steamship, the Spanish pushed south. In 1847, they permitted a Basque soldier of fortune, Oyanguren, "last of the *conquistadores,*" to mount a private expedition against the Muslims on the Gulf of Davao. He did, in fact, succeed in bringing that area under Spanish control. In 1859, the Jesuits were permitted to return to their missionary work in Mindanao, and for the next four decades they encouraged the Spanish government to subdue the remaining Muslim strongholds, especially the Sulu sultanate.

The southward advance secured Manila's claims to the south against potential European rivals, but it still fell far short of effective administrative control. Not until the Americans replaced the Spanish in the Philippines was the Muslim south finally "pacified" and integrated into the colony. The Americans, full of imperial vigor, had a more efficient army and, as Protestants representing a secular state, aroused much less religious hostility than the Spanish had in three centuries of holy war. In August 1899, an American general, John Bates, negotiated an agreement with the Sultan of Sulu, promising stipends, religious liberty, and protection in return for allegiance and for an end to the slave trade and marauding. The Bates Treaty with the sultanate seemed too lenient to men like Leonard Wood, who became commander of the "Moro" province. He viewed the Muslim leadership as "corrupt, licentious, and cruel . . . nothing more or less than an unimportant collection of pirates and highwaymen" and imposed a much harder line.[26] Diplomacy and leniency were replaced by military pressure: In 1906, for example, six hundred Muslims were killed at the massacre of Bud Dajo on Jolo Island. The Americans, however, never threatened the legitimacy of the sultan, calling him "the titular spiritual head of the Mohammedan Church in the Sulu Archipelago."[27] A Muslim south was thus incorporated into what became in time the Philippine Republic.

# 21

# Bureaucratic and Economic Frameworks

IT might seem surprising, in view of the political turmoil in Southeast Asia after 1941, that the often quite arbitrary boundaries imposed on the political map of the area by about 1910 should be virtually identical with those of today. It might also seem surprising, in view of the intensity of anticolonial feelings since 1941, that great old capitals such as Mandalay, Hue, Surakarta, and Yogyakarta have remained the secondary towns they became in the colonial period, while the capitals of independent Burma, Indonesia, and Malaysia are the upstart colonial capitals of Rangoon, Jakarta, and Kuala Lumpur.

Such curious details show how deep a reorganization took place within the political units created at first by mere conquest. Rangoon remained the capital of independent Burma because during the high colonial period it became the seat of a modern administrative network, a new judicial system, and ultimately a Legislative Council, as well as the hub of a modern sea, rail, and river transport network and the focus of a ramifying tax, banking, and credit system. The Union of Burma retained the same boundaries as British Burma because these interlocking bureaucratic and economic structures had created a new interdependence for all who lived within those boundaries and, by the same token, increasingly separated them from all who lived beyond.

At the same time, the growing bureaucratic and economic frameworks both built upon and hastened the pervasive economic transformations of the period. Growing bureaucracies became possible because of rapid economic growth, and at the same time they served to further it. Export taxes on Siamese rice and Malayan tin did much to finance the railway systems built in those countries, while the railways in turn facilitated further rapid increases in exports. Rising receipts from taxes on peasants helped to pay for irrigation works in Java and Cochinchina, and newly irrigated areas accommodated new hundreds of thousands of peasant taxpayers. In these ways, conquest, new frameworks, and sweeping economic movements reinforced each other in a cycle of revolutionary change.

## Bureaucratic Frameworks

To understand the origins of modern bureaucratic government in late-nineteenth-century Southeast Asia, one should begin not with charts in the offices of power but with the cultural milieu in which new experiments in organization were first carried out. One should look at the photographs of the time: Acehnese chiefs posed proudly and somewhat menacingly in front of a thatched hut, Siamese court ladies in the crewcut hair style of the time, Chinese with pigtails, Vietnamese mandarins in their long robes, and, alongside them, beefy Europeans in field boots or covered with sashes and medals. One should read the reports of such European visitors as Crawfurd, Pavie, and the governess Anna Leonowens and the autobiographies of Achmad Djajadiningrat and Munshi Abdullah—all, in their ways, explorers of strange lands. One should read the last section of Joseph Conrad's novel, in which Jim comes to Patusan and there finds his vocation, bringing peace and order to the small valley and becoming its Lord Jim.

Gunboats and uniformed troops established physical power—that was not new to Southeast Asians—but had nothing to say about how it would be exercised afterward. The building of modern administrations was above all a great cultural achievement—in the minds of the aliens holding the new power, who came to envision a net of administration cast over these variegated lands with their old familiar ways of government; in the meeting of these men and older indigenous elites, and the accommodations they came to; and eventually, most significant of all, in the minds of Southeast Asians themselves.

The process began with, and within, the colonial administrative elites holding power in 1870 or acquiring it soon after, and the modernizing Siamese elite grouped around Chulalongkorn and his brothers. They were tiny minorities—tinier, perhaps, than most ruling elites. But what was fundamental to their situation was the degree to which they differed culturally from their subjects. Most, of course, were Christian conquerors among Buddhists, Muslims, and Confucians, speaking foreign languages and wearing trousers. More important yet—for Chulalongkorn was Siamese, and the Spanish were Catholic like the Filipinos —they were separated from those they ruled by their modern education. Most, therefore, believed in "progress" and saw power primarily as a means to effect change. Sharing basic attitudes that set them strikingly apart, and themselves mostly civil servants in bureaucratic harness, they formed tightly knit groups with what might fairly be called revolutionary goals, though the description would have horrified them.

At the beginning of the high colonial period the goals were still only sketches of a possible future. The new administrations, even where they were not newly inaugurated or politically precarious, still did not reach very far outward or downward. Communications were poor, and both colonial governors and their subordinates in the field operated very much on their own initiative. Field officers lived far apart in their separate districts and, at a time when few European women came to Southeast Asia, took Southeast Asian mistresses and wives. In such conditions, accommodation to local practice—in way of life and style of rule

—was almost universal. In the older European-ruled areas, like the Christian Philippines and Java, such accommodation had become systematized and had the inertia of tradition. In newer colonial areas, the same circumstances led to wide variations in practice and highly personal systems of government. Conrad's Lord Jim had dozens of counterparts in real life, such as the well-known late-nineteenth-century Malayan district officer Humphrey Berkeley, the "King of Grik."

But the solidarity of the administrative elites was strong, and the germ of change was deeply planted in them. Berkeley's "kingdom," like the loose supervision exercised by the first of Chulalongkorn's royal commissioners over Lao principalities like Chiang Mai in the 1870s and 1880s, was a frontier institution in an expanding bureaucratic system. In the last decades of the nineteenth century, as administrations gained greater revenues, better communications, and more staff, the older accommodations began to give way. A new generation of colonial officers came out imbued with a stronger sense of mission and of superiority. In a series of circulars issued in the years after 1900, the Netherlands Indies government discouraged its officials from using the ceremonial appurtenances by which they had symbolized their Javanstyle rule. Colonial officials more often married European wives, creating tensions revealed in Somerset Maugham's Malayan short stories, which return obsessively to the theme of wives, "native" mistresses, and Eurasian children. In noncolonial Siam, the new elite around Chulalongkorn was Siamese to begin with, remaining so in many of its essential values. But in the 1880s, "Young Siam" was in some ways so different from the conservative bureaucratic nobility it was replacing that its representatives were like foreigners. They consciously followed European administrative organization and behavior, kept regular office hours, dressed in modified European fashion, and began to conduct business in a pattern of paperwork quite unlike the personal administration of their elders.

Such changes in life-style reflected the growing self-confidence and broadening vision of change among the small groups in the upper echelons of the new administrations. Such men were often more earnest and idealistic than their predecessors, who in the pioneer days had had a well-founded skepticism about the degree of change they could bring about. As a group, though, they lacked the personal charm of so many of the older generation, spoke local languages less fluently or not at all, and often misunderstood the societies they thought they were improving. By about 1900, almost everywhere in Southeast Asia, they had become bureaucrats in fully routinized general administrative services, which governed the countries of the area with an increasingly efficient but cold hand.

In the last decades of the nineteenth century, while the colonial and Siamese elites were being thus transformed, other changes were taking place in the relations between them and the subordinate Southeast

Asian elites with which they dealt. From their first arrival, the tiny minorities of European rulers had found it prudent, convenient, and, in fact, absolutely necessary to leave direct governance of the masses of the population to whatever traditional Southeast Asian leaders and classes would cooperate with them. Such groups varied enormously among themselves, in the nature of their ties to particular European regimes, and in the changes in these ties, but there were three main patterns in the period.

The numerous small states and societies of the Shan-Lao and Malayo-Muslim zones were in general the last to be brought under firm European (or Siamese) control, mostly in the years around 1900. In those areas, as generally elsewhere, the colonial powers began with forms of indirect rule, recognizing kings, sultans, chiefs, and other traditional leaders, harnessing them with separate treaties or agreements, and posting political agents to supervise and instruct them. Throughout those areas, with a few notable exceptions, the comparatively loose administrative arrangements continued in effect until quite recent times. Before 1900, much the same was true, for quite different reasons, of overseas Chinese communities, which largely governed themselves through "secret societies" and other institutions of their own, dealing with the ruling powers through leaders generally called—in the Malay world at least—*Kapitan China.*

A much swifter and further-reaching pattern of change in the relations between central administrations and traditional elites characterized a second group of areas, including the west-coast Malay states, Sumatra's East Coast Residency, Java, Siam, northern and central Vietnam, and, to some extent, Cambodia. All were originally governed under formulas of indirect rule, but in the course of the late nineteenth century the growing power of the colonial and Siamese governments overtook that form of political insurance. Moreover, the rapid economic change or large populations of these areas called for increasingly complex administrative methods. The central administrative elites that extended and manned these systems, eager to run things their own way and increasingly confident of their ability to do so, became less tolerant of the formalities of indirect rule. The traditional rulers, for their part, ill-equipped to govern in the new style and generally unsympathetic to what it stood for, became increasingly irrelevant in the daily administration of their own lands. In most cases, rather like European monarchs, they were bought off with substantial emoluments and encapsulated in ceremonial roles, while the colonial elites bypassed them to deal directly with traditional officials at lower levels. Javan regents continued to be treated with great deference, although, increasingly, Dutch residents gave the orders and young Dutch *controleurs* supervised Javan district and subdistrict officers in the field. The Nguyen court was infiltrated with French officials in key positions, while mandarins throughout northern and central Vietnam came under the control of French *résidents supérieurs.* The west-coast Malay sultanates were amalgamated in 1895, and a unified (British) Malayan civil service under a resident-general dropped all but the pretense of "advising" sultans, while British district officers, governing at an unusually low level of administration, dealt directly with Malay *penghulu,* themselves well on the way to becoming British-style functionaries. By 1910, the old Siamese bureaucratic nobility in the center and subordinate kings and provincial elites in the outer regions were being pensioned off, so that, from Bangkok to the district level, Siam was coming to be governed by a single national administrative elite.

The third and most thoroughgoing pattern of change was found in Cochinchina and central and southern Burma. The French severed Cochinchina from the rest of Vietnam; similarly, the British first cut off sections of the Burmese kingdom and then, after the final war in 1885, abolished the monarchy altogether. In these two areas, therefore, the Europeans never governed by indirect rule but instead dealt from the beginning with lower-level traditional leaders or, as in Cochinchina for a time, experimented with direct local rule themselves. In both cases, moreover, new nontraditional indigenous administrative classes emerged before 1900—the "interpreters" of Cochinchina and the *a-so-ya-min* in Burma. The latter were recruited through an examination system testing knowledge of English, surveying, and administrative procedures. Beginning at the bottom, they were able to rise through the ranks of the modern administrative hierarchy—the first Burmese deputy commissioner, a quite high post, was appointed in 1908. The *a-so-ya-min* class, evolving its own mixed Anglo-Burmese life style, described in Mi Mi Khaing's delightful family history, *Burmese Family,* was fully formed by 1900.

The early years of the twentieth century were a watershed in the administrative history of Southeast Asia. The last corners of the area were being incorporated into the six large states that had been constructed, and the basic administrative grids covering the six countries had been laid down. The European and Siamese central administrative services were in full running order—with graded hierarchies, regular recruitment and promotion procedures, and paperwork up to international standards. They kept a careful eye on the still indirectly ruled outlying areas and fairly closely supervised the general affairs of the major concentrations of population. By then, they had reached down below the traditional rulers in most areas to work through Southeast Asian chiefs and traditional leaders at regional and local levels of administration. There was thus a characteristic joint in the administrative systems where the lower European officials (or, for that matter, Bangkok Siamese) dealt with Southeast Asian local elites across a cultural and historical gap symbolized by the need for bilingualism or interpreters. Beyond lay the mass of the folk who still rarely dealt with a European official on any kind of business. It was here—across the bureaucratic joint and in relations between the modern state and the peasants—that the administrative developments of the decades before World War II were most striking.

The cultural gap between the Europeans and Southeast Asians in government service had appreciably widened in the decades before 1900, as the European sections of the bureaucracies had modernized themselves. That gap was largely closed during the early decades of the twentieth century, as Southeast Asian civil servants acquired a modern education. Whereas in 1900 most Southeast Asians in government service—apart from Bangkok Siamese, of course—were educated in traditional modes and held office because of traditional status, by 1940 virtually all had had a modern education, and many had achieved their positions on that basis, rather than through inherited status.

There were many reasons for the change. In the twentieth century, with larger revenues and larger goals, administrations grew enormously. as whole new specialist services—government school systems, agricultural research stations, archaeological departments—were created, to join the older and more basic general administrative services. To save money, as well as to be true to self-imposed ideas of tutelage, colonial governments aimed to fill many of the new jobs with Southeast Asians. To do so, they needed men educated in the modern way, not only for the specialist services (which was obvious) but for the general administrative services as well (by this time even village headmen were beginning to be required to keep various written records). The colonial and Siamese governments, therefore, opened an increasingly wide range of modern educational opportunities. The general European-language (or Siamese-language) government schools, which burgeoned in the early twentieth century, produced a large proportion of the Southeast Asian civil servants of the period. It was characteristic, though, that governments from the beginning provided modern schooling specifically intended for such jobs. The beginnings may be seen in the small schools founded in late-nineteenth-century Java for training vaccinators, teachers, and future administrators. Such education spread rapidly in the early years of the twentieth century, as, for example, in the schools for training district officers, police, agricultural officers, and others, which came to be established within virtually every Bangkok ministry and government department.

Southeast Asians found the new schools, and the bureaucratic jobs which they led to, increasingly attractive. Many came from old elite families which had been bypassed in the late nineteenth century. The regent class on Java was restored to relevance by the 1920s on a new basis, wearing neckties, speaking Dutch, and merging fully into the modern administration. The sons of Chiang Mai and Lao princes loosened their connections to their home areas, as they were co-opted into the national Siamese elite. Others—most often, perhaps, in Java— were the sons of lesser officials or provincial or local elite families. For them, a civil service position obtained on the basis of training and merit rather than birth represented a step toward higher status, which had been largely closed to them under the traditional order. Yet others, like many of the nineteenth-century *a-so-ya-min* in Burma, came out of still more humble or even peasant families. This was perhaps most common in the Philippines, because of the mainly English-language education system and the swift Filipinization of the bureaucracy by the Americans. But it was possible elsewhere and was the rule rather than the exception among the Minangkabau of West Sumatra, for example, where the higher-status families tended to look down on modern education and civil service jobs, while large numbers of poorer boys got their start in this way. In the early decades of the twentieth century, everywhere but in the Philippines, jobs in the expanding civil services were the single most important avenue of upward social mobility. Families scraped deeply to finance the education that could make a son into a forest officer or a postal clerk.

It would be a mistake, though, to see the phenomenon simply in terms of social ambition. The government training schools and civil service positions were opening up, but nothing compelled Southeast Asians to enter them. There is, in fact, considerable evidence from various parts of the area around the turn of the century to indicate strong family resistance to such paths. One is struck by the cultural vitality and, indeed, by the plain courage of many Southeast Asians in the early twentieth century who were willing to recast their lives to the requirements of modern civil service careers and who accepted the premises of modern bureaucratic government—so alien to their own political culture—as their own. In time, nationalists were to criticize colonial government service—accurately enough—as collaboration, but they too rejected traditional political structure in favor of a modern conception of the state.

Three broader consequences of the process require special notice. First, almost everywhere in Southeast Asia in the years after 1900, a civil service career became the dominant ambition of the new "middle sector." In this way, deep-rooted conceptions of a hierarchically graded society, with status defined in terms of relative distance from the apex of political authority, were translated into modern terms and carried forward. Such ambitions, with their wide political implications, constitute one of the most prominent features of Southeast Asian societies today.

The second consequence had more immediate political significance. By 1940, the cultural gap in the governing hierarchy had been more or less closed. Now, from governor-general to just above the village level, most of Southeast Asia was administered by bureaucratic elites, European and Southeast Asian, which shared most of the same operating assumptions about government, used one main (or sole) language of administration, and maintained similar life-styles. Nevertheless, in sharp contrast, the bureaucratic joint retained its racial aspect: Europeans on top, Southeast Asians below. Appreciation of the contrast did much to stimulate nationalist movements.

The third consequence was deeply ironical. The process described above tended inevitably to pull modern-educated Southeast Asian civil servants away from the life of the peasant. A new cultural joint had appeared, in some ways as wide as the earlier one, but now it was between the folk and the Southeast Asian bureaucratic classes that, along with Europeans, ruled over them. The consequences of that cultural gap are still an important factor in the ongoing social history of Southeast Asia.

Meanwhile the burgeoning colonial administrations were also reaching deeper and deeper into the affairs of the rural populations of Southeast Asia. The general administrative services that developed in the late nineteenth century confined themselves mainly to the fundamentals of government—maintaining order, administering the law, and collecting taxes. In this—though they differed markedly in other respects—they certainly resembled their predecessor governments and could thus, for example, incorporate traditional local elites more or less unchanged, appearing to peasants as not much more than new dynasties.

The rapid expansion of government activities after 1900, however, implied quite new relations between the state and its subjects. This was especially true of the specialist services. With few exceptions, they were established precisely to perform functions that had no local precedents. Unlike the earlier general administrative services, they rarely incorporated traditional leaders into their ranks; from the beginning, they were staffed almost exclusively with modern-educated men—Europeans, local Southeast Asians, and a characteristically high proportion of Indians, Chinese, and nonlocal Southeast Asians. Born out of the needs of European and other economic interests for various facilities, but also out of paternalist ideals, however confused, of serving the public welfare, the specialist services were dedicated by their very nature to change.

The same came increasingly to be true of the general administrative services. While they continued in the twentieth century to perform the basic functions of government, they also became much more deeply involved in programs of change, if only in coordinating the activities of the specialist services at the local level and in enforcing the latters' policies. Their ability to effect change, moreover, was greatly increased by the replacement of traditional-minded Southeast Asian administrative officials at local levels by a new generation of modern-educated men who cherished many of the same ideas of progress as the Europeans.

While some of these new government programs had nothing to do with the mass of the population (e.g., geological services) or affected them only indirectly (e.g., postal, telegraph, and telephone services, railroads, censuses), many were directed specifically at improving village life—a wide variety of public health programs, forest reserves to check erosion, village schools, rural credit services, cooperatives, agricultural extension services, the reorganization of village structure. The list seems estimable, and so it seemed to the zealous European district officers or Southeast Asian schoolteachers who introduced—not to say imposed—the measures in the villages. But peasants seldom shared the assumptions and goals of these self-defined agents of progress, and they judged the new programs by their own well-tested standards of efficiency and purpose. A few of the programs, such as public health nurses and village schools in some areas, gained wide approval. Others, such as rural credit services and agricultural extension, were well received by at least the minority who made use of them. Virtually all were at least acceptable in most villages most of the time. But all, too, aroused discontent or passive resistance in many areas, in some cases contributing directly to rebellious movements. Governments, to save money, often made villagers pay for changes they had not wanted in the first place. Forest reserves were universally disliked because they hampered the collection of firewood. The slaughter of cattle to prevent the spread of rinderpest could bring ruin to individuals whose animals were killed. The rearrangement or amalgamation of hamlets and villages, mainly for administrative convenience, broke up natural communities or submerged them in arbitrary groupings. New rules for the appointment or choice of village headmen—such as a series of village elections in northern Vietnam, which caused most of the notables to withdraw from public life—often disturbed village social structure. Everywhere new duties and closer supervision tended to draw headmen apart from village life, making them as much the lowest agents of government as leaders and members of their communities.

Well-intended programs of village welfare—not to speak of policies followed for other reasons and often quite callously applied—represented an unprecedented assault upon the ways of village life. Older rulers had extracted all the taxes and forced labor they could, but, except in time of war, they had not been able, nor had they wanted, to intrude directly upon village affairs. Twentieth-century colonial and Siamese governments were both able and eager to do so, and they drew the peasants willy-nilly into the new frameworks they were driven to create.

## Economic Frameworks

Few changes in the economic apparatus of the area in the three-quarters of a century before 1941 were more striking than those in transportation. In the land areas of Southeast Asia, transport had always been slow, expensive, and difficult. The Nguyen emperors constructed the Mandarin Road from Hanoi to Saigon, but they built and used it mainly for political communications; goods, such as tax rice to the court at Hue, went by sea. It took three months to go upriver from Rangoon

to Mandalay, a month and a half by ox cart from Nongkhai on the
Mekong to Bangkok, several weeks from Semarang to Surakarta.
Transport difficulties, in themselves, set strict limits to the intensity of
governance in the circles of influence more remote from the capitals,
and they restricted trade by land. Movement along the coasts, and particularly throughout island Southeast Asia, was much easier, and trade
played a much more important economic role generally in that region.
But in an age of *perahu,* junks, and European square-rigged vessels, the
long seaways and scattered coastal settlements of the archipelago dictated a politics of raid and vassalage rather than steady administration,
and such vessels had a limited capacity for bulk shipments.

The Irrawaddy Flotilla Company, founded in the 1860s, was the first
and largest inland steamship service in Southeast Asia. By the end of
the century it dominated inland water traffic with its large fleet, dock-
yards, warehouses, rice mills, and sawmills. It carried migrant laborers
between central Burma and the delta rice frontier and hundreds of
thousands of tons of paddy to the mills at Rangoon and Bassein. It permitted British troops to steam upriver in a few days in order to overthrow Thibaw's kingdom in 1885. Steam launches and barges played
an important but lesser role on other rivers, such as the Čhaophraya,
lower Mekong, and Solo. But the Irrawaddy, navigable from Bhamo to
the sea, had always been the most important of the inland waterways of
the area, and it remained so in the age of steam.

Elsewhere, in the land areas, it was the railroad that inaugurated the
transport revolution. The backbone line of the Burmese system ran up
the Sittang valley from Rangoon, reaching Toungoo in 1885, Mandalay
in 1889, and Lashio in the Shan hills in 1902, while a later branch connected Mandalay with Myitkyina, in the far north. The Rangoon-
Prome line opened up large areas to export rice cultivation in 1877, as
did later lines to Bassein and Moulmein. By the 1920s, Burma possessed a 2,000-mile railway network, with no outside connections,
defining in its way a distinct economic domain. Other areas where economic life was powerfully affected by railway systems were Java, with
its particularly rugged terrain for so heavily settled an area, and Luzon,
where the line from Manila north across the central plain opened up
rich areas in the twentieth century for rice and, especially, sugar production.

It was in Siam, however, that the railway was most decisive. The
Siamese government, pressed between dangerous colonial neighbors,
kept political considerations always foremost in framing its policy. It
gave the Germans a major role in the Railway Department because
Germany was no threat to Siam. Ever mindful of the survival value of
fiscal conservatism and financial self-sufficiency, it paid for all of its
early railway projects from current revenue rather than foreign loans.
The first of the three major lines, begun in 1892 and reaching Khorat in
1900, was intended to help counter the French advance through Laos.

From Khorat (Nakhǫn Ratchasima), lines were extended toward the Mekong in the 1920s and 1930s, north to Udon and Nongkhai opposite Vientiane, and east to Ubon. The second major line ran north, reaching Uttaradit in the foothills in 1909 and pausing before pushing through to Chiang Mai in 1921. The third line was begun in 1909—with a British loan accompanying the final division of the Malay states between the British and Siam—and connected Bangkok to Penang by 1922.

The economic effects of Siamese railways were impressive. The northern and northeastern lines permitted, for the first time, major rice exports from those areas. The Chinese moved outward to each new railhead in turn, reinforcing the railway network with their own commercial one. The political-economic effects were fully as significant. By 1930, a national system of 1,875 miles, centered on Bangkok, greatly enhanced the primacy of that city and the government located there. It was only after the railroad reached Chiang Mai (though not entirely because of that) that Bangkok began in earnest to collect taxes throughout the north, and it was only then that the *baht* replaced the rupee as the basic currency there. Much the same was true in the northeast, and it is clear that the railroad has been particularly important in binding modern Thailand together. At the same time, the Siamese railways, unlike Burma's, provided important links to the outside as well. The southward line reinforced an earlier tendency for parts of southern Siam to orient themselves economically toward Penang; in the nineteenth century, most Chinese tin miners had reached southern Siam via Penang, and in the twentieth century the area's tin went there for smelting—a reduction of Bangkok's economic suzerainty not effectively challenged until the 1960s. On the other hand, the northeastern lines toward the Mekong, not counteracted by any French railways into Laos, strongly reinforced a long-standing tendency of the Mekong Lao to orient themselves toward Bangkok.

By contrast, the grandiose French railway system in Indochina was of limited significance. Two lines led off into China, reflecting (rather faintly) old nineteenth-century dreams of "tapping the China market." The major line, completed just before World War II, ran along the coastal route of the Mandarin Road and, like it, was of little economic use where ships could do the job. The French were more successful with roads, opening up several new passages into the mountainous spine and along the Mekong, though not decisively enough to overcome the natural cleavages within Indochina. It was Java, which had a fine road system for its time as early as 1850, along with the Philippines and Burma, that developed the most significant road networks before World War II.

Steamships played a less revolutionary role in the sea transport of Southeast Asia than railroads and modern roads with motor vehicles did on land, for the latter were altogether new, while the steamship was simply a better version, for many purposes, of a familiar means of transport. Sailing vessels, in fact, predominated in coastal traffic until the 1890s and have continued to play an important economic role to this day. Nor did steamship lines have quite as direct and powerful an integrative effect in island Southeast Asia as railroads in Siam and railroads and roads in Burma. The newly emerging political units in island Southeast Asia incorporated great expanses of an established maritime world whose trade could move at will on the open seas. Throughout the nineteenth and into the twentieth century, in fact, the general trade of most of what became the Netherlands Indies and the southern Philippines was focused on Singapore, which belonged to another political jurisdiction.

Nevertheless, steam did bring important changes. The steamship was an important weapon in the successful piracy suppression campaigns, which in time made the region safe for other kinds of economic exploitation and political intrusion. The growing export economy of the Philippines gave rise to a busy interisland shipping, dominated by Chinese *mestizos,* and this in turn created much closer and more regular ties among the islands and peoples of that country. In the Netherlands Indies, a single far-flung shipping enterprise, the KPM, had the same kind of influence, though under much more difficult circumstances.

Unlike rail and road, of course, the steamship greatly strengthened connections with the world outside Southeast Asia as well. In this period, the numerous small, local economies that had characterized traditional Southeast Asia were not only being tied together in new "national" economic structures but also were being brought into touch with the world economy. British steam shipping lines serving Southeast Asia, at first mainly in passing, on the way to the China coast, began to appear in the 1860s. They were joined in the following decades by increasing numbers of French, Dutch, German, American, Japanese, and other lines, along with privately owned tramp shipping. The major lines often served the larger Southeast Asian ports as part of their global routes. But others provided shorter-range services, from India across the Bay of Bengal and from the China coast and Japan to the smaller ports on the Southeast Asian coasts.

International shipping, steadily increasing in tonnage, frequency, and scope of service, provided perhaps the most fundamental link between Southeast Asia and the world economy and became one of the major agents of economic change within the area. Steamships carried out the hundreds of thousands and then millions of tons of sugar and rice, bringing in textiles, canned goods, and heavy machinery. Steamships, not junks, carried most of the rising numbers of Chinese immigrants in the half-century before 1930 and almost all of the Indians to Burma and Malaya. They brought in European soldiers, colonial officials, and ambitious young men to run the plantations and, in the twentieth century, their wives and families, along with increasing numbers of tourists.

The transportation systems were the most obvious of the new economic structures, because they impinged physically on the landscape, because they carried people and bulk goods, and because—visible in a different way—they could be drawn on maps. Economic machinery of many other sorts was no less important for being less obtrusive to the eye and invisible on the map. Not the least of the preconditions for a more highly structured and efficient economic life was a standardized currency system. In Siam in 1850, to take an extreme case, the largest unit of traditional currency was the *chang,* equal to 20 *tamlüng,* or 80 *baht,* or 320 *salüng,* or 640 *füang,* or 1,280 *sik,* or 2,560 *siao,* or 5,120 *at,* or 10,240 *solot,* or 512,000 cowrie shells. In addition, Indian rupees circulated in the teak areas around Chiang Mai, and Mexican and other dollars circulated elsewhere, especially in the south. Minted coins, which circulated early in Mongkut's reign at 64 *at* to the *baht,* simplified matters somewhat, but it was not until foreign coins were made legal tender in 1857, at 5 *baht* to $3 Mexican, that the difficulties occasioned by foreign commerce and exchange were rendered manageable.

In a somewhat different case, the comparatively well-developed Vietnamese currency system was not modified but replaced, starting in Cochinchina, by a new French colonial system using the piaster as its basic unit. Colonial Burma did not even get its own currency; it got instead the Indian rupee and was thus annexed financially, as well as politically and administratively, to the Indian empire. In island Southeast Asia, which for centuries had done most of its business through a whole family of different silver dollars, the political partition completed about 1910 had its counterpart in the field of currency. In the Philippines, the silver peso carried on, tied 2 to 1 to the U.S. dollar after 1903; the guilder spread rapidly over the new Netherlands Indies after 1900; and the British sphere got its first Straits dollar notes in 1906, pegged to sterling at the rate of two shillings and fourpence.

The introduction and spread of new currency systems illustrate three types of economic linkages: to the world economy in general; to the economies of the various metropolitan powers; and among the different parts of the new colonies themselves, as economic activities within each "national" unit were increasingly expressed in terms of a single medium of exchange. New tariff systems had more limited effects. While everywhere they marked off the new political units as distinct economic domains, the most powerful consequences came where colonial policy dictated tight tariff links with the metropolitan country. This was particularly true of the Philippines and of Indochina. France enclosed Indochina in its own highly protectionist tariff system, thus forcefully cutting Vietnam's close economic association with China, just as it had also cut Vietnam's ancient but loose political subservience to China. Vietnamese were thereby forced to buy higher-priced French textiles and other goods, while large quantities of Cochinchinese rice went to France, spurred by a program of popularization that brought rice, for the first time, to an important place in the French cuisine. In the Philippines, the effects were similar and far more profound in the long run. Spanish restrictive tariffs had had little impact on Anglo-Chinese domination of Philippine foreign trade. But when virtual free trade within the United States tariff walls was established in 1913, the Philippine economy was shaped to conform to the needs of the American market. This comfortable dependence, while providing fortunes for Filipino sugar barons, among others, encouraged inefficient production methods, which priced Philippine sugar and other products out of the world market.

By contrast, the chief significance of the modern banking systems was the way they integrated the emerging export economies of Southeast Asia into the world market rather than merely into those of the metropolitan countries. The official Bank of Indochina dominated the economy of that colony, but, in general, colonial central banks, such as the Java Bank, developed rather slowly, and in most of Southeast Asia, private banks with worldwide connections dominated the field. The British ones, notably the Chartered Bank of India, Australia, and China, and the Hong Kong and Shanghai Banking Corporation, came first, establishing major branches in most of the Southeast Asian countries. They were soon followed by Dutch, American, French, Japanese, and, shortly before World War II, Nationalist Chinese banks. In individual countries, however, Europeans, a few overseas Chinese and Indians, and even fewer Southeast Asians, founded a number of banks that confined their operations within "national" spheres.

Banks, insurance firms, and all-purpose service institutions, such as the agency houses of the Straits Settlements, which dominated the export-import business, managed plantations, and did much else, were most significant as mediating institutions through which Southeast Asian economies were incorporated into the world economic system. Nevertheless, they also played a crucial role in shaping and tying together the separate economies. Banks, concentrated in the major city of each country, stood at the center of ever more complex financial systems and, alongside the more informal Chinese and Indian networks, presided over "national" credit systems. European, Chinese, and Indian chambers of commerce, while often representing export-oriented interests, served business communities whose primary frame of reference was the colony in which they operated.

Much of the economic policy of the colonial (and Siamese) governments had the same effect of reinforcing the growing "national" economic frameworks. Banking, currency, and contract laws, for example, facilitated and shaped the development of new institutions. New land laws—the issuance of title deeds and regular cadastral surveys in the nineteenth-century Philippines or twentieth-century Siam, standardized seventy-five-year plantation leases in the Netherlands Indies, new mortgage provisions in Burma or the Malay Reservation areas—

created types of access to land and strongly affected the peasant's relation to the soil. The most profound consequences of these and other
land laws were socioeconomic, but they had other effects as well. They
systematized traditional land tenure customs hitherto marked by all
sorts of local variations, and they brought the mass of the population
into much more direct and regular contact with the emerging administrative systems. More generally, new laws helped shape a distinct set of
economic practices within each "national" system.

While government tax policy, similarly, was most important for its
socioeconomic impact, it also contributed to the creation of "national"
economic structures. Periodic "land settlements" in British Burma, for
the purpose of reviewing land productivity and ownership and of
reassessing taxes, made possible a Burma-wide, impersonal system of
taxation, probably heavier in its incidence and more uniform in its
application than those which had preceded it. Everywhere in Southeast
Asia in the high colonial period there was a trend away from the more
diverse, local, and personal forms of taxation: in levies on a great variety of agricultural products and handicrafts; in different kinds of labor
services owed to patrons; and in the form of tax farms on opium and
gambling or road and river tolls sold to the highest bidder or granted to
a king's favorite in appanage. In their place came a new range of taxes:
excise taxes on salt and alcohol in Vietnam and on other consumer
goods elsewhere; head, land, and produce taxes in cash; export and
import taxes. From them emerged increasingly uniform and efficiently
enforced colonywide tax systems, expressed in the standard and impersonal medium of "national" currencies.

One thing that stands out in the administrative and economic reorganizations of the high colonial era is the unprecedented role played by
government. In traditional Southeast Asia, the main function of the
ruler was to *be,* symbolizing in his person an agreed-on social order, a
cultural ideal, and a state of harmony with the cosmos. The new colonial and Siamese governments existed primarily to *do,* providing themselves with a permanently crowded agenda of specific tasks to accomplish. They felt, by older Southeast Asian standards, a peculiar need to
tidy up casual and irregular old customs, to bring uniformity to the
numerous small, local societies in their jurisdictions, to clear paths for
economic "progress," to organize, reform, and control. To do these
things, the new governments also possessed unprecedented powers:
overwhelming military superiority; new technological tools; larger revenues; and, in the colonies at least, a freedom to innovate conferred by
conquest and by an external base of political authority and cultural reference.

The result, although by no means due entirely to government action,
was a striking historical reversal. Societies that had been rather loosely
organized politically and economically were pressed within steadily
tightening bureaucratic and economic frameworks. The same process,

however, profoundly disrupted the formerly secure social and cultural order of those societies, generating new ambitions and visions as well as social plurality, cultural alienation, degradation, and despair. One of the basic appeals of modern nationalism, when it appeared, was the solution it offered to the disorder resulting from the historical reversal: to preserve the tightening frameworks but within them, as nations, to recreate lost social and cultural harmony.

# 22

# Economic Transformation, 1870–1940

IT was said extravagantly of Java in the time of the Culture System that the island was one vast government plantation. In the same way, there has been a widespread impression that the whole of Southeast Asia's economy was given over to export production in the high colonial period. The impression is far from true. Peasant subsistence cultivation, especially of rice, remained the largest single sector of the economy. Commercial agriculture for domestic consumption, small-scale domestic industry, transportation, and credit systems all grew steadily in the period. Rapid population increase set in motion a very different train of economic events, especially among peasants. Nevertheless, the burgeoning export industries were the dominant economic force of the age and thus a major influence on developments in the other economic sectors, and indeed in society generally. The rise of export industries can therefore serve as a major theme around which one can survey the vast, complex, and as yet barely studied subject of the economic transformation that took place between 1870 and 1940.

The impetus for the export boom came from rising world market demand, felt ever more strongly in Southeast Asia after the arrival of the steamship, with its cheap bulk transport, in the 1860s. The world market, however, exerted its attraction impartially on every part of the globe. The particular way in which the Southeast Asian export industries developed was, in the beginning at least, strongly influenced by conditions in the region itself. Certain general features of the premodern Southeast Asian economic landscape were crucial. The area as a whole was sparsely and unevenly populated. Transportation was slow and difficult. Economic transactions were conducted mainly by barter; taxes were mostly in kind and labor; there was very little currency in circulation or use of credit. It was a landscape of small, local, and largely self-sufficient economies only loosely associated in provinces and kingdoms whose common bonds were more cultural and social than economic.

Southeast Asia, to be sure, had always had some export trade, particularly from the island area, where it was often locally very important. It is significant that, apart from some minerals, such as tin and gold, the exports were all tropical or subtropical agricultural commodities: cloves and nutmeg from the Moluccas, pepper from Sumatra, coffee from

West Java, to mention a few of the most important. There were good reasons for this. Southeast Asia exported raw materials, not manufactured goods, because basic economic conditions in the area precluded any but small-scale domestic industries, such as hand looms and court crafts. Instead, over the centuries, it imported large quantities of Indian textiles and Chinese ceramic wares.

This pattern of trade—tropical agricultural raw materials and some minerals for imported manufactured goods—continued through the export boom of the late nineteenth and early twentieth centuries. There were two main reasons for this: the West's rapidly lengthening lead in the industrial revolution combined with its colonial power in Southeast Asia and conditions in Southeast Asia itself.

The West, riding the tide of economic change, found ready markets in Southeast Asia for inexpensive machine-made textiles, kerosene, and locomotives. Growing and increasingly prosperous populations in Europe and elsewhere demanded more sugar, tea, and coffee; canning and electrical industries required tin; bicycles and then automobiles needed rubber tires. Increasingly powerful colonial governments, smugly confusing the selfish interests of their nationals with the cause of advancing "civilization," zealously promoted the growth of export agriculture and did little or nothing to foster local manufacturing.

Meanwhile, economic and social conditions in Southeast Asia itself made substantial domestic industrialization, in the short run at least, quite impossible, while massive agricultural exports were easily achieved.

On the eve of the export boom, the economic mobility—the willingness and ability to assume new economic roles—of Southeast Asians was in many ways limited. Most peasants, to begin with, were settled in a subsistence way of life. They had enough land, produced most of what they needed, bartered for a few necessities like salt and fish, and bargained on fairly even terms against the demands of the elites in their societies. All this, confirmed by the experience of generations, was deeply entrenched in their values and beliefs. Most of them, too, were subject to corvée labor or were attached to patrons as clients or debt-bondsmen, which restricted their economic mobility in other ways. None of this prevented peasants from responding to the possibilities of export production; quite the contrary. But it did dictate the ways in which they would do so and set limits on how far and how fast they would go in adapting to the stimulus of the world market.

Throughout Southeast Asia, their first and greatest response was smallholder production of export crops, sometimes in their home villages but more often on forest land in the vicinity or in new holdings on a nearby agricultural frontier. There was ample precedent. Some of the larger export industries of earlier centuries had started in the same way: Moluccan smallholders in the fifteenth and sixteenth centuries had traded cloves and nutmeg for textiles and rice, and peasants in central

Burma from the seventeenth century onward grew cotton for the caravans to China. The same occurred on a larger scale in the nineteenth
and twentieth centuries: Hundreds of thousands of Burmese, Thai, and
southern Vietnamese peasants moved steadily out over the deltas to
grow rice in exchange for cash and imports; hundreds of thousands of
peasants in Sumatra, Malaya, and Borneo planted stands of rubber
trees on the edge of the forests near their settlements; more tens of thousands produced many other export crops in other places.

It was a swift and massive response, a great change made easy precisely because it required so little change in peasant practices and economic values. Growing familiar crops like rice and coconuts, or new
crops like rubber and tea, whose market value had been demonstrated
by European plantations, was a natural extension of the peasants'
established subsistence agriculture. Those who produced millions of
tons of export rice remained peasants. They readily opened new land,
increased production, grew new crops, adopted kerosene lamps and
made greater use of cash, but their economic mobility did not as yet
extend much farther. They continued to be small-scale growers, almost
always leaving it to others to get the goods to the market. In 1870, very
few were willing to leave their villages to work for wages in plantations
or in the cities, and this was still true of many in 1980.

The established economic values of the comparatively few Southeast
Asians who were not peasants—the merchants, religious leaders, aristocrats, and kings—similarly restricted their response to the possibilities
of export agriculture. In traditional Southeast Asia, prestige could lead
to wealth but rarely the reverse. None of the societies, except that of the
Philippines, had a clear social image of an indigenous rich man risen to
high status merely by an accumulation of wealth. The avenues to high
status were those of birth, personal connections, Confucian study, Buddhist piety, or Islamic learning. The majesty of kings was revealed by
plenitude of manpower—the retainers, craftsmen, officials, and concubines of the palace cities—rather than by riches in goods or money.

In the Southeast Asian societies, indigenous merchants were usually
small traders operating on the fringes of the subsistence economies and
pinched in the narrow social space between lord and peasant. Almost
everywhere but in the Islamic islands they remained small traders
under the shadow of growing immigrant commercial communities, and
they took little part in the export industries.

Merchants had played a much more important role in the widespread
communities of the Malayo-Muslim world over the centuries. Trade
was more important in many areas there, and, as Muslims, the merchants had a religious motive to make money—in order to be able to go
on the *haj* to Mecca and when they returned, as *haji,* to enjoy high prestige. Such merchants continued in the years of the export boom to play
a large part in the older miscellaneous export trades of the islands, collecting small quantities of a great variety of special forest and sea prod-

ucts and bringing them to entrepôts like Singapore. In central Sumatra
and southern Borneo, they competed successfully against Chinese as
middlemen in the smallholder rubber trade. On Java, they dominated
domestic trade at the lower levels and also pioneered in many lines of
domestic industry, notably the manufacture of *batik* cloth and *kretek* cigarettes.

But everywhere in the area these *santri* merchants operated at the
outer end of commercial channels that led inward to larger and stronger
Chinese businesses in the trading centers. Forest products and smallholder rubber were assembled and shipped in bulk by Chinese (if not
European) firms, *batik*-makers and *kretek* manufacturers bought their
raw materials from Chinese wholesalers, *santri* traders in the rural areas
of Java sold their onions and soybeans to Chinese wholesalers. Various
reasons have been offered for the phenomenon. *Santri* merchants, accustomed to a less consuming struggle for existence, were not so highly
motivated. They lacked the experience of the Chinese in credit, international marketing, and other aspects of large-scale trade. Above all, their
commercial ethic was highly individualist, whereas Chinese commerce
operated through a whole range of kinship connections, secret societies,
and speech-group associations. The young Minangkabau man off with
a bit of trading capital to make some money, the Palembang peddler
walking through the hills of West Java, the Bugis trader on his *perahu*
always came in the end to deal with the wider and stronger networks
that grew from Chinese shops in the towns and great ports.

Finally, the aristocrats and kings of Southeast Asia had always
interested themselves to some extent in the export trade, though for all
but archipelago sultans and chiefs it was generally only a sideline to
their basic business of extracting rice and labor from their peasant subjects. Even the Siamese kings and nobles who had extensive interests in
the export trade from the seventeenth to the mid-nineteenth century seldom took a direct part in the trade itself. In effect, they rented out political rights to peasant production—and later provided some capital—to
Chinese and Muslim merchants, who collected the goods and did the
actual trading. For rulers and province chiefs to squeeze as much as
they could from traders in their jurisdictions was very much in accord
with elite values in those sharply stratified societies. But for the Vietnamese mandarin, the Javanese *priyayi,* and most of their counterparts,
trade itself was an occupation for lesser men. Conquest by the Europeans brought an end to their accustomed exploitation of merchants,
and the unequal treaties did the same to the more active and creative
participation of the Siamese elite. It did not, given their attitudes,
incline them to take up new, more direct roles in the growing export
industries. It was not until several generations later, with independence,
that their descendants and heirs were once again in a position to levy
tribute on export trade and incoming capital flows.

There were thus definite limits to the willingness or ability of Southeast Asians of all classes and regions to respond to the opportunities opened by the growing market for tropical export commodities. Their limited economic mobility in the face of a world economic revolution was of fundamental importance, for it opened room for immigrant entrepreneurs—Chinese, Indians, and Europeans—to play roles of unprecedented importance in the societies of Southeast Asia.

The Chinese who were drawn to Southeast Asia came almost exclusively from the coastal areas of the provinces of Kwangtung and Fukien. Though all were Chinese, they belonged to many speech-groups—especially Cantonese, Hokkien, Hakka, Teochieu, and Hainanese—whose spoken languages were unintelligible to each other, whose customs and economic specializations were often different, and who were frequently hostile to each other. But they shared certain important characteristics and attitudes. The Chinese had long had a complex economy marked by general use of money and credit, considerable manufacturing, and substantial regional and longer-distance trade. This was even more the case with the South China coast, with its thousand-year history as a region dominated economically by trade with Southeast Asia, which they called Nanyang. On the South China coast, a distinct seafaring and trading tradition had grown up over the centuries, the merchant's way of life was more highly honored, commercial skills were more highly developed, and wealth was more seriously pursued than elsewhere in China.

In earlier times, merchants from the region had traded along the shores of most of Southeast Asia, normally staying over in port towns for months waiting for the monsoon to change, but few had settled, even in the ports. In the seventeenth and eighteenth centuries, as the trade of Southeast Asia continued to grow, Chinese had begun to settle in larger numbers, especially at those places where economic opportunities were particularly good: in Siam around Bangkok and in the south, where they collaborated in royal trading enterprises and mined tin; on Java, where they organized the pepper business of Bantam in the seventeenth century and flourished under the regime of the VOC, growing sugar and farming taxes; in Manila, to which they were drawn by the silver of the galleons. In the course of the nineteenth century, their numbers steadily increased. After 1870, the influx became a flood, rising each decade to 1930—tens of millions moving back and forth, and several million ending up permanently in Southeast Asia. The migration was greatly facilitated by the rapid growth of steamship services. It was pushed from behind by the massive population growth of China in the eighteenth century, followed by the widespread disruption of the Taiping Rebellion in the mid-nineteenth century and the chaos that followed it. But above all, the Chinese were pulled by conditions in Southeast Asia, an open frontier of opportunity.

In a few places, Chinese settled down as peasants—near Bangkok and Batavia, on the lower Rejang River in Sarawak, at the northeastern

corner of northern Vietnam. Some came as merchants from the beginning, simply moving outward along their commercial channels from
China coast cities. But the great majority came, packed in the steerage
of the coolie ships, as simple laborers, owing passage money to those for
whom they first worked. They came to work on the European plantations of Sumatra's East Coast Residency, to build the 2,000 miles of
Siam's railways, to work the tin deposits of southern Siam, Malaya,
Bangka, and Billiton and the silver and lead deposits of Burma, and to
work in a variety of new jobs in the port cities and towns of Southeast
Asia, as labor for the docks, hand sawmills, rice mills, and building
trades. Those few who settled and remained as peasants were finding
only a frontier of empty land and showing only a geographical mobility.
But the rest were economically as well as geographically mobile, moving into newly opening slots that Southeast Asians were not filling. The
mobility of many led them little further; almost all intended to stay only
a few years, save up some cash, and return home; and the majority did
just that. The remainder, however, sooner or later took a further step,
becoming shopkeepers in the towns and villages and middlemen in the
growing export trades and at the same time settling down and marrying
in what became their new homes.

Like the Chinese, the Indians came from an overcrowded land with a
long history of manufacturing, of extensive and sophisticated commerce, and of a monetized economy. Their late-nineteenth-century
migration, however, did not unfold as naturally from a long history as
that of the Chinese. Merchants from many parts of India had been trading with Southeast Asia, mostly selling Indian-made textiles, for much
longer than the Chinese, and Indian textile shops have remained a
characteristic feature of many of the larger Southeast Asian cities. But it
was quite new groups of Indians who formed the bulk of the immigrants
in the high colonial age, and they went almost entirely to British Burma
and Malaya, following the lines of a new imperial connection rather
than those of their older maritime expansion. Indian migrants, too,
were more rigid in their economic specialization than Chinese. The
most important groups were the Chettyars—a South Indian moneylending caste which played a decisive role in the Burmese rice export
industry—and Telugus and Tamils, who went to Burma and Malaya as
laborers and, unlike their Chinese counterparts, seldom became shopkeepers. Finally, substantial numbers of Indians went to Burma and
Malaya as laborers, clerks, and civil servants already familiar with British ways and with the English language—a white-collar movement
entirely without a Chinese equivalent.

A final major group of immigrants to respond to the new economic
possibilities in Southeast Asia were the Westerners. The background of
their migration, which was worldwide in the period, is a familiar story.
It is enough to remark that they had considerably greater freedom of
action in their economic enterprises than their Chinese and Indian

counterparts, since they came without liens on their labor, had more capital and scientific knowledge at their disposal, and enjoyed excellent connections with the colonial regimes after they arrived.

The export industries that grew up in the different parts of Southeast Asia, particularly in the sixty years after 1870, took a great variety of forms. They were based on many kinds of soil, land rights, and crops; used widely varying amounts of capital and machinery; and were conducted by members of many different ethnic groups—combining all the elements in a host of different ways. Still, just as the hundreds of different commodities exported in the period consisted principally of agricultural raw materials and minerals, so the great variety of ways in which those commodities were produced and marketed can be reduced to a number of basic patterns. The four most important were the Chinese small capitalist, the Western capitalist, the peasant and middleman patterns, and a variant of the Western capitalist pattern in which labor was local rather than immigrant.

## Chinese Small Capitalists

The economic preferences of Southeast Asian peasants—their willingness to respond to new incentives inside the village but not to accept regular wage labor outside it—made it natural that Chinese immigrants should take up complementary economic roles. Thus, Chinese merchants served as middlemen for peasant-produced export crops, while Chinese labor was generally concentrated in the service industries, on the docks, and in the processing mills and railway construction crews, which for a long time held no appeal for Southeast Asians. The only exceptions to the rule were found in areas where the original population was very sparse. In a number of such places, there developed small Chinese frontier societies organized on *hui,* or lineage lines, and based economically on their own all-Chinese export industries. Many of the early industries—Chinese pepper plantations in Kampot and Singapore Island, gold mines in western Borneo, and sugar plantations in southeastern Siam—declined in the course of time. But Chinese tin mining in the belt of deposits running from Phuket in southern Thailand to Negri Sembilan in the southern part of the peninsula continued vigorously through the years of the export boom and beyond.

After 1870, Chinese tin mining in Siam and Malaya continued in an established pattern—many small units of production organized in partnerships or small companies and labor-intensive methods made possible by large supplies of cheap immigrant labor. Chinese miners made some changes—in Malaya, most of them went over to the much more effective European steam pump at the end of the century—but only changes that were compatible with the established many-unit, labor-intensive pattern. Their unwillingness or inability to accommodate larger change became significant when heavily capitalized European firms entered the tin business in the late nineteenth and early twentieth centuries. They built large modern tin-smelters in Penang and Singapore, driving small-scale Chinese smelters in southern Siam out of business by 1920 and forcing all tin to be shipped south thereafter. More important, the Chinese miners did not take up the tin-dredge when it was introduced by English and Australian companies after 1900. In the beginning, at least, they could not have raised the capital for the enormous and expensive machines, but it is also likely that they were not yet ready to switch to an unfamiliar industrial pattern: a few large firms using a great deal of capital and very little labor. Between the mid-1920s and mid-1930s, in both Siam and Malaya, the output from European dredges jumped from about one-third to about two-thirds of total tin production. Chinese output in those years was still well above nineteenth-century levels, but the industry had divided into two sharply different sectors, one Chinese and small capitalist, the other European and big capitalist.

## Western Capitalists

The Western capitalist mode of production, characterized by large units under a single management, wage labor, investment of money capital, and scientific methods, was in all respects quite different from prevailing methods of production in Southeast Asia. For that reason, in most parts of the area where it became established in the decades after 1870, it was not a natural outgrowth from local economic activity but imported from outside and run entirely by Westerners.

By the early twentieth century, practically all of the substantial mineral exports of Southeast Asia were being produced by Western firms using fully capitalist methods. Chinese tin from Malaya and Siam was the outstanding exception. Against it must be set Western capitalist production of tin in those countries and also in the islands of Bangka and Billiton off Sumatra; oil in Burma, Sumatra, and Borneo; coal from the Hong Gai mines in northern Vietnam; gold from Luzon; and various minerals from the Mawchi and Bawdwin mines in Burma. Though many of the deposits had been worked on a smaller scale before by Southeast Asians or Chinese, the modern, large-scale production of the minerals was dominated by European enterprises. Large-scale production of almost all minerals requires heavy equipment and advanced technology, which in turn require capital-intensive methods. It is more interesting, therefore, that the same methods were also used extensively for agricultural export production, to which no such economic imperatives apply and which was in fact carried on vigorously by millions of peasants in the same period.

To understand the place that capitalist agriculture—chiefly plantations—acquired in Southeast Asia, one must examine where it developed. Leaving aside sugar, which was always a special case, plantations were not established in the more heavily settled parts of Southeast Asia. There, the land was already occupied by peasants practicing subsistence agriculture and in many cases developing their own export production. Western entrepreneurs accommodated themselves to this reality as readily as did the Chinese. They therefore located virtually all of their plantations in areas of sparse population—particularly on west-coast Malaya, east-coast Sumatra, the interior of West and East Java, in Mindanao, and in the hilly interior of Vietnam and Cambodia.

The history of what became the East Coast Residency of Sumatra, a rectangle about 150 miles long and 50 miles deep centered on the modern city of Medan, is a classic example of the growth of a plantation system. In 1863, when an errant Dutch tobacco planter, Jacobus Nienhuys, arrived there, it resembled its coastal neighbors on both sides of the Straits of Malacca: an area of small riverine sultanates and chiefdoms set over a sparse, Malay-speaking population cultivating dry rice as a staple and exporting small quantities of pepper and other forest products. But the soil was unusually good, and the local sultans were well content, in exchange for large annual payments, to sign over great stretches of land to Nienhuys and to the planters who followed him. The plantations, prospering from the sale of what turned out to be unusually fine cigar tobacco, spread out around the new town of Medan. In the 1890s and after, new crops were added—coffee, tea, palm oil, and, above all, rubber—and the half-empty land gradually filled up with new belts of plantations. Medan became a city, and through its port, Belawan Deli, passed a quarter or more of all Netherlands Indies exports in the decades before World War II.

In the plantation system of the East Coast Residency, everything but the soil and the complaisant sultans was imported: the planters (Dutch, English, American, and Belgian), their capital ($250 million invested by 1929), their scientific techniques, and, most important perhaps, their labor along with most of its food. The original inhabitants numbered only some tens of thousands and in any case were making a perfectly adequate living; they were not interested in wage labor. The planters therefore imported their labor, first Chinese and, after about 1890, as the Chinese began to move into shopkeeping and other urban occupations, Javanese. By 1930, the population had risen to 1.8 million, of whom 645,000 were Javanese (225,000 then working on the plantations) and 195,000 were Chinese (11,000 on plantations). The various laborers lived on plantations averaging 8,000 acres in size—almost complete societies in themselves, with their own housing, staff doctors, processing plants, and, in effect, their own law and government. The East Coast Residency, made up of hundreds of enclaves, was itself an enclave, though one that exerted an increasingly strong influence on the neighboring parts of Sumatra and Malaya.

Nowhere else in Southeast Asia did plantations produce quite so great a change as in the East Coast Residency, where a whole new society, half the size of Cambodia in population, was created in sixty years. But everywhere they brought similar changes because, settling in areas of sparse population, they served as frontier institutions, creating new and much larger economic bases and importing or attracting whole new populations. In some cases, moreover—most notably in the East Coast Residency and on the western coast of Malaya, where the imported labor was alien to the area—plantation regimes contributed significantly to the development of plural societies and, in this way, to long-lasting social tensions.

Plantations began to play a decisive role in Malaya later than they did across the Straits in the East Coast Residency, and they built on an economic foundation already laid by Chinese tin mining. It was Malayan plantations that first responded to the suddenly rising world demand for rubber after 1900. In the boom years of the first three decades of the twentieth century, rubber came to dominate Malaya's agriculture and indeed its whole economy. Between 1905 and 1929, rubber acreage in Malaya increased from 50,000 to 3 million (about three times the acreage of rice, the next largest crop); rubber exports rose from 6,000 tons in 1910, as trees came into production, to 446,000 tons in 1929. Around 1914, rubber passed tin as Malaya's largest export, producing 27 percent of Malaya's export income in 1916 and 60 percent by 1929. Though smallholdings produced an increasing proportion of the totals after about 1915, it was the plantations that contributed a whole new element to the Malayan population in those years. As in the East Coast Residency, the Malays had no need or desire for wage labor; their response to the rubber boom, when they found the way, was smallholding. Chinese, though they provided some plantation labor and owned a handful of plantations, stayed mainly in their own businesses of tin and commerce; and when they, in turn, took up rubber, it was characteristically on medium-sized holdings. The English rubber planters therefore turned to the readily available supply of unskilled labor in southern India. Like the Chinese, the Indians intended to come for only a few years, sending cash home to their impoverished villages and returning later with some savings, and most followed that program. Also like the Chinese, however, some stayed on. During the first decade of the Indian Immigration Committee, established in 1907 by government and planters to organize and supervise the migration, 700,000 Indian laborers entered Malaya, and 480,000 departed. By such steady net additions, the third major element of the Malayan plural society was built up.

## Peasants and Middlemen

European-run plantations in Malaya, followed shortly by those in the Netherlands Indies, led the way in rubber-growing, as late as 1929 still producing about 50 percent of all world rubber. But smallholders in those two countries, beginning large-scale planting about a decade after the plantations, were catching up rapidly. In 1929, they were already exporting almost 40 percent of world rubber. A decade later, roughly, 1 million smallholders in Sumatra, Malaya, and Borneo had more than 4 million acres of mature trees capable of supplying most of world demand at prices that few plantations could meet. Only gross discrimination under colonial commodity control programs prevented them in the 1930s from dominating production of one of the world's most important export products.

These figures show the magnitude of the swing to smallholder rubber, but contemporary sources provide little information on the history of this peasant movement and its meaning to the societies it swept over. Word of the fabulous prices and of the success of both plantations and smallholders spread rapidly, and peasants soon saw rubber as an ideal crop for their purposes. In the boom years—1910–1920 in Malaya and the 1920s in Sumatra—they followed their conclusions with action. Rubber was ideal in many different ways. Ecologically, the rubber tree —a great success in its wild state in tropical Brazil—was very well adapted to the poor soils and fierce botanical competition of Southeast Asian forests. It required little effort to plant rubber seedlings on an already cleared and used swidden plot before moving on in the swidden cycle, or to plant an acre or two on permanently cultivated land. Once planted, the rubber trees grew just like any other secondary forest, requiring little tending. Tapping techniques were easily learned.

Rubber was also ideal in economic terms. While waiting for their seedlings to mature, and in bad times when rubber prices were low, peasants could live as before on their wet rice or swidden. In good times, a few acres of trees, tapped by the owner himself, provided cash for buying more rice than a one-family rice farm yielded with much harder work and also for taxes and imported goods. Peasant export production, of course, required middlemen to move the rubber to the market, and that part of the industry grew up as quickly and naturally as the peasant side: Chinese merchants (and some Sumatrans) moved readily to perform their complementary role. At assembly points in the rubber districts, dealers set up the inexpensive equipment necessary to prepare rubber for shipment, and from there the smoked rubber sheets moved down to the larger ports, such as Singapore, from which 300,000 or 400,000 tons of smallholder rubber were shipped each year.

Finally, rubber was ideal in social terms for subsistence peasants venturing into a cash economy. Though some peasants hired share-tappers to help them at peak periods, and others had large enough stands to require regular share-tapping, nearly all the million or so smallholders of the 1930s owned just a few acres of trees, which they operated themselves with the help of their relatives. Owning a few such plots near his village, and usually continuing to cultivate rice or other crops, the peasant could enjoy the advantages of a prime cash crop without risk and without leaving village society. It was an irresistible prospect and led quickly to a classic peasant-middleman export industry.

Rubber—plantation and smallholder—was the most spectacular export industry in early-twentieth-century Southeast Asia. Virtually none was exported in 1900, but by the 1930s it had become the most important export generally from Malaya and the Netherlands Indies and by far the most important peasant export from those countries. Its world significance was even greater: In the first four decades of the twentieth century, Malaya and the Netherlands Indies consistently supplied 75 percent or more, and all of Southeast Asia 90 percent or more, of all world rubber consumption.

Rice, the other major peasant export crop of Southeast Asia, had a much plainer record. In world terms, for example, Southeast Asia produced 70 percent or more of world exports, but they represented only a tiny fraction of world consumption. The long-term significance of rice in the economic history of Southeast Asia, however, was considerably greater than that of rubber. It was not rubber, but tin, sugar, and other products that had inaugurated the export economies of Malaya and the Netherlands Indies. Rice, however, was the first major export of Burma, Thailand, Cambodia, and Vietnam, and it remained their leading export earner through almost the whole colonial period. It was also, throughout the period, a wholly peasant-produced crop and therefore the most important of the peasant-middleman industries.

The large-scale rice export industries which grew up in British Burma, Cochinchina, and central Siam (Cambodian exports were much smaller) from around 1870 had much in common. They were made possible in the first place by the fact that the deltas of the Irrawaddy, Mekong, and Čhaophraya rivers, soggy alluvial plains very suitable for rice-growing, had never been heavily settled because the incentive to drain them had not previously existed. Unlike the Red River delta and Java, which produced large quantities of rice in the same period but also supported heavy populations and therefore could not yield an export surplus, those three deltas were able to produce large exports without any major change of growing technique. When worldwide demand increased, around 1870, peasants in or near the delta zones responded readily, moving out over the uncultivated stretches to practice a somewhat more extensive agriculture, which yielded a salable surplus. Middlemen—Chinese, Indian, and some indigenous—moved in to supply credit and imports and to assemble the rice in larger quantities for eventual milling and export.

Such was the common pattern of the industry. But the elements were mixed very differently, and the historical development and consequences diverged even more markedly, in the several countries. Since the Burma delta rice industry was the earliest, largest, and most complex, it will serve as the type case here. In 1855, just after the Second Anglo-Burmese War, in which the British seized the delta, there was an estimated total of 1 million acres under rice in the Burma delta. By 1873, a second million had been added, and thereafter the amount of land under rice increased by 1 million acres every seven years, reaching 10 million in 1930. In the same period (1855–1931), the population of the area increased from about 1.5 million to about 8 million, more than twice as fast as the population of central Burma (which suggests the social effects of the rice-export industry), but half as fast as rice acreage (which yielded an ever-increasing surplus for export).

The complex social history of the Burmese rice export industry from 1870 to 1940 may be divided into three phases: 1870–1900, the open frontier; 1900–1929, maturity and internal change; 1930–1940, depression and social collapse. The first phase was given its character by the vast amounts of good rice land readily available throughout the delta. It was dominated socially by the independent Burmese smallholder. World demand led European shippers and millers in the major ports to pay steadily rising cash prices for rice. That exciting prospect drew pioneers from the settled areas of the delta and down from central Burma to clear and plant fifty-acre holdings. The holdings were much larger than traditional peasant subsistence plots and therefore required sizable amounts of seasonal labor, which came mostly from central Burma. From the beginning, too, the whole rice industry was lubricated by an elaborate system of credit. Big mills in Rangoon and Bassein gave cash advances to the larger rice brokers, and they in turn gave advances to smaller brokers. Chettyars made mortgage loans to cultivators needing capital to pay for clearing and plow animals. Burmese and Chinese shopkeepers and Burmese moneylenders made short-term loans to cultivators to pay for migrant labor, marriage ceremonies, or *pwe* performances. At the heart of the credit system stood the Chettyar firms, a tightly knit fraternity of honest and efficient bankers who asked lower interest rates than those customary in Burma, because they confined themselves mainly to well-secured loans. It is not clear whether it was the extraordinarily rapid growth of the industry that required so vast a use of credit or the extraordinary services of the Chettyars that made possible the rapid growth. But there is no doubt that credit, especially Chettyar loans, was fundamental to the industry as it grew.

Some of the special features of the Burmese rice industry are already evident from the list of participants given above. Indigenous smallholders, immigrant Asian moneylenders, and European shippers are familiar from other Southeast Asian peasant-middleman industries. But in Lower Burma, the peasant cultivators from the beginning hired migrant labor not only for harvesting help, as in quite a few other cases, but for such jobs as clearing forest and plowing—labor long ahead of harvest and therefore usually requiring cash payment. There were also three quite distinct immigrant Asian groups occupying particular slots that elsewhere were usually all occupied by the Chinese. First were the Chettyars, who specialized in rural banking and played virtually no part in commerce. Second were the Indian (mostly Telugu) seasonal laborers, who in this phase largely confined themselves to wage labor jobs in the cities—in rice mills and on the docks—which Burmese would not take. Third were the Chinese shopkeepers, who played the more familiar role of advancing goods and cash against repayment in rice at harvest time, but on a much smaller scale than elsewhere.

The most atypical feature, however, was the vigorous thrust of Burmese into middleman functions elsewhere left almost entirely to Chinese. From the beginning, Burmese shopkeepers and moneylenders played a major role throughout the delta. Above all, Burmese did much of the brokerage by which a few dozen baskets of rice here, a hundred baskets there, were assembled into the hundreds of thousands of tons that flowed into the mills in the ports. Burmese certainly made up the great majority of the "jungle-brokers," who acquired the rice directly from the cultivators, but they apparently played a considerable part as well in larger-scale brokerage further down the veins of the system. It is not clear why. Perhaps the reluctance of Chettyars to deal in rice, coupled with the paucity of Chinese, left a gap in the chain, which Burmese came to fill. Perhaps Burmese peasant values allowed for more risk-taking and entrepreneurship than is considered "normal" for Southeast Asian peasants. Certainly, there was a land-rush atmosphere on the delta at the time, and Burmese engaged in all sorts of speculations.

In its second phase, from around 1900 to the onset of the Great Depression, the Burma delta rice industry reached full maturity, at the same time changing markedly in its internal organization. Rice acreage rose from 7 million in 1904 to 10 million in 1930; exports rose from about 2 million to 3 million tons; export income, compounded by rising prices, doubled between 1906 and 1926; annual totals of Indian labor migration into and out of Burma rose from 284,000 in 1900 to 777,000 in 1929.

The internal changes that accompanied the flowering were ominous, particularly for the characteristic figure of the previous phase, the peasant pioneer. Having committed himself in the days of the open frontier to a more thoroughly commercial mode of agriculture than most Southeast Asian peasant producers of export crops, the Burmese smallholder now faced directly the inevitable risks of this economic system. A fluctuation in the world price for rice, the death of a costly plow animal, or an impulsive extravagance could suddenly turn his precariously balanced load of credit into an unpayable debt. The same had often happened in the pioneer phase, too, but then there was plenty of land, and the peasant could simply move on deeper into the delta and start again. Now population was rising and the land was filling up; insolvent peasants slid swiftly down to tenancy or landlessness.

Tenancy had begun earlier—25 percent of the land in the thirteen main rice-producing districts of the Burma delta was already operated by cash tenants in the early twentieth century—but rents and conditions were still comparatively good. By 1928, however, the figure had risen to 42 percent; rents were much higher, tenants were more liable to eviction, and increasingly land was rented annually to the highest bidder. Some of the land that Burmese smallholders were losing passed into the hands of Chettyars and Chinese shopkeepers, but the bulk of it went to Burmese. The emerging Burmese landlord class had very heterogeneous origins, including moneylenders, former smallholders, government officials from the towns, and the owners of the hundreds of smaller Burmese-run local rice mills, which were established in the delta after 1900. Most landlords, alien or Burmese, were absentee, living in the towns or Rangoon.

In those years, moreover, the character of delta society was strongly affected by a growing influx of Indians. In the late nineteenth century, Indians had largely confined themselves to urban jobs. At that time, the typical landless laborer in the Burma delta was a seasonal migrant from central Burma who came downriver to earn some cash before returning home. After 1900, few Burmese came south. Their place was partly taken by southern Burmese peasants—former smallholders or tenants. But more and more of the field labor was now done by organized Indian work gangs, under *maistry* (crew bosses), which circulated through the rice districts, contracting for a job, doing it, and moving on to the next. Indians, too, provided a steadily increasing proportion of tenants in the rice districts, where their competition helped drive up the rents.

In the early decades of the twentieth century, these trends had not yet reached their limits. More than half the land was still owned by smallholder cultivators. Burmese landlords, especially those who lived on their properties, could have close relations with their tenants. But the social context of rice production was steadily loosening. The one-family holding of the traditional subsistence pattern was a sharply defined institution, the basic building block of a village community. The commercial smallholding of the late-nineteenth-century rice frontier—though penetrated by market forces, credit, and outside labor—was still a meaningful social unit. Now, however, the edges of even that unit were blurring; men were becoming mere factors of production, pushed about by economic forces across the expanses of an increasingly shapeless delta society.

This curious and unpleasant social machine continued to operate, producing huge exports and profits, until the Depression. Then, suddenly, it broke down, and since no one knew how to fix it properly it was allowed to carry on improperly, doing damage to almost all concerned, until the Japanese invasion wiped it out. It seems clear in retrospect that by about 1930 the system had come to the end of its rope. It had been made possible, to begin with, by the sparse population and abundance of uncultivated land in the delta. That frontier was now almost closed—rice land in the Burma delta stayed steady at just short of 10 million acres from 1931 to 1941, while population continued to rise. Pressure on the land, compounded by the peculiarly commercial character of the industry, had already been undermining established social patterns for decades. The Depression, which manifested itself in Burma by steeply falling rice prices and a sharp drop in rice export earnings, disintegrated the pyramid of credit on which the whole system was based. The Depression precipitated the crisis, but it fell on a house of cards.

The symptoms of social collapse were many. Labor gangs and annual renting of land to the highest bidder grew more common. The amount of land owned by landlords in the thirteen main rice-producing districts of Burma rose sharply from 43 percent in 1928 to 58 percent in 1935, and many of the remaining smallholders were by that time little more than debt-bondsmen on their own land. One very clear sign of crisis was the rapid increase in foreclosures by Chettyars. As late as 1930, they owned only 500,000 acres (6 percent) in the thirteen districts; by 1935, they had acquired 1.5 million acres more, holding 27 percent of the land there. Chettyars wanted land as little as mortgage bankers want houses; only catastrophic insolvency among their debtors could force them to accumulate land, and they spent the rest of the decade trying (at some profit) to extricate themselves from their Burma quagmire.

A more obvious symptom of social collapse was the cycle of anti-Indian and anti-Chinese riots in southern Burma between 1930 and 1932—the later stages of which were mixed up with the Hsaya San Rebellion—and the further anti-Indian riots of 1938. Partly as a result of this, and partly because of the general stagnation of the rice business, the volume of Indian migration into and out of Burma fell off sharply, from 777,000 in 1929 to an annual average of 483,000 in the years 1933–1938. After 1931, moreover, almost the same number left as entered Burma each year, so that the Indian minority in Burma, which had almost doubled to 1 million (7 percent) between 1901 and 1931, stayed level.

The third phase ended with serious efforts by home-rule Burmese governments to solve the delta problem, but war proved more efficient. The Japanese invasion drove several hundred thousand Indian refugees to India, and the Japanese occupation quite simply made rice exports impossible. It was left to the independent nationalist governments after the war to pick up the pieces and to try to construct a new economic order in Burma.

The other two major rice-exporting areas in Southeast Asia were the Chaophraya and Mekong deltas, each of which consistently produced about one-half as much export rice as Burma. They followed the same general pattern as in Burma, but the differences—especially in Siam— are well worth noting.

In the mid-nineteenth century, the Mekong delta was even more sparsely populated than the Irrawaddy delta. In the course of their thousand-year drive to the south *(Nam Tien)*, the Vietnamese had first reached the open delta in the seventeenth century, but two and a half centuries later their settlements were still comparatively small and were mainly confined to the eastern region around Saigon. It was that area that the French first conquered in 1858–1867, and one of the first things they did was redirect its small rice surplus from Hue to overseas markets. In the next two or three decades, there developed a peasant rice frontier moving southwest from the settled area deeper into the delta, a movement rather similar to that of southern Burma but considerably smaller and slower. Beginning in the late nineteenth century, however, vast canal and drainage projects undertaken by the colonial government brought a much more rapid expansion of the industry, and by the mid-1930s the population of Cochinchina had increased three times (to 4.5 million), rice acreage four times (to 5.5 million acres), and rice exports about five times (to 1.2 million tons).

The social and ethnic structure of the Cochinchinese rice industry was considerably simpler than in Burma, mainly because the Chinese dominated marketing and processing to the virtual exclusion of other aliens and of Vietnamese. French citizens who owned a handful of mills in Saigon did much of the shipping, but otherwise the rice business was almost entirely in Chinese hands—from the big millers and exporters in Saigon, through the large rice dealers in Saigon and their agents in the rural market towns, down to the thousands of Chinese shopkeepers and small-boat traders who sold goods on credit to the Vietnamese producers and acquired their crops in return. Like their compatriots in Siam, the Chinese in Cochinchina acquired rice-growing peasant debtors but not rice land—quite unlike the Chinese, and especially the Chettyars, in southern Burma.

The pattern of moneylending and peasant landlessness was rather like that of Burma by the 1930s, but its process of development was quite different. In the eastern delta around Saigon, the longer-established peasant society drifted under the influence of commercial export production into a pattern of medium-sized landlord holdings, built up mostly by local moneylending, of a sort more or less familiar in Vietnam. Farther west, especially in the area beyond the Bassac, the westernmost branch of the Mekong in the delta, much larger properties predominated from the beginning, as the colonial government sold off great blocks of land after completing its drainage projects there. Those estates, cheaply acquired by Saigon Vietnamese closely associated with the French regime and by French individuals, were called "plantations" but were operated like Philippine *haciendas,* with the land parcelled out among tenants. Rice was grown in small peasant units, with heavy use of seasonal labor by landless peasants living nearby or coming from the eastern delta or northern Vietnam. Since the rice itself passed through Chinese channels, the profits to the absentee landlords came from rent and moneylending to tenants. As in southern Burma, the peasants had moved out onto an almost empty frontier to clear and plant the land, but in the Mekong delta they began in a state of tenancy and landlessness that in the Irrawaddy delta took half a century to evolve. In the long run, however, Vietnamese peasants were no more willing to accept such conditions than were the Burmese. The political significance of their growing resentment was to become fully apparent after 1945.

The Thai rice industry, by contrast, had a straightforward, steady, and serene history up to 1940. One reason is that Siam was opened to world commerce not by conquest, like Burma and Cochinchina, but by the relatively conservative formula of the 1855 treaty, which entrenched the authority of the pragmatic and cautious modernizers of the Mong-kut-Bunnag school, supported by like-minded English advisers to the court. The regime moved steadily but slowly to abolish corvée and slavery (both of which inhibited the free movement of the Siamese peasant and therefore the pace of the rice industry's growth) and refused, for fiscal reasons, to invest more than small sums in irrigation and drainage (which again slowed the pace and tended to keep rice land in peasant hands). More generally, much less outside capital—from government investment and alien moneylenders—seems to have gone into the agricultural side of Thai rice than in southern Burma and Cochinchina. For these and other reasons, the rice industry in the Čhaophraya delta, from which virtually all exports came until the 1920s, grew more slowly than in southern Burma and was always far less commercial than in both southern Burma and Cochinchina. As Siamese peasants moved into the open lands of the delta, they cleared smaller cultivating units, used less seasonal labor, and above all financed the expansion very largely by themselves. The rice frontier was a great movement, as in the Burma delta and Cochinchina, but it was much more a peasant movement. The Siamese peasant remained throughout the period an independent subsistence farmer who also grew large amounts of rice as a cash crop with which to pay money taxes and to buy such imported goods as textiles, kerosene lamps, and kerosene.

Since there were few landlords—and those few mainly Thai—and since European-owned mills in Bangkok quickly gave way to Chinese competition after the 1890s, the only real partners of the peasants in the rice industry were the Chinese. In Bangkok, large Chinese mills, using Chinese labor, dominated the rice business. In the rural areas Chinese middlemen circulated in their small boats, dealing with a familiar clientele, bringing news, selling imported goods, advancing supplies, loaning money, and taking out the surplus rice at harvest time. By the 1930s, the Siamese elite in Bangkok was much exercised about Chinese commercial dominance, but the peasants found the Chinese middleman indispensable and easy to deal with. So did the Cambodian peasants in their much smaller rice industry, so closely resembling the Thai one.

Rubber and rice were the most important peasant-middleman export crops in Southeast Asia in the period and played decisive roles in the social and political as well as the economic history of large parts of the area. But peasants and foreign middlemen brought a wide variety of other crops to the world market, including rubber from Burma and Siam, abaca and copra from the Philippines, and copra from the eastern islands of the Netherlands Indies. Nor, of course, did peasant producers or middlemen confine themselves to export products and markets. There had always been a certain amount of local and regional trade, particularly in essential foodstuffs like fish and salt, and with rapidly increasing populations, improving transportation, increasing economic specialization of certain areas, and above all the growth of cities and towns throughout the area, the volume of internal trade increased enormously. In the early twentieth century, various parts of central Burma sent almost 100,000 draft animals a year to the rice areas of southern Burma; the Chinese fishing villages at Bagan Si-Api-Api in East Sumatra shipped 80,000 tons of fish a year to markets in Malaya and Sumatra; the Hindu-Buddhist Balinese sent shiploads of pigs stacked noisily in wicker baskets to feed the Chinese and Europeans in most of Islamic Indonesia and Malaya. Except for some Chinese market gardening near the larger cities and the unique Bagan Si-Api-Api fisheries, the agricultural and sea products, baskets, hats, and the like were all produced by peasant smallholders, often as a cash sideline to their subsistence farming. And except for short-distance trading of foodstuffs to markets, which peasant growers often conducted for themselves, and some of the wider activities of *santri* traders in the archipelago, the commercial side of the internal trade was largely incorporated into the Chinese middleman networks. Even rice—as urban demand grew, smaller local mills spread through the countryside and peasants developed a taste for the white milled product—ceased in many areas to be something peasants grew, stored, milled and ate themselves. It became a major item in trade, serving as one of the main levers of Chinese commercial dominance in non-rice-exporting areas such as northern and central Vietnam, Java, and the Philippines.

## Western Capitalists with Local Labor

The final group of export industries comprised those Western capitalist enterprises that for one reason or another used locally resident labor rather than immigrants housed on the premises. The distinction between them and the other capitalist industries already discussed is not always clear-cut and may even be insignificant from the point of view of economic organization, but it tells a great deal about the social history of Southeast Asia. One example was the teak industry of Burma and northern Siam—the second or third largest export earner in those countries for much of the period. On the management side, it was fully a capitalist industry, dominated by a handful of European-run firms that mobilized the large amounts of capital required by the cost of elephants and by the long waiting period between the first girdling of a teak tree and its sale as board-feet in India or Europe six or more years later. Teak labor—a gaudy mixture of Burmese, Shan and Lao, Karens and hill tribesmen—was vastly different from the company-housed, -doctored, and -schooled Tamils of a Malayan rubber plantation. The teak companies acquired labor by bringing employment to their employees rather than vice versa, just as they cut wild teak rather than grew it. For those reasons, their vast operations had very little effect (except ecologically) on the areas they moved through, while plantations were nodes of settlement and permanent economic activity in their sparsely settled areas, around which new societies grew.

   The latter point is illustrated by the second set of cases, the considerable number of plantations in the hilly and previously sparsely settled interior of East and West Java, which in the early twentieth century began to rely more and more on local peasants for labor, after having done much to build up the local population and economy themselves in the nineteenth century. In this respect, the Java plantations were only anticipating what was to become a general change in the character of plantation labor in later decades. Plantations in Malaya and the East Coast Residency of Sumatra, for example, began to hire local labor on a considerable scale in the 1850s, as population built up and local peasants began to change their economic attitudes and to accept wage labor. The plantation in Southeast Asia was a frontier institution of the high colonial period, a transplant from the industrial West, run by Westerners, set down in the emptier parts of Southeast Asia where at first no other methods were possible. As such, it was necessarily transitory. In time, Chinese and Southeast Asians, individuals, companies, and governments, were to begin taking over the management of those enterprises, and labor came more and more from local sources. The plantation began to be absorbed into its local economic environment—which it had often largely created—and lost its special historical character. In place of the sharp discontinuities of the pioneer phase (plantations utterly different from peasant subsistence at the other extreme) came a more evenly graduated spectrum (more and less capital-intensive, large- and smaller-scale) on a more homogeneous economic landscape.

   The sugar industries of Java and the Philippines were much the largest and most important of the capitalist enterprises using peasant rather than imported labor. Between 1870 and 1930, the Java sugar industry grew enormously, shipping 100,000 tons in 1865, 750,000 in 1900, 3 million in 1930, and becoming far and away the leading earner and premier export industry of the Netherlands Indies in that period. A small but substantial sugar industry developed on the Philippine island of Negros in the second half of the nineteenth century (90,000 tons by 1893), but it stagnated after that. The real growth of the Philippine sugar industry came when the Philippines was granted a sizable quota in the protected high-price U.S. market. Sugar quickly became and remained the Philippines' leading export industry, recovering its vigor on Negros and developing a second main focus on the central plain of Luzon.

Throughout its long history, sugar has almost always been a capitalist industry, if only because of the heavy costs of mill equipment (a modern Philippine centrifugal central cost about $1 million in 1920). Sugar all over the world in the past few centuries has almost always been grown on plantations with imported (often slave) labor. It was, therefore, particularly significant that in Java and the Philippines the sugar labor consisted of local settled peasants or at most seasonal migrants. In the Javanese case, the reason was that the sugar mills were built in already populated areas, where irrigated rice land highly suitable for sugar was already available. Javanese peasants in the early nineteenth century were no more interested in wage labor than other Southeast Asian peasants, but the older tradition of corvée could be modified to produce a suitable labor force.

The use of peasant labor in Philippine sugar had a somewhat different background. On Luzon, sugar became a major crop in a landscape already largely occupied by peasant cultivators. The sugar centrals, therefore, rarely had their own fields and full-time wage labor force, and they did not need them. Instead, they worked through the *hacienda* with its many tenants, contracting for certain amounts of cane and dividing the proceeds with the *hacendero* for further division down the line to his tenants, who actually grew the cane. The industry flourished under that arrangement, but it created a characteristic tension between *hacenderos* and *centralistas* over the division of the profits, a dispute that, given the great economic power of those concerned, expressed itself regularly in Philippine party politics. More important, sugar-growing under that formula exacerbated relations between *hacenderos* and tenants, contributing to the political and revolutionary movements there in the 1930s and thereafter.

Sugar began to be grown on Negros in important quantities after 1855, when the port of Iloilo, across the strait on the island of Panay, was opened to world trade. At that time, Negros was very lightly populated, but the land was highly suitable for sugar cane. With the encouragement of British export-import firms, Chinese *mestizos* from Iloilo crossed to Negros and set up small but up-to-date mills. Elsewhere that might have led quickly to plantations, but since the *mestizos* lacked the capital, and since they were more at home with the *hacienda* as a type of landowner-labor relation, the Negros sugar industry developed with millers normally owning *haciendas* and tenants growing most of the cane. With some difficulty, therefore—eased by heavy use of seasonal labor from the nearby islands—the millers of Negros managed to create on the open frontier of their island a land and labor pattern like that of the older and more densely populated areas of Luzon. Negros, however, saw much less tension between *centralistas* and *hacenderos* and between *hacenderos* and tenants, and its social and political history at least for the first half of the twentieth century was considerably calmer than that of central Luzon.

The importance of the export industries that grew so rapidly between 1870 and 1940 went far beyond the statistics by which their progress is often measured. They stood near the center of the economic and social history of the high colonial age, powerfully influencing—and also influenced by—developments in other spheres. The export industries both gained from and served to reinforce the new "national" frameworks that were developing in the same period. Their growth created in the economic life of Southeast Asia a dependence on world markets whose real long-term significance was only suggested by the painful episode of the Depression. They provided the economic base and much of the impetus for the growth of the modern urban areas and also did much to create a demand for modern-educated Southeast Asians—developments that themselves were prime determinants of twentieth-century Southeast Asian history. They also attracted large numbers of alien immigrants, thus contributing directly to the growth of the plural societies that were so typical of the area in the period and that brought such severe conflicts in the 1930s and afterward.

The export boom, nevertheless, was not the only driving force behind economic change in the period, and there were major economic movements that cannot be fully dealt with in terms of the rise of the export industries alone. This was particularly true of the changes that took place in the economic life of the great mass of the peasant population.

In 1940, after seventy years of rapid change that had created export-dominated economies throughout Southeast Asia, it was doubtful whether as many as half of the peasants played any direct part in export production. A considerably smaller proportion were anything more than part-time export growers. Even fewer had replaced the fundamental goal of subsistence with the goal of personal advancement, which so fiercely drove the Europeans, the Chinese, and some Indians. Nevertheless, the economic life of almost all Southeast Asian peasants had been profoundly altered in the previous three-quarters of a century. Economic change among the peasant millions was gradual, often almost invisible, but cumulatively massive. Within this tidal movement, peasant export production was simply one of many types of response to a variety of new forces impinging on village economic life.

There were three major determinants of economic change among peasants in the period. One was increasing exposure to the world economy—to world market demand for export products but also to imported consumer goods. As such goods became available, flowing inward from the great ports through improving transport and market networks, peasant families looked them over with the same shrewd eye they used for new opportunities for earning income, rejecting shoes as they did wage labor, accepting undershorts as they did export rubber or rice. Southeast Asian peasants had long accepted sizable quantities of Indian textiles and Chinese ceramics, and they responded as readily, and often remarkably quickly, to new imports. By the turn of the century, imported soap, for example, had already replaced homemade varieties in rural Siam; Milkmaid Brand condensed milk was so widely used in Burma that its tins became a standard of measurement in country rice transactions; kerosene, first introduced in the 1860s, was already selling in the millions of gallons a decade later, and by the end of the century the kerosene lamp was well on the way to ousting coconut oil and wick all over rural Southeast Asia. Machine-made textiles, matches, and, in the twentieth century, sewing machines and bicycles all gained wide and easy acceptance.

A second major determinant of peasant economic change was colonial government policy. British land policy in Burma made it possible for landlords and moneylenders to gain control of most southern Burma rice land by 1940, while the Malay Reservations Enactment of 1913 and the Netherlands Indies Land Law of 1870 helped preserve peasant smallholdings throughout the period—a situation not necessarily more advantageous for the peasant, but certainly very different. The more efficient collection of land, harvest, and head taxes throughout the area, particularly because they were increasingly levied in cash, required peasants to seek cash incomes in various ways. Irrigation and drainage works, disease-prevention measures, government grants of land to Europeans, salt and other monopolies, increased use or gradual abandonment of corvée levies—all had strong effects on peasant economic life.

A third major determinant was the rather sudden and very large increase in the population of Southeast Asia from about 55 million in 1870 to about 145 million in 1940. While immigration, particularly of Chinese, played an appreciable part in the increase, most of it came from slowly falling death rates and stable or slightly rising birth rates among the great mass of peasants. In 1940, as throughout history, most of the area was still lightly populated by the standards of its neighbors, India and China, but there were ample signs of the coming demographic crisis. Java, to take the extreme case, had a population of 17.5 million and a good portion of empty land in 1870; by 1940, it had 48 million, and, for practical purposes, all cultivable land was occupied. Even in less crowded areas—such as Siam, whose population rose from 6 to 15 million in the period—the rapid increase itself had powerful effects on the economic life of the peasantry.

In speaking of the effects of these strong new forces, there is a tendency to depict the peasants as objects rather than subjects, as passive beneficiaries of health measures or agricultural extension work, or as helpless victims relentlessly milked by the Indochinese salt and alcohol monopolies, losing their land in southern Burma, squeezed onto smaller and smaller plots on Java or Luzon. All that is true enough; in many ways, peasants were swept along by economic forces that they could hardly hope to deflect and never fully understood. But if the historian sees the people of a society as simply the objects of policies, the locus of problems, and the occasion for revealing his own ideas of right and wrong, he denies those people the right to enact their own history. Much of the effect of the economic changes of the period on Southeast Asian peasants can be understood only in terms of their active response to new dangers and opportunities. To simplify again, there were at least three broad types of peasant response.

One form of peasant response was adoption of the habits and assumptions of a cash economy, not necessarily the same as those of townspeople and aliens, but adapted to their own economic context. In general, Southeast Asian peasants seem to have thought of money not as an absolute standard of value but as an additional medium—just like land, rice, and socially prescribed labor obligations, for example—for use in economic transactions. As such, money had the virtue of flexibility—it was easily handled, free of social meanings that might restrict its use, and valued outside as well as inside the village. Peasants readily added it to their economic repertoire for use in an increasing number of cases where such flexibility was needed, but they did not rely on it exclusively.

They also responded in various ways to the extra-village money economy, which required them to pay taxes in cash and offered them attractive imports, which had to be bought with cash or its equivalent. Smallholder export production was one of the ways, but in many areas peasants also took up domestic cash crops and home industries in the same spirit: sesame oil and other food crops in central Burma for sale in southern Burma, sleeping mats and rattan chairs in northern Vietnam, all sorts of vegetables in Java, tobacco in northern Luzon after the end of the government monopoly. In time, too, peasants became more willing to take up wage labor outside the village.

A second major type of peasant response to the various new economic forces impinging on peasant life was migration, much of it, but not all, in the search for cash pay. Socially, the easiest form was seasonal migration, usually in the harvest season, a pattern found in the Burmese and Cochinchinese rice industries and Negros sugar but not confined to them. It was more significant when, around the turn of the century, large numbers of contract laborers from certain areas began to go to plantations: Javanese to the East Coast Residency of Sumatra and as far away as Surinam; northern Vietnamese to rubber plantations in Cochinchina and to New Caledonia and elsewhere in the Pacific; Filipinos to Hawaii, Guam, and the continental United States. The migration was partly coerced and thoroughly controlled by one-sided devices like penal sanctions to enforce labor contracts. But it was essentially voluntary, a peasant solution, in areas that had particularly dense populations, to the problem of increasing pressure on the land. In the twentieth century, another form of labor migration was to the rapidly growing urban areas all over Southeast Asia. In the early twentieth century, immigrant peasants in the towns conformed to the plural patterns of the time—they were primarily servants, trishaw drivers, office messengers, and street vendors, leaving other occupations, such as dock and factory work, to Chinese and Indians. It was only subsequently that Southeast Asians—new arrivals or by now permanent city dwellers—began to move into industrial jobs, either competing with the aliens, as in Rangoon in the 1930s, or replacing the latter as they moved up socially.

These peasants, particularly in the decade or two before 1940, gradually lost their earlier reluctance to leave their villages to seek wage labor. Meanwhile, other peasants were engaged in a quite different, and socially more conservative, form of migration, spreading out more evenly on the land and filling up unoccupied areas with peasant villages. The peasant rice frontiers of the Irrawaddy, Čhaophraya, and Mekong deltas have already been mentioned, but there were other important cases as well. Some were extensions of much older historical movements. The Vietnamese who pushed into the western delta and northward across the Cambodian border were carrying forward the thousand-year-old drive to the south. The Javanese who moved into the interior of West Java, to the Lampung area at the southern tip of Sumatra, and to parts of Borneo, Celebes, and Malaya were following predecessors who had spilled outward from the relatively heavily populated Javanese core areas, for example, to the north coast of West Java in the sixteenth and seventeenth centuries. Other such migrations were newer: Ilocanos, in the nineteenth and twentieth centuries, spread widely over northern Luzon from their overcrowded coastal lands; Bisayans began to settle heavily on the northern coast and major river valleys of Mindanao in the same period; Madurese came to occupy much of the eastern coast of Java.

A third type of peasant response, agricultural intensification, was due primarily to population pressure and manifested itself mainly inside the village. Peasants adopted crops new to Southeast Asia, or to their areas, such as peanuts, cassava, and maize. They began to grow cash crops on ricefields in the dry season, or double-cropped rice, or made more use of flooded fields to grow fish; they cultivated more intensely, pregerminating rice in their houses before planting and then transplanting; they grew cassava on the dikes between the paddies, and they harrowed and weeded more thoroughly. In such ways, by raising production per acre while the population was rising, they managed to keep per capita productivity more or less constant—a greater number of people treading water in the same pool. Throughout the area—but most of all in the extreme Javanese case of agricultural involution—intensification affected not only agricultural practices but all aspects of village life. Increasingly elaborate patterns of tenancy and subtenancy, of land-renting and crop- and labor-sharing grew up in order to accommodate more and more people on limited amounts of land. Java was and is exceptional. But even the desperate expedients of its involution—undertaken so calmly by Javanese villagers—demonstrate the creativity of peasants in devising the patterns by which their own history was lived, while they were carried along by a flood they could not hope to control.

# PART FOUR

# Social Change and the Emergence of Nationalism

# 23

---

# Preludes

As the author of a distinguished study of peasant revolt in colonial West Java has remarked, the history of the peasantry, however obscured by the activities of the great and powerful, contains currents that flow straight into modern times. No phenomenon more frequently accompanied the intensification of Western rule than sporadic, localized, and usually short-lived episodes of peasant unrest. Because the voice of the peasant is too often submerged in the roar of high affairs, such episodes have seldom received the attention they deserve, either from contemporary colonial observers—who tended to regard them as, in the main, aberrations of the misled and the fanatical—or from historians. Peasant risings, in modern times as in the past, were seldom, if ever, "nationalist." The use of this term obscures many of the more important characteristics of peasant movements. If a sense of proportion is to be maintained, they are perhaps best seen as part of a long historical continuum in which peasant discontent has at all times and in all places manifested itself, where leadership was forthcoming, in outbreaks of opposition against authority. One historian has described those occasions as the "revolution of rising irritations."[28] In the nineteenth and early twentieth centuries the irritations sprang, for the most part, from the increasing irksomeness of Western colonial rule—administrative, economic, and other interference in peasant welfare and social values. Peasant rebellion tended to reflect revolt against changing times, rather than forward-looking desire for social reconstruction. Though directed in some sense at colonial authority, peasant movements seldom had far-reaching aims beyond the improvement of the peasants' own immediate situation—the removal of the irritant. Though they are, accordingly, different in character and intent from urban-based nationalism, they have an important place alongside the latter, which they often paralleled and sometimes fed, and into which they were eventually absorbed.

Though the countless manifestations of peasant discontent in Southeast Asia resulting directly or indirectly from Western intrusion were of many different kinds, it is possible to detect features that, if not always held in common, seem to be fairly characteristic. Most obviously, all were, by definition, agrarian—that is to say, they took place in rural areas among persons engaged in agricultural occupations of a traditional kind. They tended also to be highly localized, for, although on

occasion movements amassed some thousands of followers, organization and leadership seldom extended beyond the immediate region.
Generalized peasant discontent, which was as often a response to paternalistic interference and officious welfare policies as to calculated or
careless harshness, may be assumed to have been somewhat more widespread than actual revolt. Where the latter crystallized out of the former, it was usually in response to leadership beyond the ordinary. The
leaders of peasant revolts came less often from the rank and file of the
peasantry than from what is sometimes called the rural elite—the better-off landholders, minor government functionaries at the village level,
or religious leaders. In general, leadership was characterized by an
emphasis on the traditional rather than the modern and offered a return
to previously known (or imagined) patterns of stability. Many revolts
had strong religious overtones or were explicitly religious, and some
sought by puritanism and reform, or reformulation, to create the conditions for a millenarian return to or quest for the perfect state.

A few examples may serve to illustrate the variety as well as the simi-
larities of peasant movements. In the Blora District of Central Java
around 1890, the ideas and beliefs of an unlettered but tolerably well-off
villager called Surontiko Samin began to attract followers from his own
and neighboring villages. Though later stages of the Samin movement
were certainly associated with early-twentieth-century Dutch administrative efforts at village reorganization and alterations in the tax structure, its initial impetus remains obscure. From about 1905 onward, the
Saminists came increasingly to Dutch attention as a result of their
explicit withdrawal from the existing social and bureaucratic order by
refusing to contribute to village rice banks and other communal agricultural institutions, by rejection of Islamic marriage forms, and by their
insistence that taxes, if paid, were to be regarded as donations, not obligations. At the height of the first phase of Saminism in 1907, the movement was credited with only some 3,000 members, but the Dutch,
always on the lookout for "fanaticism" and rebellion, and despite the
careful nonviolence of the movement, feared a more general rising.
Samin and his immediate followers were banished to the Outer Islands.
Though it is possible that some peasants saw in Samin the expected *ratu
adil,* or just prince, of Javanese messianic expectations, there is little
real evidence that the movement was millenarian in character. Samin's
exile did not put an end to the movement, which continued sporadically
in the district until the 1920s and beyond, usually associated with what
were seen as the harassments of new taxes, new restrictions on forest
product collection under revised forestry laws, and the like.

Newly imposed land taxes were also the immediate cause of the "To'
Janggut" peasant rebellion in the Pasir Puteh District of Kelantan in
1915, a localized rising that nevertheless prompted nervous British
administrators to see signs of a more general revolt in the state, and possibly throughout the Malay Peninsula. There is no evidence that such a
revolt was imminent. The peasant rebellion appears to have taken its

origin from a combination of circumstances. At a time when the traditional territorial chief was chafing at the loss of authority that had
attended the introduction of the British-inspired administrative system,
a fixed land rent was substituted for an earlier tax on crop production
during the incumbency of a Malay assistant district officer from another
state. Haji Mat Hassan, known as To' Janggut, an elderly peasant
landowner and peddling trader with considerable personal charisma
who had the clandestine encouragement of the territorial chief, raised a
peasant following to attack and burn the district office as a protest
against the new tax and, it was rumored, to lead an army downriver
and toward the capital of Kota Bharu. In fact, fewer than two hundred
men were directly involved, and, though there is no doubt that other
peasants in the state disliked the new tax, evidence of anything like a
general rising is lacking. Alarmed by a recent troop mutiny in Singapore and by confused reports from Kelantan, the British sent a detachment of the Shropshire Light Infantry and a gunboat to the state, where
they rapidly succeeded in putting the peasant rebels to rout. Within the
month, To' Janggut and a number of others had been killed, and an end
had been put, if not to the discontent, at least to its open expression.

Hsaya San, leader of the 1930 peasant revolt in southern Burma,
unlike Samin and To' Janggut, was not a peasant but a former Buddhist
monk who in the late 1920s had conducted a survey of peasant grievances for a branch of the General Council of Burmese Associations.
Retreating, symbolically, from the town, Hsaya San collected around
himself in the Tharrawaddy District a peasant following, organizing a
rebellion on neotraditional lines. Hsaya San, as self-proclaimed heir to
the Buddhist Burmese kings—complete with the appurtenances of royalty and a forest "capital"—gave reality to the peasantry's desire not
merely to rid itself of the ills of the present (born in part of the Depression), but to recreate an ideal past. Attacks on police stations, forestry
headquarters, and the homes of village functionaries caught up in the
colonial administration began a revolt that took the British more than a
year and a half to stamp out.

At much the same time, on the headwaters of the Rejang River in
Sarawak, a Dayak leader, Asun, who had for some years been a *penghulu*
in the Brooke administration, was organizing another armed rising.
The immediate cause of the unrest was the falling price of forest
produce (on which the Iban economy in some important respects
depended), along with the increasing incidence of administrative control in the form of restrictions on shifting cultivation, introduction of
gun licenses, and the setting up of forest reserves, which trespassed on
traditional rights to wood and water. The revolt was scarcely a major
one from the point of view of the colonial administration—a few dozen
longhouses burned, a handful of people killed—but it kept the administration occupied until 1940, eight years after Asun himself had surrendered and been banished to another part of the state.

Movements of yet another kind, with large peasant followings but originally of urban, Western-influenced beginnings, were exemplified by the Guardia de Honor in the Philippines and Cao Dai in Vietnam. The Guardia de Honor, founded in the 1880s by the Dominicans on Luzon as a confraternity devoted to the Virgin Mary, and used by the friars as a paramilitary force to combat anti-Spanish revolutionaries in 1896, transformed itself in the last years of the century into a Filipino-inspired messianic sect. Centered in the *barrio* of Cabaruan, it attracted many thousands of peasants to settle there, bringing with them their rice, which they gave to communal granaries. The leader of the sect, Baltazar, and his principal aides, were worshipped as the Trinity, the Virgin Mary, and the Apostles and ruled the *barrio* as a theocracy. Though the movement had economic overtones—landlords were regarded as sinners, and the virtues of communal economic organization were emphasized—it appears to have been primarily religious in character, offering to its adherents revitalization of their own society and salvation through faith. At the height of the movement, some 25,000 people lived in Cabaruan, but in 1901 the Americans arrested the leaders on charges of banditry and murder, and the community dispersed—only to reappear briefly thirty years later in modified form at Tayug, twenty miles away, where the Colorum Rebellion took place.

Cao Dai, which took root in southern Vietnam in the 1920s, was perhaps less a peasant movement than any of the others discussed, though it had a large peasant following. On the borderline between religious reform and nationalist movement, Cao Dai attempted at one and the same time to outmodernize the West by presenting to its adherents an ideological synthesis of several of the major world religions—Buddhism, Taoism, Confucianism, Islam, and Christianity—and to restore the traditional values of Vietnamese civilization. Ngo Van Chieu, a middle-aged civil servant in the Cochinchina colonial government, was perhaps its principal founder, though the eventual result was an amalgam with systems other than his own. Attracting hundreds of thousands of peasant adherents, as well as townsmen, Cao Dai offered a restatement of traditional values in the context of manifest needs to combat Western influence in terms the West itself employed. Anticolonial in a conservative way, many Cao Dai leaders later became monarchical nationalists, retaining the allegiance of large numbers of peasants.

But if peasant, or peasant-based, movements of a variety of kinds were in the long run to lend substance to—if not always to find common cause with—the rising nationalisms of the region, it was chiefly in the new towns that political organizations with programs directed at independent nationhood and at the substitution of indigenous for alien rulers had their origin and their being. Many of the traditional elites of Southeast Asian societies, as we have seen, were pushed aside under the impact of intensive Western rule in the nineteenth century and thereafter, leaving a vacuum which was now to be filled either by elements of the old elite made over or more commonly by the new urban intelligentsia, whose aims and ideas owed much to the West itself and to its organizational forms. The new, urban elites were influenced not only by the phenomena of urbanization and Western education but also by the presence in almost all Southeast Asian societies of powerful alien mercantile communities, principally Chinese, and by the presence in the air, as it were, of a range of new ideas, some alien in origin, others less so, which did much to determine some of the patterns that nationalist movements assumed.

It has been a persistent feature of the history and society of Southeast Asian states that many of their commercial and trading functions have been in the hands of foreigners, particularly Chinese. The earliest Chinese communities in the region—apart from the few river-based colonies in the remoter parts of Borneo and South Sumatra—were for the most part small settlements, ghettos (one writer has called them) outside the pale of the walled port towns or inland capitals. From that vantage point, in strict subordination to court or harbor officials or to the local nobility, they conducted all manner of trade and commerce, within the country and without. Many of the communities probably varied seasonally in size; where they were larger and more permanent, they usually had a form of internal self-government, whereby the leading resident merchant (known subsequently in Malay as the *Kapitan China*) ordered the affairs of the Chinese populace and answered for them to the local ruler. Though there was some intensification of Chinese trading relationships with Southeast Asia after the European powers entered the maritime commercial scene, it was not until the onset of the high colonial era in the nineteenth century that major changes took place. Then, in response to the protection afforded and to the opportunities arising for participation in wholesale economic exploitation of the hinterland, much larger numbers of Chinese took up residence in the interstices of the colonial society, as entrepreneurs, middlemen, retail merchants, domestics, and unskilled labor.

Early Chinese immigrants into the area, in the port settlement days, often married local women. In some societies—that of Siam, for example—the resulting offspring were regarded as indigenous quite as much as Chinese. Elsewhere, as with the *mestizos* of the Philippines, the *baba* Chinese of Malacca, or the *peranakan* of Java, the mixed community acquired a distinct identity of its own, although it was highly acculturated to the local society and was often regarded as a related part of it. With the greatly increased immigrations of the nineteenth century, all this began to change. Large, almost entirely male, Chinese communities appeared, frontier in character and unassimilable by local societies. As physical and economic circumstances improved in the early twentieth century, women were brought from China to join the men, sex ratios began to stabilize, and the resulting Chinese communities became biologically as well as culturally a great deal more distinct from their neighbors (as well as much more numerous) than they had been before.

Some parts of Southeast Asia saw a much greater influx of Chinese than others. The outstanding example, of course, was peninsular Malaya, which, with a total population in 1850 of perhaps 500,000, mainly Malay, saw no fewer than 19 million Chinese arrive between the early nineteenth century and World War II. Most stayed only for a time, but the residue in 1931 accounted for 39 percent of the total population. In the western coastal states, where they were most strongly concentrated, they far outnumbered the Malays. The Netherlands Indies had a much smaller Chinese component—less than 3 percent of the total population in 1931. In both areas, ethnic Chinese, because of religious and other important cultural differences, remained quite distinct from the local population, and relatively easy to count. In many of the mainland states, where past assimilation had proceeded more rapidly even if, as in Siam, a strong anti-Chinese reaction had set in in the twentieth century, it was less easy to determine who was Chinese and who was not. At a conservative estimate, some 12.2 percent of Siam's population in 1932 was ethnically Chinese; the comparable figure for French Indochina was about 1.6 percent, as it was for Burma.

But neither absolute numbers nor relative proportion were as significant as was economic role (except perhaps in Malaya, where a demographic revolution had occurred). Subject only to a bigger European share of major enterprises, the Chinese in all cases enjoyed a virtually complete ascendancy in business and commerce, from rice-milling and marketing (it has been estimated that in the 1930s nearly 90 percent of the mills in Siam, more than 80 percent in Indochina, and 75 percent in the Philippines were owned by Chinese) to urban-based wholesale and retail trade, which penetrated right into the village heart of the countryside. Their astonishing predominance had been built on the trading experience and connections of the past, on family and lineage networks that transcended state boundaries, on specifically Chinese "training" institutions (like loan associations), and on industry and thrift. It was—and in many cases remains—an unbeatable combination, and the result was the virtual exclusion from commercial or trading activity of indigenous Southeast Asians and the corresponding absence of any growth of an economic middle class based on those activities. Attention has already been drawn to the way in which the "middle class," the new bourgeoisie, in most Southeast Asian societies has been largely composed of bureaucrats and government servants.

The majority of Chinese lived in the towns. Correspondingly, a great many urban societies in Southeast Asia were substantially Chinese. It was characteristically in the towns, therefore, that modern Chinese political and cultural activity found its most lively expression. During the first three decades of the twentieth century, Chinese nationalism on the mainland—and its eventual polarization between the Kuomintang

(KMT) and the Chinese Communist Party (CCP)—generated a strong response in overseas Chinese communities. Sun Yat-sen, who visited the area more than once, was largely financed by overseas Chinese capital, and the Chinese Revolution of 1911 was accompanied—in Singapore, Bangkok, Manila, and elsewhere—by growing enthusiasm for modern education (in schools staffed mainly by teachers brought from China), by study and reading clubs with political overtones, and by a flourishing popular press. Such activities, strengthened again by the politicization that followed the KMT-CCP split in 1927, greatly fostered internal Chinese cohesion and knowledge of distinctness and helped to retard further assimilation in the host societies—a process aided in turn by suspicion and sometimes hostility on the other side. More than that, however, the material success of the overseas Chinese; their ability to organize, educate, and otherwise improve themselves; and the fervid nationalism and anti-imperialism of mainland Chinese politics as reflected in Southeast Asia acted as irritants, stimulants, and sometimes models, providing an important part of the environment in which Southeast Asian nationalism grew.

Chinese nationalism and its associated phenomena made up only one among a wide range of constellations of ideas that impinged on the intellectual world of Southeast Asia in the first part of the twentieth century. Japan's success in avoiding colonialism and becoming the first industrial power in Asia, an achievement sealed by its victory over Tsarist Russia in 1905, was much admired and later held up for emulation. The upheaval in ideas that followed World War I in Europe had many repercussions in Southeast Asia. The spread of socialism and communism, though difficult to generalize about and not yet sufficiently studied, dated from that time. Western radicalism was propagated both by the activities of European socialists in the area (like Hendricus Sneevliet and Adolf Baars in Java, engaged in trade-unionism) and by the international wanderings of such Comintern leaders as Tan Malaka and Ho Chi Minh. But the influence of Marxist-Leninist ideas concerning colonialism, and theories of finance capital and surplus value, went much wider than their immediate standard-bearers, becoming a tone, an influence, in the thinking of many educated and self-educating Southeast Asians. The same can be said of the ideas associated with the gradualist doctrines of trusteeship and mandate, which, under the auspices of the League of Nations, came to afford new rationalizations and new motivations for the activities of the colonial powers. Indian nationalism, based on ideas of *swaraj* (self-rule) and Gandhian passive resistance, though not directly reflected in Southeast Asia except within the Indian communities of Burma and Malaya, nevertheless contributed its own coloration to the mélange of ideas characteristic of the time.

The locus of new ideas was the town, the vehicle was modern education of a variety of kinds, and the recipients were the new urban elites.

# 24

# Channels of Change

## Urbanization

IF the degree of creative confusion associated with urbanization in Southeast Asia in modern times was new, the cities and towns themselves were not. Precolonial Southeast Asia had many urban communities—autonomous societies, centers of government and officials, of religious and intellectual activity, and of commerce—inhabited by a population detached from the land; townsmen rather than countrymen. The largest and most important towns, and therefore the best known, were state capitals, but there were many smaller provincial towns too. Of the bigger cities, one of the best examples is the Malacca of the fifteenth century, center of a great Malay commercial empire. The wide paved streets of the town's business section, lined with tiled or thatched wooden dwellings and warehouses and thronged with residents and traders from all over Asia, sat across the narrow canal-like river (spanned by a bridge of booths) from the fortified precinct that overlooked and commanded it, and within which were the palace of the Malay sultan, the court and its environs, and the houses of the Malay nobility and its retinue.

Another example is Bangkok, which, like its predecessor Ayudhya, was laid out in concentric circles. The innermost circle was dominated by the palaces of the king and later by the massive buildings that served as the headquarters of the major ministries. The next ring of settlements comprised the Thai portion of the city, the homes of princes and government officers and their households, retainers, and families. And beyond that was the Chinese mercantile quarter, surrounding the inner core and edging off into the countryside.

Nineteenth-century Hue, headquarters of the Nguyen court and bureaucracy, was in some respects similar. Like other major precolonial Vietnamese cities, it was rigidly divided. The principal part was the walled *thanh,* or citadel, where the court, officials, and soldiers lived. The subordinate part was the *thi,* or market, where the ordinary Vietnamese lived and where the traders hawked their wares. Observing Confucian forms of social hierarchy, in which merchants ranked below scholars and peasants, Hue confined its merchants and its bazaars to the outskirts of the city.

One of the most obvious things that colonialism and European domination did was to turn the new towns it created inside out, so that at their heart lay not the monarchy but money—the counting houses of the Chinese and other traders, the shophouses full of consumer goods from Manchester, Marseilles, Bombay, and Hong Kong. The citadel was forced to give way to the market, as mammon became king; economic gain was both the raison d'être of the new towns themselves and the motive of most of those who came to them, peasant or profiteer. Though some of the old towns also were transformed by this process, many were simply bypassed, receding in political and cultural importance like Hue and its court, which lost place in the 1880s to the colonially dominated and economically burgeoning areas of Saigon-Cholon and Hanoi-Haiphong, or like the small royal town of Kuala Kangsar in Perak in the same years, residence still of the sultan but not of the new state administration springing up on the Chinese tin fields at Taiping. In 1872, the population of Rangoon was less than 99,000, that of Mandalay at least double; thirty years later, Rangoon had swollen to nearly a quarter of a million and Mandalay had not merely stopped growing, it had begun to shrink.

Most of the new towns, then, were the focus for new or intensified economic energies and new or changing social groups. Some were frontier towns associated with rapidly developing extractive industries. In Siam, for example, as in Malaya, a number of new towns sprang up with the opening of the tin mines. An example is Phuket, probably the first town in the country to have paved roads and automobiles, toward 1910. Like Taiping and Seremban in the Malay states, it was substantially a Chinese town, with its lines of communication running mainly to Singapore and Penang. In the north of Thailand, where the major extractive industry was teak logging, towns such as Paknampho arose for the collection and milling of timber. Kuala Lumpur, which began in 1858 as a huddle of Chinese huts at the confluence of the Klang and Gombak rivers, was built from tin revenues. By 1896, it was the capital not only of Selangor but of the Federated Malay States as a whole. It had a population of more than 32,000, of whom 23,000 were Chinese and only 3,700 Malays.

Virtually all these towns produced for export, not for local consumption. To facilitate their trade, great seaports arose, funneling tin, rubber, rice, and other primary products into world markets. Some of the ports, like Manila and Batavia, were old towns transformed; others, like Haiphong and Penang, were essentially creations of the nineteenth century. But the archetype, perhaps, was Singapore, founded in 1819 to participate in older patterns of archipelago trade; it became in the course of the nineteenth century a vast export market for the produce of its immediate region as well as a transshipment port of the old kind. Singapore at the close of the nineteenth century was perhaps the most polyglot city in Asia. With nearly three-quarters of its 228,000 inhabi-

tants Chinese, it can in one sense be described as a Chinese city run by
the British for the benefit of both. But it was also a meeting place for
23,000 Malays from the peninsular states, more than 12,000 assorted
Javanese, Sumatrans, Bugis, Filipinos, Baweans, and other Southeast
Asians, numerous Muslim and non-Muslim Indians, and at least 1,000
Arabs. It thus exemplified something that was true of all the new cities
of Southeast Asia, whether or not they were dominated by aliens—the
bringing together of large numbers of people from many different social
backgrounds and varieties of experience to share a common, or at least
contiguous, life.

Finally, in listing the kinds of economic activity that gave rise to the
new cities, mention should perhaps be made of industrialization, the
force behind so much urbanization elsewhere. Because the economies of
colonial Southeast Asia were primarily, if not quite entirely, extractive,
few of the new towns could be called manufacturing or industrial towns.
The few that existed were mainly in Vietnam, where French economic
policy differed in marginal respects from that of the other colonial
powers. Textile mills were built in Hanoi and Nam Dinh in the early
1890s, and the important Haiphong cement factory dated from 1899.
Railway workshops (as also in Kuala Lumpur and at Semarang in Java)
made their appearance, as did plants (as in Manila or Singapore) for the
manufacture of carbonated waters and cigarettes. But industrialization
everywhere was minimal, and even in Vietnam the bulk of the labor
force in the 1930s remained outside the cities—on the big plantations of
Cochinchina or in the coal mines in the north.

The main function of the cities and towns was to serve the ends of
alien trade and commerce by draining out primary products and pump-
ing in consumer goods. As an adjunct to that, however, most urban
areas developed as important communications and administrative centers for the surrounding countryside. Towns like Kuala Lumpur in
Malaya, Saigon in Cochinchina, and Medan in Sumatra, became junc-
tions for networks of road, rail, and other communications, which
transported not merely rubber, tin, and powdered milk but people and
ideas. At the same time, improved communications assisted and were
indeed part of the building up of the increasingly elaborate administrative systems (ranging from land survey and police to schools and traveling dispensaries), which were regarded by colonial governments as necessary aids to economic development and proper government in rural
areas. Though the interactions between town, communications and
administrative systems, and countryside were complex, they can for
simplicity be represented as a two-way flow. From the town moved car-
riers of metropolitan values and urban culture, performing integrative
and dissemination functions similar to but much more intense than
those performed by the town in the precolonial past. In the other direction, large numbers of people from village and rural society poured into
the town, carrying with them not merely the mixture of hope and fear

that approach to the city arouses in all travelers, but their own values, ideas, and habits to throw into the urban crucible. Each side of the transaction fed and reinforced the other, making the city one of the most important single agents of change in modern times.

Most people who came to the city did so for economic reasons. The truth of that statement is most obvious in the case of the immigrant aliens, like the Chinese, who predominated in most Southeast Asian towns, and certainly in the larger ones. But it tended to be true also for the Malay, Filipino, or Javanese peasant who came to Kuala Lumpur, Manila, or Jakarta. By no means all forays into the town were permanent. Quite apart from the one-day visitors, who by definition could come from only a few miles away, perhaps to sell vegetables or eggs, there were seasonal workers (taking up agricultural slack times at home), those who left families behind for periodic spells to make a bit on the side as house servants, rickshaw pullers and casual laborers, and at all times hosts of young men who wanted to try their luck in the metropolis and might or might not go back to the village to settle down. Like the Chinese *towkay*, who, it was always said, just wanted to make his fortune and go home to die among his ancestors, the "urban peasant" usually retained close emotional (and, indeed, physical) links with his village, returning to celebrate religious festivals and hoping to make enough to buy retirement land there.

In most of the new cities, as in their older counterparts, people of one ethnic or territorial origin, or one language group, tended to live together in the same part of town. Though initially the "quartering" of towns was sometimes the result of administrative decision, people themselves tended to prefer it, for it assured them neighbors whose speech, religion, and habits of life they shared and understood, helping to perpetuate community. Sometimes, as in Manila until the late Spanish period, they even had their own form of district governing council, there known as the *gremio*. Localized patterns of residence of this kind were often found in association with specialization of occupation. The two practices together assisted newcomers to find both a place to live and work to do. Singapore, although too variegated to be altogether typical, nevertheless offers many examples of situations in some degree found everywhere. In the principal "Malay quarter" of downtown Singapore, Bugis Street was the merchandizing center for Bugis maritime traders from the eastern archipelago, and Kampong Jawa contained many of the quarter's eating houses, coffee shops, and flower stalls kept by the Javanese womenfolk. Bawean *pondok*—single houses or groups of houses in which people from the same village lived together in a semblance of the village community itself, complete with traditional institutions in microcosm—were the base from which Bawean immigrants fared forth into the city at large, mainly to become grooms and coachmen and, later, chauffeurs.

As cities grew bigger, by natural population increase and by contin-

# Cities with Populations in Excess of 100,000

## 1910

| 100,000–300,000 | | 300,000–500,000 |
| --- | --- | --- |
| Mandalay | Singapore | Rangoon |
| Hanoi | Jakarta | Bangkok |
| Saigon-Cholon | Surakarta | |
| Penang Is. | Surabaya | |
| | Manila | |

## 1930

| 100,000–300,000 | | |
| --- | --- | --- |
| Mandalay | Semarang | Saigon-Cholon |
| Hanoi | Surakarta | Singapore |
| Penang Is. | | Surabaya |
| Kuala Lumpur | **300,000–500,000** | |
| Bandung | Manila | **500,000–1,000,000** |
| Yogyakarta | Rangoon | Jakarta |
| | Bangkok | |

## 1960

| 100,000–300,000 | | |
| --- | --- | --- |
| Mandalay | Kediri | Surakarta |
| Moulmein | Pontianak | Semarang |
| Haiphong | Banjarmasin | Malang |
| Hue | Manado | Makassar |
| Da Nang | Bacolod | |
| Vientiane | Iloilo | **500,000–1,000,000** |
| Penang Is. | Cebu | Rangoon |
| Ipoh | Zamboanga | Bandung |
| Padang | Davao | |
| Jambi | | **over 1,000,000** |
| Telukbetung | **300,000–500,000** | Saigon-Cholon |
| Pemantang Siantar | Hanoi | Bangkok |
| Bogor | Phnom-Penh | Singapore |
| Ceribon | Kuala Lumpur | Jakarta |
| Pekalongan | Medan | Surabaya |
| Madiun | Palembang | Manila |
| | Yogyakarta | |

## 1980

**100,000–300,000**
Moulmein
Akyab
Songkhla
Chonburi
Nakhon Si Thammarat
Chiang Mai
Nha Trang
Qui Nhon
Hue
Can Tho
My Tho
Cam Ranh
Vung Tau
Da Lat
Georgetown
Johore Bahru
Petaling Jaya
Kelang
Kuala Trengganu
Kota Bahru
Taiping
Kuantan
Seremban
Kota Kinabalu
Ambon
Balikpapan
Bogor
Ceribon
Jambi

Kediri
Madiun
Manado
Pakan Baru
Pekalongan
Pemantang Siantar
Probolinggo
Samarinda
Sukabumi
Tanjungkarang
Tegal
Bacolod
Iloilo
Cagayan de Oro
Angeles
Butuan
Iligan
Olongapo
Batangas
Cabanatuan
San Pablo
Cadiz

**300,000–500,000**
Bassein
Vientiane
Da Nang
Ipoh
Surakarta
Yogyakarta

Banjarmasin
Pontianak
Cebu
Zamboanga


**500,000–1,000,000**
Mandalay
Phnom-Penh
Kuala Lumpur
Palembang
Ujung Pandang
Malang
Padang
Davao


**over 1,000,000**
Rangoon
Bangkok
Hanoi
Ho Chi Minh City
Haiphong
Singapore
Jakarta
Surabaya
Bandung
Medan
Semarang
Manila

ued immigration, and as rising land values and house rents combined with the decay of older areas to encourage commercial preemption and urban renewal, original patterns of residence and occupation became diversified and confused. Transitional institutions, such as the urban *kampong* or village, which, like the Bawean *pondok,* had eased peasant movement into the labor markets of Jakarta, Kuala Lumpur, and Rangoon, were pushed farther out of town or became overcrowded and unsanitary urban slums. Traditional forms of social organization, or replicas of them, became more vulnerable to the disintegrative effects of urban individualism and, more importantly, less relevant to the new quest for status and prestige in the totality of the urban social structure. But, though there were many casualties along the way, the process was by no means a wholly negative one. While it is true that urban life tended to weaken traditional societies and loosen the hold of traditional beliefs and values, it also offered much that was positive—new opportunities for specialization and skills, new relationships with others of differing social background and experience, affording new points of contact and common interest, and, in the most general way, new and enlarged liberty of thought and action. For many, particularly the young, urban life offered not the breakdown of the known, the familiar, and the secure that is so often described, but an opportunity to rid themselves of parental and other authoritarian constraints and to make life anew.

One product of the evolution of traditional institutions in the city, of the need to seek new forms of social security, of the discovery of new interest groups, and of the desire for self-improvement in a competitive environment was the emergence of "voluntary associations." Individuals joined or helped to form such clubs and societies out of choice, rather than belonging ascriptively, by accident of birth. Associations blossomed throughout Southeast Asian urban societies in the late nineteenth and early twentieth centuries. Their enormous variety reflects the complexity of city life itself, but it is possible to distinguish a few general categories. Many of the first clubs were purely recreational— especially football clubs, which in Singapore, for example, were taken to task by the more serious sections of the Malay press as time-wasting frivolities. Another early and very common form of voluntary association was the burial society, established to ensure that, by common subscription, members and the immediate families of members would be assured of a properly conducted funeral. One of the largest and, to the social historian, one of the most interesting categories was what one might call the "cultural welfare and progress" societies—debating clubs, literary circles, study groups, religious reform societies, language improvement associations. All alike, whether led by Western-educated government servants, vernacular or religious schoolteachers, or occasional members of the traditional elite, they were endowed with their own private vision, each setting out to create a new and better version of its own society.

In the circumstances of colonial rule and foreign economic dominance, which, in one way or another, afflicted all of Southeast Asia, associations of the kind just described, embodying the strivings of urban Burmese, Javanese, or Filipinos to enter and compete in the modern world on their own terms, could scarcely fail to find themselves at odds with the assumptions on which colonial rule was based. The fact of their organization, let alone the content of the largely ephemeral newspapers and journals by means of which they so frequently propounded their ideas, brought them under the surveillance of the colonial authorities, and on occasion they were suppressed—most often, perhaps, in French-controlled Vietnam. The relevance of the first associations, however, lay less in what they accomplished by means of a political confrontation seldom attempted than in the training ground they afforded for wrestling with new problems and shaping a new generation of leaders and followers—training in organizing clubs, running meetings, keeping accounts, operating elective institutions, handling information from outside, and transmitting it within. The cities of Southeast Asia were essentially foreign bodies to the societies in which they were embedded —fewer than 5 percent of all Malays, for example, lived in the towns, where they made up only 10 percent of the total population—but the importance of the city lay outside the realm of numbers or proportion. It lay in its ability to give birth to new elites.

## Education and Language

A nineteenth-century Malay writer once observed that the founding of Singapore had made "dragons out of worms and worms out of dragons."[29] Nothing contributed more to the metamorphosis, which was in one sense or another a general phenomenon in Southeast Asia, than the education systems of the colonial powers. But "the knowledge that is given to people under foreign influence," argued another Malay in 1927, "has no purpose other than to impoverish the intellect and teach them to lick the soles of their masters' boots."[30] Between those two remarks, the first sociological and dispassionate, the second political and heated, both pointing to change, lie the problems and complexities of understanding the incidence, the impact, and the intent of the process often known contemporaneously as "public instruction."

European systems of colonial rule were imposed on Southeast Asian societies with varying degrees of intensity, but most had one common purpose, the organization of the state in such a way as to maximize its potentialities, first as a producer of raw materials and foodstuffs for export to the West, and second as a market for Western manufactures. The type of control and the extent of direct interference in the administration of the state necessary to accomplish that purpose varied with the state's economic importance and promise, on the one hand, and, on the other, with the extent to which indigenous elites and systems of administration could be, or were willing to allow themselves to be, adapted to

Western organizational purpose. In the so-called indirectly ruled, economic low-pressure states—like some of those in the Malay Peninsula,
for example, and Cambodia, or for a time the outer edges of the Dutch
Indies—traditional elites continued in some measure to play an active
part in the administration, even while it was being reshaped to meet
Western needs. In many other states, however, in spite of initial efforts
to retain or work through indigenous administrative institutions, the
urgency of Western demands prompted the growth of very complex
bureaucracies that set a high premium on efficiency and technical competence of a kind either not available or not forthcoming from within
the traditional social order. In many cases, as in Burma, the indigenous
administrative hierarchy came merely to be ignored; in others, as in
Vietnam, it preferred retreat into political isolation to collaboration.

   In the directly ruled states in particular, and to a lesser extent in those
more indirectly ruled, the main need of the colonial authorities, as economic development gathered speed, was for what one might call an
administrative labor force—the overseers, deputy supervisors, clerks,
accountants, and technical subordinates, who could be provided from
the West itself only at prohibitive cost, if at all. Occasionally—especially
in British Malaya and Burma—that kind of trained assistance was
available from either resident or imported nonindigenous Asians,
mainly Indian or Chinese. In most cases, it was not and had to be
created locally.

   This, then, provided the first and most obvious motive for Western-
style training of segments of the population of Southeast Asian colonies
—and an adequate explanation of why it was often called instruction
rather than education, a process usually understood to have a nobler
purpose than mere equipment to earn a living on someone else's behalf.
But many other motives were at work, too, some of them clear and
some confused or contradictory. None of the Western powers assumed
territorial responsibilities in nineteenth-century Southeast Asia without
at the same time taking upon themselves in some degree the tasks of the
*mission civilisatrice,* or civilizing mission. Many Europeans (and Americans) really did see themselves as, in the words of Rudyard Kipling's
poem "The White Man's Burden," waiting in heavy harness "on fluttered folk and wild/ Your new-caught sullen peoples, half-devil and half-
child." Children existed to be educated, or at least toilet-trained. Intox-
icated not only by their own power and inventiveness but by currently
fashionable theories of evolution, Westerners readily accepted justifica-
tions of colonial rule based on tutelage. Notions of bringing backward
peoples into the world by teaching and example were never wholly
absent from ideas of colonial governance—except when the results of
teaching seemed likely to render colonial rule superfluous.

   For all the above reasons, then, colonial authority found itself
engaged in providing a variety of forms of educational institutions for
the peoples it ruled. Earlier in the nineteenth century, during the liberal

era of free trade in ideas as well as goods, the British in particular, who were relatively untrammeled as yet by the need to direct labor, had made some attempt to sustain or adapt indigenous educational institutions, especially in Burma. Simple literacy in the Buddhist countries of mainland Southeast Asia was far more widespread in the mid-nineteenth century than it was in Europe. In the 1860s, Sir Arthur Phayre, governor of Burma, proposed to leave the bulk of the educational task in the hands of the monastery schools, encouraging them, however, by means of the provision of books on Western subjects such as arithmetic and land-measurement, to enlarge their curricula. At the same time, the growth of lay schools of a wholly Western kind was to be restricted. Failure on each side to understand the intentions of the other rendered the policy nugatory. In Vietnam (though not in Cambodia, where traditional systems persisted), early French policies regarding education, combined with the action of the Nguyen emperor in withdrawing educational as well as other officials from the directly controlled French areas in the south, spelled the end of the Confucian examination system in Cochinchina in the 1860s. Under the sway of cultural expansionism, and in need of greater linguistic access to the society themselves, the French then attempted, by means of interpreters' schools that trained teachers as well as interpreters, to spread knowledge of at least elementary French for limited Franco-vernacular education, adopting at the same time the *quoc ngu* romanization of the Vietnamese language, which eventually became the mode of instruction in the peasant village schools. In Java, Dutch attitudes toward education in the nineteenth century were inconsistent but mainly illiberal, and by the 1860s they had clearly embarked on educational policies directed solely toward the production of a suitable range of officials and subordinates. It was partly against this wholly self-interested approach to education that the Ethical Policy was to react at the beginning of the new century.

As the twentieth century opened, then, several distinct features of colonial education had emerged, which were to do much to determine the shape of the new society then also emerging. At the base was the vernacular education offered to some proportion of the rural peasantry. Though in a few places, such as Burma and Cambodia, vernacular education was still largely supplied by traditional institutions, the colonial powers accepted at least some responsibility for financial aid or direct, government-run schemes. Answering probable critics of the small amount spent on vernacular education in the Malay states, an official remarked in 1908 that "the Government has never desired to give the children a smattering, or even a larger quantity, of knowledge which will not help them to more useful and happy lives than they now lead. To the Malay, the principal value of school attendance is to teach him habits of order, punctuality, and obedience."[31] Similar arguments were employed elsewhere; vernacular education was intended merely to make the peasant a better peasant, to reconcile him to his lot. The important thing was to avoid what was often called "overeducation," by which was meant taking people off the land and disturbing the even tenor of village life, or producing people who, unsatisfied with the dignity conferred upon them by manual labor, acquired aspirations that could not be satisfied under colonial rule. If this was true of colonial mass education in the vernacular, even more was it held to be true of education in Western languages. Too rapid an extension of English education, Malayan administrators were wont to say, would bring about "economic dislocation and social unrest."

The only colonial power seriously to dissent was the United States in the Philippines, where it was held, to the contrary, that a greater risk of social unrest lay in "a vast mass of ignorant people easily and blindly led by the comparatively few."[32] Between 1901 and 1902, more than a thousand American teachers were recruited to teach in Philippine schools, and by 1920 there were nearly a million children receiving English-language education at all levels. Elsewhere in Southeast Asia, ironically enough, it was the restricted nature of vernacular education (invariably limited to little more than the rudiments of drilling in the three R's), rather than the relatively small proportion of the peasantry granted it, that led to serious dissatisfaction among its recipients at their exclusion from the more rewarding paths of Western education.

Above the level of vernacular education, colonial administrations and Western economic enterprise alike were increasingly demanding trained subordinates. Pressures from both quarters fused with policies based on ethical recognition of past injustices and on a new desire for cultural association (as in the Dutch Indies); on the transmission to a select few of an allegedly superior culture (as in French Indochina, and less systematically elsewhere); on slightly aloof notions of trust and tutelage (as in British Burma and Malaya); or on slightly apologetic fulfillment of promises to introduce democratic institutions in return for the imposition of colonial rule (as in the American Philippines) to make available increasing amounts of Western-language education. In some areas, notably in the Malay states, in other indirectly ruled territories, and, to begin with, in Java, the principal beneficiaries were the existing traditional elites. Everywhere, in some degree, the already socially and economically advantaged were in the best position to obtain the Western education through which, it seemed clear, all future advantage lay. But gradually, in response to two factors in particular—the leveling effect of impartially applied academic standards and the virtually exclusive location of Western educational opportunity in the towns—the product became diversified, and the new elites who emerged from the system did so as a heterogeneous group, drawn from no one social class and finding identity in a common interest in the future rather than a common relationship with the past.

As systems of Western education became thoroughly established, so did they grow in complexity and in internal stratification, which they imposed upon those who passed through the various meshes of the sieve. One of the more complex examples of this was found in Vietnam, where, by the end of World War I (and after the final destruction of the Confucian examination system in the north and center, as well as the south), entry into the civil service required not merely completion of "horizontal plane" vernacular education (a graphic term) in the village, but ten years of "vertical plane" education through the three formal stages of French education. Following that, a handful of students might go on to French education overseas or to the university in Hanoi, where specialized schools gave additional training for the public service to students drawn from all of Indochina. Talented or fortunate Javanese followed a similar pattern, ending up in the engineering, law, or medical schools formed between 1919 and 1926. At each stage of the process, many fell by the wayside, and it must be recalled in any case that the total numbers affected (and even more their proportion to the populace at large) were small. Around 1937, with a population of some 23 million, Indochina had only about 500,000 children being educated, the vast bulk of them being in the first two grades of elementary school; it had only about 600 university students. In the Netherlands Indies, with a population of 68 million, 93,000 Indonesian children were receiving Dutch-language education, the vast majority in elementary schools, and there were a mere 496 students at university level. Though the Indonesian figures were probably the smallest in Southeast Asia, the general proportions were much the same throughout, save for the two important exceptions of the Philippines and Siam. In the Philippines, where mass education in English had been embarked upon early in the century, there were, by 1938, more than 2 million pupils attending schools of all levels, and more than 7,000 at local universities. In Siam, vernacular education did not have the disadvantages or colonially imposed limitations it possessed elsewhere, and in the mid-1930s there were some 45,000 students at Thai secondary schools, out of a population of 14 million, and 800 or so more at universities in the country. Both the Philippines and Siam also had considerable numbers of students studying at universities overseas, more, at any rate, than any other country in the area.

Education outside the colonial society, though intended as merely an extension rung on the ladder already described, was actually, for most of the handful of people who achieved it, an educational experience qualitatively so different as to set it quite apart. Probably the first thing that metropolitan education did was to cut the colonial powers, and Westerners in general, down to size. For Indonesians, that was literally the effect. Many have recorded their astonishment and incredulity at discovering Holland so small geographically. It had always loomed so large, appearing in schoolbooks in enormous scale maps so that they could study every rock and rill. In addition, it was a liberating experience to be treated as a human being and not as a member, however "evolved," of an inherently inferior people. It was instructive, even when it was only a matter of having one's luggage carried by an English porter, to learn at first hand that Western societies themselves were highly stratified. And finally, many of the students met Westerners who were not merely critics of the existing social order in their own societies but who argued fiercely against colonial subjugation and held theories of economic exploitation that both explained it and forecast its eventual termination. Overseas students returned to Southeast Asia not only to take up senior positions in the indigenous levels of the public service but also to provide leadership in nationalist struggles for independence.

For the Muslim societies of Southeast Asia, in which (as elsewhere except Siam) the channels opened by strictly vernacular education were blocked at a point not very far downstream from their origins—where the most one could hope for was a poorly paid teaching post in the same system or a precarious life as a journalist—there was a side-stream opening to the outside world, an opportunity similar to that afforded to a section of the Westernized elite. Following the great improvements in communications with the Middle East (which, it is sometimes forgotten, is also "West" from another point of view) at the end of the nineteenth century, greater numbers of people from the Dutch East Indies and Malaya were able to make the pilgrimage to Mecca. Though the majority spent only a few weeks there, rising cash incomes from participation as smallholders in the lower levels of the export economy made it possible for many more than in the past to stay on in Mecca or Cairo for some years, primarily to study religion. The advantage of Cairo, as one young man remarked, was that there one could study politics as well. Amid the intellectual and political ferment that possessed the Arab world at the time—engaged both in the renovation of Islam and in nationalist struggles for freedom from the West—students from Indonesia and Malaya acquired new language and new ideas with which to combat the colonial rule that possessed their own society and determined their disadvantaged position within it.

The urban intelligentsias of the mid-1920s had as vessels for their strivings and instruments of their discontent the wide range of voluntary associations already referred to—culminating in the actively nationalist political parties of Burma, the Netherlands Indies, and Vietnam, and nascent movements of a similar kind elsewhere. They also had the written word, and though some had made an extremely thorough job of assimilating Western language and culture, it was to their own in the last resort that both they and the vernacular-educated turned. Language has a peculiarly intimate relationship with cultural identity, both as the most expressive vehicle for a society's beliefs, values, and sentiments—for its innermost spirit—and as a means of self-recognition. The travail of the early twentieth century, which saw the birth of anticolonialist nationalist movements, crystallized, for many, first and foremost around concern for the language of the people or, where there was no single language, around the need to adopt one as a symbol and expression of unity in the face of cultural as well as political imperialism.

In Malaya, the first known lexicographical work by a Malay, Raja Haji Ali's *Kitab Pengetahuan Bahasa,* was compiled in the late 1850s, though it was not published until 1928. A kind of Johnsonian dictionary, in which definition is made the occasion for comment, it dwelt critically on the ways in which Malay life and language were changing under the impact of the West. One of the earliest of Malay cultural-welfare societies was started in Johore in 1888 in order to modernize Malay and make it an independent vehicle for modern systems of administration. In southern Vietnam, Huynh Tinh Cua's two-volume dictionary of the Vietnamese language, published in 1896, standardized meanings in a fashion that was to give real impetus to uniform linguistic usages throughout the country. Later, the language issue tended to center on the schools, where French cultural aggressiveness punished even the informal use of Vietnamese in institutions of higher education.

In the Netherlands Indies, the Dutch had, since the nineteenth century, used Malay as the language of "native administration" and, in contradistinction to the French, discouraged or forbade the use of Dutch by indigenous civil servants. Such attitudes, along with the almost universal use of the language in the press and organizational life of the early twentieth century, helped modernize and entrench Malay— already for centuries the lingua franca of the archipelago—and led eventually to its adoption in the 1920s as the national language, thereafter called Indonesian. In the Philippines, where the mass education policies of the American administration were doing so much to spread a knowledge of English, the desire felt by nationalists to have an indigenous national language finally led in 1936 to the establishment of an Institute of National Language and to the eventual adoption of "Pilipino," based on Tagalog, a Manila-dominated compromise among the possible alternatives. Even in Siam, fears were expressed about the purity of the language, and a special commission, which later became the Thai Royal Academy, was set up to nurture it.

Much of the force given to national language growth was expressed through the vernacular press, which everywhere in Southeast Asia played an increasingly prominent role in cultural and political life. No other medium or expression of social change is as easily accessible to study; the files of old newspapers and journals constitute an invaluable repository of the inner history of the times. Throughout the area, the first newspapers in the vernacular tended to be wholly or partly translations from the foreign language press. By the 1890s, however, and certainly in the twentieth century, most of the principal cities had at least one vernacular newspaper appearing with fair regularity and usually a host of smaller and more ephemeral weeklies and monthlies, often the product of the new voluntary associations. With the increase in basic literacy, which was fairly general in Southeast Asia, despite the unsatisfactoriness of education programs, the press became a vitally important influence in the dissemination and discussion of new ideas and in shaping the intelligentsia, training its leaders, and extending their influence. Few coffee shops or tea houses, even in the village, did not possess a newspaper from time to time, which could be read to the illiterate and argued over by budding politicians. In 1906, one of the most important of the early Malay journals listed no fewer than twenty-six different virtues of newspapers, among them that they were "the light of the mind, the talisman of the thoughts, the mirror of events, the servant of the wise, the prompter of the forgetful, a guide to those who stray, a prop to the weak, the guardian of the community, and the forum for all discussion."[33] In the hands of the new elites, that was scarcely an exaggeration.

# 25

# The Philippines

MODERN nationalism emerged first in the Philippines. The Spanish responded to the increasing pace of change by repression, pursuing a policy that one Spaniard saw as "suspicious and unenlightened but still useful for preserving the colony."[34] Endemic domestic instability in Spain and political, economic, and military weakness in the Philippines produced indecisiveness, which the Spanish hoped to hide by bravura. Nationalist sentiment found focus in 1872 as a result of Spanish repression. The *ilustrados* blamed the friars for the evils of the Spanish colonial system, because the friars were the most visible, most conservative, most able, and most permanent segment of the Spanish community. During the last quarter of the nineteenth century, the congruence of wealth, awareness, education, and discontent among these *ilustrados* led them into direct conflict with Spanish authority.

The first expression of Philippine nationalism occurred not in the Philippines itself, where censorship was rigidly imposed, but in Spain. After the mutiny at the Cavite Arsenal in 1872, many *ilustrados* were arrested; they, or their sons, subsequently went abroad to escape repression and to improve their education. The Filipino emigrés organized what became known as the Propaganda Movement. Meliorist and evolutionary in approach, it advocated equality for Filipinos, representation in the Cortes in Spain, freedom of speech and assembly, nonrepressive taxation, and staffing of the clergy with Filipinos. It contained a marked element of cultural nationalism, including emphasis on Tagalog literature and the arts, pre-Spanish Philippine history, and a self-conscious effort to search out and identify the national character. The movement was permeated with youthful moralism and romanticism, censuring unenlightened Filipino institutions like the *cacique* system, as well as Spanish repression. Its major vehicle became a newspaper called *La Solidaridad,* which began publication in 1889 in Barcelona and then moved to Madrid. Its two most famous spokesmen were Marcelo H. del Pilar (Plaridel) and José Rizal. Both men had become politicized by the Spanish suppression of the Cavite Mutiny. Rizal, a wealthy fifth-generation Chinese *mestizo,* wrote about himself that had it not been for 1872, he would have become a Jesuit, and instead of writing *Noli me Tángere*— his first and most famous novel—he would have written the opposite.

The *ilustrados* were profoundly influenced by the anticlerical traditions of nineteenth-century Europe, especially the Spanish Masonic movement. Freemasonry served as the institutional and ideological link between Spanish Liberals and these Filipino propagandists. In particular, del Pilar saw Masonic lodges as a vehicle for political action both within Spain and in the archipelago. The growth in Spain of the Filipino lodge "Revolucion" and later of its successor, "Solidaridad," led to the establishment of Masonic lodges in the Philippines itself.

As the Propaganda Movement matured, it increased its demands, especially after del Pilar took over control of *La Solidaridad.* His attack on the friars for "monastic exploitation," along with Rizal's fictional but pointed criticism of friar abuses, alarmed the Spanish. The University of Santo Tomas rector, for example, castigated Rizal's novel as "heretical, impious, and scandalous in the religious order and antipatriotic, subversive of public order," and offensive in the temporal sphere.[35] The issue of friar landholdings, in particular, became a point of controversy. In 1887, as a result of a government tax questionnaire, Rizal and his family organized a petition requesting formal and just contracts for the sale of land to the tenants. The petition became a test case for all parties: A rent strike was organized, the Dominicans instituted eviction proceedings, and the issue went to court. The governor-general, aware of the political character of the issue, sided with the Dominicans. He sent in troops, suspended the court hearings, gave four hundred tenants twenty-four hours to leave, and then burned their homes. Twenty-five people, including Rizal's father and three sisters, were deported.

By the early 1890s, the propagandists were becoming disillusioned and bitter. The goal of assimilation within the Spanish empire was abandoned, and the emigrés came to realize that their influence on events was negligible as long as they remained abroad. Propaganda and lobbying proved only marginally effective. Del Pilar abandoned all hope of peaceful change and before his death in 1896 was already contemplating revolution.

Rizal, on his return home in 1892, had at once organized La Liga Filipina. The Liga had a nonradical program, largely concerned with economic and educational advancement. Even that, however, was too much for jittery Spanish officials, who arrested Rizal and deported him to Mindanao. Spanish intransigence prompted Andrés Bonifacio, a clerk in Manila, to organize the Katipunan, a Tagalog acronym for the "Highest and Most Respectable Association of the Sons of the People." The organization was neo-Masonic and very secretive. Operating through cells, it pursued avowedly revolutionary aims. Bonifacio, acutely aware of his own educational limitations, attempted to attract *ilustrados* into the Katipunan. His revolutionary goals, however, frightened many away, including Apolinario Mabini, Antonio Luna, Rafael Palma, and, most importantly, José Rizal himself. Bonifacio eventually despaired of winning their support; instead, he plotted to implicate them through forgery in the hope that Spanish repression would radicalize them for him. The Spanish learned about the Katipunan, and on August 26, 1896, Bonifacio and his supporters had to flee to the Manila suburb of Balintawak, where he issued a call to open rebellion. Bonifacio's rebellion spread throughout the Manila area, but his tactics to win over the Manila *ilustrados* failed despite Spanish arrest and torture of many of their number.

Bonifacio needed to mobilize the *ilustrados* to succeed. Though *ilustrado* status was primarily defined by educational attainment, the sons of rich *inquilinos* or *caciques* had much greater access to educational opportunity. Bonifacio was poor, urban, and, most importantly, uneducated by *ilustrado* standards. He therefore lacked access to money, to power, and to groups beyond the Tagalog region around Manila. Only the *ilustrados* could claim a national constituency. That newly emergent intelligentsia, however, refused to accept Bonifacio's leadership, because it had already arrogated to itself the right to speak for Philippine nationalism. Rizal had noted some years earlier that "a numerous educated class, both in the archipelago and outside it, must now be reckoned with. . . . This educated elite grows steadily. It is in continuous contact with the rest of the population. And if it is no more today than the brains of the nation, it will become in a few years its whole nervous system. Then we shall see what it will do."[36]

Spanish clumsiness, however, achieved what Bonifacio could not accomplish by cajolery or forgery. Spanish officials, well aware that it was the *ilustrados* who had developed nationalist consciousness, put Rizal on trial as the principal organizer and the very soul of the Philippine insurrection. From prison, Rizal wrote a "Manifesto to Certain Filipinos," in which he reiterated that the education of the people was a prerequisite to liberty. Noting that without study and the civic virtues the Philippines could not find redemption, he stressed that "reforms, if they are to bear fruit, must come from above, for reforms that come from below are upheavals both violent and transitory." Rizal condemned "this ridiculous and barbarous uprising," but the Spanish failed to see their opportunity to isolate Bonifacio from the group he most needed.[37] Instead, they did the one thing likely to unite the *ilustrados* with the Katipunan—they executed Rizal publicly and conducted a reign of terror against his fellows. Many years earlier Rizal had written that "the day they [the Spanish] inflict martyrdom . . . farewell, profriar government, and perhaps, farewell, Spanish Government."[38]

Increases in population, dissemination of the ideas of the Propaganda Movement, rising rice prices, a business recession that lingered after 1893, a plague of locusts, an increasingly unfair tax burden, the Cuban Revolution, and the chronic inefficiency of the Spanish bureaucracy all helped the Katipunan. Bonifacio himself proved to be a very poor general, however. Indeed, it was only in Cavite, across the bay from Manila, where the friars owned half the rice land, that a young *goberna-*

*dorcillo* of Chinese-*mestizo* stock named Emilio Aguinaldo was able to win a significant battle against Spanish troops. His victory gave the Filipino revolutionaries new heart and made Aguinaldo a hero overnight. He moved quickly to challenge Bonifacio for leadership.

Kinship ties played a central part in the complex struggle that ensued. After a confused period of political friction, Aguinaldo, who had managed to gain election as leader of the movement, had Bonifacio arrested for treason in April 1897. The charge and the subsequent trial by Aguinaldo supporters were a farce. Bonifacio was not guilty of treason to Philippine nationalism; he had merely lost the struggle to retain control of the revolution. Aguinaldo's aides found him guilty, however, and condemned him to death. Aguinaldo himself issued an amnesty but was neither surprised nor upset when it failed to be delivered, and Bonifacio was shot. Though Aguinaldo emerged as the unquestioned leader, the revolution had been badly shaken by the contest for power.

The early failure of the Katipunan to mobilize the *ilustrados,* the divisive leadership struggle, the Spanish reign of terror, and Aguinaldo's reliance on friends and kinsmen from Cavite limited his ability to spark the revolution across the archipelago. The Spanish responded to armed revolt by recruiting volunteers from linguistic and geographic areas outside Manila—Pampanga, Bicol, Cagayan, Ilocos, Pangasinan, and the Bisayan Islands—and by bringing in troops from Spain. By 1897, they had increased their forces to the point where superior military technology and communications permitted them to gain the upper hand. Aguinaldo was driven out of his home province of Cavite and into the mountains of Bulacan, where he set up temporary headquarters at a small *barrio* called Biyák-na-bató. In November, one of his aides wrote what has since been known as the Biyák-na-bató Constitution in an attempt to legitimize Aguinaldo's claim to government. Despite the patriotic rhetoric contained in the document, however, it was clear that the revolution was in serious trouble.

Fortunately for Aguinaldo and the Filipinos, the Spanish had serious problems of their own. The war of national liberation in Cuba during the same years had forced them to commit most of their army and national treasure to suppress it. They knew that they could not afford to fight a similar war in the Philippines. From the Spanish point of view, it was imperative to gain time, to reduce costs, and to restore peace. From Aguinaldo's point of view, the obvious tactic was to maintain pressure. Instead, he agreed to discuss terms through a self-appointed *ilustrado* intermediary, Pedro Paterno. Aguinaldo asked for the expulsion of the friars, representation in the Cortes, equality in justice, participation in government, adjustment of property taxes, parish assignments for Filipino priests, and a bill of rights. The terms finally accepted, however, included none of those provisions. Instead, the revolutionaries were promised an amnesty, a chance to go without harm into enforced exile, and 800,000 pesos, to be paid in three installments.

While Aguinaldo subsequently claimed that the Spanish had promised much more, the only things written into the three-stage agreement concerned amnesty and money. The Spanish thereby achieved a major victory, since for a relatively small sum they had gotten Aguinaldo to end resistance and to leave the country. Though he, if not his supporters, apparently intended to use the initial payment of 400,000 pesos to buy arms in Hong Kong, the Spanish had good reason to order a *Te Deum* sung in the Manila Cathedral.

Aguinaldo's place in history was salvaged by the accident of American intervention in the Cuban revolution. The Spanish-American War that resulted suddenly altered the balance of power as Commodore George Dewey, under orders to destroy the enemy's navy in the Pacific, sailed into Manila Bay and obliterated the Spanish squadron. Though his continued presence there was ostensibly in order to await, and destroy, the Spanish relief column, Americans had already begun to realize that they had gained a Far Eastern base for expansion. The Spanish, equally aware of changed circumstances, attempted to recover Filipino loyalty by offering various concessions, including a consultative assembly to be composed of *ilustrados*. Their efforts failed both because of the residue of *ilustrado* hostility and because of the American navy's return of Aguinaldo from Singapore via Hong Kong.

His repatriation reestablished the revolution, but with a significant difference: Aguinaldo got widespread support from the *ilustrados* by surrendering his power to them. Although he continued to surround himself with relatives and Cavite supporters, he felt out of his depth and abdicated political decisions to the *ilustrados,* especially to his new adviser, Apolinario Mabini. *Ilustrados* outside the Tagalog areas were induced to join the movement out of allegiance to and confidence in their Tagalog compatriots. The radical, as opposed to the nationalist, goals of the Katipunan were abandoned as private property was guaranteed and as the suffrage was limited to those "distinguished for high character, social position, and honorable conduct." Aguinaldo's initially clumsy announcement of a "dictatorial government" was rapidly altered to the declaration of a "Philippine Republic" by Mabini, who also persuaded Aguinaldo to declare national independence on June 12, 1898.

The new government quickly took control of the countryside from the Spanish, establishing its capital at the provincial city of Malolos. Under Mabini's direction, it moved to fill the void created by the collapse of Spanish power. Throughout Mabini's writings, including his *True Decalogue* and *Constitutional Program,* runs the theme that the country required a simultaneous external and internal revolution. He was romantic, authoritarian, and nationalistic. He saw unity and discipline as essential to any social regeneration, hence he favored a strong executive and a weak, consultative legislature. The great majority of the *ilustrados,* however, were suspicious of Aguinaldo's power and favored a strong legislature as a means of insuring their control. Felipe Calderón, for example, afraid that the "military element, which was ignorant in almost its entirety, would predominate," wanted to see the military neutralized "by the oligarchy of intelligence, seeing that congress would be composed of the most intelligent elements of the nation."[39]

The question turned on whether the *ilustrados* summoned by Aguinaldo to act as a legislature at Malolos had the mandate to draft a constitution. Among the delegates were forty-three lawyers, eighteen physicians, and numerous other professional people. Mabini himself was an *ilustrado* of humble origins, a fact, together with his close association with Aguinaldo and his philosophical outlook, that put him at variance with the majority. As a result, the draft constitution that emerged made the legislature supreme. Under suasion from Mabini, Aguinaldo refused at first to sign the draft, but, faced with disaffection of the congressional *ilustrados,* he reversed this decision despite warnings from Mabini, who threatened to resign. Mabini, who knew he was beaten, reluctantly accepted the compromise draft, which was promulgated on January 21, 1899.

During the six months in which the Filipinos were establishing a government, the Americans were debating whether or not to demand final possession of the Philippines in future peace negotiations with Spain. Captain Alfred Thayer Mahan's theories, Social Darwinism, the lure of the China market, and missionary zeal encouraged the Republicans in Washington to advocate retention of what had been won. While Kipling urged America to take up the white man's burden, Mr. Dooley, less reverently, noted that it was less than two months since most Americans had learned whether the Philippines were islands or canned goods. After testing the mood of the country, President William McKinley announced that he had no choice but "to educate the Filipinos, and uplift and civilize and Christianize them, and by God's grace do the very best we could by them. . . ."[40] Maintaining that "the march of events rules and overrules" his actions, he strengthened Dewey's flotilla until the Americans had more than 10,000 troops around Manila Bay. The Spanish in Manila, preferring to surrender to the Americans rather than to Aguinaldo's Filipino troops, conducted a sham battle which ended on August 13 with capitulation to Dewey. The Philippine forces that had been blockading the city were prevented from entering, and the tenuous alliance between Americans and Filipinos collapsed as their joint enemy, Spain, surrendered.

McKinley's selection of delegates to the Paris Peace Conference with Spain, his refusal to see Aguinaldo's representative, and the actions of his field commanders made it clear to those in Malolos that a strong colonial power was about to replace a weak one. Unexpectedly, however, the Filipinos found support in rising anti-imperialist sentiment in America. The debate in Congress and in the country created strange alliances. Combining idealism with racism, the anti-imperialists polarized much of American society in a way that took the Republican leadership by surprise. McKinley, suddenly on the defensive and not sure of getting the necessary two-thirds vote for ratification of the peace treaty in the United States Senate, ordered his commander in the Philippines to promise the Filipinos a regime of "benevolent assimilation." To the Filipinos, however, that merely made clear McKinley's annexationist intentions. On February 4, 1899, under circumstances that have long been disputed, fighting broke out; the Americans made no real effort to reestablish a truce. Two days later, after narrowly defeating a number of anti-imperial and Democratic amendments, the United States Senate decided to retain possession of the Philippines by ratifying the peace treaty with Spain. The imperialist margin of victory was one vote.

Translating that decision into reality proved both costly and embarrassing. The alliance between *ilustrados* and Aguinaldo mobilized a much larger segment of the nation than had participated in the 1896 revolution. While the Americans could win set battles against Filipino troops, they were frustrated by the guerrilla techniques of a war of national liberation. As the Americans bogged down literally and figuratively on the battlefield, the Republican administration became concerned for its own political fortunes, aware that the Democrats planned to use anti-imperialism as a central campaign issue in the coming presidential election.

The Americans broke the back of Filipino resistance by splitting the tenuous alliance between the *ilustrados* and the provincial followers of Aguinaldo. Jacob Schurman, head of the newly arrived Presidential Commission, promised that America would satisfy the views and aspirations of educated Filipinos in creating a new government. The message was clearly understood. While it is far too simple to claim that all *ilustrados* became *Americanistas,* it is true that the American offer weakened the consensus forged by Aguinaldo's capitulation to the *ilustrados.* The Americans called for negotiations; Mabini, as *de facto* foreign and prime minister, took a hard bargaining position. When his negotiator proved too sympathetic to the Americans, he was arrested. The *ilustrados,* from their dominant position in the legislature, forced Aguinaldo to dismiss Mabini and to replace him with their candidate, Pedro Paterno, who advocated compromise. The generals around Aguinaldo, most importantly Antonio Luna, called Paterno a traitor. As American military power increased, and as the government of the Philippine Republic was hounded from place to place, *ilustrados* began to slip away quickly and return to Manila. General Luna, an implacable foe of appeasement and one of the few *ilustrados* in the military, emerged as the alternative leader of the republican movement. He constituted a threat Aguinaldo could not tolerate; in circumstances that are still not clear, Luna was shot by Aguinaldo's followers. Mabini openly accused Aguinaldo of ordering Luna's death. Whatever the truth of the matter, his death ended the revolution. Aguinaldo, though not captured for some time, became a harried fugitive, isolated from power.

The tension between the *ilustrados* and Aguinaldo was not simply a class struggle. It was, among other things, a contest between two world views—the urban, cosmopolitan, and educated versus the rural, unsophisticated, and innocent. Aguinaldo lost control because he lacked the range of experience needed; the *ilustrados* talked circles around him, and yet they seemed to him city slickers, men who had become so westernized that they had lost touch with the people and with the traditional verities. The *ilustrados,* for their part, saw Aguinaldo as a bumpkin, a peasant. They recognized his hold on the imaginations of the common folk but, from their urbanized and internationalized perspective, thought it foolish to continue struggling against the Americans when the opportunities were so great not only for themselves but for what they saw as the best interests of the country. In effect, the Americans made a deal with the *ilustrados.* At the price of collaboration and allegiance, they were offered the chance to fill the vacuum created by the Spanish withdrawal. The Americans ended all friar power, agreed to limit the franchise, guaranteed private property, and acknowledged the social and economic realities of Philippine life. The Americans needed the *ilustrados* to end the war, break the resistance, and demonstrate America's altruism. The *ilustrados* turned to the Americans to achieve hegemony politically, dominance socially, and security economically. Both groups had much to gain; neither was to be disappointed.

The Filipino-American War and the anti-imperialist debate combined to alter rapidly American objectives in the archipelago. Whatever the dreams of the early expansionists, the Republicans had by 1900 arrived at a policy of self-liquidating imperialism. The Americans saw their mission as providing tutelage and protection so that, in due time, the Philippines could become self-governing and independent. Whether out of guilt or by shrewdness, America rationalized its imperialist adventure by conferring upon it the benefits of American-style democracy. "The destiny of the Philippine Islands," wrote Schurman, was "not to be a State or territory . . . but a daughter republic of ours—a new birth of liberty on the other side of the Pacific," which would stand as a monument of progress and "a beacon of hope to all the oppressed and benighted millions" of Asia.[41] Implicit in William Howard Taft's condescending phrase "little brown brother" was the eventual maturation of the ward. The Americans, arguing that the colonial government had to conform to the Filipinos' customs, habits, and even prejudices, supported a strong, centralized government, dominated by educated and conservative Filipinos, to whom would be permitted increasing power as the nation developed.

By 1900, therefore, the basic pattern of Philippine national development had been established. For the next twelve years, Taft—first as governor-general, later as secretary of war, and finally as president—shaped that policy. He not only moved to minimize "the bitterness and distrust" by getting "Filipinos of education, intelligence, and property" to cooperate, but he also encouraged the *ilustrados* to alter the character of Philippine society from "the medieval-religious type" to one in which "the modern lawyer-politician" dominated.[42] Establishing civil government on July 4, 1901, Taft modeled Philippine governmental structures on American examples. Noting with satisfaction that the Filipino people, especially those he felt were of the better class, were happy with the Philippine Act of 1902, Taft went on to hold municipal and local elections and, subsequently, provincial and national ones. He encouraged *ilustrados* to hold office on the premise that no American should be appointed to any office in the Philippines for which a reasonably qualified Filipino could be found. As early as September 1901, three ranking *ilustrados* had been appointed to the seven-man ruling commission.

The emergence of Philippine nationalism was closely related to religious developments. Roman Catholicism in the islands dramatically changed as a result of antifriar hostility and the American occupation. A concomitant to the revolt against Spain had been a religious nationalist movement against Rome. During the war, a young Filipino priest named Gregorio Aglipay split the clergy along ethnic lines. Aglipay, appointed chaplain-general of the revolutionary troops by Aguinaldo, was excommunicated by the Spanish hierarchy. Although he did not at first intend to break with Rome, the intransigence of the Vatican and the seeming alliance between Madrid and Rome drove Aglipay and many others toward the creation of a Philippine national church. By 1902, the movement had become the Iglesia Filipina Independiente, with Aglipay as archbishop. Aglipayanism filled the religious vacuum created by the withdrawal of the Spanish friars. Many Filipino priests took over parishes formerly held by the Spanish and joined the new church. Within a few years, it was able to claim 1.5 million adherents, about 25 percent of the Christian population.

The Roman Church, clearly on the defensive, sought to restore its position. The Vatican agreed to Filipinize and Americanize the hierarchy, recalled the friars, bowed to the reality of separation of church and state, agreed to limit the activities of priests to ecclesiastical and charitable work, and, most significantly, accepted Taft's offer to buy the large *haciendas* of the friars and sell them out in small holdings to the present tenants—a land reform that the Americans never did see to completion. By withdrawing in some degree from its exposed position as a hated landlord, the Church freed itself from a heavy liability. During the same years, it managed to regain some of its former adherents from the Aglipayan movement. In 1906, the conservative Philippine Supreme Court —composed of Americans and *ilustrados*—ruled that all Roman Catholic properties taken over by the Aglipayans had to be returned to the Church. As a result, the Aglipayans had to find makeshift quarters, while Roman Catholic priests regained imposing stone churches. Though many Filipinos followed the Aglipayan priests, many others continued to worship where they always had, thus returning to Roman Catholicism. By 1918, the Aglipayan share of the Christian population had slipped to about 13 percent. Aglipay himself attempted to translate his position into political power, but, like Aguinaldo, he was unable to compete against the urbanized and sophisticated lawyers, politicians, bureaucrats, and professional men of the temporal *ilustrado* community. The power of the ecclesiastical world decreased, and the Philippines became a secular polity.

The seeming success of American policies in the Philippines obscured their fundamental contradiction. In order to end nationalist resistance to American rule and to extricate itself from an ideologically embarrassing situation, the Republican leadership had promised to shape colonial policy to comply with *ilustrado* aspirations and prejudices. By 1908, Taft realized that America had paid a high price to gain *ilustrado* collaboration. While theoretically committed to "popular self-government" and to the extension to the masses of sufficient education "to know . . . civil rights and maintain them against a more powerful class and safely to exercise the political franchise," Taft was alarmed that American policy might actually be "merely to await the organization of a Philippine oligarchy or aristocracy competent to administer government and then turn the Islands over to it."[43] In offering the *ilustrados* power, the Americans also accepted a particular social system and pattern of land tenure. Education, it was hoped, would in time redress the balance of economic and political power. Taft noted that the "work of instruction in individual rights will require many years before the country is rid of the feudal relation of dependence which so many of the common people now feel toward their wealthy or educated leaders. . . ."[44] Consequently, though independence might be the goal of American policy, it could scarcely come rapidly if early pragmatic expedients were to be reconciled with idealistic commitments.

The Republicans lacked the necessary luxury of time. They had been able to blunt the fighting only by reversing Clausewitz's maxim—by making politics an extension of war by other means. Under the exigencies of war, they had actively encouraged the *ilustrados* to form, in late 1900, the Federalista Party, which advocated collaboration with the Americans and eventual statehood within the American union. Pedro Paterno and others very quickly split off to form their own parties, both to establish their individual power bases and to place themselves on record as supporting eventual complete independence. During the first few years, the Americans prohibited any open advocacy of independence, but by 1907, during the National Assembly elections, politicians campaigned as Immediatistas and Urgentistas. The two groups fused into the Union Nacionalista and won fifty-nine out of eighty seats. The new Nacionalista Party, moreover, quickly turned to a group of young leaders, relegating the older *ilustrados* to positions of ceremonial impotence. Sergio Osmeña, at the age of twenty-nine, was elected Speaker of the new Assembly over Paterno, who was seen as "too Spanish." A new generation of younger men—led by Osmeña and Manuel Quezon—gained control of the nationalist movement and dominated it for the next forty years.

The key issue in both the United States and the Philippines was the timing of independence. The Nacionalistas, aware of the political value of the call for immediate independence, advocated it publicly. The opposition, eventually led by Juan Sumulong, came out for a more gradual approach. Like Taft, Sumulong believed that premature independence would establish an oligarchy rather than a democracy. His voice went unheeded, however, as nationalist rhetoric made independence the all-embracing goal. The issue became even more pressing after Woodrow Wilson's victory in the American presidential election of 1912, since the Democratic Party had consistently advocated rapid independence. Under the influence of former Democratic colleagues with a record of anti-imperialism, Wilson appointed F. B. Harrison governor-general with instructions to increase the tempo of decolonization. Harrison established a Filipino majority on the commission and increased the Filipino representation in the bureaucracy from 71 percent to 96 percent. In Washington in 1916, the Democrats passed the Jones Act, which promised independence as soon as a "stable government" could be established. The Clarke Amendment, which specified the time limit as four years, was passed in the Senate and only narrowly defeated by the Republicans in the House. Since independence seemed imminent, especially after Wilson's advocacy at Versailles in 1919 of worldwide self-determination, Harrison abdicated his supervisory functions and permitted the Filipinos to modify American institutions to satisfy indigenous desires.

Harrison actively supported the independence mission that went to the United States in 1919. Quezon and Osmeña, despite their political rhetoric, were far less eager for immediate independence than Harrison, since what they privately wanted was the benefits of self-rule without the liabilities of ultimate authority. Quezon secretly was willing to accept a twenty-five-year Commonwealth. Such an arrangement would have left problems of defense, currency, and free trade to the Americans while placing political, social, and economic power securely in the hands of the Manila elite. Quezon was spared the embarrassment of publicly admitting his plan, however, by the accident of the American election returns. Just as the fate of the archipelago had been shaped by the 1900 election, so too was its independence delayed by the Republican victory in 1920. The Warren G. Harding administration, unhappy about the lax quality of the Harrison era and about a series of economic scandals, dispatched Leonard Wood and William C. Forbes to investigate. Their mission concluded that "it would be a betrayal of the Philippine people . . . and a discreditable neglect" of national duty to withdraw "without giving the Filipinos the best chance possible to have an orderly and permanently stable government."[45] Recommending that the office of governor-general be strengthened, the Wood-Forbes mission postponed the independence that had seemed so near.

Harding's appointment of Wood as governor-general guaranteed a confrontation between the Filipino leadership and the American administration. An authoritarian, Wood served as a magnet to attract Filipino hostility. Quezon shrewdly saw great personal opportunity in the situation, using Wood's unpopularity to establish himself as the most important Filipino leader. Attacking Osmeña's allegedly dictatorial and autocratic tendencies, Quezon split the Nacionalista Party in two. He then magnified the tensions with Wood and summoned the nation to form a united front. Osmeña, caught by Quezon's appeal for a transcendental nationalism, found himself forced to accept second place in the reformed Nacionalista Party. Having established his own position, Quezon then whipsawed the opposition parties into forming an even broader coalition, which the Nacionalistas dominated. Through a whole series of incidents, including the Fairfield Bill, the Conley affair, Wood's abolition of the Council of State, and the Plebiscite Bill, Quezon exploited nationalist fervor by making Wood a foil for his own leadership. By the time Wood died in 1927, Quezon had projected himself as the embodiment of the Philippine nation.

Quezon and the Nacionalistas dominated Philippine nationalism up to World War II. Opposition critics like Sumulong were relegated to a peripheral position. The one major challenge to Quezon's position came in 1930–1933, when a concatenation of factors, including Democratic victories in the American Congress and for Franklin Roosevelt, the rise of Japanese militarism, growing opposition to retention of the Philippines by American labor and farming groups, and racial hostility toward Filipino immigrants, combined to make the American Congress again receptive to Philippine independence. The Hare-Hawes-Cutting Bill, advocating independence after a further ten-year Commonwealth period, was passed by the American Congress after Osmeña and Manuel Roxas had lobbied in Washington for it. It was vetoed by President Herbert Hoover, passed despite his veto, and then blocked in the Philippines by Quezon, who was afraid that Osmeña might regain his earlier position as the architect of independence. During the bitter pro-versus anti-independence fight in the Philippines, the Nacionalista Party again split. Quezon, the master politician, used his patronage and leverage to block the Hare-Hawes-Cutting Bill and then negotiated (as he had known he could) a slightly more favorable bill from the newly elected President Roosevelt. The measure was known as the Tydings-McDuffie Act. Osmeña, much to Sumulong's disgust, again decided not to establish himself as an opposition leader and ran as Quezon's vice-presidential candidate in the elections for the new Commonwealth government.

In summary, the forty years from 1901 to 1941 contrast sharply with the last decades of the nineteenth century. Whereas in the earlier period the political structure of society was undergoing profound reorganization, later it remained relatively stable. On the other hand, the twentieth century saw striking increases in the numbers of people involved in urbanization, in education, in the franchise, and in modernization. In the late nineteenth century, the *ilustrados* represented a minute percentage of the nation; by 1941, the actual number and the relative proportions of the educated had dramatically increased. Geographic, linguistic, and ethnic distinctions became less important as local patterns were replaced by national ones. People of every economic class and social category came to identify with Philippine nationalism—the flag the anthem, and the abstraction. Thus, while the dichotomies of tenant and landlord, urban and rural, rich and poor, elite and peasant increased rather than decreased, all strata found a common locus of loyalty in the Commonwealth. Nationalism could supply cohesion, even though it left unanswered substantive questions of direction and identity. The success of Philippine nationalism led one Filipino to write that they were "an Oriental people standing at the portals of Asia, in deep sympathy with its kindred neighbors yet with hands outstretched to the cultures of Spain and America."[46] In the prewar period, Filipinos took great pride that their nation could offer a model for other Southeast Asians to emulate. The optimism of the period was to be tempered by the problems of independence.

# 26

# Burma

THE period of less than sixty years that the British governed all of Burma, coupled with the earlier establishment of British rule in the southern frontier regions of the country, had a profound impact upon the economy and society, and not least on the relationship of the majority peasant population with the state. The revolutionary consequences of tying Burma economically to the world and politically to India were little recognized in 1886, but by the fourth decade of this century the effect was the creation of an irresistible demand for regaining the country's independence.

The established leadership groups of the old society—court officials, provincial governors, and Buddhist monks—organized a strong resistance to the imposition of British rule at the end of the nineteenth century. They were joined in this by other individuals and groups who, while benefiting from the new order, sought additional opportunities for themselves in the chaos of radical political change. The lack of centralized administration and political control over all parts of the kingdom had allowed regional leaders to contest with the capital for the use of local resources; and administrative tensions had been severe in the years immediately preceding the final annexation of Burma to India. The desires for autonomy on the part of some of the rulers of the Shan states, the *sawbwa,* reflected this most clearly. In those areas already governed by the British, the replacement of local hereditary village headmen by bureaucratically appointed officials with no traditional authority had already begun to undermine village solidarity. Monks, the alternative leaders of the old society, now arose to take a political role in their communities, abetted by the British inability to maintain the authority of the central monastic institutions.

Vagabondage and dacoity, organized actions which allowed individuals and groups to evade monarchical control of manpower, were well established as a political pattern in traditional Burma, occurring in response to official abuses or to the absence of clear authority. It was natural that such expressions of protest should continue under British rule, especially where, as in Lower Burma, new villages were founded by immigrants from the north, and where leadership, slow to develop from within, was defined artificially by British administrative fiat. But now such acts took on a different meaning, for the British state was less concerned with the control of manpower than it was with the control of land and money, as expanding the agricultural base and increasing tax revenues came to replace the religious and ceremonial functions of the monarchical state.

Another sort of resistance to the British in the late nineteenth century came from the leaders of the ethnolinguistic minorities—the Shans, Kachins, Chins, Wa, and other peripheral groups—who with great difficulty had maintained some degree of autonomy within the traditional tributary framework. As Mindon and Thibaw attempted to strengthen their control over the peripheral rulers, they provoked a resistance to central control that outlived the Konbaung dynasty. Some of the major Shan *sawbwa* viewed the collapse of the Mandalay monarchy as an opportunity to take back powers which they had lost to the royal court; the British had therefore to reimpose central control upon them by military means when diplomacy proved unsuccessful.

Some members of all these groups—village headmen, monks, dacoits, and, in outlying areas, minority leaders—actively resisted the imposition of British control throughout Burma. The resistance and rebellion that swept the country between 1886 and 1890, and continued in some more remote areas until 1895, was unquestionably political in motivation. Whether those involved were "nationalists," however, is another question. It is a mistake to dismiss them, as the British often did, as xenophobic or romantic or lawless opportunists, though doubtless some of them were. Those who had had authority under the kings naturally wanted to preserve their prerogatives against the demands of the new order and also to defend the values of a tradition which they understood and cherished. But they were unable to generate a coherent and unified force, without the focus for loyalty that a single monarch had provided in the past, against the disciplined and well-armed might of the British Indian Army and the organized and cohesive strength of the new bureaucratic order.

The changes that resulted from the imposition of colonial rule in Burma led to the creation of social formations very different from those which had existed under the traditional structure that had supported the kings. Rather than attempting to control and direct personal ambition and economic incentives as the kings had done, the colonial authorities sought to encourage individualism and to create conditions which would allow for economic expansion. Trade and profit replaced the sumptuary laws of the kings. And education useful for working as a lawyer or clerk replaced the religiously grounded learning of the village monastery.

Education was an integral part of colonial rule in Burma. It was geared to providing the civil service and modern economic enterprise with English-speaking clerks and other functionaries and providing the government with the skills a modern state requires. The cities and towns of British Burma became the centers of such schooling; its homes, shops, and offices the repositories of values communicated in the schools. Recruits into government service came primarily from the towns (especially those of Lower Burma) rather than from the villages, or from the north; the gradual colonization of Burma from the coast inward encouraged the process, at least for the period up to World War I. The British trained a bureaucracy that was nonhereditary and did not come from the old official elite; social development under British rule thus built upon new patterns established in Lower Burma prior to the fall of Mandalay. Nonofficial families that remained or emigrated to Lower Burma before 1885 and took up new land, or who went into business in the towns, or who took up service under the British, were likely to send their sons to English schools; and those young men, grown up under British rule, had both established connections with economic interests in the towns and an acquired bureaucratic position to defend against latecomers from the north after 1885.

Students in government-aided schools were exposed to a curriculum emphasizing the English language and Western arts and sciences; in time their perspectives and occupational skills became very unlike those of their village-dwelling peasant compatriots. Nonetheless, this new urban elite sought ways of bridging the gap between the old and the new in Burma's social life and at first found the means of doing so through a movement to reform and modernize Buddhist beliefs and practices. In organizational form, this effort took shape in the Young Men's Buddhist Association (YMBA). Operationally, it saw Buddhist laymen beginning to assume the moral and leadership roles held until then almost exclusively by traditionally educated Buddhist monks. The YMBA, formed in 1906, brought under one national umbrella a variety of such Buddhist modernist groups that had been formed in towns throughout the colony around the turn of the century in an attempt to assert a cultural identity distinct from the Western culture of the colonizers. At the same time, the YMBA recognized the inability of traditional Burmese culture to create an independent society capable of coping with new conditions. Though the YMBA was not organized with an avowed political intent, the political implications of such an organization were obvious, and initially the British forbade government employees to join the YMBA. Later, however, perhaps in recognition of the reformist nature of YMBA activities, the British lifted the ban and the organization for a brief time came under the control of leading members of the indigenous establishment, many of whom were closely linked with the government.

World War I and associated events in British India rapidly widened the horizons of the urban elite and led to a split between pro-British reformers and individuals more inclined to political activism. Burma's direct involvement in the war was less even than that of Thailand and Vietnam; only about eight thousand Burmese were used for labor service in Iraq. Rice exports were only temporarily disturbed by shipping shortages. The indirect effects, however, strongly influenced the new elite and made it more politically assertive. The YMBA was raising an ostensibly religious and cultural issue in 1916 when it protested the manner in which Europeans and other non-Buddhists persisted in wearing shoes when visiting Buddhist monasteries and pagodas, but, of course, the matter went straight to the heart of the colonial relationship. It was a question not merely of careless scuffing by foreigners of floors and courtyards polished by countless bare feet but rather of implicit assumptions of cultural superiority and defiant disdain for Buddhist culture, no less contemptuous than if Burmese men had insisted on visiting English cathedrals in bare feet, wearing hats and smoking cheroots. The 1916 "footwear controversy," like that of half a century earlier, was in one sense a political issue—a challenge to the British right to rule in a manner defined only by themselves. This time, after all fifty YMBA branches had mounted agitation in every town, the Burmese won. In 1918, the government ruled that abbots had the right to determine the dress appropriate to their monasteries. The importance of this victory can be gauged from the self-assurance and organization with which the YMBA tackled issues more explicitly political in the following year.

As late as 1916, despite these straws in the wind, a committee appointed by the colonial government to consider political reform saw little need for change. When changes begin in India, however, the Burmese elite was quick to see possibilities for Burma. In 1917, the British government in London announced its intention of moving toward a greater measure of self-government in India. The YMBA responded by requesting Burma's separation from India. The unrestricted immigration of Indians, the inappropriateness of Indian legislation and administration, the use of Burma's revenue surpluses to support the Indian government, and the prospect that the rule of Burma might pass into the hands of Indian politicians were among the many grievances for which the YMBA leaders felt they deserved redress. The Joint Committee on Indian Constitutional Reform, reporting in 1918, recognized the justice of such representations: "Burma is not India," it decided and stated that "the problem of political evolution of Burma must be left for separate and future consideration."[47] This consideration was apparent in the tentative scheme of reform put forward by the British governor in Rangoon later in 1918, advocating only that local self-government be strengthened at the district level by the setting up of elective governing boards, while the legislative council (61 percent indirectly elected and overwhelmingly weighted in favor of urban commercial and foreign interests) was to remain purely advisory. Those proposals were, however, overtaken by developments in India and opposition to them in Burma.

Alarmed that separation from India might mean missing out on the greater measure of self-rule to be granted to the other provinces, younger elements in the YMBA, joined by other associations, attacked the proposed reforms. In 1919 and 1920, they sent delegations to London, which gained from the British similar concessions—constitutional dyarchy under which some limited government functions would be transferred to two Burmese ministers responsible to a more representative legislative council. While the Burma delegation members talked in London, however, their compatriots were demonstrating in the streets at home for an even greater degree of self-government than the British had yet been willing to contemplate.

The agitation in Burma centered first on the proposed rules for the policies of the University of Rangoon, which were to come into effect in 1920. The YMBA, having split between its younger and more activist majority and its more conservative leaders, had taken the name of the General Council of Burmese Associations (GCBA), an action indicating its now explicitly nationalist and political purposes. The GCBA then lent its support to a student-organized strike of the new university. The strike soon spread to embrace all government and some missionary schools. At issue was whether or not the university would be exclusivist or whether a larger number of students, with lower educational standards, would be able to attend. Though unable to get the government to make fundamental changes in university admission standards or to acknowledge the right of the indigenous population to have any control over education, the strike resulted in the formation of a large number of national schools throughout the country. These schools provided a means of gaining a modern education outside of the state's control, although eventually in order to receive government financial support the national schools came under government inspection.

The political activity that began with the university strike and boycott in 1921 and continued through the decade increasingly involved the public, both urban and rural. The GCBA encouraged the organization of village-level nationalist organizations called *wunthanu athin* (own race societies). These organized peasants to boycott government officials, including village headmen, and the more radical of its leaders supported peasants who were seeking relief from economic hardships by refusing to pay taxes and rent. Both within these groups and outside them, younger Buddhist monks took an increasingly prominent role in political agitation, creating in 1922 their own national political leadership in a general council for the monkhood to direct such work. The monks who were thus active in the 1920s—attacking foreign rule, village headmen, the police and courts, tax collectors, and Indians—were in some respects similar to those who had resisted the British in the 1880s and earlier: Theirs was a defensive position that rested upon the values of traditional society, but their organization, tactics, and issues were new. Significantly, unlike many of the urban political elite in the GCBA and its many factions, the political monks remained in close contact with the peasantry in the *wunthanu athin*.

The introduction of the dyarchy constitution in 1923 strained the alliance of the urban elite and the rural leaders, whether religious or secular. Under that arrangement, a legislative council was created with 80 elected members in a total membership of 103. Of the 80, 15 were elected from communal constituencies (8 Indians, 5 Karens, 1 Anglo-Indian, and 1 British), thus reinforcing Burma's ethnic diversity. Two of the four members of the governor's council were nominated by the legislative council and put in charge of agriculture, excise, health, public works, forestry, and education. Still reserved to the governor was control over the central administration, the courts, police, land revenue, labor, and finance, as well as the "excluded areas" (Karenni, the Shan State, and the Kachin and Chin hill areas), while the central government of India kept control of defense, foreign relations, communications, immigration, and income tax. The first elections to the Legislative Council held in November 1922 split the Burmese elite over the issue of participation or collaboration in what most regarded as an unacceptable constitution. A majority of the GCBA, led by U Chit Hlaing, boycotted the election, while a minority faction led by U Ba Pe formed the "21 Party" to contest the elections, winning just under half of the noncommunal seats; but the proportion of the eligible who voted was less than 7 percent. The split in the GCBA was reflected in the organization's branches and in the village *wunthanu athin*. The result was political fragmentation, in which opportunism, generational differences, educational background, economic concerns, genuine differences in political tactics, and other forces played a part, dividing both the urban elite and village society. All agreed on the necessity of change, but many differed on its likelihood, nature, and the appropriate actions to be taken. The vast majority saw the formal political process as irrelevant to their concerns; even in the 1925 and 1928 elections, when U Chit Hlaing and other boycotters entered into the electoral game, the proportion of participating voters never exceeded 18 percent.

The ideas and interests that motivated the nationalist movement in Burma prior to 1942 reflected the dissimilar interests of the urban political elite and the village-based rural leadership. The issues that moved the elite were primarily those which were defined in terms of the political and administrative structures created by the colonial state. Their goal was to replace the British and take over these structures for themselves in the name of the Burmese people. For village leaders and their peasant followers, nationalism meant ridding the country not only of a foreign ruling class but also of the bureaucratic and economic institutions that they had introduced. Peasant unrest continued to grow during the 1920s, but there was little the urban elite could do to solve their problems and a gulf of distrust grew between the two groups. The dominance of the political elite by lawyers and others trained in the art of compromise and negotiation seemed to the bulk of the population to be a symbol of the fact that only violent action could resolve their grievances.

Politics in Burma during the 1920s were thus very lively. The elite repeatedly split into a multiplicity of parties and factions. In the Legislative Council, increasing representation of nationalist parties at successive elections served only to swing the communal representatives into the government ranks and to bring about a majority vote against the Burmese. This meant that legislation introduced to ameliorate the conditions of the peasantry had no chance of being passed. Meanwhile, rural political activity increased substantially as a result of the large number of parties and the agitational work of the political monks and other *wunthanu athin* leaders. Violence against government officials, including village headmen, increased and the government had to rely increasingly on the armed and mounted military police, often called the punitive police, to maintain control.

Political activity was further inflamed by the local effects of the world depression. Rice prices fell by more than one-half between 1928 and 1931, while land rents, payments on indebtedness, taxes, and the prices of many imported necessities dropped more slowly if at all. The foreclosure of mortgages on some 2 million acres of agricultural land between 1929 and 1934—almost 20 percent of the total agricultural land in the delta—was but the most striking symptom of a major agrarian crisis. Tensions exploded in anti-Indian riots, beginning in Rangoon in May 1930 and moving out into the countryside a year later to create general disorder of an openly anticolonial kind.

The most serious of the explosions was a peasant rebellion that broke out in Tharrawaddy District in December 1930. Its leader, Hsaya San, was a former monk, a practitioner of indigenous medicine, and an active organizer for the most pro-peasant faction of the GCBA. Under its auspices, he had undertaken in 1927–1928 an extensive survey of agrarian conditions and peasant grievances against colonial rule. His background suggests, as does the way in which his rebellion was organized, that by the late 1920s the village organizations of the GCBA and the *wunthanu athin* were seen as the only hope for ending the economic and political plight of the peasantry. Taxation, crime, rice prices, land alienation, Indian immigration, and unemployment as well as the denigration of the Buddhist religion, were all seen as direct products of colonial rule. The *wunthanu athin* had demonstrated to the peasantry that only organized protest on their own behalf held out any possibility of a change in their conditions. In this, they were joined by the political monks.

Just as peasants earlier had greeted U Chit Hlaing, the GCBA leader, with a royally caparisoned elephant to give him the dignity that, in traditional terms, set him symbolically above other men as a leader, Hsaya San was surrounded with the trappings and symbolism of royalty—the white umbrella and a capital. But while outwardly manifesting many of the symbols and beliefs of precolonial Burmese society, the rebellion was very much a revolt organized by modern means and directed at contemporary grievances. Hsaya San spent two years touring villages and encouraging the peasants to take action on their own behalf, but the rebellion apparently broke out spontaneously; although when it did, it spread with great rapidity. It began with attacks on police posts, the forestry service (which denied peasants their customary access to firewood and lumber), uncooperative village headmen, and Indians and Chinese the rebels came upon. The rebellion reached such proportions that additional forces had to be brought in from India, so that eventually there were 12,000 troops in the field to suppress it. With the capture of the leaders toward the end of 1931, the rebellion began to wane, and it was broken by mid-1932.

The Hsaya San Rebellion proved the futility of peasant rebellion to any who might have been tempted to mount one. Weapons were hard to get, and government troops were vastly superior in firepower and mobility (the rebels suffered 3,000 casualties, the government 138). It was not, however, a total failure, for it awakened public opinion, setting an example of sacrifice and anticolonial zeal that few could ignore and many romanticized. Government prestige was shaken as the seriousness of grievances was emphasized and as its own negativism and indifference were demonstrated.

When the British had begun to reexamine the Indian constitution in 1929, the issue of separation of Burma from India was also revived. The Simon Commission, which reported on the subject, recommended separation. Many Burmese distrusted British intentions, still fearful that India might be granted more autonomy than Burma and suspicious of the fact that British businessmen favored separation. However, the majority also viewed Burma's continued attachment to India with distrust, knowing that the only way that Burma could stop unfettered Indian immigration into their country was by separation. The issue of separation was tested in the general election of 1932, in which the "antiseparationists" won an important victory on the basis of GCBA, *wun-thanu athin*, and monkhood support, gaining forty-two of the eighty elective seats. At that time, representatives of Indian businesses with sizable investments in Burma contributed heavily to ensure the safety of their assets. The Legislative Council was unwilling to indicate clearly that it favored remaining in India, and when finally the British government in London decided on separation, there were no protests in Burma.

The British, in line with reforms introduced in India at the same time, gave separated Burma a more democratic constitution on April 1, 1937. This constitution provided for a cabinet responsible to a fully elected House of Representatives, with thirty-three additional general and seven additional Karen constituencies, against which was balanced a Senate of thirty-six members, of whom half were to be elected from among men of substantial property and income. Still reserved to the governor were control over the "excluded areas," defense, foreign relations, and monetary policy. Political activity approaching the 1936 elections, which were to inaugurate the new order, seemed sluggish—less meaningful and more confused than in 1932. Politicians who had campaigned in 1932 against separation returned to constituencies holding precisely the opposite view, and since little was seen to have been done to alleviate rural conditions in the meantime, their interests and those of the bulk of the peasant population seemed even further apart than before.

Increasingly the established politicians were challenged by younger men, as older parties were split by the prospects of increased power and greater opportunities for creating viable political machines, though, as soon became clear, these were unable to resolve major social grievances. A movement centered initially in the Rangoon University student union and influenced by the ideas of the Sinn Fein (Irish republican) movement, the ideas of Nietzsche and eventually, as well, by British-style Labour and Marxist ideas took formal shape in the latter half of the decade when a group of young men took control of the Dobama Asi-ayone (We Burmese Association). Originally founded in 1932 in the aftermath of anti-Indian rioting and the Hsaya San Rebellion, the Dobama Asi-ayone became a central focus of the most strongly nationalist youth. The leaders called themselves *thakin,* or "master," implying that they, not the British *thakin,* were the rightful rulers of Burma. Before taking over the Dobama Asi-ayone, many of the younger leaders gained their first political experience leading a nationwide strike in 1936 over the university act. This strike, led by then-students Aung San and Nu, along with many others prominent in government and politics in the 1940s and 1950s, was a gesture of defiance against school authorities and the colonial educational system and harkened back to the student strike of 1921. This second strike, which also reached nationwide proportions, was called off only when the university and legislature agreed to investigate student demands, ultimately bringing to the university more political independence. After leaving the university, the young nationalists then devoted their energies to writing leftist political tracts and organizing peasant and labor union protests at current conditions. The support of these young nationalists was sought by the leaders of the political parties in the legislature.

The parties that contested and won seats in the 1936 elections were still divided over the issues of cooperation with the British and the degree of reform to be demanded which had dogged party life since the early 1920s. The five-party alliance led by U Ba Pe, which won the largest bloc of seats in the legislature, was unable to form a cabinet and so, in 1937, Dr. Ba Maw—who had defended Hsaya San at his treason trial, had led antiseparationist campaigning in 1932, and had been education minister during the 1936 university strike—formed a coalition of minor parties, minority leaders, and defectors from other parties to lead the first government of separated Burma.

For the next five years, until the Japanese invasion brought to an end

British colonial rule, the politics of Burma were dominated by contests for office and power between established politicians such as Dr. Ba Maw, U Ba Pe, and others, especially the slightly younger and politically canny U Saw. Three cabinets were formed during the period, and over time a new constitutional order began to take shape. The governor, though keeping his ultimate veto power in reserve, increasingly allowed the elected ministers to decide for themselves what should be done to alleviate the country's economic and social ills. Agrarian issues including land reform, taxation, university reform, and agricultural credit, as well as immigration and "Burmanization" of government and commercial positions, were all subjects of careful study and legislation. Little had changed, however, before the Japanese invasion, and the full political implications of the late British colonial period remained to be expressed.

# 27

# Indonesia

On January 12, 1900, as the new century was dawning, a young Javanese woman called Raden Adjeng Kartini wrote, in Dutch, in a letter to a friend, "Oh, it is splendid just to live in this age; the transition of the old into the new!"[48] The exclamation point was Kartini's, but the vision was true for her time; a new age was opening in the Netherlands Indies. In the early years of the century, the many societies of the archipelago, including her Javanese one, were coalescing in a new and more comprehensive Indies society. The export economy was booming, new investment capital was pouring in, muddy-streeted towns were becoming modern cities. The government, fortified by a freshly proclaimed colonial ethos, the "Ethical Policy," was beginning to penetrate the life of the village with a host of new development programs. A new sense of change and purpose was in the air.

Kartini was aware of all this. But for her the new age was first of all in her own mind; she had needed new eyes to see the society now taking shape so rapidly around her. Her life story, as it is recorded in her published correspondence, was a voyage of self-discovery. Its special quality came not from her earliest childhood in the *priyayi* establishment of her father, the regent of Japara, but from her education in the local European primary school. There she learned Dutch, thus gaining access to all that modern European thinking had to offer. It made her voyage difficult and often painful, for she remained deeply attached to her Javanese heritage. But it enabled her to see the new Indies around her and at least to begin the task of defining a place for herself in it.

What happened to Kartini happened in many different ways to many others in the early-twentieth-century Indies; not only to Javanese, Sundanese, Makassarese, and Minangkabau but also to Eurasians, Chinese, and the Dutch themselves. The outer political history of the period was the story of how, at the height of Dutch colonial rule, the initiative passed to its subjects, who, developing a nationalist movement, challenged that rule and prepared for its demise. The inner political history of those years consisted of a series of self-transformations by all who came to play roles in that outer history. In the older Java and in the islands beyond it, numerous different societies, indigenous and immigrant, lived side by side, either having little to do with each other or, where they did interact, accommodating fairly easily to each others' cultures. After 1900, the tightening frame of modern Indies society pressed them more closely together, dissolving the old accommodations and challenging the established culture of each separate group. All came under strong pressure to redefine their cultural identities and find places for themselves in the emerging social order. Before politics, therefore, came education, both in the narrow sense of schooling and in the more fundamental sense of self-discovery.

Of all the social groups in the Netherlands Indies, it was the *totok* Dutch who found their transformation the easiest, though it went deep and was to have fateful consequences.[49] In part, the ease of this process was due simply to heavy immigration from Holland, as government and especially business expanded rapidly. *Trekkers,* as they were called, came out to the Indies, usually with Dutch wives, for a career of specified length, went home periodically on leave, and planned to retire there. Their cultural identity was already formed before they came; as their numbers increased, they found little reason to accommodate to local cultures. Thus, they differed markedly from the older, smaller group of Dutch *blijvers* (stayers), who thought of the Indies as their home. The great influx swamped the *blijvers,* and, after 1900, it was *trekkers* who set the style for the *totok* Dutch community. In the cafés, department stores, and comfortable bungalows of the European quarters of the new cities, an all-Dutch life established itself.

As Dutch *totok* in their private life drew apart into a closed community, a parallel development was taking place in the *totok*-run government. The change began in the time of the "Ethical Policy," a nickname given to the new attitudes toward colonial rule that came to the fore at the turn of the century. The leaders of the Ethical movement were high-minded men, troubled by reports of the declining welfare of the Javanese and determined to create a new class of modern-educated indigenous people to take some part in governance with themselves. To those ends, they developed a substantial Dutch-language school system and launched a series of welfare programs that thrust the government into much more direct involvement with the affairs of its subjects.

Closer involvement, however, led to greater dissociation between ruler and ruled. The Ethical Policy was a thoroughly European conception of the role of government, without roots in local political tradition. Ambitious welfare programs were necessarily administered in a bureaucratic way, through government departments and regulations rather than in the personal *priyayi* style of older Dutch officials on Java. Most of all, the Ethical Policy was founded on the cultural arrogance of *totok* Dutch. "But how glorious is the aim that we pursue!" wrote one. "It is the formation out there . . . of a social entity which is indebted to the Netherlands for its prosperity and higher Culture, and thankfully recognizes this fact."[50] Like the *totok* community in which it was rooted, *totok* government had drawn apart from its subjects to become a private club of aliens at the remote pinnacle of a bureaucratic machine.

*Totok* Dutch, for all their prominence, were only a minority among those classified as "European" by Indies law. The majority were *peranakan,* or Eurasians.[51] In the nineteenth century, all Eurasians shared in the mixed *Indisch* (Indies) culture, but they did not form so distinct and tightly knit a social community as did Chinese *peranakan.* The poorest, such as the enlisted men in the Royal Netherlands Indies Army, lived much as their Ambonese and Javanese counterparts did, using the common Malay of the barracks and back quarters of Batavia. Planters' assistants, petty clerks, and the wives and mistresses of Dutch officials spoke more Dutch and lived a petit-bourgeois life. At the top, Eurasians overlapped with Dutch *blijvers,* occupying high positions in the government, speaking mainly Dutch, and exemplifying the *Indisch* style of life at its most expansive. All, however, enjoyed the prestige of being European and the security of established social roles and cultural patterns.

Around 1900, the situation began to change. As *blijvers* gave way to *trekkers,* and as the *totok* Dutch as a group began to withdraw into a new all-European community, the social and cultural meaning of being European became more restricted, whatever the law said. An increasingly racist white community came to look on a darker skin as a sign of shame, jeered at fractured Dutch, and rejected *Indisch* culture as "native." Eurasians found it painfully necessary to redefine their cultural identity. Some merged into the poorer Malay-speaking population of the cities, ceasing for all practical purposes to be "Dutch." The majority, however, chose to define themselves culturally in *totok* Dutch terms, going to European primary schools and procuring whatever further Dutch-language education they could, abandoning *Indisch* ways, and speaking Malay only to their servants. This movement implied social and political, as well as cultural, pursuit of the fast-receding *totok* Dutch in the early decades of the century. For a brief period after 1912, however, one group of Eurasians attempted a different definition of themselves. In that year, E. F. E. Douwes Dekker founded the Indies Party, an avowedly revolutionary movement whose slogan was "the Indies for those who make their home there." Though his cofounders were Javanese, most of the party's few hundred members were Eurasians, like Douwes Dekker. In turning against *totok* Dutch, they were trying to establish a specifically Indies nationalism that would be broad enough to encompass Eurasians as well as modern-educated Javanese and other indigenous people.

Somewhat similar social groups had succeeded in just the same enterprise in the late-nineteenth-century Philippines, but it failed in the Indies. Mild government repression was hardly necessary; the movement limped on under a variety of names until the end of the decade and then collapsed. In the troubled year 1919, Eurasian opinion moved decisively in another direction, symbolized by the name of their major organization, the Indo-European Union, founded in that year. They had now defined themselves—as a distinct and lesser kind of Dutch, wedded to continued *totok* rule—and, like the *totok* Dutch, had withdrawn into a clearly demarcated community of their own.

There were many more Chinese than Dutch in the Indies, but they numbered only about a quarter of a million (1 percent) in 1870, a million and a quarter (2 percent) in 1930. Like the Dutch, they too were divided into *totok* and *peranakan,* and the historical development of the two elements in the early twentieth century in some ways paralleled that of their Dutch counterparts. But their internal social divisions were more elaborate, the routes of cultural change open to them were longer and more numerous, and their minority position in an alien-dominated society did not permit the kind of political allegiance to both homeland and colony simultaneously that *totok* Dutch and even Eurasians achieved easily. In all respects, then, the self-transformations of Chinese in the early twentieth century were more complex, dangerous, and exciting than those of the Dutch.

Before 1900, almost all established Chinese communities in the Indies were *peranakan,* formed originally by the intermarriage of male Chinese immigrants and local women, stabilized by the formation of all-*peranakan* families, and marked by varying degrees of accommodation to their host societies and cultures. By far the largest and most important of these was the *peranakan* community of Java. Compelled by Indies law to live in special quarters of the towns; dominated by a wealthy and often hereditary hierarchy of Dutch-appointed majors, captains, and lieutenants; organized in families whose kinship patterns were more Javan than Chinese; and originating almost exclusively from just one of the many South China speech groups, the Hokkiens, Java *peranakan* formed a clearly demarcated community. At the same time, they had a secure and important place in the larger society, for *peranakan* middlemen and shopkeepers were indispensable to peasants and townsmen, while the majors and captains ran the opium monopoly and other tax farms for the government.

In the first decade of the twentieth century, this comfortable and well-established community was rather suddenly faced with a series of converging pressures and new opportunities, and its members set forth on a quest for new cultural and social identities that is not yet concluded today. On one side, the pressures came from the establishment by *totok* Dutch, in the cities where *peranakan* lived, of a modern European way of life and a new standard of social status. On the other side, pressure came from events in China itself, as new revolutionary movements gathered strength after 1900. Emerging Chinese nationalism provided a second and more emotionally powerful model of cultural and political identification, which, like the Dutch one, made *peranakan* feel ashamed of what had a decade earlier been so satisfying a style of life.

The opportunities, as for all groups, were first of all in new schools. In the late nineteenth century, small but increasing numbers of Java *peranakan* began to go to new Christian missionary schools. It was mostly missionary-educated *peranakan* who founded the first modern pan-Chinese association, the Tiong Hoa Hwe Koan (THHK), in March 1900, and it was the THHK a year later that opened the first modern Chinese school in the Indies, in Batavia, an example quickly followed in the other major cities of Java. In such schools, *peranakan* were taught by young nationalist teachers imported from China, and they used textbooks from China. Above all, *peranakan*—who spoke only Hokkien and Malay and who were fully literate only in Malay in the Latin script—were taught in *Kuo-yü,* the Chinese national language, and they became literate in Chinese characters. They thus garbed themselves in a new cultural identity—modern, nationalist, and Chinese in the fullest sense.

The section of the *peranakan* community that set out on this route was first accompanied and then overtaken by Chinese *totok.* Rapid economic growth after 1870 brought ever-increasing numbers of Chinese immigrants to Java, as elsewhere in the Indies. In areas like East Sumatra, with no previously established *peranakan* communities, the immigrant society was *totok* in character from the beginning. On Java the established process of absorption of newcomers into the *peranakan* community continued until the turn of the century and then broke down. One reason was the steadily increasing weight of new immigrants, accompanied for the first time by substantial numbers of *totok* women, who now formed all-*totok* families more resistant to incorporation. More important, in a time of rising Chinese nationalism, *totok* had every reason to hold on to their Chinese-ness and to see *peranakan* ways as an ignoble compromise. Enrolling their children in the growing Chinese school system, they could in fact do more than hold fast, for, through education in *Kuo-yü,* they could begin to submerge their own particularisms as Hakka, Cantonese, or Teochieu in modern pan-Chinese culture.

From that process, there had emerged by about 1915 a new and specifically Chinese community in the Indies, dominated by *totok* but also incorporating substantial numbers of Chinese-educated *peranakan.* The members of this community oriented themselves politically not to the Indies but to China. They contributed to famine relief there and, at times of threat, organized boycotts against Japanese, British, or other imperialists. Even more than *totok* Dutch and Eurasians, *totok* Chinese had drawn themselves into a tight little cell in one corner of the larger Indies society.

Many *peranakan,* like Eurasians, followed the lead of their *totok* into a new national identity focused on the homeland outside the Indies. But *peranakan* were long-established residents of the Indies with deep roots there. In the twentieth century, one large group of them went to missionary schools, acquiring the knowledge of Dutch and English, and often the Christianity, which opened the way to a modern identity on European cultural grounds. A still larger group went to the government

Dutch-Chinese Schools launched in 1908. In the following years, Indies law was revised to give *peranakan* a legal position closer to Europeans, and they gained access to higher Dutch-language education, the civil service, and the various advisory legislative bodies, such as the Volksraad. Most of the new leaders of the *peranakan* community took that route, and Dutch-educated *peranakan* showed a strong tendency in the following decades to move toward white-collar occupations, government service, and the professions, while *totok* remained overwhelmingly in commerce. As the majors and captains faded away, a new *peranakan* social order appeared, headed by the best-educated—doctors, professors, and lawyers.

In a sense, these *peranakan* were perpetuating their old special community in new cultural dress. But the *peranakan* community never closed in upon itself as the *totok* Dutch, Eurasians, and *totok* Chinese did; it could still contain Dutch-educated doctors, Chinese-educated shopkeepers, and Malay-speaking traders within its broad net of family ties. A man like Kwee Kek Beng, the editor of the newspaper *Sin Po,* had had a Dutch education, was active in Chinese nationalist causes, and wrote his autobiography in *peranakan* Malay. And, in East Java in the 1930s, a small group of *peranakan* founded the Partai Tionghoa Indonesia (Chinese Indonesian Party), which supported the Indonesian nationalist cause—a portent of new *peranakan* movements to come.

The transformations among the Dutch and Chinese showed how general and powerful were the social forces at work in the Netherlands Indies in the early years of the twentieth century. They also illustrate a striking paradox, for, as these groups became more tightly interlocked within an ever more complex Indies economy, they tended to draw apart into their own private compartments. That was eventually to prove a fatal weakness, but, in the age of high colonialism, it had a more immediate significance. These dominant minorities, by thus isolating themselves from the subject population, were abdicating their power to influence developments within that population and to absorb whatever new movements and elites might emerge from it. Compelled —and freed—to seek their own new cultural identities and social roles, the weak in time found ways to be strong.

But it was a stupendous task. The Indies of the early twentieth century incorporated a whole world of indigenous societies: large and small; Islamic, Hindu-Buddhist, Christian, and animist; wet-rice growers, swidden cultivators, and traders; kingdoms and kin-groups; literate and nonliterate. There were certain commonalities in the historical experience, artistic traditions, and religious assumptions of those societies, but each had its own integrity, a distinct cultural tradition defined and enforced by its own language and shared by aristocrats and commoners alike. Members of those societies, as they sought to come to terms with modernity, had models to use, but they were foreign and difficult to translate. There were no preexisting versions of modernity for any of the indigenous societies of the Indies, let alone for all of them in common. This was something that members of those societies had to do for themselves, if they chose to, an immense job of creating and re-creating their identities.

In a population that counted 40 million in 1905 and was divided into dozens of distinct societies, the range of choices offered and paths of change to be followed were innumerable. Different societies varied widely in their need for change. The Balinese, for example, remained emphatically Balinese. Left entirely alone by Dutch planters and sugar-growers, and well satisfied with their uncommonly intricate cultural order, they reacted in quite their own way by appropriating a handful of admiring Western artists as a catalyst to bring forth new schools of Balinese painting and sculpture, an artistic revolution unparalleled in the Indies at the time. Elsewhere, Bugis and Makassarese, for example, were less bold in their experiments than their fellow Muslims on Suma-tra. In general, peasants, particularly in the larger and more stratified societies, moved more slowly than the small elites, which obtained mod-ern schooling and ventured into self-change.

Such transformations led off in many different directions, but for vir-tually all they began in one of three modes of education—in the deeper sense as well as the narrower one of schooling. One was Christian, the second Islamic, and the third was in the classrooms of modern Dutch-language schools.

Christianity had very little influence in the archipelago before 1800, but the worldwide missionary movement of the nineteenth and twenti-eth centuries spread out widely among the societies of the Indies. Mis-sions had their greatest impact in non-Islamic areas outside Java. Many of these regions were inhabited by scattered swidden-cultivating popu-lations like the numerous groups in the interior of Borneo, in central Celebes, and on the island of Flores. The missions provided the peoples there with their first opportunity to acquire literacy and the wider vision opened by a world religion—experiences that most Southeast Asians had undergone centuries or millennia earlier. Before 1940, most were fully occupied with developing the possibilities of this kind of transfor-mation: creating new and larger communal identities as Dayak, Toraja, and Florinese or building new religious and, in effect, political bulwarks against their historically exploitative Muslim neighbors.

The effects were more far-reaching among the Toba Batak in north-central Sumatra. The Toba formed a large, compact, wet-rice-growing society with a strong tradition of territorial expansion. After the 1860s, this dynamic found new expression in the channels opened up by the German Protestants of the Rhenish Mission. Younger Toba, in particu-lar, quickly sought a newly created prestige as evangelists and school teachers in mission schools. By 1917, the process had reached one cli-max with the founding of the Hatopan Kristen Batak (HKB), or Batak Christian Association, which gave concrete form to their new identity as modern Christian Bataks and which took the lead in a quarter-century struggle against the old-fashioned and authoritarian rule of the Rhenish Mission. But the HKB proved just a way-station, in the political sense at least, for it represented only a Toba Christian "nationalism" directed against an equally parochial "colonialism" of the mission. Even as it was being founded, Toba were pressing eagerly into newly established Dutch-language schools in the vicinity and spreading out in increasing numbers to the nearby Medan plantation region and to Batavia and other cities on Java. On those new frontiers, they gained jobs as civil servants, schoolteachers, and doctors and took an active part in creating wider identities.

The Islamic mode of education and self-change was far more important, if only because so many of the peoples of the Indies were at least nominally Muslim. Before 1900, with few exceptions, Islam was practiced throughout the islands as a traditional folk religion. Boys went to Kuranic classes to learn the established practices of the adult Muslim community; for this purpose, it did not matter at all that they learned to recite in a language—Arabic—that they could not understand, for that very fact assured the sanctity of the mysteries whose outward forms they were memorizing. Muslim scholars found intellectual challenge and enlightenment in their study of an immense religious literature and served in an indispensable role as legal experts and spiritual leaders. Everywhere Islam had gracefully united with local beliefs.

Life in the Indies of the early twentieth century, however, brought new experiences that became increasingly difficult to comprehend within the frame of thought provided by the traditional versions of Islam. It was not only that the more direct intrusion of a Christian government threatened or challenged the old ways. There were new opportunities as well, and, to seize them, men needed new images of who they were and what they were doing. Increasing numbers of Muslims began to doubt the adequacy of what had been perfectly satisfactory identities; in their need, they were presented with an outside model of modernity —Reform Islam, which had risen in the Middle East in the last years of the nineteenth century as a response to precisely the same urgent needs. Reform Islam stood for a return to what it called the fundamental truths of the Kuran, discarding both the accretions of medieval scholasticism and the compromises with local animism, thus clearing the way for a thoroughgoing modernization of Islam. It offered self-respect and a guide for new times without a denial of one's identity, a way to become modern while remaining Muslim. This gave it great appeal and roused strong resistance in the Islamic societies of the Indies.

These Islamic societies were diverse, and the Reform movement took very different forms in different areas. Among most of the Muslim peoples of Sumatra, for example, its development was closely associated with the old and powerful *rantau* pattern. *Rantau* has many meanings: It can refer to movement out to a frontier of settlement, to traders off seeking their fortunes in distant lands, and also to men who set out on the road to deeper religious knowledge. In all its meanings, it connotes a drive outward from one's present situation to embrace new opportunities.

In such societies, Reform Islam provided not only its general program for a Muslim modernity but also a new and wide channel for the *rantau* drive. Reform ideas supplied the base for the most important Acehnese movement of modern times, the PUSA (Persatuan Ulama Seluruh Aceh, All-Aceh Union of Religious Scholars), founded in 1939 by Daud Beureueh, which embodied a singularly intense drive to reformulate Acehnese Islam and to remake the whole of Acehnese society in that image.

A Reform movement also dominated the life of Minangkabau after 1900, vigorously attacking both Minangkabau matrilineal custom and traditional Islamic practice and arousing strong counterattacks in turn. The movement produced notable figures, such as the novelist and controversialist Hamka and Haji Agus Salim, the leading national exponent of Reform Islam in the political sphere. With PUSA, Reform Islam and the *rantau* drive were turned inward, while among the Minangkabau they were associated with expansive movements: the rubber-planting boom of the early twentieth century, and a remarkable migration of Dutch-educated intellectuals to Batavia and other cities on Java.

The religious pattern of the Javanese was different from those on Sumatra—and, for that matter, those of other peoples on the island—and consequently Reform ideas had a different role to play there. Virtually all Javanese professed themselves Muslims, but within that unity there were two distinct variants whose roots went back to the sixteenth century. The majority of Javanese, peasants and *priyayi* alike, were *abangan,* who had responded to the coming of Islam by absorbing it, along with much that was Hindu, Buddhist, or animist in origin, into a larger complex of belief—the "Javanese religion," as it is often called. The minority, the *santri,* took their self-identification as Muslims more seriously, distinguishing themselves from *abangan* by their more exacting performance of such requirements as the five daily prayers and abstinence from food and water during the daylight hours of the fasting month.

Javanese, however, place a high value on harmony; *santri* and *abangan* had lived together amicably enough for centuries. *Abangan,* after all, were Muslims too, while *santri* Islam, as taught in the *pesantren* scattered about the countryside, was a folk religion containing many pre-Islamic elements. That social harmony, like so many others, was destroyed by the relentless quest for new identities and social roles in the twentieth century.

The process began quickly enough, in the changing economic conditions of the late nineteenth century. After 1870, the steamship made it possible for much greater numbers of *santri* to make the pilgrimage to Mecca, and they returned more conscious of their Islam and wearing a modified version of Arab dress. In the rural areas, from which most came, returned *haji* often established new *pesantren,* and around them the rural *santri* community grew in numbers and piety. Some also grew in wealth: rural traders, peasants saving for the pilgrimage, *pesantren* heads using the labor of their students in fields they accumulated. While the great majority of rural *santri* remained no better off than other peasants, the accumulative ethic of the minority gave rise in time to the hostile *abangan* image of all *santri* as rich, stingy, sanctimonious "Arabs." Rural *santri*'s religious beliefs changed little in the process; they were not so much seeking a new identity as expanding the scope of an old one. But their increasing consciousness of themselves as members of a distinctly Muslim community had the same effect as the economic behavior of the richer few. Rural *santri* as a group drew slowly apart from their *abangan* neighbors.

In the longer run, this slowly expanding gap was to have profound consequences in Javanese rural society. But after 1900 it was overtaken for a time by a more dramatic development, an altogether new and deep cleavage inside the Javanese *santri* community itself. The economic changes of the late nineteenth century had affected urban *santri* more deeply than rural ones. Urban traders expanded their businesses, moving into new lines. *Santri* groups built up substantial *batik* cloth and *kretek* cigarette industries in towns like Yogyakarta, Surakarta, and Kudus. In the towns, they felt the pressure of Chinese competition; at the same time, they saw at first hand the transformations of the Chinese and the Dutch communities. By around 1900, many had come to feel the need for a new image of the world and their place in it. It was they who welcomed Reform Islam and claimed it as their own.

Most urban *santri,* particularly in the larger towns and cities, went over quickly to Reform Islam in the first two decades of the century. As they did so, they spread out from commerce and small industry to a wider range of urban occupations—as journalists, schoolteachers, and white-collar workers—laying the base for a self-confident, modern, and specifically Muslim urban community. The community's character was exemplified by the activities of its most important organization, Muhammadiyah, founded in Yogyakarta in 1912, which grew very rapidly in the following decades. Muhammadiyah was modern by its very nature, for Indies Muslims had not previously organized themselves in associations with boards of directors, branches, and the like. It carried on its work through further organizations: youth and women's associations, clinics, orphanages, and above all a large school system, which presented academic subjects along the lines of the contemporary government Dutch-language schools and taught Islam not by recital and exegesis but as a basic system of religious, ethical, and social beliefs. Most important, perhaps, Muhammadiyah soon developed branches in the non-Javanese areas of the island, in Sumatra, and elsewhere. From the beginning it was not a Javanese organization but a specifically Muslim one; the new identity it embodied transcended ethnic particularism —and traditional local variants of Islam—in the various societies of the Indies.

It also inevitably opened a wide gap within the Javanese *santri* community, as in Minangkabau and elsewhere. Everywhere in the smaller towns, and sometimes in the countryside itself, small but militant groups of modernists attacked what they called the meaningless ritual of Kuranic chanting and the quibbles of traditional scholasticism, and they demanded that Javanese Islam be purged of its non-Islamic "superstitions." Such attacks threatened the identity of rural *santri* for the first time and, in particular, challenged the leadership of *pesantren* heads and traditional scholars. They responded in kind, calling the modernists Christians and unbelievers.

The battle raged through the 1910s and 1920s; half a century later the wounds still had not fully healed. But in time traditionalists founded modern Islamic schools and modern organizations—the first and greatest of the latter, the Nahdatul Ulama, being established in 1926 precisely to use the modernists' own methods against them. For their part, modernists drew back from the more extreme of their views. Together, too, they felt the increasing pressures of new movements among *abangan* —both peasants in the countryside and the rising Dutch-educated intelligentsia in the cities.

It was the third major mode of education, in Dutch-language secular schools, that was most significant for the depth, and especially the breadth, of the transformations it engendered among the peoples of the Indies. The beginnings were slow. In the nineteenth century, the government developed a small but good system for its European nationals, but before 1900 only a handful of high-ranking "natives," such as Kartini, were allowed to attend European primary schools. The number increased in the years of the Ethical Policy, reaching 4,000 in 1905 and 6,000 in 1920. Those privileged students, still largely from the traditional elite classes in the different Indies societies, also predominated among the very small numbers of indigenous people who went on through the new European secondary schools and colleges (Engineering School, 1920; Law School, 1924; Medical School, 1927) or to study in Holland.

Meanwhile—alongside this European school system always intended primarily for the Dutch themselves—a separate government system of Native schools was growing. Most of the Native schools of the nineteenth century, as well as the very large system of village schools developed after 1907, used local languages as the medium of instruction and hence had much less cultural impact. But the "Dokter Djawa" School, which came in time to graduate fairly completely trained "native doctors," used Dutch as the language of instruction after 1875. For that reason, its few hundred students played a disproportionately large role in the political and cultural movements of the first two decades of the twentieth century. It was after 1900, however, that the government Dutch-language Native system really developed. Between 1907 and 1914, the existing Native primary-level schools evolved into Dutch Native Schools (DNS), which provided primary education for "natives" entirely in the Dutch language. During the following decade, a latticework of new schools was built above the DNS to provide higher education for a few "natives" and transfer routes to advanced training in the parallel European system. But it was the government Dutch Native Schools, with 20,000 students in 1915 and 45,000 in 1940, that were decisive—perhaps the most important single institution in twentieth-century Indies history.

Dutch-language secular education had many consequences. Most obviously it opened a new route for upward social mobility into urban positions as civil servants, teachers, white-collar workers in private business, journalists, lawyers, and doctors. It also provided a new criterion of social status, which had a double effect. On the one hand, Dutch education placed all those who had it above those who did not, graduates from the European system above those from the Native system, and so on upward to the handful who had advanced degrees from the Netherlands. It was a new, easily calculated hierarchy of standing, which put those lower down in an often painful position and left the peasant an outcaste. On the other hand, this criterion necessarily challenged the old status hierarchy, which was based, within each indigenous society, mainly on birth. A lower *priyayi* official who had an education as good as, or better than, that of the hereditary regent he served under found it difficult or unpleasant to use the humble "high" Javanese when speaking to him, as required by traditional status ranking. Virtually all of the modern movements of the early twentieth century, therefore, had a strong anti-"feudal" aspect. By the same token, the new criterion increasingly called into question the high status the Dutch inherited with their skin. The engineer Sukarno was fully as well educated as the lawyer governor-general who exiled him in 1933, but he could not possibly have attained that office. Dutch education, finally, gave easy access to the self-proving truths of modern science, to new and conflicting political visions, to whole schools of literature not necessarily better but certainly different and stimulating. More deeply, the very fact of thinking in a foreign language, as several tens of thousands came to do, imposed a new geometry on what they thought.

The experience of these changes defined, in both social and cultural terms, a new group that rose in the early-twentieth-century Indies, the secular urban intelligentsia of indigenous origin. But that educational experience did not of itself provide them with a new identity. They were no longer traditional Bugis, Minangkabau, or Javanese—though they continued to think in those languages too, with all that that implied.

Nor, evidently, in a racist Indies, were they Dutch or Eurasians or *peranakan* Chinese—though they shared a language and much else with them. Their predicament gave rise to a whole series of efforts in the early decades of the century to create new identities. This quest was not in origin a political one, but the politics of the time were very largely determined by it.

One avenue that many groups explored was that of ethnic identity redefined on a modern basis. The first and most important of the organizations formed on this basis was the Budi Utomo, founded in 1908 on the initiative of a group of Javanese students in the "Dokter Djawa" School. Throughout its twenty-seven years, Budi Utomo stood for an effort by Dutch-educated Javanese *priyayi* to create a modernized Javanese cultural foundation on which they could base a more secure self-respect and from which they could, somehow, claim a greater say in affairs. But the difficulties inherent in this project were reflected in a complicated history marked by persistent difficulty in deciding between a purely cultural program and experiments with various political postures. Budi Utomo was moderate in tone, for many of its *priyayi* members were reluctant to go too far in abandoning their traditional culture, which, among other things, assured them a high status. It often showed uncertainty in defining the identity it represented; thus it spoke frequently of "Greater Java," a notion that Sundanese and Madurese, understandably, found not at all attractive.

In all these respects, Budi Utomo was typical of numerous similar organizations established by other ethnic groups in the 1910s. Student organizations, beginning somewhat later, tended to be more militant. It is revealing that, while they continued to organize along ethnic lines, their names almost all began with the Dutch word "Jong" (young), thus neatly symbolizing the poles of their cultural and political dilemma: Jong Java, Jong Sumatranen Bond, Jong Minahassa, Jong Celebes. The Jong Islamieten Bond of the same period represented the same phase in the thinking of Dutch-educated Reform Muslims.

The Indies Party and its successor organizations represented a second avenue explored by some of the Dutch-educated. Two important members of the intelligentsia, Suwardi Suryaningrat and Tjipto Mangunkusumo, were cofounders of the party, playing a major role in its early life. Few other non-Eurasians ever joined the party, but it exerted a wide influence nevertheless, for, at a time when other organizations were speaking of self-improvement and a greater degree of autonomy, it came boldly forth with a demand for the end of Dutch rule. What was for Eurasians their last chance, in effect, to escape a cultural and political second place was for Javanese and others their first chance to experiment with a much broader definition of their political identity. "Indies" nationalism—which included Eurasians and in principle Dutch *blijvers* and Chinese *peranakan*—did not long survive, but the idea of nationalism did.

Unlike the Indies Party and such ethnic associations as Budi Utomo, the Sarekat Islam (Islamic Union) did not stand for any single identity, however loosely defined. Its significance was precisely the opposite. It was the first mass movement in Indies history (the only one before 1945), and, at one time or another in its fourteen years, groups of almost every persuasion enrolled under its banner. The extraordinary confusion and excitement of its career reflected the confusion and venturesome spirit of the times.

Sarekat Islam (SI) was founded in 1912, the same year as Muhammadiyah, and by members of the same social group, the urban Reformist *santri*. Both were influenced by the new winds blowing through the Chinese community at the collapse of the Manchu dynasty in 1911; urban *santri,* who had close contacts with Chinese, felt both a threat and a stimulus to their own growing sense of community. But while Muhammadiyah stood for the religious interests of such *santri,* the Sarekat Islam—founded by a prominent Surakarta *batik* merchant, Haji Samanhudi—stood mainly for their economic interests at a time of increasing pressure from Chinese wholesalers and competitors.

But the SI did not long remain confined to its original economic aims and to the particular social group those aims served. In a Muslim Java and a predominantly Muslim Indies, "Sarekat Islam" was a rallying cry, implying a wider movement for change. The organization quickly attracted members of a second group, disaffected intelligentsia, which within a year had taken over leadership. The most important of them was Umar Said Tjokroaminoto, a Dutch-educated *priyayi* and an extraordinarily eloquent orator who was largely responsible for the mass following that SI quickly acquired.

Two other important groups soon emerged within the SI's leadership. One was a small group of Dutch-educated Reformist Muslims around Haji Agus Salim, who became Tjokroaminoto's right-hand man and the leader of the organization's specifically Muslim wing. The other was an equally small and able group of socialists. A handful of *totok* Dutch immigrants had established an Indies Social–Democratic Association (ISDA) in Semarang in 1914, and their views—Western but anticolonial and anticapitalist—had the same formative influence on some Dutch-educated Javanese and others as reformist doctrines from Cairo had on urban *santri.* Some, such as Alimin Prawirodirdjo, Darsono, and a young railway employee, Semaun, joined the ISDA. Semaun and others were active in the radical wing of the growing trade-union movement of the late 1910s. From that organizational base, working mainly through the Semarang branch of the Sarekat Islam, they came to play an increasingly important role in the central SI after 1916.

The SI's mass following, which was what attracted these and other disparate and often hostile groups to the SI leadership, was not created by their efforts. It developed, instead, out of a curious interplay among three elements: government policy, inchoate folk feeling, and Sarekat

Islam, acting not as an organization with a program but as a symbol and a voice—especially the voice of Tjokroaminoto himself. The Ethical government of those years was inclined to look indulgently on "native" movements for self-improvement, and despite strong pressure from Dutch opinion, it gave the SI wide latitude. Tjokroaminoto spoke of wrongs to be righted, and millions flocked to follow his charismatic lead: urban *santri* in Kudus, traditional rural *santri* in West Java, *abangan* peasants, Muslims throughout Sumatra, the Celebes, and elsewhere, even Toba Christians. They had grievances—a greater number than usual, because those were rapidly changing times—and they reported them to local SI branches in a great flood, expecting redress. Moreover, the Sarekat Islam took on a messianic significance. Tjokroaminoto's name, by what appeared to be more than coincidence, was one of the traditional Javanese names of the expected deliverer, Prabu Heru Tjokro. SI membership cards were widely believed to guarantee salvation. Tjokroaminoto criticized *priyayi* officials, even the regents and the remote Dutch government itself, and they appeared too weak to stop him. That could mean only one thing: The *wahyu*, the magical potency of rule, was passing to new hands.

Sarekat Islam membership grew to more than 2 million in 1919, but the figures meant little, since only a few tens of thousands were members in the sense of joining an organization, while many more than 2 million felt the pull of what was a great folk movement. Tjokroaminoto and other members of the leadership felt that pull too; SI propaganda became steadily more militant between 1916 and 1919. So, by the same token, did the government. A number of local rebellious incidents in 1919 broke its tolerance forever. In short order, some members of the central SI and the ISDA were brought to trial or exiled. Local officials, both Dutch and indigenous, harassed SI branches and repressed strikes everywhere.

The year 1919 marked the end of the Ethical Policy. Some of its slogans and programs remained, but from then until the end of colonial rule in 1942, the government never hesitated to suppress whatever it considered subversive native movements. That year also marked the end of the Sarekat Islam as a mass movement. Its founders, the non-Dutch-educated urban *santri,* had already largely gone back to Muhammadiyah. Now the secular intelligentsia also withdrew to join other organizations and to look in other directions. And much of the folk following simply looked the other way, not really leaving because they had never really joined.

What was left was the organization's symbolic name, its leader Tjokroaminoto, and the more deeply committed fraction of its original mass following—mostly local leaders and vernacular-educated men who could no longer be content with village life but lacked the credentials for good urban jobs. The two remaining wings—Muslim and socialist—of the central leadership immediately fell into bitter dispute.

As they did so, each found it necessary to define its political identity more clearly. The socialists were more successful. As non-Dutch members of what had been a Dutch-founded organization with a Dutch name (the ISDA), and likewise at best nominal Muslims in an organization called Sarekat Islam, they had good reason to sharpen their self-image. Meanwhile, the Russian Revolution provided an attractive new model and the Comintern a strong framework in which to reorient themselves. In 1920, the socialists, still including a few not yet exiled Dutch, changed the name of their organization to the Perserikatan Komunis di India (PKI, Indies Communist Party) and joined the Comintern. They thus defined for themselves a new and explicitly international identity. Haji Agus Salim's Muslim wing also moved in an internationalist direction during the early 1920s. It needed an ideological counterweight to the PKI and found it in the worldwide pan-Islamic movement of the time, focused on the idea of restoring Kemal Ataturk as the caliph of all Islam.

The Muslim wing soon won Tjokroaminoto and control over the name Sarekat Islam, forcing the PKI out of the central SI in 1921. In the course of the next few years, on the other hand, the PKI gradually gained the support of the great majority of the remaining branches and followers. But the cost of the intense struggle was high for all concerned. In many Javanese areas, the dispute, expressed in new ideological terms, gave a new and bitter meaning to the slowly growing gap between rural *santri* and *abangan*—a focusing of opposed identities that was to bear terrible fruit after 1945. And elsewhere the tension kept alive the fervor of the remaining faithful, who stumbled on toward the final disaster. A scattered and easily suppressed revolt broke out in December 1926, led in most areas by local PKI members. In the repression that followed, the government rounded up 13,000 "subversives" of various political colors, exiling 1,000 to the malarial swamps of New Guinea. The PKI was broken for a generation, Sarekat Islam was left holding the by now dead cause of the caliphate. It was the end of the great folk movement of the SI and the end of a political era.

Over the wreckage of the old movement, the idea of Indonesia rose suddenly and, within a few quick years, implanted itself forever in the minds of men who now became Indonesians.[52] In July 1927, a small group led by Sukarno founded the Partai Nasional Indonesia (PNI, Indonesian National Party). As its name made clear, the PNI stood for a new political identity that on the one hand transcended and encompassed the many societies of the Indies, and on the other declared the end of waiting for "an airplane from Moscow or a Caliph from Istanbul." In October 1928, a congress of youth organizations brought the idea forth in one echoing phrase, "one nation—Indonesia, one people —Indonesian, one language—Indonesian." The congress also adopted the red over white national flag as its own and sang for the first time the newly composed national anthem, "Indonesia Raya." The wave spread swiftly through public life: The SI became the Partai Sarekat Islam Indonesia, Budi Utomo merged into a new Partai Indonesia Raya, hundreds of new organizations with "Indonesia" in their titles were established in the next few years. More deeply, in the privacy of their own thoughts, virtually all modern-educated men and women came in those years to identify themselves as Indonesians.

The idea of Indonesia spread so easily, once launched, that it seemed to later historians as if it had always existed, if not actually explicitly then inchoate in the hearts of the people. But it was, in fact, a new creation, the product of a great and difficult leap of the imagination. The idea of Indonesia required the denial of the political meaning of the societies into which the first Indonesians had been born. It required also the acceptance of the new reality of the Dutch Indies, and then the transmuting of that into "Indonesia." In the first decades of the century, in effect, only the Dutch-educated had the kind of experience that made this creative leap possible and ultimately necessary. In Dutch-language schools, members of all ethnic groups underwent the same transforming education together and came out with as much in common as any had with the non-Dutch-educated of their own ethnic background. The jobs they took were mostly unknown to the traditional societies, with meaning only in an Indies-wide frame of reference. The modern cities where they studied and worked were in many ways closer to each other than to their respective hinterlands.

Even so, up to the mid-1920s, the politically active few among them joined organizations such as Budi Utomo, Sarekat Islam, and Jong Minahassa, which were certainly not Indonesian. It was a tiny minority of a minority, students in Holland, who actually took the lead in creating the idea of Indonesia. In Holland, they were liberated from the daily reality of the Dutch-run Indies and enabled to view it as a whole but not necessarily as the Indies. They were also liberated more fully from ethnic ties; it was inconceivable for their dozens, among millions of Dutch, to divide up into Jong Java, Jong Celebes, and the rest. Their first organization, founded in 1908, was called the Indies Association, itself an ready and clear indication of a common identity. The decision in 1922 to reconstitute that organization as the Perhimpunan Indonesia (PI), or Indonesian Association, was the first unambiguous declaration of the birth of the Indonesian identity.

The term "Indonesia" was beginning to be used in discussion at home as well, but it took several years for the implications to sink in and for the PI's program to be widely accepted. Students, with less stake in established organizations and identities, responded more quickly; two youth groups with "Indonesia" in their titles and straight nationalist programs were founded in 1927 before the PNI. But it was the PNI—catching the growing trend at the right moment and riding on the remarkable personality of Sukarno—that brought Indonesian nationalism into the open in the Indies and did most to ensure its success.

Indonesian political life in the 1930s took place in a context of rigorous police surveillance and infrequent but effective repression, which made mass movements impossible and helped to keep a majority of civil servants and others out of public activity. Within that narrow political space, great numbers of different organizations grew, split, merged, and quarreled among themselves, but not on fundamentals. Some ethnic associations continued actively, but, with few exceptions, they came to see themselves as representing parts of a larger Indonesian whole rather than separate entities. Muslim organizations, insofar as their activities were political, had given up the pan-Islamic movement, seeking instead to define Indonesia in Islamic terms. The small minority of "non's" (noncooperators), who refused to work within colonial institutions, such as the largely powerless electoral bodies of the time, fiercely attacked the great majority of "co's," who were willing to do so. But the controversy concerned only tactics. When the Japanese arrived in 1942, the members of the urban elite—and to a great degree the hereditary elites most closely attached to the Dutch—shared a common and by then well-established Indonesian national identity.

During the same two decades in which the political idea of Indonesia arose and gained general acceptance among the modern-educated elite, a parallel process of creating an Indonesian national culture was under way. The major symbol of the movement was the transmutation of the universal Malay of the islands into the national language, Indonesian—an act of re-creation strikingly similar to the political one and quite as significant. But in other respects there were greater differences. The political idea of Indonesia had emerged in the minds of men who had their roots in one or another of the many regional societies and who through education—primarily in Dutch—had grasped the reality of the modern Indies. At that point, they were bipolitical, for they were at home in two different political worlds—fairly comfortably in the case of the Ambonese and Minahassans and the traditional elites close to the Dutch, uncomfortably in the case of the new urban intelligentsia. But when the leap had been made and the Netherlands Indies redefined as Indonesia, it was quite easy for the intelligentsia to commit themselves unambiguously to that new political identity. The Indies as a working system was already there; they needed only to appropriate it as their own, first symbolically and later actually. In so doing, they also directly served their own political interests, since they would be the ones who would have the best opportunity of rising to political leadership in an independent Indonesia.

The same education had also made them bicultural, specifically bilingual, in their home languages and in Dutch. This tension, however, was not so easily surmounted. On the one side, they could not simply decide to stop thinking in Javanese or Madurese or to erase the cultural assumptions of their childhood, as they could change their political commitments. On the other side, they could not simply rename Dutch "Indonesian," nor could they ever take over Dutch culture from its original possessors to make it theirs only, as they could hope to do with the political unit, the Dutch Indies.

It was out of this tension that the Indonesian language was born, what one writer has aptly called "Revolutionary Malay" and "an enterprise for the mastery of a gigantic cultural crisis." Malay was in many ways highly appropriate for the role it was to play. It was the home language of only a few scattered peoples in the Indies, and thus it had the great political advantage of belonging to no one. In another sense, Malay belonged to all, for it had been the lingua franca of commerce and Islam in the whole archipelago for centuries. As such it had many virtues: flexibility, a "democratic" character marked by the absence of elaborate status distinctions, a simplicity that left it open to the infusion of modern terms and concepts.

Those attributes had already given Malay wide currency in the century or so before 1920. The Dutch had used it for convenience as a secondary language of administration; *peranakan* Chinese used it for commerce and also in their homes, and so did most Eurasians; from the very beginning, around 1900, the indigenous press had used it almost exclusively. It was quite natural, therefore, for the emerging Indonesians of the 1920s to adopt it as their national language and to rename it Indonesian—a vessel into which to pour their discontents and their hopes.

The very qualities that made Malay so suitable for transformation to Indonesian, however, also made this a precarious enterprise in its first two decades, and in some ways long after. A modern literature in Indonesian began to appear from the 1920s, mainly from writers connected with the government-run popular publishing house, Balai Pustaka, and from the Indonesian literary journal *Pudjangga Baru* of the 1930s. But it is remarkable how many of the authors were Sumatrans, especially Minangkabau, whose language is closely related to Malay; it proved difficult for Javanese and others to do creative work in the national language. The public life of Indonesian organizations was conducted almost entirely in Indonesian, but few thought in it; committee meetings, draft writings, and most of the private life of the intelligentsia continued to be carried on in Dutch, or a regional language. Moreover, only a very small part of the Indies school system of the time used Indonesian as the language of instruction. Indeed, before 1942, it was used only in the Taman Siswa school system, founded by Ki Hadjar Dewantoro in 1922, and some of the informal and quasi-political "wild schools" of the 1930s, which might qualify as the beginnings of a fourth major mode of education for modern Indonesians. Meanwhile, students who were Indonesian by political conviction and committed to the ideal of an Indonesian national culture, continued like their elders to be educated largely in Dutch. By the end of colonial rule, the Indonesian cultural identity, unlike the political one, had only been sketched in principle and was as yet fully practiced only in limited circles.

In a larger sense, however, the same was true of both. The idea of Indonesia, in both the political and the cultural sense, had been achieved and had set down its roots. But it was still confined to a very small proportion of the population, those who had themselves been transformed in one of the modes of modern education: Dutch, Muslim, Christian for a few, and Indonesian for even fewer. Beyond and around them remained the mass of the peasants, still living mainly in the traditional political and cultural worlds defined by the languages of the many societies of the islands. In fact, one of the chief consequences of the remarkable changes of the previous forty years had been to open up a new and dangerously wide gulf between the Indonesian elite and the folk of the land, whom they also called Indonesians.

# 28

# Vietnam

RADICAL absorption of Western institutions and philosophies, a growing individualism among the elite, and the appearance of strains
between old values and new ones were not prominent features of Vietnamese life before 1900. If nationalism in the Southeast Asian context
means ideologies that simultaneously stress the rediscovery and preservation of a distinctly non-Western cultural identity and the assimilation
of modern Western material techniques and revolutionary ideas, then
Vietnamese resistance to French colonialism before the 1900s was not
nationalistic but a compound of xenophobia and Confucian loyalism. It
was nonetheless a vital forerunner of Vietnamese nationalism. It is
desirable, perhaps, to distinguish between prenationalistic traditionalist
ideologies of resistance and change-absorbing ideologies of resistance in
modern Vietnamese history.

Southern resistance to the French conquest of "Cochinchina" in the
1860s had been led by men of different backgrounds: sons of court military commanders (Truong Cong Dinh), scholars (Nguyen Huu Huan),
and fishermen (Nguyen Trung Truc). By the summer of 1861, the most
famous of these leaders, Truong Cong Dinh, had recruited a volunteer
army of perhaps ten thousand men to fight the French. Southern political self-consciousness was also stimulated in the 1860s by the celebrated
"writing-brush war" between two southern scholars, Ton Tho Tuong
and Phan Van Tri. Tuong collaborated with the French, serving them as
a provincial official and political middleman. Tri, on the other hand,
invoked the Confucian tradition that "the loyal minister does not serve
two princes," declining French invitations to serve in the Cochinchina
colonial government. The two men exchanged brilliant, heavily allegor-
ical poems justifying their respective positions of collaboration and
resistance in a savage polemical battle that was designed not as private
correspondence but as an appeal to the public opinion of the southern
scholar class as a whole. The outstanding southern apologist of collaboration with the French, Tuong went so far as to compare himself to a
woman (Sun Fu-jen) in the medieval Chinese novel *Romance of the Three
Kingdoms (San kuo chih yen i)* who must live with her husband (the
French) even though he is the archenemy of her own father (the Vietnamese court). Tri, in turn, argued in a poetic response that the obligations of a woman to her husband and of a man to his political morality

were intrinsically incomparable, and that Tuong's use of *Three Kingdoms* political mythology to objectify—or give an artificial historicity to— transparent time-serving was unconvincing.

From the 1870s to the 1890s in northern and central Vietnam, the provincial intelligentsia swung between philosophic disillusionment and militant anti-Catholic xenophobia. A provincial governor-general who was also one of the most sensitive writers in Vietnam in the 1880s, Nguyen Khuyen, saw the Vietnamese court's collapse not so much in terms of technological inferiority as in terms of a strange moral paradox: namely, that until 1885 France had conquered separate regions of Vietnam while outflanking, rather than attacking, the traditional structure of political loyalties, which remained oddly untouched at the very moment that the state was losing its sovereignty. For until 1885, active resistance to the French had often meant disloyalty to the negotiation-prone court. Analyzing the conquest, Khuyen focused upon the growing discrepancy between forms (the mandarin class was still intact, with its books, gowns, and seals) and realities (it had lost its power and supposed moral invulnerability). As Khuyen put it of himself, in a famous "self-satire" written perhaps about 1885: "When I open my mouth, I speak strongly and with a bookish authority. Yet my soft, flaccid lips can also drink me into drunken stupors. When I think of myself I am disgusted with myself, yet even with all this . . . my name has appeared upon the gold examination list."[54]

After the death of the Tu-duc emperor in 1883, an anti-French "war party" of officials led by a strongman regent named Ton That Thuyet became the masters of Vietnamese court politics. Thuyet and his allies disposed of a succession of youthful emperors (Duc-duc, Hiep-hoa, Kien-phuc) in 1883–1884 but were unable to block the establishment of the French protectorate over northern and central Vietnam. In July 1885, however, after launching an unsuccessful surprise attack against the first French *résident supérieur* for central Vietnam, Thuyet fled from Hue, taking the Ham-nghi boy emperor with him. He now had Ham-nghi issue a decree calling for general insurrection in the provinces. Although the French captured Ham-nghi in 1888, transported him to exile in Algeria, and found another prince to serve as emperor at Hue (Dong-khanh, 1885–1889), the decree finally galvanized the provincial elite into action. Their movements of resistance to the French, which began in 1885 and merged eventually with the newer nationalist struggle, rallied initially under the slogan "aid the king" *(can vuong)*, a Sino-Vietnamese adaptation of a Chinese concept more than twenty centuries old.

The two most celebrated leaders of the provincial resistance movements were Phan Dinh Phung in the Ha Tinh area and Hoang Hoa Tham in the northern mountains. "Aid the king" partisanship had a character both ideological and racial-political. Its theme was to "exterminate the religion and drive out the French," the former objective being accomplished by the indiscriminate slaughter of Vietnamese Catholics. The movements, heavily dependent upon their leaders, were fragmented by region. High-ranking provincial officials were often less responsive to "aid the king" sentiments than were notables on the outer fringes of the bureaucracy—village chiefs, former officials, examination system students. In at least five provinces, the governors and financial and judicial commissioners fled, were imprisoned, or were murdered by "aid the king" bands. One consequence of the royalist movement of 1885 was, therefore, the near-collapse of the indigenous provincial bureaucracy, which French colonialists were never completely able to restore qualitatively. A second fateful consequence of the movement was its aggravation of Vietnamese Catholics' traditions and feelings of separateness.

The "aid the king" movement was ethnocentric without having any real concept of Vietnam as a nation-state in competition with other nation-states. Authentic nationalism, however, emerged after 1900, receiving its inspiration by way of China. By 1900, the works of Rousseau, Voltaire, and Montesquieu and of Social Darwinists like Herbert Spencer had begun to appear in China in classical Chinese translations. Since Vietnamese scholars could still easily read classical Chinese but rarely any European languages, they first became familiar with European ideas as translated by Chinese intellectuals like Yen Fu. Two Chinese ideologues in particular enjoyed a tremendous popularity in Vietnam in the early 1900s through their writings—K'ang Yu-wei and Liang Ch'i-ch'ao, leaders of the abortive 1898 reform movement in Peking. Liang's works were certainly sources from which a few Vietnamese scholars at this time gained an awareness that the world was not, as they had thought, a place of harmony governed by a hierarchy of the unequal but rather a battleground of competition between strong and weak but legally equal nations. Liang's example helped Vietnamese reformers to discard some of their Confucian outlook and to adopt social Darwinist concepts instead. Here was the beginning of an important change in values.

The two giants of early nationalist politics were Phan Boi Chau (1867–1940) and Phan Chau Trinh (1871–1926). The two men came from different regions and further diverged in that Chau flirted with revolutionary monarchism while Trinh became an antimonarchical democrat. Chau, born into a Confucian scholar family, organized an "aid the king" military company in 1885 and was, in a sense, a bridge to the later nationalistic age. Although he entered the examination system and passed the regional examinations in 1900, he fell under the spell of Liang Ch'i-ch'ao, embarking upon a lifetime of anticolonial activities. In 1902–1903 he wrote a tract entitled "A New Book about the Tears of Blood of the Ryukyu Islands," perhaps the first book ever written in Vietnam expressing the nationalistic idea that all Vietnamese were fellow countrymen who should be united in love of country. At the same time, the indirect model of the Ryukyus, recently annexed by Japan, was used to persuade other members of the mandarin class of the evils of the loss of independence. In another tract, "Idolizing Beautiful Personages," Chau exalted the story of George Washington, arguing that Washington had become a soldier in the British army so that he could acquire the proper methods and background for fighting it. One moral was that Vietnamese revolutionaries should attempt to infiltrate the Indochina colonial militia in order to enlighten Vietnamese militiamen ignorantly serving the French.

After the Japanese victory in the Russo-Japanese War, from 1905 until about 1912, the encouraging Meiji Japanese example of progressive, modernizing monarchism became paramount in Vietnamese revolutionary politics. The most consistent Vietnamese admirer of the Japanese model—of nationalism and modernization combined with a "restored" monarchy—was probably Prince Cuong De (1882–1951), a descendant of Prince Canh, the eldest son of Gia-long, who had visited Paris in 1787. In a polemic he wrote in classical Chinese, Cuong De proclaimed that French rule in Vietnam was impermanent and that the Japanese army would help him recover the country. By 1908, two hundred Vietnamese students had gone to Japan to study at Japanese universities. Phan Boi Chau himself, by this time the leader of a political group known as the "Renovation Society" (Duy Tan Hoi) initiated this so-called Eastern Travel (Dong Du) Movement, arriving in Japan in 1905. He immediately came under the tutelage of Liang Ch'i-ch'ao, who was living in exile in Japan as the editor of a Chinese newspaper published there, and wrote, with help from Liang, a history of Vietnam's recent loss of independence. Copies of the book were smuggled back to Vietnam by returning Vietnamese students, who formed, in Saigon, Hanoi, My-Tho, and other places, secret regional organizations of the "Renovation Society" that went by the names of hotels, business cooperatives, and village associations. The disguises were intended to fool the colonial secret police, for whom liberty, equality, and fraternity were not adoptable ideals in Vietnam.

The Dong Du movement itself lost its momentum in 1908–1909 when the Japanese government, responding to French diplomatic pressure, formally expelled the Vietnamese students. But the real climax of those early stirrings of Vietnamese nationalism had come not in Japan but in Hanoi, with the opening there of the famous Dong Kinh Free School in March 1907. Indeed, the Dong Kinh Free School marks one of the major watersheds of the modern Vietnamese revolution. As an institution, it was a Vietnamese imitation of Keio School, later Keio University, in Tokyo, founded in 1868. It was Vietnam's first university. Education was free to all comers, the expenses of the school being paid by patriotic elite families in northern Vietnam. At its height, it attracted about a thousand students. It had a number of divisions specializing in "education," "literature," "economics," and, significantly, "propaganda." It remained open for less than a year, since French colonial authorities suppressed it in November 1907, arresting some of its leaders and banishing them to the prison island of Poulo Condore.

Expressing the dogmatism of cultural revolutionaries in its most fastidious form, teachers at the Dong Kinh Free School commenced their mission by attacking the use of Chinese characters in Vietnam. They demanded the use of romanized Vietnamese instead, because it would allow the elite to teach literacy to, and communicate with, Vietnamese peasants, and thus win the mass support that eluded them as long as they isolated themselves by writing esoterically in classical Chinese. Dong Kinh teachers also attacked the Confucian civil service examinations, which perpetuated an anachronistic elite culture and produced mandarins, untainted by nationalism, who would serve the puppet court and thus the colonialists. Since the traditional institutions had been captured by the French, they had to be undermined, Yet the sudden reversal of values was indicated by the fact that the school's principal, Luong Van Can, held a degree from the very examination system he was attacking. Although the examinations survived until 1918–1919, they received their death blow in 1907 from the Dong Kinh scholars, who now molded the opinion of the more enterprising students. The program of the Dong Kinh School did not exclude anticolonial activism: Its vice-principal, Nguyen Quyen, and some of his colleagues were implicated in a plot to poison French army officers as a means of seizing Hanoi. Above all, the Dong Kinh School pioneered the teaching in Vietnam of all the newest Western theories of the nation, of the social contract and the general will, of evolution. It even called for the adoption of Western clothing as a means of losing old-fashioned appearances. One of the jingles that students at the school recited, the "Cut Your Hair Now Song," suggested: "Your left hand should clasp a comb, your right hand should clutch a pair of scissors. Cut off your bun of hair at the back now. . . . Do it leisurely so that your haircut will be skillful. Cast away your stupidities, throw away your foolishness. Today we'll have a haircut, tomorrow we'll have a shave."[55]

After the expulsion of Vietnamese students from Japan, and after the October 1911 revolution in China, the Chinese model of revolutionary change became more attractive to Vietnamese nationalists. In February 1912, Phan Boi Chau and more than a hundred other Vietnamese, in exile in China, replaced the "Renovation Society" with a new organization called the Vietnamese "Revival Society" (Quang Phuc Hoi). The purpose of the organization, it was decided after a vote (and despite Chau's own monarchism), was to create a democratic republic in Vietnam similar to the one Sun Yat-sen was trying to achieve in China. South China Kuomintang leaders like Hu Han-min gave financial aid to the "Revival Society." More important, the society decided to create its own army in order to liberate Vietnam, drawing its military cadres from Vietnamese graduates of cadet schools in China and Japan. The strategy of reconquering Vietnam from China border bases, crucial to nationalist history, was born at this time. But despite a windfall the army received in 1915, when the German consul in Siam supplied it with 10,000 piasters, it remained bedeviled by a lack of funds. Chau decided that a premature uprising in Vietnam, even if it were unsuccessful, would garner enough publicity to improve the movement's financial prospects. The attacks the army did launch in 1915, from South China, against seemingly vulnerable centers in the north (Mong Cai, Lang Son) were badly defeated. It was typical of the lack of power of the "Revival Society" army—a far-flung, tenuous organization with cells scattered from Yunnan to Hanoi—that its own internal circumstances and needs as an organization, and not Vietnam's inviting revolutionary potentialities, had dictated its 1915 insurrectionism.

Furthermore, Phan Boi Chau himself was a Confucian revolutionary, more at home with Mencius than with Montesquieu. As he wrote in his book, *Khong hoc dang (The Lamp of Confucian Scholarship)*, he admired the unhurried mythological "democracy" of the Chinese sage-emperors, who acknowledged that their throne belonged to the people, not to themselves. What was wrong with colonial Vietnam, in his eyes, was not just its inability to modernize itself but its loss as well of the self-regulating moral education and social rituals of its classical past. It now had the worst of both worlds: Its residual Eastern spirit of "government by men" had long since disappeared, yet the colonial regime had not given it all the requisite institutions of "government by law"—habeas corpus, labor codes, taxation through genuine representation, and others. With its ossified Confucian education, its corruption, and its arbitrary political controls, it was a society neither of perfectly preserved cultural obsolescences nor of freely acquired constitutional modernities, but an eccentric half-way house between two civilizations.

The other father of early Vietnamese nationalism, Phan Chau Trinh, was a more straightforward advocate of a Western-style written constitution and of a republican presidency, whose incumbent could be impeached. After being active as the sponsor of a celebrated tax resistance movement in central Vietnam in 1908, Trinh spent the 1911–1925 period in France, sometimes in prison. He was especially famous in the 1920s, both in France and in Vietnam, for his attacks upon the concept of monarchy in general ("the emperor is the man who takes other people's rights and makes them his own, who takes public powers and makes them private powers") and upon the Khai-dinh emperor (who reigned from 1916 to 1925) in particular. When Trinh died in the spring of 1926, his funeral in Saigon turned into an unprecedented mass demonstration, with Vietnamese students striking their classes all over the country in order to attend memorial gatherings. A new phase of nationalism, involving greater popular participation than that of the Phan Boi Chau–Phan Chau Trinh era, was now at hand.

Before 1926, Vietnamese nationalism had faced two significant limitations. First, the surviving Confucian mystique of public service, the desire of literate Vietnamese not to rebel but to acquire government positions, perfectly suited the purposes of the French. Nationalists had to prove that the colonial regime was using educated Vietnamese, in the words of Phan Boi Chau, as "bottles for storing French wine in, as clotheshangers for hanging French clothes on, as puppets for sitting in French cars and living in French buildings," and that entering the civil service was not, as in the past, a legitimate means of social advancement but rather a form of enslavement to an alien colonial power.[56] The absence of many occupational opportunities for Vietnamese youth outside the civil service and the failure of industry and commerce to develop extensively under indigenous control further undermined their cause.

Second, the decline of the monarchy as the unifying symbol of Vietnamese society, the administrative fragmentation of Vietnam into three regions and sixty provinces, and the efficiency of the French secret police combined to make it difficult for Vietnamese politicians to build nationwide associations or movements of any kind. It was characteristic of a situation in which patriotic mass mobilization seemed hardly possible that the term "socialism" *(chu nghia xa hoi)* became very popular among nationalists by the 1920s; instead of suggesting specific policies, like state control of economic enterprises or expropriation of land owned by landlords, to them the term simply represented a gospel of togetherness, an ideal of collective action. Phan Chau Trinh noted in 1925:

> In Europe, socialism is so extremely popular and so greatly developed, yet people over here are indifferent to it like sleepers who do not know anything. . . . If you have understood how to live, then you must protect each other—in the old days even our forefathers understood it. Only through that did the expressions arise: "Nobody breaks chopsticks which are in a bundle," and "many hands make a big repercussion."

He commented that in the ancient period "the Vietnamese people knew group action and . . . their situation was not like the current deplorable one of mutual abandonment. . . . In a village today, there may be a hundred people, but the relationships of people on this side of the village with people on the other side are all magnetized by considerations of power." He concluded that "if we want the Vietnamese nation one day to achieve freedom and independence, then before all else the Vietnamese people must have community spirit and action. But if we want to have community spirit and action, is there anything better than to preach socialism among the Vietnamese people?"[57]

By the late 1920s and early 1930s, Confucian familism had begun to dissolve, and the individual had begun to be less dependent upon his elders and other relatives. While such a development temporarily

increased that fragility of social relationships which Trinh had condemned, it also reduced the attractions of the civil service career as a
means of satisfying traditional family (rather than individual) ambitions. In his controversial novel, *Doan tuyet (A Severance of Ties)* the brilliant writer Nhat Linh, founder of the influential Self-Reliance Literary
Group (Tu luc van doan), attacked the passivity created in other family
members by the absolute authority of the traditional family head and
warned that Vietnam was falling behind, that "in all the Far Eastern
countries, Japan, China, and Siam, the scope of the family now is no
longer what it was in the past."[58]

In 1927, the Nationalist Party (Kuomintang) came to power in China
as a result of Chiang Kai-shek's "Northern Expedition." The Chinese
Revolution seemed finally to have supplied Vietnamese political ideologues with a definitive, conclusive model of a revolutionary party suitable to East and Southeast Asia. In December 1927, a Vietnamese
Nationalist Party (known as the Quoc dan dang, the Sino-Vietnamese
equivalent of the Chinese term *kuo-min-tang*, and hereafter referred to as
the VNQDD) was secretly created in Hanoi. It grew out of a small
Hanoi book club, whose purpose had been to write and translate, and
above all to publish, books that could be cheaply purchased by a wide
audience. As of 1927, the VNQDD had a secret society cast, using the
traditional method of sworn brotherhood, including a ritual act before
an altar, to cement its membership. A new recruit had to be introduced
by two party members, who guaranteed him. Many of its idealistic but
inexperienced founding members were students from higher-level commercial schools of the Hanoi area, like the party chairman himself,
Nguyen Thai Hoc (1901–1930). A feature of the VNQDD, from the
very beginning, seems to have been the immobility of its borrowed
political symbols. Although it held discussions with other revolutionary
groups, including the early Communists, in attempts to unify the Viet
namese nationalist movement, agreement foundered upon two issues.
First, the VNQDD rather incautiously insisted that the central committee of any unified party should operate inside colonial Vietnam,
whereas the Communists, in Canton, Hong Kong, and Siam, preferred
to operate outside. Second, the VNQDD's deference to the prestige of
its Chinese model was so literal-minded that it balked at entering any
amalgamation of nationalist groups that would force it to sacrifice its
name.

The structure of the VNQDD was a secondhand copy of Leninist
democratic centralism (collective discussions of party policy at many
levels, combined with the hierarchical imperative that the lower ranks
of the party obey the higher ranks), an imitation of the Chinese
Kuomintang's own incomplete reflection of Russian Communist organization. There were, on paper, local cells, provincial committees,
regional committees, and a central committee at the summit. A party

rule insisted that the executive of each group, from local cells to the central committee, be elected or re-elected every six months—a utopian organizational requirement for a secret, illegal revolutionary party under police surveillance. Unlike its Chinese namesake, the VNQDD lacked the support of a large treaty-port merchant class, of a group like the Shanghai bankers who could combine nationalism with specific, pragmatically defined non-Communist political objectives. Perhaps partly for this reason, the VNQDD also lacked any specific image of what future Vietnamese society should be like after colonialism had been overthrown. In its three-stage revolutionary program of the late 1920s, stage one was the "embryo period" when new members were recruited, stage two was the "strategy preparation period," and stage three, the final stage, was the "destruction period" of the colonial regime. The very idea of violent revolution had become an end in itself. The party newspaper was called *The Soul of Revolution (Hon cach mang)*, and a whole subcommittee of the party central committee was charged with "assassinations," the murders of key colonial authorities. The ghost of Blanqui reigned with that of Sun Yat-sen.

By the 1920s and 1930s, the Vietnamese reaction to French colonialism exhibited a dichotomy of form between northern political parties and southern religious movements. Of the latter, the Cao Dai religion, claiming converts at the rate of a thousand a day by 1926–1927 and preaching the virtues of spiritualism, Confucian piety, and vegetarianism, displayed an anticolonial bias of a conservative kind. (The term Cao Dai means "high platform," a platform so high that it has no roof; above it exists the Supreme Being, which cannot be designated by any one name and which expresses itself in this world only through a medium.) Many Cao Dai leaders soon became monarchical nationalists, willing to collaborate loosely with the Japanese army when it arrived in the early 1940s. Another southern religious movement, Hoa Hao Buddhism, founded in 1939 and dedicated to the elimination of idol worship and expensive ceremonies in Vietnamese temples, had for its founder a charismatic faith-healer (Huynh Phu So, 1919–1947) who deliberately grew his hair long in the nineteenth-century manner to demonstrate that he was not under Western influences. Yet for the leaders of political parties more dependent upon Western political theories than upon the cultural mystique of the past to resist Western imperialism, political recruitment possibilities in the south did nonetheless exist. The development of plantations in the south, for example, had created a landless agricultural worker class that was more mobile and slightly more likely to support revolution than parochial landholding peasants. Circulating through the south, rural wage laborers might serve a number of employers, less commonly owing noneconomic, particularistic loyalties to one employer or one village. Their circumstances were miserable, yet they were free of the domination of the notables of their native villages back in the north.

The VNQDD was weak in southern Vietnam. In 1928, it had twenty-two cells in the south, with a total of 256 armed members. Nonetheless, in early 1929, attempting to win the allegiance of the agricultural workers there, party members in Hanoi assassinated a Frenchman named Bazin who was the chief labor recruiter throughout Indochina for the southern plantations. The French response was a reign of terror, which saw the arrest and brutal liquidation or maltreatment of 225 VNQDD members and the destruction of most of the party's cells. Hoc, the VNQDD leader, escaped but decided to launch armed uprisings immediately, even against hopeless odds, in order not to lose whatever resources he still controlled. In February 1930, the VNQDD briefly seized the northern town of Yen Bai, engineering an uprising of the Vietnamese garrison. In the repression that followed, the French captured and guillotined the VNQDD leaders, including Nguyen Thai Hoc. That was possibly a turning point in Vietnamese history, for with the liquidation of so many non-Communist revolutionaries, the Communists were in a favorable position to regroup the forces of Vietnamese nationalism under their own banner.

The man who always had the clearest title to wave that banner learned his Marxism in France during World War I. Born in 1890 in a Nghe An village that was a hotbed of "aid the king" and subsequent scholarly resistance to the French, Ho Chi Minh (to use his best-known pseudonym, in vogue since the early 1940s) had traveled to Europe as a messboy on a French ship. First reading the works of Lenin in the French Communist Party newspaper *L'Humanité*, he went as a convert to Moscow in 1923 and then to Canton in 1925 to serve in South China as a Comintern agent. At Canton, he founded an organization known as the Vietnamese Revolutionary Youth League, whose newspaper *Thanh Nien (Youth)* translated Marxist terminology into Vietnamese and some of whose members, drawn from Vietnamese exiles, enrolled in the Chinese Whampoa Military Academy. And in 1930, while in Hong Kong, Ho persuaded the leaders of several other Vietnamese Communist-oriented political parties to join him in founding the Indochina Communist Party. From then until the early 1940s, in and out of jail, Ho spent his time in exile in Russia or organizing Vietnamese revolutionaries in areas like South China and northeastern Siam. In its early stages, his work should be seen as contributing not merely to the evolution of Vietnamese nationalism but also to an international plan to foster communism throughout all of Southeast Asia—among Malays, for example, as well as among Vietnamese.

In some respects, Ho Chi Minh differed remarkably from Mao Tsetung, his Chinese counterpart. While the Chinese Communist revolution seems ultimately to have called for the leadership of a provincial radical from inland China sensitive to the moods of the peasantry and antagonistic to all forms of treaty-port intellectuality, the Vietnamese one drew instead on the leadership of a peripatetic, cosmopolitan mas-

ter of the coordination of geographically scattered anticolonial enterprises. Yet Ho became a Communist for the same nationalistic reasons
as Mao. The Leninist doctrine of imperialism offered a convincing
explanation of French behavior in Vietnam and suggested at the same
time that colonialism was ultimately doomed. And Leninist elitist organizational theory supplied a methodology capable of confounding even
the secret police. In the 1930s, however, all orthodox Communists in
Vietnam had to coexist or compete with so-called Trotskyist Communists. The Trotskyists were a group of radical teachers, students, and
journalists, strong in the south, who claimed a following of some three
thousand enthusiasts in Vietnam by 1939. They attacked the Indochina
Communist Party for its acceptance of the patronage of the French
Communists, whom the Trotskyists correctly believed did not entirely
yearn for the disintegration of the French colonial empire. The Trotskyists also denounced the gradualism of the regular party's two-stage
blueprint for a limited bourgeois-democratic revolution for national
independence, involving a broad coalition of social classes, as the
appropriate precursor of the proletarian socialist revolution. Profiting
by the accession to power of a left-wing government in France, which
relaxed political controls in the colony briefly, Trotskyists and Communist regulars fought each other in municipal council and colonial council
elections in southern Vietnam in the middle and late 1930s. The
Trotskyists, who functioned far better in the towns than in the countryside, where the Vietnamese revolutionary struggle was to be transferred
in the 1940s, usually won these contests. *La Lutte,* a Saigon French-
language newspaper, commonly presented the Trotskyist viewpoint.

Except during this strange interlude (roughly, 1936–1939) when, as a
result of domestic politics in France, legal political activity could be carried on through front groups, the Indochina Communist Party expected
and received the savage repression of the colonial government. In 1930,
at the height of the world depression and upon the collapse of the price
of rice, it made its first violent bid for power—the creation of rural
"soviets" in the north-central provinces of Nghe An and Ha Tinh.
Communist sources claim that in 1930–1931, 535 peasant demonstrations, involving 500,000 people in twenty-five provinces, took place in
Vietnam. The soviets, created in the vacuum left by local administrators fleeing from party-organized intimidation, published their own
clandestine newspapers—for example, *Nghe An Do (Nghe An the Red)*—
and began the domestication of international Communist symbols in
Vietnam, like May Day and red flags. More important, they informally
promised the peasants land redistribution, the land issue being one the
VNQDD had neglected. Preaching the solidarity of urban workers and
rural peasants, party committees transported Communist workers of
factories in the city of Vinh to rural areas to augment the ranks of politically active peasants. By the summer of 1931, however, French troops
had crushed the soviets. It was only in 1941, ten years later, that the

party's prospects, more closely than ever associated with those of Vietnamese nationalism in general, began meaningfully to improve.

Up until the 1940s, in fact, nationalism was more or less confined to the intelligentsia. It could be plausibly argued that the socioeconomic condition of the Vietnamese peasant was worse in 1935 than it had been a century before—because of the new and unprecedented taxes, especially those on salt and rice wine; because of the collapse of dynastic restraints, however ineffective, on landlordism; because of the unprecedented export of rice that in precolonial days had been consumed entirely in Vietnam; because of the pressure of a rising peasant population on the land in the north; and because of the new vulnerability of the peasant to world price changes in rice and other commodities. Yet the situation in the countryside remained so peaceful as late as World War I that almost 100,000 Vietnamese were transported, with little significant resistance, to France to serve as soldiers and war workers, while the French military garrison in Indochina itself dwindled to fewer than 3,000 men. Even in the late 1930s, the Vietnamese proletariat—including miners and plantation workers—could not have numbered more than 200,000 people, its modest size forcing the Communists to devise at the time of the soviets the sociologically expansive but doctrinally questionable slogan, "poor people are proletarians."

# 29

## Siam

THE history of Siam between the death of King Chulalongkorn in 1910 and the outbreak of World War II in 1941 is essentially the political working out of the social consequences of the reforms of Chulalongkorn's reign. Chulalongkorn and his ministers fundamentally changed the structure of the kingdom. They revived royal authority as against that of the old nobility, directed a thoroughgoing formalization and depersonalization of the administration, and created a new class of civil servants whose status was legitimized by education and by function within a hierarchical bureaucracy. They reduced the power of local ruling families in the provinces and of the noble families in the capital. Ironically, however, the system had come nearly full circle; the stability and effectiveness of government still rested heavily on the king's personal control over the bureaucracy. The king had partially freed himself of the wickerwork of ceremony that had enveloped his person, engaging directly in the day-to-day workings of the government. While his personal authority was thereby enhanced, it was also more exposed to challenge. The extension and elaboration of the bureaucracy made it more directly responsive to the royal will, but its westernized ideals and functions also made it, in the long run, virtually impossible to control within the traditional framework of royal authority.

It is useful to conceive of modern Siamese, or Thai, history in generational terms, according to which the successive groups of men who come to prominence in Siamese public life may be defined in relation to changes in ideas and experience. The intellectual and psychological distance separating successive generations is particularly important in such times of great change as the century following the Burney Treaty of 1826. The generation of Mongkut and Suriyawong, which came to power in the 1850s, was the first to experience the West and to adjust to it. It did so primarily in terms of traditional values. Chulalongkorn's generation, on the other hand, was a modernizing one. It fell to Chulalongkorn, Damrong, and Devawongse to found a modern state on Western lines, selecting from the West whole institutions and sets of ideas, the value of which they did not question, but which they knew only from a distance, secondhand. It was within the framework they constructed that the third generation grew up, to face the problems of reconciling the contradictions Chulalongkorn never quite recognized.

The contradictions were the consequences of modernization begun from the top down, a superstructure of modern administrative bureaucracy and economic institutions set atop a society and state whose lower portions no longer fitted comfortably within the old mold of the absolute monarchy. The cabinet ministers and department heads of 1910 wore European suits, lived amidst grand pianos and printed books in modern houses with indoor plumbing, drank iced beverages and ate with European silver, worked with modern law codes and administrative regulations, and invested their personal savings in modern banks or businesses. At the same time, Siamese peasants still lived much as they had a century earlier, in rude houses on piles with no conveniences, growing their rice and marketing their surpluses. The discontinuity between the two realms of experience was most evident to those in the middle—junior army officers, schoolteachers, doctors, and merchants—who could see both sides of the modern-traditional division within Siamese society. Theirs was the first generation of Siamese who in substantial numbers were trained abroad. However enlightened their bureaucratic superiors, there was a deep gulf in ideas and experience between them. By virtue of their trained skills, their modes of thought, and their generally liberal political commitments, the members of the foreign-trained group felt they deserved a greater share of power than the existing order granted them. Their "nationalism" was, essentially, the sets of ideas—and the rhetoric—in which they expressed that demand, in both positive and negative terms. Positively, they expressed their commitment to modernity, to keeping up with the rest of the world, against which they constantly measured Siam and found it wanting, or at best too slow. They thought, too, in terms of a unified Siamese nation enclosed within defined frontiers and peopled by Siamese speaking a single language and pledging their loyalty to a single monarch and state. Negatively, they thought their power should be directed against economic, political, and social divisions remaining—and growing—within the nation and against the injustice they felt their country had suffered and continued to suffer at the hands of the imperialist West.

The ideas and experience of the "new men" of the 1910s were shaped by the general acceptance of the West that King Chulalongkorn and his brothers had forced upon the nation, and they saw more clearly than either their royal patrons or the peasantry the fundamental problems of unfinished business and incomplete change—political, economic, and intellectual or cultural—that still faced their nation. Politically, they felt Siam's most serious problem to be the distribution of political power, and specifically the relationship of the absolute monarchy to increasingly aware political interests in the bureaucracy, which could not be contained within the narrow channels of the administrative hierarchy. Economically, Siam's Chinese minority, which occupied a commanding position in the economic life of the country by 1910, was more and more felt to be alien in its life and methods. The power of the Chinese was demonstrated forcefully to the Siamese in the course of a short Chinese strike in 1910 against a tax rate the same as that imposed on the Siamese. The ensuing reaction against the Chinese was to a considerable extent negative, directed against the supposed materialism of the Chinese and their un-Siamese behavior, but it was also positive, affirming the younger generation's commitment to Siamese values.

One important bridge across generational and class lines that helped to hold society together was Buddhism. Religious modernism in Siam was shaped only in part by contact with the West. Whereas in Burma the refusal of the colonial government to sanction authority in the monkhood meant that no modernist sects could organize and gain recognition, though some monks—like the Ledi Sayadaw—were influential exponents of modern religious and social ideas, the case was quite different in Siam. There, Buddhist modernism even antedated the influence of Western ideas. The prince-monk Mongkut, in his personal quest for a meaningful religious experience, founded in 1829 an intellectual movement within Buddhism based upon a critical rationalism, universalism, and careful textual study of the Buddhist scriptures. Its effect was to create a tradition that advocated a self-conscious, living religion composed of the essential values and ideas of Buddhism and unencumbered by inherited local tradition. Here was an intellectual framework within which Mongkut and his fellow monks could accommodate Western science and a world broader than that encompassed by traditional cosmology and morality. For reasons essentially political, the brotherhood of monks Mongkut established in the 1830s did not gain formal status as a separate sect, the Dhammayut, until Chulalongkorn's reign, by which time it had expanded into the provinces, Laos, and Cambodia. Though it remained a minority within Siamese Buddhism, the Dhammayut Sect was disproportionately active and influential from the 1880s on. Under the leadership of Prince Wachirayan Warorot (King Chulalongkorn's younger brother), it was an extremely important force for educational and ecclesiastical modernization, as Prince Wachirayan and his brother monks organized provincial schools and created a national ecclesiastical hierarchy in the decade following 1898. It was a Dhammayut monk, Phra Thammathiraratchamahamuni (Čhan), who spoke out against Siamese entry into World War I. Others, in sermons and writings, were influential in giving Siamese Buddhism an intellectual strength that weathered the general acceptance of modern science and Western ideas. The vigor of the Siamese monkhood (Sangha) was a product not only of the Dhammayut Sect's activities but also of a religious institution that could tolerate dissent and divergence and could serve the whole of a population increasingly disparate in education and daily concerns.

Siamese secular culture, however, remained threatened by the widespread influence of European ideas. It was some decades, for example, before the elite could be certain that its language might retain its vitality in the face of foreign words (new words were coined from Sanskrit roots) or that Siamese literature could hold its rightful place in the intellectual firmament of the Siamese gentleman. It was only in the reign of King Vajiravudh, Chulalongkorn's son, that such problems and fears were tackled head-on.

Vajiravudh (r. 1910–1925) was one of the younger generation—educated abroad at Oxford University and committed to the same ideas as others of his generation. He did more than any other individual to make such national sentiments a part of the ideas of every educated Siamese. A prolific writer and ardent dramatist and actor, he promoted those ideas on the stage and in the public press through voluminous writings, numbering well over two hundred pieces, which ranged from translations of Shakespeare and Molière and trenchant bits of romanticized Siamese history to political essays directed against the Chinese ("The Jews of the East") or Germany during World War I ("Freedom of the Seas"). Through several organizations he founded and headed, the Wild Tiger Corps (an adult paramilitary movement), the Boy Scouts, the Royal Navy League, and his dramatic and literary groups, the king was the nation's most vocal advocate of cultural nationalism, its most effective propagandist, and the creator of organizations of lasting social and political importance.

Vajiravudh, however, was a poor politician. Anxious to escape the domination of his father's generation, he had forced all but one of Chulalongkorn's ministers from office by 1915 and surrounded himself with a government made up of his personal favorites, most of them from nonroyal families and many of them younger men educated abroad. Personal alliances and favorites shaped many of his choices, and his lack of interest in administration left them beyond his direct control. He thereby alienated many. The Wild Tiger Corps in particular was, in effect, the king's private army, and it sorely antagonized, among other groups, the regular army.

An early reaction against Vajiravudh came in 1912, when a group of junior military officers in their early twenties planned a coup against the king. They claimed to have been reacting against the incomplete modernization of the administration, against its unfinished business in the countryside, against the degree to which personal relationships still governed administrative acts, and against the low moral caliber of many they saw about them. Their ideas had been shaped in part by the Russo-Japanese War of 1905 and by the Chinese Revolution of 1911, from which they gained both a sense of their own national identity and a sense of shame in comparing their country with what they knew of more advanced Asian and Western nations. Quietly subverting military posts in the Bangkok area and upcountry, they planned to carry out a revolution at the annual oath of allegiance ceremony in April 1912. Their activities were, however, uncovered in February, and ninety-one men were given prison sentences ranging from twelve years to life.

It is possible that another military coup was forestalled in mid-1917, when there was a wave of arrests in the army at the time Siam entered World War I on the side of the Allies, but it is more likely that those events reflected simply internal army politics. In any case, by participating in World War I, the kingdom gained a voice at Versailles and sufficient diplomatic momentum to end, by 1925–1926, extraterritoriality and all but a few clauses of the unequal treaties.

Vajiravudh died without an heir in 1925. He was succeeded by a much younger brother, Prajadhipok (r. 1925–1935), who had never expected to become king and was unprepared for his new tasks. While he had strong liberal-democratic sentiments, he had neither the personal nor the political power to put them into action. His government was one in which Chulalongkorn's generation and the royal family enjoyed a return to power at the expense of the younger nonroyal men Vajiravudh had favored. Unlike his elder brother, Prajadhipok made regular use of advisory councils composed of princes and high officials, and it is clear that he seriously considered turning them gradually into a parliament. He was dissuaded by his uncles, the senior princes, the more easily because popular demand for representative government was not strong.

The demand for political change did exist, however, even though there were no well-defined channels for its expression. Over the course of the preceding forty years, the kingdom had been building a new elite of civil administrators, professionals, and soldiers. For some time, their upward movement in society and government was continual and satisfying, but it was checked and even reversed during Prajadhipok's reign, when many princes were returned to high office, and when promotions and salary increases were held back at a time of retrenchment in the late 1920s.

The world depression also helped to reawaken the sentiments expressed, and afterwards muted, in the unsuccessful rebellion of 1912. A small group of radicals had been quietly organizing for some years, beginning with meetings when they were studying in Europe. The royalist tone of Prajadhipok's reign, together with retrenchment, made many more receptive to the idea of revolution against the absolute monarchy—young military officers deprived of promotions, students returned from training abroad to find jobs not up to their expectations, and older men no longer so certain about the dignity and generosity of the monarchy. Younger radicals and older moderates joined together to plan and execute the bloodless revolution of 1932.

After the tanks rolled out on June 24, 1932, and after the government had been taken over by what the challengers called the "People's Party," they asserted their Western political ideas in a letter to the king asking that he submit to a constitution and in another to the general public explaining their actions. Both were written in terms strongly condemning absolute monarchy and the previous reign and proclaiming the party's own intention to rule for the good of the people. The initial republican radicalism of some civilian members of the group was soon toned down so that the group's leaders might bring in senior civil officials from the old regime favorable to their cause for the purpose of heading the new provisional government, thereby reducing the chances of any immediate conflict. The balance of power remained, however, unmistakably in the hands of the People's Party when a constitution was inaugurated in December 1932. The radical civilian wing of the party, the leader of which was the university law lecturer, Luang Pradit Manutham (Pridi Phanomyong), made a brief attempt to carry out the early ideals of the coup in an economic plan of March 1933, but the king and the conservative nobles who had continued in government moved against them, forcing Pridi from office and muting the voice of the radicals. A few months later, in June, the military staged another coup to install their own man as prime minister, Phraya Phahon (Phot Phahonyothin). When a royalist countercoup led by Prince Boworadet failed in October, the military group was left firmly in control, having defeated all its rivals, left and right—Pridi's civilian radicals, the conservative civilians carried over from the prerevolutionary regime, and the royalists. Their success was confirmed with the abdication of King Prajadhipok in 1935 and with the accession of a boy-king, Ananda, still at school in Switzerland.

The constitutional regime then inaugurated was not a great advance on the previous period in democratic terms. Power was still concentrated in the hands of a few, the members of the People's Party, who, in the initial stages of constitutional development, maintained their primacy through an appointive monopoly of seats in the Assembly and the Cabinet, although appointees were supposed to be replaced gradually by elected representatives when educational levels permitted or ten years had passed. Indirect elections in 1933 and 1937 gave the Assembly a membership of which half was elected, keeping the pressure on the government to fulfill its liberal program and to maintain its expressed democratic ideals. Despite a shortage of funds during the period, the government was able to make considerable progress in social welfare, particularly in the area of education and public health, and, to a lesser extent, in economic affairs. Universal and compulsory primary education finally was extended throughout the kingdom. The government was particularly alert to the impact of its taxation policies on the village, making efforts to reduce taxes when economic conditions were poor. The *quid pro quo* for those programs was the support of the elected members for continued strong military budgets, which the army justified first in terms of internal threats and later by external ambitions and fears. From mid-1933 to the end of 1938, Phraya Phahon, as prime minister, steered the government along a course that by Siamese standards was moderate and certainly progressive. His government finally fell in December 1938, when strong questioning of the budget by the elected members of the Assembly resulted in a vote of no confidence. Luang Phibun Songkhram, a colonel popular in the army for his strong championing of its cause and more widely for his role in breaking the royalist forces in 1933, came to power. He was a vigorous exponent of Thai—and not just Siamese—nationalism and the logical choice of the ruling group.

Phibun's first government (1938–1944) is understandable principally in terms of the world environment in which it was set. At a time when the prestige of the Western democracies was low and when the capacity of Western ideas and values to solve grave economic crises and to survive international strife seemed spent, assertive, ultranationalist, and militarized states such as Japan were attractive to the Siamese. And so Siamese politics took a turn to the right, with open glorification of the army, assertion of national values, and strong attacks upon Western culture, Western imperialism, the Chinese position in the Siamese economy, and the regime's own critics. Siam carefully cultivated relations with the Japanese government, establishing strong economic and political ties. Once France had fallen to German armies in June 1940, Phibun stepped up pressure on French Indochina with irredentist territorial claims, associated with a more general pan-Thai movement best expressed in the change of the name of the kingdom to "Thailand." This led to full-scale war with France in 1940–1941. The war was popular in Siam but ended with Japanese mediation and with the cession to the Siamese of western Cambodian provinces and some Lao territories. Phibun's government was undoubtedly strengthened by the outcome of the war, but he had found himself more heavily dependent on Japanese aid than he could have anticipated. The limits of Siamese military power were now as clear as the real predominance of Japan in Southeast Asia. When on December 8, 1941, Japanese forces suddenly disembarked at six points along the coast of peninsular Siam, crossed into the country from Cambodia, and landed at the airfield near Bangkok, they met with the automatic resistance of local Siamese garrisons. But Phibun, informed of the landings, could see no alternative but to capitulate and join the Japanese. There were, after all, some Siamese goals that could be served in the process. Although, at Japanese urgings, he agreed to declare war on the American and British governments, it was not a Siamese affair: The war was between Japan and the West. With two such ponderous elephants fighting, the ant of Siam scurried to avoid being crushed.

The increasing prominence of the military in Thai public life stemmed primarily from the unique advantages of military organization, which helped the army to maintain strong hierarchical and personal (patron-client) relationships while inculcating cohesive and modern values. They were much better organized than their competitors, they had had less exposure to the West, and they were somewhat more conservative and formalistic in their approach. The civilians, who were disorganized to the point of inability to function consistently as a unity and who lacked physical force, were more willing to see radical change. Their numbers were small, and they were distributed in small pockets through the society of the capital, while the military was neatly organized in a single hierarchy. Together, the two elements were the young elite of the society, their status clearly defined in the public view. Peasants and townsmen expected them to act as "big men"—government was their business, not the public's. When these men began to talk directly to the peasant in the language of equality, on new radios and through the press, it took time for some people to realize that the game of politics had really changed—that it was now about "us" and not simply "them."

# 30

# Malaya

THOUGH the protectorate control established by the British in the peninsular Malay *negeri* was based on earlier patterns of suzerain relationship and was seen by some of the Malay rulers as a means of obtaining powerful and knowledgeable assistance in the profitable governance of their territories, it rapidly came to entail a great deal more than that and to introduce radical changes in the life of the states. On the west coast in particular, with the Federated Malay States (FMS) in the lead, there took place large-scale development of European and Chinese entrepreneurial and extractive economic activity, with a startling increase in alien immigration. In the FMS, population rose from 218,000 in 1891 (at the time of the first full census) to 1.7 million in 1931. Already, by 1891, as the result of accelerating Chinese (and to a lesser extent Indian) immigration during the previous two decades, Malays, including immigrants of Malay stock from elsewhere in the archipelago, could muster only 53 percent of the total population. By 1931, a mere 34.7 percent of the population was of Malay stock, while the Chinese had risen to 41.5 percent, and there were, in addition, 22.2 percent of Indians. Though the census-taker in 1931 argued that most Chinese remained transient, which may well have been true, there was already a substantial residue who regarded the peninsula as their permanent home, as well as many thousands who had been born there. Even in the Unfederated Malay States (UMS), Johore, the state most developed in relation to the export economy, was by 1931 very similar in racial composition to the FMS, and Kedah, too, had a large alien component. Down the whole of the west coast, with Penang and Singapore as the northern and southern nodal points and Kuala Lumpur as the federal capital in the center (all three demographically Chinese cities), stretched a complex system of roads, railways, telephones, and telegraphs, which provided the bones and sinews for an export economy whose earnings had risen from 10 million Straits dollars in the late 1880s to more than 300 million dollars just before the depression of 1930.

Much of the change, however, despite its revolutionary and lasting character, did not immediately or directly affect the Malays. Not that Malay life continued in uninterrupted tranquility—for, manifestly, much happened to shift the peasant view of the world—but the changes that did take place did not coincide with or take their direction solely from the incidents of British rule, and change occurred within (or coexisted with) a remarkable persistence of traditional patterns of social organization. The relative sparseness of the Malay population and its involvement in a traditional social order based on the village and cultivation of the land meant that few Malays were available or willing to engage in the wage labor needed for rapid development of export industries and their ancillary facilities. British policy in the peninsula was, accordingly, based on a mutually profitable alliance with the Malay ruling class, by which, in return for the right to develop a modern extractive economy within the *negeri* by means of alien immigrant labor, the British undertook to maintain intact the position and prestige of the ruling class and to refrain from catapulting the Malay people into the modern world. This symbiotic relationship certainly deprived the Malay sultans and territorial chiefs of most of their decision-making or policy-making powers, but it was furthered with a tact that carefully preserved the fiction that the sultans were autonomous rulers acting under advice from Residents, who were in some sense their servants. Though this fiction wore threadbare less rapidly in the UMS than in the FMS (where mild protests at procrustean amalgamation were to result in a measure of decentralization in the 1920s), it nowhere completely concealed the fact that the rulers, in direct proportion to the value of their states to the export economy, were bound hand and foot to British policies.

To say that the sultans lost all substantial powers of decision and control, however, is to take something of a Western view. Within Malay society itself, they not only remained paramount but had their position considerably strengthened by the improvement, under the aegis of the British, of the centralized apparatus of government, by the reduction of previously competitive territorial chiefs to the status of titled courtiers and pensioners or government-salaried bureaucrats, and by the strengthening of their customary but previously unexercised control over religion. The saving clause in the protectorate agreements concluded between the Malays and the British, excluding from residential "advice" matters touching upon "Malay religion and custom," encouraged both a turning to the ceremonial trappings of Malay life and, more importantly, the creation in most states, in one form or another, of elaborate administrative and judicial establishments for the governance of Islam. Known generically as Councils of Muslim Religion and Malay Custom, the establishments were largely appointed by, dependent on, and answerable to the rulers. They became important repositories of traditional and usually conservative authority in relation to Malay society as a whole.

Nor were the effects of British rule seriously disruptive of the role played in Malay society by the aristocracy, once the initial period of adjustment to deprivation of taxation rights and other privileges of territorial independence had passed. It is true that, for the most part, they

ceased to be politicians, and the importance of this should not be discounted. But senior chiefs in particular, who stood to lose most, played
a deliberative role in the State Councils (a more meaningful task in the
unfederated states than in the federated), and the territorial structure of
the traditional Malay aristocratic establishment was maintained alongside the new centralized bureaucracy in sufficient degree to afford district chiefs some continuing responsibility for Malay customary life. In
return, they were rewarded with state pensions or salaries and had, by
reason of their position and influence, other economic advantages, such
as access to the disposal or acquisition of land, of mining rights, and the
like.

In the FMS after the turn of the century, the Malay aristocrats of the
younger generation received special education and training, reserved
largely for the sons of the traditional elite, and were recruited into the
colonial bureaucracy. Though the positions they occupied were subordinate in relation to the European civil service, the Malay administrative
cadre thus created had a dual advantage—over their fellow Malays of
peasant origin, who had not had the same educational opportunities,
and over all non-Malays, who were by policy barred from the administrative or executive ranks of the public service. Malay Officers, as they
were styled, were almost invariably employed in rural administration
among their own people, where the tasks they performed, though different in detail, were at least comparable to those of the territorial Malay
administration of an earlier time, insofar as the nexus between peasant
and prince was concerned. The prestige and authority conferred by traditional social status were thus re-emphasized by administrative authority derived from the colonial regime. The pattern was repeated, and
indeed intensified, in the UMS, where the incidence of direct British
participation in local administration was less. Only in Kedah was there
something like a truly autonomous Malay administration of a modern
kind acting under British advice, though in Johore the strong Malay
aristocratic establishment retained a firm hold on Malay affairs, even as
the direction of administrative matters in general came to rest only
nominally in their hands. In the east-coast states of Kelantan and
Trengganu, which approached the modern world only slowly, the Malay
aristocracy remained largely untouched.

The maintenance of the traditional Malay elite throughout the peninsula, either in its customary form or as the new bureaucracy, was paralleled by a striking absence of Malay peasant involvement in the
mushrooming export economy, either as part of the work force or as
entrepreneurs. The British sought actively to shield Malay peasant society from the disruptive effects of the new economic order, partly in the
interests of the protectorate relationship and of a sentimental view of the
idylls of village life, partly as a means of ensuring continued food production, and partly in order to avoid the political consequences thought
likely to follow any substantial disorganization of the peasant economy.

The traditional Malay ruling class actively concurred in the measures that resulted. The problem of providing the work force (clerical and technical as well as manual) for expanding export industries and burgeoning government services was met by the wholesale importation of immigrant workers from South China, British India, and Ceylon. Relative abundance of unoccupied land made it possible to allot large tracts to European and Chinese plantation enterprises without trespassing seriously on Malay holdings. Land policies were framed to give the Malay individual title to his land, to keep the peasant in possession of his patrimony, and to encourage his continuing cultivation of traditional crops, in particular wet rice. Such measures were reinforced by a system of elementary vernacular education (in Malay, and, effectively, for Malays only) which, though fairly widespread in incidence, at least in the FMS, had as its principal objective the creation of a "vigorous and self-respecting agricultural peasantry," conscious of the dignity that attaches to hewing wood and drawing water.

Though the effect in general of these policies and practices was to reduce the impact and the rate of socioeconomic change at the village level, this is not to say that changes did not occur, but rather that they were neither radical in extent nor structural in implication. Individual land title tended to encourage both the sale and the mortgaging of peasant lands, though the government attempted, in the interests of prevention and reduction of rural indebtedness, to curtail transactions in certain types of land by the creation of Malay Reservations, within which land could be disposed of only to other Malays. One effect was to hold down the price of Malay land and to encourage Malay, at the expense of non-Malay landlordism, economic developments of doubtful value to the peasant. The only substantial participation of the Malay in the export economy—the adoption by large numbers of peasants after 1910 of rubber smallholding as a means of earning cash income—led to more intensive monetization of the peasant sector of the economy. But after some years, the government, in the interests of food production and later of plantation-biased rubber restriction schemes, introduced legislation that drastically limited new Malay rubber planting. In addition, the presence of non-Malay middlemen, in control of preparation, marketing, and profit-taking, seriously reduced the stimulant effect that rubber-growing might otherwise have had upon Malay economic life. Despite this, rubber incomes (until the slump in the late 1920s) did enable some Malays from the first generation of smallholders to purchase for their sons a better education than was possible in the village and thus a chance to enter the upwardly mobile ranks of the government civil service.

One of the principal results of the wholesale retention of the Malay peasant within the matrix of the traditional agricultural society was the small part played by the Malay in the urban life of the developed western states or the Straits Settlements and his consequent isolation from social change arising within the urban environment. In numerical terms, Malays constituted in 1921 only some 10 percent of the urban population of the peninsula, a figure corresponding to perhaps 4 or 5 percent of the total Malay population. Those proportions rose only very slowly in the course of the next two decades, despite the eventual introduction of policies designed to lessen non-Malay predominance in the urban-centered subordinate ranks of government employment. Though the small Malay component of urban society was to be of great significance for eventual nationalist movements, the great majority of Malays continued to find the town alien and strange, if indeed they had any acquaintance with it at all.

Despite the slow pace and limited extent of social change among the peninsular Malays, in comparison with peoples more rudely embroiled in colonial economic development, the relatively brief period of British rule before 1941 witnessed the appearance of a nascent Malay nationalism, appealing at first to loyalties to religion, race, and language and seldom effectively transcending traditional state boundaries but coming ultimately to seek a specifically political community that would safeguard Malay interests against those of the culturally alien myriads who now claimed residence in the peninsula. In the course of this process of growing self-recognition, it is possible to discern the emergence of three new elite groups in Malay society, each associated with a particular educational environment and each in turn offering its own vision, based on interest and background, of what Malay society must become to survive and prosper in the modern world. The first of the groups was grounded in the Islamic-educated religious reform movement; the second was the largely Malay-educated radical intelligentsia; and the third was the English-educated bureaucracy, its upper echelons drawn from within the traditional elite itself.

The religious reform movement had its ideological origins in the Islamic renaissance, which took place in the Middle East around the end of the nineteenth century. Malaya-born Muslims, sometimes of Arab or Sumatran descent, returning from sojourns in Cairo or the Hejaz, brought with them a burning desire to renovate Islam in their own society and to make it a fit instrument with which to respond to the social and economic challenges posed by alien domination. In propagating doctrines of the essential unity of the Islamic community without regard to potentates and powers, of the need to cleanse local Islam of accretions of custom standing in the way of progress, and of the essential equality of all Muslims before God, they came into immediate conflict with well-entrenched elements in Malay society, especially the separate state rulers and their religious establishments, newly developed under British rule. Though the strength of the movement lay in the urban centers, particularly Singapore and Penang (where its individualistic ethic proved attractive to those engaged in modern economic competition), it found adherents also among religious teachers and others in rural village society. The contest between the reformers and the traditional establishment was essentially unequal, but its many-sided and protracted argument acted as an important modernizing force within Malay society. In the long run, the religious reform movement failed to create or to lead a mass movement among the Malays, primarily because of opposition from the traditional establishment (religious and secular), which still held the loyalty of the great majority of the people, but also to a considerable extent because the issues on which it fought were being overtaken—or taken over—by a secular nationalism more concerned with pragmatics than piety.

Already, in the mid-1920s, a number of young Malays who had had their introduction to anticolonialist ideas in Egyptian Islamic reform circles were voicing overtly political, pan-Indonesian nationalist sentiments with little religious content in two journals published in Cairo. On their return to Malaya, they joined forces with the more numerous, secular, Malay-educated intelligentsia, which formed the second of the three new elite groups in Malay society. In large part teachers and journalists, products of the Sultan Idris Training College for vernacular schoolteachers and of two similar institutions for technical and agricultural education, the radical Malay intelligentsia was strongly influenced by the left wing of the Indonesian nationalist movement and looked to the creation of a Greater Malaysia or Greater Indonesia, which would embrace both the British and the Dutch colonial territories. With few exceptions, the radical intelligentsia was drawn from the peasant class, and though its ideology was in many ways confused, it criticized alike, mainly by way of the flourishing town-based vernacular press, the traditional elite and the new English-educated bourgeoisie (whose privileges it often envied), as well as British colonialism. It attracted to its cause some English-educated journalists and public servants, but its program was unformed and never really achieved organizational coherence. The Kesatuan Melayu Muda (Young Malay Union), an embryo political organization formed by the radicals late in 1938, spent the last year or two before the war under cautious surveillance by the British. It was mistrusted or feared by the majority of Malays who came into contact with it for its radical social views and its pan-Indonesian political aims. Though it served as a valuable training ground for left-wing nationalists later active during the Japanese occupation and after the war in radical Malay political movements, it failed utterly before the war to gain anything like a mass or solidly peasant-based following.

The leadership of the third new elite group in modern Malay society sprang for the most part from within the traditional ruling class itself, among the English-educated administrators and public servants. Essentially, this group was reacting against increasingly vociferous claims in the 1930s from the local-born elements of the Chinese and Indian communities (in 1931, 31 percent and 21 percent, respectively) for a larger share in government and administration and in the public life of a unitarily conceived British Malaya. The economic depression of the early 1930s, coming on the heels of revised policies aimed at increasing the Malay share of urban-based subordinate government employment, placed great strain on the neat plural society formulae by which Malaya had lived up to then. Many Chinese and Indian mine and estate workers, thrown out of employment, sought to settle on the land as agriculturalists, previously an entirely Malay preserve. Aspiring Malays in the towns, in receipt of slightly increased measures of English education, were vying with local-born Indians and Chinese for government clerical and technical posts at a time of general retrenchment of staff. The leaders of both the Straits Chinese and the local-born Indian communities were arguing strongly that, in the new Malaya, non-Malay residents must be afforded equal rights with Malays, at least in proportion to their contribution to the economy—to which a frequent Malay response was: "If you get someone in to build a house, you don't ask him to live with you afterward." Simultaneously, other Chinese, looking more obviously to metropolitan China for political satisfactions, were engaged in Kuomintang politics in the peninsula (despite the proscription of the KMT in 1930), or in the founding of the Malayan Communist Party (1930), an almost wholly Chinese organization with links nevertheless to Indonesia and Vietnam.

From the late 1920s onward, the traditional Malay ruling class—both those who, like the rulers and their immediate establishments, were still part of the old structure and those who had become absorbed in the new colonial bureaucracy—showed concern at the obviously disadvantaged position of the Malay in the modern world. Periodic gatherings of rulers (durbars), begun in 1927 as part of a token devolution of federal authority to the states, became the occasion, especially toward the end of the 1930s, for proposals by the rulers to encourage Javanese and to limit Chinese immigration, to strengthen Malay rights to the soil, and similar measures. In the Federal and State councils, the Malay members— all of high status within the traditional establishment—argued civilly for more jobs in the administrative apparatus for English-educated Malays or for more Malay Reservations for the peasants, but they were hampered in expressing (or perhaps holding) views directly critical of government policies by reason of the fact that most were also in the upper ranks of the bureaucracy. It was in part to meet that situation, to provide alternative forums for Malay opinion, and to organize "constituency support" for council representatives that elements of the English-educated elite began in 1938 to form avowedly political Malay Associations on a state basis. Conservative in bias, loyal to the rulers (who in most states had given their blessing to the enterprise), and displaying an almost equal enthusiasm for British colonial rule—bulwark for the time being against the clamorous demands of Malaya-born and domiciled aliens—the Malay Associations movement, linked as it was with the traditional leadership to which the bulk of the Malays still gave their loyalty, was the only prewar movement that showed real signs of gaining anything like mass support. Though little success attended efforts, made at national conferences in 1939 and 1940, to unite the associations in a single organization, and though state loyalties remained powerful, the growth of a genuine Malay nationalism after the war owed much in both ideology and structure to the Malay Associations movement and its leadership.

# 31

## Laos and Cambodia

In the years preceding World War II, French administrators in Laos and Cambodia, gratified by the apparent docility of the kings and people under their protection, hinted that both kingdoms were approaching an unspecified kind of renaissance. To assist in bringing it about, the French concentrated their resources on public works, primarily the extension of all-weather roads, and on cultural projects like the restoration and maintenance of Angkor Wat. In both protectorates, the French worked through princely families and bureaucratic elites. The generation of Lao and Cambodian leaders that matured under the French worked comfortably with them, seldom urging any modifications of French control. Because they lacked enough power to alienate anyone, and because the largely rural population was politically passive and geographically dispersed, the leaders themselves were unchallenged. Moreover, the rudimentary condition of the French-controlled educational system delayed the appearance of qualified rivals. Finally, the mechanisms through which French and elite rule could have been challenged, such as a vernacular press, elected assemblies, and voluntary associations, barely existed among the Cambodians and Lao.

In both protectorates, the events of World War II played a crucial part in the emergence of nationalist sentiment and organizations. French policy toward Laos and Cambodia was forced into a more positive stance by the Indochina War of 1940–1941, when the loss of sizable portions of territory to Thailand forced the French to renegotiate the loyalties of the protected monarchs. In Laos, the renegotiation took the form of strengthening and expanding the powers of the king of Luang Prabang; in Cambodia, where the newly installed King Sihanouk was considered more malleable than King Sisavangvong of Laos, the new policy took the form of increasing the king's visibility to his people.

### Laos

In any formal sense, Laos was swamped within the larger unity of French Indochina—it contained only 7.3 percent of the population, generated only 1 percent of its foreign trade, and employed only 167 French administrators. Moreover, much of its economic and administrative activity was carried on by foreigners—mainly Vietnamese immigrants, who constituted three-fifths of its urban population of 50,000 in 1943. However, the French political and emotional commitment to Laos was much stronger than such quantitative indices would suggest. It was based upon the situation of helplessness that beset the divided Lao elite in the later years of the nineteenth century and, perhaps, on some French feeling that more was owed to the Lao than the French could do for them with limited colonial budgets and, eventually, limited power.

There was no Lao society as such, apart from local societies in each *müang,* when the French took control in 1893. At the vortex of a tributary system in the extreme north was the ruling family of Luang Prabang, trying with difficulty to fend off bands of marauding Chinese in order to maintain its suzerainty over nearby vassals and to sustain its autonomy in the face of increasing Siamese interference. In the far south, at Champassak, was a ruling family recognized as governors by the Bangkok monarchy, similarly maintaining a weak hold over nearby *müang* to the north and east. With their officers and vassals, they constituted a clearly defined ruling class of royalty and nobility. The French position of rule in Laos was founded upon the personal relationship between King Oun Kham (r. 1872–1894) of Luang Prabang and Consul Auguste Pavie and on the Franco-Siamese Treaty of 1893, by which Siam gave up its "pretensions" to the east bank of the Mekong River. No written agreements between the French and Lao regulated their relations. The French had little difficulty working on the basis of such an ephemeral legal situation, because they simply assumed the role of a suzerain power—in this case, making real their claim to act in the name of the court of Hue. For their part, the Lao elite could enjoy an order, security, and prosperity denied them since the end of the seventeenth century, accepting French rule because they derived "modern" benefits from it, such as education and heightened administrative authority.

In a sense, the French froze Laos in the *status quo*—particularly by maintaining the powers and prerogatives of the ruling families of Luang Prabang and its provinces. But they did more than that: The French declared their mission to be "to create . . . a sufficiently numerous and aware elite . . . so as to form a national consciousness."[59] The effort involved the delicate task of selective education of the princely and governing elite to French values and the neglect of Lao traditions. Its political effect was to strengthen the monarchy as an institution and to fortify the existing distribution of political power in Laos, while working to increase the elite's dependence on French power.

The political history of Laos under French rule up to the Japanese *coup de force* of March 1945, is primarily constitutional. French rule was extended in the south with the posting of French commissioners to seven chief provinces to superintend the administration, while six more were posted in the major provinces of Luang Prabang. The indigenous administration, however, remained intact and indeed was strengthened by the creation of a unified Laos in 1899 (to which the Lao territories opposite Luang Prabang and the remainder of Champassak were added by treaty with Siam in 1902 and 1904), under the authority of a *résident supérieur* in Vientiane. Gradually, the continuing participation of the Lao elite in government was regularized by the formal creation in 1920 of provincial consultative councils to advise the French government on "all questions of economic and social interest . . . which were submitted to them, and especially the program of public works . . . for the succeeding year."[60] Shortly thereafter, the Royal Council in Luang Prabang, which the French had attempted unsuccessfully to abolish in 1915, was reorganized along functional lines, three high dignitaries being put in charge of interior; justice, education, and religion; and finance, public works, commerce, and agriculture.

For such executive functions, various members of the Lao elite—the royal family of Luang Prabang and the provincial ruling families—were provided with full French education, beginning in Vientiane and continuing in high school in Hanoi, Saigon, or Paris before university or technical education in France. King Sisavangvong (r. 1904–1959) of Luang Prabang spent a year in France as early as 1900–1901, and many of his sons and nephews followed him there. One indication of the size and composition of the Lao elite might be gained from the fact that nearly all of Laos's educated political leaders as late as 1945 could be represented on a single genealogical chart, composed of the direct male line of the kings of Luang Prabang and the line of the *upahat* (viceroy) Boun Khong (whose son Phetsarath was refused succession to that office in 1914). Trained as engineers and lawyers, these young men were employed in technical positions—less frequently in administration—throughout the French colony. Prince Souvanna Phouma, as a young engineer, for example, superintended the restoration of Vientiane's most important religious center, Vat Phra Keo, between 1937 and 1940, and Prince Souphanouvong was put to work building bridges in Vietnam.

The French attitude toward Lao culture was ambivalent. Both traditional and modern cultural interests made natural the resort of the Lao elite to Thai newspapers, books, and radio, all in a language they could understand, and many Lao monks sought Buddhist higher education in Siam. To counter that attraction, the Kingdom of Laos participated in the founding of the Buddhist Institute in Phnom Penh in 1930 (Laos later had its own institute, in 1937), and the French started a weekly newspaper and radio broadcasts in Lao in 1941. It was on the initiative of the Lao elite, however, that the critical break with Thai culture was attempted in 1941, with the introduction of romanized script for the Lao language to replace the Thai-style script previously employed. The attempts, none of which endured, had their immediate origins in circumstances directly political.

After the fall of France in 1940, the French and Lao were virtually helpless in the face of the pan-Thai pretensions and irredentist claims of Phibun's government in Thailand. At the conclusion of the Indochina War of 1940–1941, France was forced to cede to Thailand the Lao provinces on the west bank of the Mekong opposite Luang Prabang and Pakse. The former territory, the province of Sayaburi, was a particularly painful loss, as the mausoleum of the Luang Prabang royal family was situated there. For those territorial losses, France—as Laos' protecting power—was held responsible. A reaction against Thai culture followed, as did an attempt by France to repair the damage done to its reputation. The present-day provinces of Xieng Khouang, Vientiane, and Nam Tha—areas the monarchy had not controlled since the seventeenth century—were transferred from direct French administration to the king. Furthermore, a formal treaty establishing the French protectorate was finally concluded, replacing the informal agreement with Pavie and a nondiplomatic agreement with the governor-general of Indochina concluded at the beginning of the French period. The king was given a new cabinet with five functional posts. Prince Savang Vatthana was named heir-apparent, and Prince Phetsarath finally succeeded to his father's post as viceroy, as well as becoming prime minister. The two main branches of the royal family—the line of the king and that of the viceroy—were brought back together. The elite, however, small as it was, was still divided by the uncertain position of the house of Champassak in the south, just as both royal and French authority were administratively divided. Some members of the elite were so awakened politically by the events of 1940–1941 and their consequences that they began to envisage a future for Laos of which the French would not be a part. One French official in Luang Prabang warned his government to "Be careful of this prince [Phetsarath] when the war is over, because he will join with Thailand to seek independence."[61]

## Cambodia

In terms of Cambodian nationalism, the most significant institutional innovation of the years preceding World War II was the Buddhist Institute, founded in Phnom Penh in 1930 under the joint patronage of the Cambodian monarchy, the king at Luang Prabang in Laos, and the French. The Institute was intended to focus and encourage Buddhist studies throughout Cambodia and Laos; it had the effect of intensifying the relationship between the Cambodian monarch and his people. Using printing equipment supplied it by the French, the Institute soon began to issue editions of Buddhist texts in Pali and Cambodian, collating material sent to it from provincial monastic libraries. The Institute's output of printed matter, although not large by absolute standards, far exceeded what had been previously available. As the Institute's reputation grew, enhanced by frequent conferences, it became a rallying point for an emerging intelligentsia. The Institute's librarian, Son Ngoc

Thanh, who had been born in southern Vietnam of Vietnamese-Cambodian parents, founded a Cambodian-language newspaper, *Nagaravatta (Angkor Wat)* in 1936. The pressure of events, like the war with Thailand in 1940–1941 and the coronation of Prince Sihanouk as king soon afterward, obscured but failed to extinguish the kinds of ideas that the paper set in motion.

The brief war with Thailand and the subsequent losses of Cambodian territory coincided with the final illness of the sixty-five-year-old Cambodian monarch, Sisowath Monivong, who had reigned since 1927. The French were eager, as in Laos, to arrange the succession in a way that would strengthen their hand vis-à-vis the Thai, seeking a candidate for the throne whom they could manipulate. For these reasons, when Monivong died in April 1941, French officials had already successfully proposed to the colonial office in Paris that Monivong's thirty-two-year-old son, Monireth, be passed over in favor of Prince Norodom Sihanouk, the eighteen-year-old son of Monivong's eldest daughter and, on his father's side, the great-grandson of King Norodom. The young prince, then in his last year at the French lycée in Saigon, was totally untrained for his new position. In October 1941, he received his crown from the governor-general of Indochina, Admiral Decoux, who took pains to note that Sihanouk's great-grandfather had also been crowned by a French naval officer. Sihanouk's reply, probably written by the French *résident,* was suitably humble about himself and grateful to the French.

Over the next few months, as war spread across most of Southeast Asia, the components of Indochina remained isolated from their neighbors and from the war itself, for French policy was formulated in France by the neutralist Vichy government. The French maintained day-to-day control over Indochinese affairs until March 1945. Internal disturbances in the meantime were severely dealt with. The most important of them, in Cambodian terms, took place in July 1942, shortly after the French had arrested two monks on charges of "spreading discord" among members of the Cambodian militia. Approximately a thousand people, roughly half of whom were monks, assembled outside the headquarters of the French *résident supérieur* to demand that the monks be released. When the French authorities temporized, elements of the crowd (including a large number of monks) stormed up the steps of the building, hitting out at the French with sticks, umbrellas, and sandals. More than twenty people were injured before order was restored. Lay spokesmen for the demonstration were arrested, accused of treason, and shipped to the penal colony France maintained off the coast of southern Vietnam. Son Ngoc Thanh, a friend of the detained monks and of the lay spokesmen for the demonstration, later denied any involvement in the disturbance. Nonetheless, he left Cambodia for Thailand soon afterward, gaining asylum in Bangkok at the Japanese Embassy, which arranged for him to be flown to Tokyo, where he remained until the spring of 1945.

The demonstration probably surprised the French, accustomed since Norodom's death to treating Cambodia with a drowsy kind of paternalism that took for granted Cambodian acquiescence to French rule. The French were aware, of course, that religious movements, such as the Cao Dai in Vietnam, contained a potential for subversion and, in the 1920s, had prohibited proselytization in Cambodia by heterodox religious sects. They had also assumed, however, that the Cambodian Sangha's loyalty to the monarch was indistinguishable from the monarch's loyalty to the French. The idea that the Buddhist Institute might provide a platform for Cambodian nationalism seems to have been overlooked. In any case, the French now believed, rightly as it turned out, that the platform provided by the Institute was not very wide and that discontent among the Sangha as a whole did not run very deep. As a result, under a vigorous young *résident* appointed in 1943, the French moved to reduce the generally conservative influence of the Sangha while integrating Cambodia more closely with other components of Indochina and enhancing the public role of the young Cambodian king. A royal decree of 1943 made the use of a romanized Cambodian script mandatory for official documents; another regulation replaced the Buddhist calendar with the Gregorian. Both moves were deeply resented by the Sangha, however, and never took full effect.

Another facet of French policy at the time was to make King Sihanouk more visible throughout the protectorate than his forebears had been and to bring him in touch with the similarly protected monarchs of Vietnam and Laos. Within Cambodia, Sihanouk's increased activity consisted largely of sponsoring the paramilitary youth organizations encouraged throughout Indochina by the Vichy regime. The groupings, the first of their kind in Cambodia, gave Sihanouk ideas about political organizations that he used after the kingdom gained independence. Under the policy that brought him face-to-face with his people, the young king's self-confidence increased. Although he was still hemmed in by protocol and by French and pro-French advisors, it is likely that in those years Sihanouk glimpsed the kinds of power and prestige the French had allowed to reside in the institution of the monarchy.

The liberation of Paris in late August 1944 further isolated the Vichy-oriented French administration in Indochina, which had been physically cut off from France for more than two years. On March 9, 1945, the Japanese throughout Indochina moved to imprison all French military and civilian personnel, turning day-to-day administration over to the largely unprepared Cambodians, Lao, and Vietnamese. On March 10, the Japanese commander in Phnom Penh informed King Sihanouk that Cambodia was independent. The monarch cautiously replied by requesting diplomatic recognition from Tokyo (which never arrived) before proclaiming Cambodia's independence himself on March 12. At this point began a new phase, in many senses the first, in the development of Cambodian nationalism.

# PART FIVE

# Southeast Asian Nations in a New World Order

# 32

# War, Independence, and Political Transition

THERE have been few events in the history of Southeast Asia that affected the region as profoundly or as rapidly as World War II. During a period of just over three and a half years, the foundations of the colonial era were destroyed, and the peoples of the region began first thinking of, then planning on, and finally fighting (and sometimes dying) for a future that they could see as their own rather than something determined for them by colonial rulers. What provoked this dramatic change was not the physical toll exacted by the war—the innumerable deaths, the material damage, the interrupted lives, serious as these were—but rather the subjective effects of the war: the effects that wartime developments had upon the thoughts and feelings of Southeast Asians. These effects were so deeply felt that to the present day those who lived through that period treat it as marking a dramatic break—in their personal history and also in their history as a people—when they use such phrases as "before the war," "during the war," and "after the war." The experiences of the wartime period greatly accelerated change and the expression of nationalism in Southeast Asia. Intent on freeing their societies and leading them toward a new era, many nationalists who gained power during the war did not intend to surrender their newly achieved authority. In that sense, the Japanese prophecies of "a new dawn for Asia" and an "Asia for the Asiatics" came true.

From the beginning of World War II in Europe in September 1939, it seemed certain to most people that Southeast Asia would become involved, and there was little that Southeast Asians could do about it. The Burmese, for example, were simply told that they were at war with Germany. The foodstuffs and raw materials of the region—especially metals, petroleum, and rubber—constituted important war materiel not only for the colonial powers fighting for their survival in Europe but also for industrial Japan, since 1937 bogged down in its war against China.

With the fall of France and the Netherlands to Germany in June 1940 and the prospect of an imminent end to the war in Europe, some leading Japanese pressed for an early move into Southeast Asia—both to prevent the Germans from succeeding to the British and Dutch empires in the region and to secure the region's resources for the prosecution of their war in China. Immediately after the fall of France, Japan exerted diplomatic pressure on the government of French Indochina that gained it bases and a strategic position in northern Vietnam, severing the Red River route by which Nationalist China had been supplied; that action led to the creation of the "Burma Road" by which China was supplied through Rangoon across Burma to Yunnan. Japan further expanded its position with bases in southern Indochina by mid-1941 and stepped up pressure against the Netherlands East Indies and British Malaya for increased supplies of vital raw materials.

It was at this point that Allied resistance to Japan's expansion into Southeast Asia stiffened, in a curious way that was to presage events a quarter-century later. In effect, the United States drew the line at southern Vietnam. When Japan took over military bases in southern Indochina, the United States imposed an embargo on the export of petroleum and scrap steel to Japan, and the British and Dutch followed, resisting Japanese demands for increased exports of petroleum and rubber. Through diplomatic negotiations over the next five months an accommodation was sought, but they ran aground on the issues of Allied support for China and the Western stake in Southeast Asia's war supplies. Japan proceeded to plan for war in the region—a plan which finally committed Japan to a southern and maritime strategy rather than a land-based effort to attack the Soviet Union from Manchuria.

The Japanese design for a "Greater East Asia Co-prosperity Sphere," encompassing East and Southeast Asia, envisioned a combination of states in the region that in detail was much like the British Commonwealth (with the equivalents of "dominions" and "crown colonies"), the achievement of which depended upon a startlingly ambitious military plan. In the few hours preceding and following dawn on December 8, 1941 (December 7 east of the International Date Line), Japanese forces attacked the United States naval fleet at Pearl Harbor, Hawaii; American military installations in the western Pacific, the Aleutians, and the Philippines; the British at Hong Kong, Singapore, and several towns on the northern coast of Malaya; and Thailand at seven points on the Gulf of Siam, across the border from Cambodia, and by air against the main Thai air base north of Bangkok. The chief military objectives of these attacks were control of the international shipping lanes through the Malacca and Sunda Straits; access to the tin, petroleum, rubber, and rice resources of Malaya, Burma, and the Netherlands East Indies (and denial of these to the Allies); and the attainment of a strategic position from which to threaten Australia and India and to close off the flow of supplies to Nationalist China through Burma.

Thailand capitulated and aligned itself with the Japanese within hours of the attack. The British, Americans, and the Dutch navy resisted, but against superior forces and in the face of European military distractions that limited the men and materiel available to them, they could not long survive. For four months, the world's newspapers almost weekly reported the fall of yet another important city to the Japanese: Hong Kong on December 25, Manila on January 2, Kuala Lumpur on January 11, Singapore on February 15, Rangoon on March 7, and the entire Dutch East Indies on March 9. By the end of April, Western power—established for decades or even centuries—had been completely evicted from the region, save for the Vichy government of French Indochina, which shared power with the Japanese.

The intrusion of Japanese power into Southeast Asia shattered the mystique and the institutions of Western colonialism. The expansion of the Japanese empire dramatized the vulnerability of the West. The suddenness, rapidity, and force of the Japanese conquest jolted Southeast Asians out of their acquiescence, fear, or awe in the face of European power—and the fact that the Japanese were Asians was not lost upon them. They may have felt that it was one thing to be dragged reluctantly, over many decades, into the international economic order but quite another to be thrown into the maelstrom of international politics with little more than a token defense and no power to affect their own security. And here, perhaps, lay the seeds of a much more determined nationalism in the postwar period.

Despite the widely varying effects of the Japanese occupation in different parts of Southeast Asia, certain common features stand out. Through almost all of the region the Japanese encouraged the formation of indigenous military or paramilitary forces that formed the core of many postwar national armies and anticolonial struggles. Japanese military administration also effectively demonstrated a principle of army participation in politics that would be remembered in the postwar period. The revival of indigenous military traditions and the demise of the myth of Western omnipotence were two of the legacies of the Japanese occupation. Intentionally or not, the occupation policies of the Japanese in a number of Southeast Asian countries also afforded practical experience to local political leaders and scope for the expansion of popular participation in politics. At a lower social level and in a different way, thousands of ordinary peasants, rudely forced by the Japanese army to abandon their villages and join the "Sweat Army" of conscripts toiling on the construction of the Burma-Thailand railway or transporting military supplies, were shaken out of their village isolation and shocked into a recognition of the possibilities of change.

Japanese patronage of Southeast Asian nationalism was not disinterested. To many Southeast Asians, it seemed to be as much a profanation of their desires for emancipation from colonialism as an international legitimation of them. Kamei Katsuichiro, a postwar Japanese critic of Japanese expansion into Southeast Asia, argued that Japanese contempt for other Asian countries, a psychological by-product of Japan's more rapid modernization than that of its neighbors, was his country's great modern tragedy. For although Japanese wartime propaganda belittled the West and its colonialist political mythology, many Japanese occupation officials shared the Western condescension toward the Southeast Asians they governed. Furthermore, the Japanese occupation in Southeast Asia was economically ruinous. The decline of exports as Allied submarines sank more and more Japanese ships, the sudden unemployment of plantation labor, the requisitioning of rice and other commodities by the Japanese army, followed by serious rice shortages, the sabotage of tin mines and oil fields, the bombing of roads, bridges, and rail lines, and brutal programs of forced labor, produced extreme social and economic distress. Rampant inflation further exacerbated the suffering.

At the same time, the changing situation of the Japanese worked indirectly to stimulate political change. They had invaded Southeast Asia anticipating that the war in Europe might end in 1942, but by mid-1943 the tide of battle had begun to turn against them with the failure of their attempt to invade India and the Battle of Midway, which destroyed much of the Japanese fleet and opened the way for the American thrust northwards from the southwest Pacific. In an attempt to rally indigenous support, the Japanese military began to make political concessions to Southeast Asian nationalists, setting up quasi-independent regimes in Burma and the Philippines and transferring some of the Shan states and portions of northern Malaya to Thailand. The pressure on the Japanese to take more radical steps increased as the military pressure on them intensified from the latter half of 1944 as British troops began moving across northern Burma, American forces began the reconquest of the Philippines, Allied bombing of Japanese supply routes increased, and British- and American-sponsored resistance movements gained strength in Burma, Thailand, French Indochina, and Malaya. Through the first half of 1945, especially after Burma was retaken by the British in May, harried Japanese military officials worked desperately to mobilize Southeast Asian support for their war effort and began to allow many nationalists yet further scope for action to that end.

But even as late as July 1945 hardly anyone realized that the war would end a few weeks later, when atomic bombs were exploded on Hiroshima and Nagasaki on August 6 and 9 and Emperor Hirohito broadcast Japan's unconditional surrender on August 14. No one was politically prepared for this, least of all the exiled colonial authorities. It was not just that they were militarily and administratively unready; they also lacked understanding of the strength of Southeast Asians' determination to resist the reimposition of colonial rule. With the exception of the United States, which a decade earlier had negotiated its postcolonial relationship with the Philippines, the colonial powers expected to return to Southeast Asia and resume their powers and perquisites almost as if nothing had happened; or, worse, that because of wartime damage they would even have to roll back such meager political reforms as they had begrudged the region's nationalists in the 1920s and 1930s until its economies and societies could be put "back on their feet." The stage was set for a violent conflict between an increasingly assertive nationalism and a sanctimonious and self-interested colonial paternalism.

In the pages that follow, we will examine the histories of the countries of Southeast Asia in the decades since World War II. Before turning to the details of this tumultuous period, however, we should consider the context in which this history is set and suggest a periodization that makes Southeast Asia a coherent region and not just a collection of nations.

The postwar period can be roughly divided into four phases, with the divisions between phases marked by events or processes that were perceived and felt through most of the region. The first phase begins with the end of World War II and in most countries ends around 1954. This period encompasses the successful struggles of the peoples of Burma, Indonesia, Cambodia, Laos, Vietnam, and the Philippines for national independence and the maturation of Malaysian nationalist politics to the point where the working out of an end to colonial rule was only a matter of time (to be completed in 1957). During this phase, local Communist movements mounted major challenges to governments in almost every country of the region. Leaders wrestled with the enormous problems of postwar reconstruction and economic rehabilitation, while attempting to build new social and political institutions. The postwar economic recovery fed by consumerism in the West, and then by the Korean War (1950–1953) boom, contributed to economic growth in the region; but domestic insurgency, the revival of age-old political divisions, and the beginnings of new forms of external interference began to erode the euphoria engendered by nationalist success.

The second phase began following the Korean War, around 1954, in the aftermath of the success of the Communists in China in 1949 and in the midst of the climactic struggle that led to the Geneva Conference of 1954 and an end to the First Indochina War as well as the formation of the Southeast Asia Treaty Organization (SEATO) in 1954. It ended with a violent escalation of conflict in much of Indochina in the mid-1960s. This phase is characterized by fresh and growing foreign intrusion into Southeast Asian life and politics, motivated for the West—and for many Southeast Asians—by an almost panic-stricken fear of communism and for China and the Soviet Union by a fear of encirclement. This was a period of intense rivalry between the superpowers in Southeast Asia. While Thailand, North Vietnam, and the Philippines took sides in this contest, others, like Indonesia and Cambodia, joined the nonaligned movement that took shape at the Bandung Conference (1955). Both East and West bestowed enormous amounts of economic and military aid upon their clients in the region, while at the same time attempting openly and covertly to influence their politics and policies. In order to strengthen Japan after the loss of China as a market and

source of raw materials, the United States encouraged Japan to improve its economic relations with Southeast Asia. This was a period of
growing prosperity, fueled by aid and trade, but it was also a time when
the political and other institutions so eagerly and optimistically fashioned at independence began to come under stress that led, for example, to Sukarno's "Guided Democracy" in Indonesia and in many cases
erupted in violence and brought more authoritarian regimes to power in
several countries in the early 1960s.

The third phase coincides with the period of the Second Indochina
War and extends from 1965 to 1975. This conflict involved Vietnam,
Cambodia, and Laos, and virtually all of the region was affected by it.
It brought a massive intrusion of American military and economic
power into Southeast Asia, and the strong political pressures and interference that went with it, as well as considerable aid to the Communist
nations from China and the Soviet Union. The American intrusion provoked retaliatory challenges to the power and stability of the other countries of the region through insurgency and other attempts at destabiliza-
tion. Meanwhile, the economic impact on the region of American
military and economic spending fed the region's economies and stimulated further social and economic change that made "privileged"
groups millionaires and deepened political discontent.

The fourth phase began with the withdrawal of United States forces
and the end of the Second Indochina War in the early 1970s, culminating in Communist victories in Vietnam, Cambodia, and Laos in 1975.
The political events of these years allowed Burma's emergence from
self-imposed isolation; the beginnings of intraregional cooperation that
grew into the Association of Southeast Asian Nations (ASEAN, formed
in 1967); and the broadening of the region's international relations.
The aftermath of the Communist victories was surprising; the world's
first open military conflicts between allegedly Marxist regimes took
place when Vietnam invaded Cambodia and China attacked Vietnam
in 1978–1979. The most pressing problems felt by the region's leaders,
however, were local and regional. Many of the nations went through
major political upheavals—Thailand (1973–1977), Cambodia (1975–
1979), Laos (1975), Philippines (1972–1986); while Malaysia (1969–
1971) and Indonesia (1965–1966) experienced them earlier—and all
were hard-pressed to maintain control over increasingly complex and
contentious societies. Economically, most of the region, like the rest of
the world, had to adjust to the serious effects of skyrocketing energy
prices following the OPEC cartel's escalation of petroleum prices in
1973–1974, a situation that hurt poorer countries more than the prosperous West, and then their rapid decline in 1986. (Oil-producing Indonesia, Malaysia, Burma, and Brunei, of course, suffered the opposite
ends of the oil-price swings.) The rise and fall of petroleum prices
revealed the increasing volatility of international commodity prices and
the region's vulnerability to these swings. Its economic stability was

unsettled even more by the growing protectionism of the industrial world. At the same time, however, it benefited in the 1970s and 1980s from a boom in "offshore" manufacturing and huge American and Japanese investments that to a considerable degree helped at least the ASEAN countries weather what might otherwise have been a crippling economic storm.

Through the decades since World War II, then, the countries of Southeast Asia—whose peoples may have been sustained through the struggle for national independence by the hope that they might achieve some insulation from the dangers of the international environment into which the colonial powers had thrown them—increasingly found that the world was an even more hostile and dangerous place than it had been in the 1940s.

# 33

# Vietnam

THE Japanese occupation of Vietnam from 1941 to 1945 transformed the unpromising revolutionary prospects there as completely as did Japanese occupying armies elsewhere in Southeast Asia. In addition to undermining the reputation of French military power in Vietnamese eyes, the Japanese invasion gave the Vietnamese Communists an opportunity to blend their esoteric dogmas with the more easily understood nationalist cause of resistance to both the French and the Japanese.

Ho Chi Minh returned to Vietnam from the Soviet Union in February 1941, visiting the Chinese Communists' stronghold at Yenan in north China on his way. Making his headquarters at Pac Bo in the northern border province of Cao Bang, he convened the meeting of the Communist Party central committee in May 1941 which founded the Vietnamese Independence Brotherhood League, more popularly known as the Viet Minh. By itself, the tiny Indochina Communist Party (which had only 20,000 members as late as 1946) could never have hoped to attract the support of politically engaged Vietnamese who hated colonialism but who as yet had no fondness for an imported Western creed like Marxism-Leninism. By itself, the ICP could also never have hoped to attract significant foreign assistance, for the purpose of fighting the Japanese invaders of Vietnam, from the British, the Americans, or from the anti-Communist Chinese government led by Chiang Kai-shek. Ho Chi Minh's unequalled knowledge of the world outside Vietnam apparently convinced him that Vietnam was too small a country ever to generate a successful revolution, in such a predatory age, without some outside help and that serene and persistent manipulation of foreign governments and foreign political parties sooner or later might give the Vietnamese Communists enough internal and external political leverage to achieve Vietnam's independence. The Viet Minh was a "front" organization. It was sponsored by the ICP but designed to accommodate patriotic Vietnamese from a variety of social classes.

The Viet Minh had to compete with other forces in a country whose spiritual foundations were shifting unpredictably. Marshal Petain, the leader of wartime Vichy France, had called for a French "national revival" based upon patriotism, familism, and work and opposed to individualism. This appeal, when overheard by a colonized people, had anticolonial effects. Vietnamese intellectuals began to study their own society and its past for the secrets of a Vichy-like "national revival," and mass action, they hoped it might contain. The "Clear Counsel" *(Thanh nghi)* journalists began to publish for the first time from June 1941 relatively independent Vietnamese-language discussions of such subjects as the restoration of Vietnamese agriculture, as seen by French-educated intellectuals with modern legal training who were nevertheless outside the colonial civil service. Radical thinkers associated with the Han Thuyen publishing house (1941), some of whom the Viet Minh were to attack as "Trotskyists," tendentiously reinterpreted Vietnamese historical figures, such as the Quang-trung emperor of 1788, whom they now saw as a representative of the "peasant class" struggling against feudalism. Young writers began to produce emotive fictional close-ups of the miseries of the peasants, as in Ngo Tat To's "Affairs of the Village" *(Viec lang,* 1940). In this more restless ethos, the Viet Minh struggled against the intellectuals who tried to upstage it, against the remnants of the Vietnamese Nationalist Party, against the big religious sects of the south, and against newer political formations sympathetic to the Japanese promotion of a "Greater East Asia." But the Viet Minh alone had a detailed political program that looked beyond independence, to the creation of a "bourgeois democratic republic" (the first stage in a multistage Communist revolution) with a large, efficiently organized popular following.

Until January 1945, the Japanese armed forces had no more than 35,000 men in Indochina. They were content to let the colonial government, responsible to the neutral Vichy regime in France, preserve order. The disappearance of the Vichy regime by the fall of 1944, and the American invasion of the Philippines, changed Japanese calculations. In early 1945, Japan increased its forces in Indochina, achieving absolute military superiority. And on March 9, 1945, the Japanese struck. They overthrew French colonialism and eliminated the French army as any sort of threat in "French Indochina" in less than twenty-four hours. The Japanese ambassador hardly improved France's stricken prestige when he commented, after this coup, that the French community in Vietnam was like a wounded bird which had fallen into the hands of its hunters and that Japanese warrior ethics regarded it as contemptible to mistreat the weak and defenseless. The emperor Bao Dai signed a proclamation, under Japanese guidance, which reclaimed Vietnam's rights of independence but said that Vietnam now considered itself to be an "element" in Japan's Greater East Asian system.

But the Viet Minh were the ultimate beneficiaries of the Japanese coup. Viet Minh leaders had been planning an uprising in Indochina, in order to seize power in a colony strangely divided between the French and the Japanese, for almost a year. They had created a "liberation army" in the Cao Bang hill country in December 1944. It comprised some thirty-four people on the day it was formed and was commanded by Vo Nguyen Giap, a brilliant former Hanoi schoolteacher. By the spring of 1945, the small but growing Viet Minh forces had carved out a "liberated zone" which ran right across the north's mountainous borderlands and had also infiltrated the Red River delta. American officers who were attached to the U.S. Office of Strategic Services in China wanted Ho Chi Minh's cooperation in rescuing American pilots shot down over northern Vietnam. To get it, they aided the Viet Minh army and trained its technicians. There is an extant letter from Ho to two such Americans, dated May 9, 1945, which says in English, "I will be very much obliged to you of taking care of our boys. I wish they can learn radio and other things necessary in our common fight against the Japs. . . . Yours sincerely Hoo."

Apart from the prestige they gained in being associated with the increasingly victorious Americans, the Vietnamese Communists were also able to take advantage of a terrifying famine which ravaged northern Vietnam from the end of 1944. Hundreds of thousands of Vietnamese starved to death; Tonkinese rivers were full of corpses. Survivors were reduced to eating the roots of plants. Giap's new army entered northern villages, seized the fatally prominent granaries which were storing rice for landlords or for the Japanese army, and distributed their rice to hungry peasants. The Viet Minh combined the slogans "National independence" and "Destroy the paddy granaries and resolve the famine," under the conscious inspiration of the 1917 Bolshevik slogan, "Peace, bread, and land." The famine thus enabled them to overcome conservative village notables who had previously opposed them. Village chiefs were invited or compelled to destroy their own seals of office. "People's committees" replaced them.

After Japan surrendered to the Allies in August 1945, Viet Minh forces seized major cities and towns, sometimes by mobilizing scythe-carrying peasants to invade them. The Communists were determined to gain superficial control of as much of Vietnam as they could before the French could return to resume their rule. Bao Dai's government at Hue, although it enjoyed support from civil servants and other members of the urban intelligentsia, had no military power of its own. Bao Dai later wrote that he "felt isolated in a dead capital city" in 1945. Being impressed both by Viet Minh arms and by Viet Minh connections with the Western powers, he therefore abdicated his throne when the Viet Minh demanded this, handing over the dynastic seal to Ho Chi Minh's representatives in a remarkable public ceremony. Fortified by the emperor's acceptance of his legitimacy, Ho announced the birth of a Communist-run Democratic Republic of Vietnam (DRV) in Hanoi on September 2, 1945, with himself as president. As he did so he quoted from the U.S. Declaration of Independence and referred also to the French Revolution's Declaration of the Rights of Man of 1791. This entire performance reflected Ho's belief (not shared by some of his politburo colleagues) that the Vietnamese revolution would be destroyed if it could not muster the support of many diverse constituencies inside and outside Vietnam. Buoyed by the genuine outpouring of popular patriotism that the events of 1945 had encouraged, but aware as well that Chiang Kai-shek's Chinese government would crush the DRV if it thought Ho's new government was vulnerable, Ho and the Viet Minh carried out an "August Revolution," which appealed to the "extremely festive" soldiers and peasants and shopkeepers in Hanoi (as one American military eyewitness described them). But they stopped far short of communism. The colonial tax system was abolished. Mass education was introduced. The course of this moderate revolution was, however, also darkly punctuated by a series of political murders, as Communist assassins killed a number of distinguished non-Communist intellectuals.

Ho Chi Minh's great political skills were tested to the utmost to save his revolution in 1946. In the fall of 1945, a Chinese army of 180,000 men occupied northern Vietnam as if it were a conquered country, bringing with them worthless wartime Chinese currency and a disorderly crowd of porters, wives, and children. Their pretext was that they were exercising Nationalist China's mandate, as one of the major allied powers, to receive Japan's surrender. But they also undoubtedly hoped to replace Ho's government with anti-Communist politicians more favored by Chiang Kai-shek. Instead of attacking the Chinese invaders, Ho cunningly welcomed them as "friends." To enlarge his Vietnamese support, and also to confuse the Chinese, he announced (November 1945) the outright dissolution, on paper, of the Indochina Communist Party itself as a "sacrifice" to the need for a "national union" government in which non-Communists would feel at home. The party then went underground and publicly reappeared in 1951.

Most daringly of all, Ho invited the French armed forces to return to northern Vietnam, so that he could use them as a counterweight to the Chinese occupation. (The French had already reentered southern Vietnam, aided by the British.) By an arrangement of March 1946, France recognized the DRV as a free state and negotiated the withdrawal of the Chinese army from the north. In return, Ho's government accepted membership in a proposed French Union (an ambiguous commonwealth version of the old French empire) and allowed the French army to reoccupy northern Vietnam for five years. Viet Minh orators, significantly, compared this 1946 deal with France to the Treaty of Brest-Litovsk of 1918, when Bolshevik Russia had accepted a shameful treaty with a decaying German empire in order to consolidate its political system. But the French now dreamed of using Cochinchina as the fulcrum of a French-controlled Indochinese Federation that would permit the preservation of their Southeast Asian empire, except northern Vietnam. In the summer of 1946, Ho made his last effort to flatter the French into peaceful decolonization. As president of the DRV, he paid a state visit to France in which he explained patiently that Cochinchina was as much a part of Vietnam as Brittany was a part of France and that Vietnamese independence would serve the "greater honor" of France. His effort failed. War between the Viet Minh and the French broke out at the end of 1946 and lasted until 1954.

The French colonial regime thus won the opportunity to perish in a revolutionary war which it never really understood. The military thinking of the Vietnamese Communists, as explained trenchantly by Vo Nguyen Giap, included such principles as the value of continuous attack over stationary defense (because attacking deepened the political consciousness of the people and more passive defensive postures did not); the importance of learning how to use small resources, cleverly deployed, to defeat larger resources not so wisely managed; the value of surprise; the flexible use of different types of forces, ranging from a main army equipped with the most modern weapons available to local self-defense forces armed with hoes and pickaxes; and, most crucial of all, the total involvement of the population, old and young, male and female, in fighting the enemy. To get such popular involvement, the Viet Minh launched a drive against illiteracy. Everyone was to be taught how to read, from prostitutes to fishermen to monks and nuns to highland minorities. The education itself was an odd mixture of information and indoctrination. Viet Minh "Library for the Masses" primers dealt with such diverse topics as the evils of fascism, the importance of having a national assembly, the nature of railway locomotives, and the futile superstitiousness of praying for rain. The French soon found themselves submerged in a strange guerrilla war in which peasant children could be spies and toothless old women could be laying mines.

By 1949, Mao Tse-tung's Communists had seized power in China, vanquishing Chiang Kai-shek. The Viet Minh gained a strong if possessive ally. In 1953, the increasingly desperate French tried to lure the Viet Minh into fighting a classic set-piece battle, of the sort the Western military mind could understand and Western artillery and air power could dominate, in the Dienbienphu valley near northern Vietnam's border with Laos. Giap's peasant army, supplied by coolies who transported to Dienbienphu—by animal carts and bicycles—everything from heavy artillery to rice, unexpectedly surrounded the French garrison there by the spring of 1954 and forced them to surrender. Dienbienphu was the worst defeat any Western colonial power ever suffered on the battlefield at the hands of an Asian people it had once ruled. Yet the Viet Minh still failed to reunify Vietnam on their own terms. At an international peace conference at Geneva, convened soon after the collapse of Dienbienphu, the Vietnamese Communist government was pressed by its allies, the Soviet Union and China, to accept less than it thought was its due. The Geneva Agreement of 1954 required a final French withdrawal from Indochina. But the agreement arranged a partitioned Vietnam in which the Communist regime, based in Hanoi and confined to north of the seventeenth parallel, had to coexist for at least two years with an anti-Communist southern Vietnamese state based in Saigon. At the time the Geneva Agreement satisfied the Chinese desire to exclude American military interference in Indochina and the post-Stalin Soviet formula that Asian revolutionary movements should develop peacefully. It anticipated nationwide reunification elections in Vietnam in 1956. The new South Vietnam and its American patron refused to sign the Geneva Agreement and resisted these elections, which were not held.

The leader of the new government in the southern half of Vietnam, which had evolved in the last five years of the war, was Ngo Dinh Diem. Diem was a devout Catholic mandarin whose father had been a court official at Hue. His own political career had included brief service as a cabinet minister to the young Bao Dai emperor in 1933. As to the U.S. government, after 1950 it had helped finance the French war in Indo-china out of a deep fear of southward expansion by Communist China, whose huge armies had confronted the United States in the Korean War (1950–1953) and whose submissive underlings the Vietnamese Com-munist leaders in Hanoi were thought to be. Now the United States hoped to make Diem the Winston Churchill of Southeast Asia (as Vice President Lyndon Johnson publicly hailed him in 1961) and thus work through him to reform those bewildering Vietnamese political habits which most facilitated communism and frustrated the realization of Washington's world-view. In his 1953 inaugural address, President Eisenhower had found that a common anti-Communist faith conferred "a common dignity upon the French soldier who dies in Indochina . . . [and] the American life given in Korea." Eisenhower regarded Vietnam as a land shaped "roughly like a bent dumbbell" whose sur-render to "Communist enslavement" would "threaten" Thailand, Burma, and Malaya and would mean the irreparable loss of "valuable deposits of tin and prodigious supplies of rubber and rice." The Ken-nedy administration continued the Eisenhower policy of regarding the suppression of communism in South Vietnam as geopolitically indis-pensable. As his secretary of state and his secretary of defense told Pres-ident Kennedy in November 1961, "the loss of south Vietnam would make pointless any further discussion about the importance of South-east Asia to the free world; we would have to face the near certainty that the remainder of Southeast Asia and Indonesia would move to a com-plete accommodation with Communism."[62]

Accordingly, American advisers, ranging from political science pro-fessors to Central Intelligence Agency paladins (Edward Lansdale) to land reform experts (Wolf Ladejinsky), descended upon Saigon in order to share "the best possible American political thinking" (as Lansdale put it) with Ngo Dinh Diem and to help supply Diem with a decent republican constitution (1956), a bureaucracy, a police force, and schools. It must be kept in mind that the Communists did not challenge such outside efforts to introduce new, American-flavored institutions to the south until the end of 1959, when they finally launched their "synchronized uprisings" *(dong khoi)* against Diem and the Americans in the Mekong delta and in the hill country of central Vietnam. At first, therefore, the results of such efforts looked much better than they were. But the president of South Vietnam, as Diem became by 1955 in a referendum that was rigged more heavily than it needed to be, was difficult to advise. He had intractably Vietnamese cultural values and social class characteristics. At his best, Diem the mandarin saw politics in essentially Confucian rather than American liberal terms as an arena in which any political opposition, no matter how fervently anti-Communist it was, called into question by its very existence the moral authority of the ruler, who supposedly governed through superior virtue. At his worst, and strongly prompted by his more sordid brother who became his real political manager, Diem debased his residual Confucian ideals by resorting to the procedures of a police state, arbitrarily arresting and mistreating tens of thousands of political prisoners, many of whom were not even Communists.

For all these reasons, there was never much chance that Diem would carry out the Americans' wish that South Vietnam be made a nursing-ground of vital non-Communist "grass roots political organizations." Diem eliminated provincial and municipal council elections. He tried to relocate grumbling peasants into large fortified villages. And he converted his presidency into a sort of artless informal monarchy, buttressed by a network of brothers and other relatives (a dynastic house being one part of his political heritage) if not by a reliable non-family civil service (another part of that heritage). The old rural social structure in the south, with its rich landlords, remained unscathed by Diem's token 1956 land reform. Diem's politically inept police raids upon Buddhist temples, in the summer of 1963, climaxed his hostility as a Catholic and Confucian ruler to the rise of intermediate organizations, like the General Association of Vietnamese Buddhists (founded in 1951), which he could not control. The raids ended the Americans' romance with him. The U.S. ambassador in Saigon intrigued with dissident Vietnamese military officers who were plotting against Diem and even proposed the island of Saipan as a convenient place for the "removal of key personalities."

The Vietnamese Communists, north and south, had not formally challenged the Diem political machine until 1959, partly because they initially underestimated it. They were restrained as well by Soviet and Chinese pressure upon Hanoi to defer any major uprising in the south and by Hanoi's preoccupation with the restoration and transformation of the north's economy. But they were in a strong position to preach social revolution in the south. Most of the Vietnamese landlord class lived there. During the war against France, the Viet Minh had won adherents by redistributing 630,000 hectares of land to poorer peasants; southern peasants had been major beneficiaries. After 1954, land-owners who supported the Saigon government had reclaimed redistributed lands, angering peasants to a degree dangerous to Diem's survival.

In December 1960 the Communists formally resurrected the southern branch of the Viet Minh, in the form of a new patriotic coalition which called itself the National Liberation Front (NLF). Known to its enemies by the derisively over-simple term "Viet Cong" (an abbreviation of the Vietnamese term for "Vietnamese Communists"), the NLF certainly included implacable veteran Communists but also at least a few liberal intellectuals whom a less autocratic Diem might have been able to win over. Fighting a skillful guerrilla war, the Viet Cong soon created a state within a state in the south. By November 1962 they controlled or influenced, by U.S. estimates at the time, some two-thirds of all the south's villages. The Diem government had centralized decision-making power above the villages and relied for its revenues upon colonial use and consumer taxes (market taxes, sales taxes, fees for the issuance of documents) it had inherited from the French, and which most heavily victimized the poor. The NLF in its early years gave considerable decision-making authority to people who actually lived in the villages and pursued tax and property distribution policies which favored the poor. In the towns its satellite organizations, such as the "Committee for the Preservation of the National Culture," appealed to some teachers and students who feared that the progressive "Americanization" of southern institutions, as seen in the penetration of teaching colleges and the National School of Administration by American money and advisers, might eventually turn them into "yellow-skinned Americans." By 1969, although it was past its prime, the NLF formed a "Provisional Revolutionary Government." It had its own schools, newspapers, and broadcasting service.

To respond to this threat, the Americans began their overt military intervention in the south with the development in 1961–1962 of a "Military Assistance Command Vietnam" (MACV). The U.S. secretary of defense stated in November 1961 that even if Hanoi and China attacked "overtly," the "maximum U.S. forces required on the ground in Southeast Asia" would not exceed "about 205,000 men." MACV was the nucleus of what was to become, by 1967, an American armed force in South Vietnam of 525,000 men. American-supported Saigon military officers murdered Diem in a successful coup against him in November 1963. After the general who immediately replaced Diem made it clear that he did not want U.S. advisers installed in Vietnamese villages—because this would look too much like colonialism—he was removed in another coup (January 1964) that U.S. officials knew about in advance and did not discourage. By 1965, when Major-General Nguyen Van Thieu became the leader of the Saigon government, the Saigon military elite, less well educated, less steeped in classical traditions, and thus more willing to experiment with Western political and economic techniques than Diem, had seized control of the non-Communist power structure. Armed with a new constitution in 1967, which replaced the Diem constitution and called for American-style presidential elections every four years, General Thieu served as the president of the southern republic from 1967 until its collapse in 1975.

With the murder of Diem, the war expanded. By 1965 its nature had changed and it became a direct confrontation between the conventional military power of the United States and the disciplined and tenacious army of North Vietnam. Advised by the U.S. ambassador in Saigon that U.S. bombing of north Vietnam might "bolster morale and give the population in the south a feeling of unity," President Lyndon Johnson contrived a congressional resolution, which authorized him to use "all necessary measures" in Indochina, and began to bomb Ho Chi Minh's republic systematically from February 1965. General William Westmoreland, the U.S. commander in South Vietnam, was allowed to deploy a large American conscript army which embarked on open-ended "search and destroy" assaults throughout the southern country-side. Such assaults, when combined with bombs and napalm, drove much of the rural population into the cities as refugees and succeeded by sheer firepower in damaging the political connection between the Viet Cong and the peasantry. In response, the regular northern Communist army came south, eventually overwhelming the largely southern membership of the NLF. And in February 1968, the Vietnamese Communists, following the precedent of the Taysons' surprise attack upon an invading army from China during the lunar New Year of 1789, launched their "Tet" (New Year's) offensive. They briefly penetrated even the grounds of the U.S. embassy in Saigon and seized the old imperial capital of Hue, from which they were not dislodged for weeks. The Tet offensive, gruesomely televised in millions of American living rooms, was a turning-point in the war. On the one hand, its dramatic if temporary success exposed the falseness of President Johnson's claims that he was firmly managing, and even winning, what was supposed to be a "limited" American war in Asia. On the other hand, the offensive's failure to trigger large pro-Communist uprisings in southern cities, let alone any pro-Communist inclinations in the Saigon army itself, made it clear to leaders in Hanoi that popular support for the revolution they had envisaged in the south was stagnating. Representatives of the Hanoi and Washington governments therefore agreed to meet for peace talks in Paris later in 1968.

The Paris peace talks did not reach a conclusion until January 1973, after four more years of slaughter. President Richard Nixon and his chief foreign policy adviser, Henry Kissinger, even reversed more than two decades of unrelenting U.S. hostility to Mao Tse-tung's China, in 1971–1972, partly to encourage this Communist superpower to press its ally in Hanoi to accept U.S. peace terms. Although this move successfully irritated the historically difficult relations between China and Vietnam, which Washington had belatedly discovered, it did not prevent the 1973 peace treaty from being a triumph for the Vietnamese Communists.

The original American objective in the peace negotiations had been the mutual withdrawal from South Vietnam of "external forces," both North Vietnamese and American. Washington's central ideological proposition had been that American and North Vietnamese soldiers were equally "external" when they fought in the south, that the Vietnamese south was a legitimately separate nation-state. Acceptance of this proposition would have meant the de facto annulment of the Vietnamese Communists' claim to be leading a national revolution. Having more at stake than Washington, the Vietnamese Communists resisted and prevailed.

The 1973 treaty allowed Hanoi to keep its army in the south indefinitely, after American ground forces had been removed. In Saigon, President Thieu had little difficulty in seeing what Nixon and Kissinger refused to acknowledge: that the parallel legitimation of the Viet Cong's "provisional revolutionary government" (which was a partial signatory to the treaty with Thieu); the permanent presence of northern troops in the south; and the withdrawal of American forces all portended his downfall. The United States poured more weaponry into Saigon to enable the humiliated Thieu government and its army, by now one of the world's biggest, to hold their own. This proved to be impossible. In the spring of 1975 a Vietnamese Communist offensive, propelled by the 264,000 fresh combatants Hanoi had sent south since 1973, finally destroyed the non-Communist republic of Vietnam and reunited north and south on the Hanoi government's terms.

Such was the end of a bleak and bloody episode in Vietnamese history. Millions of Vietnamese were killed and wounded; about 58,000 Americans also died. Superficially, it seemed to be a Vietnamese encounter with the operations of an American neocolonialism that ultimately lost both its stamina and the consistency of its world-view. The United States did not perfectly control any Saigon government between 1954 and 1975. But it is also true that no Saigon government ever survived without enormous American economic and military aid. And no Saigon government whose behavior the U.S. government seriously distrusted remained in office for very long.

But there was another side to this story, which explains why the passions aroused by the war did not cool quickly. The south's 1967 constitution had conveyed the hope that a meaningful multiparty democracy might be born in Vietnam, despite the Saigon military elite's often ill-disguised admiration for the manipulative Leninist political methods of its northern adversaries. Although President Thieu rigged elections and ignored the principle of the separation of powers expressed in this constitution, a complex assortment of Catholic priests, Buddhist monks, religious sect theoreticians, lawyers, teachers, economists, and labor union organizers, based usually in the cities and towns, worked courageously and against very great odds to achieve a real democracy in the south. They were under no illusions about the obstacles. The French colonial police had helped prevent the emergence of large, public, non-conspiratorial political parties in Vietnam. There were twenty-four non-Communist parties in Saigon at the end of 1970. The unsympathetic Thieu government's command of the foreign aid-based economy, and of conscription, denied the parties necessary financial and human assets. Their more enlightened members still persevered in a struggle for political freedom that could somehow tap the instincts of a very ancient Vietnamese humanism.

Historians should also remember that Saigon between 1954 and 1975 was the home of a subtle and variegated literary culture whose intellectuals stood for a cosmopolitan emancipation of Vietnamese energies. As one example, young women novelists suddenly flourished during this period. They wrote fiction about prostitutes, decaying landlord families, and "dust of life" street people, as if such fiction were a desperate form of "ghost raising" (in the words of one such writer, Tuy Hong). In such a literature-loving nation, the fact that three women won the top literary prizes in South Vietnam in 1970 demonstrated the growth of a significant new female cultural freedom. After 1975, the Communist leaders of the reunified Vietnam were too autocratic and too insecure to accommodate such women, or tireless and versatile Saigon literati like Vo Phien, with their expert knowledge of Camus and Kafka and Stephan Zweig—and of dissident Soviet literature. The repression of this critical middle-class intelligentsia, or their forced flight to the West to become Canadian grain elevator workers or American government clerks or overseas journalists, was a Vietnamese national disaster of incalculable proportions. But although such people lost, the history of modern Vietnam belongs to them as well as to the Hanoi politburo and the Saigon militarists.

As for the winners, in a region of the world long used to imported notions of sultanates, kingships, and presidencies, the Communist political system that governed North Vietnam from 1954, and all of Vietnam from 1975, was still one of the most arcane. Communist states are not supposed to stand still but to mobilize their people for bureaucratically regimented programs of economic development. Thus the 1980 constitution of Vietnam asserted that the "historical mission" of the new Vietnamese state was to organize its people to accomplish "three revolutions" (in the relations of production, in science and technology, and in thought and culture); to end exploitation of man by man; and to oppose counterrevolutionaries. The apparatus of such a state was far-flung. There were a State Council and ministries; a government bureaucracy; secret police or "public security" machinery (created as

early as February 1946); a network of representative organs, not democratic by Western standards, which ranged from a National Assembly to
more local people's committees; and controlled mass organizations such
as labor unions or women's federations which the Communist Party
used as "transmission belts" for expounding its policies and soliciting
support for them.

The Communist Party itself dominated and led this state and its
armed forces. The party resembled a paramilitary formation. It had
chains of command and an all-powerful general staff of leaders at its
very summit, known, in faithful imitation of Soviet practices going back
at least to 1919, as its "Political Bureau" (Politburo, *Bo chinh tri*). After
Ho Chi Minh died in 1969, and even before, the general secretary of
the Vietnamese party, Le Duan, exercised increasingly decisive authority over the politburo, which usually comprised ten to fifteen people.
Through much of this period, the Vietnamese Communist Party as a
whole bore a startling resemblance to the elderly male Confucian oligarchy that had traditionally ruled Vietnam. It was small (3 percent of the
population in 1976) and far from youthful. In 1979, after nearly fifty
years of being a "proletarian vanguard," fewer than 10 percent of its
members were workers, and only 17 percent were women. In the 1980s,
close relatives of Le Duan and of another politburo grandee, Le Duc
Tho, held strategic offices not far outside the politburo. This evoked
another tradition of dynastic Vietnam: the absence of a clear dividing
line between government based on merit and government based upon
family loyalties.

From 1941 to about 1965, Communist politics in Vietnam were
loosely interlocked with the Communist revolution in China as led by
Mao Tse-tung. Indeed, the inherent susceptibility of Vietnamese
thought to Chinese political and philosophical trends was one of the
things that had helped the Vietnamese Communists to win, along with
French repressiveness (which had led to the success only of tightly
organized, conspiratorial political parties), the absence before 1954 of a
middle class large enough to create a Vietnamese version of the Indian
Congress Party, and the perceived need for social revolution. The keystone of Mao's thought was the belief that human willpower could create a revolution even where the orthodox requirements for such a revolution—capitalism or an industrial working class—did not exist. But
Mao's idealized revolutionary will, or consciousness, could be attained
only through such measures as the ideological remolding of intellectuals. This meant their subordination to the peasant masses, who supposedly possessed spontaneous revolutionary energies. Land reform
campaigns as conducted by Mao deliberately stimulated the supposedly
inherent class conflict within each village, as a means of eliciting the
innate political wisdom of the poor. In the 1940s, one leader of the Vietnamese party, Truong Chinh, whose pseudonym actually meant "Long
March," tried to bring some of Mao's principles to Vietnam. He

demanded the creation of a "new democratic" culture in Vietnam that would serve the masses by being "national, scientific, and popular." This language was taken from Mao's "New Democracy" treatise of 1940. In his "Marxism and Vietnamese Culture" (1948), Truong Chinh further made it clear that solidarity with the revolutionary poor was more important than conventional learning: he said that the Vietnam of the Viet Minh should not "dream of using the classical methods of advanced industrial countries" but should rather freely draw upon the experiences of its own "laboring masses" to improve the limited understanding of its elite scientists and technologists. In 1950, the DRV government introduced an educational reform in the areas it controlled which reduced examinations, replaced subjects like foreign languages with lessons in increasing farm production, and even allowed parents and pupils to review the competence of teachers. Such policies were gradually abandoned, as unsuitable "guerrilla warfare" education, only after 1956.

But the land reform campaign that the DRV launched in 1953 brought Maoist influences to their zenith. To carry out the redistribution of farmland owned by landlords or "counterrevolutionaries" to more than two million peasant families, the DRV leaders created "special tribunals," composed of poor peasants, to punish all dissenters and even began to purge the Communist Party itself of many old cadres, replacing them with "good" peasants in order to guarantee "purity." (The party had grown from 20,000 members in 1946 to 700,000 members by 1950; by 1960, it was down to 500,000 members, some indication of the scope of the purge.) Revolts against such a land reform campaign, which had been based upon Maoist caricatures of rural society, led to bloody violence. Truong Chinh was briefly demoted from the politburo, as the regime expressed ritual contrition for "grave errors."

But Hanoi did not fully renounce its qualified attraction to Mao's revolution until the late 1960s. Then the DRV government's war with the United States compelled it to seek advanced weapons technology from the Soviet Union. It became more fully converted to the Soviet Union's more orthodox and more elitist commitment to international scientific and industrial civilization, and it grew displeased at the disruptive propaganda of Mao's Cultural Revolution, which was spread inside Vietnam itself by the 30,000 Chinese soldiers sent there temporarily after 1965 to repair the roads and railways the United States was bombing. Even before then, Soviet economic aid had undergirded Hanoi's first five-year plan (1961–1965), notably by helping build power plants and by reviving the north's coal mines. In so doing, it had provided a counterpoint to Maoism, allowing Hanoi to balance between the two Communist superpowers.

Between 1958 and 1964, most of the north's peasants lost their private farm plots. The peasants were compelled to become the employees of some 31,908 small agricultural cooperatives, whose average size in

1964 was eighty-three families. The purpose of this rural collectivization was the substitution of planned group production for individual production, as a means of overcoming the acute fragmentation of prerevolutionary northern agriculture. The north's "commercial capitalists" (a paltry group of fewer than 1,500 merchant families) were ordered to become members of joint public-private business enterprises. But by this time, the north's remaining independent intellectuals had begun to rebel. They took advantage of the political uncertainty which followed the troubled land reform. Led by such men as the illustrious journalist Phan Khoi, who had been writing sensitive polemics about the modernization of Vietnam since the 1920s, these intellectuals demanded an end to dictatorship and, significantly, urged that "socialism" be postponed until Vietnam had become richer through capitalism. Such writers and their journals were suppressed in 1957. But in 1963 the party dictatorship was again confronted, not just by "dogmatists" who wanted to borrow even more from Mao's China, but by "rightists" within the party itself who were suggesting that the agricultural cooperatives had been introduced "too early."

Of the fledgling Communist state's achievements which no one seriously disputed, the most important were the inculcation of literacy and the modernization and social expansion of Vietnamese public health care. By 1964 a network of village public health stations, unprecedented in Vietnamese history, had been installed throughout the north, and the average life-span of a northern Vietnamese person began to rise, from only thirty-five years in 1940 to fifty-eight years by 1975. The regime also tried to introduce a post-Confucian order of more equal rights for women with a Marriage and Family Law (December 1959), which struck at concubinage; forced or early marriages; the delay of marriage during extended family mourning for the dead; the denial to widows of the right to keep their property and remarry; and other "feudal" customs. Decades after its promulgation, however, this law had shown only a limited capacity to transform the popular culture.

In 1976, less than a year after the Americans had evacuated themselves from Saigon, the Vietnamese Communist leaders formally reunited the two halves of Vietnam. The entire country was renamed the Socialist Republic of Vietnam. The city of Saigon already had been renamed Ho Chi Minh City. Student youths in southern cities, many of whom had long been antagonistic to the United States–backed Saigon governments, were organized to uproot all vestiges of "neocolonialism" and its "servant culture." In Hue alone, private households and coffee shops alike were persuaded to deliver 160,000 "reactionary" books and magazines to a new Bureau of Information and Culture, which presumably destroyed them. New people's libraries, whose book collections had been stockpiled in the north before 1975, were quickly set up in southern cities to fill the contrived literary vacuum. Hundreds of thousands of southerners, ranging from anti-Communist army officers to hospital directors and monks, and including relatives of the Viet Cong themselves, were imprisoned in "reeducation camps." The camps violated human rights in shocking and ugly ways and often meant prolonged detention in circumstances of malnutrition and maltreatment. When the Hanoi politburo abruptly dissolved the southern Communists' "provisional revolutionary government," thus ending the dream of some of its members of a federal Communist state in which the south retained some decision-making powers, anguished Viet Cong veterans held a "funeral" for the Viet Cong at the old Rex Dance Hall in Saigon.

The postwar rural revolution in the south turned into the theoreticians' mirage. To work, it had needed two human elements: an oppressive landlord class, more than a century old, whom peasants hated, and party activists who were close to, or themselves, peasants. Both had been eliminated by the war. The fighting, and such campaigns of terror as "Operation Phoenix," which the U.S. Central Intelligence Agency had first unleashed in 1967 against supposed Viet Cong village "operatives," had killed tens of thousands of low-level party organizers. The Communist revolution failed to enjoy enough popularity in southern villages in the 1970s to enable it to replace them. As for the old Cochinchina landlord class, the transfer of power in Saigon from the landlord-based government of Diem to a government run by military officers with lucrative business ties, after 1963, had meant a severe decline in their influence. Another land reform law of 1970; the destructive effects of the fighting itself; and the gestation through lavish American aid of a modern capitalist farm economy, featuring miracle rice and plowing machines, in which many peasants could participate, had all helped to reduce the old rural "feudalism." After 1975, the Mekong delta provinces were dominated instead by skilled "middle peasants." Such people owned their lands, relished marketing their produce on free markets, and had little interest in Communist-style collectivization, which they resisted. The Communist government redistributed 265,400 hectares of land to more than 440,000 southern peasant families between 1975 and 1984. But, a decade after the war, it still had not got control of the south's village markets and had managed to entice little more than half of the south's peasants into even rudimentary forms of cooperative farming, such as joint machinery-using groups. Moreover, once the social stimuli of the revolution in the south diminished, the discipline and appeal of the party itself became clouded. (The party had a mere 34,900 members among more than nine and a half million southern peasants in late 1983.) Southern merchants and farmers were able to corrupt party cadres by offering them "shares" in their businesses, in a modern echo of the traditional relationship between mandarins and merchants.

A brief but shocking war with China, in February 1979, further battered the Vietnamese revolution. Up to 200,000 Chinese troops were involved in an invasion of Vietnam's northern border provinces. They seized several provincial capitals but were withdrawn in March after a fierce struggle in which Vietnamese soldiers performed so well that the Vietnamese army then occupying Cambodia did not need to be diverted to defend Hanoi, as the Chinese undoubtedly had hoped.

The war had a variety of immediate causes. China and Vietnam had competed with each other for the right to be the chief foreign patron of the revolutions in Laos and Cambodia. But after 1976 the Pol Pot regime in Cambodia had showed intense enmity to Vietnam and assaulted the borders of southern Vietnam. Vietnam thereupon invaded Cambodia and installed a more manageable government in Phnom Penh ( January 1979), reminding the world as it did so of imperial Vietnam's recurrent colonial manipulations of Khmer politics and greatly embarrassing Pol Pot's Chinese patrons. Truong Chinh, once the preeminent apostle of Maoist thought in Vietnam, revealed something of the fantastic fears which lay behind this invasion when he charged China, in 1979, with wishing to encircle Vietnam from the rear and even absorb it, through such stratagems as pouring Chinese immigrants into Cambodia once Pol Pot had obediently "liquidated" many of his own people.

Apart from Cambodia, Sino-Vietnamese relations foundered upon the two governments' increasingly provocative contradictory involvements in the interminable global duel between the American and Soviet superpowers. China feared the Soviet Union and sought greater intimacy with the United States, even before the Vietnamese Communists' war with the United States had ended. Vietnam allied itself with the Soviet Union, alarming China. There were also border disputes, on land and at sea, and a tragic controversy over the nature and behavior of the overseas Chinese people in Vietnam, who had enjoyed double citizenship privileges there until 1978. For overseas Chinese merchants had now become the scapegoats for Hanoi's inability to impose its revolutionary blueprints readily upon the conquered south after 1975. As Sino-Vietnamese tensions mounted, ethnic Chinese refugees, including veterans of the Vietnamese army and Communist Party, as well as factory workers, hospital doctors, booksellers and peasants, fled from Vietnam. They went either to southwest China or by sea to Hong Kong and non-Communist Southeast Asia, as part of a disheveled stream of "boat people." Beyond the immediate causes of the 1979 war, the leaders of China undoubtedly still had a vestigial notion of the Vietnamese as ungrateful "Annamites" who owed their civilization to China. The Vietnamese leaders doubtless remembered Le Loi.

The consequences of the war were grim. Marxists pretend that socialism, being devoid of monopoly capitalism and thus of imperialism, guarantees peace; this was the first wholly undisguised war in history between two major Communist states. As such, it called into question the ideological purity of both regimes, at least for serious Chinese and

Vietnamese Communists, and party purges were inevitable. The most conspicuous in Vietnam was Hoang Van Hoan, a longtime associate of Ho Chi Minh who had served in the Hanoi politburo itself until 1976. Hoan fled from Vietnam to China in the summer of 1979. In China, as one of the most senior defectors in history from an established Communist government, he vainly summoned Vietnamese to a "second revolution" against the Le Duan regime. Such events, and the prolonged deprivation of normal relations with the United States, drove Vietnam into a suffocating dependency upon the Soviet Union. This worsened Sino-Vietnamese relations still more. Hanoi signed a friendship treaty, which implied military cooperation, with the Soviet Union in November 1978; it had previously (June 1978) joined the Council for Mutual Economic Assistance (COMECON), the Soviet-run trading bloc. Vietnamese trade with the other COMECON countries, which had been less than half the value of Vietnam's external trade in 1976, had climbed to roughly 75 percent of the value of that trade by 1985.

Apart from the eternal, impassioned, and discordant duet with China, the central problem in contemporary Vietnamese history is the appropriateness of the Marxist-Leninist formula of economic development to the world's third most populous Communist state. (The Vietnamese population doubled, from thirty million people to sixty million people, between 1960 and 1985.) The chief prescriptions of this formula are the increase of the state's investable surplus, through the elimination of the excess consumption of the prerevolutionary upper classes; the investment of this surplus, when combined with tax revenue from farming, predominantly in the modernization of industry; and the use of an intricate process of central planning to direct the economy. But the traditional Vietnamese kingdom commanded a far smaller surplus in taxes and tribute, and its upper classes were far poorer, than those of the ancestral societies of any other major Communist government. When it began its industrialization in 1954, North Vietnam had far fewer modern industrial assets than China or North Korea. The early political and military triumphs of the Vietnamese revolution, however, favored the exaltation of the imagined capacities of the Vietnamese economy in the minds of its leaders.

Soviet and Chinese aid, especially between 1960 and 1975, acted to replace the domestic economic surplus which North Vietnam had really needed when it began to industrialize. The aid enabled the north to invest in industries (power plants, cement factories, machine tool factories), and to transfer millions of workers from farming to industry, in the illusion that it was making a permanent breakthrough to the proper modern sort of division of labor between agriculture and industry as described by orthodox Marxist-Leninist (and Western capitalist) economists. After 1975, as foreign aid declined and the population boom continued, the Vietnamese economy regressed to its real level of development. When the state continued to commit scarce capital to industry but not to the purchase of farm products at tolerable prices, its peasants rebelled. As de facto public employees, rather than the dismissible tenants of private landlords, they ironically had greater power to do so. Disgruntled peasants abandoned their lands, or mixed sand into their compulsory rice deliveries, or held back their sugar cane harvests and boiled them into wine, which they could then drink. The state's taxable surplus shrank catastrophically. It was unable to supply enough subsidized food to its privileged elite of cadres. Their real salaries fell; they had to take second jobs to earn enough money to buy necessary goods on free markets; public administration deteriorated.

Reforms in the 1980s at least briefly rescued the Vietnamese government. The increasingly unreal official price system to which Hanoi leaders had clung between 1960 and 1981, with many of its attendant subsidies, disappeared. Peasants were no longer tied to work contracts which paid them arbitrarily, and modestly, through work points; they were now allowed output contracts in which they rented farmland from their cooperatives and sold privately, and at better prices, the surplus food they grew. The national rice crop increased, the amount of it the state was able to collect as a surplus did also, and Vietnam was able to feed itself without grain imports for the first time in 1983. But two different conceptions of Vietnam still jostled each other at the end of the Le Duan era: that of a centralized, autarkic, revolutionary nation in arms and that of a slightly more open, decentralized society of different urban and rural interest groups and income levels. Under the shadow of the party dictatorship, critical economic thinkers in the universities and research institutes whose commitment to the narrow orthodoxy of the Le Duan politburo was far from unlimited (in 1985 only 26 percent of the principal teaching cadres at Vietnam's ninety-three universities and high-level educational institutions were Communist Party members) continued to try to push Vietnam more rapidly toward the second conception.

The economic liberalization of the 1980s did not dissipate the fears of such thinkers that the historical problem of capital accumulation for economic growth would remain far more difficult in Vietnam than in China, the Soviet Union, or eastern Europe. They complained that Vietnam's long addiction to foreign aid had obscured this fact; and they hinted that Vietnam's unusually "low economic starting-point" required more changes in the Marxist-Leninist state orthodoxy than were being allowed. Thus the future of the Socialist Republic of Vietnam is likely to present a spectacle every bit as Vietnamese as brilliantly playful poetry, or conical hats: the interaction between an imported, publicly consecrated model of political and philosophical action and intellectuals who worry about at least some of this model's Vietnamese validity.

# 34

## Cambodia and Laos

### Cambodia

IN May 1945, two months after King Norodom Sihanouk, with Japanese encouragement, had declared Cambodia's independence, Son Ngoc Thanh returned from Tokyo to become foreign minister in the new regime. In September, after the Japanese had surrendered to the Allies but before the French had returned in force to Indochina, Thanh became Cambodia's first prime minister, but his days were numbered, for on October 15, French officials flew into Phnom Penh, arrested him, and flew him off to eventual exile in France.

The seven-month interregnum between March and October made it difficult for the French to resume governing Cambodia as they had done before March 1945. In early 1946, they signed a *modus vivendi* with Sihanouk and delegates selected from the pro-French bureaucratic elite. The document was vague about independence but proposed that a consultative assembly be elected to draft a constitution and allowed political parties to be formed, for the first time in the country's history.

Two important parties took shape in 1946. Both were headed by members of the royal family. The larger one, the Democrats, drew support from the middle ranks of the bureaucracy, from educated young people, and from the Buddhist monastic order. Many of them were associates of Son Ngoc Thanh. The Liberals tended to be more conservative, less republican, and more pro-French.

In the elections for the consultative assembly, the Democrats captured two-thirds of the seats and the Liberals the remainder. The constitution, drafted by the Democrats, called for a strong legislature and saw the king, like the president of France at that time, playing a ceremonial role. Soon after it was promulgated in 1947, the Democrats won fifty-four of the seventy-six seats in the newly formed National Assembly.

For the remainder of the 1940s, the Democrats presided over a series of regimes which were powerless vis-à-vis the French and increasingly quarrelsome with King Sihanouk, whose own advisers were drawn from the bureaucratic elite and from relatively right-wing political groupings not represented in the Assembly.

In 1951, politics became more volatile. The Democrats won another Assembly election; the French *résident* was murdered by his Vietnamese house-boy, who escaped and was proclaimed a patriot by the Viet Minh; and Son Ngoc Thanh returned from France to be welcomed by crowds estimated by the French as exceeding a hundred thousand people. Five months later, Thanh fled the capital with a handful of supporters to form a guerrilla movement hostile to Sihanouk and France. Shortly afterwards, the king dissolved the National Assembly; for the next three years he ruled Cambodia by decree.

Dissatisfied with the pace of French concessions, Sihanouk embarked on what he called a crusade for independence, aimed at embarrassing the French, by calling attention to their recalcitrance in public statements he issued while traveling abroad. He was aided in these efforts by the deteriorating military situation inside Cambodia; by the middle of 1953, more than half of the countryside was effectively under insurgent control.

In November, the French caved in and granted Cambodia nearly all the trappings of independence, including command over its armed forces and the right to send diplomats abroad. Sihanouk and his advisers interpreted these concessions as giving him a mandate to rule without political parties. At the Geneva Conference in 1954, Cambodia emerged as a "winner," at least in anti-Communist terms, partly because its delegation was more independent than those of Laos and southern Vietnam, partly because the military situation in Cambodia still was not as favorable to the Communists as it was elsewhere in Indochina, and partly because its delegation stood up to the Great Powers at the conference, insisting on getting their own way on several issues.

Sihanouk took credit for everything Cambodia had gained. However, agreements reached at the conference required Cambodia to conduct elections before the end of 1955. Fearful of the Democrats, and bemused by his own "mandate," Sihanouk set in motion a scenario which, by the end of the year, had placed him even more firmly in control.

First, he staged a referendum on his crusade for independence. One ballot, colored white, had his own picture on it and the word for "yes." The other was black, with the word "no" inscribed on it. Balloting was open, and over a million citizens handed white ballots to the government officials who manned the voting tables. According to official statistics, fewer than two thousand had the temerity to oppose the king.

Sihanouk's second step was to attempt to amend the constitution so as to grant sweeping executive powers to himself. The proposal encountered strong opposition from the elite, and in a tactical master-stroke, the king then abdicated the throne so as to enter politics as a "private citizen." He allowed the monarchy to remain ineffectual by installing his own father, the affable Prince Suramarit, on the throne, which he occupied until his death in 1960.

Sihanouk's final move was to assume the leadership of a recently formed national political movement, the Sangkum Reastr Niyum, usu-

ally translated as People's Socialist Community. Members of the movement could not belong to any other political party but were eligible to
stand as candidates for the Assembly.

In the elections of October 1955, Sangkum candidates, all hand-
picked by Sihanouk, captured over 80 percent of the vote and all the
seats in the Assembly. Official statistics gave the Democrats 12 percent
of the vote and the pro-Communist People's Group another 4 percent.
It seems likely that the actual vote was closer than this, particularly in
areas where Communist guerrillas had recently been active; but Sihanouk's popularity with the electorate was genuine enough, and the elections spelled the end of party politics in Cambodia. The resentment of
Democrats out-maneuvered by Sihanouk, and of pro-Communist candidates and voters roughed up by the police, were to have serious
denouements in the 1960s and contributed to Sihanouk's fall from
power.

Scholars and journalists writing about Cambodia before 1970 tended
to accept Sihanouk's assessment of his popularity and his characteriza-
tion of the Cambodian Communists as a miniscule grouping subservi-
ent to Vietnam. More recently, however, scholars seeking the roots of
the Communist regime which took power in Cambodia in 1975 have
built up a more nuanced picture of Cambodian radicalism in the "Sihanouk years."

Few if any Cambodians joined the Communist Party of Indochina
when it was founded in Hong Kong in 1930, but several hundred did so
in the late 1940s, at the outset of the First Indochina War. In 1951, a
separate Cambodian party was formed, under Vietnamese guidance,
and several thousand Cambodian guerrillas, hundreds of them members of the party, fought alongside the Vietnamese to throw the French
out of Indochina.

When the war was over, the party was in disarray. Many of its members saw no point in fighting, now that the French had gone. Others,
fearing reprisals, went off to northern Vietnam to await developments.
Still others found themselves swept up in Sangkum politics. Sihanouk's
political style often involved over-reacting to real or imagined threats
and at the same time seeking, on the surface at least, to preempt ideological positions to both right and left. Thus he was consistently anti-
Communist at home, while increasingly pro-Communist abroad. Surrounded by right-wing advisers, he favored state intervention, under
the rubric of "Buddhist Socialism," rather than unfettered private
enterprise.

Sihanouk's foreign policies, domestic popularity, and his police gave
Cambodian radicals in the 1950s little room for optimism or maneuver.
By 1960 the Communist Party appeared to its members to be losing
ground. At this time, a thirty-two-year-old schoolteacher named Saloth
Sar took up a position on the party's Central Committee. From a privi-
leged background, he had studied in France in the early 1950s. In 1962

he became secretary of the Cambodian party's Central Committee, a post he was to keep for over twenty years. When the party seized state power in Cambodia in 1976, Saloth Sar began to call himself Pol Pot.

By 1962, meanwhile, Sihanouk's popularity had probably reached its highest point. Cambodia was at peace, and relatively prosperous. Young members of the elite, returning from tertiary education abroad, took up positions in the government. Aid flowed in from many sources, particularly the United States, but also from China, France, and the Soviet bloc, in sufficient quantities to offset annual budget deficits. Assembly elections in 1958 and 1962 confirmed the Sangkum's domination of political life.

By 1963, however, pressures against Sihanouk's government had begun to build up. An anti-Sihanouk demonstration in Siem Reap led to repression of leftists in Phnom Penh; Saloth Sar and some of his colleagues went into hiding, at this point, and three leftist ministers in Sihanouk's cabinet, vilified by the prince, resigned. At the same time, Sihanouk stepped up his attacks on the United States, blaming Washington for plotting against him (he later wrote a book entitled *My Wars with the CIA*); he cut off U.S. military aid in 1963, and diplomatic relations were broken in 1965.

In the 1960s, the intensifying war in Vietnam had several important effects on Cambodia. By trading rice with the Communists (rather than selling it to the government, at artificially low prices) many farmers and entrepreneurs became wealthy, while the government lost its customary earnings from rice exports. By charging commissions for transporting Vietnamese military goods overland from Cambodia's deep-water port at Sihanoukville, the Cambodian officer corps, far from radical in ideology, became one of the richest segments in the society. At the same time, austerity measures introduced by Sihanouk and his advisers had little effect on the elite, while angering ordinary people. Opposition to the prince, particularly among students, became widespread.

In public, Sihanouk spoke out against border violations on the part of U.S. and South Vietnamese forces and military aircraft. In private, he was also worried by the increasing use made of his territory by Vietnamese Communist forces.

In 1966, his response to the deepening crisis was to allow Sangkum candidates for the National Assembly to compete openly for votes, rather than to await his nomination. The results revealed a pattern of local patronage and loyalty in many parts of the country, but the most representative Cambodian election since the early 1950s also was marked by a large number of electoral offenses. By and large, relatively right-wing candidates, often after distributing largesse, won seats in the Assembly; however, two leftists, Hu Nim and Hou Youn, although attacked persistently by the prince, also held their seats in areas where people were being recruited in large numbers to assist the Communist Vietnamese.

Although the Cambodian Communist Party kept its existence a secret from outsiders until 1977, we now know a good deal about its activities in the 1960s. By 1966, Saloth Sar and his colleagues, still in hiding, had begun to advocate a policy of armed resistance to Sihanouk and his "feudal" entourage. They may well have been moved to do so in part by the debacle that had overtaken the comparatively cooperative Communist Party in Indonesia in 1965–1966. Others in the party, more attuned to long-term international goals, perhaps, than to short-term Cambodian ones, argued unsuccessfully that the Cambodian revolution should be postponed until Vietnam's had been achieved. To Saloth Sar's faction, neither the Vietnamese nor Sihanouk could be trusted to put Cambodia's interests ahead of their own, a view they shared, ironically, with many of the politicians, students, and military figures whom they also proposed to destroy.

In early 1967, a peasant uprising in Samlaut in the northwest was brutally suppressed by Sihanouk's forces; perhaps as many as ten thousand people were massacred before order was restored. The uprising accelerated the momentum of Saloth Sar's faction, and over the next three years, insurgency against Sihanouk's government, as distinct from occasional clashes between Vietnamese forces and those of Sihanouk's army, spread throughout much of the kingdom, creating a situation reminiscent of the early 1950s.

Under these increasing pressures, Sihanouk lost much of his political *élan*. He spent his time producing and starring in feature-length films, travelling abroad, and denouncing his opponents. This behavior alienated many of Cambodia's elite, while Sihanouk himself was unhappy about the austere policies and pro-American leanings of the cabinets he put together to cope with Cambodia's malaise. Internationally, he drifted slightly to the right, restoring diplomatic relations with the United States in 1969, because he believed—incorrectly, as it turned out—that the Cambodian Communist insurgency was being orchestrated by the Vietnamese.

Several months earlier than this, perhaps with Sihanouk's permission, but without informing the American people, the United States had begun to bomb Vietnamese positions inside Cambodia in a systematic way. These attacks helped to radicalize many Cambodians who were unwittingly subjected to them. They also pushed Vietnamese military enclaves deeper into Cambodia.

In March 1970, while Sihanouk was abroad, he was removed from office as chief of state by his own National Assembly. The United States may have been tangentially involved in the coup, but the main impetus came from the Cambodian elite and from the army officer corps, verbally encouraged to take such action by their counterparts in Indonesia and South Vietnam. In Beijing, Sihanouk adroitly announced the formation of a coalition government, which included the radicals he had been trying to exterminate only a few weeks earlier. In Phnom Penh, a new regime under General Lon Nol allowed mobs to burn down Vietnamese Communist diplomatic missions while declaring itself neutral in the war inside Vietnam. This ambiguous position failed to restrain the United States and South Vietnam, whose forces invaded Cambodia in May and devastated the border region before pulling back to Vietnam after about a month.

The politicians who had brushed Sihanouk aside were in many cases nostalgic for the relatively open politics of the 1950s; some of them had been Democrats; and many had grown contemptuous of the monarchy as an institution. In October 1970, Cambodia renamed itself the Khmer Republic. Party politics resumed for a time (and Son Ngoc Thanh, who had supported the coup from his offices in Saigon, became prime minister for several months) but they guttered out as Lon Nol became repressive and as the war in the countryside, for Republican forces, went from bad to worse.

Until the Paris Agreement and the cease-fire in Vietnam in 1973, Communist forces inside Cambodia were often trained and largely equipped by Vietnamese, and by Cambodian cadre sent back into the country after many years of residence in Vietnam. After 1972, this aid diminished, and there is evidence that many of the returnees were assassinated under orders from the party's Central Committee. Even with this drop in aid, Communist forces effectively controlled more than two-thirds of Cambodia by the end of 1972, including the ruins at Angkor.

In early 1973, Cambodia was the "only war in town" for U.S. forces, and to prop up the Khmer Republic, U.S. B-52 bombers began carpet-bombing Communist-controlled areas of the country in order to retain control of Cambodia's besieged provincial cities for Lon Nol's government. When the campaign was stopped by the U.S. Congress at the end of the year, the B-52s had dropped over half a million tons of bombs on a country with which the United States was not at war—more than twice the tonnage dropped on Japan during World War II.

The effects of the bombing on Cambodian rural society and the number of casualties incurred cannot be systematically assessed. It seems clear from oral testimony, however, that the Cambodian Communists used the bombings to recruit new followers among survivors, enraged by a war about which they previously had known little or nothing.

In Phnom Penh, the ineptitude of the Lon Nol regime was compounded by the influx of perhaps two million refugees from rural areas who had fled the bombing and subsequent depredations. Public services gradually broke down; Republican forces, despite infusions of U.S. aid, were unable to loosen the grip of Communist units around the capital. By the beginning of 1975, Phnom Penh was cut off from the rest of the country. The Communists closed in and seized control of the capital soon after Lon Nol, a few of his advisers, and the staff of the American embassy had flown out to safety.

The appearance of the people who occupied Phnom Penh and Battambang (Cambodia's second largest city, which had also held out until
April 1975) shocked many urban Cambodians cut off by choice or circumstances from Cambodia's backwoods. The newcomers were silent,
dressed in peasant black, heavily armed, and often very young. What
they did next was even more disturbing. Within twenty-four hours in
Phnom Penh, and seven days in Battambang, they ordered all the people in these cities—perhaps three and a half million in all—to walk away
from their homes and take up work indefinitely in the countryside. The
exodus in both cases was costly in lives and dislocation, but instant and
total ruralization fitted closely with the ideas Saloth Sar and his colleagues had developed at war and in hiding over the past ten years
or so.

As millions of displaced Cambodians criss-crossed the country, they
soon found that money, postal services, markets, schools, and Buddhist
temples had been extinguished by what they knew only as the "higher
organization" *(angkar loeu),* perhaps a pseudonym for the Communist
Party's Central Committee. Other reforms, in language, clothing,
female hair-styles, adornment, courtship and other matters, generally
puritanical and rural in orientation, soon went into effect throughout
the country; in new villages, political education, emphasizing the speed
and purity of Cambodia's revolution, without acknowledging any foreign models or inspiration, now took up several hours a week.

In early 1976, when Cambodia's third constitution was promulgated,
the country began to call itself Democratic Kampuchea, and Sihanouk,
hitherto nominally the chief of state, was eased into retirement, indistinguishable from house-arrest, in his former residence in Phnom Penh.

Democratic Kampuchea had some of the trappings of a socialist state,
but the party itself continued to keep its existence a secret, although we
now know that it planned to announce its role at celebrations of the party's twenty-fifth anniversary in September 1976. The celebrations never
took place, and the party's Four-Year Plan that was to be inaugurated at
the same time was apparently shelved, although the document itself has
survived, and provides interesting insights into the Cambodian revolution.

The plan called for a "super great leap forward" which would carry a
collectivized Cambodia swiftly through several evolutionary stages
toward socialism. Essential to this progress were self-sufficiency and
independence, which could be achieved by increasing agricultural production to the point where export earnings from crops, particularly rice,
could pay for imports of machinery and for a long-term program of
industrialization. The targets set by the plan sprang from the idea that
collectivized, revolutionary people could accomplish miraculous things.
The plan called for yields and exportable surpluses more than twice as
high as any in prerevolutionary times—and called for them by the end
of 1977, which is to say immediately after a war, using a largely inexpe-

rienced work force (for the brunt of the work fell on "new people," evacuated from the towns) and with severe shortages of livestock, seed,
insecticides, and tools.

At political meetings, cadre stressed the slogan "three tons per hec-
tare," and the collectivization of eating and property called for by the
plan took effect in early 1977, more humanely in some parts of the
country than in others. Serious malnutrition soon occurred, particularly in the west and northwest, where cadre cut down on people's
rations (but seldom on their own) to obtain the "surpluses" demanded
by higher echelons of the party. The regime's dependence on traditional
medicine meant that hundreds of thousands of Cambodians probably
died between 1976 and 1979 from untended or misdiagnosed diseases or
from diseases formerly under control with Western medicine, like
malaria.

Executions also took tens of thousands of lives. In the early days of
the regime, victims tended to be those from the "exploiting" classes of
prerevolutionary Cambodia. These included army officers, civil servants, and particularly teachers. By the middle of 1976, this wave of
killings had subsided, and party officials seem to have believed that
their problems with "internal enemies" were under control. However,
in September and October 1976 a mysterious sequence of events caused
Pol Pot to announce his retirement as prime minister. He seems to have
been absent from Phnom Penh for about a month, perhaps in hiding
following an abortive coup or stepping aside tactically to watch his
enemies emerge inside the party. In October and November, hundreds
of party members were herded into the regime's interrogation center at
Tuol Sleng in the capital, where they were tortured, forced to confess to
"treason," and put to death. More than four thousand of these confes-
sions, transcribed between 1976 and 1978, have survived; the crimes
which people admit in them are so sweeping as to be difficult to believe.
Some victims, for example, claim to have been working simultaneously
for the United States, the Soviet Union, and Vietnam. By the end of the
year, party documents indicate that Pol Pot and his associates believed
that their enemies were everywhere, and particularly in the lower echelons of the party.

A complicating factor was the growing antagonism of Democratic
Kampuchea toward Vietnam. Until the end of 1976, relations between
the two countries were chilly, but correct. By early 1977, perhaps with
encouragement from China, Cambodian forces started to attack Vietnamese targets along the border, and we now know that cadre urged
Cambodians at this time to attack Vietnam in order to regain territory
that had been under Vietnamese control for several hundred years but
which sheltered a sizable Cambodian minority. This warfare was kept
secret by both sides for several months but escalated sharply at the
beginning of 1978, when a Vietnamese attack by six divisions was
repelled. At this stage, if not earlier, the Vietnamese Communist Party

appears to have decided to lend support to forces inside the Cambodian party antagonistic to Pol Pot. These were particularly numerous in the eastern part of the country, bordering on Vietnam.

By the middle of 1978, therefore, Democratic Kampuchea was fighting a civil war as well as an international one. The regime's response, internally, was to intensify its policy of terror. Tens of thousands of people, throughout the country, were executed at this time. These executions, following years of disease, overwork, and malnutrition, which probably killed over a million men, women, and children, de-legitimized Pol Pot's regime in the eyes of the population at large; when the Vietnamese forces attacked in early 1979, no one outside the retreating Communist army offered them any resistance. Phnom Penh fell in January 1979, and within a month a pro-Vietnamese regime, calling itself the People's Republic of Kampuchea, had been installed, while Pol Pot's forces had been forced into sanctuaries in the forest along the Thai border.

By the end of 1979, the Vietnamese and their proteges were firmly in control of most of the country, but given the opportunity to flee, hundreds of thousands did so, eventually finding refuge in France, Canada, the United States, and other Western countries. Pol Pot's forces, supported logistically by Thailand and China, remained a threat to the regime's stability, while it was unable to attract support or recognition from the United Nations. Democratic Kampuchea, formed into a coalition with anti-Communist groups in 1982, was for many years the only government in exile recognized by the United Nations.

The People's Republic of Kampuchea was slow to exert strong economic or political controls, while accepting the protection of over a hundred thousand Vietnamese military "volunteers" and assiduously following domestic and international policies meshed with the interests of Vietnam. Because of the odium attached to Pol Pot's regime, the Vietnamese at first relied for leaders on people who had gone to Vietnam from Cambodia in the 1950s, and on others, like the president, Heng Samrin, who had rebelled against Pol Pot in 1977 and 1978. By 1986, however, the Cambodian Communist Party Central Committee included at least twenty members (out of forty) who had neither Vietnamese connections nor pre-1979 Communist affiliations. Like Laos, Cambodia was the beneficiary of what the Vietnamese referred to as a "special relationship" with Vietnam, but Vietnamese advisers, and Cambodian officials, were unwilling to impose excessive economic controls on the Cambodian people. As in Laos, Buddhism was encouraged, although monks and monasteries were monitored closely, as they had always been, by the state.

Ironically, the coalition government in exile was nominally headed by Prince Sihanouk, who was released from house arrest in the last days before the Vietnamese army occupied Phnom Penh. Since 1941, the prince has been completely out of power in Cambodia for only two and a half years.

## Laos

The political history of Laos since 1945 has been dominated by the efforts of various Lao and foreign groups to construct a political entity named "Laos" where none existed before. Until 1975, when a Communist regime assumed power in Vientiane, these groups and outsiders were thwarted by deeply embedded habits of regionalism and family rivalries among the Lao elite, poor communications and backwardness throughout the country, and most importantly by the political pressures and physical devastation that came to Laos as a result of the Second Indochina War.

Regional and foreign rivalries were compounded by ethnic differences between the Buddhist lowland Lao and minority populations inhabiting hilly and wooded areas of the country. In the south, these were referred to disparagingly as *kha,* the Lao word meaning "slave"; in the north, tribal groups such as the Hmong and Yao, fiercely independent, eked livings from unreported trade across the border with China, from cultivating opium, and in the 1960s and 1970s as mercenaries paid by the United States to fight Lao Communist forces.

Like Cambodia and parts of Vietnam, Laos in the 1940s, 1950s, and 1960s was swept up in a conflict to which few of its people at first at least gave strong support to any side. The few who did were concentrated largely in the ranks of the Indochina Communist Party and its successor parties, which in the Lao case grew from less than a hundred members in 1945 to over forty thousand in the 1980s. What differentiated the Lao Communists, supported by the Vietnamese, from their domestic rivals since World War II, was that they were optimistic about gaining and holding political power throughout the country. For nearly forty years, this optimism seldom wavered, but in the 1940s, at least, the Communist victory of 1975 would have been nearly impossible for non-Communist observers to predict.

In March 1945, when the Japanese informed Sisavangvong, the Lao king at Luang Prabang, of his country's independence, his heir, Prince Savangvatthana, rejected the offer, proclaimed that Laos would always remain a protectorate of France, and was arrested. The viceroy, Prince Phetsarath (1890–1959) then gathered a nucleus of independence-minded members of the elite and made the old king declare independence. In the confusion that followed—the French did not reoccupy Vientiane until April 1946—Phetsarath and his entourage, calling themselves the Lao Issara (Free Lao), took control of much of central and northern Laos. In the south, the hereditary prince of Champassak, Boun Oum (b. 1900), aided the French. When French administration resumed in 1946, the king was rewarded by being named the ruler of the "Kingdom of Laos"—an invented entity—encompassing all of the French-controlled areas, including Champassak. Phetsarath then fled with his full brother, Souvanna Phouma, and their half-brother, Souphanouvong, to exile in Thailand.

Over the next four years, French willingness to negotiate the issue of independence gradually drew many Lao Issara, including Souvanna Phouma, back from Thailand. Phetsarath, in disfavor with Luang Prabang, remained in Bangkok until 1957. Souphanouvong also refused to return home peacefully, preferring to take to the hills and to ally his military following, the Pathet Lao (Lao Nation), with the Viet Minh fighting the French in eastern Laos and in northwestern Vietnam.

Souphanouvong was joined at this stage by other Lao radicals who were to assume important roles in the Communist Lao government. These included Kaysone Phomvihan (b. 1920), who in 1975 became prime minister of Laos, and Nouhak Phoumsavan (b. 1913), who was to become deputy prime minister. All three men had, like other leaders of the party, family and working ties with Vietnam; Kaysone's mother, in fact, was Vietnamese.

In October 1953, France granted Laos its independence within the framework of the French Union, promising to defend it militarily. France was forced to honor its pledge almost at once, after a Viet Minh–Pathet Lao feint into central Laos late in 1953 threatened to cut the kingdom in two. The French then hastened to fortify the valley of Dienbienphu in northwestern Vietnam, hoping to withstand a Viet Minh–Pathet Lao attack on Luang Prabang, which never came. Instead, Dienbienphu itself fell—after a long siege and heavy losses—in May 1954, just as the Geneva Conference on the Far East turned its attention to Indochinese affairs.

Under terms agreed upon at Geneva, the Pathet Lao were allowed to "regroup temporarily" in two northern provinces of Laos, which became a Communist stronghold until their assumption of power throughout Laos in 1975. At the time of the Geneva Conference, ethnic Lao Communist forces thus regrouped numbered fewer than two thousand men—probably fewer than their counterparts in Cambodia—but the disarray of the Lao royal government at that stage, the collapse of French military power, and Vietnamese insistence on these concessions meant that the Lao Communists benefited far more than their fellow-insurgents in either southern Vietnam or Cambodia at the end of the French war in Indochina.

For the remainder of the 1950s, the United States sought persistently but with little success to assemble and shore up governments in Vientiane capable of preventing a Communist victory in Laos. Some of these governments were more pro-American than others, but none captured more than fleeting loyalty from the predominantly rural population of the country. This was partly because none of the governments had the time or inclination to focus their attention on rural issues, partly because the benefits (and the cash) flowing from U.S. economic aid seldom got very far from Vientiane, and partly because the Cold War itself, of such crucial importance to bureaucrats in Washington, seemed far away from the lives of ordinary Lao men and women.

In 1960, probably with French connivance, a Lao army captain named Kong Le staged a neutralist coup d'état that attracted widespread popular support and made both the Americans and the Pathet Lao nervous about the possibility of their "winning" Laos. Communist military offensives following the coup caught U.S.–financed Lao forces off guard. To salvage what it could, the United States agreed in 1961 to attend a second international conference at Geneva, which was convened to declare the neutralization of Laos, backed by international guarantees.

Although the United States was unwilling to go to war over Laos, its policies after 1962, like those of the Communists, were to undermine the viability of a neutralist regime while seeking to defeat their own opponents. Because of bad faith on both sides—and the high stakes involved—agreements reached at Geneva rapidly came apart, and by 1963 Laos was engulfed in a civil war which intensified over the remainder of the decade, along with fighting in Vietnam.

Increased Vietnamese military support for the Lao Communists, and their use of Lao territory after 1965 to funnel men and materiel southwards, led to a prolonged and ruinous U.S. bombing campaign. By 1970, an estimated seventy thousand North Vietnamese troops were stationed in Laos or in transit through the country. Bombing, Vietnamese conscription, and uncertainty caused nearly a million men, women, and children, particularly from the highlands, to flee their villages and to become refugees in camps administered by the United States. By the early 1970s, Laos was still only nominally a nation-state.

Following the Paris Peace Talks between the United States and Vietnam in 1973, the Vietnamese were able to impose a cease-fire on their followers in Laos, as they were unable to do in Cambodia. This meant that in Laos at least, the next two years were relatively free from full-scale warfare. In Laos, more than in Vietnam, where no genuine coalition government was established, these two years saw the erosion of non-Communist state power, the eclipse of the six hundred-year-old Lao monarchy as an institution, and the gradual institutionalization of Communist control. In the months following the Communist victory in southern Vietnam, and Pol Pot's victory in Cambodia, Lao Communists in the coalition government in Vientiane increased their pressure on their colleagues, until the coalition government collapsed, more or less peacefully, and the monarchy was abolished at the end of 1975. Scholars have drawn parallels between what happened at that point and events in Czechoslovakia in 1948. In both cases, the Communists took power without violence (but not without threatening to use it) and were able to draw at first at least on widespread support. In the Lao case, this derived largely from the reservoir of disillusionment, bitterness, and fatigue with warfare that affected all strata of society, as well as from the fact that the Communists, in the zones that they controlled, had not instituted unjust or particularly severe social programs.

However, in the first few months of 1976, much of this good will evaporated, as Communist cadre earnestly attempted to collectivize much
of lowland Laos and as thousands of former government workers were
herded into brief, but unnerving, "re-education" courses. In the process, hundreds of thousands of lowland Lao, including large numbers of
the educated elite, fled across the Mekong River into Thailand, where
many of them remained in the 1980s. Tens of thousands of Hmong
tribespeople, many of whom had been fighting the Communists for
years, also sought refuge in the West. The fledgling administration
could not afford the loss of so many trained personnel, although its
leaders may well have welcomed the departure of the Hmong. Over the
next few years, acting often on Vietnamese advice, the Lao administration followed Vietnamese initiatives in foreign policy, particularly those
after 1979 that sought to bind the constituent parts of Indochina more
closely to each other. At the same time, collectivization efforts having
failed so frequently were gradually relaxed, market forces were allowed
to re-emerge, and an uneasy truce was maintained with Thailand and
other ASEAN states. Leadership at the center remained remarkably
constant, with Kaysone Phomvihan exercising close control over the
powerful party apparatus into the late 1980s as he had done for forty
years. Because, unlike Cambodia, Laos retained diplomatic relations
with many non-Communist states, the country benefited from a somewhat wider range of foreign aid programs than Cambodia did. As an
institution, the Buddhist Sangha seems to have operated more openly in
Laos than in Cambodia. By the late 1980s it seemed unlikely that any
foreseeable Lao regime would be able or willing to shake the country
free from a subordinate relationship with Vietnam. The Vietnamese, in
fact, had replaced the French as the patron of the Lao, much as the
French, in turn, had taken the place of the Thai at the end of the nineteenth century and drawn lines on the map which created the boundaries for the state of Laos.

# 35

## The Kingdom of Thailand

THAILAND's wartime policy of collaboration with the Japanese was useful to the Thai only so long as Japan's power was paramount. It spared Thailand extensive damage and left the power of its government unimpaired. When the course of the war turned against the Japanese, however, Thai policy had to change. Accordingly, in August 1944 the National Assembly forced Phibun Songkhram's government to resign and installed a new government led by a civilian politician, Khuang Aphaiwong, and directed from behind the scenes by Pridi Phanomyong. Since early in the war, Pridi had acted as regent for the absent boy-king Ananda Mahidol, organizing from the regent's office an underground movement of resistance against the Japanese—the Free Thai Movement—which was supported by the British Force 136 operating from Ceylon and by the American Office of Strategic Services through Yunnan. Those connections were used in an attempt to gain the good graces of the Allies, especially when some Thai offered to mount an uprising against the Japanese in May 1945, an offer later rejected.

At the end of the war in August, the gravity of Thailand's international position was exposed by the victorious Allies. At that time, Thailand still held Lao and Cambodian territories annexed after the Indochina War of 1940–1941, as well as the four states of northern Malaya and two Shan states of Burma granted them by the Japanese in 1943. Britain attempted to impose what amounted to a protectorate over Thailand by advancing eighteen demands, the acceptance of which would impose controls over the Thai economy, government, and army, and requiring that Thailand furnish the Allies 1.5 million tons of free rice "as a special measure of reconcilement and aid by Thailand toward those who had suffered because of Thai denial of rice exports during the war years." With the assistance of strong American diplomatic pressure hastily mobilized by the new prime minister, Seni Pramoj (the wartime Thai ambassador to the United States, who had personally decided not to inform the American government officially of Thailand's declaration of war against the United States), the most extreme demands were moderated, but Thailand still had to agree to furnish the Allies rice at low fixed prices. French demands for the retrocession of Lao and Cambodian territories were even more strongly resisted, but it was the mini-

mum price the French charged for allowing Thailand admission to the
United Nations, a symbol of international respectability that the Thai
felt they needed to secure. After the signature of treaties with Britain
and France in January and November 1946, Thailand was admitted to
the United Nations in December, expressing from the first a strongly
pro-Western foreign policy.

Postwar politics in Thailand were influenced heavily by considerations of external affairs; the period immediately following the war set
patterns that persisted. The army, whose prewar predominance reflected the coherence of the military elite and the weakness of its divided
rivals, was at least temporarily discredited by its association with the
Japanese (although it had never fought the Allies). The willingness of
the Allies to settle their claims on terms favorable to the Thai was due in
part to an apparent resurgence of parliamentary democracy. A new constitution providing for a fully elective legislature came into force early in
1946, when Pridi left his protected position as regent to become prime
minister. He encountered serious difficulties in making the new parliamentary system work. Postwar economic dislocation and the attendant
problems of inflation and corruption were more than he or his successors could manage without jeopardizing their parliamentary position.
Pridi was forced from office in the aftermath of the violent death of King
Ananda on June 9, 1946—an event never satisfactorily explained but
for which public opinion seemed to hold him accountable—and Tha-
wan Thamrongnawasawat, who succeeded him, lacked the strong following that would have made effective government possible. The politicians drifted in indecision until an army conspiracy seized power late in
1947 to establish a nominally independent civil government under
Khuang. The army was reluctant to show its full presence as long as
Western disapproval threatened, but Western distrust of military rule
began to lessen in mid-1948, when other countries of the region were
beset by Communist insurrection. At that point, Khuang was forced
from office, and Field Marshal Phibun again became prime minister.

For the first three years of Phibun's rule, the army restrained itself,
and a semblance of parliamentary government remained. The civilian
politicians, however, were divided. The radicals, led by Pridi, were in
disrepute as the investigation of King Ananda's death dragged on,
while the Democrat Party led by Khuang resented its exclusion from
real power. The armed forces were split on service lines, while the army
itself was divided and younger officers were still distrustful of Phibun.
The government needed foreign support and aid, but it was anxious not
to incur American disapproval by establishing an avowedly military
government. Phibun gradually won a substantial measure of American
support when he committed Thai troops in Korea and kept Thailand
relatively stable. Four abortive military coups between 1948 and 1951
reduced Phibun's rivals to two men: General Phao Siyanon, director-
general of the paramilitary police force, and General Sarit Thanarat,

who commanded the First Army in Bangkok. Caught between the two rivals, as well as between them and the parliament, Phibun saw his grip on power begin to loosen in the early 1950s.

The successes of the Viet Minh in Indochina in 1953 and early 1954 and the possibility of Communist-dominated regimes in Cambodia and Laos made the government receptive to the efforts of the American secretary of state, John Foster Dulles, to bolster the region's military security by organizing the Southeast Asia Treaty Organization (SEATO) in 1954. In addition, American military and economic aid to Thailand was increased. The civilian politicians were worried by the advantage this gave the army; General Phao's arbitrary acts of imprisoning government opponents, together with rampant official corruption, brought the government under increasing attack. Phibun visited Europe and America in 1955 and returned enthusiastic about the possibilities of strengthening his own position by democratization. He legalized political parties and lifted press censorship in preparation for general elections early in 1957. A massive government party pledged to Phibun conducted an intense campaign managed by Phao, while the major opposition came from the weak Democrat Party and smaller leftist parties in the poor northeast. Despite flagrant electoral corruption, however, the government was able to win no more than a bare majority of the seats in the election. Sarit, who ostentatiously avoided full participation in the campaign and election and criticized its outcome, became the focal point of agitation against the conduct of the elections, and, on September 16, 1957, he led a bloodless coup d'état, which ended the long political career of Phibun.

The new parliamentary government inaugurated after elections in December 1957 had but a short life. The parliament reflected the grave divisions stemming from personal feuds, disparate ideological and economic interests, and the clash of traditional and modern political styles and outlooks within Thailand's urban elite. When the new government proved in the army's eyes incapable of acting decisively on the many domestic and international policy problems facing it, Sarit returned from medical treatment abroad to reimpose military rule in October 1958. Sarit commanded political support on a national base much broader than that of his predecessors. He was respected throughout the armed forces, as well as by conservatives of the civil service and the business community, and he raised many professional civil servants to prominent positions in the government. He moved firmly against the radical opposition, especially the mostly ethnic-Chinese Communist Party of Thailand, and attempted at the same time to minimize its appeal by embarking on strong policies of economic development, public welfare, and education. Not so antimonarchical as members of the generation that had ended the absolute monarchy in 1932, he enhanced the authority of the government by encouraging King Bhumibol Adulyadej to play a stronger role in the public life of the nation. Promulgating an authoritarian interim constitution based on those of Gaullist France and Nasser's United Arab Republic, he appointed a Constituent Assembly composed of representatives of all wings of public opinion to draft a permanent constitution.

By the time of Sarit's premature death in 1963, the era of the Vietnam War was beginning immediately next door, and the forces set in motion by that long conflict worked profoundly to change Thailand. Since the end of World War II, Thailand's security concerns have focused primarily on the states of former French Indochina. The resurgence of Vietnam awakened Thai fears for the country's eastern frontiers, especially as the Viet Minh and its successor in Hanoi have come to be seen by the Thai to be fighting and thinking in terms of the whole of Indochina, and not just of Vietnam alone. Naturally, the Thai army, which was the main proponent of pan-Thai nationalism in the Indochina War of 1940–1941, has been acutely aware of the dangers of Vietnamese encroachments on the sovereignty and territory of Laos and Cambodia, particularly as Thailand's natural defense perimeter (as opposed to its borders) is not the Mekong River, which is a highway, but rather the chain of mountains that divides Vietnam from the rest of the Southeast Asian mainland. Thus, the Thai government was long anxious about the desperate "neutralism" of Cambodia in Sihanouk's time, and it has taken a strong interest in events in Laos, where the Thai early supported rightist military factions. Thai disquiet over the inability of SEATO to act in the Laos crisis of 1960–1962 and over the outcome of the Geneva Conference of 1962, which established a neutralist government in Laos, led to quiet agreements with the American government providing for a direct commitment by the United States to come to Thailand's defense, should its security be seriously threatened. And in return, Thailand became deeply involved in the Vietnam conflict, to the point of providing air bases from which Indochina could be bombed and sending troops to fight in southern Vietnam and Laos.

But the impact of the Vietnam War on Thailand was much more than military, it was also economic and social. Ultimately the effects would be political as well. The direct effects were fairly obvious at the time. American spending (and investment) in Thailand was enormous, amounting to several hundred million of dollars. Forty thousand U.S. military personnel stationed in Thailand spent, by Thai standards, lavishly. Servicemen on "rest and recreation" (R & R) leaves from Vietnam spawned a thriving service sector (hotels, prostitution, bars, and nightclubs) in the Thai economy. Highrise hotels and office buildings interrupted the Bangkok skyline, dwarfing the spires of Buddhist monasteries, and the population of the city mushroomed from 1.7 million in 1960 to almost 3 million by 1975.

Furthermore, the rural countryside shared to some extent in the city's prosperity. Upcountry air bases stimulated the growth of nearby towns like Udon, Nakhon Ratchasima (Khorat), and Phitsanulok. Rail service extended to serve provincial military needs and roads improved to open military access to border areas could also carry farmers' produce to market. The result was impressive economic growth, which by the late 1960s was running at an annual rate in excess of 7 percent.

The apparent successes of Sarit and his hand-picked successor, Thanom Kittikachorn, however, were not accompanied by the political stability at which they had aimed. A generation earlier, in the 1940s and early 1950s, Phibun was worried about Thailand's Chinese minority, numbering in excess of 2 million, particularly when Pridi took up exile in Communist China and became the leader of a Thai Patriotic Front and when the membership of the Communist Party of Thailand was composed almost entirely of ethnic Chinese. By the 1960s, however, most Thai Chinese were well along the road to assimilation, and the military rulers of the kingdom now feared political discontent and rural revolution like that they could see occurring in Indochina. In particular, the impoverished northeast, with an ethnic minority akin to the Lao exceeding 10 million, was of major concern to the government. Sarit—himself a northeasterner—began a considerable program of economic development in the northeast, which promoted agricultural production; the building of roads, wells, and irrigation systems; and the expansion of educational opportunities. The government's approach to ruling seemed to be to buy political acquiescence with the currency of social and economic improvements. They could point to statistics and congratulate themselves—and yet the challenges to their dominance steadily mounted. By the late 1960s, they faced serious rural insurgency in the northeast, north, and south led by a Communist Party of Thailand that was now predominantly ethnic Thai in its composition.

As if to repair its political support in the cities, where economic growth and expanded educational opportunities had dramatically enlarged the middle class, the government promulgated a new constitution in 1968, providing for an elected lower house of parliament. Elections held early in 1969 initiated a brief period of democratic relaxation before Thanom again stepped in to reinstitute military rule in late 1971, motivated perhaps by a deteriorating situation in Indochina and the beginnings of an American withdrawal from the region that would leave Thailand to face heightened dangers alone. But in this situation the dashing of democratic hopes, artificially raised, worked against the military. Student unrest, building through the late sixties in Thailand as elsewhere in the world, grew until hundreds of thousands demonstrated in the streets of Bangkok in October 1973, erupting into violence. Leading figures within the military and elsewhere refused to send troops against youthful demonstrators that included their own sons and daughters, and Thanom and his close associates were forced to flee the country, yielding power to a civilian government. Here, perhaps, was the closest thing Thailand had ever had to a "revolution," for it was mass power mobilized on a far greater scale than any Thai had seen before.

Its immediate objective—the end to authoritarian military rule—was far easier to achieve than the students' long-term goal, the institution of the democratic government that had been talked about, but seldom seen, in Thailand since 1932. Over the next few years, Thailand experienced democracy of the most thorough-going sort, with a frenetic anarchy of political parties, demonstrations, strikes, debates, activism, and turmoil. All shades of political commitment were expressed, from the communism of Che Guevara, Kim Il Sung, and Mao Tse-tung to an ultra-rightist monarchism. Students organized to study the economic plight of rice farmers or to assist striking factory workers, and youth everywhere challenged the privileged, the established, the taken-for-granted. The political left came out into the open, and the right, increasingly alarmed, counterattacked. Tempers and violence escalated as a society that a few years earlier had been thought placid was now shown to be riven with cleavages between rich and poor, city and countryside, management and labor, monarchist and anarchist, revolutionary and conservative.

The time for political change could hardly have been worse. World events over which the Thai could have no control inflamed their situation. The world petroleum crisis of 1973–1974 curtailed economic growth and fueled general inflation, while world commodity prices slumped. And as if that were not enough, early in 1975 the long Indochina War finally reached its climax as Communists took full power in Vietnam, Cambodia, and Laos. Kukrit and Seni Pramoj, two brothers who led contending political parties, each tried to forge coalitions that could govern and manage Thailand's multiplying problems. The task was more than they, or anyone, could have been expected to handle. On October 6, 1976, demonstrations that had begun weeks earlier on the return of General Thanom to Thailand exploded into a riot at Thammasat University in Bangkok in which rightist elements abetted by the police and some military factions embarked on an orgy of violence, lynching, beating, burning, and killing demonstrating students. The military establishment then interceded and imposed a regime far more authoritarian than any that had gone before, ironically presided over by a civilian law professor as prime minister, Thanin Kraivichien. In the suppression of the left that followed, thousands of youth fled the city to join guerrilla movements in the forests. But before this awful political polarization could be driven to its extreme, the army yet again stepped in, in October 1977, to replace Thanin with General Kriangsak Chomanand. Through the next decade there was only one further prime minister, General Prem Tinsulanonda (1980-   ). The Thai military, itself now much less unified than it was when Phibun or Sarit or Thanom could act as a military strongman, has proven to be more accommodating of various interests within the society and more moderate in its treatment of dissent. The insurgents in the countryside have dwindled and a modestly lively—if not so exuberant—political life goes on.

It has become increasingly clear that the analytical categories once used to examine Thai society are no longer adequate to the task. Only a generation ago, Thai and scholars who studied them spoke in terms of a few monolithic, hierarchical structures in Thai society, the interplay between which shaped its politics, economics, and intellectual life. As late as the time of Sarit, we could speak of the army, the monarchy, the Buddhist monkhood, the bureaucracy, the Chinese business community, and the peasantry and conclude that we had covered all the elements of Thai society that "mattered." We explained military dominance by referring to the unity of the army in the face of a disunited and even fractious urban population (the bureaucracy and the Chinese) and an amorphous, subsistence-oriented peasantry. All these elements were held to be rigidly structured in an authoritarian fashion, with those wearing uniforms lording it over those without, those with more stripes on their shoulders ordering around those with fewer, and the king and Buddhist monks serving as the upholders of eternal values while everyone else could attend to more immediate material concerns.

All that has changed, because Thailand has changed. What a generation ago was a small society with a miniscule elite and an invisible (because Chinese or obedient bureaucratic) middle class has now doubled in size to more than 50 million persons. The percentage of people who live in cities has doubled to more than 10 percent. Where 85 percent of the population once were rice farmers, now barely half the households in the country gain their livelihood from agriculture. And where there were ten thousand university graduates in 1947, there are now more than a million. The society is now too large, too diverse, too well-educated, too cosmopolitan to be neatly boxed into a few clear-cut hierarchical, vertical structures—or, for that matter, into horizontal "class" structures.

The Thai experience of the mid-1970s may someday be viewed in retrospect as cathartic; but for those who lived through it, it was a period of intense pain and shock. People awakened to a Thailand that they did not realize was there: a nation of conflict, contention, incivility, outrage, and injustice, whether viewed from the left or from the right. The task of the next generation of Thai to wield political power will be to determine, by the exercise of their wisdom and humanity, whether the wounds from that experience would fester or heal.

# 36

# The Union of Burma

THE political order of Burma that the British had presided over collapsed after the Japanese imperial army invaded Burma in January 1942. The British-Indian army was too weak to put up more than a token resistance, and as it retreated toward India at the end of March, several hundred thousand Indians and Britons who had taken up residence under the colonial government fled. The Japanese were accompanied by a small group of young Burmese, the "Thirty Comrades," led by Thakin Aung San, who had been trained by the Japanese to form the officer corps of a new Burma army. The new force, known initially as the Burma Independence Army (BIA), grew as it passed through lower Burma to number about 23,000 untrained but politically inspired youth. The pro forma participation of the BIA in the defeat of colonial rule gave its officers and men great status and popular respect. For the first time Burmese were perceived to be successfully attacking the British. The BIA's power and prestige were further enhanced when the young officers and their *thakin* colleagues assumed the conduct of local administration, especially in rural areas, after the collapse of the British administration. By July 1942, however, the BIA was largely demobilized at Japanese insistence, renamed the Burma Defense Army (BDA), and reduced to 5,000 men.

The Japanese then sought to establish an indigenous administration which would not interfere with their military operations but would help keep the population under control. With Japanese support, Dr. Ba Maw and other prewar politicians established a central administration in collaboration with some of the leading *thakin*. Aung San was made minister of defense, the future prime minister Thakin Nu was made foreign minister, and the future leader of the Communist Party, Thakin Than Tun, was made minister for agriculture. The Japanese granted Ba Maw's government a limited measure of administrative authority and then, in August 1943, nominal independence as an ally. The limited nature of that independence was soon obvious, and coupled with the hardships of the wartime economy and Japanese military demands for goods and services, including the forced drafting of labor, the government and its Japanese allies became increasingly unpopular.

The left wing of the *thakin* movement had refused to countenance collaboration with the "fascist" Japanese, and at the commencement of the war they set about organizing an underground resistance movement. This became identified with the Communist Party that Thakin Soe established in the delta region in 1943. The Communist leaders met with Aung San and other military and non-Communist leaders, known later as the Socialists, to form the Anti-Fascist Organization (AFO) in August 1944. Their intention was to find a means of driving out the Japanese in collaboration with the Allies and then to regain Burma's independence under a genuinely leftist government. They were aided in this effort by the contacts made in India with the British army and the Special Operations Executive's secret intelligence organization, Force 136, by another Communist *thakin,* Thein Pe.

Thus, when British troops reconquered Burma in the first months of 1945, they were joined by elements of the Burma army under Aung San's command and received assistance from the various resistance cells organized by the Communists. Both groups were operating under the nominal authority of the AFO, which had been renamed the Anti-Fascist People's Freedom League (AFPFL). Recognizing the popular support of the AFPFL, the British military administration tried to find a means of ensuring that they did not turn their forces against the British before the Japanese had been defeated in the rest of Asia. Even though the British refused to acknowledge the AFPFL's claim to have established a provisional government, the League cooperated by and large with the British because of the "peaceful development" policy advocated by the leading Communists and the skillfully managed negotiations with the army's leadership by the British supreme commander, Admiral Lord Louis Mountbatten.

The military administration was withdrawn in October 1945, and power was officially returned to the last prewar British governor, Sir Reginald Dorman-Smith. Despite the obvious popularity of the AFPFL leaders, Dorman-Smith refused to give the AFPFL a majority on his advisory Executive Council, arguing that consideration of the League's demand for a prompt grant of independence under an AFPFL government would have to be postponed until "more settled conditions" had been established. He then embarked upon policies designed to revive the prewar economic order by bringing in Indian labor and reinstating Indian and British business interests. In the following months the AFPFL organized well-disciplined demonstrations and strikes with massive public support throughout Burma until they made clear to the British Labor government in London that Dorman-Smith was unable to implement its policies and maintain order within the country. In particular, the increasing prospect of armed rebellion with a consequent shift to the left in AFPFL policies forced the recall of Dorman-Smith in July 1946 and the initiation of conciliatory policies under a new governor, Sir Hubert Rance.

Rance, without conceding that independence would be granted shortly, offered Aung San and other non-Communist members of the

AFPFL's leadership the majority of the positions in his Executive Council. In acknowledgment of his position as the president of the League, Aung San was made the council's vice-chairman and effective premier. However, the acceptance of office by some of the League's leaders led to a split in the national front. The Communist members, except very briefly, received none of the seats on the council and relations between them and the non-Communist leaders became strained. Toward the end of 1946 an increasing number of non-Communist and conservative leaders from the prewar period had joined the League and the Communists had been eased out of their previous leading positions.

However, after the expulsion of the Communists, the League entered into negotiations with the British government, which in January 1947 resulted in an agreement that following elections for a constituent assembly that would draft a constitution, independence would be granted within one year. In April, the AFPFL won 171 of the 182 seats up for election and dominated the drafting of the country's first independent constitution.

An important problem that faced the drafters of the constitution was the status of the "excluded areas" where a variety of ethno-linguistic communities had remained remote from colonial Burma's nationalist politics and modern economy. These groups were still governed indirectly through their traditional authorities. The situation of some of the Christian Karens was different. Their leaders were apprehensive as to their future under an indigenously controlled popular state. Many sought to maintain the special position they had achieved under the colonial administration and demanded a separate government for themselves. With some difficulty, the assembly drew up a constitution that provided for a semi-federal "union" of Burma. Nominal states were granted to the Shans, Kachins, and Kayah (Karen-ni), which were to have very limited administrative autonomy. The Shan and Karen-ni states were given the option to secede from the Union after ten years. Many of the lowland Karens, however, lived intermingled with other Burmese and a separate administration for them was impossible.

On July 19, 1947, an event occurred that shattered what hopes there were that an independent government of Burma might be able to control the various conflicting forces in Burmese society. The assassination that day of Aung San, along with seven associates, at the apparent behest of former premier U Saw, removed from the political scene the one figure who had been able to bridge the warring political factions. The vice president of the AFPFL, U Nu, who was named to succeed the fallen leader, had neither the support of the army nor the trust of the Communists that Aung San had managed to hold. Nonetheless, preparations for independence proceeded on schedule.

Within three months of Burma's independence on January 4, 1948, the new indigenous rulers and their one-time Communist allies in the independence struggle became locked in a civil war for control of the state. Insurrections had begun as early as 1946 when the British declared illegal the "Red Flag" Communists under Thakin Soe. In March 1948, the "White Flag" Communists, led by Aung San's erstwhile colleague, Than Tun, took the offensive after the government home secretary, U Kyaw Nyein, ordered their arrest. They were joined in July by the largest faction of Aung San's veterans' organization, the "White Flag" People's Volunteer Organization (PVO) as well as by about half of the former BIA troops in the government's army.

Scarcely had the government begun to develop plans to cope with these leftist opponents than Karen rebels under the leadership of the Karen National Union, and including some defecting government troops, went into rebellion at the end of 1948. In 1949 the government found itself in control of only a few urban centers. The civil war had its extraordinary aspects. The edge of Rangoon saw young children taking turns shooting at the other side while individuals were permitted to cross the no-man's-land between them. Gradually the government's armed forces began to regain the ascendancy, although the intrusion into the Shan hills of defeated Kuomintang troops at the end of China's civil war complicated and prolonged the conflict. Not until 1951 was security sufficiently established to permit the holding of elections.

The government and the Union survived the civil war but never defeated their opponents, who nearly forty years later continue to deny the central state control over perhaps 10 percent of Burma's territory. The government was able to regain control over most of the country for several reasons. Among these were the creation of a strong national army; a small amount of aid received from Britain, India, and other states; and the support anti-Communist elements in the bureaucracy and middle class gave the socialist AFPFL leaders who during the height of the conflict actually abandoned office to the army and more conservative politicians, as well as the ideological and other incompatibilities of the various insurgent forces that made it impossible for them to unite against the government. Once the possibility that the Communists might assume control or the Karens might dismember the state had collapsed, the AFPFL resumed power, but by the early 1950s its efficacy as a political organization had declined and the government's legitimacy became more and more dependent upon the charisma of the devoutly Buddhist prime minister, U Nu.

The AFPFL had been formed as an anti-fascist united front and by 1946–1947 had become a coalition of forces—peasant and workers' unions, ethnic organizations, political parties, and independent members—bound together by opposition to the British and by the common goal of independence. Soon, however, it was riven by splits. The first split occurred with the expulsion of the "Red Flag" and "White Flag" Communists in 1946–1947; more support was lost in 1950 with the expulsion of the pro-Soviet Burma Workers' and Peasants' Party (BWPP) when the latter disputed the government's approval of the

United Nations' entry into the Korean War. Although the AFPFL and
its affiliates won about 200 of the 239 seats contested in the 1951–1952
elections, the opposition parties drew large votes. The prestige of the
AFPFL declined further as pre-independence hopes remained unful-
filled, the economy failed to recover rapidly, and internal unrest continued. Sharp policy divergences worked further to divide the ruling
coalition. To maintain his position as the 1956 elections approached, U
Nu was increasingly under pressure to satisfy one special interest or
another, to reinvigorate the bureaucracy, and to raise the morale of his
followers. U Nu and his socialist cabinet colleagues strove to combine
Buddhist and Marxist values in a new national ideology. Buddhist
Socialism, as it was named, represented a return to fundamental ethical
principles and an attempt to avoid the abuses that capitalism was
alleged to have inflicted upon the country during the colonial period,
without allowing power to fall to the Communists.

The 1956 elections revealed the continuing erosion of AFPFL popularity. The AFPFL and its affiliates won 173 of 230 seats, while the
largest opposition party, the National Unity Front (NUF, successor to
the BWPP) gained only 47; but the AFPFL received only 48 percent of
the total vote while the NUF had 30 percent. U Nu recognized the dangers facing the AFPFL and retired from office for a period in order to
reassert some organizational discipline in the League. The effect, however, was to fuel factional tendencies in the government, as his reform
efforts attacked the power bases of his political opponents in the government. Thus, shortly after Nu's return to office in 1958 the League
underwent a major split: the two deputy prime ministers, the Socialists
U Ba Swe and U Kyaw Nyein, formed themselves and their followers
into the "Stable" AFPFL, while Nu, with Thakin Tin and others,
formed the "Clean" AFPFL. Nu and his group were able to remain in
power, thanks to support from the former opposition parties of the left
and right. But to maintain his majority, Nu yielded substantial concessions to minority interests, including the left-wing NUF, the Shan
*sawbwa,* and wealthy Arakanese nationalists. But when total amnesty
was promised to all insurgents and Nu stated his willingness to consider
the formation of separate Arakanese and Mon states, political tensions
became too great for the normal parliamentary processes to resolve.
Hampered by bureaucratic paralysis caused by political interference in
the administration of government programs, by the disaffection of ethnic minorities, and by the threat of civil war within the armed forces of
the government itself, Nu handed over the government to the army
commander, General Ne Win, in October 1958, for a six-month period
of "caretaker" rule. This was extended to eighteen months, during
which preparations were made for new elections, held in February
1960.

U Nu's faction of the AFPFL, renamed the Union Party, was returned to power with a strong parliamentary majority. However, the

political and symbolic concessions he made during the campaign, which he proceeded to implement, again endangered national unity. Nu antagonized religious minorities by the establishment of Buddhism as the state religion and then antagonized Buddhist militants by passing a constitutional amendment guaranteeing freedom of religion. And when Nu announced his intention to resign as party leader in 1962, and as prime minister in 1964, his supporters began to fight over the succession. The party began to divide over membership questions, and Shan insurgency broke out in the east. Nu could no longer provide effective leadership, but none of his civilian rivals could fill his role. To the army, it appeared that Burma was heading back to the bitter conflicts of 1958. Because the army's period of rule as a caretaker government had been marked by some success in combating corruption and inflation, in restoring law and order, and in promoting economic growth, the army and General Ne Win could not ignore what they saw to be a clear need to reimpose military rule in order to maintain political stability and national independence. They carried out a coup d'état on March 2, 1962, imprisoned many civilian politicians, suspended the constitution, and again set about reconstructing the state and its relations with civil society under the auspices of an army-led Revolutionary Council.

The army began by dismantling the political structures that had arisen in the first fourteen years of independence and replacing them with others that the Revolutionary Council could supervise. The two chambers of the legislature were dissolved, the president was removed, the separate state governments were abolished, and the courts were centralized under a new supreme court. More gradually, many of the administrative arrangements first introduced in the colonial period were also removed or radically modified. The Revolutionary Council was the government for the next twelve years. Its chairman, General Ne Win, was given full executive, legislative, and judicial powers. At the local level, control of the implementation of government policies was taken away from various ad hoc organizations and passed to Security and Administration Committees (SACs) which, led by local military commanders, coordinated and supervised the activities of the civil bureaucracy and political activities as well.

Initially the Revolutionary Council government attempted to gain the cooperation of the leaders of the political parties that had been active in the 1950s. However, except for the left-wing NUF, they all refused, apparently believing that the military eventually would hand power back to them as it had done in 1960. Such a belief proved to be illusory. None of the leading politicians of the 1950s has ever returned to power and most were forgotten within a few years. Failing in 1962 to get the cooperation of civilian political leaders, the Revolutionary Council established its own political party, the Burma Socialist Programme Party (BSPP, or *Lansin* Party) in order to mobilize support for the government and dominate rival political forces. The BSPP, founded on

July 4, 1962, and made the sole legal party in 1964, remained a "cadre" party until the early 1970s when it was declared a mass party. Until then its membership remained essentially synonymous with the membership of the Revolutionary Council. By 1972, there were still only 79,459 full members of the party, 58 percent of whom came from the army. Membership has expanded rapidly since then, and in 1981 there were a million and a half members, about 5 percent of the total population. Advancement in government employment and preferment in other regards such as scholarships and paid holidays have become increasingly linked with party membership.

The Revolutionary Council implemented economic policies much more radical than those of the 1950s. All foreign and larger domestic businesses were nationalized and several thousand Indians and Pakistanis returned to South Asia when their means of livelihood was taken from them in 1963–1964. All internal trade in essential commodities such as rice and other grains was declared a government monopoly and both internal and external trade came officially under government control. Though many of the Revolutionary Council's economic policies were unpopular, especially among the urban middle class, which lost the most in terms of wealth and security by its program, peasants initially benefited when the government declared all their debts to be void in 1963 and abolished land rents in 1965. However, as all ownership of land was formally held by the state, the peasants came increasingly under government control, and as government rice purchase prices declined, so also did production, so that Burma lost its position as one of the preeminent rice-exporting countries of the world. Foreign revenues also declined, and through the 1960s economic growth was minimal.

The rationale for the Revolutionary Council's economic policies was published in 1962 in a statement known as "The Burmese Way to Socialism." This was explained further in 1964 in a major ideological document called *The Correlation of Man and His Environment*. The latter combined some of the analytical categories of Marxism-Leninism with the basic philosophical ideas of Theravada Buddhism, including impermanence and the concept that evil in this life is caused by man's inherent greed, which only a strong state can and must control in the name of man's higher spiritual needs. Thus, the outwardly radical socialist economic and political doctrines of the Revolutionary Council came to be explained to the people of Burma in terms of the conservation of historically received moral and religious doctrines.

In 1974 a new constitution was introduced in Burma establishing a socialist one-party state which in many ways is similar to its counterparts in Eastern Europe or China. However, there are significant differences. The bulk of economic activity remains in private hands, especially the peasantry, and the country's foreign policy is not aligned to either the East or West in global politics. The BSPP remains the sole governing body, and its subordinate organizations for peasants, workers, youth, women, and veterans are intended to serve as the means through which the people's will is expressed. The local SACs have been replaced by elected People's Councils, which have a large role in carrying out central government policies. The party's chairman, former General Ne Win, remained in the mid-1980s the leading figure of politics, but much of his power was by then wielded by subordinates, most recruited from the army.

The creation of a one-party socialist state was not as free from conflict as this chronological summary would suggest. Students, who played a large role in anti-British demonstrations in the colonial period, and provided a constant critique of the government in the 1950s, demonstrated in July 1962 against the Revolutionary Council's policies. The army responded with a quick and oppressive display of power, arresting student leaders and blowing up the university students' union, a center and symbol of political activism for several generations. Students again demonstrated in 1974 when they used the occasion of the return of the body of former United Nations general secretary U Thant to express not only their dissatisfaction with the fact that this world leader was not given a state funeral (he had been a close associate of former prime minister U Nu) but also their personal sense of isolation and lack of opportunities. University education after 1962 was no longer a key to success and unemployment among the educated had risen to high levels, as the economy had not expanded rapidly enough to absorb all the new graduates. Moreover, the standard of education had declined following the decision in the mid-1960s to require that all education be in the Burmese language. Adequate textbooks were no longer available and a sense of gloom had settled around the university, previously one of the intellectually liveliest institutions of higher learning in Southeast Asia.

The students' complaints were matched by others'. Workers demonstrated for higher wages at about the same time, and for a period in early 1975 Rangoon was under martial law. Discontent also developed within the ranks of the armed forces during this time and plots against General Ne Win and other leading officers were reported. These and other subsequent attempts to change the nature of the leadership failed, however, because of the fundamental loyalty that most of the officers maintained toward the longest surviving head of state in postwar Southeast Asia.

The army throughout the period since 1962 was faced with two essential tasks. One was the creation of the new political order and, as noted above, serving and retiring army personnel were given leading posts in the major and many of the minor political, administrative, economic, and educational institutions of the country. The other was the continual battle against the insurgent forces, ethnic and Communist, which the government had been fighting since 1948. By the ruling party's own account, the army faced four major and eleven minor armed opposition groups in 1981. Its strategy toward them was one that combined both continual armed pressure as well as political and organizational work to undercut their recruitment bases. By the mid-1980s, several of these groups, including the Karen National Liberation Army (KNLA) and the Burma Communist Party (BCP), were being severely tested. The KNLA, the armed force of the Karen National Union, had survived for many years through its control of the smuggling "gates" between Thailand and Burma. There the KNLA extracted a 10 percent levy on all goods smuggled in and out of Burma. By 1985, however, because of improved cooperation from the government of Thailand and greater control by the army on the Burma side of the border, the KNLA had lost most of its financial resources and thus was unable to purchase arms and ammunition, as well as medicines and food, from Thailand.

In the northern parts of the country, the Burma Communist Party, due in part to changes in the attitude of the Communist Party of China toward antigovernment Communists in Southeast Asia, was also much weakened. The BCP, like its allied ethnic insurgent force, the Kachin Independence Army (KIA), was strongly backed by China during the Cultural Revolution of the 1960s when China called the Ne Win–BSPP government a reactionary force similar to the former Chinese Nationalist government of Chiang Kai-shek. However, as China's relations with Burma improved from the early 1970s, external support for the BCP and the KIA apparently waned and the government was able to reassert its control over much of northern Burma. By the mid-1980s China was once more, as in the 1950s, providing economic aid to the government in Rangoon and cooperating in re-demarcating China's long border with Burma, first agreed upon in 1960.

Burma's foreign policy from a year or so after independence has been marked by a consistent policy of neutrality. The government has never entered into any military alliances; aid has been accepted only when no obvious strings were attached and the government has been willing to forego aid when it appeared, as in 1963, to compromise Burma's international position. Except for the Communists and several of the ethnic insurgent groups, all shades of political opinion in the country have endorsed this policy. The Revolutionary Council's first statement after taking power in 1962 was to reaffirm its commitment to nonalignment. A glance at the map and a quick review of the foreign policy orientations of Burma's many neighbors demonstrates the logic of such a policy.

Burma stands at the point of the Asian map where East, South, and Southeast Asia meet. It is bordered by several larger powers, particularly India and China, who were at war in the 1960s and who subsequently developed good relations with opposing superpowers, the Soviet Union and the United States. If Burma were to choose to ally itself with any one of its bigger neighbors, or with either of the superpowers, the effect would be, at a minimum, to create a potential opponent along one of the borders. Burma is located along major "fault lines" of Asian international politics and has managed to avoid being dragged into one or another of the continent's wars since 1945 by making clear that it will assist no other state in that state's designs against one of Burma's other neighbors. The depth of the Burma government's belief in the efficacy of nonalignment was demonstrated most clearly in 1979 when it withdrew from the Non-Aligned Movement itself at the Havana summit because too many of the movement's members, such as Cuba and the Philippines, were too obviously aligned. Similarly, Burma has never joined ASEAN, though it has remained a participant in the United Nations Organization and its affiliate regional and functional bodies as long as these have maintained universal qualities.

Because of its noninvolvement in the major international conflicts of Asia for many years and, especially after 1962, of the government's policy of avoiding close contacts with international economic, educational, and cultural bodies, Burma was often criticized during the 1960s and 1970s for being hypernationalistic if not xenophobic. For some years it was impossible to get a visa for more than twenty-four hours and even in the mid-1980s stays of more than seven days in Burma were extremely difficult to arrange. Foreign multinational corporations were unable to invest in the country and it remained one of the few in the world where one could buy neither Coca-Cola nor Pepsi-Cola. Burmese students were rarely seen at foreign universities and Burmese scholars almost never attended international conferences. Clearly, Burma's self-imposed isolation made it difficult to maintain the country's educational system or to obtain the imported technology or consumer goods that much of the rest of Southeast Asia took for granted by the fourth decade of independence.

These costs, many in Burma would argue, have to be put against certain advantages. While most Burmese do not enjoy the possibility of purchasing many consumer goods available elsewhere or seeing Hollywood first-run films, neither do they have to worry about their land being taken by a moneylender or a landlord. While they may have to fulfill a government quota for rice sales, they receive their fertilizer at a price only a quarter or so of that paid by farmers in Thailand or Malaysia. While they may not be able to consider sending their children abroad for an education or to take a holiday in another country, neither do they have to worry about having their fields collectivized and having cadre tell them where to live or when to work. The institutions of the Buddhist faith thrive and families still trek during the dry season to pagoda festivals and fairs just as their ancestors did. The government has made available more medicines and hospitals than were provided under the British, though not necessarily up to contemporary Western standards, and does test and use indigenous forms of medicine.

For the urban resident also, the advantages of the political system since 1962 are not to be found in consumer items such as air conditioning and BMWs. Most of Rangoon in 1986 still went to work each day in buses that began life as trucks in the 1940s and 1950s. But even critics of the government will say that they can sleep safely in their beds at night. In the late 1940s and early 1950s Burma was a country in the throes of civil war, and in the late 1950s and early 1960s much of it was still ruled by a variety of men who could command the allegiance of gangs of gunmen. Not all of Burma was peaceful by 1980, but by then more people were ruled by the pen than by the gun. A network of administrative and political structures had been imposed upon the country that gave individuals a role, and if these institutions tended to stifle creativity, they also provided stability and predictability. The certainty of the political order seemed so obvious even to severe critics of the regime that many who had gone underground or abroad in opposition in the years after 1962 returned to Rangoon in 1980, received medals for their previous service to the nation, and were granted state pensions.

Compared with the rest of Southeast Asia the history of Burma since independence seems different, but in many ways it is more like that of other Southeast Asian societies such as Vietnam or Indonesia than might first appear. Political order has been won at great cost to other human values. Economic growth has had to wait upon the creation of political order. Political leaders have made serious mistakes. Well-intentioned plans have had to be abandoned when leaders confronted human realities not first acknowledged. The government has had to attempt to balance competing and often incompatible sets of demands and has achieved stability at the expense of economic development.

# 37

## Malaysia, Singapore, and Brunei

### Malaysia

WHEN the British returned to Malaya in September 1945, some of its inhabitants looked forward to early release from colonial rule, while others thought such aspirations premature. The Japanese occupation, though it had broken many of the psychological bonds that had permitted the continuance of Western domination, had greatly exacerbated social and political tensions only latent in the 1930s. Toward the Malays the Japanese had been, if scarcely paternalistic, somewhat conciliatory, pursuing as the British had policies directed toward minimal disturbance of the indigenous society in the interests of economic exploitation. Toward the Chinese the invaders had been initially brutal, in memory of Nanyang assistance to China during the Sino-Japanese war, and subsequently mistrustful and harassing. The Chinese, in turn, had provided most of the active guerrilla resistance to Japanese rule, organized through the Malayan Peoples Anti-Japanese Army (MPAJA), the nucleus of which was the prewar Malayan Communist Party (MCP). Some Indians became caught up in the enthusiasms of the Indian National Army (INA), but thousands of others were carried off to work, and die, on the Burma railway. Many Malays, at least for a time, filled positions in the civil administration to which they had not been permitted to aspire under the British. Those from all communities who "collaborated" with the new rulers found themselves targets of MPAJA hostility, and the eventual Japanese surrender was followed by a settling of scores on both sides. Throughout much of the occupation the only common experience was of hunger, sickness, misery, and demoralization, with a marked decrease in standards of social trust and an increase in corruption.

Malaya's gradual achievement of independence during the decade that followed the British return, though sometimes derogated as "non-revolutionary," was the product of new and hard-won understandings between the then-accepted leaders of the communities of Malaya. The nature of the compact reached in the early 1950s was to underlie not merely the forms the new state would take but the manner of its politics (and much else) during the first decades of independence. It was a compact reached between two groups: on the one hand, the Western-educated Malay leadership, composed largely of bureaucrats and public officials drawn from the traditional elite and its fringes, and on the other, a small group of Western-educated Chinese, drawn mainly from among wealthy, Malaya-born businessmen. In essence, the understanding reached was that in the interests of both leadership groups, and, it was argued, of the society as a whole, Malay entitlement to political and administrative authority—premised on their better claim to be "sons of the soil"—should be accepted unchallenged, at least for the time being, in return for non-interference in Chinese control of the economy. With those understandings as a starting point, a process of reconciliation of interests would be embarked upon, aimed explicitly, for the Malays, at measures intended to redress the balance of economic power and implicitly, for the Chinese, at gradual admission to the franchise and to the political power flowing from this. Subsequent problems have centered upon two issues—the extent to which the two leadership groups have continued to be acceptable to the communities for which they professed to speak and the fact that one side of the bargain (the increment of political power for the Chinese) operated largely by passage of time, while the other (the increment of economic power for the Malays) did not.

During the war years, while Malays and Chinese had been coming to a new appreciation of the complexities of their continued relationship, the British had been planning a reorganized version of the Malayan polity. Unveiled in London in a White Paper in January 1946, the intention was to create a unified Malayan state—excluding only Singapore, which was to remain a separate colony—by cession of all separate jurisdiction from the sultanates to the British crown and by conferring citizenship upon all born there or resident for ten out of (effectively) the preceding nineteen years.

Malay opinion was grievously affronted by this Malayan Union plan because of the loss of Malay sovereignty it involved and the extension of full participatory rights in the state to hundreds of thousands regarded as sojourners with external loyalties—though in fact out of the 2.5 million Chinese in Malaya at the time, comprising 38 percent of the population, some 64 percent were locally born and presumably intended to stay. Publication of the plan elicited from the Malays a remarkable political response, far exceeding any demonstration of national feeling manifested before the war. Resurrecting and building upon prewar state Malay Associations and similar organizations, Malay leaders—preeminent among them Onn b. Jaafar of Johore—brought into being within a few weeks a mass Malay movement, the United Malays National Organization (UMNO), to fight the union scheme.

Within eighteen months, the scheme had been abandoned and a federal system of government restored, based on continuance of the traditional state structure, greatly restricted citizenship, and the introduction of a nonelective legislative council in which government officials and the Malay rulers together outnumbered unofficial members. The new Federation of Malaya was inaugurated on February 1, 1948, with Singapore remaining a separate colony under direct British rule.

When, at the end of the war, the MPAJA had laid down its arms and disbanded, it appeared that the Malayan Communist Party was, at least for the moment, prepared to pursue by constitutional means its opposition to the restoration of colonial rule. In this it was joined by a rather unstable coalition of broadly left-wing groups, led by the multiracial Malayan Democratic Union and the pan-Indonesianist Malay Nationalist Party. Postwar economic dislocation and social unrest, especially in Singapore, encouraged the MCP to turn its attentions to the industrial labor unions, and during 1946 and early 1947 it established a convincing hold over the labor movement there and in the peninsula. Most industrial labor remained Chinese, and as before the war the MCP became primarily identified with the Chinese community, at some cost where Malays in particular were concerned. Strict British regulation of union practice, combined with an upturn in the economy and factional disarray within the party, led the MCP to abandon constitutionalism for armed struggle in mid-1948. The resulting "Emergency," as it became known, lasted for twelve years, though the back of the revolt was broken by the mid-1950s.

The initial aim of the MCP, and of the Malayan Races Liberation Army (MRLA) it shortly set up, was to subvert the economy by disrupting the rubber plantations and tin mines that provided most of Malaya's wealth, to destroy authority by attacking and defeating government security forces, and to win mass support from the populace. Though some early successes were recorded in assassinating European and Chinese rubber planters and tin miners, and in isolated acts of sabotage, the MRLA by 1949 was forced to retire to the jungle, where it engaged in a sporadic guerrilla war. Protracted though this struggle became, it early proved an unequal one. While numbers of Chinese were prepared to give aid and encouragement to the MRLA, through a combination of disaffection and fear of reprisals, most Malays saw the war as preeminently a Chinese attempt to gain control of the state and not only remained loyal to the colonial power but fought actively against the MRLA. Government successes in the field, coupled with evidence of intention and ability to protect most of the populace most of the time, encouraged Chinese resistance to MCP demands, and the so-called Briggs Plan of forcibly regrouping in "New Villages" vulnerable Chinese peasant squatter communities from the jungle fringes did much to restrict support for the Communists. Between 1950 and 1952 no fewer than half a million Chinese were resettled, in more than four hundred areas. During the same period, nearly ten thousand Chinese were deported to mainland China.

But the war was above all a political one, and it became increasingly clear to Malays, non-Communist Chinese, and British alike that the only real way to repudiate the MRLA's claim to be a liberation army was by moving toward self-government and independence. The British, however, refused to consider self-government until greater unity of purpose had been achieved by the Malay and Chinese communities. The stringent detention and other security measures prompted by the Emergency—leading, among other things, to the virtual extinction of the democratic socialist parties, Malay and multiracial alike—stifled most overt political activity. Leading Chinese became concerned that the Chinese community lacked any politically acceptable organization, comparable to UMNO, to speak for it. In February 1949, with the encouragement of the British, a number of wealthy, Western-educated Chinese (led by the millionaires Tan Cheng Lock and H. S. Lee) were successful in forming a Malayan Chinese Association (MCA). While the MCA's constitution described its first aim as "the promotion and maintenance of interracial harmony in Malaya," Tan Cheng Lock, in an inaugural address in Malacca, said that its chief task would be to work to secure justice for the Chinese community. Though the two objectives were not necessarily incompatible, simultaneous pursuit created considerable problems of accommodation.

Paradoxically, the existence of two strong communal groupings was greatly to assist the process of compromise. Already, early in 1949, shortly before the formation of the MCA, a British-sponsored Communities Liaison Committee had taken the first steps toward a reconciliation of interests, formulating somewhat more liberal citizenship proposals for the Chinese in return for promises of special economic assistance for the Malays. In 1952, with the first democratic elections under the Federation constitution approaching—for the municipality of Kuala Lumpur—the Selangor state branches of UMNO and MCA agreed to form a temporary pact, largely in the interest of defeating the Independence of Malaya Party (IMP), a noncommunal party formed by Onn b. Jaafar after his break with UMNO over communal questions the previous year. The electoral pact was highly successful—UMNO and the MCA between them took all but two of the contested seats—and the arrangement rapidly proved so politically productive at similar elections in Johore Baharu, Muar, and Malacca that its continuance was assured. In August 1953 the National Alliance was formally constituted, and in September a year later the makeshift "Round Table Conference" that had assisted internal bargaining gave way to a thirty-member National Executive Council. In October 1954 the Malayan Indian Congress (MIC) agreed to join the Alliance, thus completing the communal spectrum.

In the first full-scale federal elections in July 1955, the Alliance, campaigning on a platform demanding immediate self-government and early independence, won 51 out of 52 elective seats in a newly organized, 98-member Legislative Council, with 81 percent of the vote. Thirty-four of the Alliance seats went to UMNO Malays, 15 to MCA

Chinese, and 2 to MIC Indians. Tengku Abdul Rahman, leader of UMNO and of the Alliance, was appointed chief minister and formed a cabinet.

The way was now open for *merdeka* (independence). The character and interest of the leaders of the Alliance—moderate, administration-minded Malays and well-to-do Chinese and Indian businessmen—seemed to the British to offer future political and economic stability and a reasonable insurance for their own investments. During the long series of constitutional talks that ensued (conducted by the Reid Commission), there was considerable difference of opinion among the communities on certain crucial issues relating to citizenship, language, the status of the Malays, and other questions. UMNO and the MCA, recognizing that neither community could successfully go it alone, finally presented to the British a joint set of Alliance proposals embodying compromises made by both sides. With little further demur, the British accepted them, and on August 31, 1957, the independent Federation of Malaya came into being. Insofar as they can be briefly summarized, the essential elements of the constitution were these: (1) continuance of the Malay sultans in each state, acting as constitutional monarchs on the advice of ministers chosen from the majority party in fully elected state legislative assemblies; (2) quinquennial appointment by the rulers from among themselves of a paramount ruler (Agung) who would likewise act on the advice of ministers responsible to a fully elected national parliament; (3) establishment of Islam as the state religion, within the framework of individual freedom of religion; (4) extension of citizenship to all born in the Federation from then on and increasingly, by registration or naturalization, to much larger numbers of Chinese and Indians resident there; (5) determination of Malay as the sole national language at a date to be fixed after the elapse of ten years, with English accorded concurrent status in the interim; and (6) recognition of the special position and needs of the Malays by reservation to them of quotas of entry into the public services, of scholarships, and of certain sorts of economic opportunity.

Independent Malaya had more than a decade of stable government and relatively smooth economic growth before some of the contradictions implicit in the pre-1957 compact had serious and, eventually, explosive effect. A start was made at diversifying an economy based almost entirely (85 percent before 1957) on export earnings from rubber and tin, but less success was had in reducing economic disparities between and within the major ethnic groups. By 1966, the country had become the world's largest producer of palm oil, timber was a growing source of export earnings, and there was a steady increase in manufacturing. The Malay peasant economy was assisted by the establishment of institutions such as the Federal Land Development Authority (FELDA), which opened up large tracts of new land for settlement, and by improvements in rural credit and marketing. An attempt was made by control of licenses and similar means to encourage Malay entrepreneurial participation in transport, commerce, and industry.

Throughout this first decade, which saw several major changes in the external and internal political environment, the Alliance remained unchallengeably in charge of affairs. Registered in 1958 as a political party independent of its member parties, it was able through its inner council (under the strong leadership of Tengku Abdul Rahman) to determine parliamentary representation among its constituent groups and to control in large part the emergence of divisive issues by a process described by one observer as "democracy in camera." Central to such issues were questions relating to the cultural as well as the political character of the new state, expressed in argument about access to citizenship, about special privileges of various kinds, and not least about education and language policies, matters of deep concern to Malays and Chinese alike. Though the Alliance continued to be successful at the polls in the general elections of 1959, 1964, and 1969, its share of the popular vote declined, and opposition parties often of a more explicitly communal character—notably the Democratic Action Party (DAP), modeled on Singapore's People's Action Party (PAP), and the Pan-Malayan Islamic Party (PAS)—made considerable inroads in both state and federal assemblies.

At least some of the tensions that came to the fore in the course of the 1960s related to processes and events external to the peninsula. As early as May 1961, Tengku Abdul Rahman, with British knowledge but probably at his own initiative, proposed the federation of the existing Federation of Malaya with Singapore and the three British-controlled territories in northern Borneo—Sarawak, Sabah, and Brunei—to form a united "Malaysia." The merger of Singapore and Malaya alone, in recognition of their long economic and political interdependence, had often been urged by Singapore politicians and others but was unattractive to Malay opinion in the peninsula because of the great increase it would have meant in the overall Chinese population. In the proposed Malaysia, this would be counterbalanced by the indigenous tribal and Malay peoples of the Borneo territories. At the same time, both the Malayan and the British governments felt that left-wing elements in Singapore might be controlled more successfully if the state were to come within the security ambit of the central government in Kuala Lumpur. The two years following Tengku Abdul Rahman's Malaysia proposals were marked by much international politicking, especially on the part of Indonesia, which embarked on a policy of "confrontation" with Malaya, and the Philippines, which laid prior claim to Sabah. Despite this opposition, the new state came into being in September 1963, minus, however, Brunei, which had opted to stay out.

The internal politics of peninsular Malaya were at once affected by the new arrangements, for the Singapore PAP decided to participate in the 1964 general elections on the basis of the slogan "a Malaysian Malaysia," by which was meant a Malaysia in which no one community (the Malays were clearly intended) should have a monopoly in nation-building and its prerogatives. This struck at the heart of the implicit compact between the Malay and Chinese partners in the Alliance and prompted a sharp Malay response. Finally, for fear that Malaya's own delicate communal balance would be irremediably upset if matters continued to deteriorate, Kuala Lumpur in August 1965 asked Singapore to leave the Federation, and the island was thereafter an independent city-state. Though the rhetoric of the time spoke of "separation, not divorce," and of eventual reunification, developments since have continued to emphasize separate identity.

Singapore's expulsion from Malaysia, and its implications for the dominant Malay role in federal politics, led to some disquiet in Sarawak and Sabah, the remaining "new members." Both had large, non-Malay (and non-Muslim) indigenous populations that were becoming politically active. The Ibans in Sarawak and their counterparts the Kadazans in Sabah accounted for some 30 percent of the population, against much smaller groups of Malays and considerable numbers of Chinese. Though both states enjoyed a greater degree of autonomy than any of the peninsular states, especially in relation to immigration and initially to language and education policies, there was resentment at what was seen as Kuala Lumpur's insistence on the export of the Alliance pattern of politics. The adoption throughout Malaysia of the term *bumiputera* ("son of the soil") and the extension thereby to Kadazans, Ibans, and other indigenes of the constitutionally protected privileges secured to Malays did little to lessen this resentment.

But the political center of gravity in Malaysia remained in the peninsula and in Kuala Lumpur, as became abundantly clear in 1969. At the general elections in May of that year, the Alliance, its share of the popular vote falling from 58 to 48 percent, lost 23 of its seats in the Dewan Rakyat to opposition parties and thereby lost also the two-thirds majority that had in the past enabled it to secure the passage of constitutional amendments. Similar swings took place at the state level. The beneficiaries included the Pan-Malayan Islamic Party, which drew on substantial Malay dissatisfaction with UMNO and Alliance policies and achievements, but the principal gainers were the DAP and Gerakan parties, which saw mainly Chinese voters, especially in the cities, desert the MCA and elect no fewer than twenty-one of their candidates to the federal parliament, and many more to state assemblies. DAP and Gerakan victory processions in Kuala Lumpur the next day, amid reports that at least one and possible three state governments would end up with non-Malay chief ministers, led to a counter-demonstration by UMNO supporters on 13 May and eventually to four days of communal rioting in the city and environs (and sporadic outbreaks in the weeks immediately following) that left some two hundred dead.

The events of "13 May," though local and fairly rapidly contained, deeply shocked most segments of Malaysian society and were perceived by many as a rude questioning of the bases on which political and economic life had been conducted since 1957. With a state of emergency declared, and parliament suspended and replaced by a National Operations Council (NOC), which had military and police as well as political and civil service members, the task began of assessing why the social order had begun to unravel and what do about remedying the situation.

Diagnoses were numerous but, at least in official quarters, tended to suggest that significant numbers of Malays, especially, had lost faith in the capacity of the pre-independence compact and its political managers to deliver what had been promised: prospects of a greater share in the country's wealth and, less tangibly, in important cultural determinants of the new society, such as language. Considerable numbers of Chinese, for their part, frustrated by constitutionally guaranteed Malay access to certain kinds of privilege or opportunity but with new found strength at the ballot box, had turned to more chauvinist forms of political expression in search of redress. The solutions proposed by the government and the ad hoc, broadly representative National Consultative Council (NCC) established in 1970, resulted in the resumption of parliamentary government in February 1971, but on terms and in pursuit of policies in many ways markedly different from what had gone before.

The major changes can most conveniently be summarized under constitutional, ideological, economic, and political headings. Constitutionally, return to parliamentary government was premised on the passage of a Constitution (Amendment) Act which, though complex, may be seen as having two main ends: to remove from public discussions (including in parliament) certain sensitive issues already entrenched in the constitution (in particular, the special position of the Malays and the status of the rulers); and to improve the numbers of Malays and other Bumiputera receiving university education. Ideologically, a new Department of National Unity having enunciated a set of "Principles of State" *(Rukunegara)* to which allegiance was to be promoted (consisting of Belief in God, Loyalty to King and Country, Upholding the Constitution, Rule of Law, and Good Behavior and Morality), efforts were to be made through formal and informal institutions to foster a sense of common national identity and purpose. In addition, the constitutional position of Malay as the sole national language was strengthened, and a new policy for acceleration of its adoption as the medium of instruction at all school levels was put into effect.

Some of the most far-reaching changes, at least in their intended long-term effect, lay in the economic sphere. Embodied in what became known as the New Economic Policy (NEP) and set out in successive four-year Malaysia Plans, the NEP had two principal objectives: the reduction and eventual eradication of poverty, irrespective of community; and a restructuring of society so that identification of community with economic function (and fate) would be progressively reduced until eliminated. The central element in the second of these objectives was a proposed redistribution of ownership and control of the Malaysian economy in such a way that, by 1990, Malays and other Bumiputera should own and manage 30 percent of the share capital in commerce and industry, other Malaysians 40 percent, and foreigners 30 percent, contrasting with an estimated 1.9 percent, 22.5 percent, and 60.7 percent, respectively, in 1970. Though a great variety of stratagems has been employed to attain these ends—such as creation of a range of state-sponsored statutory authorities to purchase and hold shares in public companies, including many large foreign-owned concerns, on behalf of Bumiputera—it was still unclear in the mid-1980s how far there was to go or what the social costs of new forms of inequity might be.

Politically, the principal development after the resumption of parliamentary government, manifested at regular general elections in 1974, 1978, 1982, and 1986, was the evolution of the Alliance model of political compromise into a Barisan Nasional (National Front) model. Begun pragmatically as an electoral strategy in the early 1970s by Tun Abdul Razak (Tengku Abdul Rahman's successor as prime minister until his death in 1976), somewhat as the Alliance had begun in 1951, the Barisan Nasional was an UMNO-dominated coalition of some ten parties (membership has fluctuated), several previously in opposition but now given an opportunity to share in government. The principal advantage of the Barisan co-optative model for UMNO was that it allowed it to form partnerships with Chinese leadership groups other than those represented within the seriously weakened MCA. It also worked, at least for a time, to mute the political effect of increasing differences within the Malay community itself, partly on Islamic and partly on other grounds, by offering the possibility of direct participation in government, outside UMNO, though the resulting decline of the Pan-Malayan Islamic Party as a political force in the late 1970s pointed to the perils of this kind of embrace.

The Malaysia that entered the last half of the 1980s was very different from that of the mid-1940s. It was a much more urbanized society (with a significantly higher proportion of Malays especially living in towns), and though most of its income still came from primary production, it had an important and growing industrial sector. Petroleum products had displaced rubber as the main revenue earner, and even after the downturn of the early 1980s Malaysia was more prosperous than most of its neighbors, though with considerable persistent rural poverty. Increasing state intervention in the economy in pursuit of the ownership and control goals of the NEP had resulted, as some saw it, mainly in the growth of a largely Malay "bureaucratic bourgeoisie" without directly assisting the bulk of the Bumiputera population, and at some cost in non-Bumiputera discontent. Ethnicity remained a major dynamic for political allegiance and social action (along with the *dakwah* Islamic revivalist movement among the Malays), despite the striking growth of Malay as a common language and other evidences of cultural integration. Problems abounded, but as the "nation-building" of the previous forty years had shown, the "New Malaysians" had considerable reserves of ingenuity, industry, and compromise to carry with them into the future.

## Singapore

Singapore moved a good deal more slowly toward independence than Malaya, principally because of British fears that the overwhelmingly Chinese island and its military base would succumb to Communist subversion. Limited representative institutions were introduced in 1951, and a constitutional commission three years later recommended larger measures of participation and self-government. Following elections in 1955, the moderate left-wing Labour Front, led by David Marshall, a Singapore Jewish lawyer, was able to form a coalition government with local UMNO and MCA members. Tengku Abdul Rahman's successful visit to London in early 1956, during which he obtained the assurance of independence for Malaya, prompted Marshall to make a similar trip in December. He was offered, he complained, only "Christmas pudding with arsenic sauce"—limited independence with continued British control of defense and internal security. His case had not been helped by widespread middle school and labor disorders. Marshall resigned and was replaced by the colony's first Chinese chief minister, the trade unionist Lim Yew Hock, who in the course of the next year, by pursuing policies of rigor toward dissidence and reassurance toward the British, was able to get a firm promise of independence for 1959.

At elections in that year, the Labour Front lost the support of the Chinese-educated and victory went overwhelmingly to the People's Action Party (PAP). Led by a Cambridge-educated lawyer, Lee Kuan Yew, the PAP, a pragmatic socialist party which in later years was to move markedly to the right, gained wide support from the Chinese proletariat by working closely with more doctrinaire left-wing and Communist groups. The uneasy alliance between the right and left wings of the party, however, started to unravel when the leadership found that socialist tenets were ill-matched with the state's heavy dependence for its very existence on servicing local and international capital and finally came apart in 1961. The divisive issue at that point was the proposal to join Malaysia, strongly favored by Lee Kuan Yew and those closely associated with him, and bitterly opposed as a neocolonialist plot by the party's left wing, which seceded and formed a new party, the Barisan Sosialis (National Front). Though the PAP continued in power, it learned to exercise a much tighter control over emergence of factions within the party and began at this time to establish the grass-roots organization which enabled it to enjoy the remarkable social control that through the 1980s continued to be its hallmark.

Consolidation of PAP authority in the period leading up to merger with Malaysia in August 1963 (and to elections the following month, in which it gained 37 of 51 Legislative Assembly seats) was greatly assisted by the arrest and long-term detention early that year of a large part of the Barisan Sosialis leadership, on grounds of complicity in the Brunei revolt the preceding December and of sympathy toward Indonesia's confrontation policies. Membership in Malaysia, however, was to bring its own problems, and attempts by the PAP to engage in federal politics without due sensitivity to the complexities of peninsular Malaysia's very different ethnic and rural-urban mix earned it increasingly strong animosity from Malaysia. When this culminated in Singapore's ouster from the federation in August 1965, the now wholly independent city-state (population 1.75 million) was faced with a future in which it was at odds with its much larger and more powerful neighbors and had few resources other than its inherited role as a regional entrepôt and the talents and energies of its people.

To add to Singapore's difficulties, Britain announced in 1968 that beginning in 1970 it would withdraw from its "East of Suez" military role and close down its Singapore military base, a major contributor to the state's economy. The PAP rose to these challenges by embarking on a "politics of survival" and self-discipline for the state's "rugged society" and by instituting measures directed both toward total social mobilization and social control and toward economic growth based on attracting foreign capital to industrial development in the fields of electronics, shipbuilding and repairing, petroleum processing, and global as well as regional communications. The two decades from 1965 saw singular success on both political and economic fronts.

At four- and five-yearly elections from 1968 through the mid-1980s, the PAP increasingly swept the board, Singapore becoming in effect a one-party state. This process was assisted at the outset by the continuing detention of opposition leaders, by a Barisan Sosialis boycott of the electoral system, and by some manipulation of constituency boundaries. But the party's strength came increasingly to depend on its careful articulation with nominally non-party Citizens' Consultative Committees and People's Associations at all local levels, on efficient and noncorrupt if increasingly authoritarian government, and on the provision of a wide range of social services unmatched elsewhere in Southeast Asia.

In economic terms, the PAP provided Singapore with one of Asia's most burgeoning economies, achieving an overall standard of living second only, in Asia, to that of Japan and well in excess of anything else in Southeast Asia. The shift from entrepôt to manufacturing and service industries, together with stringent controls on labor—through the Employment Act and Industrial Relations (Amendment) Act of 1968— enabled the state to maintain double-digit rates of growth in gross domestic product throughout much of the period, declining somewhat only in the world recession of the early 1980s. Along with this growth, and made possible by it, came heavy investment by the state in urban renewal; land use planning and reclamation; and infrastructural development in transport, communications, and public utilities.

Singapore's transition from colonial dependency in 1945 to Southeast Asia's most thriving entrepreneurial state and a major world communications center in the 1980s, though made at some cost in personal liberty and self-expression, carried many obvious benefits for its citizens. Nearly two-thirds of its people live in government-built housing provided with a wide range of social, cultural, and health-care amenities. An integrated national education system, basically English and mother-tongue in emphasis and with a strong premium on performance in the upper levels, prepares them for entry into a technologically demanding work force. Relatively successful family planning programs promise to hold population growth down to replacement level at or near the end of the century. Though questions remain about the manner of transition from Lee Kuan Yew's generation of PAP leadership to the next, and self-conscious attempts in the mid-1980s to establish a more central place for "Confucianism" within the national culture suggest to some observers underlying uncertainties about social identity and direction, Singapore continues to be in material terms one of the region's success stories.

## Brunei

The British administration that returned uncontested to Brunei after the Japanese surrender in 1945 had as its main aims a resumption of colonial protectorate rule in the name of Sultan Omar Ali Saifuddin III and rehabilitation of the Seris oilfields. By 1950 the fields were producing 100,000 barrels a day and a revenue of some $7 million annually. Just over thirty years later, shortly before its reluctant attainment of independence, with a population still under a quarter of a million, Brunei had amassed foreign reserves totaling more than $9 billion, making it, even among oil-rich states, one of the wealthiest in the world on a per capita basis. It was also, while not despotic, still one of the least democratic.

Provision of a constitution in 1959, with a partially elected legislature, was the stimulus for the emergence of popular political expression, principally through the left-wing Partai Rakyat (People's Party) led by A. M. Azahari. Though the party won all 16 elective seats in the August 1962 elections, it differed radically with the sultan (and, separately, with the Federation of Malaya) over plans for the future of the territory, preferring a local merger with Sabah and Sarawak to absorption in the proposed Malaysia. Thwarted in this, the party led an armed revolt in December 1962, which was rapidly put down by British troops from Singapore.

Subsequent constitutional progress was slow, despite British urgings, and Brunei became a fully independent state on January 1, 1984, under Sultan Hassanal Bolkiah (Sultan Omar having abdicated in favor of his son in 1967), without a fully elected legislature or a government responsible to the people.

# 38

# The Republic of Indonesia

AT the outbreak of war in 1941, the Netherlands Indies was in a nearly perfect state of what the Dutch called *rust en orde,* calm and order. The rapid changes of the previous decades, while creating deep social tensions, had not shaken colonial stability. Dutch rule, occasionally disturbed earlier in the century, was secure and nowhere effectively challenged from within. Indies society—a mosaic of numerous folk societies and small ethnically defined urban communities—was intact in its complex order. The small, mainly Dutch-educated elite of "Indonesians" was itself just another such urban community embedded—alongside similar Dutch, Eurasian, and *totok* and *peranakan* Chinese ones—within the frame of the plural Indies structure.

The Japanese occupation ended the old order, overturning the politically and economically dominant elites, herding the *totok* Dutch into concentration camps, and harassing Chinese and Eurasians in various ways. By hasty improvisation, the Japanese drastically simplified the Indies' plural legal structure and, more important, the plural education system, which it replaced with a unitary system using Indonesian as the medium of instruction. The export industries collapsed, unbacked occupation currency caused a huge inflation, and rationing led to black markets and widespread corruption. Hundreds of thousands of peasants were marched off as slave labor to die in various parts of Southeast Asia.

In one sense Japanese rule simply exchanged one externally based colonial power for another. The Japanese maintained the basic Dutch administrative system, continuing to rule through established elites like the Javan *priyayi.* But their political style was fundamentally different: Where the Dutch were conservative and aimed to keep their subjects quiet, the Japanese were totalitarian and sought to stir them up. They mounted a relentless, provocative propaganda campaign designed to enlist the energies of their new subjects in their own desperate war effort. On Java, where the occupation had its strongest impact, the Japanese set out to enlist the Muslim and secular nationalist elites in their cause. In particular, a succession of widely publicized Japanese-controlled mass organizations gave the nationalist intelligentsia opportunities inconceivable in Dutch times to build connections and gain access to a broad public. Established prewar leaders, such as Sukarno and

Mohammed Hatta, publicly supported Japan in order to spread the nationalist idea of Indonesia. The Japanese actively indoctrinated young people in schools and a host of special organizations. In PETA (*Pembela Tanah Air,* Defenders of the Fatherland), finally, the Japanese built up a well-trained military force of 65,000, officered up to the battalion level by Indonesians—a development quite without colonial precedent.

Japanese rule ended in August 1945, as abruptly as it had begun and before most of the Indies had been reconquered by the Allies. Competing forces moved quickly to fill the vacuum of power thus created. The first to act were the older-generation nationalists who had built up a momentum of leadership during the Japanese occupation. In Jakarta on August 17, two days after the Japanese surrender, Sukarno and Hatta proclaimed the independence of Indonesia. In the next two weeks, a small committee quickly sketched the outlines of the new Indonesian state: a constitution, a cabinet, Sukarno as president, and Hatta as vice-president. The colonial response came soon enough; on September 29, the first British army units began landing at Jakarta. Representing the victorious Allies, they supported Dutch administrators whose task was to restore Dutch colonial rule.

The ensuing collision opened a long and bitter struggle, which lasted until the achievement of Indonesian political independence in December 1949. Specifically, in September 1945 it precipitated a mass movement, a violent upheaval that swept over most of Java and Sumatra where three quarters of all Indonesians lived, and pinned British troops and Dutch officials to their coastal footholds. It was this social upheaval, and not simply the political struggle for independence, that made the Indonesian revolution the central event and experience in modern Indonesian history.

The mass movement rose first because of the sudden disappearance of effective government. The Japanese administration had collapsed overnight; the British had few troops available and were only marginally interested; the Dutch had the motive and precedent for rule but, until 1947, few troops; the Republic, finally, was at first only an idea, with almost no machinery for enforcing its will. In any society, absence of government stirs deep fears and generates powerful impulses aimed at recovering the lost commonwealth. In Indonesia, in September 1945, those emotions were fixed most immediately and massively on the symbol of the Indonesian Republic, and the mass movement, which arose with startling suddenness, was founded on an impassioned Indonesian nationalism.

It was above all men and women in their teens and early twenties who responded in this way, and hence the outpouring is called the *pemuda* movement. (*Pemuda* literally means youth, but in the revolution it took on a deeper connotation of activism, militance, and patriotism.) The movement swept over *pemuda* of all classes and ethnic groups, uniting them in a common commitment to the cause of independence and a powerful sense of liberation and idealism. *Priyayi pemuda* dropped their titles and abbreviated their aristocratic names; men vowed not to cut their hair until freedom had been achieved; young women left home to work in the Indonesian Red Cross; a cult of heroes sprang up. These primarily political energies, moreover, spilled over into other domains, producing a flowering of specifically Indonesian painting, fiction, and poetry inconceivable a few years earlier.

The other side of idealism is fanaticism. The political significance of the *pemuda* movement lay in the violence it mobilized and sanctioned. It began in mid-September with ever-larger parades and demonstrations; shifted to attacks on Japanese posts, offices, and garrisons; progressed to fighting the British; and reached one climax in the battle of Surabaya in early November, in which the larger part of a British division would have been destroyed had Sukarno not intervened. The movement's domestic political impact, however, was more significant. In the extreme disorder it created throughout Java and Sumatra, all established claims to political and social leadership were subject to a drastic test. Those unable to justify themselves, to adapt to revolutionary conditions, or to defend themselves were abused, driven out, or killed. Minority groups—Dutch, Chinese, Eurasians, and Ambonese—suffered particularly heavily from looting and atrocities. A wave of local "social revolutions" spread over the area between Aceh and Surakarta, challenging the traditional local elites on which Dutch, Japanese, and now Republican rule rested, destroying some and driving most into cautious retreat.

The most violent, and politically significant, phase of the *pemuda* movement lasted from September 1945 to mid-1946. During that period, and long after, *pemuda* associated themselves loosely in what were called *badan perjuangan,* spontaneous local groupings usually formed around a leader with charismatic qualities. Hundreds of such groups emerged, dissolved, and combined in the tumult; the *badan perjuangan,* one of the key institutions of the revolutionary years, was the most characteristic manifestation of the *pemuda* movement. During the same period, certain *pemuda* leaders and groups began to build a national army. In some cases PETA companies—which had all been disbanded by the Japanese immediately after the surrender—reconstituted themselves; in other cases, PETA officers or others organized their own units. Over the years, as local units aggregated into battalions and regiments, the army slowly created itself.

The enormous but unchanneled power of the *pemuda* movement decisively influenced political developments at the national level. It brought what was from one viewpoint a struggle between two small elite groups —the Dutch and the Dutch-educated Indonesian nationalists—out into the arena of mass politics. In particular, it greatly complicated the affairs of the small group of older nationalists who had founded the

Republic. These men had declared independence and created the Republic, but they lacked a mass organization like the Viet Minh because they had been isolated from the masses both by Dutch and Japanese design and by their own precocious cultural and political development. Nor did they have much taste or aptitude for military organization. During the first months of the revolution, they made no effort to establish a national army, which left the field wide open for *pemuda*. As a group, the founders and leaders of the Republic were urban politicians —committee men and orators. Characteristically, they organized themselves in terms of political parties, which grew in great profusion in late 1945 and after. Few if any of their parties gained mass followings during the revolution; like their predecessors, the prewar parties, they were mainly vehicles of intra-elite politics.

During the revolution, cabinets rose and fell regularly without changing the basic policy of the Republic. That policy was *diplomasi,* a program for attaining independence by negotiating with the Dutch and by appealing to international opinion. *Diplomasi* was the antithesis of the *pemuda* ideal of *perjuangan,* an uncompromising armed struggle for total independence. The question of *diplomasi* or *perjuangan* became the overriding issue of domestic politics throughout the revolution. Each of the five cabinets that fell during the revolution resigned because of a public outcry against the concessions it had made to the Dutch—a protest always supported by parties and factions out of power. Each of the succeeding cabinets carried on the same basic *diplomasi,* with the support of former advocates of *perjuangan* currently in power and, always, of Hatta and Sukarno.

Until mid-1947, the Dutch were quite as willing as the Republicans to negotiate. Holland was exhausted by the German occupation. The Dutch had been lucky, with the help of the British and the Republic itself, to be able to hold out against the *pemuda* in their enclaves in the major cities of Java and Sumatra. The negotiations themselves dragged on until November 1946, when they produced a compromise satisfactory to neither party. Meanwhile, the Dutch had reoccupied the more sparsely populated islands outside Java and Sumatra with little resistance. In December 1946 they established the state of East Indonesia—comprising the Celebes, Bali, and the rest of the eastern archipelago—as the first in a series of regional member states in a projected federal system, which they could expect to control from the center.

By July 1947, the Dutch had assembled enough divisions to launch a "Police Action" in which they easily seized West and East Java and the plantation and oil areas of East and South Sumatra. Though the United Nations began to intervene at that point, the Dutch were able, in January 1948, to compel the government of the Republic to acquiesce in those conquests. In the occupied areas, they quickly established new federal member states based politically on more conservative social groups—hereditary elites, former cooperating nationalists, Chinese,

Eurasians, and others—which had been badly shaken by the *pemuda* movement. The next step was logical: in December 1948, the Dutch launched their second "Police Action," quickly occupying most of the remaining Republican territory and capturing Sukarno and Hatta.

The success of the campaign proved fatal for the Dutch. The Indonesian army, released from the restraints of *diplomasi,* turned to guerrilla war; the United Nations swung sharply against Dutch policy; and the leaders of many of the Dutch-made federal states—nationalists, too—took a more independent line. The Netherlands had to give way; the Republican leaders, as ever, were ready to negotiate. The Hague Agreement of November 2 brought a settlement: political independence for Indonesia; temporary retention of Western New Guinea by the Netherlands; and guarantees for Dutch investments in Indonesia. On December 27, 1949, the Dutch flag was hauled down for the last time.

In the course of the revolutionary upheaval most inhabitants of what the early nationalists had christened "Indonesia" came to think of themselves as Indonesians—a supra-ethnic national identity not to be found elsewhere in Southeast Asia except the Philippines. During the same years the Indonesian language—also supra-ethnic—acquired a new emotional significance, while the unitary Indonesian-language school system was permanently built in. It would be difficult to overrate the importance of these developments in the long run for the future of the sprawling multiethnic nation of Indonesia.

In the short run, however, the newly sovereign Republic faced formidable difficulties on all fronts. Economically, Indonesia was a shambles after eight years of assault by Japanese and Dutch. The economic provisions of the Hague Agreement, surprisingly easily accepted by the Indonesian delegation, implied a continuation of the prewar colonial economy. Indeed, during the early 1950s the Dutch and Chinese carried on their business very much as before the war. Socially, the revolutionary upheaval had created new expectations and old scores to settle. The veterans of the *perjuangan* expected personal prosperity with the independence they felt they had assured. The graduates of the rapidly expanding school system of the 1950s pressed into an equally rapidly expanding bureaucracy. At the same time, the revolution had sharply accentuated internal divisions. Chinese and Indonesians each had much stronger grounds for mistrust than they had had five years earlier. New Indonesian institutions—the army, political parties, government departments—had emerged, but their interests often clashed. In some areas, such as East Sumatra, ethnic differences had become open ethnic hostilities after clashes in the revolution. In West Java, South Celebes, and Aceh, Islamic groups, stirred up by the revolution and hostile to the triumphant secular state, launched rebellions in the cause of an Islamic state. The Communist Madiun Rebellion in 1948, rising mainly out of party politics at the national level, had led to savage fighting between Javanese *santri* and *abangan* in the villages.

Politically, in the early years of independence, the long dominant nationalists led by Sukarno and Hatta held all the formal levers of power: the numerous political parties, the provisional parliament, the presidency, and the upper levels of the central bureaucracy. But these institutions were centered in Jakarta. Outside the capital an immense variety of local elites, hereditary or otherwise, lords or headmen, had much or everything to say about actual government. Both in Jakarta and beyond, in the regions, the army—proud of its *perjuangan,* disdainful of the nationalist elite's *diplomasi,* poorly funded and not taken seriously by the civilian elite—nursed its resentment.

During the early years of independence a series of cabinets working through the provisional parliament set out to construct a proper, full-scale government on a broadly Western European model and to repair the ravages of a decade of turmoil. Their task was eased by the general optimism in the new-born republic, the patronage they commanded in establishing the organs of a new state, and the Korean War boom for Indonesian export products.

Those favorable circumstances came to an end in late 1952, and the intensity of conflict grew steadily over the next three years. Party politics became more bitter and divisive; Muslim reformists and traditionalists split into two separate parties, while the PKI (Communist Party) made a remarkable recovery from its debacle at Madiun. More important, the political parties, up to that point representing mainly small urban elites, made their first serious efforts to build up mass support in preparation for the elections to be held in 1955; they thus introduced the conflicts of urban politics directly into village life. Meanwhile governments, faced with falling export revenues and rising demands from their urban constituents, moved steadily toward deficit financing and antiforeign, and especially anti-Chinese, economic nationalism.

The long-awaited national election of 1955, though a great success as an act of popular franchise, led quickly to the end of parliamentary democracy in Indonesia. Between 1956 and 1958, the parties, parliament, and the cabinet collapsed as major political institutions, and new political forces rose in their stead. In Sumatra and Celebes, export areas whose foreign exchange went primarily to feed Java and to support urban elites concentrated there, local army commanders asserted local autonomy in a series of coups beginning in December 1956. By early 1958, the movement had proclaimed a rebel Indonesian government, which took Jakarta several years to suppress. Meanwhile the PKI grew rapidly, and the army gained wide administrative powers with the declaration of martial law in March 1957. After December 1957, when the United Nations rebuffed Indonesia's claims to western New Guinea, all Dutch enterprises in Indonesia were expropriated and the army gained control of a large new pool of patronage.

As Indonesia began to unravel politically, President Sukarno, a formidable and still intact symbol of Indonesian unity, moved steadily toward the center of national politics. In mid-1959 he abrogated the existing provisional constitution and inaugurated a regime called Guided Democracy. During the next six years Indonesian political power rested in a competitive alliance between the army, with most of the machinery in its hands, and Sukarno with his vintage charisma along with the loyal support of the PKI. This oddly constructed political tripod remained surprisingly stable during the descent into chaos. Exports shrank as army officers made away with the assets of former Dutch plantations, Java no longer reliably supplied the staple foods its growing population required, inflation rose faster and faster. The government launched two major "confrontations," the first (1960–1962) against Holland for recovery of West New Guinea, which it successfully achieved in 1962, the second (begun in 1963) against the newly formed state of Malaysia. For these campaigns, among other reasons, Sukarno's government imported a great deal of Soviet military equipment. In due course it proceeded also to expropriate British and Indian assets, in addition to the earlier Dutch ones. Sukarno himself propagated a stream of new slogans which became part of an official ideology in which all civil servants and students were indoctrinated. In 1964 the PKI, more and more openly sponsored by Sukarno in alliance against the army, shocked the rural leadership of Java, and especially the *santri* part of it, with a vigorous land reform and rent reduction campaign.

As Guided Democracy moved into 1965 the mounting inflation turned into a classic hyperinflation. The army worried about what Sukarno might do next for the PKI and stood by its guns. The PKI, unable to do anything but mount another strident campaign, agitated for a people's militia, which might arm some of its supporters, and clung ever tighter to Sukarno. As for Sukarno, his extraordinary talent seemed spent.

The crisis burst before dawn on October 1, 1965, when a group of middle-rank officers assassinated six senior generals and proclaimed their own assumption of power under Sukarno's aegis. In Indonesia the coup is officially attributed to the PKI; foreign scholars diverge widely in their interpretations. At any rate it was the aftermath of the coup—suppressed within a day by forces shrewdly deployed by General Suharto—that was decisive.

With both Sukarno and the PKI shaken by apparent complicity in the coup, and the martyrdom of the six generals for a rallying cry, the army set out to destroy the PKI forever. In late October, after an ominous three-week silence, the massacres began, in Central Java, then East Java, then Bali. Army units themselves seem to have killed comparatively few people; they provided assurance of support and sometimes firearms, but it was mostly neighbors and youth bands who did the killing. Hundreds of thousands were massacred, systematically and—most awfully—without resistance. (Estimates of the number of victims range, shakily, from fewer than a hundred thousand to a million. The main killings outside Java and Bali were in North Sumatra. In Aceh and West Borneo large numbers of Chinese were also massacred.)

Amid these horrors, on March 11, 1966, Sukarno was tactfully compelled to transfer effective authority to Suharto, and Indonesia passed from what later came to be called the "Old Order" into the "New Order." On the one hand Suharto moved swiftly on economics and foreign policy. At home, aware that he could do nothing with hyperinflation raging, he built a strong connection with a group of U.S.-trained Indonesian economists, his "technocrats" of the sixties, seventies, and eighties. Abroad, he promptly cancelled Sukarno's two major foreign policy initiatives of the moment, military "confrontation" with Malaysia and intimate association with China. These steps opened the way to closer connections with the West and Japan and therefore to the possibility of help for Indonesia's ravaged economy. As the capitalist bloc warmed to these overtures, Suharto and his technocrats promptly took steps to return Dutch and other nations' expropriated assets and to promulgate an attractive law on foreign investment. There followed a steady and generous flow of aid from abroad.

On other matters, especially domestic politics, Suharto moved slowly and with great care. He understood the enormous appeal of Sukarno's political language and persona and was careful to copy much of the former and back away from direct confrontation with the latter during the arcane constitutional maneuvers of 1966 to 1968. It was not until March 1968 that Suharto was elected president and until June that he was able to appoint his own cabinet.

Once properly established, Suharto's Indonesia has been run, rather like Singapore, as if it were a corporation rather than a nation. The most familiar example is the nearly perfect uniformity of the government party's percentage of the vote in the three elections of 1971, 1977, and 1982: 62 percent to 64 percent. It is easier, therefore, to describe the constructions than the history of New Order Indonesia. We may begin with politics.

The politics of Suharto's military regime is centered in the officer class of the Indonesian armed forces. When most of the officers are content, as they generally have been since, roughly, 1967, the New Order runs as it is designed to. Not surprisingly, this has required a good deal of careful work by Suharto. He inherited an army that was much larger, politically far more important, and much richer than the other military services and hence eyed jealously by them. Over the years, though still relying most on the army, Suharto has scrupulously reduced its salience, merging it more and more into the armed forces as a whole to facilitate his control. Over the long haul Suharto has cut the relative budget share of the military and made clear that its function is domestic security, not national defense. Finally, by regular and thorough reorganizations of the military structure and personnel he has kept the reins in his own hand.

The visible politics of New Order Indonesia, a complex, multilayered parliamentary system with general elections and special presidential elections in staggered years, is strictly for show. The Indonesian state runs its own political "party," Golkar, in the election campaign. Golkar, short for "Functional Groups" in Indonesian, was first organized by the army in Guided Democracy times to counter the innumerable unions and associations of the PKI. In the New Order it has become a compulsory political affiliation for government employees. In election years the apparatus of the territorial civil service under the Ministry of the Interior, along with the parallel local military hierarchy, turns out to deliver the vote. The rival, so to speak, genuine, political parties are subject to a great deal of formal and informal manipulation by the state; among other rules they are allowed to campaign in the villages for no more than a couple of weeks in each election, so as not to disturb the tranquillity of the peasant "floating mass" too much.

The New Order's foreign policy has been as understated as Sukarno's was excitable. The Suharto regime, having embraced the West and Japan so promptly in 1966, has seen no need to change its friendships. It has made a special point of hostility to China, not so much because China is Communist as because it is Chinese. For this reason it has differed from the rest of ASEAN in seeking good relations with Vietnam and would presumably welcome the latter as a barrier to any Chinese inclination to expand to the south. Given that Indonesia consists entirely of islands it is perhaps understandable that the Indonesian foreign minister, Mochtar Kusumaatmadja, has played a particularly large role in the worldwide debate on the limits of national territorial waters. The one flagrant breach of the regime's cool foreign policy style came in 1975 after the sudden collapse of Portuguese authority in the eastern half of the island of Timor at the far end of the chain of islands stretching eastward from Java and Bali. For reasons never made very clear, and despite repeated declarations by Indonesia for almost three decades that it made no claims on East Timor, Suharto ordered the invasion of the territory. The result was, and is, a more than usually brutal counterinsurgency operation well into its second decade.

As early New Order overtures to the West continued to be warmly received, Suharto and his technocrats set about reconstructing the Indonesian economy. It is convenient to deal here first with the political-economic machine constructed mainly by Suharto and to turn later to the more narrowly economic policies of the technocrats that were so salient in the 1970s. Economics as it affected the general public will appear below under the heading of social developments in the New Order.

In 1965–1966 Suharto, seizing power amid inflation and universal corruption, as well as the great massacre he had triggered himself, sought stability for himself and his regime. As he maneuvered to get and maintain control of a badly divided armed forces officer class, he concluded that he needed a great deal of money to help keep them in line politically and satisfied with their standard of living. Suharto used familiar devices, but his political-economic machine was exceptionally large and well made. Though in setting up his apparatus Suharto relied on many different sources of funds—including, for example, the state oil corporation Pertamina and the government bureau charged with stabilizing rice prices—the most important and reliable flows were from Indonesian-Chinese businessmen and multinational corporations of all sorts. Suharto and his technocrats seem to have held much the same assumptions about the economic aptitude of indigenous Indonesians as Sukarno, Hatta, and their generation: that Indonesians could not be expected to compete successfully with Chinese at home or Westerners abroad. The two political generations, however, differed sharply in how heavily they were able and willing to tax foreign and Chinese business. In the early and middle 1950s the elites and governments of the older generation got little in taxes from the dominant Dutch firms, and when Sukarno expropriated the Dutch holdings in 1957 the assets went mainly to the army under martial law, rather than to the government as such. The New Order, by contrast, has encouraged the multinationals to invest in Indonesia and has collected regular taxes from them. It has also, and this is machine business, blessed the flow of further sums from the foreign companies to deserving military officers who become sleeping partners in those companies' operations.

The older-generation leaders and governments also got very little from the Chinese merchants—either in legal taxes, which were poorly organized, or from payoffs, which went mostly to low and middle civil servants. Under the New Order petty bribery has increased markedly, if only to accommodate the much larger numbers of civil servants, but the important change was at the higher levels of the system. In the years of parliamentary democracy it was not unusual for individual Indonesian officials to exchange their signatures for a modest share of profits generated by Chinese capital. The economic chaos of Guided Democracy lowered standards and raised the size of the payoffs but left them still largely ad hoc arrangements between individuals. The New Order, as always bold and clear-eyed where its direct interests are concerned, has greatly enlarged and systematized such arrangements in what is known as the *cukong* system. A limited number of *cukong*—Indonesian-Chinese businessmen controlling great conglomerates—are matched with one or more major figures in the higher reaches of the military pyramid, starting with President Suharto. With protection of the highest quality each *cukong* makes fortunes for both himself and his patron.

These economic/political arrangements have played a large part in maintaining a remarkable political stability in Indonesia over more than two decades. Meanwhile in the 1970s, with continuing heavy development aid from the Inter-Governmental Group on Indonesia (Japan, the United States, European nations), further multinational investment and much higher oil prices, the Indonesian economy grew at an average rate of some 8 percent. The regime meticulously controlled rice prices, especially for the politically critical urban areas, and brought Indonesia to self-sufficiency in rice. When the top-heavy oil-based conglomerate Pertamina fell apart spectacularly in 1975 the technocrats nursed it through its crisis and back to a leaner and healthier state. They did the same for the economy as a whole in the early 1980s. The 1980s have in general been darker, elsewhere in Southeast Asia as well, and prospects for Indonesia to the end of the century, with oil reserves drawing down and population going up, are unclear.

The New Order also brought striking changes in the social sphere, of which two were especially significant for the longer run. One was the quite sudden collapse of social agreement between haves and have-nots in rural Java—that is, about half of all Indonesians. The other, with which we may begin, was the consolidation of a new bureaucratic middle class.

After 1900 the hereditary *priyayi* of Java and the lords of the outer islands lost some of their majesty as they came to wear neckties and speak faultless Dutch. The egalitarianism of the 1945 revolution completed the transformation: men born to rule were followed by middle classes. First were the nationalists of the 1920s who towered over Indonesia between 1945 and 1959 (in Sukarno's case until 1966). Then came the officers of the self-created Indonesian Army who first touched political power in 1957 and took the whole of it in 1966. And, over the decades—not to be ignored because they never held power—there were the four hundred thousand civil servants of 1957 and the 1.4 million of 1968. The galloping urban prosperity of the 1970s, above all in Jakarta, entrenched the new and newly self-confident middle class, which turned itself over to pursuit of car or motorcycle, TV or refrigerator, along with the all-important advanced education for its children.

Over the years, members of the bureaucratic middle class, especially students in Jakarta and Bandung, set off a number of substantial protests. But these regularly faded away when the military applied pressure, and even the extraordinarily cautious Suharto regime does not seem to have worried very much. The regime knew very well that it was the only significant source of middle-class employment for indigenous Indonesians. It also knew that it could count on the indigenous middle class to share its own racial hostility to the only economically significant middle class in Indonesia—that of the Chinese. The flourishing Indonesian middle class, in short, was a natural ally of the regime. In other ways, too, it made its mark—most notably in its contribution to the lively developments in Indonesian music, poetry, and the theater from the 1970s on.

In the late 1960s and early 1970s, as the bureaucratic middle class was stepping rather noisily onto the stage in the cities, millions of landless peasants were suddenly disappearing from sight on the landscape of rural Java. The underlying force behind this development was a steady growth of population on the island, long one of the most densely populated areas in the world: 42 million in 1930, 63 million in 1961, roughly 100 million in 1990. As rural population densities increased in the 1950s and 1960s, some families added a bit of riceland to their holdings, rarely much over an acre, while others lost their last patches of land. So long as the political elites paid little attention to the Javanese peasantry, as was the case from 1945 to 1964/1965, old customs giving the poor some claim to assistance in return for service given and respect paid to better-off patrons could leave the rural world intact, in charge of its own affairs.

But as soon as the army took full political control of rural Java in the aftermath of the 1965 massacres, Javanese villagers—whatever their politics—were no longer free to conduct their village affairs by themselves. The state broke in and it stayed. Landless peasants could no longer hint that they might turn to violence if they did not get customary kinds of assistance; better-off peasants had less reason to defer to old values requiring them to pay attention to the needs of their poor neighbors. At the same time, beginning with the official opening of the first five-year plan in 1969, the government set out for straightforward economic reasons to make Indonesia self-sufficient in rice. It introduced and vigorously pushed the planting of high yield rice varieties from the International Rice Research Institute (IRRI) in the Philippines. Getting the full potential from IRRI strains, however, requires substantial investment in fertilizer and pesticides—something a riceland owner could manage, and expect a good profit on, but beyond the capacity of a poor peasant, let alone a landless one.

The combination of these two forces, political and economic—and not just continuing population—brought abrupt changes in rural Java. Landowners became less willing to cut their poorer neighbors in. They were less likely to enter sharecropping arrangements. If they could not do all the necessary work themselves they hired labor for cash rather than shares. When they opened their fields of ripe grain to crowds of women harvesters, as traditionally, they retained a larger proportion of the grain each harvester had gathered than had been normal earlier. Others, wanting to dispense entirely with the traditional claim of poorer fellow-villagers to partake in the harvest on shares—but wishing to avoid embarrassment at so crass a breach of custom—sold the standing grain in their fields to people from outside the village. At harvest time these outsiders brought in small crews of their own people, men now, rather than women, and working with the more efficient sickle rather than the *ani-ani,* a finger-length blade for cutting each head of grain separately and reverently.

In the same years of the early 1970s riceland owners also began to cut labor costs in the most direct way by turning to machinery: mechanical threshers, powered tillers for preparing soil and weeding, and mechanical rice-hullers. The hullers spread particularly fast and wide; within a few years they had put an end to a major source of paid work for women in poor families. When Masri Singarimbun asked five of these women what alternative employment they would seek, they answered that there was no alternative work for them. " 'Then what will you do?', I asked. 'We will eat more carefully,' they replied."[63]

The appearance of labor-saving devices of these sorts, in the densely packed villages of Java, marked a parting of ways. Peasant landowners turned from the old ideals of rice sufficiency and good reputations as generous patrons of their less fortunate neighbors and set out to acquire more land and motorbikes and television sets. Landless peasants ate cassava, competed for the much fewer ricefield jobs, and spent even longer hours making and peddling petty trade items such as mats and palm sugar. In the early 1970s large numbers of them migrated to the cities of Java, especially Jakarta, to work as pedicab drivers, prostitutes, street vendors, and scavengers.

The government, for its part, did not want masses of poor peasants pressing into the capital city and took steps to keep the number of migrants down. It launched a fairly tough birth control program in rural Java but this still left the population increasing at not much below two million a year. Inevitably, it also returned to the perennial dream—first conceived by the Dutch early in the century—of exporting Java's masses to sparsely populated islands elsewhere in the archipelago. It will be a long time before any government is able to put Java together again.

# 39

## The Republic of the Philippines

AT the outbreak of World War II, Commonwealth president Manuel
Quezon summoned his nation to fight against the Japanese, noting that
"no nation is worth anything unless it has learned how to suffer and
how to die." But rapid Japanese victories doomed U.S. general Douglas
MacArthur's defense, and the American relief fleet was rusting at Pearl
Harbor. Just prior to the surrender of the Fil-American forces, MacArthur, Quezon, and Sergio Osmeña were evacuated—MacArthur to
plan reconquest, Quezon and Osmeña to maintain a government in
exile.

The Japanese, who had in the meantime occupied the city of Manila
on January 2, 1942, persuaded most of the prewar Manila politicians to
collaborate with them. With the notable exceptions of Chief Justice José
Abad Santos, the opposition leader Juan Sumulong, and a few others,
the elite rallied to Jorge Vargas, Quezon's former executive secretary, in
joining the Philippine Executive Commission and, subsequently, the
Japanese-sponsored Philippine Republic led by José P. Laurel. Most
Filipinos, however, actively supported or joined the guerrilla movement.

Not all guerrillas were motivated by lofty ideals; people joined for
complex reasons, including severe economic dislocation, starvation,
and misery, as well as greed and political opportunity. Old grudges and
wanton violence could be hidden under a patriotic mantle, and prewar
factionalism played a key role in determining who became a guerrilla
and who a collaborator. Nevertheless, the will to fight the Japanese was
genuine, and sacrifice sprang from a sense of standing on the front line.

Victory was won, but at a very high price. At the end of the war,
many people were homeless and most were starving. Medical and sanitation facilities were shattered; transportation was paralyzed; industrial
output was at a standstill. Manila bore the brunt of the destruction.
Since the modern sector of the economy was almost exclusively within
this urban environment, precious resources of facilities and skilled personnel were lost. The Filipinos were left limping through the rubble of
all they had built from 1901 to 1941.

The war broke the hermetically sealed isolation created by colonialism and gave Filipinos a sense of their place in Asia. The wartime use of
the Tagalog language and the glorification of indigenous institutions

generated a new pride. In 1935, Pio Duran, an apologist for Japan, had been considered a pariah for advocating the idea that the Philippines was "inextricably linked" to Asia, yet after the war his message became a key component in the thinking of establishment leaders like Claro Recto, Ferdinand Marcos, and Carlos P. Romulo.

The war also heightened social, political, and economic tensions between tenants and landlords, patrons and clients, exiles and captives, city dwellers and rural *tao* (peasants), guerrillas and collaborators. Thus the Hukbalahap (People's Anti-Japanese Army), while a guerrilla resistance movement in central Luzon, was equally a peasant effort to redress grievances with landlords. Not all guerrillas were radicals, not all conservatives were collaborators, not all peasants were Huks, and not all landlords were absentee landlords. But the disruptions of war and of occupation gave the Huks a special opportunity.

The war shattered the preponderant Nacionalista Party. After Quezon's death in 1944, Osmeña, who had become president, returned to the islands burdened by the Americans with the responsibility of prosecuting his peers who had served in the Japanese-sponsored Republic of the Philippines. Osmeña's position was awkward. He was forced by the Americans to be the chief inquisitor rather than a forgiving leader. The issues he faced included the legitimacy of a recall of the 1941 legislature, the fitness of Quezon's cabinet appointments, the need for a People's Court to try collaboration cases, the priorities to be established in regard to postwar planning and economic rehabilitation, and factional issues that dated back a decade or more. When MacArthur personally asserted that Manuel Roxas was free from wartime guilt, he established Roxas as Osmeña's rival for the post of president.

The April 1946 election was bitter. Roxas won with a modest majority. The emoluments of office seemed to triumph over the liabilities of public trust. Politicians and bureaucrats, whether they were collaborators, exiles, or guerrilla leaders, often seemed to be corrupt, self-seeking opportunists.

The problem of collaboration was complex. How could a nation unquestioningly believe that by enduring it had reached its finest hour, when its most prestigious and educated segment of society, its own elite, was accused of treason? How could the suffering of Filipinos during the war serve as a model for future generations, if those charged with the defense of national ideals not only seemingly flouted those ideals but survived in power after the war? The wartime experience made it seem that to obey was to abandon the good fight and that to resist the law was heroic. Nations that have been put in this terrible situation have discovered that they cannot turn on or shut off respect for the law as if it flowed from a spigot. Here, violence was institutionalized, and the use of weapons, whatever the reason, was justified as patriotic. The war spawned an armed society, and the readiness to resort to force has been a pervasive and disturbing feature of postindependence Philippine life.

Those under indictment for collaboration claimed to be vindicated by Roxas's victory. While presidential amnesty for political collaboration was declared early in 1948, the issue has lingered for decades.

The war years also led to disillusionment with the United States. Dissatisfaction began as early as 1942, when Quezon had bitterly complained to Charles Willoughby that "America writhes in anguish at the fate of a distant cousin, Europe, while a daughter, the Philippines, is being raped in the back room." Most Filipinos felt that the United States owed them generous postwar support, not merely because they had been allies but especially because they had fulfilled handsomely the obligations of *utang na loob* that cemented the "special relationship." Instead, the Filipinos were crushed to discover that the United States seemed preoccupied and insensitive. The relative meagerness of postwar economic aid, especially in comparison with the far more substantial support given Germany and Japan, and the crude way in which the United States tied its aid to postwar concessions, soured many Filipinos. They expected American gratitude; instead, the United States proved to be niggardly, calculating, and neocolonial.

The United States had retained the giant military installations at Subic Bay and at Clark Air Field on 99-year leases. These bases and the American claim to have made the Philippines a "showcase for democracy" were threatened by the Hukbalahap rebellion. As communism triumphed in China and Vietnam, America became increasingly afraid that it could triumph in the Philippines as well. Cold War ideology, therefore, helped to shape the areas of continuing involvement. Military and geopolitical concerns came to dominate Washington's priorities, angering Filipino nationalists like Senator Claro M. Recto. Such concerns led the Americans to endorse the political oligarchy and to address socioeconomic issues with military solutions.

Corruption, low morale, inflation, and economic exhaustion prevented the Manila government from defeating the Huks. Roxas, prior to his death in office in 1948, and his successor, Elpidio Quirino, simply lacked the strength or appeal to break the agrarian uprising led by a charismatic peasant, Luis Taruc, even though the United States was supplying increasing military and economic aid. The 1949 presidential election, in which Quirino defeated the wartime president, José Laurel, through bribery, fraud, and violence, weakened democracy. In 1950, the country went through an economic, moral, political, and military crisis. In October of that year, the Central Bank had to borrow to meet government payrolls.

The emergence of Ramon Magsaysay altered the history of the Philippines. Born in a bamboo hut, the son of a teacher who became a blacksmith, he was no scion of an elite family. Magsaysay, a guerrilla leader during the war, became Quirino's secretary of defense. He made three great contributions in his years as secretary. First, he infused a corrupt and demoralized army with a new sense of purpose and esprit

de corps. Second, Magsaysay's intelligence network enabled him to
arrest en masse the Communist Party Politburo and to seize documents
that listed sympathizers. Third, and most important, he got the army to
guarantee that the 1951 congressional elections would be honest. By
protecting the ballot box he restored a degree of confidence in the electoral process. He won an easy victory in the presidential election of
1953. Gathering a brain trust of bright young men, he broke the
Hukbalahap uprising by a combination of heavy military pressure
against those who refused to surrender, amnesty for those who did, and
a series of resettlement schemes to ease tenancy in the Huk areas. By
the time of his death in a plane crash in 1957, he had done much to
restore vitality and cohesiveness to the nation.

His immediate successors, however, lacked the vision and political
power to maintain the momentum. Carlos Garcia, Magsaysay's vice
president, was elected in 1957, and Diosdado Macapagal in 1961. This
era, subsequently known as the "old order," clearly revealed the structural contradiction of the postindependent, oligarchic society. It was a
working democracy, in the sense that people out of office could through
the electoral process win power. It was dominated, however, by a single
elite, whose members jumped parties with dizzying speed. It was a
period of private armies, growing lawlessness, and uneven economic
development.

Land reform was much talked about but never implemented. The
elite had no intention of abolishing the source of its wealth; and, even
had it wanted to, it lacked the economic resources to fund the program.
At the same time, it was also an era of substantial business growth.
Multinational corporations entered the Philippines in large numbers as
world prosperity, fueled by the American economy, sought new markets
and opportunities. It was in this era that the modern sector of the society moved out to Makati, the new city built just outside Manila.

Under the entrepreneurial management of the Zobel family, highrise
buildings, broad boulevards, shopping centers, and residential subdivi-
sions all sprouted on land previously trampled by carabao. To misquote
Marx, if the rich got richer and the poor got children, there was also a
sense of optimism, prompting large numbers of youngsters to seek college education as the vehicle for upward mobility to the good life. The
free press limited some of the excesses of the system by spotlighting
them, and there was a growing sense of national pride, a growing
awareness of the Asian-ness of the Philippines.

In 1963, an ambitious senator, Ferdinand Marcos, successfully challenged the prewar oligarch, Eulogio (Amang) Rodriguez, for the presidency of the Senate. Two years later, Marcos jumped parties, became a
Nacionalista, and won a landslide presidential victory. In his 1965 inaugural address, he said, "The Filipino, it seems, has lost his soul, his dignity, and his courage. Our people have come to the point of despair. We
have ceased to value order." Marcos continued by noting that the "gov-

ernment is gripping the iron hand of venality, its treasury is barren, its resources are wasted, its civil service is slothful and indifferent, its armed forces demoralized and its councils sterile."

Marcos, the creature of the "old order," claimed to be the savior of the nation. In 1969, running on the slogan, "Rice and Roads," and liberally spending money from the public treasury, Marcos was reelected president, the first man ever to win a second full term. His claim to be a distinguished war hero enhanced his glamor and his flamboyant, beautiful wife Imelda made them seem like Philippine versions of the Kennedys. This was an era of prosperity, fueled in large measure by the growing American presence in Indochina.

What distinguished Marcos from his immediate predecessors was his interest in a new political ideology for the Philippines. Marcos saw democracy as not only wasteful but licentious, as not only corrupt but paralyzing. In his view, "Constitutional authoritarianism" should supplant the "old order." The authoritarian instinct had been articulated by Apolinario Mabini at the Malolos Constitutional Convention in the 1890s. During World War II, José Laurel, Marcos's mentor, took the presidency in his belief that the Philippines needed a fundamental reorganization in keeping with a world-wide trend in which "totalitarianism [was] gradually supplanting democracy."

Throughout his career, Ferdinand Marcos was obsessed with constitutions. To his last days in office, he clung to the notion that there had to be a law to justify an action. This made his regime increasingly like that of the Queen of Hearts in *Alice in Wonderland.*

On September 21, 1972, Marcos proclaimed martial law. Claiming he was exercising his power "to protect the Republic of the Philippines and our democracy," Marcos moved rapidly to end all forms of dissent and opposition. Thousands of persons were arrested, habeas corpus was suspended, the media was drastically curtailed, the courts substantially weakened, and the army strengthened. Marcos justified this declaration by claiming there was a serious threat of a Communist takeover led by a new generation of radical Maoist students, many of whom were upper middle class by birth.

In fact, Marcos was motivated by a broader set of issues. He viewed the constitutional convention that was then debating the future of the government structure as a threat to society. He was in his seventh year as president, constitutionally banned from running for a third term. Moreover, as his power began to slip away, he was being challenged by members of the oligarchy, including the powerful Lopez family, owners of the *Manila Chronicle,* television stations, and the Manila Electric Company. A young Senator Benigno Aquino was the likely next president. The last issue of the *Free Press,* the leading opinion magazine at the time, carried a prophetic cover bearing a picture of Aquino targeted through the crosswires of a rifle sight with the caption, "Senator Benigno S. Aquino: TARGET?"

Marcos's declaration of martial law won the strong support of the modern business community and of U.S. president Richard Nixon. In the first three years, tourism and government revenues tripled, and the economy grew at an average annual rate of 7 percent. The private armies of the oligarchs were disbanded and some 500,000 privately held weapons were confiscated. In those early years, Marcos often was compared to Lee Kuan Yew of Singapore. If he violated human rights with impunity, his was a less brutal dictatorship than some others. People indeed were arrested and tortured and murdered. The total story of brutality has yet to be told, and yet, many Filipinos saw these years as a time of progress and seemed willing to surrender liberty for economic development.

Marcos dramatically expanded the army's role in society, tripling its size. The officer corps was given opportunities to acquire great wealth, and the tradition of a nonpolitical military disappeared. Marcos issued a new constitution, replaced Supreme Court justices and changed the court system, created people's organizations at the mass and local level, and built a new political party, the KBL (Kilusang Bagong Lipunan). Manipulating patronage and the power of government effectively, and using referenda, constitutional amendments, and other techniques, Marcos built a dominant political organization which stifled dissent. In 1976, while amending of the constitution, Marcos inserted Amendment Six, which gave him transcendent political power no matter what structure might subsequently be put into place.

By 1975, however, the ideological fervor dissipated and it became apparent that the new order was a vehicle for Marcos's personal aggrandizement. Crony capitalism gave close friends of the First Family vast economic opportunity. Sugar and coconut areas were made exempt from the land reform which had begun with such fanfare in 1973. The obvious growing greed of the cronies and of Imelda Marcos substituted profit for ideology. This was the period known as the Conjugal Dictatorship. With her jewels, her jet-set friends, and her many projects, Mrs. Marcos became the symbol of corruption. Known as Nuestra Señora de Metro Manila because, among many other posts, she was also governor of Metropolitan Manila and minister of human settlements, she chaired no fewer than twenty-three government councils, agencies, and corporations. She controlled hundreds of millions of dollars annually through their budgets, and it was during this period that she built eleven five-star hotels, the Manila Cultural Center and the 5,000-seat International Convention Center, a $21 million Film Center, and a sprawling terminal at the airport. Increasingly, she became the most visible representative of the regime, and speculation centered on her succession to the presidency upon her husband's illness or death. The aimless drift of the Marcos government was perfectly summarized during a press conference with Mrs. Marcos in 1982 when she said, "The Philippines is in a strategic position—it is both East and

West, right and left, rich and poor." After a pause she went on to note, "We are neither here nor there."

While the Marcoses and their friends were growing richer and more complacent, others in the society were less satisfied. In the Mindanao and Sulu regions of the southern Philippines, a rebellion erupted in the Muslim-Filipino community. The sources of this revolt were deep, dating back to centuries of hostility between Christians and Muslims (Moros) in the Philippines and around the world, and aggravated by a policy first begun by the Americans and continued by Magsaysay of resettling landless Christian lowland Filipinos on homesteading sites in Mindanao. The policy changed the demography of the region, leaving the Christians in the majority. The rise of Arab and Southeast Asian nationalism, new Muslim oil wealth, and local factional politics all contributed to the ferment.

In 1968, a group of Muslim leaders organized the Moro National Liberation Front (MNLF), with full independence as their stated objective but with increased autonomy as their real goal. The constitutional convention in 1972 spent much time debating the role of the Muslim areas. After the oil shock of 1973 and the declaration of martial law, more and more Muslim youth joined the MNLF, and at its peak the rebels were able to field fifty to sixty thousand guerrillas. The key leader of the Muslim hard-liners was Nur Misuari, in exile throughout this period; but Marcos skillfully bought off many of the local leaders and, simultaneously, granted many of the concessions they demanded for the purpose of protecting their autonomy. By 1981 the Moro National Liberation Front had fallen to approximately ten thousand guerrillas. Marcos directed substantial development money into Muslim areas, including the Cotabato-Agusan River Basin Development Program.

If money and political compromise blunted the secessionist fervor of the Muslims, it did nothing to stem the growth of the New People's Army (NPA), the radical guerrilla arm of a reorganized Communist Party of the Philippines. Marcos, who had cited the Communist threat as the justification for martial law, was the best recruiter the NPA could have had. His mismanagement of the economy, his greed and the greed of his associates, and the growing contradictions of Philippine society drew the hungry, homeless, and hopeless to the NPA. Functioning at first in remote rural areas and skillfully manipulating local grievances, tensions, and desires, the NPA established armed units and networks of supporters. Over fifteen years, approximately twelve to fifteen thousand hard-core guerrilla soldiers were mobilized, and by 1985 American and Filipino military observers felt that the NPA was reaching a critical stage of development that would permit it to launch larger military engagements, posing a direct threat to the survival of the government.

In January 1981, Marcos technically lifted martial law in order to defuse growing worldwide criticism. He felt confident of his position politically but also understood that he would need increasing American military and economic assistance if he was to defeat the NPA. U.S. president Jimmy Carter's focus on human rights and the growing attention of the mass media to human rights abuses made martial law appear an unnecessary and cumbersome impediment. Marcos wanted to be invited to pay a state visit to Washington and calculated that lifting martial law would win strong support from his old friend Ronald Reagan. The world was very different in 1981 from what it had been in 1972, and through his many plebiscites and constitutional manipulations Marcos already had secured all the continuing authority he felt he required. Thus, in June 1981, he held a presidential election, running against a weak and virtually unknown candidate, Alejo Santos. It was perhaps significant that a fringe candidate, Bartolome Cabangbang, won 4 percent of the total national vote on a platform advocating statehood in the United States. It was following this totally fraudulent election that Vice President George Bush toasted Marcos, saying, "We love your adherence to democratic principles—and to the democratic processes."

Although Marcos dominated the Philippines, his regime was in fact being seriously eroded by increasing army abuses, the proliferation of warlordism, growing corruption, and his own deteriorating physical health. The president suffered from lupus, a degenerative disease attacking, in his case, perhaps mortally, his kidneys. As it became clear that he was ill, the jockeying for power and the growing influence of Imelda Marcos created palace intrigue worthy of Ch'ing dynasty China. Secretary of Defense Juan Ponce Enrile, among others, lost out to Marcos's cousin and loyal supporter, General Fabian Ver. The oil crises of 1973 and 1979, the collapse of world commodity prices, and the increasing tendency of the elite to send capital abroad doubled the nation's foreign debt between 1979 and 1983. Inflation was rampant, and the technocrats and entrepreneurs came to see Marcos and his cronies as the problem, not the solution.

Confident, however, of his own hold on society and eager to avoid world criticism, Marcos permitted opposition news to be printed and broadcast, including on Radio Veritas, a station run by the Roman Catholic Church. It was during this same period that Marcos, under pressure from the United States, allowed his arch rival, Benigno Aquino, to go from jail into exile in Boston with his wife and children. Aquino was the one figure in the opposition capable of rallying the splintered opposition into a coherent political front. In 1978, while still in solitary confinement in jail, Aquino had formed the Laban ("Fight") Party, had run for an Assembly seat, and probably would have won, had the election been fair.

In August 1983 Aquino decided to return to the Philippines because he believed that Marcos was undergoing a kidney transplant and was in grave risk of dying. He sensed that this was a period of great fluidity and that his presence in Manila would be the one thing that would keep General Ver and Imelda Marcos from seizing power.

In a murder most foul, Aquino was shot in the back of the head by one of the guards escorting him off the plane at the Manila International Airport. The army's version of what happened was a transparent fabrication. Whether Marcos himself knew or whether it was a deed ordered by Mrs. Marcos and General Ver was hotly debated. The political martyrdom of this leader of the opposition, however, began brutally the final years of decay. Under heavy pressure domestically and internationally, Marcos appointed a Commission of Inquiry in October 1983, ostensibly to search out the truth. After extensive hearings, the Agrava Commission issued its report in which it discounted the army's story, accusing instead a conspiracy of army and air force officers including General Fabian Ver. In the following trial, held in front of a military tribunal, however, all of the officers and enlisted men were found not guilty. This clear travesty of justice was a warning signal that drove increasing numbers of Filipinos away from the Marcos government. Immediately following Aquino's assassination there was a major flight of capital in which those with money, including the middle class as well as the rich, sent their funds abroad. In June of 1983 the peso was devalued to six pesos to the dollar; the exchange rate later fell to twenty. Moreover, any Filipino who could, attempted to leave the country. Some 300,000 emigrated from the Philippines to the United States during the Marcos years, and Filipinos became the second largest Asian-American group in the United States. In all, 1.5 million Filipinos were in a diaspora, scattered from the Arab and Persian Gulf states across Asia to the United States, Canada, and Europe.

The flight of brains and money, the loss of confidence in the regime, and the growing impatience of international financial institutions, including the World Bank, accelerated the economic collapse. In effect, the Philippine nation was bankrupt. There was rampant inflation, insufficient funds to service the debt, and a risk to the world monetary system through a collapse of the Philippine banking system. Thus, the *Economist* predicted in 1985 that the "country's economy may now be locked into a decline that only radical change can save from ending in complete disaster." The economy declined approximately 15 percent during these three years of disarray, and individual Filipinos were acutely affected. The government was forced to try and sell, without success, more than 150 government-owned corporations to raise revenue.

With the state $27 billion in debt, 483 creditor banks and the International Monetary Fund insisted upon reform before any further cash would be advanced. Fourteen sugar mills built in the early years of the Marcos era were bankrupt and shut. Coconut mills stood empty; and cement plants, automobile factories, and textile mills were foreclosed by the government which, assuming their debt, jeopardized the government itself. The Development Bank of the Philippines and the Philippine National Bank held over 100 billion pesos of non- or underperforming assets. In 1981, to cite one example, a textile magnate, Dewey Dee, disappeared with outstanding debts of $80 million. That pattern accelerated as the Construction and Development Corporation of the Philippines (CDCP) was absorbed with 5 billion pesos of debt, and Delta Motor Corporation was nationalized, with 2 billion pesos of debt. Both of these companies were, of course, owned by close friends of the president. Twenty thousand people worked for CDCP, and it had been earning more foreign exchange than any other company in the Philippines.

In this growing chaos, there was a scramble for power. Marcos himself, periodically seriously ill, dropped from sight only to reappear seemingly well again. General Ver was under a dark political cloud, although it was obvious that the president relied more and more on him and the army. Others fluttered like moths around a flickering lamp.

Meanwhile, the opposition was attempting to regroup following Aquino's assassination. In February 1984, Marcos called Assembly elections. The moderate opposition divided between those who advocated an electoral boycott and those who urged participation. Aquino's brother advocated boycott while his widow Corazon strongly supported participation. The burgeoning of the National Movement for Free Elections (NAMFREL); the increasingly outspoken activism of the Roman Catholic Church, which urged participation; and the emergence of Mrs. Aquino altered the outcome so that, despite Marcos's political leverage and financial muscle, he suffered a substantial defeat. Approximately one-third of the new legislature belonged to the opposition, and had the vote been truly fair, most experts speculate that it would have won a majority.

The American government at this time was becoming more and more anti-Marcos. At first, it was the Democrats in the House of Representatives, led by Congressman Stephen Solarz. Then, the Department of State, the Department of Defense, and the Central Intelligence Agency came to see the Philippines as threatened by such instability that the bases could be lost, the Communists would win, and American interests could be seriously damaged.

During most of the Marcos era, the Roman Catholic Church had been split into factions. Conservative traditionalists accepted the status quo and did not intervene "in temporal matters," "radicals" engaged in social action, while moderates avoided "liberation theology." The Church collectively, however, had been the most outspoken defender of human rights. Nuns and clergy were themselves tortured and killed, while others were forced into exile. After Aquino was assassinated, the Church coalesced behind the Chinese *mestizo* Archbishop of Manila, Jaime Cardinal Sin. With his colleague, Cardinal Vidal, he became a spearhead of an opposition that Marcos could neither quell nor silence.

Corazon Aquino also became a political force that Marcos could neither fathom nor control. A shy, retiring woman, born into one of the wealthiest Chinese *mestizo* families of central Luzon, the Cojuancos, she had been a private, pious wife to her martyred husband. After his death, however, she discovered inner strength that had been developing during the eight years when she and her husband were forced to endure much humiliation. With transcendent grace, she was drawn, reluctantly, into political leadership.

With the arrogance of a long-standing dictator, Ferdinand Marcos believed that he had the political machine, the powers of government, and the popularity to withstand any storm. Prodded by a series of visits by high-level Americans and by television interviews, on November 3, 1985, the president called for a snap election. On December 2, General Ver and the twenty-five others were acquitted. The president immediately restored Ver to his former position as chief of staff. The following day, Mrs. Aquino announced that she would run against Marcos. NAMFREL, jointly led by a Makati businessman and Bishop Fortich of Negros, organized to insure the fairness of the election, eventually mobilizing half a million poll watchers, people who served at great risk, since the president used every trick to steal the election. With the misguided notion that press attention would reaffirm his legitimacy, Marcos permitted the election to become a media sideshow, not only inviting and welcoming literally hundreds of foreign reporters into the country but also permitting the opposition, including Radio Veritas, to continue its daily attacks on him, his government, and twenty years of corruption. Cardinal Sin increasingly played a central role on behalf of the opposition, forging the political compact that joined Mrs. Aquino and her chief rival, Senator Salvador (Doy) Laurel. Moreover, he used the power of the pastoral letter to counterbalance presidential patronage, bribery, and intimidation.

The election itself, held on February 7, 1986, was one part television show, one part *Portrait of Dorian Gray*, two parts *Macbeth*, four parts Passion play. The skill of Marcos's operatives, the massive use of vote buying and intimidation, the combat between Marcos's warlords and the half-million citizen army of NAMFREL, and the passionate expression of political concern by the great majority of Filipinos, riveted the world's attention via television. Mrs. Aquino clearly won the election, but Marcos's machine claimed the victory. As the fraud became more apparent, in part because of Marcos's key miscalculation in permitting the media to function freely, the political crisis deepened. The Church became the refuge and "People Power" became a secular restatement of a crusading fervor. Rarely have good and evil been so unambiguously portrayed in politics, and the postelection weeks saw increasing pressure on Marcos to resign or abdicate. The Americans, international funding agencies, and the world community watched with alarm as the society drifted into anarchy. The New People's Army, which had openly supported Marcos in the hope that that very anarchy would sweep them to power, seemed the great winners, while moderate social reformers seemed the losers.

Both Mrs. Aquino and Marcos were planning competing inaugurations, when a reform faction of the army broke with the government. Juan Ponce Enrile and the second-ranking army officer, General Fidel Ramos, fled to a military base to revolt. Cardinal Sin summoned the people into the streets.

The army refused to attack the demonstrators, the Americans convinced Marcos to leave the country, and on February 25, 1986, a joyful, peaceful transfer began a new order with staggering problems, including malnutrition, underemployment, and unemployment. The bottom 20 percent of the nation got approximately 5.5 percent of the national income, while the top 2 percent got 53 percent. The nation owed $27 billion. The standard of living for the individual Filipino had fallen 5 percent per year during the late Marcos era.

Mrs. Aquino opened the prisons, offered amnesty to the NPA, and attempted to enter into political dialogue, not only with the dissidents but also with the army—especially the so-called "reformists"—other sectors of the society, and Marcos loyalists. She made an early political decision that she needed to form a government that included some key Marcos holdovers, most crucially Juan Ponce Enrile and General Fidel Ramos. Enrile's personal ambition and the military's deep anxiety about a policy of rapprochement and conciliation with the Communists put her in a complex bind. The stability of her government was challenged from both the left and the right. Personal ambition had been pitted against national priorities. The key question was whether the center could hold. Whether there would be a social revolution to reorder the nation's priorities and make the society more just remained to be seen.

In 1974, Benigno Aquino wrote a poem entitled "Maria Corazon" which began, "You are love—earnest, genuine, sincere, womanly, humanly divine! Unruffled by trouble, undeterred by the burden though heavy the load." Little did he know that his description of her as "anchorage of the troubled, the worried, the frightened," would be the burden she assumed as she led her nation toward the twenty-first century.

# 40

# Transforming Southeast Asia

SINCE the end of World War II, the political changes flowing from de-colonization have for the most part been matched or overtaken by social, economic, and cultural ones. The international context in which political and economic relations were conducted by Southeast Asians after 1945 underwent a bewildering series of mutations. In the political sphere, these affected the relations between Southeast Asian states and their former colonial masters, the acceptance or refusal of patronage from larger powers, and the relationships among Southeast Asian states themselves, as well as conditions within these diverse societies.

Between 1945 and 1960, Southeast Asian states responded in varying ways to the departure of colonial powers from the region. Some responses were abrupt. Burma, for example, refused as early as 1947 to join the British Commonwealth, though it continued in the sterling bloc for some time longer. Other responses were colored by prolonged anti-colonial wars to drive out the European powers. Relations between Indonesia and the Netherlands, and between Vietnam and France, are cases in point. In still other countries, including Malaya, Laos, and Cambodia, government-to-government relations remained cordial for some time after decolonization, partly because of the aid that Great Britain and France provided to incumbent rulers faced with insurrections. In the Philippines, the colonial relationship with the United States was modulated at the formal level into a network of treaties and a military alliance.

The polarization of world politics after World War II forced Southeast Asian nations to adopt a neutral position or to take sides with the United States and its allies on the one hand or, on the other, with the Soviet Union and its allies, including China after 1949. In 1954, Thailand and the Philippines chose to join the Southeast Asia Treaty Organization (SEATO), devised by the United States as a response to the French defeat in Indochina and surviving until 1976. They were the only Southeast Asian states to do so. Partly in response to the formation of SEATO, the Democratic Republic of Vietnam chose to remain aligned with China and the Soviet Union.

Most of the states in Southeast Asia, along with decolonized states elsewhere, responded to the transformation of international politics by choosing to be "nonaligned" in the Cold War. This policy became internationally established following the 1955 Bandung Conference in Indonesia of Asian leaders, including Sukarno, Sihanouk, Nu, Nehru, and Chou En-lai. Burma, Indonesia, and Cambodia actively pursued neutralist policies, perceived as"immoral" by the American secretary of state, through most of the period. In Laos and Vietnam, men and women who may have preferred a nonaligned response to international animosities they knew little about were swept into murderous conflicts by governments within and outside Southeast Asia that had more dogmatic perceptions of international affairs.

Another significant change flowing from decolonization was the reestablishment of relations between Southeast Asian states themselves. In some cases, the advent of independence reopened rivalries and disagreements which had preceded the colonial era. For the most part, these involved quarrels over the frontiers imposed on Southeast Asia by the colonial powers. Philippine claims to Sabah were matched by Cambodian claims to portions of Vietnam, and Thai claims to parts of northwestern Cambodia echoed Malay irredentist sentiments toward southern Thailand. The armed conflict that broke out between Malaysia and Indonesia in the early 1960s, *Konfrontasi,* was also partly territorial in nature.

Vietnamese and Thai relationships with Laos in the 1950s and 1960s were also colored by the ways in which nineteenth-century Thai and Vietnamese rulers had acted in the region; once again, the buffer states between the two became a battleground. Vietnamese attempts to secure their western frontier in the early nineteenth century were reenacted, in some ways, when Vietnam established its hegemony over Laos and Cambodia in the late 1970s. On a larger scale, the consolidation of China under Communist rule in 1949 soon led to the reassertion of official Chinese interest in Southeast Asia, not only along its frontiers, particularly with Laos and Burma, but also further afield, especially in the nonaligned nations and among ethnic Chinese who had been settled in the region, often for generations.

In the 1950s and 1960s, Southeast Asia's entrance into a larger world was accompanied by substantial foreign intrusions into Southeast Asia. At this stage such intrusion took the form mainly of military and economic aid to parties favored by one or another external power. Many Southeast Asians perceived this as a way of reasserting some form of neocolonial control; certainly the largest programs, those of the United States, were framed in political and strategic quite as much as in altruistic terms. Throughout the region, the United States and to a much lesser extent the Soviet Union and China vied for client governments. By the late 1950s, Laos was receiving more aid per capita, US$1,500, than any other country in the world at a time when per capita income in Laos was equivalent to only US$800 per year. For a time Burma, Indonesia, and Cambodia were able to play the great powers off against each other, accepting aid wherever it appeared, provided strings were not too visibly attached. The direct entry of over half a million United States troops into the Vietnam War in the 1960s brought a new dimension to the structure of superpower involvement in the region.

The war in Vietnam, and the failure of SEATO to respond to it as the United States wished, led the government in Washington to encourage several states of Southeast Asia to form an Association of Southeast Asian Nations (ASEAN) in 1967. Composed of Thailand, Singapore, Malaysia, the Philippines, Indonesia, and (from 1985) Brunei, the ASEAN member states have been generally receptive to involvements of a political and economic kind with the nations of the West. Burma chose not to join the association and, in a comparable move, resigned in 1979 from the Non-Aligned Movement (NAM) on the grounds that its members were in fact aligned in one way or another in world politics.

The Socialist Republic of Vietnam (SRV), frozen out of ASEAN and unable to receive assistance from the United States and international lending agencies, chose in 1978 to affiliate itself with the Soviet-led Council for Mutual Economic Assistance (COMECON), composed of the Soviet Union, the states of eastern Europe, Cuba, and Mongolia. Since 1979 China has refused to provide assistance to the Vietnamese economy.

In the international political context, therefore, Southeast Asian states in the last forty years have developed self-consciously in regional terms, reaching out to larger powers and, with the exception of Burma, frequently allowing larger powers to influence their international alignments. Similarly, these years have seen fundamental changes in the economic relations of the region with the rest of the world. Independent governments, unlike their colonial predecessors, have begun to develop their domestic economies in ways that have had significant consequences on the structure of their societies, the nature of employment patterns and lifestyles, and the ecology of the region. By the 1980s the economic transformation speeded by decolonization had resulted in several Southeast Asian countries making a partial entrance into the industrial world. The rate of change in others, however, has been much slower because of the development strategies adopted or the existence of internal disorder. With the ability to mobilize significant amounts of domestic capital for investment severely limited, the ASEAN states have welcomed foreign investment as well as aid and loans for development projects, whereas Burma and the Communist countries have remained dependent on the latter for most of their development capital.

Decolonization ended the domination of trade and investment by the European powers in the region. As Britain, France, and the Netherlands were no longer able to control the flow of capital into and primary products out of Burma, Malaya, Indonesia, and Indochina, and as the United States gradually lessened its protective economic relationship with the Philippines, their governments were forced to look for markets elsewhere. The postwar economic power of the United States allowed it to replace Europe as the major economic partner of many Southeast Asian states, in terms of trade, investment, and aid at the cost of maintaining its special relations with the Philippines.

But after the mid-1970s, Japan became the dominant economic partner of many of the countries of Southeast Asia. By the end of 1982, one-fifth of Japan's total overseas investment was directed to the ASEAN members; Japan imported large quantities of minerals and timber, as well as oil and natural gas, from Southeast Asia; and nearly half of Japan's total world trade was with the region. Southeast Asia's economic dependence upon Japan was equally impressive: in the 1980s more than half of Indonesia's oil production and more than two-thirds of the Philippines' copper production was exported to Japan.

The Japanese wavered between an economic view of the region as a source of raw materials and a market for Japanese goods and a moral sense that Southeast Asia was the place where Japan had a special responsibility to solve the schism between "developed" and "underdeveloped" countries. The Southeast Asian view of Japan was also ambivalent. Between 1970 and 1975 university students in several countries launched anti-Japanese demonstrations, and in the 1980s the leaders of Indonesia and the Philippines complained about American pressure upon Japan to expand its military defense force and strategic power in the region. In Malaysia, however, Prime Minister Mahathir launched a "Look East!" campaign and expressed admiration of the Japanese economic system, in which the government was alleged to be the "coach" of its own national capitalism rather than being merely the "referee," as was sometimes said of the English-speaking countries, or the "manager," as in planned socialist and communist economies. The dependent relationship of the Southeast Asian states with Japan or the United States was exacerbated by the latters' domination of international economic institutions such as the World Bank and the Asian Development Bank, which exist to loan capital and facilitate the transfer of technology to the region.

A goal shared by all the postcolonial elites was the rapid industrialization of their societies. The dependence of Southeast Asian economies on the export of primary commodities such as rice, tin, and rubber in exchange for manufactured goods such as toothpaste, automobiles, and textiles led all the governments of the region, with the exception of Laos, to launch ambitious industrialization plans in the 1950s and early 1960s. In the hope of getting rid of the need to import such things as paper, clothing, and the like, these plans initially concentrated on the development of import-substitution industries. In a familiar pattern, the finance for this development was to come primarily from the income earned from the export of primary products. Behind high tariff barriers designed to protect nascent industries, and by tapping pools of low-wage labor, several states achieved a measure of success as private or government-owned industry developed, often in collaboration with foreign firms. In the late 1960s and 1970s, however, in response to pressures from interests in the United States and Japan and a desire to develop more rapidly an industrial sector which would absorb many more unemployed and underemployed workers, import substitution gave way to strategies of export-oriented industrialization in the ASEAN countries. Foreign capital would be invited into a country to build assembly plants for the production of manufactured goods primarily for export. Initially states developed their textile and shoe industries before launching into the production of radios, television sets, chemicals, and silicon chips. Singapore led the way in this process as its earnings as an entrepôt and British naval base declined. By the 1970s the other ASEAN states had adopted similar strategies, and textiles, clothing, and shoes from Indonesia, the Philippines, Thailand, and Malaysia became common sights in the shopping centers of the Western world. However, much foreign investment in the ASEAN economies such as Japan's, as we have seen, was still concentrated in the production and extraction of primary products such as timber, rubber, tin, petroleum, and natural gas. The fluctuating international prices of rice, palm oil, teak, copra, and other agricultural products placed millions of Southeast Asians at the mercy of the outside world, much as they had been at the height of the colonial era.

The economic growth of the ASEAN states during the 1970s and 1980s had been dependent upon their being able to provide a stable climate for investment; foreign capital is highly competitive, after all, and can seek homes anywhere in the world. The need for such stability encouraged the political elites in several ASEAN states, enamored of the status quo in any case, to attempt to control wage rates and maintain political order so as not to frighten away foreign multinational investors. Such policies have been criticized for curtailing the rights of labor unions and leading to the further exploitation of labor in the region. As we shall see, the introduction of thousands of peasant women into factories, particularly in Malaysia, Thailand, and Singapore, as well as the occasional use of child labor, has been a matter of concern to opposition groups in several ASEAN countries.

Whatever the consequences for particular sectors of society, the economic development of most of the Southeast Asian states has been impressive. As a world market, the region bought more from the West in the 1980s than did either China or India. Throughout the 1970s and early 1980s, several countries achieved annual growth rates as high as 8 percent. Per capita gross national product (GNP) in Singapore stood at US$5,910 in 1982, making it wealthier than some countries in the European Community. Malaysia by the same year had achieved a per capita GNP of US$1,860, while Thailand and Indonesia stood at US$790 and US$580, respectively. The economic development of the Philippines was delayed by mismanagement and political turmoil in the early 1980s after having led the region in some respects for several years. In contrast, Burma, Laos, Cambodia, and Vietnam, measured in terms of GNP per capita, remained among the poorest countries of the world. Comparable data for the Communist countries is not available, but GNP per capita in Burma in 1982 was US$190.

Despite the growth of several of the region's economies, they have remained highly dependent on international market forces and foreign capital supplies outside their control. Much more than the industrialized countries of the West, government and individual incomes and security in Southeast Asia are still determined by decisions made in the boardrooms of international banks and commodity markets in New York or London and multinational boardrooms in Tokyo, Frankfurt, and elsewhere. The collapse of international prices for tin, rice, and petroleum, which occurred in the mid-1980s, caused severe worry to the governments of the region, fearful of the political consequences flowing from a lowering of standards of living for people who have been promised for years that their sacrifices would be rewarded in the future with better lives for themselves and their children and who were starting to see their personal situations improve. These changes have affected countries in different ways: falling oil prices, for example, tend to alarm Indonesia and Malaysia, which have substantial oil deposits to exploit, but are welcomed by Thailand, the Philippines, and the Indochinese states, which must import oil.

Also of concern to the governments has been the growth of their national debts, both public and private, to foreign banks and multinational lending agencies. In the 1980s these debt problems were not yet as severe as in some parts of South America, with the exception of the Philippines, where mismanagement and chicanery led to a debt of more than US$27 billion in 1986 before the fall of the Marcos regime. The obligation to export 30 to 40 percent of their primary and manufactured goods in order to pay back the capital and interest on their loans—the so-called debt-service ratio—may well have crippling effects on Southeast Asian economies in the future. Even in the economies where the debt service ratio had reached only about 25 percent in the mid-1980s, such as Thailand, development projects were halted until concessionary financial arrangements could be made with foreign lending agencies.

The ASEAN states, while often expressing their eagerness to cooperate, have not opened up their economies to each other. Instead, they have persistently competed with each other for access to markets in the rest of the world. This is hardly surprising, for they possess the same kinds of resources and similar human skills, and all wish to develop more or less independent industrial capacities.

Throughout the 1970s and 1980s, the government of Burma pursued a development strategy different from that of the ASEAN states. During the 1950s joint ventures with foreign capital were encouraged, but after 1962 stringent autarky was perceived as the only way of maintaining the country's economic independence while increasing peasants' and workers' economic equality with other classes. The result has been a slower rate of economic expansion than in the ASEAN states and very little change in the structure of the economy. Industrialization, largely financed by Japanese war reparations and aid and loans from international bodies, has led to increased production of some consumer items, but many remained in short supply in the 1980s. A significant parallel or "black" market grew up in the 1960s and 1970s next to the government-controlled market to provide luxury and better quality goods often smuggled into the country at high prices.

The Communist states of Indochina, excluded from major trading opportunities with their ASEAN neighbors and with the United States, evolved into an economic bloc of their own. Vietnam, profiting both from its greater size and its greater acquisition of educational and economic facilities during the colonial period, cultivated "special relationships" with Laos after 1975 and with Cambodia after 1979. Vietnam, despite being one of the poorest countries in the world, made interest-free loans to Laos in the late 1970s. The"marriage" of Vietnamese and Cambodian cities and provinces to each other (with Ho Chi Minh City adopting Phnom Penh, for example) was a symbolic consummation of Vietnam's multilayered hegemony at that time. Yet in the same period Vietnam itself became the economic pensioner of the Soviet Union, depending on the USSR for most of its imported oil, iron and steel, chemical fertilizer, and even cotton. The Vietnamese debt to the USSR became so great that in 1981 Vietnam agreed to repay part of it by sending thousands of workers to labor in Soviet factories and mines.

Economic changes in Southeast Asia since World War II have radically affected the ecology of the region. For example, the rapid expansion of the timber industry, particularly in Indonesia, Thailand, Malaysia, the Philippines, and Vietnam, has denuded large areas of forest, causing soil erosion and a decline in water supplies. Probably one-third of Vietnam's forest was destroyed between 1945 and 1980 for reasons similar to those found in Indonesia—the extraction by a variety of official agencies plus unchecked use by local people. The unrestrained use of chemical fertilizers and pesticides required to grow new forms of "miracle" rice, a factor leading to the ability of most states in the region to export food despite growing populations, has caused the contamination of fishing ponds and rivers. The development of industrial plants without proper waste disposal arrangements has resulted in the polluting of streams and has created groundwater problems Uncontrolled economic development has resulted in problems familiar to people living in more industrialized societies who are now accused by many Southeast Asians of exporting their dirty chemicals and polluting industries to the region. In the 1980s environmental protection groups played an increasingly important part in the politics of Malaysia, Thailand, and the Philippines, where the nearly completed nuclear plant at Bataan was the target of frequent demonstrations at the end of Marcos era.

As we have seen, the domestic political context throughout Southeast

Asia changed dramatically in the decades following the end of World
War II. Throughout the region, a wide range of political doctrines,
compromises, and institutions were tried, modified, rejected, or opposed by the governments of Southeast Asia, but in very general terms
the era could be seen, at the end of the 1980s, to be characterized by a
gradual drift toward greater authoritarianism. In the 1940s and early
1950s, hastily conceived and erected Western-style political institutions
grew unpalatable to the more or less charismatic leaders who had come
to power at independence. People like Nu, Sukarno, and Sihanouk
attempted to govern through the force of their personalities, trusting a
small group of advisers and buttressed by such eclectic ideologies as
Sukarno's notion of Guided Democracy or what Sihanouk called Buddhist Socialism. Ngo Dinh Diem was a somewhat similar figure, and his
philosophy of Personalism owed little to the adversarial politics of western Europe or the United States.

For a time, political elites and particularly military leaders went
along with these novel attempts to weld newly independent nations into
something more formidable than large collections of people with lines
drawn around them on a map. However, to many military leaders, having a charismatic individual running the nation as a private fief was
anathema, and sooner or later many countries succumbed to the imposition of military regimes justified in the name of the national interest.
In sharp contrast to the rest of Southeast Asia, it should be noted that
politics in the Philippines, Singapore, and Malaysia remained remarkably open throughout the 1960s, as their governments were free of the
sorts of challenges to central authority experienced in Burma, Indonesia, and Vietnam and their leaders felt more confident of their positions.

In the 1970s, after the imposition of martial law in the Philippines,
the institutionalization of more or less single-party rule in Indonesia,
and the Communist victories in Indochina, the drift toward authoritarianism which had been perceptible earlier now accelerated. Ferdinand
Marcos of the Philippines coined a phrase that characterized this period
when he referred to "constitutional authoritarianism." Throughout the
region, governments desirous of adhering or appearing to adhere to the
idea that they were subordinate to constitutions have used the documents themselves, often amended or written entirely afresh, to secure
their own perpetuation. "National unity" has usually been given as the
rationale for this behavior. The Philippines from 1972 to 1986 is perhaps the clearest example of constitutional authoritarianism, but the
term can also be applied to Suharto's Golkar movement, to several Thai
military governments, and to the Lansin Party in Burma. The actions
taken by the Malaysian government after 1969, using a parliamentary
majority to amend the constitution so as to limit freedom of speech and
to increase executive powers vis-à-vis those of the judiciary, can be seen
as fitting this authoritarian model.

By the 1980s, militarized political parties controlled the governments of Burma and Vietnam, while politicized armies held power in Thailand and Indonesia. The opening up of the Philippines after the fall of Marcos in 1986, like the brief opening of the Thai political scene in 1973–1976, were exceptions to the rule, and by the end of the 1980s, it was fair to say that the daily lives of the men and women of Southeast Asia were more thoroughly affected and overseen by government agents and agencies than ever before in the region's history. This is not to say that these developments should be seen as heralding a kind of political twilight in Southeast Asia any more than the same trend in Western societies necessarily would do. For one thing, the peoples of Southeast Asia are not merely the objects of governmental exploitation; they are the subjects of their own histories, making individual and collective decisions not necessarily in the interests of those who have been chosen, or more often have chosen themselves, to govern the states of the region.

One of the ways in which the people of Southeast Asia have shaped their lives, sometimes in opposition to the wishes of the government, has been through the growth in the size of their families. No country since World War II has escaped this phenomenon. For example, the population of the areas that now comprise Malaysia was in 1947 only 5.78 million people but by the 1980s had grown to 13.75 million. By the mid-1980s the total population of Southeast Asia had reached almost 400 million, roughly 10 percent of the world's total, although the populations of the component countries varied greatly. Tiny Brunei had fewer than a quarter-million inhabitants, and Singapore only 2.5 million, while Indonesia, the fifth most populous country in the world, had a population of over 162 million people.

The rapid increase in the region's population flows from a variety of factors, of which improved health care since the 1940s has probably been the most significant. Every country in the region, except Singapore and, for reasons of war and genocide, Cambodia, had average annual population growth rates for the years 1976 through 1983 of 2 percent or higher. At these rates of growth the populations of most of the countries of Southeast Asia will double in the next thirty years or so.

Expansion of this order inevitably results in a population where, in contrast to those of industrialized countries with lower birth rates, women aged fourteen to forty form a disproportionate share of the population, making a rapid decrease in population growth, regardless of what governments do, extremely difficult. With the exception of Singapore, every country in the region in the mid-1980s had at least 37 percent of its total population under the age of fifteen years; the figure for Indonesia and the Philippines was over 60 percent. Declining rates of infant mortality, below 100 per thousand in every country except Cambodia, Indonesia, and Laos, and increased life expectancy, over sixty years everywhere except in these countries and Burma, suggests that zero population growth, if that should be the goal, will remain impossible for many years to come.

These gross figures do not, however, reveal the great varieties of population issues that face the peoples of Southeast Asia. Density of settlement varies as widely within countries as between them. On the island of Java, for example, there were more than 60 million people in the mid-1980s. The only way to recognize the implications of the relationship of such a population to the land upon which it must live is to imagine a man/land ratio something like the so-called Boston-Washington urban belt in the United States or that of the suburbs of an industrial city elsewhere in the West. In contrast, other regions are largely unpopulated, such as the inhospitable mountains of northern Burma, inland Kalimantan (Borneo), or the forest areas along the borders shared by Laos, Cambodia, and Vietnam.

Efforts at population control have also varied from state to state. In Thailand, for example, there was in the 1970s and 1980s an active and popular nonofficial campaign to limit family size. The government of Singapore created a system of legal disincentives to having families with more than two children by denying social and educational benefits to additional children. In Vietnam and Indonesia, government officials and political organizations have been instructed to implement population planning programs, whereas in Burma, where the government feels isolated and outnumbered by its huge Indian and Chinese neighbors, family planning has not been encouraged but men and women themselves have sought to limit family sizes. In September 1982, the prime minister of Malaysia caused a great stir by saying that his country should aim for an ultimate population of 70 million, five times the existing one, and this has been adopted as a policy aim and embodied in development plans, to be achieved by the year 2100.

Not only has the population of Southeast Asia expanded rapidly since World War II, but that population has become increasingly mobile. In the colonial era, very few people moved away from their villages, to say nothing of their provinces, islands, or countries, except in the Philippines where the urbanization process was well underway in the American era. Elsewhere in the region, however, during the first years of independence the dominant pattern was little changed, but in more recent times millions of Southeast Asians have moved from the countryside into the cities. They have also travelled and emigrated to other countries. By 1985, several hundred thousand Southeast Asian workers, most of them from the Philippines, but with sizable numbers from Thailand and Indonesia as well, were working under contract in the Middle East, and their cash remittances played an important role in many urban Philippine communities, as well as providing significant amounts of foreign exchange for the government.

Similarly, in recent years more and more Southeast Asians, especially from the ASEAN countries, have travelled abroad to study or for pleasure. More than thirty thousand tertiary students from Malaysia, for example, were pursuing studies abroad in 1982, while some five thousand Thai students were enrolled in colleges and universities in the United States alone. With the exception of Burma, the larger Southeast Asian countries all had thousands of tertiary students pursuing courses abroad at any point in the 1980s.

Increasing affluence and improved communications meant that by the mid-1980s, many more Southeast Asians were travelling within the region than before. Nearly half the tourists visiting Singapore, for example, came from other Southeast Asian countries, and nearly a quarter of the two million visitors to Thailand each year crossed into the country from Malaysia.

Migration and tourism, of course, represent choices freely made by families or individuals. The transmigration program in Indonesia falls into a different category. Since the 1960s, over a million men and women in more than three hundred thousand family groups have been moved at government expense from densely populated islands, like Java and Bali, to remote or sparsely populated parts of the archipelago, such as Kalimantan and Irian Jaya. Despite the high priority the Indonesian government has placed on the program, obstacles encountered have included the reluctance of many Indonesians to move away from their homes, the high expense of the program and, more recently, resistance to newcomers on the part of local people, particularly in Irian Jaya. In the Philippines, internal migration has not only filled in the Mindanao land frontier but has created a volatile situation in which, by the mid-1980s, there were more Christians on the island than Muslims.

The most dramatic movement of people in recent Southeast Asian history has been the exodus of refugees from Cambodia, Laos, and Vietnam since 1975. In the decade after Communist regimes seized power in these countries, more than a million men and women fled by land, sea, and, more rarely, air to seek resettlement, largely in Europe, Australia, and North America. For the most part, the refugees have been people with close ties to the United States before 1975, ethnic Chinese frightened by the policies of the Vietnamese government since 1979, and others pessimistic about their chances under a socialist state. By the late 1980s, the flow of refugees from all three countries abated somewhat, partly because they were no longer welcome overseas, but the loss of so many well-educated people has had severe economic and cultural effects on the Indochinese states. Refugee movement within Southeast Asia has also increased. Several thousand Karens from Burma fled into Thailand in the 1980s, as did tens of thousands of Cambodians. In both Laos and Cambodia immigrants from Vietnam seeking economic opportunity numbered in the hundreds of thousands in the mid-1980s.

The broadening of horizons and expansion of opportunities normally assumed to accompany increasing mobility were only part of the new experiences that growing numbers of Southeast Asians, particularly youths, enjoyed in the decades of the sixties, seventies, and eighties. The expansion of educational opportunities and facilities in Southeast Asia was one of the most dramatic changes to affect the region after World War II. This expansion, in turn, raised the levels of literacy and technical competence throughout the region, as well as the level of young people's material expectations. Confronted with expanding younger populations, many countries responded by designating larger and larger portions of their national budgets to education. For example, Burma devoted about 17 percent of all government current expenditure on education in the mid-1980s, second only to defense spending.

In the colonial era, the Dutch and the French, as we have seen, were particularly parsimonious in the field of education. The British were somewhat more generous in Malaysia and Burma, though education above the primary level remained very much the preserve of urban and wealthier sectors of society. In the Philippines, however, America's emphasis on expanding facilities and access meant that by 1945 the archipelago, which already contained the oldest university in Southeast Asia, had the widest range of educational institutions and a relatively large pool of educated men and women. The trend continued into recent times; in 1982, the Philippines had 1.3 million college and university students compared with only 616,000 in Indonesia, though the latter country's population was more than two-and-one-half times that of the former.

Spending on primary education in post-World War II Southeast Asia has been most significant, since less than half the eligible population, particularly in rural areas, tended at that time to go to secondary schools. Primary school enrollments in countries with similar sized populations were strikingly consistent in the 1980s, when roughly 8 million boys and girls were enrolled at this level in the Philippines, Thailand, and Vietnam. The number of students enrolled in secondary schools was higher in Vietnam (3.7 million) than in the other two countries (roughly 2.3 million apiece), and differences were even more marked in the tertiary sector, with Thailand having about half as many students as the Philippines and Vietnam less than half as many as Thailand.

All countries took part in the educational boom that characterized the second half of the twentieth century. In Vietnam, for example, in 1985 more than 13 million people, or almost one of every four members of the population, were going to school; some 130,000 were attending some sort of college or university. Hanoi, which had only two institutions for higher learning in 1954, thirty years later had thirty-one such institutions. In order to cope with a demand for greater regional equality in education, governments have also attempted to decentralize learning and in Burma, for example, have developed extensive systems of instruction by correspondence. Television has also been used as a medium of instruction.

Outside of the Philippines, where Catholic schools continued to play an important role, the expansion of education in Southeast Asia tended to be in the hands of state authorities. This meant, among other things, that state-sponsored ideologies were emphasized in school curricula, reinforcing the tendencies throughout the region toward democratic authoritarianism as well as national uniformity in views as well as knowledge. In Malaysia, for example, ethnic Malays were favored in the upper reaches of the system, in keeping with the constitution and an acknowledged need to redress past imbalances, while Confucianism has more recently become prominent in English-language Singapore schools. By the 1980s, Marxism-Leninism was taught throughout the secondary schools of Indochina. In Southeast Asia, as in the much of the remainder of the modern world, governments often turned to the schools first as a device for social engineering to "solve" obvious social and economic inequalities by opening opportunities for groups previously discriminated against or to socialize potentially dissident groups into an official national culture.

In the early 1970s in Thailand, Cambodia, and Indonesia, however, the fit between state ideology and curricula broke down, and university students demonstrated against their governments. In Thailand they succeeded in creating the conditions for the fall of a government. Somewhat more obliquely, student involvement in the *dakwah* Islamic revivalist movement in Malaysia (notably through the Malaysian Islamic Youth Movement, ABIM) has been an important part of that movement's strength, in criticism of government policies of a variety of kinds. Students were directly active in toppling Ferdinand Marcos in the Philippines in 1986, but by and large a government's capacity to close down the system or to pull students out of colleges and universities, and worsen their career chances, acted as a brake on student activism.

An important intellectual development that intensified after 1970 or so was the growth of national forms of history and political science, and localized theories of economic development, which sought to explain the human condition in new ways and to benefit Southeast Asian states and the men and women who inhabit them. Tens of thousands of Southeast Asians have undertaken graduate study in the West, while thousands from Vietnam, Laos, and Cambodia (as well as several hundred from Burma in the 1960s and 1970s) have studied in the USSR and Eastern Europe. Returning to university posts, some of these students, as teachers and scholars, developed graduate and undergraduate programs in the humanities and social sciences that are responsive to local needs and eclectic in their adaptation of foreign theories. For example, in the 1970s and 1980s, there was a renewed interest in Thai history in Thai universities, and similar developments could be noted in universities in the Philippines, Vietnam, and, to a lesser extent, Indonesia. The intellectual ferment of these universities was not, however, matched elsewhere, and in Burma and Malaysia, for example, historiography changed only slowly from the style of the 1950s.

The adumbration of national histories and identities went along with a growing sense of Southeast Asia as a region, a process enhanced by the success of ASEAN and the intellectual leadership provided by the universities and by such research bodies as the Institute of Southeast Asian Studies in Singapore, founded in the 1960s, and national centers for strategic studies as well as by innumerable regional conferences for academics, businessmen, and government officials. However, one should not overemphasize the degree of change. For most Southeast Asians in the mid-1980s, the world was still limited by local and national horizons.

The dramatic expansion of educational opportunities in postwar Southeast Asia was in keeping with developments elsewhere in Asia, Africa, and Latin America. A World Bank Report of 1980 estimated that the average percentage of age-eligible children attending primary schools in "Third World" countries had reached 62 percent, an increase of one percent per year since 1960. Islamic, Confucian, Roman Catholic, and Theravada Buddhist countries of Southeast Asia have always revered education but generally viewed it in terms of individual enlightenment rather than as a talisman of collective progress—the Philippines being something of an exception to this generalization.

As noted above, demographic projections for Southeast Asia, with the exception of Singapore, point to younger populations for the countries of the region for the rest of the twentieth century. This will obviously strain existing educational facilities and place burdens on planners and national budgets. At the same time, it seems likely that leaders in Southeast Asian countries, as well as ordinary men and women, will continue to place high priorities on increasing educational opportunities for their children. Although the proverbial volatility of college-age students poses a threat to the authoritarianism that has entrenched itself throughout the region, by the late 1980s the authorities of most countries were willing to take this risk in order to reach their social, economic, and security goals.

Despite the economic development of Southeast Asia and the consequent growth of employment in factories and offices, as well as the profusion of educational opportunities, more than half of the men and women working in Southeast Asia in the 1980s earned their living from agriculture and fishing. Most of the rest of the population was dependent upon them in two ways: as well as providing the nation's food, they were also the main market for the manufactured goods and services provided by the urban minority. Of the larger countries by 1983, only in Malaysia did fewer than half the people till the land. In Burma and Vietnam, despite the efforts of their governments to restructure their economies, about 65 and 71 percent, respectively, of the people lived off the land in the mid-1980s.

Historically, the people of Southeast Asia who grew their own food were referred to as peasants, and often they still are, but in fact the conditions under which they work, and the networks of economic and political linkages they now must master, are very different from those of only fifty years ago. And whereas one might have generalized in the 1880s about the "economic life of the peasantry throughout monsoon Asia," no one can do so now. The consequences of colonialism and postwar government economic and agricultural policies, plus changes in the available technology of crop production and harvesting, have created great variations in the lives of Southeast Asia's farmers. It is no longer primarily the weather that determines whether a farm family eats well or poorly in a single year; a wide range of factors is at work.

Nonetheless, there has been one trend in the past one hundred years or so that has continued and even accelerated in the recent transformation of Southeast Asia. The consequences of this trend can be found throughout the region. We refer to the breakdown of the various forms of patron-client ties which formed the basis not only of peasant economics but also of government and other forms of social life in the precolonial world and which have been described earlier in this book. Industrial agriculture, based upon profit and loss rather than usage and consumption, undermined many of the patron-client ties of the peasants in the Burma delta, for example, and led to the establishment of a peasant economy based upon cash and market value.

The rapid transformation of Burma was typical of other countries, though changes took place in different ways. The peasants of Java were momentarily "protected" from the destructive forces of the market by the Dutch, as were the Malay rice farmers of peninsular Malaya by the British. The large landowners of the Philippines also persisted in displaying a paternalistic attitude toward their tenants, protecting them to a modest degree from economic deprivation while establishing personal ties of loyalty between themselves and the families of their labor force. Even the rapacious French government in the north, if not in the south of Vietnam, did not disturb the relative continuity of the relationship of man to land in the colonial period.

The growing commercialization of the economies of Southeast Asia since 1945, however, has changed these relationships in radical ways. The peasant of the central plains of Thailand began to experience in the 1960s and 1970s the same insecurity of tenure and livelihood that rice farmers in Burma had known in the 1920s and 1930s. Urbanites with money to invest in land as a hedge against inflation or developers of "agro-businesses" sought to consolidate landholdings in the belief that this would increase gross productive efficiency. Thousands of peasants then found themselves forced off their land by individuals, backed up by the law of the state, who had money and experience in the ways of government.

The Thai experience was not duplicated precisely elsewhere, but the

growing insecurity of the farmer can be seen under different circumstances throughout the region. In the Philippines, for example, as large
landlords became increasingly concerned with maximizing profits, they
invested more time and effort in capital intensive than in labor intensive
agriculture. Fewer people were thus needed in the landlord's fields, and
migrant farm workers often were used as a cheaper form of labor. The
landlord's own interest was now to please a bank manager more than to
make certain that the people who lived on his lands had enough to eat,
were cared for in times of distress, and were able to enjoy their traditional rights of sharing with the landowner in religious and social occasions. Growing commercialization made rural life in the Philippines
increasingly anomic; one result was growing peasant distrust and
organized opposition to landlords and the government that stood
behind them. Even land reform, when carried out, often did not
improve the security of the farmer and his family, for rather than providing him with the network of security that the old system had provided, he now had to turn himself into an individual entrepreneur.
Because he was a small and undercapitalized one, he was the first to fall
victim to a bad harvest or an increase in interest rates, dictated by more
remote forces and ameliorated neither by networks of sympathy nor by
traditional loyalties.

James Scott, in his perceptive book *Weapons of the Weak,* provides a
detailed study of the consequences of economic change on the lives of
Malay farmers in peninsular Malaysia in the 1970s and early 1980s. In
the village he studied in Kedah, "economic progress" came in the form
of increased irrigation, and consequently double cropping, and in the
use of mechanized equipment, especially the combine harvester, to alleviate the drudgery of hand reaping and threshing of the local rice crop.
The consequences have been very mixed. For those farmers with larger
fields and some capital, as well as political affiliations through the ruling
party to loan authorities and other government agencies, the advent of
the combine harvester has meant greater profits and a more stable and
predictable life. It allowed them and their families to enjoy new religious and consumption benefits such as the pilgrimage to Mecca and
motorbikes or pickup trucks. For the poorer sections of the village, however, technical change has meant a declining level of security and
greater need to seek employment elsewhere. Women are no longer able
to supplement the family's income by joining in the harvest, and for the
poorest, the rice that was provided by the landlords has now to be
obtained through other means. Whether the village was ever a unified
and harmonious human settlement is debatable; by the 1980s, however,
the village Scott studied and many others like it throughout the market
economies of Southeast Asia had developed their own version of the
class conflicts that divide the better off from the poor in all societies.

However, the fraying of patron-client ties in the market economies of
the region has led to more obvious forms of discontent and inequality;

much the same thing ha , happened in the planned economies. In
Burma the government set out from the 1950s to ensure that the peasants would be spared the consequences of capitalist agriculture they had
suffered under the British. Although in the initial years socialist agriculture seemed to mean little more than replacing the Indian or British rice
miller with a government rice purchasing agency, in 1963, the government took more radical steps to change the economic condition of peasant families and by law abolished all peasant debts. In 1965 the payment of land rent was similarly abolished. Instead of market forces,
peasants were now to produce for the state, and the state would in turn
undertake to ensure that the manufactured and imported goods peasants needed would be readily and cheaply available. For a variety of
reasons, the latter part of the exchange did not take place. The farmer
was still left on his own and had to invent new ways of making a living;
production fell and so did consumption, as farmers refused to sell at the
low price the state set for the crops and the state was unable to supply
the goods farmers and their families wanted to buy. A parallel economy,
or black market, grew up which the government had to devote a great
deal of attention to trying to control through such measures as the
demonetization of larger denomination banknotes in 1985.

Vietnam's attempt to change the condition of its peasantry was
another controversial example of social engineering. There Communist
theoreticians liked to contrast what they regarded as the anarchic individualism of traditional peasant "small producers" with the disciplined
economic collectivism they were trying to impose. Premodern Vietnamese villages were famous for the importance they attached to the public
management of property; as late as 1932, village communal lands
accounted for about one-fifth of all cultivated farm land in the Red
River delta. The point was not that collectively owned property did not
exist, but that it had different purposes. In Vietnam, traditional village
communal lands had been used as a government salary system (they
were distributed to bureaucrats as appanages); or as a means by which
villagers could honor and share in the wealth of distinguished mandarin
households (who would voluntarily add some of their estate to the existing public lands in return for the villagers' promise to hold rituals of
commemoration for them in succeeding centuries). Consequently, the
notion of publicly owned land was not alien to the Vietnamese peasants
who were being collectivized. What was alien to them was the invitation
to think of such land in narrowly utilitarian terms as a purely economic
asset—as a capital-generating instrument of modernization—rather
than in more broadly social and religious terms as in the past.

The isolation of the traditional Vietnamese village, concealed (in the
north) behind its green bamboo hedges, has now vanished. Villagers
are now much more likely to leave home, temporarily or permanently,
to serve in the army; to attend youth league meetings; to take courses in
the use of machinery at district tractor stations; to become workers in

city factories; to migrate, with or without their relatives, to "new economic zones"; and even perhaps, if fortunate, to go to universities or teachers' colleges or at least to middle schools in district towns. Male youths are more likely to leave the village than middle-aged women, who do most of the farm work.

Regardless of the forces at work behind the scenes, the same can be said for the conditions of the peasantry throughout the region. The breakdown of patron-client ties and more traditional attachments of farmers to their land for several generations have been replaced by a high degree of mobility and individuals seeking, legally or otherwise, to find what they consider to be best for themselves and for their families. In so doing, they often come up against new forms of authority relationships and officials unlike those their grandparents experienced.

The development of new class and other social conflicts within Southeast Asian societies have placed great strains on the ability of various societal institutions to maintain both social order and a sense of purpose in the lives of the population. By and large, the maintenance of social order depends only in extreme circumstances upon the conscious compliance of individuals with the orders of the government. Rule without coercion is easier for the managers of the state than the use of force, for, as many rulers have found, resorting to violence may ultimately destroy the society that the forceful measures were intended to uphold. The compliance of the politically aware citizen results from his or her feeling a stake in the government and society, and such a sense of allegiance can exist only where there is a set of values that is widely shared across the class, ethnic, and religious cleavages that exist.

In societies with a perceptible historical continuity, there is an established terminology to portray these values. In societies that have lost the momentum of historical continuity, new sorts of symbols must be found. In all cases, the process of inculcating elite values in the habits of thought of the people at large is a slow one, requiring the use of communications media, the emergence of transitional intermediaries such as teachers and agricultural extension workers to bridge the gaps in society, and the demonstration of political and cultural sensitivity by the elite. In the postindependence period, some Southeast Asian elite groups demonstrated a tendency to monopolize the formation and expression of their nations' values. Though men like Sukarno, Sarit, and Sihanouk were populists in theory, they were oligarchs in fact. Nonetheless, they were aware of the necessity to create a sense of community in the minds of their subjects if they were to govern in peace. For this reason, all the governments of the region have devoted much attention to the development of national ideologies such as Panca Sila in Indonesia, the Burmese Way to Socialism, or the trinity of "Nation, Religion, and King" in Thailand. Nonetheless, governments also have to be staffed with officials who wield the authority of the state, and it is to these and their relationship with the governed that we now turn.

In many Southeast Asian countries, a new political and administrative class emerged in the postwar period. This class drew its precedents from the precolonial as well as from the colonial world. The result, however, is in many ways *sui generis*. What most obviously set this group off from the rest of society was its penchant for uniforms. Men, and much more rarely women, in uniforms with gold braid and epaulets became figures of authority who outwardly and ostentatiously possess the ability to call up the coercive power of the state. These men are often army officers, although they are occasionally uniformed civilians in government departments concerned with such things as taxation, irrigation, birth control, sanitation, transport, or education. Educated in the cities or even abroad, they have ideas about authority that owe more to notions of imperial right than to the notion of public service which their titles imply. By the 1980s, this phenomenon was as prevalent in the ASEAN states as in socialist Burma or Communist Indochina, although in each society the characteristics of the new ruling group vary.

In Vietnam, for example, the people who manage the affairs of the state are referred to as "cadres." These men and women are simply officials who, like their Confucian mandarinal predecessors, rarely do manual work. The creation of a large class of this kind has been, in its own eyes, one of Communist Vietnam's greatest achievements: North Vietnam had only 18,400 cadres in 1960 who had graduated either from university of from middle school, but it claimed to have 356,700 such people in 1975. Similarly, in Indonesia, by the mid-1980s, an estimated 15.4 percent of the work force, or 8.3 million people, worked for the government.

The expansion of government employment has been a common phenomenon throughout Southeast Asia, for it provides jobs for politically powerful groups and ensures a core of citizens whose economic well-being depends directly on the state. Elite government employees enjoy the greatest power and privileges. Again, the example of Vietnam illustrates the point. The educated elite of cadres not only recalls the traditions of the old Vietnamese mandarinate but it also accords with the general Western, and specifically Marxist-Leninist, exaltation of science and of managerial planning. In its early stages, the Vietnamese Communist state had only two types of cadres, political organizers and military specialists, but by the 1980s, the ranks of the most prestigious cadres were increasingly dominated by academic degree-holders. And just as in the old mandarinate the higher degree-holders were to be found at court, not in the villages, so too in the new Vietnam, the educational qualifications of the cadres became more impressive the farther away from the villages they were.

The desire of the better-educated cadres of Vietnam not to serve in more remote agricultural communities is a general phenomenon throughout Southeast Asia. By and large, educated officials want to live in the cities where educational opportunities for their children are better and where better health services, shops, and entertainment are to be found. This is true of all kinds of officials, and only the government of Burma was so bold as to conscript doctors into the armed forces in 1962 in order to deploy them outside the cities against their, or their families', will.

The governing class of bureaucrats, army officers, and technicians sit on top of society issuing orders and filing reports while enjoying benefits such as special shops or perhaps foreign travel not available to the average citizen. Much of the actual governing of local communities is carried out by individuals who achieve the position of rural village headman or, under a more contemporary nomenclature, chairman of the Village People's Council or town councillor, because of the respect with which they are held by their fellow villagers or, more likely, because of the belief on the part of the central rulers that they are reliable and will carry out instructions. Thus, for example, in Burma and Indonesia, retired army sergeants often become the heads of village governments, and commissioned officers retire to become heads of larger units of local government. These positions are often thankless, for their holders are obliged to keep the upper wheel of the central government satisfied and are thus ground against the nether wheel of people desiring neither to pay taxes nor to provide other services to the state.

Nevertheless, most Southeast Asians perceive government service as a desirable occupation. It provides a guaranteed income and often carries with it considerable prestige and usually a job for life. While women may continue to dominate in petty trading and alien groups still have a large say in big business, for the modestly ambitious young man seeking a good marriage and security, government employment provides the answer. The level of pay cannot always be the reason for this choice, as the salaries provided by the state in much of Southeast Asia do not cover living costs, especially in urban areas. If, as was the case in the mid-1980s, a used Toyota sedan, after the payment of import duties of 300 percent, cost a resident of Rangoon about US$30,000, and a typical government employee's salary was equivalent to about US$1,000 per year, how could he afford to have such a private car?

The answer, of course, is that government employment is widely used to create additional income. This is often perceived as corruption or, in the Philippines, as "anomalies." Foreign and, when permitted, domestic newspapers often report such examples, the most flagrant being President Marcos of the Philippines, who apparently managed to accumulate more than US$10 billion on an official salary of US$5,000 per year. This pervasive form of "anomalies" results from the fact that public employment, either for reasons of personal gain, minimal subsistence, or familial or community obligation, motivates an individual to use his or her official position in ways which are illegal.

One should not draw the conclusion from these remarks, however, that corruption and cynicism have dominated the politics of Southeast

Asia after independence any more thoroughly than they had done before. There were probably as many incorruptible People's Court judges in Burma in the 1980s as there had been magistrates in the 1930s. What perhaps changed more was the level of dissatisfaction on the part of much of the population with the excesses of corruption, which became more and more obvious and onerous to farmers and small businessmen who realized that they were working hard so that others could do little and still enjoy greater benefits from the public coffers than the taxpayers did. This realization and the appearance of publicly aware lawyers, journalists, academics, and college graduates willing to articulate this dissatisfaction caused the growth of public advocacy groups and support for more broadly based antigovernment movements. In those Southeast Asian societies with large and growing urban, educated middle classes in particular, the consequences of such movements could be seen in public protests against the construction of polluting factories and in the formation of groups concerned with civil liberties. While it may be too much to claim that students brought down the military government in Bangkok in 1973 by themselves or that President Marcos fled from Manila in 1986 because of "people power," nonetheless the governments of the region have had to become more aware after forty years of transforming Southeast Asia that power does not always or uniquely grow out of the barrel of a gun.

One important source of power in Southeast Asian society since the Second World War has been religion. By the 1980s, three trends were perceptible in the religious life of Southeast Asia. Perhaps the most important was an increasing secularization along American lines of a good deal of urban culture, particularly among the middle class. This was accompanied throughout the region by a reduced emphasis, on the part of government spokesmen, on the importance of religion in peoples' daily lives. The Americanization of the socialist states was checked to a large extent by ruling parties, and the rulers of the Communist countries eschewed religious ceremonies and discouraged others from attending them. In Indonesia, likewise, although the philosophy of Panca Sila included "belief in God" as a requirement for good citizenship, Suharto's Golkar regime was often standoffish and saw fundamentalist Islam as a threat to its values.

A second trend, operating particularly at the popular level, was the revival of religious practices, perhaps partly in response to the secularization of daily values as well as the perceived behavior of the political elite. This was especially noticeable among Muslims in Malaysia, Indonesia, and the southern Philippines. In Catholic areas of the Philippines, there was aroused interest in charismatic services, and in relatively radical Catholic social teachings stemming from "liberation theology," while Buddhist practices in Thailand and Burma were being modified to meet new social and economic needs.

A third, less important trend, was some growth in religious tolerance and heterogeneity in the region, reflected by the progress made by evangelical Christians working in Indonesia and the Philippines and by the increased interest among some Javanese in the teachings of Buddhism and Christianity. In countries where such missionary activities were excluded, however, little change could be perceived.

These trends can be seen in part as responses, individually or en masse, to some of the economic, social, and political pressures we have discussed. The Islamic revival among ethnic Malays, for example, can be connected with the rapid rate at which these predominantly rural people have been brought into culturally alien cities as part of the work force or as students at colleges and universities. To these young men and women, the *dakwah* (call, propagation) of Islam often had a strong appeal, buttressed by a resurgence of ethnic pride vis-à-vis the Chinese in particular and by links with Islamic resurgence elsewhere.

This enlargement of Islam has encouraged religiously based opposition parties, such as the Party Islam (PAS) in Malaysia and the United Development Party (PPP) in Indonesia, to link their own ideologies with a worldwide Islamic revival, seen as far purer than the day-to-day shenanigans of most elected and appointed state officials. Similarly, in southern Thailand and Mindanao, beleaguered Muslim minorities have clashed violently with what they perceive as the colonialism and intolerance of Buddhist or Catholic officials.

In the Catholic Philippines, the boundary between politics and religion is blurred. The ironically surnamed Jaime Cardinal Sin, Catholic archbishop of Manila in the 1980s, played a decisive role in the overthrow of President Marcos. The Catholic radio station, Radio Veritas, was openly anti-Marcos, while priests, nuns, and members of religious orders were encouraged by their superiors to demonstrate against the Marcos regime. In this context, the meaning of "liberation theology," often associated with radical Catholicism in Latin America, broadened to include a democratic center.

Theravada Buddhism has been greatly affected by the nature of the regimes under which it existed during the 1960s, 1970s, and 1980s. Buddhists in urban Thailand were drawn away from strenuous adherence by the strong pulls of "modernization"; fewer and fewer young men felt obliged to become monks, even for a short time, while the number of men choosing to remain monks for longer periods has declined even more sharply. In Laos and Cambodia, Buddhists found religion closely monitored by socialist regimes, but in Burma and Thailand, monks gifted at preaching, healing, and giving advice, as well as hermits renowned for ascetic practices, attracted large followings, and some monks in Bangkok curried favor with the new conservative middle class by vehemently attacking the "devilish" character of communism. Theravada Buddhism enjoyed a revival in Burma after independence, encouraged by official and unofficial state support, and there were in particular renewed forms of private practice, such as meditation, which became increasingly important to the urban devout. Although Burmese found it difficult to invest money in manufacturing or agriculture, religious edifices, especially after 1962, have been given vast sums of gold, silver, and money by the laity. In six years over 3.25 million dollars' worth was donated for the construction of a single new pagoda in Rangoon.

Secularization and religious revivals throughout the region have forced the elites of Southeast Asia to look at religion in different ways. The attachment of elites to a new gospel of science based on "progress," for example, has led many to make distinctions between "religion" (by which they mean scholarly, intellectually higher religions), on the one hand, and "superstition" (by which they mean less scholarly, more autonomous forms of popular religious thought) on the other. Traditional Asian rulers, even in colonial times, would not have made such a distinction. In Vietnam in the 1980s, however, Buddhism is no longer seen as a single spectrum of higher and lower traditions, both of which may be involved in peasant life; instead, it is divided into two categories, one tolerated while the other is not. As part of its conciliatory but managerial approach to the Buddhism of more urbane, educated people, the regime permits a Central Committee of the Buddhist Church in Vietnam to exist and in 1981 opened a High Level School of Vietnamese Buddhist studies. The government, however, is hostile to manifestations of popular Buddhist millenarianism, even those which are wholly nonpolitical. Soothsayers, sorceresses, and shamans who under traditional dynasties (and the French) might have been watched but not forcibly converted to other occupations are now condemned not just for being potentially subversive but for being "backward"—obstacles to a more scientific, economically rational culture. The turbans, imperial robes, and paraphernalia of traditional rural sorceresses are confiscated. The women are forced to renounce their occupations and are relocated to new work sites. Despite pressures of this kind, a number of Vietnamese as late as 1982 proclaimed themselves prophets of the "dragon flower assembly of messianic Buddha," and their following seems to have included not only temple watchmen, soothsayers, and traders but students and Communist Party cadre as well.

A similar example in Indonesia took place in the early 1980s. Called the "Sawito affair," it had strong overtones of Javanese Hindu-Buddhist mysticism but also involved opposition to the government. From such episodes it might be inferred that a "little tradition," or rather a popular amalgam of little and great traditions, has persisted in Southeast Asia in spite of or perhaps because of the assaults on Southeast Asia thinking and society which we have noted since the end of World War II. Certainly, popular cults persisted in the Philippines, alongside or "underneath" Catholicism; and hundreds of Buddhists, on a daily basis, ask the Buddha not for enlightenment but to be cured of ailments or bailed out of crises. In Burma, where government censorship of publications existed in the 1980s, cosmology and fortune-telling magazines had a wide circulation, as they did in Thailand also. Except in places where the state is antagonistic to religion, and where revivalist Islam, for example, demands orthopraxy among its adherents, most Southeast Asians have persisted in religious practices which meet their social and spiritual requirements, while modifying or abandoning those which fail to do so, once again refuting simplistic notions about the "timelessness" of religious behavior.

Religions are, of course, affected by the cultural context in which they exist. In Southeast Asia, urbanization has begun to reshape the milieux of an increasingly large proportion of the people. Visitors returning periodically to Southeast Asia, particularly by air, are often impressed by what they take to be the rapid urbanization of the region. The pace of urbanization has indeed increased dramatically in comparison to colonial times when the region was one of the least urbanized of the world. The primate cities, especially Jakarta, Bangkok, Kuala Lumpur, and Manila, have been transformed into very large, "modern" metropolitan areas, but in fact a far smaller proportion of Southeast Asians have come to live in the cities recently than their counterparts have done elsewhere, particularly in Latin America, East Africa, and South Asia. Except for the anomalous states of Brunei and Singapore, which claim to be 71 percent and 100 percent urban, respectively, only peninsular Malaysia and the Philippines, in the 1980s, had more than a third of their people living in cities; on the other hand, more than half of the people of Argentina live in the conglomerate of Buenos Aires.

Although contemporary "international" style architecture has raised the skyline and reshaped a good deal of Jakarta, Manila, Bangkok, and Kuala Lumpur, following a style set by Singapore, the sheer size of these once modest colonial cities is even more impressive. In the mid-1980s, roughly 7 million people lived in greater Bangkok, 8.5 million inhabited Jakarta, and the sprawl of Metropolitan Manila, a 246-square mile creation of Ferdinand Marcos, housed 13 percent of the Philippines population, or nearly 9 million people.

There is nothing particularly surprising about the reasons for this growth. In addition to high birth rates, they include the hope of gaining economic benefits and steady employment in service or industrial jobs, increased educational opportunities, and the excitement of urban life. Scholars have argued inconclusively whether Southeast Asians are "pushed" from rural environments or "pulled" into urban ones. Where land is short and rural populations relatively heavy, as in Java, the "push" factor often predominates; where recently opened employment opportunities abound, as in the industrial estates in Malaysia, people are "pulled" toward them.

Arguments of this kind are complicated by the large number of so-called circular migrants in Southeast Asia, men and women who come into the cities during the slack agricultural season to supplement their incomes. In Jakarta, these transients often live in work-site boarding houses, or *pondok,* where conditions are austere; elsewhere they tend to settle in areas hospitable in earlier times to fellow villagers or members of linguistic subcategories, as in the Cebuano quarters of Manila. Since the mid-1960s, many of these migrants have tended to spend longer periods in the cities, merging with permanent residents. The majority of them, however, maintain their links with the countryside and return to their villages to get married, or when urban employment opportunities are scarce. Studies have revealed that for the most part, only people with strong rural support networks, or prosperous urban connections, take the risk of moving permanently into a city.

Two aspects of Southeast Asian urban life have been singled out as relatively new, though hardly surprising. These cities, unlike during the colonial era, now serve as more than foreign entrepôts and have developed social structures and employment patterns consequent to their serving the rural areas with goods and services. There has been a proletarianization of segments of the work force, with implications of alienation, solidarity, and class consciousness on the one hand, and, on the other, the appearance of a recognizable, Western-oriented, bureaucratic and entrepreneurial middle class. While wage laborers are often housed in squatter shanties in urban centers, or commute long distances in crowded trucks and buses to the center from the outskirts, the wealthiest and most powerful sectors of the new middle class tend literally to be insulated from the poor inside their air-conditioned, tinted-windowed cars and in elegant suburban enclaves where the poor, unless they are household servants, are unseen and unwelcome. In Makati in Manila and Pondok Indah in Jakarta, visitors might imagine themselves in an extension of Houston or on the outskirts of San Diego.

Between these two strata can be found millions of people who less readily fit into these conventional analytical class categories. The response of the new urban laboring class to the conditions of wage labor in Southeast Asia has varied and is controlled to an extent by the democratic authoritarianism already discussed, or by more stringent socialist regimes, and mitigated by the continuing rural character of a great deal of urban life. Trade unionism in Southeast Asia is not fully developed; strikes are rare, if not illegal, and horizontal ties across job categories have not often taken place. The rural factor is also important. In Southeast Asian cities, words for "village," e.g., *kampung, barrio, ban, ywa,* are often used to describe an urban quarter where people often share rural and kinship ties, as well as the feeling that they are citizens of the "village" rather than of anything larger such as the city or a trade union. Neighborhood loyalties of this kind are not peculiar to Southeast Asia, of course, but are notable there because, for the most part, they are comparatively recent. And, unlike in the colonial period, the consumption patterns and expectations of the city have spread to the villages and the plastic goods and soft drinks found there come to be more universally expected.

In Vietnam, at least, the rural flavor of urban life has entered official statistics. The 1979 census recorded the population of Hanoi as 2.6 million, but classified nearly two-thirds of these people as "villagers." Interestingly, comparable figures for the conglomerate of Ho Chi Minh City, formerly Saigon, came to barely a quarter of the total. In colonial times, as we have seen, the centers of primate cities were often the home of ethnic minorities, particularly the Chinese, and in Burma, Indians. This is no longer as noticeable, since hundreds of thousands of Chinese Southeast Asians have moved to suburban areas, or, in the Vietnam case, have left the country, while millions of indigenous people, particularly in Malaysia and the Philippines, have taken their places "downtown." The departure of ten of thousands of Indians from Burma in the 1950s made Rangoon for the first time in its modern history a city populated mainly by Burmese.

Perhaps, as some studies have shown, the capacity of these urban communities to pull together and to pool resources has diminished what would otherwise be a severe crisis in the provision of services. Despite what some have called the urban bias of Southeast Asia's national planning, and the middle-class bias implicit in thinking about cities, most of the men and women in Southeast Asia's cities, as distinct from the new ruling groups, suffer periodically from shortages of water, sewerage, and power; from seasonal floods, particularly serious in Bangkok, and from delays and breakdowns in urban transportation.

Southeast Asian cities also contain what economists call an "informal sector" made up of petty traders, small scale entrepreneurs, messengers, pedicab drivers, and the like. The lives of these people on the margins of the work force are taken up with the struggle of making ends meet. For example, in Jakarta, once they have paid for food and transport, on a daily basis, very few of them manage to clear more than $20 per month, most of which is remitted to their families in rural areas.

Socialist and nonsocialist regimes alike tend to view these people as a threat and a disgrace, capable of developing antistate loyalties, on the one hand, and, on the other, of bringing the state's ideals of capitalist or socialist modernization into disrepute. In Jakarta, Rangoon, and Hanoi in the late 1970s, unauthorized peddlers were swept out of city centers by the central government, often to return a few hours or days later.

Periodic efforts at "slum clearance" invariably spill men, women, and children from these informal sectors into the outskirts of the cities, where services are even more unpredictable, if they exist, jobs are hard to find, and neighborhood solidarity must be developed from scratch, in anonymous apartment blocks or more frequently in jerry-built squatter communities that are themselves subject to periodic government raids.

Unless the population of Southeast Asia declines dramatically in the remainder of the century, a most unlikely prospect, it is probably safe to predict widening and deepening fissures between the rich and the poor in urban Southeast Asia, a continuing decline in services, and continuous migration into the cities from rural areas. Whether this potentially explosive mixture will transform people's perceptions of themselves and of the political order along class lines, and what the results will be if this happens, is much less easy to predict.

The urbanization phenomenon is but one part of the process of transformation under way in the region. Since decolonization, most Southeast Asian states have tried to reduce the tensions between their linguistic, ecological, cultural, and historic ethnic variety and their expressions, on the one hand, and the notions of political solidarity and monoloyalty which are considered as fundamental to the creation and maintenance of modern nation-states on the other. Vietnam, for example, is officially composed of fifty-three ethnic groups; the mountain and midland regions where the "minority" peoples of Vietnam live occupy three-quarters of Vietnam's national territory and account for 250 of the 400 districts (huyen) in the administrative system. As an example of how arbitrary much of the classification of such ethnic groups is, often being derived from nineteenth-century European officials' fascination with minor linguistic or dress variations, Burma, which contains more linguistic minorities than Vietnam, is often thought to contain only five minority groups. Both notions are fanciful.

The issues that indigenous "minorities" posed for the governments of the region stemmed from two phenomena. One grew out of the ideological justification for the state in the twentieth century. States and nations are often mistakenly thought to be the same thing, and therefore every state in the international system should represent a nation. On the other hand, all of the states of Southeast Asia contain within their territories individuals and groups who claim, or have it claimed for them, that they are different from the "majority" group from which the state almost always takes its name, such as Thailand, the land of the Thai. Some states, such as Indonesia or the Philippines, are more "artificial" than others. There were no Indonesians, after all, until the Dutch created the Netherlands East Indies. For the rulers of Indonesia, therefore, though the state has often been dominated by individuals born on the island of Java, it was easy to proclaim as the national motto "Unity in Diversity" and claim that as many linguistic and cultural groups as wished to be created could safely reside in the territory of one state. Attempts at federalism, such as tried in Indonesia in the first years of independence, have all failed and unitary states have become the norm throughout the region.

The problems were more difficult for other states where the idea of ethnicity became intimately linked with notions of political power during the colonial period. For example, in Burma after 1945 claims to the right to possess autonomous political authority seemed plausible to individuals claiming to speak for the Karens, Shans, Karenni, Kachins, Chins, and other groups which had had no notions of political autonomy a hundred years earlier. After the Second World War such views were given credence because they fit with the statements on "the nationalities question" enunciated by many Marxist thinkers, including Stalin, on the problem of nationalism in Europe. Thus, the drafters of Burma's first constitution allowed for the illusion of autonomy for the minorities. In fact, no more autonomy was granted than any other central state permits its constituent parts, and when some of the leaders of regions on the periphery began to threaten to secede from the union and possibly seek alliances with the United States or another state, the government responded by removing them from power. Since 1962, the illusion of regional autonomy has been removed from Burma, and though seven states with regional or ethnic names exist, they are governed in the same manner as the rest of the country.

The denial of what they thought to be their just rights to "national self-determination" led some Burmese leaders to seek a separate state after 1948, as discussed in Chapter 35. Since 1958 other groups have sought by armed struggle to establish separate international identities for themselves. None has been successful, and indeed nowhere in the world have such efforts been successful in recent times without the armed intervention of a third state, as in the case of the creation of Bangladesh after the Indian Army intervened against the government of Pakistan. It is, of course, the possibility of such action that makes the question of minorities and national integration so important for governments in Southeast Asia. The threat of Libyan backing for the Moros in the southern Philippines in the 1970s raised a similar specter for the government in Manila.

The Vietnamese Communist Party announced in 1976 its determination to "solve" Vietnam's "nationalities problem"; the solution was to be a more intensive integration of highland and lowland economies and cultures. An important conference on Vietnamese nationalities held at Nha Trang in 1978 defended such integrationist policies by proposing that most ethnic groups in Vietnam were the components of a "common mass" of a "great family" of peoples who had fought together against nature or foreign aggressors since the "dawn" of Vietnamese history. The economic integration of Vietnam's northern mountain minorities often meant their conversion from swidden farming to membership in lowland-state agricultural cooperatives and state farms. But the mountain minorities have resisted permanent cooperatization as alien to their traditions and tastes. Many of their cooperatives broke up and had to be put back together by the state.

These cooperatives seem to have failed because they were artificially divorced from the traditional economic strengths of the mountain and midland regions (animal breeding, the cultivation of such crops as aniseed, oranges, and soybeans rather than just rice); because they violated the peoples' notion of the ideal size of an economic community (the cooperatives, like lowland Vietnamese villages, were larger than traditional mountain hamlets); and because the highland peoples did not regard cooperative chairmen as exercising specialized managerial functions, viewing them rather as rotating elected chiefs who could be readily changed.

In Vietnam, the educational integration of the minorities was major national policy. (The very term for "culture" in Vietnamese means "the change that literature brings about.") In 1982, to encourage Khmer pupils in Vietnam to enter Vietnamese schools, for example, Khmer children who completed primary school were, unlike their Vietnamese counterparts, allowed to enter middle school without having to pass "transfer examinations." The Vietnamese language was decreed to be the language of "transmission" by which all minorities "received" the cultural and material achievements of all other peoples. Nonetheless, pupils from northern mountain minorities failed to stay in school as long as Vietnamese children.

Other governments approached the question differently. For example, in Thailand many of the insurgents in the northern hills in the 1960s and early 1970s were mobilized in protest against being pushed off their lands by lowlanders seeking farms. The government's initial response to these people who had no other form of power at their disposal was to resort to the force of arms, even napalming villages and thus creating greater discontent. The government subsequently changed tactics and began programs designed to integrate the economies and cultures of the hill peoples with those of the rest of the country. The king's involvement in these programs emphasized their importance for the government. In Malaysia, the ethnic tensions which divide the majority Malay population from the minority Chinese and Indian communities are of a different nature, and the government has sought to alleviate them by trying to distribute wealth more equally throughout the nation.

In Burma, the government also placed much emphasis on economic and educational programs to try to alleviate the causes of minority discontent. Recognizing that one of the bases of regional antagonism toward the center was the fact that the most remote areas of the country were the poorest, efforts were made to locate development projects in areas of unemployment and limited opportunities, while trying to improve agricultural yields in order to lower consumer prices. Another program was established in 1965 to bring young men and women from the border areas to study together at an Academy for the Development of National Groups; people trained there would return to their homes, or other areas of the country, and work as teachers and officials to encourage national solidarity. At the annual Union Day celebrations, there are cultural performances by individuals displaying the styles of dress, music and dance common in their regions. To a European who may hold nationalism to be an outmoded idea or a cause of war, the sight every year of Burmese officials bowing solemnly to the national flag as it is carried through every state and division before Union Day may seem anachronistic, but to the government of Burma it is a way of instilling in its citizens the idea that their primary loyalty must be to the central nation-state rather than to any subordinate minority identity.

The complexities of the processes of change at work in the different nations and localities of Southeast Asia are so formidable, by any general synoptic reckoning, that only a foolhardy scholar would attempt to give a final schematic exposition of them. Attainment of an understanding of the developments in education, communications, religion, and language discussed above is only a prelude to the gaining of greater wisdom. Because of this, it would be artificial to draw up a balance sheet of the supposed successes and failures that all Southeast Asian countries have experienced in their efforts to reconstruct their political and social systems for the purposes of reducing their vulnerabilities in the shrinking world community. Confronted with any attempt to make far-wandering judgments about the future of the region, historians are probably best served by remembering how recently they and other scholars have begun to study Southeast Asia and by invoking for a time the Vietnamese proverb: "If you know something, speak, but if you don't know, lean against the pillar and listen."

* This map includes only places
  mentioned in the text.

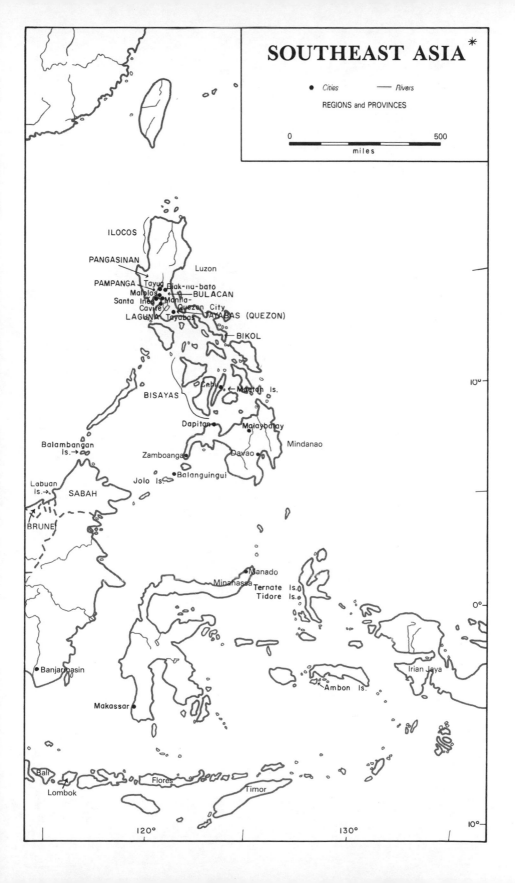

SOUTHEAST ASIA

- Cities     —— Rivers

REGIONS and PROVINCES

0               500

miles

ILOCOS

PANGASINAN

Luzon

PAMPANGA — Tayug Biak-na-bato
Malolos — BULACAN
Santa Inés — Manila
Cavite — Quezon City
LAGUNA Tayabas TAYABAS (QUEZON)

BIKOL

BISAYAS

Cebu — Mactan Is.

Dapitan — Malaybalay

Balambangan
Is. →

Zamboanga — Mindanao

Davao

Labuan
Is. →

SABAH

Jolo Is. — Balanguingui

BRUNEI

Manado

Minahassa

Ternate Is.
Tidore Is.

0°

Banjarmasin

Irian Jaya

Ambon Is.

Makassar

Bali

Flores

Lombok

Timor

10°

120°                   130°

10°

# APPENDIX

## SOUTHEAST ASIAN LANGUAGES

Some of the languages of Southeast Asia are written in roman alphabets, while others employ writing systems ultimately deriving from those of India. The following paragraphs are intended to assist the reader in coping with the pronunciations of Southeast Asian names and words that occur in the text. Most terms used more than once appear in the Glossary.

None of the languages of Southeast Asia forms plurals by adding -s as in English. In such cases, it is conventional in English-language scholarship not to add -s to indicate plurality. Thus the word *dalang* in the text may refer to one or more of these Javanese shadow-play puppeteers.

### Burmese

English speakers should generally have no difficulty pronouncing Burmese as it is transcribed in the latin alphabet. Note, however, that gy is pronounced as English *j* (*gyi* is pronounced *jee*); all final -*n*, -*m*, and -*ng* are pronounced as the final nasal -*n* in the French *vin;* and final -*t* and -*k* are not aspirated (being sounded like the -*t* of "set" in the phrase "set to" and the -*k* of "talk" in "talk clearly"). In the interest of making pronunciation easier, words like *myo-za* (often rendered *myosa*) and *bo-gyok* (often *bogyoke*) have been divided.

### Cambodian

Not enough Khmer words appear in this book to warrant a discussion of pronunciation, although the rules for Thai governing *ph* and *th* (e.g., in the Cambodian word *phnom*) generally apply. A helpful transliteration system for the Cambodian language was proposed by Saveros Lewitz in the *Bulletin de l'Ecole Française d'Extrême Orient* 55 (1969). The language itself is most closely related to those spoken in the upland regions of southern Vietnam, southern Laos, and eastern Thailand. Unlike Burmese, Thai, Lao, and Vietnamese, Cambodian has no tones.

### Lao

The only Lao words that appear in this book are proper names which are so well known in French transcription as to resist any attempt to make them more amenable to English pronunciation. Note, however, that *th* and *ph* are pronounced as in Thai (e.g., *thao* like the "tow" in "tower" and *ph* as a *p*, not an *f*); and Vientiane and Luang Prabang are pronounced as if transcribed Viang Chan and Luang Phrabang.

## Malay/Indonesian

Malay is a member of the Indonesian or western branch of the Austronesian (or Malayo-Polynesian) language family, which is geographically one of the most widespread of language families, second only to the Indo-European. Malay is spoken as the mother tongue in Malaya and certain parts of southern Thailand, Sumatra, and Borneo. It has for centuries, however, performed the role of lingua franca throughout a major portion of the Indonesian archipelago and has functioned as the medium of communication for traders, itinerants, and immigrants of all races and creeds.

The earliest records of Malay are found in inscriptions written in an Indian script and dating from the seventh century A.D. The language of these inscriptions is often termed "Old Malay." The language of most Malay literary works prior to the twentieth century is generally termed "classical Malay." These works emanated mainly from the sphere of the palace, forming what is sometimes called a court literature. The term "classical" is, however, somewhat misleading and should not be understood to mean that there existed one standard form of literary Malay, for, although "classical" Malay is usually identified with Riau-Johore Malay, the language of the literary works of various regions—for example, Aceh, Kutai, and Brunei—all possessed distinctive features.

In Malaysia today, Malay is spoken as mother tongue in a number of dialects, delimited by isoglosses that to some extent coincide with state boundaries. Throughout the country, there is one form of speech that is understood by most Malays and is the language of school instruction, of the radio, and in general of formal occasions. This form of speech may be termed "standard Malay." Most educated Malays speak both standard Malay and their own dialect. Since 1957, standard Malay has been the national language, termed (since 1968) Bahasa Malaysia, and government policy encourages its widespread adoption and use by all sections of the population.

The national language of Indonesia is Bahasa Indonesia (or, in proper English usage, simply Indonesian). This is not a distinct language, for Bahasa Malaysia and Bahasa Indonesia are dialects of the same language, Malay. Standard Malay and Indonesian grew apart in the twentieth century as the former slowly absorbed English loanwords and the latter more rapidly added Dutch (or, after 1945, English) ones. Each, however, is still easily intelligible to speakers of the other. Although Indonesian is the mother tongue of only a small minority of Indonesians, Dutch colonial practice, Indonesian nationalist adoption, and present policy have had the result that virtually all everyday public affairs are conducted in this language. Almost all Indonesians speak a regional language in the home, such as Javanese, Sundanese, Madurese, Batak, or one of many others.

For most of the early and much of the colonial period, Malay in the mother-tongue areas of Malaya, Thailand, Sumatra, and Borneo was written in the *jawi*, or modified Arabic, script, though in Indonesia, and increasingly in Malaysia since independence, the Latin script has tended to displace it. As one of the products of colonialism, the spelling systems adopted in the Latin script in Indonesia and Malaysia differed in certain respects, but agreement has since been reached on a unified system. A variant of it is used in this book, except in the case of a number of well-established proper names. Malay/Indonesian spelling is, in general, closely phonemic.

## Pilipino

The national language of the Philippines is a modern effort to create an indigenous lingua franca. Tagalog, the language of the area around Manila, has been broadened to include words and idioms both from the scores of other vernaculars and from Chinese, Spanish, and English.

Many Filipinos acquired Spanish names over the long colonial period, even though they had no Spanish blood and could not speak Spanish; thus, a Spanish name is today no guarantee of *mestizo* parentage. Some Chinese chose to adopt Spanish names, while others merely continued to use their Chinese ones, for example, Teehankee or Locsin. The only difficulty readers of this book may have in pronouncing Filipino names is in those which have a tilde *ñ*. The name Osmeña, for example, should be pronounced Oz-main-ya.

## Thai

The "General System of Phonetic Transcription of Thai Characters into Roman" of Thailand's Royal Institute has been employed here. It contains a number of pitfalls for English readers. First, note that *h* following a consonant means that that consonant is aspirated. *Kh* is pronounced like the *c* in car, while *k* alone is pronounced like the *g* in *glockenspiel.* Similarly, *th* and *ph* are pronounced like the *t* in table and the *p* in power. *Čh* is pronounced as if written *tj,* while *ch* is pronounced as the *ch* in chair.

"Thailand" and "Thai" have been the name of the country, the people, and the language only since 1939. In the strict sense, both these terms have political connotations, implying a unity that transcends the historically separate ethnic groups that make up the modern nation—the Siamese of the Central Plain, the Lao of the Northeast, and the Northern Thai (or Lao) of the North. By contrast, the older names of "Siam" and "Siamese" have narrower connotations, referring primarily to the society and culture of the Central Plain. We have used "Siam" and "Siamese" in those parts of the book referring to the period prior to 1939.

Most Thai names appearing in this book are prefixed by a bureaucratic rank, which ascends from *luang* to *čhaophraya.* The main name by which a person was known was the bureaucratic title which follows; but as many different individuals were known by the same title at different times, the personal (given and family) names of the individual are inserted after rank and title in parentheses. Thus, *Čhaophraya* (rank) Si Suriyawong (title) is followed by the man's personal name (Chuang Bunnag). In modern times, men generally are called by their given names, rather than their family names—thus Pridi rather than Mr. Phanomyong.

## Vietnamese

Because of the unreasonable cost, it has not been possible for us to write Vietnamese names and terms in this book in the full glory of their diacritical marks. It is necessary to apologize for this omission, because those marks indicate the tones of words and the correct pronunciation of their vowels, and tones and vowel pronunciations are crucial to an understanding of the meanings of Vietnamese words. Even when the vowel pronunciation of a word is obvious, and no tone marks are required, the romanized Vietnamese language requires special markings for it to be intelligible. To take a simple example, when the word *dinh* is written without a stroke through the stem of the *d,* it is pronounced *zinh* and means "military camp" or "palace of an official." Only when *dinh* is written with a *đ,* is it pronounced the way it looks without the stroke to a Western reader, and it then means "adult male taxpayer" or "nail."

Vietnamese names are complicated. The first word in a three-word sequence like Cao Ba Quat indicates the family or lineage to which the person belongs. The second word, known as a "cushion" or "lining" word, may indicate the sex of the person and may also be used for all the male members of one family or, less commonly, may designate one generation of the male members of a family. The third and final word in the sequence is the given name of a Vietnamese individual. But unlike Western usage, and even unlike Chinese usage, a Vietnamese person is ordinarily cited by his given name, not by his family name. Thus Ngo Dinh Diem is referred to in these pages as Diem, Nguyen Truong To as To. Very rarely are there exceptions to this rule. The most famous exception is the bearer of the artificial Sino-Vietnamese pseudonym Ho Chi Minh, who is referred to as Ho.

# NOTES

1. Chapter 38 of the Malacca Code, as given in T. J. Newbold, *Political and Statistical Account of the British Settlements in the Straits of Malacca* (London, 1839), 2:275–276.

2. *Dai Nam thuc luc chinh bien* [Primary Compilation of the veritable records of Imperial Vietnam], I, 43:15.

3. *Minh Hanh in Phat-giao Viet-Nam* [Vietnamese Buddhism] (Saigon, n.d.), pp. 8, 22.

4. From Vietnamese texts in Pham Van Dieu, "Viet Nam Van Hoc," *Giang Binh* [Lectures on Vietnamese literature] (Saigon, 1960), pp. 74, 77–78.

5. H. de la Costa, *Readings in Philippine History* (Manila, 1965), pp. 87–91.

6. Dorothy Woodman, *The Making of Burma* (London, 1962), p. 139.

7. Henry Yule, *A Narrative of the Mission Sent by the Governor-General of India to the Court of Ava in 1855* (London, 1858; repr. Kuala Lumpur, 1968), p. 109.

8. Sir John Bowring, *The Kingdom and People of Siam* (London, 1857), 1:226.

9. Charles Meyniard, *Le Second Empire en Indo-Chine* (Paris, 1891), p. 461.

10. G. Finlayson, *Mission to Siam and Hue, the Capital of Cochinchina, in the Years 1821–1822* (London, 1826), p. 366.

11. Do Thuc Vinh, *Ho Xuan Huong: tac gia the ky XIX* [Ho Xuan Huong: nineteenth-century writer] (Saigon, 1956), p. 63.

12. *Dai Nam thuc luc chinh bien*, II, 79:29b ff.

13. *Dai Nam thuc luc chinh bien*, II, 205:12b ff.

14. Quoted in Rupert Emerson, *Malaysia, A Study in Direct and Indirect Rule* (New York, 1937), p. 81.

15. There were and are three major ethnic groups on Java: the Javanese (much the largest), Sundanese, and Madurese. Although the term "Javan" is sometimes used to refer to all of them together, so, more often, if less correctly, is "Javanese."

16. Soepomo Poedjosoedarmo and M. C. Ricklefs, "The Establishment of Surakarta, a Translation from the Babad Giyanti," *Indonesia* 4 (Oct. 1967): 94. The original and translation are in verse, rendered here in prose format.

17. Maria Lourdes Diaz-Trechuelo, "The Economic Development of the Philippines in the Second Half of the Eighteenth Century," *Philippine Studies* 11, 2 (April 1963): 228.

18. Nicholas Loney to Consul W. Farren, July 10, 1861, cited in Robert MacMicking, *Recollections of Manila and the Philippines* (Manila, 1967), pp. 245, 250.

19. Cited in Edgar Wickberg, "The Chinese Mestizo in the Philippines," *Journal of Southeast Asian History* 5, 1 (March 1964): 75.

20. Sinibaldo de Mas, *Secret Report of Sinibaldo de Mas* (Manila, 1963), p. 133.

21. Quoted in H. de la Costa, "Development of the Native Clergy in the Philippines," *Studies in Philippine Church History* (Ithaca, 1969), pp. 99–100.

22. Austin Craig, *The Filipinos' Fight for Freedom* (Manila, 1933), p. 400.

23. Trinh Van Thanh, *Giang luan Viet Van* [An exposition of Vietnamese literature] (Saigon, 1962), p. 687.

24. *Recueil des traités conclus par la France en Extrême-Orient: 1648–1902* (Paris, 1902–1907), 1:209.

25. *The Times* (London), May 11, 1927 (obituary for Sisowath).

26. Report of General Wood as to Abrogation Bates Treaty, Zamboanga, Mindanao, December 16, 1903, cited in *Report of the Philippine Commission* (1903), 1:489–490.

27. William Cameron Forbes, *The Philippine Islands* (New York, 1928), 2:31.

28. Harry J. Benda, "Peasant Movements in Colonial Southeast Asia," *Asian Studies* [Manila], 3, 3 (Dec. 1965): 433–434.

29. Quoted by R. J. Wilkinson, "The Education of Asiatics," *Special Reports on Educational Subjects,* vol. 8, published as Cmd. 835, Great Britain, Parliamentary Papers, 1902, p. 687.

30. Tengku Abdullah Ahmad, "Apa-Kah Faedah Merdeka?" ["What is the advantage of freedom?"], *Seruan Azhar* [Cairo] 3 (Oct. 1927): 492–493.

31. Frank Swettenham, *British Malaya* (London, 1907), p. 248.

32. *Report of the Philippine Commission,* 1903, 1:59.

33. *Al-Imam* [Singapore], 1, 6 (Nov. 1906).

34. Sinibaldo de Mas, *Report on the Condition of the Philippines in 1842* (Manila, 1963), p. 169.

35. John N. Schumacher, "The Filipino Nationalists' Propaganda Campaign in Europe, 1880–1895," Ph.D. diss., Georgetown Univ., 1965, p. 191.

36. José Rizal, "Filipinas dentro de cien años," (1890), cited in de la Costa, *Readings in Philippine History,* p. 229.

37. W. E. Retana's transcription of *The Trial of José Rizal,* trans. and ed. H. de la Costa (Manila, 1961), pp. 102–103.

38. José Rizal to Mariano Ponce, April 1889, cited in Schumacher, "Filipino Nationalists' Propaganda Campaign," p. 547.

39. Maximo M. Kalaw, *The Development of Philippine Politics, 1872–1920* (Manila, 1926), p. 128.

40. Richard Hofstadter, "Manifest Destiny and the Philippines," in Theodore P. Greene, ed., *American Imperialism in 1898* (Boston, 1955), p. 91.

41. G. A. Grunder and William E. Livezey, *The Philippines and the United States* (Norman, Okla., 1951), p. 2.

42. *Report of the Philippine Commission* (1902), 1:3–4.

43. Special Report of the Secretary of War, William H. Taft to President Theodore Roosevelt, January 23, 1908, 3:238–239.

44. *Report of the Philippine Commission* (1902), 1:4.

45. William Cameron Forbes, *The Philippine Islands* (Boston, 1928), 2:520–44.

46. Maximo M. Kalaw, *Introduction to Philippine Social Science* (Manila, 1937), p. 185.

47. The Report was published as Cmd. 9109, Great Britain, Parliamentary Papers, 1918, vol. 8.

48. Raden Adjeng Kartini, *Letters of a Javanese Princess* (New York, 1964), p. 63.

49. *Totok* is an Indonesian term for foreign-born immigrants. As used in this chapter it refers to (in principle) pure-blooded individuals identifying themselves, and identified by others, as Dutch and Chinese, respectively.

50. Quoted in Robert Van Niel, *The Emergence of the Modern Indonesian Elite* (The Hague, 1960), pp. 38–39.

51. The Indonesian term *peranakan* (from the root *anak,* child) means local-born foreigner. As used in this chapter, it refers to Dutch or Chinese *mestizos* of mixed blood and, before their transformations at least, of mixed culture.

52. The word "Indonesia" (Latin: island India) was not commonly used at the time. It was a technical term coined by nineteenth-century anthropologists to refer to island Southeast Asia in general.

53. Benedict Anderson, "The Languages of Indonesian Politics," *Indonesia* 1 (1966): 89.

54. Trinh Van Thanh, *Giang luan Viet Van* [An exposition of Vietnamese literature] (Saigon, 1962), p. 375.

55. Nguyen Hien Le, *Dong Kinh Nghia Thuc* [The Dong Kinh Free School] (Saigon, 1956, 1968), p. 83.

56. Lam Giang, *Giang luan ve Phan Boi Chau* [A disquisition on Phan Boi Chau] (Saigon, 1959), pp. 96–97.

57. Translated from the text in Pham Van Dieu, *Viet Nam van hoc giang binh* [Lectures on Vietnamese literature] (Saigon, 1960), pp. 474–476.

58. Nhat Linh, *Doan tuyet* [A severance of ties] (Saigon, 1967 ed.), p. 187; first published in 1935.

59. *Indochina*, September 2, 1943.

60. Jean B. Alberti, *L'Indochine d'autrefois et d'aujourd'hui* (Paris, 1934), p. 447.

61. "3349," i.e., Prince Phetsarath Ratanavongsa, *Iron Man of Laos: Prince Phetsarath Ratanavongsa,* trans. John B. Murdoch (Ithaca, 1978), p. 23.

62. *The Senator Gravel Edition: The Pentagon Papers* (Boston, 1971), 2, 111.

63. Quoted by Benjamin White, "Population, Involution, and Employment in Rural Java," in Gary E. Hanson, ed., *Agricultural and Rural Development in Indonesia* (Boulder, Colo., 1981), p. 165.

# GLOSSARY

*abangan:* the variant of Javanese religion characterized by an eclectic blend of Islamic, Hindu-Buddhist, and earlier beliefs and practices. Used in contrast to the *santri* variant.

*adat:* custom in the widest sense, and customary law in general, in Malaysia and Indonesia

*ahmudan:* that portion of the population in monarchical Burma who rendered labor service to the king and his officers and were bound personally to the king by virtue of their hereditary status and occupancy of royal lands, usually near the capital

*alcalde-mayor:* a Spanish provincial governor in the Philippines

*alun-alun:* the central square of a Javan royal capital or other town, on which the court of a king or *bupati* looks out

*amphoe:* Thai term for the administrative districts into which a province is divided

*atap:* the Malay term for roof thatch, usually made from the leaves of the nipa palm

*athi:* the portion of the population in monarchical Burma who rendered labor service to local officers rather than to the king and were free of obligations from the use of royal land

*atwin-wun:* the "inside ministers" or palace privy councilors who presided over the Burmese king's privy council *(byè-daik),* and who directed the service corps at the palace

*audiencia:* the highest tribunal of justice, and the advisory council to the governor of the Spanish Philippines

*baba:* colonial-born; the community of Chinese in the Malay Peninsula (especially Malacca) who, through intermarriage with Malays and long residence, have acquired a distinct identity of their own. Also used for the analogous group of *peranakan* Chinese on Java.

*bach lang:* "blank coins," a traditional Vietnamese term for inflation

*badan perjuangan:* "struggle groups," a term from the Indonesian Revolution; armed groups spontaneously formed in the post-1945 struggle for independence

*bahasa:* language, hence Bahasa Melayu (Malay), Bahasa Indonesia (Indonesian), and Bahasa Nasional

*baht:* the basic unit of the Thai currency

*balai:* the audience hall of a Malay *raja*'s palace

*barangay:* a kinship unit in the pre-Spanish Philippines that consisted of from 30 to 100 families, which the Spanish preserved as the basic unit of local administration in the Philippines

*barong tagalog:* a loose-fitting embroidered shirt worn without neck ornaments in the Philippines

*barrio:* a village in the Philippines

*batik:* a type of Indonesian or Malay dyed cloth

*bay buom:* "butterfly flights," an atmosphere of carefree elegance and freedom sought by some Vietnamese higher-education students

*bekel:* "tax farmer," the individual who did the actual tax collecting for the princes or officials granted appanages by the Mataram king

*bendahara:* the "treasurer" of a Malay *raja;* honorific given to one of the most senior of Malay chiefs

*bilal:* the mosque official who makes the daily calls to prayer

*binh hoa qui:* "vase of precious flowers," a tradition in Vietnamese education—attacked by revolutionaries—in which the village school is considered an outpost of the Confucian elite, not an agency for mass education

*blijvers:* "stayers," those Dutch who thought of the Indies as their home (used in contrast to *trekkers*)

*bodhi:* "great awakening," part of the name of middle and elementary schools sponsored by the General Association of Vietnamese Buddhism for the children of Buddhist families in Vietnam

*bodhisattva:* a man, lay or ecclesiastical, who has become a Buddha-to-be and who compassionately helps others to reach Nirvana before entering it himself

*budak-budak raja:* the "bully boys" or armed retainers of a Malay *raja*

*bundok:* Tagalog for "mountain"

*bupati:* Javan local lord or leading territorial official, called "regent" in Dutch and English

*byè-daik:* the Burmese king's privy council

*cabecilla:* "boss," "foreman," or "ringleader"—a system of distributing and purchasing goods in the Spanish Philippines in which a Chinese central agent with his provincial factors provided a link between the *indio* producer and the foreign export community

*cabeza de barangay:* the Spanish term for the hereditary headmen (formerly *datu*) of the smallest unit of local administration in the Philippines

*cacah:* term used for revenue purposes in the Mataram period to indicate the head of a Javanese peasant family subject to tax

*cacique:* a member of the privileged landholding elite in the Spanish Philippines

*central:* a sugar refinery in the Philippines

*cetiya:* a tower-like Buddhist monument usually containing relics

*čhangwat:* province, in twentieth-century Thailand

*čhaomüang:* the "lord" of a town and its territory; used throughout the Thai-Lao world

Chettyar: a caste of Indian money-lenders, originating in Madras, who played an important role in colonial Burma

*chu nghia xa hoi:* "socialism"—the Vietnamese term

*co mat vien:* the Vietnamese privy council created by the Emperor Minh-mang

*cofradia:* a term for a religious brotherhood in the Philippines

*consulado:* "consulate," or "guild." Such a guild was established in the Philippines in 1769. It consisted of Spanish merchants in

Manila who supervised the galleon trade, subject only to the control of the governor.

*controleur:* subordinate Dutch administrative official in the Indies

Cortes: the Spanish parliament in Madrid

*creoles:* a term for Spaniards born in the Spanish empire, in contrast to those born on the Iberian Peninsula *(peninsulares)*

*dakwah:* literally (from Arabic) call; hence proselytization, propagation of Islam

*dalang:* the puppeteer for the Javanese shadow-play *(wayang kulit)*

*dalem:* the court of a *bupati* on Java

*datu:* (also spelled *dato, datuk*) aristocratic title used throughout island Southeast Asia

*daulat:* the mystical powers conferred by kingship on a Malay *raja*

Dayak: a loose term for various swidden-cultivating ethnic groups on Borneo. The best-known "Dayaks" are the Iban, sometimes also called "Sea Dayaks."

*devaraja:* "god-king"

*Dhamma:* Pali term for the teachings of Buddha; Dharma to Mahayana Buddhists

*diplomasi:* in Indonesian, literally "diplomacy." In political disputes of the Indonesian Revolution, the term stood for a policy of negotiating for independence, in contrast to *perjuangan*.

*Do sat vien:* the Censorate in traditional Vietnam; a body of officials who scrutinized the conduct of other mandarins, and sometimes that of the emperor himself

*Dong Du:* "eastern travel," a movement of Vietnamese who went to Japan to study between 1905 and 1908

*filipino:* prior to the nineteenth century, a term applied to Caucasians born in the Philippines *(creoles),* as opposed to Caucasians born in the Iberian Peninsula. During the nineteenth century it came to include *mestizos* and *indios* born in the Philippines as well.

*gobernadorcillo:* "petty governor," the chief magistrate of a municipality in the Spanish Philippines, and the highest *indio* official in the Spanish bureaucracy

*gremio:* a district governing council in Manila during the late Spanish period

*guru:* a teacher in Indonesia and Malaysia

*hacienda:* an estate in the Philippines

*haj:* the rites performed during the pilgrimage to Mecca

*haji:* one who has performed the *haj*

*hakim:* Malay/Indonesian word for "judge," one of the principal officials of a Malay *raja,* sometimes also his chief religious dignitary

*halus:* "refined" or "polished," a Javanese concept defining one polar type of life-style and behavior, particularly for *priyayi.* The opposite is *kasar.*

*Hlutdaw:* the supreme council of state in traditional Burma

*hoi chu ba:* associations of temple nuns in Vietnam

*hoi dong hao muc:* the village council of notables in Vietnam

*hui:* "secret society," a type of social organization common among overseas Chinese in Southeast Asia

*hukum adat:* Malay customary law

*hukum akl:* Malay principles of natural justice based on the intellect

*hukum faal:* Malay principles of right conduct

*hukum shera:*  *shar'ia* law; the canon law of Islam

*ilustrado:*  "enlightened one," a member of the indigenous intelligent-sia in the late nineteenth-century Philippines, which spoke for the emerging Filipino community

*imam:*  the leader of a mosque congregation and, by extension, of any Muslim community

*indio:*  a Spanish term for the indigenous population of the Philip-pines

*Indisch culture:*  literally "Indies" culture; the mixed Dutch-Javan culture pattern adopted by most Eurasians and *blijver* Dutch on Java in the nineteenth century

*indulto de comercio:*  a fine paid in advance by the Spanish provincial governors of the Philippines who expected to transgress the legal pro-scription on commercial activity

*inquilino:*  "lessee," an *indio* or *mestizo* to whom was given a concession to clear and improve Church land in the Philippines. The land remained the property of the Church and the lessee would sublet it to tenants for a percentage of their crop yield.

*istana:*  Malay/Indonesian word for "palace." In particular, the palace of the *raja* of a Malayo-Muslim *negeri*.

*jago:*  an Indonesian term for bandit

*jawi:*  Malay (modified Arabic) script

*Jawi Peranakan:*  a Muslim of mixed South Indian and Malay descent born in Malaysia

*kalahom:*  originally the ministry of military affairs in fifteenth-cen-tury Siam, it came to denote the ministry of the southern provinces in the eighteenth and nineteenth centuries, and became the modern ministry of defense in 1894

*kamma* (Pali) or *karma* (Sanskrit):  the Buddhist law of action, which affirms that deeds in one's existence determine one's situation in a later incarna-tion

*kampung:*  a Malay/Indonesian term for village, also used in Indonesia to describe an urban neighborhood

*kanmüang:*  "the business of the province," a Thai word for politics in general

*Kapitan China:*  a Malay/Indonesian term for the leading resident Chinese merchant

*kasamahan:*  the landholding system in the Spanish Philippines whereby an *inquilino* leased land from the church and sublet it to ten-ants for a percentage of their crop yield

*kasar:*  "coarse," or "unrefined"; a Javanese concept defining one polar type of life-style and behavior, typical for peasants or uneducated people generally. The opposite is *halus*.

*kathi:*  an Islamic magistrate in Malaysia and Indonesia

*Kempeitai:*  the Japanese military police in World War II

*kerah:*  Malay term for tribute labor (corvée)

*kha:*  "savage," or "slave"; a term sometimes used in Laos and Thailand to refer to upland peoples whose linguistic affilia-tion is Mon-Khmer (the Lamet, Khmu, P'u Noi, and others)

*khao tich:*  the triennial rating reports on Vietnamese officials, a device by which the emperor kept watch over his provincial offi-cials

*khatib:* the reciter of the *khutbah* (address) at the Friday mosque service

*khau phan dien:* "allotment lands," lands given to local officers of Emperor Gia-long's armed following

*kongsi:* generically, an association of any sort. Used especially for working communities of Chinese miners in the Malay Peninsula and Indonesia.

*kraton:* the sacral palace-city of the Javanese kings

*kretek:* Indonesian cigarette, with cloves mixed into the tobacco

*krom müang:* the ministry in charge of the districts around the capital, and of metropolitan law and order, in Siam through the nineteenth century

*krom na:* the ministry of lands in Siam, superseded in 1892 by the ministry of agriculture

*kuasa:* the supreme temporal authority embodied in a Malay *raja*

*Kuo-yü:* Mandarin Chinese, the official "national speech" of China

*kyaung:* a Buddhist monastery in Burma

*laksamana:* "warden of the seas," honorific given to one of the most senior of Malay chiefs

*langgar:* a small prayer house in Java, sometimes attached to the home of one of the wealthier peasants in a village

Lansin Party: short name for the Burma Socialist Programme Party, or *Myanma Hsoshelit Lansin Pati*

*luc bo:* the Six Boards, which crowned the traditional Vietnamese administrative structure

*lukčhin:* a term for Chinese born in Thailand

*mahatthai:* originally the ministry of civil affairs in fifteenth-century Siam, it came to denote the ministry of northern and eastern provinces in the eighteenth and nineteenth centuries and became the ministry of the interior in 1894

*maistry:* recruiter of an Indian work gang in Burma

*manca negara:* the third administrative circle of Mataram, which consisted of most of Java outside the palace city and the core administrative area

*menteri:* "minister," officer of state in the Malay *negeri*

*merdeka:* "freedom" or "independence" in Malay and Indonesian

*mestizo:* a Spanish term for people of mixed blood

*monthon:* the "circles" into which King Chulalongkorn grouped Siam's provinces in an effort to expand the control of the central administration over the provinces

*müang:* in Thailand, a town or city, and by extension the area administered or controlled by it

*myei-taing:* see *ywa thu-gyi*

*myo:* in Burma, a town or city, and by extension the area controlled or administered by it

*myo-thu-gyi:* a township headman in Burma

*myo-wun:* a provincial governor in pre-British Burma. Unlike the *myo-thu-gyi*, the *myo-wun* derived his authority from the royal court rather than from local allegiance.

*myo-za:* a province or town "eater" in pre-British Burma; a prince or high official to whom was awarded the revenue from a designated town or province

*nam giao:* the "southern altar" of the Vietnamese emperor

*Nam Tien:* the 1,000-year Vietnamese drive from the Red River delta to present-day central and southern Vietnam

Nanyang: "the southern region," a Chinese term for Southeast Asia

*nat:* term for animist spirit in Burma

*negara:* from Sanskrit *nagara,* for "kingdom" or "capital." See *kra-ton,* and *negeri.*

*negara agung:* the second administrative circle in the kingdom of Mataram. It consisted of the core area immediately outside the palace-city.

*negeri:* A Malay/Indonesian word for "state." In particular, a riverine or coastal principality in the Malayo-Muslim world.

*nhap the:* "participation" in worldly affairs as a course of action in Vietnamese Buddhism. Used in contrast to *xuat the.*

*Nirvana:* the final transcendence of the self, which is the goal of Buddhists

*noi cac:* the Grand Secretariat created by Emperor Minh-mang in 1829 in order to improve the coordination of the central Vietnamese administrative structure

*noi vu phu:* the Vietnamese Household Affairs Office, which served as the private treasury of the imperial household

*nom:* the indigenous Vietnamese writing system

*pacto de retro:* a system in the Spanish Philippines used by moneylenders to gain ownership of land. A Chinese *mestizo* would buy land from an *indio* owner, granting him the option to repurchase later. Because the original owner usually was unable to repurchase, the moneylender usually kept the land.

paddy: unmilled rice and the irrigated fields in which it is grown; from Malay *padi*

Pali: classical scriptural language of Theravada Buddhism, closely related to Sanskrit

Panca Sila: the five basic principles of an independent Indonesia as outlined by Sukarno in 1945: nationalism, internationalism, democracy, social justice, belief in one God. The Panca Sila has served ever since, and especially since the late 1970s, as the official national ideology of Indonesia.

*pasisir:* "coast"; in particular, the north coast of Java and the historical complex based on Islam and trade that developed there in the fifteenth and sixteenth centuries

*patih:* the chief minister of the kingdom of Mataram or, later, of a Javan *bupati*

*payung:* the Javanese ceremonial parasol, which symbolized high rank

*pemuda:* Malay/Indonesian word for "a youth," "youths." In the Indonesian Revolution, the term acquired powerful overtones of militancy and patriotism.

*penghulu:* a Malay or Sumatran village headman

*peninsulares:* a term for Spaniards born on the Iberian Peninsula, in contrast to those born in the Spanish empire *(creoles)*

*perahu:* Malay/Indonesian word for a small sailing vessel

*peranakan:* "locally born foreigner," a Malay/Indonesian term for people of mixed local and foreign blood, born in the region

*perjuangan:* Malay/Indonesian word for "struggle." In the Indonesian Revolution the term acquired a deeper significance: struggle for the revolutionary cause. In the political disputes of the time it stood for uncompromising armed struggle, as opposed to *diplomasi.*

*pesantren:* Javanese term for a community of students formed around an Islamic scholar and holy man

*phi:* animist spirits in Thailand and Laos

*phrai luang:* those in premodern Siam who rendered labor service impersonally to the king and his designated representatives, rather than personally to local officials

*phrai som:* those in premodern Siam who rendered labor service personally to local officials, rather than to "the government"

*phrakhlang:* the Siamese ministry, and minister, responsible for finance and foreign affairs (and also, in the nineteenth century, for the administration of the provinces at the head of the Gulf of Siam). Its functions were divided at the beginning of King Chulalongkorn's reign.

*picul:* a variable unit of weight, usually about 60 kg. (132 lbs.)

*piezas:* the shares into which the Manila galleon space was divided. Each galleon was supposed to be divided into 4,000 shares.

*polo:* a term for draft labor (corvée) in the Spanish Philippines

*pondok:* literally "hut" or "shanty," a Malay/Indonesian term for a community of students formed around an Islamic teacher

*pongyi:* "great glory," a Buddhist monk in Burma

*principalia:* the village elite in the Spanish Philippines

*priyayi:* the Javanese and Sundanese hereditary aristocracy or gentry; also, a member of the same

*pueblo:* an administrative unit in the Spanish Philippines which consisted of a church and several *barrios* with a combined total of at least 500 tribute-tax-payers, centered on a plaza

*pwe:* a popular dramatic performance in Burma

*quan lo:* the "mandarin road" in nineteenth-century Vietnam

*quoc ngu:* the Vietnamese "national language," written in romanized form rather than in Chinese and Vietnamese characters

*quoc tu giam:* the National College in traditional Vietnam

*raja:* the ruler of a Malay *negeri*

*Ramakian:* Thai versions of the *Ramayana*

*rantau:* a term for a strong outward drive—for trade or for settlement, for example—typical of many Sumatran societies

*ratu adil:* the "just prince" of Javanese messianic expectations

*regent:* see *bupati*

*regulares:* the friars, those ecclesiastics in the Spanish Philippines who belonged to a religious order, as opposed to the *seculares,* or diocesan priests

*residencia:* the judicial and public review faced by all Spanish officials in the Philippines at the termination of their service and prior to their departure from the colony

Resident: title of a high Dutch or English territorial official in the Netherlands Indies or Malaya

*rijsttafel:* the Dutch term for a Javan meal of rice with many side dishes

*Rukunegara:* Principles of State (Malaysia)

Sangha: Pali term for the Buddhist monkhood

*Sangharaja:* the supreme patriarch of Buddhism in Burma, and also in Siam, whose decisions and injunctions on affairs respecting the Sangha were enforced by civil authority

*sangley:* the Spanish term for Chinese immigrants to the Philippines

Sanskrit: ancient classical language of India, in which most of its texts were transmitted. It is an Indo-European language, distantly related to Latin and many European languages, including English.

*santri:* the variant of Javanese religion characterized by more self-conscious identification as a Muslim and stricter observance of Islamic requirements such as the daily prayers and the fasting month. Used in contrast to *abangan.*

*sawah:* Malay/Indonesian term for the wet-rice paddy field and, by extension, for the whole wet-rice pattern

*sawbwa:* Shan rulers of principalities

*seculares:* diocesan priests in the Spanish Philippines, in contradistinction to the friars *(regulares)* who belonged to religious orders

*senabodi:* ministers of state in Siam

*shahbandar:* an officer of trade who acted as liaison between the *raja* of a Malay or Indonesian *negeri* and the foreign traders in his port

*shaykh:* an honorific given to (or assumed by) many Malayan Hadrami Arabs other than *sayyids* (those tracing their descent back to the Prophet Muhammad), and to men of unusual religious learning

*situado:* the annual subsidy sent to the Philippines from the Spanish treasury in Mexico

Straits Settlements: Singapore Island, Penang and Province Wellesley, and the territory of Malacca, including Naning

*sultan:* Islamic honorific given to the ruler of a Malay or Indonesian *negeri*

*surau:* a building in Malaya that is not a mosque of general assembly but is otherwise devoted to religious or quasi-religious purposes

*susuhunan:* Javanese term for ruler

*swaraj:* a Hindi term for "self-rule," hence, independence

*swidden:* an anthropological term for the worldwide agricultural pattern characterized by slash-and-burn, shifting cultivation; used in contrast to the wet-rice pattern

*tam cuong:* the "three principles" or "three bonds" that were the operative ideal of traditional Vietnamese life: a subject's loyalty to his ruler, a son's obedience to his father, and a wife's submission to her husband

*tam giao:* "the three religions," a formula describing the syncretistic existence of Buddhism, Taoism, and Confucianism in traditional Vietnam

*tanah sabrang:* the fourth administrative circle of Mataram, consisting of the coastal states overseas that acknowledged the suzerainty of Mataram and sent tribute

*tarekat:* literally (Arabic), "path" or "way"; used to denote Sufi mystic orders

*temenggong:* a Malay chief of high rank

*thakin:* "lord, master"; a word originally used by Burmese when addressing an Englishman. It was adopted in the 1930s by Burmese nationalists in the Dobama Asi-ayone as a way of addressing each other.

*thanh:* "walled citadel," the walled part of a traditional Vietnamese city, where officials lived

*thi:* the market area of Hue, where the ordinary Vietnamese lived

*Tipitaka:* the Pali scriptures of Theravada Buddhism; *Tripitaka* in Sanskrit Buddhism

*totok:* an Indonesian term for foreign-born, pure-blooded immigrants. Used in contrast to *peranakan.*

*towkay:* a Malay/Indonesian term for rich Chinese

*Tran Tay:* the province name given Cambodia by the Nguyen court during Cambodia's subjection by Vietnam, 1834–1841

*trekkers:* Dutch who came out to the Indies, usually with Dutch wives, for a career of specified length and who planned to retire in Holland. Used in contrast to *blijvers.*

*trung quoc:* "middle kingdom," a term for Vietnam used by the Vietnamese court to differentiate its society from the nonsinicized societies of Indochina

*tulisanes:* bandits in the Philippines

*ulama:* those learned in Islam

*ummat:* the Islamic community

*uposatha:* a building for ordinations and rites in the Theravada Buddhist monastery

*utang na loob:* "debt of gratitude," a norm of social behavior in the Philippines. A recipient of a favor is obliged to return the favor with interest in order to discharge his debt of gratitude.

*uy tin:* a Vietnamese term meaning "prestige," a combination of *uy* (fearsomeness) and *tin* (capacity to inspire trust)

*van te:* a Vietnamese funeral oration, a particularly popular literary form in the 1790s and early 1800s

*vihara:* a small preaching hall in a Theravada Buddhist monastery

*wahyu:* the divine radiance, manifesting itself in various ways, which marks its possessor as a Javanese king, and whose departure signals his fall

*wang:* the ministry of the palace in traditional Siam

*wayang kulit:* Javanese shadow-play, which uses puppets to dramatize stories from the Javanese versions of the *Mahabharata* and *Ramayana*

*wayang orang:* the Javanese dance drama derived from *wayang kulit*

*wedana:* a court official of Mataram; in the nineteenth and twentieth centuries, a Javan administrative official below a *bupati*

*wong cilik:* Javanese for the "little man," or peasant

*wun-gyi:* the chief royal ministers in Burma, members of the *Hlutdaw*

*wunthanu athin:* "own race societies," village nationalist societies created in Burma in the 1920s, which attempted to gain peasant support for anti-British and anti-Indian boycotts

*xa:* the Vietnamese village, the basic unit of peasant life in Vietnam, composed of a number of hamlets *(thon)*

*xa truong:* a village chief in Vietnam

*xuat the:* "abstention" from worldly affairs as a course of action in Vietnamese Buddhism. Used in contrast to *nhap the.*

*Yam Tuan:* short for *Yang di-Pertuan*

*Yang di-Pertuan:* "he who is made Lord"—the ceremonial title of a Malay ruler

*ywa thu-gyi:* a village headman in Burma

# BIBLIOGRAPHY

## A Note of Explanation

Aside from the general works on Southeast Asia and the section on introductory works for Southeast Asian societies, the bibliography follows the format of the book itself, beginning with Part I, "The Eighteenth-Century World," and continuing through Part V, "Southeast Asian Nations in a New World Order." Individual monographs, when considered useful for more than one topic or chapter, have been cited more than once. Although this makes for a bulkier bibliography, it is hoped that citing important studies wherever they apply will make the bibliography easier to use.

The bibliography has been compiled primarily from English-language materials, although essential French materials have been included. The basic literature of the field, however, includes a great deal of material in Southeast Asian and other languages, and the reader is encouraged to carry studies beyond English-language monographs to the wealth of primary and secondary materials available in Western and Southeast Asian languages.

## Bibliographies of Southeast Asia

**General Guides:** Among the many bibliographic reference works, see G. Raymond Nunn, *South and Southeast Asia: A Bibliography of Bibliographies* (1966); John F. Embree and Lillian O. Dotson, *Bibliography of the Peoples and Cultures of Mainland Southeast Asia* (1950); Karl J. Pelzer, *Selected Bibliography on the Geography of Southeast Asia* (3 vols., 1949–1956); Donald Clay Johnson, *A Guide to Reference Materials on Southeast Asia* (1970); Donald Clay Johnson, *Index to Southeast Asian Journals: A Guide to Articles, Book Reviews, and Composite Works* (2 vols., 1977–1982); and D. R. SarDesai and Bhanu D. SarDesai, *Theses and Dissertations on Southeast Asia* (1970). The nine parts of *Southeast Asian Research Tools* published by the University of Hawaii Southeast Asian Studies Program in 1979 are cited separately below. The annual *Bibliography of Asian Studies* is an essential cumulative source for recently published books and articles; and the annual *Doctoral Dissertations on Asia* fulfills the same function for dissertations.

## Bibliographies for Individual Countries

**Burma:** Though now dated, the best available bibliography on Burma is Frank N. Trager, *Burma: A Selected and Annotated Bibliography* (1973). The 2,086 entries are annotated, and there is an index of entries by topic. Michael Aung-Thwin, *Southeast Asian Research Tools: Burma* (1979), is a helpful guide to unpublished and other research materials. Frank Joseph Shulman, *Burma: An Annotated Bibliographical Guide to International Doctoral Dissertation Research 1898–1985* (1986), is particularly well annotated.

**Thailand:** The best place to begin is Donn V. Hart's *Thailand: An Annotated Bibliography of Bibliographies* (1977), which usefully surveys the field. Other useful compilations are Charles F. Keyes, *Southeast Asian Research Tools: Thailand* (1979); and Michael S. Watts, *Thailand* (1986).

**Vietnam:** Henri Cordier's massive *Bibliotheca Indosinica* (4 vols., 1932) contains much bibliographical information. Cordier's work was carried forward by Paul Boudet and Rémy Bourgeois, *Bibliographie de l'Indochine française, 1913–1935* (4 vols., 1929–1967). Cecil C. Hobbs, et al., *Indochina: A Bibliography of the Land and the People* (1950), is still useful; see also Michael Cotter, *Vietnam: A Guide to Reference Sources* (1978).

Nguyen The Anh, *Bibliographie critique sur les relations entre le Viet-Nam et l'occident* (1967), covers the history of Vietnamese-Western contacts. See also Roy Jumper, *Bibliography of the Political and Administrative History of Vietnam* (1962); Tran Thi Kimsa, *Bibliography of Vietnam, 1954–1964* (1965); Richard D. Burns and Milton Leitenberg, *The Wars in Vietnam, Cambodia and Laos: A Bibliographic Guide* (1984), which lists over six thousand titles but is still remarkably incomplete; and Phan Thien Chau, *Vietnamese Communism: A Research Bibliography* (1975), which cites English- and French-language work as well as much Vietnamese-language material.

**Cambodia:** The best bibliographic introduction to Cambodian studies, overtaking previous efforts (while mentioning them) is Charles F. Keyes, *Southeast Asian Research Tools: Cambodia* (1979). For French-language sources, students might consult the special issue of *France-Asie* (1955) entitled *Presence du Cambodge*. See also Mary L. Fisher, *Cambodia: An Annotated Bibliography of its History, Geography, Politics and Economy since 1954* (1967), and Zaleha Tamby, *Cambodia: A Bibliography* (1982).

**Laos:** Students of Lao history should consult Charles F. Keyes's helpful *Southeast Asian Research Tools: Laos* (1979), which supplements Bernard Lafont's *Bibliographie du Laos* (2 vols., 1964–1978). The most recent compilation is William W. Sage and Judith A. N. Henchy, *Laos: A Bibliography* (1986).

**Malaysia:** The best guide to source materials of all kinds is Ding Choo Ming's *A Bibliography of Bibliographies on Malaysia* (1981), but William R. Roff and M. L. Koch's *Southeast Asian Research Tools: Malaysia* (1979) is also useful. The fullest bibliography is R. S. Karni, *A Bibliography of Malaysia and Singapore* (1980); but see also Karl J. Pelzer, *West Malaysia and Singapore: A Selected Bibliography* (1971). A recent bibliography is Ian Brown and Rajeswary Ampalavanar, *Malaysia* (1986). For the Borneo territories, see Conrad P. Cotter, *Bibliography of English Language Sources on Human Ecology, Eastern Malaysia and Brunei* (1965). Two excellent bibliographies attached to other works should also be mentioned: C. M. Turnbull's bibliography of writings in English on the history of British Malaya from 1786 to 1867, in L. A. Mills, "British Malaya, 1824–67," *Journal of the Malayan Branch Royal Asiatic Society* 33, 3 (1960): 327–424; and the bibliography of economic works appended to T. H. Silcock, *The Commonwealth Economy in Southeast Asia* (1959), pp. 216–250.

**Indonesia:** Char Lan Hiang's *Southeast Asian Research Tools: Indonesia* (1979) provides a broad introduction to scholarship on Indonesia which includes an annotated survey of bibliographies on the country. Two major general bibliographies are W. Ph. Coolhaas, *A Critical Survey of Studies on Dutch Colonial History* (2nd rev. ed. 1980), and Raymond Kennedy's anthropological *Bibliography of Indonesian Peoples and Cultures* (2nd rev. ed. 1962), which is somewhat dated.

**The Philippines:** The literature on the Philippines in English is extensive. Among the more recent reference bibliographies are a *Selected Bibliography of the Philippines,* topically arranged and annotated, prepared by the Philippine Studies Program at the University of Chicago (1973); Shiro Saito, *Philippine Ethnography: A Culturally Annotated and Selected Bibliography* (1972); E. R. Baradi, *South-*

*east Asian Research Tools: The Philippines* (1979); Belen B. Angeles, *A Bibliography of Theses and Dissertations, 1965–1979* (1981); and W. H. Scott, *A Critical Survey of the Prehispanic Source Materials for the Study of Philippine History* (1984). Among those dealing with more specialized topics are A. T. Tiamson, *The Muslim Filipinos: An Annotated Bibliography* (2 vols., 1979–1981); Michael P. Onorato, *Philippine Bibliography, 1899–1946* (1968); Shiro Saito, *Philippine-American Relations: A Guide to Manuscript Sources in the United States* (1982); M. J. Netzorg, *The Philippines in World War II and to Independence: An Annotated Bibliography* (1977); and C. See, *A Bibliography of the Chinese in the Philippines* (1970).

## Historiography

An early survey of Southeast Asian historiography was edited by D. G. E. Hall, *Historians of South-East Asia* (1961). A more recent collection is C. D. Cowan and O. W. Wolters, eds., *Southeast Asian History and Historiography* (1976). The collection of essays edited by Soedjatmoko, *An Introduction to Indonesian Historiography* (1965), has no equivalent for the other countries of the region, although K. G. Tregonning, *Malaysian Historical Sources* (1962), is frequently useful. In the early 1960s, a series of important articles appeared in the *Journal of Southeast Asian History,* by such scholars as D. P. Singhal, John R. W. Smail, F. J. West, and Harry J. Benda. Benda's contributions to the field may be sampled in the posthumous collection of some of his articles, *Continuity and Change in Southeast Asia* (1972). The most important recent explorations into the field are in a fine collection edited by Anthony Reid and David Marr, *Perceptions of the Past in Southeast Asia* (1979). For samplings of recent work, see Ruth T. McVey, *Southeast Asian Transitions: Approaches Through Social History* (1978); and D. K. Wyatt and A. Woodside, eds., *Moral Order and the Question of Change: Essays on Southeast Asian Thought* (1982). Donald K. Emmerson, "Issues in Southeast Asian History: Room for Interpretation," *Journal of Asian Studies* 40 (1980): 43–68; and Theodore Friend, "Southeast Asia: Integration, Development, and the Terror of Time," *Journal of Interdisciplinary History* 3, 3 (Winter 1975): 159–168, are among those who critically reviewed the first edition of *In Search of Southeast Asia.*

## Academic Journals

The journals listed below contain scholarly articles and, in most cases, reviews of recent books dealing with Southeast Asia in whole or in part. A first group consists of the journals with the broadest and most comprehensive coverage of the area and/or the largest numbers of book reviews:

*Asian Survey* (monthly, Berkeley)
*Bulletin of Concerned Asian Scholars* (quarterly, Berthoud, Colo.)
*Contemporary Southeast Asia* (quarterly, Singapore)
*Journal of Asian Studies* (quarterly, Ann Arbor)
*Journal of Southeast Asian Studies* (succeeds *Journal of Southeast Asian History;* semiannual, Singapore)
*Modern Asian Studies* (quarterly, Cambridge)
*Pacific Affairs* (quarterly, Vancouver)
*Asiaweek* and *Far Eastern Economic Review* (weekly, Hong Kong). These weekly news magazines provide reportage on current events in Southeast Asia, political as well as economic.

A second group consists of a sampling of important journals, most of which concentrate on just one part of the area:

*Archipel* (Paris)
*Bulletin of Indonesian Economic Studies* (Canberra)

*Indonesia* (Ithaca)
*Journal of the Malaysian Branch, Royal Asiatic Society* (Kuala Lumpur)
*Journal of the Siam Society* (Bangkok)
*Philippine Historical Review* (Manila)
*Philippine Studies* (Manila)
*Prisma: Indonesian Journal of Social and Economic Affairs* (Jakarta)
*Review of Indonesian and Malayan Affairs* (Sydney)
*The Vietnam Forum: A Review of Vietnamese Culture* (New Haven)

## General Works on Southeast Asia

**General Histories:** The single most comprehensive history of Southeast Asia is D. G. E. Hall's *A History of South East Asia* (4th ed., 1981). This work by one of the region's greatest historians is especially valuable to the specialist. John Bastin and Harry J. Benda wrote a volume of interlocked essays entitled *A History of Modern Southeast Asia* (1968). More recent general histories include Lea E. Williams, *Southeast Asia: A History* (1976); Milton Osborne, *Southeast Asia: An Introductory History* (1979); and D. J. M. Tate, *The Making of Modern South-East Asia* (2 vols., 1971–1979). The 1940s are treated in Jan M. Pluvier, *South-East Asia From Colonialism to Independence* (1974). O. W. Wolters' extended essay, *History, Culture and Region in Southeast Asian Perspectives* (1982), is a thoughtful and provocative attempt to define the dynamics of the region. For an even shorter introduction to Southeast Asian history, W. F. Wertheim's essay entitled "Southeast Asia," in *International Encyclopedia of the Social Sciences* 1 (1968): 423–438, is sinewy, shrewd, and full of ideas. Harry J. Benda and John A. Larkin prepared a very useful book of readings based on primary sources—both Southeast Asian and foreign—called *The World of Southeast Asia* (1967). Jan M. Pluvier's *A Handbook and Chart of Southeast Asian History* (1967) is a valuable compendium of chronology and succession.

Three related works address the question of the nature of the premodern state in Southeast Asia: Anthony Reid and Lance Castles, eds., *Pre-Colonial State Systems in Southeast Asia* (1975); Lorraine Gesick, ed., *Centers, Symbols, and Hierarchies: Essays on the Classical State of Southeast Asia* (1983); and Clifford Geertz, *Negara: The Theatre State in Nineteenth Century Bali* (1980).

**Geography:** Among the many Southeast Asian geographies, see Charles A. Fisher, *Southeast Asia: A Social, Economic and Political Geography* (1966); Ernest H. G. Dobby, *Monsoon Asia* (3rd ed., 1967); and Charles E. Robequain, *Malaya, Indonesia, Borneo and the Philippines* (1954). Lee Yong Leng, *Southeast Asia: Essays in Political Geography* (1982), considers the origins of the region's modern boundaries, and it is usefully complemented by J. R. V. Prescott, *Map of Mainland Southeast Asia by Treaty* (1975).

A useful but by no means exhaustive atlas of Southeast Asia is Djambatan Uitgeversbedrijf, *Atlas of South-East Asia* (1962), with an introduction by D. G. E. Hall.

**Ethnography:** Two excellent specialized studies are Frank LeBar, Gerald Hickey, and John Musgrave, *Ethnic Groups of Mainland Southeast Asia* (1964); and Peter Kunstadter, ed., *Southeast Asian Tribes, Minorities and Nations* (2 vols., 1967). Frank LeBar, *Ethnic Groups of Insular Southeast Asia* (1972), is complemented by Ben J. Wallace, *Village Life in Insular Southeast Asia* (1971), and R. M. Koentjaraningrat, *Introduction to the Peoples and Cultures of Indonesia and Malaysia* (1975).

**Social and Economic Development:** Excellent introductions to life in mainland Southeast Asia can be found in Lucien M. Hanks, *Rice and Man: Agricultural Ecology in Southeast Asia* (1972), and Charles F. Keyes, *The Golden Peninsula: Culture and Adaptation in Mainland Southeast Asia* (1977). John S. Furnivall's *Colo-*

*nial Policy and Practice: A Comparative Study of Burma and Netherlands India* (2nd ed., 1956) has profoundly influenced subsequent thinking about Southeast Asia's economic and social development. Terence G. McGee's *The Southeast Asian City: A Social Geography of the Primate Cities of Southeast Asia* (1967) makes a unique contribution to the literature. John T. McAlister, Jr., has pulled together a useful though now somewhat dated collection of essays in his *Southeast Asia: The Politics of National Integration* (1973), to which a collection edited by Robert O. Tilman, *Man, State, and Society in Contemporary Southeast Asia* (1969), provides a useful adjunct. On Chinese communities in the region, Victor Purcell, *The Chinese in Southeast Asia* (1964), is a useful overview, and Mary F. Somers Heidhues, *Southeast Asia's Chinese Minorities* (1974), is a brief but much respected study. Robert C. Lester, *Theravada Buddhism in Southeast Asia* (1973), is one rare attempt to look at religion in a substantial portion of the region.

Annual reviews of recent events in Southeast Asia appear in the January and February issues of *Asian Survey* and in the annual *Southeast Asian Affairs* published by the Institute of Southeast Asian Studies in Singapore.

## Individual Societies: General Studies

**Burma:** James George Scott (Shway Yoe), *The Burman: His Life and Notions* (1882, repr. 1963), though written over a hundred years ago, remains a fascinating introduction to village life in central Burma. Mi Mi Khaing's *Burmese Family* (1946, repr. 1962), is a good introduction to the more urbanized life of some segments of colonial society, and her *The World of Burmese Women* (1985) is helpful. Studies of postcolonial village and urban society are few, but of value are Manning Nash, *The Golden Road to Modernity: Village Life in Contemporary Burma* (1965), and Melford E. Spiro, *Burmese Supernaturalism* (1967).

Though now conceptually questionable, the two oldest histories of Burma in English, G. E. Harvey, *History of Burma* (1925, repr. 1967), and Arthur P. Phayre, *History of Burma* (1883, repr. 1967), remain valuable introductions. Htin Aung, *A History of Burma* (1967), is an idiosyncratic nationalist history by a lawyer and dramatist. John F. Cady's *A History of Modern Burma* (1960) has yet to be replaced for the modern period; it is limited, however, by its reliance primarily upon official and English language sources. *The State in Burma* (1987) by Robert H. Taylor attempts to explicate the nature of the relationship between state and society in Burma from the 1700s to the present. Precolonial history is better served thanks to the publications of Michael Aung-Thwin, *Pagan: The Origins of Modern Burma* (1985); Khin Maung Kyi and Tin Tin, *Administrative Patterns in Historical Burma* (1973); and Victor B. Lieberman, *Burmese Administrative Cycles: Anarchy and Conquest, c. 1580–1760* (1984). Of these, Lieberman's is the most carefully drawn, but all are valuable; Khin Maung Kyi and Tin Tin's ideas can be usefully applied to the present period. E. Michael Mendelson, *Sangha and State in Burma: A Study of Monastic Sectarianism and Leadership* (1975) is the most complete, though in places sketchy, study of the relationship between the Buddhist monkhood and government in Burma, on which see also Donald Eugene Smith, *Religion and Politics in Burma* (1965). F. S. V. Donnison, *Burma* (1970), is a fine but dated introduction to the country by a British writer who knew it well.

**Thailand:** John de Young, *Village Life in Modern Thailand* (1955), was among the first systematic studies of Thai village society. Lauriston Sharp and Lucien M. Hanks, *Bang Chan: Social History of a Rural Community in Thailand* (1978), is an extraordinary work that treats the history of a Thai village from the early nineteenth century to the present. A range of important scholarship is represented in *Change and Persistence in Thai Society*, ed. G. William Skinner and A. Thomas Kirsch (1975). The works of *Phya* Anuman Rajadhon, long the dean of scholarship in Thailand, are of enduring value: Some, like *Life and Ritual in Old Siam* (1961) and *Five Papers on Thai Custom* (1952), are available in translation. Thai religion is much more complicated than canonical Buddhism as such. Kenneth Wells's *Thai Buddhism: Its Rites and Activities* (1960) is a descriptive introduction, while A. Thomas Kirsch, "Complexity in the Thai Religious System: An Interpretation," *Journal of Asian Studies* 36, 2 (Feb. 1977): 241–266, introduces the complexities produced by religious syncretism. The most widely read works on Thai Buddhism have become the various books of Stanley J. Tambiah, including *World Conqueror and World Renouncer: A Study of Buddhism and Polity in Thailand Against a Historical Background* (1976). A more solid historical treatment is given in Yoneo Ishii, *Sangha, State and Society: Thai Buddhism in History* (1986).

Among the better reference works dealing with Thailand are Frank J. Moore, *Thailand: Its People, Its Society, Its Culture* (rev. ed., 1974); *Thailand: A Country Study* (1980); and the government's own *Thailand in the 80s* (1984), which has exceptionally fine photographs. The standard statistical reference is the biennial *Statistical Yearbook of the Kingdom of Thailand*. For geographical reference, the classic is Robert L. Pendleton, *Thailand: Aspects of Landscape and Life* (1962), updated by Larry Sternstein, *Thailand: The Environment of Modernization* (1976).

The most recent general history of Thailand is David K. Wyatt, *Thailand: A Short History* (1984). Another recent but incomplete work is B. J. Terwiel, *A History of Modern Thailand, 1767–1942* (1983). A stimulating survey and critique of Thai studies is to be found in Eliezer B. Ayal, ed., *The Study of Thailand: Analyses of Knowledge, Approaches, and Prospects in Anthropology, Art History, Economics, History, and Political Science* (1978).

**Vietnam:** A study of their literature is one of the most satisfying ways for foreigners to begin to acquaint themselves with the mind and values of the literature-loving Vietnamese people over the centuries. By far the best place to begin doing this is with Huynh Sanh Thong's magnificent *The Heritage of Vietnamese Poetry: An Anthology* (1979). The greatest single Vietnamese poem itself is also masterfully translated by Huynh Sanh Thong, *The Tale of Kieu: A Bicultural Edition of Nguyen Du's Truyen Kieu* (1983). Readers also may consult with profit Maurice Durand and Nguyen Tran Huan, *An Introduction to Vietnamese Literature*, trans. D. M. Hawke (1985), and Nguyen Ngoc Bich, Burton Raffel, and W. S. Merwin, *A Thousand Years of Vietnamese Poetry* (1975).

Pierre Huard and Maurice Durand, *Connaissance du Vietnam* (1954), summarizes aspects of traditional Vietnamese civilization. Louis Bezacier, *L'Art Vietnamien* (1955), brilliantly surveys art and architecture; B. P. Groslier, *The Art of Indochina* (1962), is less useful but is available in English. On Vietnamese religion, see the classical writings of Léopold Cadière, *Croyances et pratiques religieuses des Vietnamiens* (1958). See also Maurice Durand, *Technique et panthéon des médiums Vietnamiens* (1959). The Asia Society's *Vietnam: Essays on History, Culture, and Society* (1985) has stimulating introductory-level essays.

The most important general history of Vietnam written in a Western language is Le Thanh Khoi, *Histoire du Viet Nam des origines à 1858* (1981), a revision of his *Le Viet-Nam, histoire et civilisation* (1955). In English, there is Joseph Buttinger, *The Smaller Dragon: A Political History of Vietnam* (1958), which gives only the sketchiest treatment of Vietnamese history before Vietnamese relations with the West became critical, and Buttinger's *Vietnam: A Dragon Embattled* (1967), which continues the story. Buttinger's *Vietnam: A Political History* (1969), is a compressed version of these two works and hardly treats Vietnamese history before France conquered the country in the 1800s. Stanley Karnow's popular *Vietnam: A History* (1983) is similarly misnamed, being more interested in the French and Americans who intervened in Vietnam than in the Vietnamese themselves. Readers may also turn to an interesting oddity, Thomas Hodgkin's

*Vietnam: The Revolutionary Path* (1981). Hodgkin's "intelligent young Third World radical's guide to Vietnamese history" looks at early and medieval Vietnamese history in some detail, with a Hanoi-guided Marxist viewpoint. Ralph Smith, *Vietnam and the West* (1968), is a lucid but brief introduction to tradition and change in Vietnam. William J. Duiker, *Vietnam: Nation in Revolution* (1983), deals essentially with Vietnam's history since the 1940s, but the first two chapters survey Vietnam's peoples and religions and their premodern history. Alexander Woodside's *Community and Revolution in Modern Vietnam* (1971) is an excellent overview.

**Cambodia:** The best general view of prerevolutionary Cambodian society is the sumptuously illustrated volume *Cambodge,* produced by the Cambodian Ministry of Information in 1964. See also Solange Thierry's *Les Khmers* (1964), a sensitive analysis. For the specialist, Eveline Porée-Maspero's *Rites agraires des Cambodgiens* (3 vols., 1962–1969) is indispensable, as is Jean Delvert's *Le Paysan Cambodgien* (1961). For a more recent perspective, see Ben Kiernan and Chanthou Boua, *Peasants and Politics in Kampuchea, 1942–1981* (1982), a valuable collection of documents, and David P. Chandler and Ben Kiernan, eds., *Revolution and its Aftermath in Kampuchea: Eight Essays* (1983). Charles Meyer, *Derriere le sourire khmere* (1971), is bitter but perceptive.

Of the histories of Cambodia, the only one to deal with the nineteenth and twentieth centuries in detail is David P. Chandler's *A History of Cambodia* (1983), whose narrative stops in 1953. For more recent times, Milton Osborne's *Politics and Power in Cambodia* (1973) is helpful, and so is Michael Vickery, *Cambodia, 1975–1982* (1983). Martin Herz's *Short History of Cambodia* (1958), although essentially a cold war document, is valuable for its comments on Cambodian politics in the 1940s and 1950s.

**Laos:** The best introductions to Lao society are Frank M. LeBar and Adrienne Suddard, eds., *Laos: Its People, Its Society, Its Culture* (rev. ed., 1971); Nina S. Adams and Alfred W. McCoy, eds., *Laos: War and Revolution* (1970); the wide-ranging collection of René de Berval, ed., *The Kingdom of Laos* (1959); and *Laos: A Country Study* (1985), prepared by Foreign Area Studies of American University. See also Joel Halpern's two studies, *Economy and Society of Laos* (1964) and *Government, Politics and Social Structure in Laos* (1964).

Paul Levy's concise and helpful *Histoire du Laos* (1974) supersedes Paul le Boulanger's earlier *Histoire du Laos français* (1931). See also Maha Sila Viravong, *History of Laos* (1964).

**Malaysia:** A general introductory account of the peoples of peninsular Malaya is given by B. W. Hodder, *Man in Malaya* (1959). Ooi Jin-Bee, *Land, People and Economy in Malaya* (1963), contains substantial sections on population, as does his *Peninsular Malaysia* (1976). The standard demographic work for the Malay Peninsula is T. E. Smith, *Population Growth in Malaya: An Analysis of Recent Trends* (1952), and for East Malaysia, L. W. Jones's *The Population of Borneo: A Study of the Peoples of Sarawak, Sabah and Brunei* (1966).

There are some useful studies of the different communities of Malaysia. For the Malays, see the iconoclastic work of Sayyid Hussein Alatas, *The Myth of the Lazy Native* (1977), and on a different sort of theme, Shaharuddin b. Maaruf, *Concept of a Hero in Malay Society* (1984). David Banks, *Malay Kinship* (1983), deals with an important aspect of Malay culture; and S. Husin Ali's *The Malays: Their Problems and Future* (1982) is a perceptive contemporary study. Older works, now dated in approach, include R. O. Winstedt, *The Malays: A Cultural History* (5th ed., 1958), and *The Malay Magician* (rev. ed., 1951). Tom Harrisson's *The Malays of Southwest Sarawak* (1970) is the sole work of substance on the Malays of East Malaysia.

For the Chinese in Malaysia, the most useful general account, now rather out of date, is Victor Purcell's *The Chinese in Malaya* (new ed., 1967); an interesting nineteenth-century account is J. D. Vaughan, *The Manners and Customs of the Chinese of the Straits Settlements* (1971). C. S. Wong's *A Cycle of Chinese Festivals* (1967) describes many aspects of contemporary Chinese cultural life.

Descriptive material on the Indian communities of Malaysia includes Kernial Singh Sandhu, *Indians in Malaya, 1786–1957* (1969); S. Arasaratnam, *Indians in Malaysia and Singapore* (1979); and see also Sharon Siddique and N. P. Shotam, *Singapore's Little India: Past, Present and Future* (1982).

The best introductory history of Malaysia is Barbara W. Andaya and Leonard Y. Andaya, *A History of Malaysia* (1982); but see also C. M. Turnbull, *A Short History of Malaysia, Singapore and Brunei* (1980), and, for the modern period, J. M. Gullick, *Malaysia: A Survey* (1969). R. O. Winstedt's narrative, *A History of Malaya* (rev. ed., 1962), was first published in 1935. Histories of most of the individual Malay states were published in the *Journal of the Malayan Branch Royal Asiatic Society* between 1932 and 1949, and may be found in the general index to that journal. Many have since been separately published.

**Indonesia:** Indonesia's past contains scores of distinct cultures and histories such as those of the Hindu Javanese/Muslim Javanese, the Muslim Sundanese, the Protestant Toba Bataks, the Catholics of Flores, the Hindu-Buddhist Balinese, the animist Dayaks, and a wide range of Malayo-Muslim coastal peoples who have more in common historically with the Malays of the peninsula than with any of the foregoing. Two works are particularly useful in surveying this multiplicity of societies: Hildred Geertz's masterly essay, "Indonesian Cultures and Communities," in *Indonesia,* ed. Ruth McVey (1963); and *Villages in Indonesia,* ed. Koentjaraningrat (1967).

There is no complete and fully satisfactory single history of Indonesia or any of its constituent societies. Taken in conjunction, however, seven works in English cover much of the ground. J. D. Legge's *Indonesia* (3rd ed., 1984) is a lively essay on the main themes and interpretations of the history of the vast archipelago which became Indonesia in the twentieth century. W. F. Wertheim's *Indonesian Society in Transition* (rev. ed. 1959) is a study of the social history, organized in topical, rather than chronological, chapters. J. S. Furnivall, *Netherlands India* (1944), surveys the details of administrative and economic history, particularly for the nineteenth and early twentieth centuries, in superb prose. Claire Holt's *Art in Indonesia: Continuities and Change* (1967), the only work on the general cultural history of Indonesia, encompasses both Java and the "Outer Islands," both tradition and modernity, in a remarkable synthesis. Three more recent works are also useful: Ailsa Zainu'ddin, *A Short History of Indonesia* (1968), and the multiauthor works, Haryati Subadio and Carine A. du Marchie Sarvaas, eds., *The Dynamics of Indonesian History* (1978), and Harry Aveling, ed., *The Development of Indonesian Society* (1980). Two books on the history of the Netherlands Indies, which is Indonesian history seen from a different point of view, are still useful: E. S. de Klerck's two-volume political narrative, *History of the Netherlands East Indies* (1938), and J. J. van Klavaren's analytical *The Dutch Colonial System in the East Indies* (1953).

Major reference works include the annual statistical volumes of the colonial *Indisch Verslag* (Indies Report) and its successor in independent Indonesia, the *Statistical Pocketbook of Indonesia.* The classic large-format *Atlas van Tropisch Nederland (Atlas of the Tropical Netherlands),* provides copious social, cultural, and economic information in its many broad and detailed maps. All the above have full English subtitles. The multivolume *Encyclopedië van Nederlands Indië* (1917–1932) is in Dutch.

**The Philippines:** A good introduction to the Philippines is in the Foreign Area Studies Handbook, *Philippines, A Country Guide* (3rd ed., 1983). The Center for Southeast Asian Studies at Northern Illinois University has been surveying "the state of the art" for each discipline of Philippine studies. Publications include Frederick Wernstedt et al., *Philippine Studies: Geography, Archaeology, Psychology, and Literature—Present Knowledge and Research Trends* (1974); Donn V. Hart, ed., *Philippine Studies: History, Sociology, Mass Media, and Bibliography* (1978); and Kip Machado, Richard Hooley, and Lawrence Reid, *Philippine Studies: Political Science, Economics, Linguistics* (1981). A good introduction to the geography and people is F. L. Wernstedt and J. E. Spencer, *The Philippine Island World: A Physical, Cultural, and Regional Geography* (1978). See also *Filipino Tradition and Acculturation: Reports on Changing Societies* (1983), and the anthology of primary sources and scholarly articles with an emphasis on Philippine culture prepared by Cynthia N. Lumbera and Teresita G. Maceda, *Rediscovery* (1982). Alfred W. McCoy and E. C. de Jesus have collected an important sample of outstanding scholarly articles on various aspects of culture and society in *Philippine Social History* (1982). William Henry Scott has written *Cracks in the Parchment Curtain and Other Essays in Philippine History* (1982). Damiana L. Eugenio has compiled *Philippine Folk Literature: An Anthology* (1981).

There are many general histories of the Philippines varying from mediocre to appalling. One of the best is by the prolific, staunchly nationalist Teodoro A. Agoncillo, *History of the Filipino People* (1977). See also the ten-volume encyclopedia, *Filipino Heritage* (1977–1979). The late and great Jesuit, Horacio de la Costa, prepared a collection of very useful sources in Philippine history entitled *Readings in Philippine History* (1965). The most important source for English-language readers on the Spanish era is the fifty-five volumes of annotated documents prepared by E. H. Blair and J. A. Robertson, *The Philippine Islands, 1493–1898* (1903). See also Gerald H. Anderson, ed., *Studies in Philippine Church History* (1969). E. A. Manuel's *Dictionary of Philippine Biography* (1955) is a very useful biographical reference.

## PART ONE: THE EIGHTEENTH-CENTURY WORLD

There is very little material explicitly on Southeast Asian societies in the eighteenth century. The historian, therefore, is dependent in large part on studies of nineteenth- and twentieth-century Southeast Asian societies and must use great care when drawing conclusions for the eighteenth century from them.

### Chapter 1: The Peasant World

**Peasants:** Perhaps the best general work on peasant society is Eric Wolf's *Peasants* (1966); but see also Teodore Shanin, ed., *Peasants and Peasant Societies* (1971). Both James C. Scott, *The Moral Economy of the Peasant* (1976), and Samuel L. Popkin, *The Rational Peasant: The Political Economy of Rural Society in Vietnam* (1979), analyze precolonial villages, although they are not exclusively concerned with them. A stimulating treatment is Lucien M. Hanks, *Rice and Man: Agricultural Ecology in Southeast Asia* (1972), which though based on research in Thailand is of more general interest. On mainland communities in general, see also Charles F. Keyes, *The Golden Peninsula*, already cited.

**Burma:** For village life in Burma, good introductions are to be found in Manning Nash, *The Golden Road to Modernity: Village Life in Contemporary Burma* (1965); David E. Pfanner, "Rice and Religion in a Burmese Village" (Ph.D. diss., Cornell Univ., 1962); Sir James George Scott (Shway Yoe), *The Burman: His Life and Notions* (1882, repr. 1963); and Mi Mi Khaing, *Burmese Family* (1946, repr. 1962). See also J. A. Mills, "Burmese Peasant Response to British Provincial Rule 1852–1855," in D. B. Miller, ed., *Peasants and Politics* (1978), 77–104. The works by Frank N. Trager and William J. Koenig, eds., *Burmese Sit-tans 1764–1826: Records of Rural Life and Administration* (1979), and Mya Sein,

*Administration in Burma: Sir Charles Crosthwaite and the Consolidation of Burma* (1938; repr. 1973), are especially good at noting first the structure of precolonial society and then the efforts of colonial administration to change it.

**Thailand:** It is hard to imagine a better treatment of traditional peasant life in Thailand than *Phya* Anuman Rajadhon's "The Life of the Farmer," in his *Life and Ritual in Old Siam,* trans. William J. Gedney (1961). A fine historical treatment is Lauriston Sharp and Lucien M. Hanks, Jr., *Bang Chan: Social History of a Rural Community in Thailand* (1978). Lucien M. Hanks, Jr., has also written an important article entitled "Merit and Power in the Thai Social Order," *American Anthropologist* 64 (1962): 1247–1261. Herbert Phillips' *Thai Peasant Personality* (1965) also merits attention.

**Vietnam:** The classic English-language study of the Vietnamese village, Gerald C. Hickey, *Village in Vietnam* (1964), deals with southern village life of the post-1954 period but contains themes of historical importance. Charles F. Keyes, *The Golden Peninsula: Culture and Adaptation in Mainland Southeast Asia* (1977), 188–192, has a brief, incisive account of traditional Vietnamese village life. Pierre Gourou's *Les paysans du delta Tonkinois* (1936), and its English translation by Richard R. Miller, *The Peasants of the Tonkin Delta* (1955), is a fascinating pioneering French study of the lives of northern peasants. Also on northern villages, see Paul Ory, *La commune annamite au Tonkin* (1894), and Vu Van Hien, *La propriété communale au Tonkin* (1939). Paul Kresser, *La commune annamite en Cochinchine* (1935), describes traditional villages of the south.

**Cambodia:** Jean Delvert's *Le paysan Cambodgien* (1961) is a thorough and interesting study, covering all aspects of Cambodian rural life. It complements Henri Monod's more impressionistic *Le Cambodgien* (1931)). Guy Porée and Eveline Maspero's *Moeurs et coutumes des Cambodgiens* (1938) is a good general work, as is Solange Thierry's *Les Khmers* (1962). See also May Ebihara, "Svay: A Khmer Village in Cambodia" (Ph.D. diss., Columbia Univ., 1968). On housing in rural Cambodia, see Eveline Porée-Maspero, "Kron Pali," *Anthropos* 56 (1961): 179–251. On Cambodian village organization, see May Ebihara's contribution to Frank LeBar, Gerald Hickey, and John Musgrave, *Ethnic Groups of Mainland Southeast Asia* (1964). See also Ben Kiernan and Chantou Boua, eds., *Peasants and Politics in Kampuchea, 1942–1981* (1982), a useful anthology focused on recent historical events.

**Laos:** For Lao peasants and village life, see George Condominas, "The Lao," in Nina Adams and Alfred W. McCoy, eds., *Laos: War and Revolution* (1970), 9–28; and Joel M. Halpern, *Aspects of Village Life and Cultural Change in Laos* (1958).

**Malaysia:** There have been a number of excellent studies of contemporary Malay peasant society by social anthropologists, among them Rosemary Firth, *Housekeeping Among Malay Peasants* (1943, repr. 1966); Michael G. Swift, *Malay Peasant Society in Jelebu* (1965); and S. Husin Ali, *Malay Peasant Society and Leadership* (1975). G. E. Shaw, "Rice Planting," in R. J. Wilkinson, ed., *Papers on Malay Subjects: Malay Industries,* vol. 3 (1911), gives some account of traditional rice agriculture on the peninsula. Patterns of land ownership in the west-coast Malay states are examined in W. E. Maxwell, "The Law and Customs of the Malays with Reference to the Tenure of Land," *Journal of the Straits Branch Royal Asiatic Society* 13 ( June, 1884): 75–220. Although R. N. Hilton's article, "The Basic Malay House," *Journal of the Malayan Branch Royal Asiatic Society* 29, 3 (1956): 134–155, is of recent date, his detailed discussion of house types refers to many patterns of construction that were common in the eighteenth century.

**Indonesia—Java:** Clifford Geertz has provided an excellent general exposition of the contrast between wet-rice and swidden society in his book *Agricultural Involution* (1963). Another useful general study is Koentjaraningrat, ed., *Villages* *in Indonesia* (1967). The most comprehensive anthropological study of Javanese peasant life is found in the published works of a team that investigated the east-central Javanese district of "Modjokuto" in the early 1950s. These include *The Religion of Java* (1960) and the poignant essay "Ritual and Social Change: A Javanese Example," *American Anthropologist* 59, 1 (1957): 32–54, by Clifford Geertz; *The Javanese Family* (1961), by Hildred Geertz; Robert Jay's *Religion and Politics in Rural Central Java* (1963) and *Javanese Villagers: Social Relations in Rural Modjokuto* (1969); and Alice Dewey's *Peasant Marketing in Java* (1962). The articles in B. Herring, ed., *Indonesian Women: Past and Present* (1977), cover a good deal of time and territory.

**Indonesia—Outside Java:** Among the state/peasant societies in "Outer Indonesia," Bali is the most thoroughly covered in the literature. Chapter 3 in Clifford Geertz, *Negara: The Theatre State in Nineteenth Century Bali* (1980), provides an excellent short description of traditional agriculture, irrigation, and politics in Balinese village life. The same author, in his *The Interpretation of Cultures* (1973), surveys the remarkable complexities of "Person, Time, and Conduct in Bali." Jane Belo, ed., *Traditional Balinese Culture* (1970), is a useful introduction to the prodigious artistic energies of the Balinese—above all the peasant Balinese.

**The Philippines:** There is an extensive literature on what has been called "Christian lowland village life" in the Philippines. See, for example, F. Landa Jocano, *The Ilocanos: An Ethnography of Family and Community Life in the Ilocos Region* (1982); Brian Fegan, "Folk-Capitalism: Economic Strategies of Peasants in a Philippines Wet-Rice Village" (Ph.D. diss., Yale Univ., 1979); and Marshall S. McLennan, *The Central Luzon Plain: Land and Society on the Inland Frontier* (1980). To get a sense of the traditional *barrio*, see Mary R. Hollnsteiner's perceptive *The Dynamics of Power in a Philippine Municipality* (1963). See also Richard W. Lieban's *Cebuano Sorcery: Malign Magic in the Philippines* (1967); Ethel Nurge's *Life in a Leyte Village* (1965); and Akira Takahashi's *Land and Peasants in Central Luzon: Socioeconomic Structure of a Bulacan Village* (1969).

Since the mid-1960s there has been a fascinating debate attempting to define Philippine social values. Among the most important publications are *Four Readings on Philippine Values*, ed. Frank Lynch (1964), and Donn V. Hart, *Compadrinazgo, Ritual Kinship in the Philippines* (1977). See also the articles by Fred Eggan and George Guthrie in *Six Perspectives on the Philippines* (1968). Emma Porio, Frank Lynch, and Mary Hollnsteiner are the authors of a report submitted to the Philippine Social Science Council by the Institute of Philippine Culture, *The Filipino Family, Community, and Nation: The Same Yesterday, Today, and Tomorrow* (1975).

The principal minority group of the Philippines, the Muslims, have also received substantial attention over the past two decades. A good introduction is Peter G. Gowing's *Muslim Filipinos: Heritage and Horizon* (1979). F. Landa Jocano edited *Filipino Muslims: Their Social Institutions and Cultural Achievements* (1983). See also Samuel K. Tan, *Selected Essays on the Filipino Muslims* (1982); Michael O. Mastura, *Muslim Filipino Experience: A Collection of Essays* (1984); Ruth Moore, "Women and Warriors Defending Islam in the Southern Philippines" (Ph.D. diss., Univ. of California, San Diego, 1981); Kenneth E. Bauzon, "Islamic Nationalism in the Philippines: Reflections in Socio-Political Analysis" (Ph.D. diss., Duke Univ., 1981); and Antonio Martel de Goyangos, *The Island of Mindanao* (1977). See also Thomas M. Kiefer's case study, *The Tausug: Violence and Law in a Philippine Muslim Society* (1972), and Cesar Adib Majul, *Muslims in the Philippines* (1973).

**Fishermen:** The most instructive works about peasant fishermen describe Malay coastal fishermen, concerning whom one of the classics of social anthropology has been written, Raymond Firth's *Malay Fishermen: Their Peasant Economy* (rev. ed., 1966). Thomas M. Fraser, *Rusembilan: A Malay Fishing Village in Southern Thailand* (1960), is more generally ethnographic.

**Slavery and Bondage:** A recent and comprehensive work on slaves and bondsmen is Anthony Reid, ed., *Slavery, Bondage and Dependency in Southeast Asia* (1983), the articles in which summarize the current state of knowledge. Each article includes extensive bibliographical references.

## Chapter 2: Non-State Peoples

**General:** A good introduction to non-state societies and their life is Robbins Burling's *Hill Farms and Paddy Fields* (1965). J. E. Spencer's *Shifting Cultivation in Southeastern Asia* (1966) is an excellent analysis of swidden agriculture and is complemented by H. C. Conklin, "The Study of Shifting Cultivation," *Current Anthropology* 2 (1961): 27–61, which contains a good bibliography. A fine short analysis of swidden ecology may be found in Clifford Geertz, *Agricultural Involution* (1963), 16–28. The best introductions to the study of individual groups are Peter Kunstadter, ed., *Southeast Asian Tribes, Minorities, and Nations* (2 vols., 1967), and Frank LeBar, Gerald Hickey, and John Musgrave, *Ethnic Groups of Mainland Southeast Asia* (1964).

**Burma:** Together with his stimulating essay, "The Frontiers of 'Burma,'" in *Comparative Studies in Society and History* 3, 1 (Oct. 1960): 49–68, E. R. Leach's *Political Systems of Highland Burma* (rev. ed., 1965) is the best analysis of the upland peoples of Burma. On contacts between upland and lowland peoples, the best documentation for Burma, as far as the eighteenth and nineteenth centuries are concerned, is to be found in *Gazetteer of Upper Burma and the Shan States,* edited by J. G. Scott and J. P. Hardiman (5 vols., 1902–1905).

**Thailand:** Surveys of upland groups in Thailand include Gordon Young, *The Hill Tribes of Northern Thailand* (2nd ed., 1962); Joanne L. Schrock et al., *Minority Groups in Thailand* (1970); and John McKinnon and Wanat Bhruksasri, eds., *Highlanders of Thailand* (1983). The study of highlanders is considered in Charles F. Keyes, "Ethnography and Anthropological Interpretation in the Study of Thailand," in Eliezer B. Ayal, ed., *The Study of Thailand* (1978), 1–60.

**Indochina:** For the histories and cultures of the highland peoples of Indochina, the paramount work in English-language scholarship now is Gerald C. Hickey, *Sons of the Mountains: Ethnohistory of the Vietnamese Central Highlands to 1954* (1982), and its companion volume, *Fire in the Forest: Ethnohistory of the Vietnamese Central Highlands, 1954–1976* (1982). On the Hmong people, see William R. Geddes, *Migrants of the Mountains: The Cultural Ecology of the Blue Miao* (1976); Jacques LeMoine, *Un village Hmong Vert du haut Laos* (1972); and F. M. Savina, *Histoire des Miao* (1930). Among the best studies of individual groups are those of the Mnong Gar of southern Vietnam by Georges Condominas, *We Have Eaten the Forest,* trans. Adrienne Foulke (1977), and K. G. Izikowitz's study of a Laotian group, *Lamet: Hill Peasants in French Indo-China* (1951). See also R. Baradat, *Les Samre ou Pear* (1941); J. Boulbet, *Pays des Maa'* (1967); and Georges Condominas, *L'exotique est quotidien* (1967).

**Malaysia:** An early standard work on the aboriginal peoples of the Malay Peninsula is W. W. Skeat and C. O. Blagden, *Pagan Races of the Malay Peninsula* (1906, repr. 1967). The anthropologist I. H. N. Evans, in addition to his study of one particular group in the peninsula, *The Negritos of Malaya* (1937), published also two useful collections of papers, *Studies in Religion, Folk-Lore and Custom in British North Borneo and the Malay Peninsula* (1923) and *Papers on the Ethnography and Archeology of the Malay Peninsula* (1927). An excellent discussion of the historical relationship between the inland, aboriginal peoples of the peninsula and the coastal Malays may be found in F. L. Dunn, *Rain Forest Collectors and*

*Traders: A Study of Resource Utilization in Modern and Ancient Malaya* (1975); for the aborigines today, see Iskandar Carey, *Orang Asli: The Aboriginal Tribes of Peninsular Malaysia* (1976).

Together, Benedict Sandin, *The Sea Dayaks of Borneo before White Rajah Rule* (1968), based on oral tradition, and J. D. Freeman, *Iban Agriculture: A Report on the Shifting Cultivation of Hill Rice by the Iban of Sarawak* (1955), give a good systematic description of the Iban swidden-cultivating society. For other descriptions of tribal life in Borneo, see Henry Ling Roth, *The Natives of Sarawak and British North Borneo* (1896, repr. 1968); C. Hose and W. McDougall, *The Pagan Tribes of Borneo* (1912); and W. R. Geddes, *The Land Dayaks of Sarawak* (1954). Geddes has also published a more popular account of Dayak life entitled *Nine Dayak Nights* (1957). A useful and detailed account of the nomadic *orang laut* of the Malayan coast, the only one of its kind, has been published by David E. Sopher, *The Sea Nomads: A Study Based on the Literature of the Maritime Boat People of Southeast Asia* (1965).

**Indonesia:** Among the medium-sized wet-rice growing non-state societies so characteristic of Indonesia are the Minangkabau of west-coast Sumatra, the various subgroups of the Bataks in north-central Sumatra, and the Toraja in central Sulawesi. Useful introductions to the Minangkabau, well known for their matrilineal kinship system and long-standing tension between Islam and their indigenous custom, can be found in Taufik Abdullah, "Adat and Islam: An Examination of Conflict in Minangkabau," *Indonesia* 2 (1966): 1–24; B. J. O. Schrieke's classic "West Coast Report" of 1927, translated partly in Schrieke, *Indonesian Sociological Studies,* Part I (1955), and partly in Harry Benda and Ruth McVey, eds., *The Communist Uprisings of 1926–7* (1960); and in Elizabeth Graves, *The Minangkabau Response to Dutch Colonial Rule in the 19th Century* (1981). For the Toba branch of the Batak, see J. G. Vergouwan, *The Social Organization and Customary Law of the Toba-Batak of North Sumatra* (1964). The best history of the Toraja is Terance Bigalke, "A Social History of 'Tana Toraja' 1870–1965" (Ph.D. diss., Univ. of Wisconsin, 1981).

Since the 1960s, anthropologists have produced a copious literature on the innumerable small and mostly nonliterate ethnic groups of eastern Indonesia as well as Borneo, concentrating mainly on ecological adaptations, beliefs, and kinship. A representative selection of such studies may be found in James Fox, ed., *The Flow of Life: Essays on Eastern Indonesia* (1980). Fox's own *Harvest of the Palm: Ecological Change in East Indonesia* (1977), one of the few dissertations in this field to have been published yet, explores the remarkable reliance of the people on the small island of Roti on palm sugar as their basic foodstuff. Alfred Hudson's "The Padju Epat Ma'anjan Dayak in Historical Perspective," *Indonesia* 4 (1967): 8–43, is particularly useful in exploring the historical relationship between this animist group on Borneo and the nearby Muslim state of Banjarmasin.

**The Philippines:** Among the best studies of upland peoples in the Philippines are R. C. Ileto, *Magindanao, 1860–1888* (1971); William H. Scott, *The Discovery of the Igorots: Spanish Contacts with the Pagans of Northern Luzon* (1974); Michelle Z. Rosaldo, *Knowledge and Passion: Ilongot Notions of Self and Social Life* (1980); Renaldo Rosaldo, *Ilongot Headhunting: A Study in Society and History* (1980); and Stuart Schlegel, *Tiruray Justice: Traditional Tiruray Law and Morality* (1970) and *Tiruray Subsistence: From Shifting Cultivation to Plow Agriculture* (1979). See also Karl L. Hutterer and William K. Macdonald, eds., *Houses Built on Scattered Poles: Prehistory and Ecology in Negros Oriental, Philippines* (1982); Felix M. Keesing, *Taming Philippine Headhunters: A Study of Government and Cultural Change in Northern Luzon* (1984); Yasushi Kikuchi, *Mindoro Highlanders: The Life of the Swidden Agriculturalists* (1984); and Violeta Lopez-Gonzaga, *Peasants in the Hills:*

*A Study of the Dynamics of Social Change Among the Buhid Swidden Cultivators in the Philippines* (1983). Some of the best essays on the subject appear in B. Babcock, ed., *The Reversible World* (1978).

## Chapter 3: Authority and Village Society
(See bibliography for Chapter 1)

## Chapter 4: Provincial Powers
(See bibliographies for Chapters 7–11)

## Chapter 5: Religious Life and Leadership

MAHAYANA BUDDHISM: In Western languages, perhaps the most useful introduction to Vietnamese Buddhism is Mai Tho Truyen, "Le Bouddhisme au Viet-Nam," published independently and in the special issue "Presence du Bouddhisme," of *France-Asie* 16 (1959). Thich Nhat Hanh, *Vietnam: Lotus in a Sea of Fire* (1967), contains a very brief summary of Vietnamese Buddhism's history. For a discussion of the political potentialities of Buddhism in Vietnam, and methods of court control, see Alexander Woodside, "Vietnamese Buddhism, the Vietnamese Court and China in the 1800's," in Edgar Wickberg, ed., *Historical Interaction of China and Vietnam: Institutional and Cultural Themes* (1969), 11–24.

THERAVADA BUDDHISM: On the region in general, see Robert Lester, *Theravada Buddhism in Southeast Asia* (1973).

**Burma:** Burmese Buddhism is particularly well-studied in the works of E. Michael Mendelson, especially his *Sangha and State in Burma: A Study of Monastic Sectarianism and Leadership* (1975). Donald Eugene Smith, *Religion and Politics in Burma* (1965), examines the changing political relationship between the Sangha and the state during and after the colonial period. A more sweeping and debatable thesis about the role of Buddhism in Burma's history is offered by E. Sarkisyanz in his *Buddhist Backgrounds of the Burmese Revolution* (1965). The role of religion in precolonial society was first described fully in the West by Father Vincentius Sangermano, *Description of the Burmese Empire* (5th ed., 1966), which is understandably unsympathetic. More recently the relationship between merit-making, state finances, and the place of the monkhood in Burmese society has been debated by Michael Aung-Thwin, "The Role of *Sasana* Reform in Burmese History: Economic Dimensions of a Religious Purification," *Journal of Asian Studies* [ *JAS* ] 38 (1979): 671–688, and Victor B. Lieberman, "The Political Significance of Religious Wealth in Burmese History: Some Further Thoughts," *JAS* 39 (1980): 753–769, two enjoyable essays which must be read together. Melford Spiro provides one anthropologist's view of religion in Burmese life in *Buddhism and Society: A Great Tradition and Its Burmese Vicissitudes* (1972).

**Thailand:** On popular, village Buddhism see *Phya* Anuman Rajadhon, "Popular Buddhism in Thailand," in his *Life and Ritual in Old Siam*, trans. William J. Gedney (1961). Kenneth Wells, *Thai Buddhism: Its Rites and Activities* (1960) is outdated but still clear and useful. On an analytical level, one is better served by A. Thomas Kirsch, "Complexity in the Thai Religious System," *Journal of Asian Studies* 36, 2 (Feb. 1977): 241–266; and S. J. Tambiah, *World Conqueror and World Renouncer: A Study of Buddhism and Polity in Thailand Against a Historical Background* (1976). Craig J. Reynolds, "The Buddhist Monkhood in Nineteenth Century Thailand" (Ph.D. diss., Cornell Univ., 1972) has no equal. Yoneo Ishii, *Sangha, State and Society: Thai Buddhism in History,* trans. Peter Hawkes (1986) is well-informed and wise. Simon de la Loubère, *A New Historical Relation of the Kingdom of Siam* (1693, repr. 1969), includes a very early sympathetic treatment of Siamese Buddhism.

**Cambodia:** Adhémard Leclère's *Le Bouddhisme au Cambodge* (1899) is still a useful source. See also May Ebihara's perceptive contribution to Manning Nash et al., *Anthropological Studies in Theravada Buddhism* (1966). François Bizot, *Le figuier à cinq branches* (1976), and his *Le don de soi-même* (1980), break new ground.

**Laos:** Perhaps the best introduction to Buddhism in prerevolutionary Laos is the special issue of the *Bulletin des amis du royaume Lao,* no. 9 (1973), entitled *Aspects du Bouddhisme Lao.* Students might also consult G. Condominas, "Notes sur le bouddhisme populaire en milieu rurale lao," *Archives de sociologie des religions* 25, 6 (1968).

ISLAM: A historical introduction to Islam in Southeast Asia is provided in the appropriate chapters of *The Cambridge History of Islam* (1970), by H. J. de Graaf, William R. Roff, and Harry J. Benda. *Islam in South-East Asia,* ed. M. B. Hooker (1983), contains six useful survey articles. Clifford Geertz, *The Religion of Java* (1960) is an ambitious study of the "variants" of Islamic belief and practice in Java. See also the same author's synoptic *Islam Observed: Religious Development in Morocco and Indonesia* (1968); but compare William R. Roff, "Islam Obscured? Some Reflections on Studies of Islam and Society in Southeast Asia," *Archipel* 29 (1985): 7–34. M. B. Hooker, *Islamic Law in South-East Asia* (1984) is a reference work focusing mainly on positive law and the colonial period. On the early period of Islamization in Southeast Asia, see A. H. Johns, "Islam in Southeast Asia: Reflections and New Directions," *Indonesia* 19 (1975): 33–55, and "From Coastal Settlement to Islamic School and City: Islamization in Sumatra, the Malay Peninsula, and Java," *Hamdard Islamicus* (Karachi) 4, 4 (1981): 3–28; and M. C. Ricklefs, "Six Centuries of Islamization in Java," in Nehemia Levtzion, ed., *Conversion to Islam* (1979), 100–128. An important article on the pilgrimage to Mecca, as it affected Indonesians and Malays, is Jacob Vredenbregt's "The Hadj: Some of its Features and Functions in Indonesia," *Bijdragen tot de Taal-, Land- en Volkenkunde* 118 (1962): 91–154. Most of the writings of the great Dutch Islamicist, C. Snouck Hurgronje, have not been translated into English, but his classic description of Indonesian and Malay sojourners in *Mekka in the Latter Part of the 19th Century* (1931) is of great importance for historical studies.

A number of useful works deal with particular parts of the region, though some have more historical perspective than others. C. Snouck Hurgronje's *The Achehnese* (2 vols., 1906) is a classic work on one of the area's most staunchly Muslim peoples; and for Aceh, see also James Siegel, *The Rope of God* (1969). On Minangkabau, in Sumatra, see Christine Dobbin, *Islamic Revivalism in a Changing Peasant Economy: Central Sumatra, 1784–1847* (1983), with which it is useful to compare Taufik Abdullah, "Adat and Islam: An Examination of Conflict in Minangkabau," *Indonesia* 2 (1966): 1–24. The small number of works that deal historically with Islam in Malaya include R. J. Wilkinson, *Malay Beliefs* (1906, repr. in the *Journal of the Malayan Branch Royal Asiatic Society* 30, 4 [1957]: 1–40); R. J. Wilkinson and W. J. Rigby, *Malay Law,* in R. J. Wilkinson, ed., *Papers on Malay Subjects* (1908); Naguib al Attas, *Some Aspects of Sufism as Understood and Practised Among the Malays* (1963); and the excellent study by Clive S. Kessler, *Islam and Politics in a Malay State: Kelantan, 1838–1969* (1978). Among the handful of works on Muslims in the southern Philippines, the following are noteworthy: Najeeb M. Saleeby, *Studies in Moro History, Law and Religion* (1905); Cesar Adib Majul, *Muslims in the Philippines* (2nd ed., 1973); Peter G. Gowing, *Muslim Filipinos: Heritage and Horizon* (1979); and Peter G. Gowing and Robert D. McAmis, eds., *The Muslim Filipinos: Their History, Society and Contemporary Problems* (1974). Moshe Yegar's *The Muslims of Burma: A Study of a Minority Group* (1972) is the only monographic study for that country. For elsewhere on the mainland, see Raymond Scupin, "Islam in Thailand Before the Bangkok

Period," *Journal of the Siam Society* 68 (1980): 55–72, and Pierre-Yves Manguin, "The Introduction of Islam into Champa," *Journal of the Malaysian Branch, Royal Asiatic Society* 58, 1 (1985): 1–28.

CHRISTIANITY: Much of the extensive literature about the Roman Catholic Church in the Philippines has been written by clerics past and present. An excellent place to begin is *Readings in Philippine Church History*, ed. John N. Schumacher (1979). Among the extensive works of Horacio de la Costa, see his posthumous *Church and State: The Philippine Experience* (1976). Pablo Fernandez, *History of the Church in the Philippines (1521–1898)* (1979), is less critical and less useful. Also useful is Gerald H. Anderson, ed., *Philippine Church History* (1969). Esperanza B. Gatbonton, *A Heritage of Saints: Colonial Santos in the Philippines* (1979), and Fernando Zobel de Ayala, *Philippine Religious Imagery* (1963), both present the artistic achievement of a religious tradition which used Chinese craftsmen to carve many religious objects. One of the most fascinating subjects is the interaction between the high tradition of global Catholicism and the folk traditions of traditional peasant life. See, for example, F. Landa Jocano, *Folk Christianity: A Preliminary Study of Conversion and Patterning of Christian Experience in the Philippines* (1981). Perhaps the most important recent study on the relationship of nationalism and Christianity is Reynaldo C. Ileto, *Pasyon and Revolution* (1979).

Concerning Catholicism in Indochina, volume one of Georges Taboulet's two-volume *La geste française en Indochine: histoire par les textes de la France en Indochine des origines à 1914* (1955–1956) is a compendium of important documents, accompanied by analysis, revealing the evolution of missionary-sponsored Catholicism from the seventeenth century in Vietnam. Adrien Launay, *Histoire de la Mission de Siam, 1662–1881* (2 vols., 1920), remains the definitive study on the Catholic Church in Thailand.

HINDU-BUDDHISM: The Hindu-Buddhism of Bali has been extensively studied and is best approached through *Bali: Studies in Life, Thought and Ritual* (1960) and C. Hooykas, *Religion in Bali* (1973). Robert W. Hefner's *Hindu Javanese: Tengger Tradition and Islam* (1986) surveys a variant group in East Java still committed to the Hinduism of older Java.

FOLK RELIGION: In the area of folk religion, the literature is extensive. For Burma, Melford E. Spiro's *Burmese Supernaturalism* (1967) is the best. Eveline Porée-Maspero's *Les rites agraires des Cambodgiens* (3 vols., 1962–1969) is a good study of folk religion in Cambodia. See also Charles Archaimbault, *Structures religieuses lao (rites et mythes)* (1973), a collection of perceptive articles. W. W. Skeat's *Malay Magic* (1900, repr. 1967) remains a classic account of Malay folklore and popular religion. Folk religion in Java is analyzed by Clifford Geertz in *The Religion of Java* (1960). Leopold Cadière's *Croyances et pratiques religieuses des vietnamiens* (1959) includes a description of family ancestor worship in Vietnam. Richard W. Lieban's *Cebuano Sorcery: Malign Magic in the Philippines* (1967) is a vivid analysis of popular religion in lowland Philippines.

## Chapter 6: Traders and Markets

**Internal Trade:** Late but extremely useful references to trade between lowlands and highlands in Burma are contained in Henry Yule's *A Narrative of the Mission to the Court of Ava in 1855* (1857, repr. 1968). The most extensive works on the premodern Siamese economy are Constance M. Wilson, "State and Society in the Reign of Mongkut, 1851–1868" (Ph.D. diss., Cornell Univ., 1971); Lysa Hong, *Thailand in the Nineteenth Century: Evolution of the Economy and Society* (1984); and see also C. M. Wilson's important *Thailand: A Handbook of Historical Statistics* (1983).

The best short analysis of the Philippine economic structure during the Spanish era is Benito Legarda y Fernandez, "The Philippine Economy under Spanish Rule," *Solidarity* 2, 10 (Nov.–Dec. 1967): 1–21. See also Maria Lourdes Diaz-Trechuelo, "Philippine Economic Development Plans, 1746–1779," *Philippine Studies* 12 (Apr. 1964): 203–231; and "Eighteenth Century Philippine Economy: Commerce," *Philippine Studies* 14 (Apr. 1966): 252–279, and her other publications. The most carefully researched work to date is Edelberto C. de Jesus, *The Tobacco Monopoly in the Philippines: Bureaucratic Enterprise and Social Change, 1766–1880* (1980). Finally, there are many translations of contemporary accounts; see, for example, Jean Mallat, *The Philippines: History, Geography, Customs, Agriculture, Industry and Commerce of the Spanish Colonies in Oceania,* trans. Pura Santillan-Castrence (1983).

**Trading Networks:** Henry Yule, *A Narrative of the Mission to the Court of Ava in 1855* (1857; repr. 1968) remains a good source on the caravans that plied between Yunnan and Burma in the eighteenth century; the background to which is presented in Ralph Crozier, "Antecedents of the Burma Road in the Nineteenth Century," *Journal of Southeast Asian History* 3, 2 (Sept. 1962): 1–18. Victor Lieberman's *Burmese Administrative Cycles* (1984) also has valuable insights on trade in precolonial Burma and the rest of the region. Note also Kuo Tsung-fei, "A Brief History of the Trade Routes between Burma, Indochina and Yunnan," *T'ien Hsia Monthly* 12, 1 (1941): 9–32. On Siam's trade with China, see Sarasin Viraphol, *Tribute and Profit: The Sino-Siamese Trade, 1652–1853* (1977), which is complemented by Jennifer W. Cushman, "Fields from the Sea: Chinese Junk Trade with Siam during the Late Eighteenth and Early Nineteenth Centuries" (Ph.D. diss., Cornell Univ., 1976). For inland connections, see Ann Maxwell Hill, "Familiar Strangers: The Yunnanese Chinese in Northern Thailand" (Ph.D. diss., Univ. of Illinois, 1982). For the South China Sea network, Yi Yi's unpublished University of London doctoral dissertation on "English Trade in the South China Sea, 1670–1715" (1958) is of considerable interest, although it by no means exhausts the field, particularly on Chinese trade. D. S. Richards, ed., *Islam and the Trade of Asia* (1970), contains several essays important for understanding the long-distance maritime trade of Southeast Asia.

The classic study, *The Manila Galleon,* was written many years ago by William L. Schurz, reissued in paper in 1959, and reprinted as recently as 1985. Schurz wrote with verve and accuracy, and the book is fun to read. For a shorter and more recent treatment of the galleon trade, see Benito Legarda y Fernandez, "Two and a Half Centuries of the Galleon Trade," *Philippine Studies* 3 (1955): 345–372.

A book that is full of information on the Dutch East India Company trade is Kristoff Glamann's *Dutch-Asiatic Trade 1620–1740* (1958). The key work on the trade of the English East India Company is K. N. Chaudhury, *The Trading World of Asia and the English East India Company 1660–1760* (1978). C. N. Parkinson's *Trade in the Eastern Seas, 1793–1813* (1937) is a good, readable survey. W. J. M. Buch's important study of the Dutch trade with Indochina is translated into French as "La Compagnie des Indes Néerlandaise et l'Indochine," *Bulletin de l'École Française d'Extrême-Orient* 36 (1936) and 37 (1937). For British trade, see C. N. Parkinson's compilation, *The Trade Winds: A Study of British Overseas Trade during the French Wars, 1793–1815* (1949). H. P. Clodd, *Malaya's First British Pioneer: The Life of Francis Light* (1948), is a brief account of the founder of Penang; and K. G. Tregonning, *The British in Malaya: The First Forty Years* (1965), also deals extensively with British trading at this time. D. G. E. Hall's *Early English Intercourse with Burma, 1587–1743* (rev. ed., 1968) merits attention, and the broader study of M. A. P. Meilink-Roelofsz, *Asian Trade and European Influence in the Indonesian Archipelago between 1500 and about 1630*

(1962), though referring to an earlier period, certainly is applicable generally to the seventeenth and eighteenth centuries as well. J. A. E. Morley, "The Arabs and the Eastern Trade," *Journal of the Malayan Branch Royal Asiatic Society* 20, 1 (March 1949), although concerned largely with later years, devotes considerable attention to the period before 1800. Recent scholarship has revealed that there was far more trade between the Philippines and the rest of Asia than earlier believed. See, for example, W. E. Cheong's "Anglo-Spanish-Portuguese Clandestine Trade between the Ports of British India and Manila, 1785–1790," *Philippine Historical Review* 1, 1 (1965): 80–94, and Serafin D. Quiason's *English "Country Trade" with the Philippines, 1644–1765* (1966). For a glimpse into the French trade with Manila, see H. de la Costa's "Early French Contact with the Philippines," in *Asia and the Philippines* (1967).

**Overseas Chinese:** A useful overview is C. P. FitzGerald, *The Southern Expansion of the Chinese People* (1972). On the subject of the early history of the overseas Chinese in Vietnam, see Paul Boudet, "La Conquête de la Cochinchine par les Nguyen et le rôle des émigrés Chinois," *Bulletin de l'École Française d'Extrême-Orient* 42 (1942). For Thailand, the first chapter in G. William Skinner's *Chinese Society in Thailand: An Analytical History* (1957) is essential reading. The two volumes edited by Alfonso Felix, Jr. (1966), *The Chinese in the Philippines, 1570–1770* (1966), and *The Chinese in the Philippines, 1770–1898* (1969), are useful introductions to aspects of Chinese life in the past. See also S. S. C. Liao, ed., *Chinese Participation in Philippine Culture and Economy* (1964). Much information on the Chinese in early Batavia (Jakarta) may be gleaned from Johannes T. Vermeulen, "The Chinese in Batavia and the Troubles of 1740," *Journal of the South Seas Society* 9, 1(1953): 1–68.

## Chapter 7: The Buddhist Kings

A good introduction is Robert von Heine-Geldern's *Conceptions of State and Kingship in Southeast Asia* (1956 [first published in *Far Eastern Quarterly* 2 (Nov. 1942): 15–30]), which gives a brief but important account of traditional ideas concerning monarchy and society, principally in the mainland states.

**Ava:** The standard histories, which include analyses of Burma in the eighteenth century, are G. E. Harvey, *History of Burma* (1925, repr. 1967); Arthur P. Phayre, *History of Burma* (1883, repr. 1967); and Htin Aung's idiosyncratic *A History of Burma* (1967). More recent monographs that treat the eighteenth century include Victor Lieberman, *Burmese Administrative Cycles* (1984), and William Koenig, "The Early Kon-baung Polity, 1752–1819: A Study of Politics, Administration and Social Organization in Burma" (Ph.D. diss., Univ. of London, 1978), the flavor of which can be gained from his introduction to Trager and Koenig, eds., *Burmese Sit-tans* (1979). On the Burmese sources, see Tet Htoot, "The Nature of the Burman Chronicles," in D. G. E. Hall, ed., *Historians of South-East Asia* (1961), 50–62. Several of the essays of Michael Aung-Thwin, including "Divinity, Spirit and Human: Conceptions of Classical Burmese Kingship," in Lorraine Gesick, ed., *Centers, Symbols, and Hierarchies: Essays on the Classical State of Southeast Asia* (1983), 45–86, and "Hierarchy and Order in Pre-Colonial Burma," *Journal of Southeast Asian Studies* 15, 2 (Sept. 1984): 224–231, give this literature in a more contemporary understanding.

**Ayudhya:** W. A. R. Wood's *A History of Siam* (1924, repr. 1959) is superseded by David K. Wyatt, *Thailand: A Short History* (1984). H. G. Quaritch Wales has written two helpful studies: *Ancient Siamese Government and Administration* (1934, repr. 1965) and *Siamese State Ceremonies* (1931). The origins of the kingdom are treated in Charnvit Kasetsiri, *The Rise of Ayudhya* (1976). Pertinent information first published in the *Journal of the Siam Society* (1904–present) is made available in the *Selected Articles from the Siam Society Journal* (10 vols., 1954–1959). The best of the contemporary accounts from the seventeenth century are

Simon de la Loubère, *A New Historical Relation of the Kingdom of Siam* (1693, repr. 1969); *The Ship of Sulaiman*, trans. John O'Kane (1972); and E. W. Hutchinson, trans. and ed., *1688 Revolution in Siam: The Memoir of Father de Beze* (1968). Hutchinson also has provided us with the best narrative of that period in his *Adventurers in Siam in the Seventeenth Century* (1940). Relations with the Dutch were important: see George Vinal Smith, *The Dutch in Seventeenth-Century Thailand* (1977). Akin Rabibhadana, *The Organization of Thai Society in the Early Bangkok Period, 1782–1873* (1969), has some extremely important things to say about Thai society and the extent to which political struggles were affected by problems in the control of manpower. The chief Thai sources for the Ayudhya period are, of course, the multiple versions of the royal chronicles, *Phraratchaphongsawadan*, little of which have been translated; but see Jeremias van Vliet, *The Short History of the Kings of Siam* (1975). Classical Thai literature is surveyed by Paul Schweisguth, *Étude sur la littérature siamoise* (1951). The role of provincial towns in premodern Thailand has only just begun to be studied. Some of their chronicles have been translated: *Hikayat Patani: The Story of Patani*, ed. and trans. A. Teeuw and David K. Wyatt (1970); and *Crystal Sands: The Chronicles of Nagara Sri Dharrmaraja*, trans. David K. Wyatt (1975) are of interest.

**Phnom Penh:** Eighteenth-century Cambodia has received little attention from scholars, but students of earlier periods are well served by Mak Phoeun, *Chroniques royales du Cambodge (de 1594 à 1677)* (1981); Adhémard Leclère, *Les codes cambodgiens* (2 vols., 1898); and Saveros Pou, *Ramakerti* (1977). See also B. P. Groslier, *Angkor et le Cambodge au XVIe siècle* (1958); Michael Vickery's contribution to Anthony Reid and David G. Marr, eds., *Perceptions of the Past in Southeast Asia* (1980); and the articles by David P. Chandler and May Ebihara in the September 1984 issue of the *Journal of Southeast Asian Studies*. Popular views of the Cambodian monarchy are discussed in Solange Thierry's "La Personne sacrée du roi dans la littérature populaire cambodgienne," in *Studies in the History of Religions*, vol. 4, *The Sacral Kingship* (1959). See also David P. Chandler's contribution to Lorraine Gesick, ed., *Centers, Symbols, and Hierarchies: Essays on the Classical State of Southeast Asia* (1983), which deals with precolonial kingship. On the role of provincial officials in precolonial Cambodia, see David P. Chandler, *A History of Cambodia* (1983), chap. 6.

**The Lao and Shan World:** Paul le Boulanger, *Histoire du Laos français* (1931); and *Maha* Sila Viravong, *History of Laos* (1964), are general histories of the Mekong Lao. The work of Charles Archaimbault in translating Lao chronicles is extremely important: "L'Histoire de Campasak," *Journal Asiatique* 249 (1961): 519–595, and "Les Annales de l'ancien royaume de S'ieng Khwang," *Bulletin de l'École française d'Extrême-Orient* 53 (1967): 557–673. Two works are especially useful to the study of the middle Mekong region: James B. Pruess, *The That Phanom Chronicle* (1976), and Charles Archaimbault, *Contribution à l'étude d'un cycle de légendes lau* (1980). Chiangmai and northern Thailand are the subject of the third volume of Camille Notton's translations of *Annales du Siam* (1926–1932), which will have to suffice until a more systematic study of the rich vernacular sources is undertaken. Some of these are delightfully exhibited in George Coedès, "Documents sur l'histoire politique et religieuse du Laos occidental," *Bulletin de l'École française d'Extrême-Orient* 25 (1925): 1–202, and *The Nan Chronicle*, ed. David K. Wyatt (1966). Also see Nigel Brailey, "The Origins of the Siamese Forward Movement in Western Laos, 1850–92" (Ph.D. diss., Univ. of London, 1968). The early history of the Shan states generally is known mainly through the *Gazetteer of Upper Burma and the Shan States*, ed. J. G. Scott and J. P. Hardiman (1900–1905); but see also *Sao* Saimong Mangrai, *The Shan States and the British Annexation* (1965), the first chapters of which treat earlier periods, and also the same author's translation, *The Padaeng Chronicle and the Jengtung State Chronicle Translated* (1981).

**Chapter 8: The Vietnamese Emperors**

Keith Weller Taylor's outstanding *The Birth of Vietnam* (1983) is indispensable to an understanding both of early Vietnamese history and of the Vietnamese sense of identity, which is deeply historical. For an excellent analysis of one famous text connected to the Vietnamese national identity, as it was expressed within the medieval Confucian world system, see Stephen O'Harrow, "Nguyen Trai's *Binh Ngo Dai Cao* of 1428: The Development of a Vietnamese National Identity," *Journal of Southeast Asian Studies* 10, 1 (March 1979): 159–174. See also the contributions by John Whitmore and Pham Cao Duong, "The Vietnamese Sense of the Past," in *The Vietnam Forum* (Winter–Spring 1983): 4–16. The literature translated in Huynh Sanh Thong's *The Heritage of Vietnamese Poetry*, already mentioned, is most useful to an understanding of traditional elite political values.

For the more immediate background to eighteenth-century Vietnam, John K. Whitmore, *Vietnam, Ho Quy Ly, and the Ming 1371–1421* (1985), examines the impact of the short-lived Chinese occupation of the Vietnamese kingdom in the fifteenth century. There are articles by Whitmore, D. Haines, A. Woodside, and N. Jamieson on medieval Vietnamese social organization and our conceptualization of it in the September 1984 issue of the *Journal of Southeast Asian Studies*, 296–329. Ta Van Tai, "The Status of Women in Traditional Vietnam: A Comparison of the Code of the Le Dynasty with the Chinese Codes," *Journal of Asian History* 15, 2 (1981): 97–145, studies the limits of Vietnamese elite borrowing from China in the critical realms of legal history and women's rights. Nguyen Ngoc Huy, "On the Process of Codification of the 'National Dynasty's Penal Laws'," *The Vietnam Forum* (Winter–Spring 1983): 34–57, looks at the questions of when and how Vietnam's oldest extant and historically most influential law code was compiled. M. G. Cotter, "Towards a Social History of the Vietnamese Southward Movement," *Journal of Southeast Asian History* 9, 1 (March 1968): 12–24, explores very briefly the expansion of medieval Vietnam.

For the eighteenth century itself, there is an introduction to some but not all of the political and social thought of Vietnam's greatest Confucian philosopher, Le Quy Don, in Alexander Woodside, "Conceptions of Change and of Human Responsibility for Change in Late Traditional Vietnam," in D. K. Wyatt and A. Woodside, eds., *Moral Order and the Question of Change: Essays on Southeast Asian Thought* (1982), 104–150. Nguyen Thanh Nha, *Tableau économique du Vietnam aux XVIIe et XVIIIe siècles* (1970), remains the best social and economic history of Vietnam in this period in a Western language, but the whole subject of the premodern Vietnamese economy has just begun to be investigated. The Tayson rebellion, for Vietnamese the most important eighteenth-century topic of all, awaits Western attention; however, see Truong Buu Lam, "Intervention versus Tribute in Sino-Vietnamese Relations, 1788–1790," in John K. Fairbank, ed., *The Chinese World Order: Traditional China's Foreign Relations* (1968), 165–179.

**Chapter 9: The Malay Sultans**

J. M. Gullick's study of the *Indigenous Political Systems of Western Malaya* (1958) examines peninsular Malay society in the mid-nineteenth century, but it is relevant to the eighteenth century as well. An important revisionary treatment of the subject is A. C. Milner, *Kerajaan: Malay Political Culture on the Eve of Colonial Rule* (1982); and see also the same author's "Islam and Malay Kingship," *Journal of the Royal Asiatic Society* (1981), 46–70. For a more Marxist (and controversial) account, see Patrick Sullivan, *Social Relations of Dependence in a Malay State: Nineteenth Century Perak* (1982). The several articles on Malay states in Anthony Reid and Lance Castles, eds., *Pre-Colonial State Systems in Southeast Asia: The Malay Peninsula, Sumatra, Bali-Lombok, South Celebes* (1975), offer useful comparative perspectives. For Brunei, see D. E. Brown, "Brunei: The Structure and History of a Borneo Malay Sultanate," *Brunei Museum Journal* 2, 2 (1970).

## Chapter 10: The Javanese Kings

Theodore Pigeaud's *Java in the Fourteenth Century: A Study in Cultural History* (5 vols., 1960–1963) is an elegant reconstruction with much that is relevant to later centuries. B. J. O. Schrieke, "Ruler and Realm in Early Java," published as *Indonesian Sociological Studies*, Part II (1957), is a pioneering effort to elucidate the ill-documented structure of Javanese political life using mainly seventeenth-century Dutch sources. Soemarsaid Moertono used hitherto untouched Javanese sources in his *State and Statecraft in Old Java: A Study of the Later Mataram Period, Sixteenth to Nineteenth Century* (1968) to comment on Schrieke and further develop the picture. Benedict R. O'G. Anderson's "The Idea of Power in Javanese Culture," in Claire Holt, ed., *Culture and Politics in Indonesia* (1972), is a wide-ranging essay on the patrimonialism of Old Java, as well as some of its more recent manifestations. P. J. Zoetmulder's *Kalangwan: A Survey of Old Javanese Literature* (1974) is the standard work on its subject. Many of the complex questions relating to the Islamization of Java can usefully be approached through G. W. J. Drewes, "New Light on the Coming of Islam to Indonesia?" *Bijdragen tot de Taal-, Land- en Volkenkunde [BKI]* 124 (1968): 433–459; A. H. Johns, "Islam in Southeast Asia: Reflections and New Directions," *Indonesia* 19 (1975): 33–55; and S. O. Robson, "Java at the Crossroads: Aspects of Javanese Cultural History in the Fourteenth and Fifteenth Centuries," *BKI* 137 (1981): 259–292.

For those who do not read Dutch, *Islamic States in Java, 1500–1700: A Summary, Bibliography and Index* (1976), by Theodore Pigeaud and H. J. de Graaf, provides an invaluable, compact guide to de Graaf's life-work in the history of seventeenth-century Javan politics. M. C. Ricklefs' admirable *Jogjakarta Under Sultan Mangkubumi, 1749–1792, A History of the Division of Java* (1974) is the standard work on its subject. *The Social World of Batavia: European and Eurasian in Dutch Asia* (1983), by Jean Gelman Taylor, opens up previously unimagined vistas on the marital and social ways of the elite and not-so-elite of Batavia (now Jakarta) in the seventeenth to nineteenth centuries.

## Chapter 11: The Spanish Governors

Onofre D. Corpuz's *The Bureaucracy in the Philippines* (1957) is still perhaps the best introduction to the power structure of the Spanish colonial administration. Nicholas P. Cushner's *Spain in the Philippines: From Conquest to Revolution* (1970) complements Corpuz's strong focus on administration and political structure with a broader concern. A more speculative analysis can be found in John Leddy Phelan, *The Hispanization of the Philippines: Spanish Aims and Filipino Responses, 1565–1700* (1959). Cushner also has published a more detailed study, *Landed Estates in the Philippines* (1976); on which also see Dennis M. Roth, *The Friar Estates of the Philippines* (1977).

Over the past decades there have been a great many contemporary sources translated or reissued to further complement the source materials in Blair and Robertson (cited above). See, for example, Tomás de Comyn, *State of the Philippines in 1810* (1969), and J. Martinez de Zuñiga, *The Status of the Philippines in 1800* (1973).

## PART TWO: NEW CHALLENGES TO OLD AUTHORITY

### Chapter 12: Burma, 1752–1878

The general works of John F. Cady, *A History of Modern Burma* (1958), G. E. Harvey, *History of Burma*, and Arthur P. Phayre, *History of Burma*, as well as

Frank Trager and William Koenig, eds., *Burmese Sit-tans* (1979), are useful for this period. More detailed studies, especially of British Indian and Burmese relations, are found in H. H. Wilson, *Narrative of the Burmese War in 1824-26 as Originally Compiled from Original Documents* (1852); J. J. Snodgrass, *Narrative of the Burmese War* (1827); W. S. Desai, *History of the British Residency in Burma, 1826-1840* (1939); Dorothy Woodman, *The Making of Burma* (1962); and D. G. E. Hall, *The Dalhousie-Phayre Correspondence, 1852-56* (1932).

For the politics of the Burmese court during this period, see Thaung, "Burmese Kingship in Theory and Practice Under the Reign of King Mindon," *Journal of the Burma Research Society* [*JBRS*] 42, 2 (1959): 171-185; Kyan, "King Mindon's Councillors," *JBRS* 44, 1 (1961): 43-60; Myo Myint, "The Politics of Survival: Burma Under King Mindon, 1853-1878," (Ph.D. diss., Cornell Univ., 1987); Vincentius Sangermano, *Description of the Burmese Empire* (1833; 5th ed., 1966); D. G. E. Hall, ed., *Michael Symes: Journal of his Second Embassy to the Court of Ava in 1802* (1955), which has a long introduction of great use; John Crawfurd, *Journal of an Embassy from the Governor General of India to the Court of Ava in the Year 1826* (1828); and Henry Yule, *A Narrative of the Mission to the Court of Ava in 1855* (1857, repr. 1968). The Burmese sources are discussed by Yi Yi in two articles: "Burmese Historical Sources, 1752-1885," *Journal of Southeast Asian History* 6, 1 (1965): 48-66, and "Additional Burmese Historical Sources (1752-76)," *Guardian* 15, 11 (Nov. 1968): 33-35, and in subsequent numbers. The most complete synthetic study of this period unfortunately is unpublished, William J. Koenig, "The Early Kon-baung Polity, 1752-1819: A Study of Politics, Administration and Social Organization in Burma" (Ph.D. diss., Univ. of London, 1978), although much of the flavor of this work is in the introduction to Trager and Koenig, eds., *Burmese Sit-tans* (1979). Oliver B. Pollack, *Empires in Collision: Anglo-Burmese Relations in the Mid-Nineteenth Century* (1979), is the most recent and perhaps fairest study in English of British-Burmese relations before the final annexation and disbanding of the court.

## Chapter 13: Thailand, 1767-1868

David K. Wyatt, *Thailand: A Short History* (1984), provides a general introduction to the period and may be supplemented by B. J. Terwiel, *A History of Modern Thailand, 1767-1942* (1983), and Prince Chula Chakrabongse, *Lords of Life: The Paternal Monarchy of Bangkok, 1782-1932* (1962). Klaus Wenk, *The Restoration of Thailand Under Rama I, 1782-1809* (1968), is interpretively weak, and might be read in conjunction with David K. Wyatt, "The 'Subtle Revolution' of King Rama I," in *Moral Order and the Question of Change*, ed. D. K. Wyatt and A. Woodside (1982). On Buddhism and religious change, see Craig J. Reynolds, "The Buddhist Monkhood in Nineteenth Century Thailand" (Ph.D. diss., Cornell Univ., 1972) and "Buddhist Cosmography in Thai History," *Journal of Asian Studies* 35 (1975-1976): 203-220; and Yoneo Ishii, *Sangha, State and Society: Thai Buddhism in History* (1986). David K. Wyatt's "Family Politics in Nineteenth-century Thailand," *Journal of Southeast Asian History* 9, 2 (1968): 208-228, casts some light on the politics of the period and is importantly supplemented by Akin Rabibhadana, *The Organization of Thai Society in the Early Bangkok Period, 1782-1873* (1969). Walter F. Vella's *Siam Under Rama III* (1957) is the standard source for the period 1824-1851. The most important modern studies of King Mongkut are Abbot Low Moffat, *Mongkut, the King of Siam* (1961), and Constance M. Wilson, "State and Society in the Reign of Mongkut, 1851-1868: Thailand on the Eve of Modernization" (Ph.D. diss., Cornell Univ., 1971). The treaty of 1855 is discussed by Nicholas Tarling, "The Mission of Sir John Bowring to Siam," *Journal of the Siam Society* 50, 2 (1962): 91-118. Economic and social effects of Siam's opening to the world are explored in Lysa Hong, *Thailand in the Nineteenth Century* (1984), and James C.

Ingram, *Economic Change in Thailand, 1850–1970* (1971); while documents on the subject are translated in two collections by Chatthip Nartsupha and Suthy Prasartset, *The Political Economy of Siam 1851–1910* (1981), and *Socio-Economic Institutions and Cultural Change in Siam, 1851–1910* (1977). The best of the contemporary sources of this period in Western languages are John Crawfurd's *Journal of an Embassy to the Courts of Siam and Cochin China* (1828, repr. 1986); Vajirañana National Library, comp., *The Burney Papers* (5 vols., 1910–1914; repr., 1970); Jean Baptiste Pallegoix, *Description du royaume thai ou Siam* (2 vols., 1854; repr. 1969); and Sir John Bowring, *The Kingdom and People of Siam* (2 vols., 1857; repr. 1969). Two of the standard Thai chronicles for the period are available in translation: Chaophraya Thiphakorawong (Kham Bunnag), *The Dynastic Chronicles, Bangkok Era, The First Reign* (1978), and *The Dynastic Chronicles, Bangkok Era, The Fourth Reign* (5 vols., 1965–1974).

For Laos in this period, see David K. Wyatt, "Siam and Laos, 1767–1827," *Journal of Southeast Asian History* 4, 2 (1963): 13–32; John K. Whitmore, "The Thai-Vietnamese Struggle for Laos in the Nineteenth Century," in Nina S. Adams and Alfred W. McCoy, eds., *Laos: War and Revolution* (1970), 53–66; and Walter F. Vella, *Siam Under Rama III* (1957). Also useful are Paul le Boulanger, *Histoire du Laos française* (1931), and *Maha* Sila Viravong, *History of Laos* (1964).

## Chapter 14: Cambodia, 1779–1863

The most detailed treatment of the period is probably David P. Chandler, "Cambodia before the French: Politics in a Tributary Kingdom, 1794–1848" (Ph.D. diss., Univ. of Michigan, 1973), which draws on Khmer, Thai, Vietnamese, and Western-language sources. See also his *History of Cambodia* (1983), chaps. 6–7. For the eighteenth century, Jean Moura's *Royaume du Cambodge* (2 vols., 1883), and Etienne Aymonier's *Le Cambodge* (3 vols., 1901–1905), are generally more reliable than Adhémard Leclère, *Histoire du Cambodge* (1914), but all draw uncritically on Cambodian chronicle sources, which are laconic for the early nineteenth century.

There is a good chapter on nineteenth-century Cambodia in Walter F. Vella's *Siam Under Rama III* (1957), which synthesizes Thai-language chronicle materials. For French diplomatic efforts in the 1850s, see Charles Meyniard, *Le Second Empire en Indochine* (2 vols., 1891), and the relevant documents in Georges Taboulet's *La geste française en Indochine* (2 vols., 1955). Precolonial society and the imposition of French control is discussed in Chandler, *A History of Cambodia* (1983), chap. 8, which draws on Milton Osborne's pioneering study, *The French Presence in Cochinchina and Cambodia: Rule and Response, 1859–1905* (1969). Osborne's *River Road to China* (1974) captures the spirit of French exploration in nineteenth-century Cambodia, and so does Christopher Pym's translation of Henri Mouhot's *Diary: Travels in the Central Parts of Siam, Cambodia and Laos During the Years 1858–61* (1966).

## Chapter 15: Vietnam, 1802–1867

Alexander Woodside, *Vietnam and the Chinese Model* (1971), considers the politics and organization of the Nguyen state and bureaucracy from 1802 through 1847. The foreign relations which preceded and were important in the consolidation of the nineteenth-century Nguyen dynasty have begun to be studied in a new French work by Pierre-Yves Manguin, *Les Nguyen, Macau et le Portugal: aspects politiques et commerciaux d'une rélation privilégiée en mer de Chine 1773–1802* (1984). P. L. F. Philastre, *Le code annamite* (2 vols., 1909; repr. 1968) translates the new Nguyen dynasty law code. John Crawfurd, *Journal of an Embassy to the Courts of Siam and Cochin China* (1828, repr. 1986) is an interesting English-language eyewitness account of Vietnam in the early 1800s.

Vietnam's loss of sovereignty to the French colonialists after 1858 is best studied from the Vietnamese side through the translations offered in Truong Buu Lam, *Patterns of Vietnamese Response to Foreign Intervention 1858–1900* (1967), and from the French side through the documents presented in Georges Taboulet, *La geste française en Indochine* (2 vols., 1955). Vo Duc Hanh, *La place du catholicisme dans les relations entre la France et le Viet-Nam de 1851 à 1870* (2 vols., 1969), studies the expansion of Catholicism in nineteenth-century Vietnam from a Vietnamese Catholic point of view, based upon French and Church (but not Vietnamese) archives. Much of the history of the long Tu-duc reign is still a mystery, but Nguyen The Anh, *The Withering Days of the Nguyen Dynasty* (1978), gives a brief account of the Hue court's anguish and collapse after 1883; see also his essay on nineteenth-century reform in Pierre Brocheux, ed., *Histoire de l'Asie du Sud-est: révoltes, réformes, révolutions* (1981).

## Chapter 16: The Malay Peninsula to 1874

L. A. Mills, *British Malaya, 1824–67* (1925; repr., 1967), is a good introductory study for this period; but see also the scholarly monograph by C. M. Turnbull, *The Straits Settlements, 1826–1867: Indian Presidency to Crown Colony* (1972). The principal Malay source for the period, now translated into English, is Raja Ali Haji, *Tuhfat al-Nafis (The Precious Gift)* (1981). Two major studies of the region in the seventeenth and eighteenth centuries are Leonard Y. Andaya, *The Kingdom of Johore, 1641–1728* (1979), and Barbara Watson Andaya, *Perak, the Abode of Grace: A Study of an Eighteenth Century Malay State* (1979). For two slightly later studies, see Rollins Bonney, *Kedah, 1771–1821: The Search for Security and Independence* (1971), and Carl Trocki, *Prince of Pirates: The Temenggongs and the Development of Johore and Singapore* (1979).

Perhaps the best of numerous studies of Raffles is C. E. Wurtzburg's *Raffles of the Eastern Isles* (1954). A collection of Raffles's correspondence, with a commentary, was published by his widow, Lady Sophia Raffles, *Memoir of the Life and Public Services of Sir Thomas Stamford Raffles* (2 vols., 1830–1835). A Malay view of Raffles, and of a great deal else of importance in the British settlements and Malay states of that time, may be found in Abdullah bin Abdul Kadir, *Hikayat Abdullah,* of which an English translation by A. H. Hill appeared in the *Journal of the Malayan Branch Royal Asiatic Society* [*JMBRAS*] 28, 3 (1955). An interesting account by Abdullah of a visit to the east-coast peninsular states is contained in his *Kesah Pelayaran Abdullah,* translated into English by A. E. Coope as *The Voyage of Abdullah* (1949). See also the account of the west-coast states by Abdullah's son, *The Voyages of Mahamed Ibrahim Munshi,* trans. Amin Sweeney (1975). Descriptions of the settlements and the peninsular and Borneo states by European observers in the first half of the nineteenth century are numerous. Some of the more important are the following: John Anderson, *Political and Commercial Considerations relative to the Malayan Peninsula and the British Settlements in the Straits of Malacca* (1824; facs. repr. in *JMBRAS* 35, 4 [1962]); P. J. Begbie, *The Malayan Peninsula* (1834; repr. 1969); T. J. Newbold, *Political and Statistical Account of the British Settlements in the Straits of Malacca* (2 vols., 1839); Sherard Osborn, *Quedah, or Stray Leaves from a Journal in Malayan Waters* (1857); Henry Keppel, *The Expedition to Borneo of H.M.S. Dido for the Suppression of Piracy* (2 vols., 1845); Hugh Low, *Sarawak: Its Inhabitants and Productions* (1848); Spenser St. John, *Life in the Forests of the Far East* (2 vols., 1862); and Charles Brooke, *Ten Years in Sarawak* (2 vols., 1886). J. M. Gullick's *Indigenous Political Systems of Western Malaya* has already been referred to.

Direct British intervention in the affairs of the western peninsular states in 1874 has been the subject of a number of studies, notably Nicholas Tarling's *British Policy in the Malay Peninsula and Archipelago, 1824–1871,* published in *JMBRAS* 30, 3 (1957); C. Northcote Parkinson, *British Intervention in Malaya, 1867–87* (1960); and C. D. Cowan, *Nineteenth Century Malaya: The Origins of*

*British Political Control* (1961). Khoo Kay Kim, *The Western Malay States, 1850–1873: The Effects of Commercial Development on Malay Politics* (1972), deals with the economics of intervention in the west-coast states.

## Chapter 17: The Archipelago, 1785–1870

Scholars have largely ignored the nineteenth-century history of the island world reaching from Sumatra to Mindanao and the Moluccas. Much of G. J. Resink's pioneering work in defining and evoking this historical field can be found in his *Indonesia's History between the Myths: Essays in Legal History and Historical Theory* (1968). A large part of Joseph Conrad's fiction, such as his novels *Lord Jim, Almayer's Folly,* and *The Rescue,* is located in the "Outer Islands," and provides an excellent introduction to the historical setting. See also Norman Sherry, *Conrad's Eastern World* (1966). Anglo-Dutch rivalries in maritime Southeast Asia have been the subject of a number of studies, among them Nicholas Tarling, *Anglo-Dutch Rivalry in the Malay World, 1780–1824* (1962), and Graham Irwin, *Nineteenth Century Borneo: A Study in Diplomatic Rivalry,* no. 15 of the *Verhandelingen van het Koninklijk Instituut voor Taal-, Land- en Volkenkunde* (1955). A typical far-away community's story is well told in James C. Jackson's *Chinese in the West Borneo Goldfields: A Study in Cultural Geography* (1970). On West Sumatra at this time, see J. Kathirithamby-Wells, *The British West Sumatran Presidency (1760–85): Problems of Early Colonial Enterprise* (1977), and Christine Dobbin's important contribution to the political economy of Islamic revivalism, *Islamic Revivalism in a Changing Peasant Society: Central Sumatra 1784–1847* (1983); and see also two influential articles, Taufik Abdullah, "Adat and Islam: An Examination of Conflict in Minangkabau," *Indonesia* 2 (1966): 1–24, and Tsuyoshi Kato, "Rantau Pariaman: The World of Minangkabau Coastal Merchants in the Nineteenth Century," *Journal of Asian Studies* 39, 4 (1980): 729–752. For the eastern archipelago, see two outstanding works by anthropologists writing as historians, Clifford Geertz, *Negara: The Theater State in Nineteenth Century Bali* (1980), and James J. Fox, *Harvest of the Palm: Ecological Change in Eastern Indonesia* (1977).

## Chapter 18: Java, 1757–1875

Apart from sections of broader works, such as D. H. Burger, *Structural Changes in Javanese Society: The Village Sphere/The Supra-Village Sphere* (1956–1957); J. S. Furnivall, *Netherlands India: A Study of Plural Economy* (1944); and the now rather controversial *Agricultural Involution: The Processes of Ecological Change in Indonesia* by Clifford Geertz (1963); more recent monographic studies include M. C. Ricklefs, *Jogjakarta under Sultan Mangkubumi, 1749–1792: A History of the Division of Java* (1974); P. B. R. Carey, *Babad Dipanagara: An Account of the Outbreak of the Java War (1825–1830)* (1981); R. E. Elson, *Javanese Peasants and the Colonial Sugar Industry: Impact and Change in an East Java Residency, 1830–1940* (1984); and Jean Gelman Taylor, *The Social World of Batavia: European and Eurasian in Dutch Asia* (1983). Robert Van Niel's article, "The Effect of Export Cultivation in 19th Century Java," *Modern Asian Studies* 15, 1 (Feb. 1981): 25–58, is an important work by a leading specialist on this controversial question. The fine volume by Sartono Kartodirdjo, *Protest Movements in Rural Java* (1973), is the most useful work on its subject. Onghokham's remarkable "The Inscrutable and the Paranoid: An Investigation of the Brotodiningrat Affair," in Ruth T. McVey, ed., *Southeast Asian Transitions: Approaches Through Social History* (1978), has for very nearly the first time given scholars a picture of nineteenth-century Javanese society in color rather than black-and-white. The same is true of Claude Guillot's *L'affair Sadrach: un essai de Christianization au XIXe siècle* (1981). "Social Control and Influence in 19th Century Indonesia: Opium Farms and the Chinese of Java," *Indonesia* 35 (April 1983): 53–64, will introduce James R. Rush's important research on the neglected subject of the great Chinese tax farms. The gorgeous photographs in E. Breton di Nijs, *Tempo Doeloe; Fotographische Documenten uit het Oude Indie 1870–1941* (1961), are invaluable for historical understanding.

## Chapter 19: The Philippines, 1762–1872

Eliodoro G. Robles has written one of the most detailed accounts of *The Philippines in the Nineteenth Century* (1969), based primarily on the extensive holdings of the Newberry Collection at the University of Chicago. Benito F. Legarda y Fernandez, "Foreign Trade, Economic Change and Entrepreneurship in the 19th Century Philippines" (Ph.D. diss., Harvard Univ., 1955), remains one of the most important scholarly works on the economy in that era. There is extensive literature in Spanish including Jose Montero y Vidal's *Historia General de Filipinas desde el Descubrimiento de Dichas Islas hasta Nuestras Dias* (1887), a classic. There are also many first-hand accounts in English; see, for example, Thomas R. McHale and Mary C. McHale, *Early American-Philippine Trade: The Journal of Nathaniel Bowditch in Manila, 1796* (1962). The Filipiniana Book Guild has published many memoirs and contemporary accounts; for example, Paul P. de la Gironière's *Twenty Years in the Philippines* (1962), and Robert MacMicking's *Recollections of Manila and the Philippines, during 1848, 1849, and 1850* (1967). During the early years of the American occupation, T. H. Pardo de Tavera, one of the leading *ilustrados* and political leaders of his day, wrote the history section of the *Census of the Philippine Islands, 1903*, no. 1 (1905). In the early 1840s, Sinibaldo de Mas wrote a *Report on the Condition of the Philippines in 1842*, vol. 3 (reprint, 1963) in which, with perception and bluntness, he described the importance of repression as a tool to control the Philippines.

Edgar Wickberg's *The Chinese in Philippine Life, 1850–1898* (1965), and his article, "The Chinese Mestizo in Philippine History," *Journal of Southeast Asian History* 5, 1 (March 1964): 62–100, are among the most important works on modern Philippine history. James Francis Warren, *The Sulu Zone, 1768–1898: The Dynamics of External Trade, Slavery and Ethnicity in the Transformation of a Southeast Asian Maritime State* (1981), is the most important work on this key aspect of the period. See also Jonathan Fast and Jim Richardson, *Roots of Dependency: Political and Economic Revolution in 19th Century Philippines* (1979), especially for their introduction to political and economic change in the period. The literature attacking and defending the friars is extensive and usually polemical. A good example of anti-friar writing can be found in M. H. del Pilar, reprinted as *Monastic Supremacy in the Philippines* (1958). For a more sympathetic defense of the friars' role, see Vicente R. Pilapil, "Nineteenth Century Philippines and the Friar Problem," *The Americas* 18, 2 (Oct. 1961): 127–148.

Among the most important trends of Philippine historiography since the mid-1970s has been the growth of interest in regional history. Moving away from a Manila-centric focus on national and colonial institutions, a group of younger historians has explored the wealth of regional and local experience, detailing the fascinating mosaic that previously had been all but ignored by both Filipino and foreign scholars. For a good introduction, see Norman G. Owen's "Trends and Directions of Research on Philippine History," *Asian Studies* (Manila) 12 (1974): 1–17. Among the best regional histories, many of which cut across the periodization of this book, are John A. Larkin, *The Pampangans: Colonial Society in a Philippine Province* (1972); Robert Bruce Cruikshank, *A History of Samar Island, the Philippines, 1768–1898* (1985); and Norman G. Owen, *Prosperity Without Progress: Manila Hemp and Material Life in the Colonial Philippines* (1984). See also Bruce L. Fenner, *Cebu Under the Spanish Flag, 1521–1896: An Economic-Social History* (1985); Robert R. Reed, *City of Pines: The Origins of Baguio as a Colonial Hill Station and Regional Capital* (1976); Howard T. Fry, *A History of the Mountain Province* (1983); Rosario Mendoza Cortes, *Pangasinan, 1572–*

*1800* (1974); Maria Fe Hernaez Romero, *Negros Occidental between Two Foreign Powers (1888–1909)* (1974); Marshall S. McLennan, *The Central Luzon Plain: Land and Society on the Inland Frontier* (1980); and Willem Wolters, *Politics, Patronage and Class Conflict in Central Luzon* (1983).

## PART THREE: FRAMEWORKS FOR NATIONS
### Chapter 20: The Making of New States

**The Province of Burma:** John F. Cady, *A History of Modern Burma* (1958), remains the standard source and is a good place to start. Works that concentrate on the initial response of different sectors of Burma's societies to the coming of British rule are E. C. V. Foucar, *Mandalay the Golden* (1963); Horace Brown, *Reminiscences of the Court of Mandalay* (1907); D. P. Singhal, *The Annexation of Upper Burma* (1960); Philippe Preschez, "Les relations franco-birmanes aux XVIIIe et XIXe siècles," *France-Asie* 21, 3 (Sept. 1967): 275–425; Htin Aung; *The Stricken Peacock: Anglo-Burmese Relations, 1752–1948* (1965); Sao Saimong Mangrai, *The Shan States and the British Annexation* (1965); Dorothy Woodman, *The Making of Burma* (1962); and Ni Ni Myint, *Burma's Struggle Against British Imperialism (1885–1895)* (1983). Study of each of these works will illuminate the variety of interests and how they chose to adapt to, or oppose, colonial rule.

**The Kingdom of Siam:** The study of this complex period might begin with the more general and move to the particular. David K. Wyatt, *Thailand: A Short History* (1984), and *The Politics of Reform in Thailand* (1969), cover the central administration. The best treatment of administrative reform, and internal Siamese "colonization" of the outlying provinces, is the subject of Tej Bunnag's *The Provincial Administration of Siam 1892–1915* (1977). Important documents are translated in Chatthip Nartsupha and Suthy Prasartset, *The Political Economy of Siam 1851–1910* (1981), *Socio-Political Institutions and Cultural Change in Siam 1851–1910* (1977), and *The Political Economy of Siam 1910–1932* (1981). On relations with the West, see Neon Snidvongs, "The Development of Siamese Relations with Britain and France in the Reign of Maha Mongkut, 1851–1868" (Ph.D. diss., Univ. of London, 1961); Constance M. Wilson, "State and Society in the Reign of Mongkut, 1851–1868" (Ph.D. diss., Cornell Univ., 1971); Pensri Duke, *Les Relations entre la France et la Thaïlande (Siam)* (1962); Chandran Jeshurun, *The Contest for Siam 1889–1902: A Study in Diplomatic Rivalry* (1977); and Thamsook Numnonda, "The Anglo-Siamese Negotiations 1900–1909" (Ph.D. diss., Univ. of London, 1966). On the internal politics of the reign of Chulalongkorn, see David B. J. Adams, "Monarchy and Political Change: Thailand Under Chulalongkorn, 1868–1885" (Ph.D. diss., Univ. of Chicago, 1977); and Noel Alfred Battye, "The Military, Government, and Society in Siam, 1868–1910" (Ph.D. diss., Cornell Univ., 1974).

**French Indochina—Vietnam:** Milton Osborne, *Rule and Response: The French Presence in Cochinchina and Cambodia* (1969), traces the establishment of French colonial institutions in southern Vietnam. The same author's *River Road to China: The Mekong River Expedition 1866–1873* (1975) is a very readable account of the career of Francis Garnier. Nguyen Van Phong's excellent *La société vietnamienne de 1882 à 1902* (1971) is indispensable, being much more than its title suggests: it is both a social history of early colonial Vietnam and an intellectual history of influential early colonial "Orientalist" interpretations of Vietnamese institutions. On colonial Catholic institutions in Vietnam, see the article by Jean-Raoul Clementin in Jean Chesneaux, G. Boudarel, and D. Hémery, eds., *Tradition et révolution au Vietnam* (1971). On French colonial policy and its background, the reader could consult such works as R. F. Betts, *Assimilation and Association in French Colonial Theory, 1890–1914* (1961), and

Stuart M. Persell, *The French Colonial Lobby 1889-1938* (1983). There are also the discussions in the textbooks by Le Thanh Khoi and Joseph Buttinger already mentioned.

**French Indochina—Cambodia:** Milton Osborne's perceptive *Rule and Response: The French Presence in Cochinchina and Cambodia* (1969) is indispensable for students of the early years of French "protection." See also David P. Chandler, *A History of Cambodia* (1983), chaps. 8 and 9. The years just after those dealt with by Osborne are covered in Alain Forest's *Le Cambodge et la colonisation française: histoire d'une colonisation sans heurts (1897-1920)* (1981). Forest can be supplemented by Milton Osborne, "Peasant Politics in Cambodia: The 1916 Affair," *Modern Asian Studies* 12 (1978): 217-243, and David P. Chandler, "The Assassination of Resident Bardez (1925): A Premonition of Revolt in Colonial Cambodia," *Journal of the Siam Society* 70 (1982): 35-49. See also A. Pannetier's caustic attack on French administration in Cambodia, *Notes cambodgiens. Au coeur du pays khmer* (1921, repr. 1983).

**French Indochina—Laos:** The various volumes issued under the auspices of the Mission Pavie (1898-1919) are a rich source of data on Laos at the end of the nineteenth century, as is Auguste Pavie's *A la Conquête des Coeurs* (1947). Etienne Aymonier's *Voyage dans le Laos* (2 vols., 1897) is also useful; and see the first chapter of Hugh Toye, *Laos: Buffer State or Battleground* (1968).

**British Malaya and Borneo:** Emily Sadka, *The Protected Malay States, 1874-1895* (1968), gives an extremely detailed picture of the workings of the Resident system in the western peninsular states. See also her edited version of "The Journal of Sir Hugh Low, Perak, 1877," *Journal of the Malayan Branch Royal Asiatic Society* 27, 4 (1954). Sir Frank Swettenham, *British Malaya: An Account of the Origin and Progress of British Influence in Malaya* (1907), gives the point of view of a participant; see also P. L. Burns and C. D. Cowan's edition of *Swettenham's Malayan Journals, 1874-1876* (1975). Of accounts by contemporary observers of the early Resident system, three are outstanding: J. F. A. McNair, *Perak and the Malays: "Sarong and Kris"* (1882); Isabella L. Bird (Mrs. Bishop), *The Golden Chersonese* (1883, repr. 1967); and Emily Innes, *The Chersonese with the Gilding Off* (2 vols., 1885). Two late nineteenth-century administrators in Malaya, Hugh Clifford and Frank Swettenham, published a number of lively descriptions of Malay life at the time, of which Clifford's *In Court and Kampong* (1899) and *Studies in Brown Humanity* (1898), and Swettenham's *The Real Malay* (1900), may be mentioned. Collections of their works have been compiled and introduced by William R. Roff: *Stories by Sir Hugh Clifford* (1966) and *Stories and Sketches by Sir Frank Swettenham* (1967). The further expansion of British control at the beginning of the twentieth century is discussed in detail in Eunice Thio, *British Policy in the Malay Peninsula, 1880-1910* (1969). Chai Hon Chan's *The Development of British Malaya, 1896-1909* (1964) is based largely on the annual reports of the several states. The only substantial studies of the transformational effects of colonial rule on particular peninsular states are Sharom Ahmat, *Tradition and Change in a Malay State: A Study of the Economic and Political Development of Kedah, 1878-1923* (1984); and Shaharil Talib, *After Its Own Image: The Trengganu Experience, 1881-1941* (1984); but see also the collection of essays in William R. Roff, ed., *Kelantan: Religion, Society, and Politics in a Malay State* (1974).

For British rule in Borneo, K. G. Tregonning's *Under Chartered Company Rule* (1958 [2d ed., entitled *A History of Modern Sabah, 1881-1963* (1965)]) deals with the politics and administration of the chartered company, while Steven Runciman's *The White Rajahs: A History of Sarawak from 1841 to 1946* (1960) performs a similar task for Brooke rule in Sarawak. Two contemporary accounts of real value and interest to the historian are Spenser St. John, *Life in the Forests of the Far East* (2 vols., 1862), and Charles Brooke, *Ten Years in Sarawak* (2 vols., 1866). Robert Pringle's *Rajas and Rebels: The Ibans of Sarawak under Brooke Rule, 1841-*

*1941* (1970) is the first social history of modern Sarawak. Two critical but balanced works by American scholars give an account of the processes and effects of British administration in the peninsula prior to World War II: Rupert Emerson, *Malaysia: A Study in Direct and Indirect Rule* (1937, repr. 1964); and Virginia Thompson, *Postmortem on Malaya* (1943).

**The Netherlands East Indies:** Apart from sections of the broader works— J. S. Furnivall, *Netherlands India* (1944), and G. J. Resink, *Indonesia's History between the Myths: Essays in Legal History and Historical Theory* (1968)—included in the bibliography for previous chapters, there is virtually nothing in English on the military or administrative details of the making of the Netherlands Indies. The old-fashioned colonial history by E. S. de Klerck, *History of the Netherlands East Indies,* vol. 2 (1938), is still valuable for factual information on the incorporation of the islands outside Java. Wicki Baum's fine novel, *Tale of Bali* (1938), tells the story of the conquest of Bali from a Balinese point of view.

**The Philippines:** The story of how the Americans integrated the Muslim areas of Mindanao and Sulu into the Manila orbit is related in detail in the various reports filed by the United States Army. It is also described by two principals in the effort, Dean C. Worcester, *The Philippines Past and Present* (1930), and William Cameron Forbes in his two-volume *The Philippine Islands* (1945). See also the scholarly work by Peter G. Gowing, *Mandate in Moroland: The American Government of Muslim Filipinos, 1899–1920* (1983).

## Chapter 21: Bureaucratic and Economic Frameworks

(NOTE: For more on bureaucratic development, see Part Five, Chapter 40.)

**Burma:** Though somewhat overdrawn and mechanical, James Guyot, "Bureaucratic Transformation in Burma," in Ralph Braibanti, ed., *Asian Bureaucratic Systems Emergent from the British Imperial Tradition* (1966), 354–443, remains the best introduction to British administrative policy; almost as good but more sympathetic to the British is F.S.V. Donnison, *Public Administration in Burma* (1953). Furnivall's studies emphasize the importance of bureaucratic rationalization for the rest of Burma's society and its economic structure. Good introductions to his views are found in his "The Fashioning of Leviathan," *Journal of the Burma Research Society* 29, 3 (1939): 1–138, which is a marvelous read; his drier *The Governance of Modern Burma* (1959); and his classic but often misunderstood *Colonial Policy and Practice* (1948; 2nd ed., 1956). Though primarily concerned with the development of local government in the South Asian subcontinent, Hugh Tinker, *The Foundations of Local Self-Government in India, Pakistan, and Burma* (1954), has important things to say about why local self-government did not develop under the British in Burma.

**Siam:** For Thailand, the vitally important efforts at reform in the provincial administration are the subject of Tej Bunnag, *The Provincial Administration of Siam 1892–1915* (1977). Case studies are given in Nigel Brailey, "The Origins of the Siamese Forward Movement in Western Laos 1850–92" (Ph.D. diss., Univ. of London, 1968), which deals with the north; Kennon Breazeale, "The Integration of the Lao States into the Thai Kingdom" (Ph.D. diss., Oxford, 1975); and Rujaya Abhakorn, "Ratburi, an Inner Province: Local Government and Central Politics in Siam, 1868–1892" (Ph.D. diss., Cornell Univ., 1984). Civil service reform is brilliantly handled by William J. Siffin, *The Thai Bureaucracy* (1966). Fred W. Riggs's *Thailand: The Modernization of a Bureaucratic Polity* (1966), is stimulating but historically unreliable. Note also the documents edited by Chatthip Nartsupha and Suthy Prasartset, cited under Chapter 20 above.

**Vietnam:** The first chapter of Alexander Woodside, *Community and Revolution in Modern Vietnam* (1976), analyzes changes in bureaucratic and legal life and consciousness in colonial Vietnam. Truong Buu Lam, *New Lamps for Old: The*

*Transformation of the Vietnamese Administrative Elite* (1982), looks at the transformation of Vietnamese officials in the 1920s and 1930s who were moving toward "modernity, and increasing powerlessness." Robert Lingat, *Les régimes matrimoniaux du sud-est de l'Asie: essai de droit comparé indochinois* (2 vols., 1952–1955), discusses the construction of colonial civil law codes for different Vietnamese regions and shows how the codes were compromises between French and traditional Vietnamese law.

**Cambodia:** See Alain Forest, *Le Cambodge et la colonisation française: histoire d'une colonisation sans heurts (1897–1920)* (1980), especially chap. 10. See also Roger Pinto, *Aspects de l'evolution gouvernementale de l'Indochine française* (1946), and Achille Silvestre's massive "handbook," *Le Cambodge administratif* (1924).

**Laos** is very poorly studied in this period; but see the official *Notice sur le Laos française* (1900) by Lt. Col. Tournier. Joel Halpern's *Government, Politics, and Social Structure in Laos: A Study of Tradition and Innovation* (1964) traces the roots of Laos's modern government and bureaucracy in some detail.

**British Malaya:** The principal studies are Rupert Emerson, *Malaysia: A Study in Direct and Indirect Rule* (1937), and, on the early years of the Resident system, Emily Sadka, *The Protected Malay States, 1874–1895* (1968). Decentralization in the 1920s and 1930s has been the subject of two studies, Yeo Kim Wah, *The Politics of Decentralization* (1982), and Kalyan Kumar Ghosh, *Twentieth-Century Malaya: Politics of Decentralization of Power, 1920–1929* (1977). James de Vere Allen, "Malayan Civil Service, 1874–1941: Colonial Bureaucracy/Malayan Elite," *Comparative Studies in Society and History* 12 (1970): 149–178, is an examination of the ambiguous role of the European bureaucracy in Malaya, while Robert Huessler, *British Rule In Malaya: The Malayan Civil Service and Its Predecessors, 1867–1942* (1981), and Khasnor Johan, *The Emergence of the Modern Malay Administrative Elite* (1984), deal at length with the two sides to this equation. A nuts-and-bolts description of the administrative system is given in S. W. Jones, *Public Administration in Malaya* (1944), and a critical account of the juridical relationship is provided by R. St. J. Braddell, *The Legal Status of the Malay States* (1932).

**The Netherlands East Indies:** The best work in English is still J. S. Furnivall's *Netherlands India* (1944). Furnivall's *Colonial Policy and Practice* (1948; 2d ed., 1956) is a systematic comparison of the administrative systems of British Burma and the Netherlands Indies. The official Dutch view is rendered in A. D. A. de Kat Angelino's *Colonial Policy* (2 vols., 1931). See also Clive Day, *The Policy and Administration of the Dutch in Java* (1904, repr. 1966), and J. J. van Klaveren, *The Dutch Colonial System in the East Indies* (1953).

**The Philippines:** In addition to Onofre D. Corpuz, *The Bureaucracy in the Philippines* (1957), see Joseph Ralston Hayden, *The Philippines: A Study in National Development* (1942). Hayden deals with the development of Philippine government under American rule. Also helpful for the early period of American hegemony is James H. Blount, *American Occupation of the Philippines, 1898–1912* (1912, repr. 1968).

ECONOMIC FRAMEWORKS: There is a vast literature on this subject, portions of which are referred to both below and above. Two works in particular might serve as an introduction to it, without by any means definitively answering the many questions that remain. Thomas B. Birnberg and Stephen A. Resnick, *Colonial Development: An Econometric Study* (1975), includes treatment of Thailand and the Philippines and raises interesting hypotheses about the economic effects of colonialism and dependency. R. Higgott and R. Robinson, eds., *South-East Asia: Essays in the Political Economy of Structural Change* (1985), asks important questions about class, capital, and state, even if its answers are not always convincing.

**Burma:** In addition to J. S. Furnivall's classic *Colonial Policy and Practice* (1956), James R. Andrus, *Burmese Economic Life* (1947), and B. O. Binns, *Agricultural Economy in Burma* (1948), three more recent works deal with the Burmese economic framework in greater detail: U Tun Wai, *Economic Development of Burma from 1800 to 1940* (1961); Aye Hlaing, "Trends of Economic Growth and Income Distribution in Burma, 1870–1940," *Journal of the Burma Research Society* 47, 1 (1964): 89–148; and Maung Shein, *Burma's Transport and Foreign Trade in Relation to the Economic Development of the Country* (1964).

**Siam:** James Ingram's *Economic Change in Thailand 1850–1970* (1971) is an excellent general account. More specific information is provided in Lysa Hong, *Thailand in the Nineteenth Century: Evolution of the Economy and Society* (1984); David H. Feeny, *The Political Economy of Productivity: Thai Agricultural Development, 1880–1975* (1982); David B. Johnston, "Rice Cultivation in Thailand: The Development of an Export Economy by Indigenous Capital and Labor," *Modern Asian Studies* 15 (1981): 107–126; Clyde Michael Douglass, "The Political Economy of Regional Integration: The Central Plains of Thailand, 1855–1980" (Ph.D. diss., Univ. of California at Los Angeles, 1982); and in the marvellous village history by Lauriston Sharp and Lucien M. Hanks, *Bang Chan: Social History of a Rural Community in Thailand* (1978). The documents collected by Chatthip Nartsupha and Suthy Prasartset have been mentioned for Chapter 20. More analytical treatments are offered by Norman Jacobs, *Modernization Without Development* (1971); Takashi Tomosugi, *A Structural Analysis of Thai Economic History* (1980); and Yoneo Ishii, ed., *Thailand: A Rice-Growing Society* (1978).

**Vietnam:** The peasant economy of colonial Vietnam is a controversial and increasingly studied subject. A. Woodside, *Community and Revolution in Modern Vietnam* (1976), chap. 4, looks at village life, including certain features of village economic activity. Charles Robequain, *The Economic Development of French Indochina* (1944), is a by-now somewhat musty general account of its subject from the French, but not from the Vietnamese, point of view. Martin J. Murray, *The Development of Capitalism in Colonial Indochina* (1980), is not a general economic history but rather an extremely complex and strongly theoretical exploration, with a Marxist flavor, of such things as how the continued existence of noncapitalist agrarian class relations helped block the accumulation of capital in Vietnam. Ngo Vinh Long, *Before the Revolution: The Vietnamese Peasants Under the French* (1973), is an eloquent study of the deterioration of peasants' lives under colonial rule, culminating in the 1940s famine; this book is important also as an introduction to the writings of Vietnamese writers of the colonial period who interested themselves in the countryside. Pham Cao Duong, *The Vietnamese Peasants Under French Domination 1861–1941* (1985), is a slightly revised translation of one of the most important and useful postcolonial Vietnamese surveys of this subject. Tran Tu Binh, *The Red Earth: A Vietnamese Memoir of Life on a Colonial Rubber Plantation,* trans. John Spragens, Jr. (1985), by a northerner who enrolled as a rubber plantation worker in the south in 1927 and eventually became a Communist Party cell leader there, is an invaluable, if biased, source of social and economic history.

**Cambodia:** The best study of the Cambodian economy is Remy Prud'homme, *Economie du Cambodge* (1969), which supersedes Pierre Dreyfus, *Le Cambodge économique* (1910). For two Marxist perspectives, see the contributions of Hou Youn and Hu Nim in Ben Kiernan and Chantou Boua, eds., *Peasants and Politics in Kampuchea, 1942–1981* (1982), and Khieu Samphan, *Cambodia's Economy and Industrial Development,* trans. Laura Summers (1979). See also Jean Delvert, *Le paysan cambodgien* (1961).

**Malaysia:** K. M. Stahl, *The Metropolitan Organisation of British Colonial Trade* (1951), contains substantial material on Malaysia, and T. H. Silcock, *The Com-*

*monwealth Economy in Southeast Asia* (1959), discusses the basic economic patterns of the colonial era and also has an excellent bibliography. Wong Lin Ken, "The Trade of Singapore, 1819–69," *Journal of the Malayan Branch Royal Asiatic Society* 33, 4 (1960), is also helpful. Lim Chong-yah, *Economic Development of Modern Malaya* (1967), is an account by a leading Malaysian economist of economic development in the peninsula in the twentieth century; and see also P. P. Courtenay, *A Geography of Trade and Development in Malaya* (1972). Amarjit Kaur, *Bridge and Barrier: Transport and Communications in Colonial Malaya, 1870–1957* (1985), is a major contribution to the study of infrastructural change. For studies of more specific aspects of the Malayan economy, see the following: C. K. Meek, *Land Law and Custom in the Colonies* (1946), which has two chapters on Malaya; two pioneering monographs on the peasant economy under colonial rule by Lim Teck Ghee, *Origins of a Colonial Economy: Land and Agriculture in Perak, 1874–1897* (1976), and *Peasants and Their Agricultural Economy in Colonial Malaya, 1874–1941* (1977); and J. J. Puthucheary, *Ownership and Control in the Malayan Economy* (1960), which is a stimulating and sometimes controversial study with a marked historical perspective. A collection of important articles on many of the more important features of the Malayan economy may be found in T. H. Silcock, ed., *Readings in Malayan Economics* (1961).

**Indonesia:** For the Netherlands East Indies and British Malaya, G. C. Allen and Audrey G. Donnithorne, *Western Enterprise in Indonesia and Malaya: A Study in Economic Development* (1957), examines the instruments and methods of European economic penetration. Works specifically on the economic framework of the Netherlands East Indies include: J. H. Boeke, *Indonesian Economics: The Concept of Dualism in Theory and Policy* (1961); *The Structure of the Netherlands Indies Economy* (1942), by the same author; J. O. M. Broek, *The Economic Development of the Netherlands Indies* (1942); and G. Gonggrijp, *Schets Ener Economische Geschiedenis van Indonesië* [Sketch of an economic history of Indonesia] (1957).

**The Philippines:** For a leftist view of Philippine economic development, see Rene E. Ofreneo's *Capitalism in Philippine Agriculture* (1980) and Jonathan Fast and James Richardson's *Roots of Dependency: Political and Economic Revolution in 19th Century Philippine Agriculture* (1979). A. V. H. Hartendorp's *Short History of Industry and Trade of the Philippines* (1953) is a good introduction to Philippine economic development but is very weak on pre-twentieth-century issues. Among the many specialized studies, see Frederick Wernstedt, *The Role and Importance of Philippine Interisland Shipping and Trade* (1957). Documentary data on the economy during the American period are extensive and readily available, especially in the annual reports of the governors-general to the U.S. Congress. *The Records of the Bureau of Insular Affairs Relating to the Philippines, 1898–1935* (1942), compiled by Kenneth Munden, and the companion *Preliminary Inventories of the Records of the Office of the High Commissioner to the Philippines* (1963), compiled by Richard S. Maxwell, are introductions to the archival material at the Library of Congress, which is the greatest single repository of Philippine materials.

Of the numerous studies of Philippine economic history, one of the most important is Norman G. Owen, *Prosperity Without Progress: Manila Hemp and Material Life in the Colonial Philippines* (1984), since Owen's goal is to trace the interaction of economic development and social change. See also Vicente Valdepeñas and Gemilino M. Bautista, *The Emergence of the Philippine Economy* (1977). There are a number of more traditional economic histories, including Carlos Quirino, *History of the Philippine Sugar Industry* (1974), and Albert John Nyberg, "The Philippine Coconut Industry" (Ph.D. diss., Cornell Univ., 1968). Frank H. Golay's many writings on the Philippine economy are important reference works. See, for example, *The Philippines: Public Policy and National Economic Development* (1961). See also George L. Hicks, *Trade and Growth in the Philippines: An Open Economy* (1974).

## Chapter 22: Economic Transformation, 1870–1940

EXPORT INDUSTRIES: Jonathan Levin, *The Export Economies: Their Pattern of Development in Historical Perspective* (1960), is a good general study of this subject, and it includes a case study of the Burma export-rice industry, which Furnivall described as industrial agriculture. An excellent overview of the rice-export industry in general is provided in Norman G. Owen, "The Rice Industry of Mainland Southeast Asia, 1850–1914," *Journal of the Siam Society* 59, 2 (July 1971): 75–143; while a more contemporary view is given in V. D. Wickizer and M. K. Bennett, *The Rice Economy of Monsoon Asia* (1941). More detailed studies of the Burma rice industry are Cheng Siok-hwa, *The Rice Industry of Burma, 1852–1940* (1968), and Michael Adas, *The Burma Delta: Economic Development and Social Change on an Asian Rice Frontier, 1852–1941* (1974). The effects of the rice-export industry on other aspects of Burma's economic life are drawn in Tun Wai, *Burma's Currency and Credit* (1962). The Thai rice industry is discussed in James C. Ingram, *Economic Change in Thailand, 1850–1970* (1971), and in David Feeny, *The Political Economy of Productivity: Thai Agricultural Development, 1880–1975* (1982).

On the rubber export industry, P. T. Bauer has written *The Rubber Industry: A Study in Competition and Monopoly* (1948), and another volume, *Report of a Visit to the Rubber Smallholdings of Malaya* (1948), which is one of the few, extended discussions of that important section of the economy. A view of the industry in more recent contexts is Voon Phin Keong, *Western Rubber Planting Enterprise in Southeast Asia* (1976). A full-scale study of plantation rubber in Malaya has been made by J. H. Drabble, *Rubber in Malaya, 1876–1922* (1973), supplemented by the industrial study of C. Barlow, *The Natural Rubber Industry, Its Development, Technology and Economy in Malaysia* (1978). Also see James C. Jackson's *Planters and Speculators: Chinese and European Agricultural Enterprise in Malaya, 1786–1921* (1968), which is a general discussion of a changing agricultural economy. B. J. O. Schrieke's "West Coast Report," in his *Indonesian Sociological Studies*, Part I (1955), deals with the coffee and rubber industries of Sumatra in the 1910s and 1920s. Karl J. Pelzer, *Planter and Peasant: Colonial Policy and the Agrarian Struggle in East Sumatra, 1863–1947* (1978), is a more recent study. The definitive account of the early tin industry in Malaya is Wong Lin Ken, *The Malayan Tin Industry to 1914* (1965). Clifford Geertz, *The Social Context of Economic Change: An Indonesian Case Study* (1956), together with other Geertz works, and R. E. Elson, *Javanese Peasants and the Colonial Sugar Industry: Impact and Change in an East Java Residency, 1830–1940* (1984), cover the sugar industry in Java. Benito F. Legarda y Fernandez, "Foreign Trade, Economic Change, and Entrepreneurship in the Nineteenth-Century Philippines" (Ph.D. diss., Harvard Univ., 1955), is perhaps the best study of economic change in the early Philippines.

SOCIOECONOMIC TRANSFORMATION: Works on the economic development of the individual countries of Southeast Asia have been listed in the bibliography for Chapter 21. Among the socioeconomic changes experienced by Southeast Asians was the tremendous rise of population. Charles Fisher, "Some Comments on Population Growth in South-East Asia with Special Reference to the Period Since 1830," in C. D. Cowan, ed., *The Economic Development of Southeast Asia* (1964), provides a general discussion of this problem. Internal migration is the subject of Robin J. Pryor, ed., *Migration and Development in South-East Asia: A Demographic Perspective* (1979). Another aspect of the socioeconomic transformation was the influx of aliens into Southeast Asia. For Chinese immigration, G. William Skinner's study of *Chinese Society in Thailand* (1957) is excellent; see also W. L. Blythe, "Historical Sketch of Chinese Labour in Malaya," *Journal of the Malayan Branch Royal Asiatic Society* 20, 1 (1947): 67–114. A pioneering and important study of an immigrant ruling group is John G. Butcher, *The British in*

*Malaya 1880–1941: The Social History of a European Community in Colonial Southeast Asia* (1979). (NOTE: For more on overseas Chinese, see the Bibliography for Chapters 6, 23, and 40.) Other works on the influx of immigrants include: R. N. Jackson, *Immigrant Labour and the Development of Malaya, 1786–1920* (1961), and Kernial Singh Sandhu, *Indians in Malaya: Immigration and Settlement, 1786–1957* (1969). On immigration from India to Burma, see Michael Adas, "Immigrant Asians and the Economic Impact of European Imperialism: The Role of the South Indian Chettiars in British Burma," *Journal of Asian Studies* 33, 3 (May 1974): 385–401; and N. R. Chakravarti, *The Indian Minority in Burma: The Rise and Decline of an Immigrant Community* (1971). On effects on sex-roles, see Norman G. Owen, "Textile Displacement and the Status of Women in Southeast Asia," in Gordon Means, ed., *The Past in Southeast Asia's Present* (1978), 157–170.

Southeast Asian peasants adapted to these changes in various ways. The classic work on the peasants of Java is Clifford Geertz's historical treatment, *Agricultural Involution* (1963), which subsequently stimulated an important debate. The best way to follow this debate is in Benjamin White's " 'Agricultural Involution' and its Critics: Twenty Years After," *Bulletin of Concerned Asian Scholars* 15, 2 (1983): 11–31 (with a comprehensive bibliography), along with Geertz's rejoinder, "Comments on White 1973," *Human Ecology* 1 (1972): 237–239. Among the more important works coming out of this mass of research covering the past several centuries on Java are: Jan Breman, *The Village on Java and the Early-Colonial State* (1980); Peter Carey, "Waiting for the *ratu adil:* The Javanese Village Community on the Eve of the Java War (1825–1830)," *Anglo-Dutch Conference on Comparative Colonial History* (1981); W. Collier, "Declining Labour Absorption 1878–1980 in Javanese Rice Production," *Kajian Ekonomi Malaysia* (1981), 102–136; H. Kano, "Land Tenure System and the Desa Community in Nineteenth Century Java," Institute of Developing Economies (Tokyo), *Special Paper* 5 (1977); R. E. Elson, "Sugar Factory Workers and the Emergence of 'Free Labour,' " *Modern Asian Studies* 20 (1986): 139–174; G. Knight, "From Plantation to Padi-Field: The Origins of the Nineteenth Century Transformation of Java's Sugar Industry," *Modern Asian Studies* 14, 2 (1980): 177–204; and Robert Van Niel, "Measurement of Change under the Cultivation System in Java, 1837–1851," *Indonesia* 14 (1972): 89–109, which is one of a long series of papers by Van Niel on this subject.

Other useful works on the subject include Clark Cunningham, *The Postwar Migration of the Toba-Bataks to East Sumatra* (1958); and S. Husin Ali, *Social Stratification in Kampong Bagan: A Study of Class, Status, Conflict and Mobility in a Rural Malay Community* (1964), among others. In *Le problème economique indochinois* (1934), Paul Bernard examines the Vietnamese situation during the World Depression. On the Depression, see also Ian Brown, "Rural Distress in Southeast Asia During the World Depression of the Early 1930s: A Preliminary Reexamination," *Journal of Asian Studies* 45 (1986): 995–1025; and William J. O'Malley, "Indonesia in the Great Depression: A Study of East Sumatra and Jogjakarta in the 1930s" (Ph.D. diss., Cornell Univ., 1977). Articles in the *Bulletin économique de l'Indochine* explore some basic areas of colonial Vietnamese socioeconomic history.

## PART FOUR: SOCIAL CHANGE AND THE EMERGENCE OF NATIONALISM

### Chapter 23: Preludes

NATIONALISM: As a product of the interest aroused within the past two decades, there are now many general studies of nationalism and its processes in the non-Western world, though few with adequate historical perspectives.

Among those relevant to the early stages of nationalism in Southeast Asia are Clifford Geertz, ed., *Old Societies and New States: The Quest for Modernity in Asia and Africa* (1963), and Benedict Anderson, *Imagined Communities: Reflections on the Origin and Spread of Nationalism* (1983). Harry J. Benda's articles, several of which bear directly on this subject, are collected as *Continuity and Change in Southeast Asia* (1972).

PEASANT RISINGS AND PRENATIONALISM: For some stimulating studies of peasant unrest and similar phenomena in general, see E. J. Hobsbawm, *Primitive Rebels: Studies in Archaic Forms of Social Movement in the Nineteenth and Twentieth Centuries* (1959, repr. 1971); Michael Adas, *Prophets of Rebellion: Millenarian Protest Movements Against the European Colonial Order* (1979); and the same author's "From Avoidance to Confrontation: Peasant Protest in Precolonial and Colonial Southeast Asia," *Comparative Studies in Society and History* 23 (1981): 217–247. For works dealing generally with peasant revolts in Southeast Asia, see Harry J. Benda, "Peasant Movements in Colonial Southeast Asia," *Asian Studies* (Manila) 3, 3 (1965): 420–434. Much argument on the subject has been stimulated by the debate between James C. Scott, *The Moral Economy of the Peasant: Rebellion and Subsistence in Southeast Asia* (1976) and *Weapons of the Weak: Everyday Forms of Peasant Resistance* (1986), and Samuel Popkin, *The Rational Peasant: The Political Economy of Rural Society in Vietnam* (1979). See the symposium edited by Charles F. Keyes, "Peasant Strategies in Asian Societies: Moral and Rational Economic Approaches—A Symposium," *Journal of Asian Studies* 42, 4 (1983): 753–868.

**Burma:** The peasant movements of colonial Burma were closely linked both with the economic transformation of the country and the precolonial patterns of moral thought that suffused the countryside. Buddhism and ideas of social equity played a large role in such movements, and these themes are explored, in various ways, in E. Sarkisyanz, *Buddhist Backgrounds of the Burmese Revolution* (1965); Donald Eugene Smith, *Religion and Politics in Burma* (1965); E. Michael Mendelson, "A Messianic Buddhist Association in Upper Burma," *Bulletin of the School of Oriental and African Studies* 24 (1961): 560–580; Patricia Herbert, *The Hsaya San Rebellion (1930–1932) Reappraised* (1982); and Maung Maung, *From Sangha to Laity: Nationalist Movements of Burma 1920–1940* (1980).

**Siam:** In Siam, there were rebellions similar to those mentioned in the text, the chief among them occurring in 1902 in Patani, the north, and the northeast, spilling over into Laos. See Tej Bunnag, *The Provincial Administration of Siam 1892–1915* (1977); Charles F. Keyes, "Millennialism, Theravada Buddhism, and Thai Society," *Journal of Asian Studies* 36 (1977): 283–302; Yoneo Ishii, *Sangha, State, and Society* (1986), chap. 9; and John S. Murdoch, "The 1901–1902 'Holy Man's' Rebellion," *Journal of the Siam Society* 62, 1 (1974). On Laos, see also Georges Condominas, "Phibun Cults in Rural Laos," in G. W. Skinner and A. Thomas Kirsch, eds., *Change and Persistence in Thai Society* (1975).

**Vietnam:** Peasant unrest in colonial Vietnam was a central feature of the Vietnamese revolution, and it is increasingly well studied. Phan Chu Trinh, *A Complete Account of the Peasants' Uprising in the Central Region,* trans. P. Baugher and Vu Ngu Chieu (1983), is an account, written in Paris in 1911 by a major early nationalist, of peasant protests in 1908. Readers should also consult the works already mentioned by Ngo Vinh Long, Tran Tu Binh, Pham Cao Duong, and Alexander Woodside. James C. Scott, *The Moral Economy of the Peasant,* and Samuel Popkin, *The Rational Peasant,* both also previously cited, have much of critical importance to say about how and why peasant unrest occurred in colonial Vietnam.

Standing in a class by itself for excellence is Hue-Tam Ho Tai, *Millenarianism and Peasant Politics in Vietnam* (1983). Her analysis of the Hoa Hao movement and its antecedents has been hailed as the best study of any Southeast Asian millenarian movement to date; it is indispensable to learning how a sect "institutionalized" itself, and the differences between millenarian and revolutionary outlooks. For the Cao Dai movement, see Victor Oliver, *Cao Dai Spiritism: A Study of Religion in Vietnamese Society* (1976); the articles by R. B. Smith, "An Introduction to Cao Daiism," *Bulletin of the School of Oriental and African Studies* 33 (1970): 335–349 and 573–589; and Jayne S. Werner, *Peasant Politics and Religious Sectarianism: Peasant and Priest in the Cao Dai in Vietnam* (1981).

**Cambodia:** On disturbances in rural Cambodia, see David P. Chandler,"An Anti-Vietnamese Rebellion in Early Nineteenth-Century Cambodia," *Journal of Southeast Asian Studies* 6, 1 (1975): 16–24; Milton Osborne, "Peasant Politics in Cambodia: The 1916 Affair," *Modern Asian Studies* 12 (1978): 217–243; and David P. Chandler, "The Assassination of Resident Bardez (1925): A Premonition of Revolt in Colonial Cambodia," *Journal of the Siam Society* 70 (1982): 35–49. See also Ben Kiernan, "The Samlaut Rebellion, 1967–1968," in Ben Kiernan and Chantou Boua, eds., *Peasants and Politics in Kampuchea, 1942–1981* (1982), 166–205; and the last chapter in Michael Vickery, *Cambodia 1975–1982* (1983), a theoretical analysis of peasant rebellions generally.

**Malaysia:** The "To' Janggut" movement in Malaya is the subject of James de V. Allen's article, "The Kelantan Rising of 1915: Some Thoughts on the Concept of Resistance in British Malayan History," *Journal of Southeast Asian History* 9, 2 (1968): 241–257. For other peasant movements in Malaya and Borneo, see Dato' Seri Lela Di-Raja, "The Ulu Trengganu Disturbance, May, 1928: Extracts from the Diary of Dato' Seri Lela Di-Raja," *Malaysia in History* 12, 1 (1968): 21–26; and Robert R. Pringle, "Asun's 'Rebellion': The Political Growing Pains of a Tribal Society in Brooke Sarawak," paper delivered to the International Conference on Asian History, Kuala Lumpur, 1968 (mimeo.).

**Indonesia:** Studies of peasant movements in Indonesia include Justus M. van der Kroef, "Javanese Messianic Expectations: Their Origin and Cultural Context," *Comparative Studies in Society and History* 1 (1959): 299–323, and Sartono Kartodirdjo, *Protest Movements in Rural Java* (1973). For the Samin movement, see Harry J. Benda and Lance Castles, "The Samin Movement," *Bijdragen tot de Taal-, Land- en Volkenkunde* 125 (1969): 207–240; and The Siauw Giap, "The Samin and Samat Movements in Java: Two Examples of Peasant Resistance," *Revue du Sud-Est Asiatique* no. 2 (1967); no. 1 (1968). See also Harry J. Benda and Ruth T. McVey, eds., *The Communist Uprisings of 1926–1927 in Indonesia: Key Documents* (1960).

**The Philippines:** Perhaps the single most important monograph to have appeared on modern Philippine history is Reynaldo C. Ileto's *Pasyon and Revolution: Popular Movements in the Philippines* (1979). Ileto explores the connection between the peasant religious tradition centered around the Passion of Christ and peasant movements. For more conventional analyses, see David R. Sturtevant, *Popular Uprisings in the Philippines 1840–1940* (1976), and Willem Wolters, *Politics, Patronage and Class Conflict in Central Luzon* (1983). See also William H. Scott's *Cracks in the Parchment Curtain and Other Essays in Philippine History* (1982) and his "The Igorot Struggle for Independence," *Solidarity* 5 (May 1970): 18–27.

THE CHINESE IN SOUTHEAST ASIA: The principal compendium of information on the overseas Chinese communities is Victor Purcell, *The Chinese in Southeast Asia* (rev. ed., 1965), which also has a substantial bibliography. A recent brief survey of the Chinese in Southeast Asia may be found in C. P. Fitzgerald, *The Southern Expansion of the Chinese People* (1972). Mary F. Somers Heidhues, *Southeast Asia's Chinese Minorities* (1974), is an excellent account from a more sociological point of view. On the particular question of Chinese economic capacities, see Maurice Freedman, "The Handling of Money: A Note on the Background to the Economic Sophistication of the Overseas Chinese," *Man* 59 (1959): 64–

65; and on the general problems of association and assimilation, see Alice Tay Ehr Soon, "The Chinese in South-East Asia," *Race* 4, 1 (Nov. 1962): 34–48.

**Thailand:** The classic work, superior to all others, is G. William Skinner, *Chinese Society in Thailand: An Analytical History* (1957), which for Thailand should be used to the exclusion of Purcell. His *Leadership and Power in the Chinese Community of Thailand* (1957) is also useful. Also of importance are R. J. Coughlin, *Double Identity: The Chinese in Modern Thailand* (1960), and K. P. Landon, *The Chinese in Thailand* (1941). Also note G. W. Skinner's comparative essay "Change and Persistence in Chinese Culture Overseas: A Comparison of Thailand and Java," *Journal of the South Seas Society* 16, 1–2 (1960): 86–100.

**Indochina:** Three helpful works on the Chinese in Indochina are W. E. Willmott, *The Chinese in Cambodia* (1967); Joel Halpern, "The Role of the Chinese in Lao Society," *Journal of the Siam Society* 49, 1\ (1961): 21–46; and Tsai Maw-Kuey, *Les Chinois au Sud-Vietnam* (1968).

**Malaysia:** Descriptions and studies of the Chinese in Singapore and Malaysia are numerous. Some of the most useful may be listed (alphabetically) as follows: W. L. Blythe, *The Impact of Chinese Secret Societies in Malaya* (1969), and "Historical Sketch of Chinese Labour in Malaya," *Journal of the Malayan Branch Royal Asiatic Society* 20, 1 (1947): 67–114, by the same author; John M. Chin, *The Sarawak Chinese* (1981); John R. Clammer, *Straits Chinese Society: Studies in the Sociology of the Baba Communities of Malaysia and Singapore* (1980); Maurice Freedman, *Chinese Family and Marriage in Singapore* (1957), "Immigrants and Associations: Chinese in Nineteenth century Singapore," *Comparative Studies in Society and History* 3 (1960–1961): 25–48, and "Chinese Kinship and Marriage in Singapore," *Journal of Southeast Asian History* 3, 2 (1962): 65–73, by the same author; L. A. P. Gosling, "Migration and Assimilation of Rural Chinese in Trengganu," in J. S. Bastin and R. Roolvink, eds., *Malayan and Indonesian Studies* (1964), 201–221; R. N. Jackson, *Pickering: Protector of Chinese* (1965); Barrington Kaye, *Upper Nankin Street Singapore: A Sociological Study of Chinese Households Living in a Densely Populated Area* (1960); Edwin Lee, *The Towkays of Sabah: Chinese Leadership and Indigenous Challenge in the Last Phase of British Rule* (1976); Lee Poh Ping, *Chinese Society in Nineteenth Century Singapore* (1978); Mak Lau Fong, *The Sociology of Secret Societies: A Study of Chinese Secret Societies in Singapore and Peninsular Malaysia* (1981); S. M. Middlebrook, "Yap Ah Loy, 1837–85," *Journal of the Malayan Branch Royal Asiatic Society* 24, 2 (1951); William H. Newell, *Treacherous River: A Study of Rural Chinese in North Malaya* (1962); Png Poh Seng, "The Kuomintang in Malaya," *Journal of Southeast Asian History* 2, 1 (1961): 1–32; Victor Purcell, *The Chinese in Malaya* (1948, repr. 1967); Lawrence K. L. Siaw, *Chinese Society in Rural Malaysia: A Local History of the Chinese in Titi, Jelebu* (1983); Song Ong Siang, *One Hundred Years History of the Chinese in Singapore* (1923, repr. 1967); Eunice Thio, "The Singapore Chinese Protectorate: Events and Conditions Leading to Its Establishment, 1823–1877," *Journal of the South Seas Society* 16, 1–2 (1960): 40–80; T'ien Ju-Kang, *The Chinese of Sarawak: A Study of Social Structure* (1953); J. D. Vaughan, *Manners and Customs of the Chinese of the Straits Settlements* (1879); and C. S. Wong, *A Cycle of Chinese Festivals* (1967) and *A Gallery of Chinese Kapitans* (1963).

**Indonesia:** The literature on the Chinese in Indonesia is both extensive and of high quality. It includes: Mary Somers, *Peranakan Chinese Politics in Indonesia* (1964); Donald E. Willmott, *The Chinese of Semarang: A Changing Minority Community in Indonesia* (1960); Tan Giok-Lan, *The Chinese of Sukabumi: a Study of Social and Cultural Accommodation* (1963); Lea Williams, *Overseas Chinese Nationalism: The Genesis of the Pan-Chinese Movement in Indonesia, 1900–1916* (1960); and G. W. Skinner, "The Chinese Minority," in Ruth T. McVey, ed., *Indonesia* (1963). Skinner's "Change and Persistence in Chinese Culture Overseas: A Comparison of Thailand and Java," *Journal of the South Seas Society* 16, 1–2

(1960): 86–100, is instructive and is commented on by The Siauw Giap, "Religion and Overseas Chinese Assimilation in Southeast Asian Countries," *Revue du Sud-Est Asiatique* no. 2, (1965): 67–84 (see also the latter's "Group Conflict in a Plural Society," *Revue du Sud Est Asiatique* (1966) no. 1, pp. 1–31, and no. 2, pp. 185–217). Kwee Tek Hoay, *The Origins of the Modern Chinese Movement in Indonesia* (1969), is the translation by Lea Williams of an important pre-World War II work. Recent work of importance includes J. A. C. Mackie, ed., *The Chinese in Indonesia* (1976); Charles A. Coppel, *Indonesian Chinese in Crisis* (1983); and several books by Leo Suryadinata, including his edited volume of readings, *Political Thinking of the Indonesian Chinese, 1900–1977* (1979).

**The Philippines:** Edgar Wickberg's study of *The Chinese in Philippine Life, 1850–1898* (1965), and his article "The Chinese Mestizo in Philippine History," *Journal of Southeast Asian History* 5, 1 (March 1964): 62–100, are essential reading. Also see Alfonso Felix, Jr., ed., *The Chinese in the Philippines, 1570–1770* (1966), and *The Chinese in the Philippines, 1770–1898* (1969). Among other useful works are Antonio S. Tan, *The Chinese in the Philippines 1898–1935: A Study of their National Awakening* (1972); John T. Omohundro, *Chinese Merchant Families in Iloilo: Commerce and Kin in a Central Philippine City* (1981); Gerald A. McBeath, *Political Integration of the Philippine Chinese* (1973); and Marr Wai Jong Cheong, *The Chinese-Cantonese in Manila: A Study in Culture and Education* (1983).

INTRUSIVE IDEOLOGIES: Frank N. Trager, ed., *Marxism in Southeast Asia: A Study of Four Countries* (1959), discusses Marxist influences and movements in Burma, Thailand, Vietnam, and Indonesia. The early history of the Communist movement in Southeast Asia is dealt with in J. H. Brimmell, *Communism in Southeast Asia: A Political Analysis* (1959), and Malcolm Kennedy, *A Short History of Communism in Asia* (1957).

**Burma:** For a brief account of the history and development of the Communist movement in Burma, see Robert H. Taylor's introduction to *Marxism and Resistance in Burma, 1942–1945: Thein Pe Myint's Wartime Traveler* (1984), or his "The Burmese Communist Movement and Its Indian Connection: Formation and Factionalism," *Journal of Southeast Asian Studies* 14, 1 (March 1983): 95–108.

**Siam:** On communism in Siam, see E. Thadeus Flood, "The Thai Left Wing in Historical Context," *Bulletin of Concerned Asian Scholars* 7, 2 (1975): 56–67, and Wongtrangan Kanok, "Communist Revolutionary Process: A Study of the Communist Party of Thailand" (Ph.D. diss., Johns Hopkins Univ., 1982).

**Indochina:** On Vietnamese communism, William J. Duiker, *The Communist Road to Power in Vietnam* (1981), is a sensible and painstaking account of its subject from its beginnings to about 1978. Huynh Kim Khanh, *Vietnamese Communism 1925–1945* (1982), is an incisive analysis of trends and factions in the Vietnamese movement in its earlier years. The Lao Communist Party is definitively treated in MacAlister Brown and Joseph J. Zasloff, *Apprentice Revolutionaries: The Communist Movement in Laos, 1930–1985* (1986). On the early stages of communism in Cambodia, see Ben Kiernan, *How Pol Pot Came to Power* (1985), chaps. 2–3; and David P. Chandler, *A History of Cambodia* (1983); as well as Michael Vickery, *Cambodia 1975–1982* (1983), chap. 2, and Elizabeth Becker, *When the War Was Over* (1986).

**Malaysia:** J. H. Brimmel's pamphlet, *A Short History of the Malayan Communist Party* (1956), and Gene Z. Hanrahan, *The Communist Struggle in Malaya* (1954), provide some background to the growth of the party on the peninsula. On Singapore, see Lee Teng Hui, *The Communist Organisation in Singapore: Its Techniques of Manpower Mobilization and Management 1948–66* (1976).

**Indonesia:** Takashi Shiraishi, "Islam and Communism: An Illumination of the People's Movement in Java, 1912–1926" (Ph.D. diss., Cornell Univ., 1986), and Ruth McVey, *The Rise of Indonesian Communism* (1965), deal in great detail with the early years of the Indonesian Communist Party, and Harry J.

Benda and Ruth McVey, eds., *The Communist Uprisings of 1926–1927 in Indonesia: Key Documents* (1960), provides some of the source materials for this period, as does B. Schrieke, "The Causes and Effects of Communism on the West Coast of Sumatra," in B. Schrieke, *Indonesian Sociological Studies,* Part I (1955).

On the influence of Islamic reform in Indonesia, the best work is Deliar Noer's *The Modernist Muslim Movement in Indonesia 1900–1942* (1973). The first half of Harry J. Benda, *The Crescent and the Rising Sun* (1958), is especially helpful on relationships between Dutch policy and Islamic reform. For Malaya, see William R. Roff, *The Origins of Malay Nationalism* (1964). For some account of ideological life in the Middle East, see William R. Roff, "Indonesian and Malay Students in Cairo in the 1920s," *Indonesia* 9 (1970): 73–87.

OVERSEAS NATIONALISM: For Chinese nationalism in Southeast Asia, a number of the studies on the overseas Chinese are valuable, particularly G. William Skinner's *Chinese Society in Thailand* (1957); Png Poh Seng, "The Kuomintang in Malaya," *Journal of Southeast Asian History* 2, 1 (1961): 1–32; and Lea Williams, *Overseas Chinese Nationalism: The Genesis of the Pan-Chinese Movement in Indonesia, 1900–1916* (1960). The only work that sets out to examine Indian nationalism in Southeast Asia is Usha Mahajani, *The Role of Indian Minorities in Burma and Malaya* (1960). For the influence of Chettyars in Burma, see Chester L. Cooper, "Moneylenders and the Economic Development of Lower Burma: An Exploratory Historical Study of the Role of the Indian Chettyars" (Ph.D. diss., American Univ., 1959); and Philip Siegelman, "Colonial Development and the Chettyar: A Study in the Ecology of Modern Burma, 1850–1941" (Ph.D. diss., Univ. of Minnesota, 1963). Kernial Singh Sandhu, *Indians in Malaya: Immigration and Settlement, 1786–1957* (1969), may also be read with advantage. The influence of the overseas Japanese was perhaps most strongly felt in the Philippines, and this subject has been extensively studied by Grant K. Goodman in his *Davao: A Case Study in Japanese-Philippine Relations* (1967) and *Four Aspects of Philippine-Japanese Relations, 1930–1940* (1967). See also Serafin D. Quiason, "Some Notes on the Japanese Community in Manila: 1898–1941," *Solidarity* 3, 9 (Sept. 1968): 39–59.

For the Philippines, a scholarly debate has examined whether Masonry is distinct from other rural movements of a peasant tradition. Ileto sees Masonry in an indigenous context, while others have stressed its alien, Spanish origins. See John N. Schumacher, "Philippine Masonry to 1890," *Asian Studies* (Manila) 4 (1966): 328–341; and Teodoro M. Kalaw, *Philippine Masonry* (repr. 1956). See also Richard L. Deats, *Nationalism and Christianity in the Philippines* (1967).

## Chapter 24: Channels of Change

URBANIZATION: Increasing interest has focused in recent times on the city as an important agent of social change, an interest reflected in studies of the sociology of cities and the processes of urbanization. Two bibliographies give an introduction to the extensive literature: Erik Cohen, *Southeast Asian Urban Sociology: A Review and a Selected Bibliography* (1973), and Robert Lawless, *The Southeast Asian City: An Introductory Essay and an Annotated Bibliography* (1975). A. J. S. Reid provides a historical perspective in "The Structure of Cities in Southeast Asia, Fifteenth to Seventeenth Centuries," *Journal of Southeast Asian Studies* 11,2 (1980): 235–250; and Paul Wheatley's *Negara and Commandery: Origin of the Southeast Asian Urban Tradition* (1983) is of interest. The only full-scale study of modern urbanization in the region is T. G. McGee, *The Southeast Asian City* (1967); but useful readings on the subject are to be found in Y. M. Yeung and C. P. Lo, eds., *Changing Southeast Asian Cities: Readings on Urbanization* (1976). A very thoughtful and provocative re-thinking of the idea of the city in Southeast Asia is Richard O'Connor, *A Theory of Indigenous Southeast Asian Urbanism* (1983). A number of articles dealing with general phenomena rather than particular cities are worth attention, and the following may be instanced: D. W. Fryer, "The Million City in Southeast Asia," *Geographical Review* (Oct. 1953): 474–494; Norton S. Ginsburg, "The Great City in Southeast Asia," *American Journal of Sociology* 60 (1955): 455–462; and Nathan Keyfitz, "Political-Economic Aspects of Urbanization in South and Southeast Asia," in Philip M. Hauser and Leo Schnore, eds., *The Study of Urbanization* (1965).

**Burma and Thailand:** Urbanization is covered only in the secondary accounts listed elsewhere, most notably through the details in Virginia Thompson, *Thailand: The New Siam* (1941, repr. 1967); Kenneth P. Landon, *Siam in Transition: A Brief Survey of Cultural Trends in the Five Years Since the Revolution of 1932* (1939); John Christian, *Burma and the Japanese Invader* (1945); and B. R. Pearn, *History of Rangoon* (1939, repr. 1971). On Bangkok, a good starting place is Larry Sternstein, *Thailand: the Environment of Modernisation* (1976).

**Indochina:** On urban trends in colonial Vietnam, see Alexander Woodside, "The Development of Social Organizations in Vietnamese Cities in the Late Colonial Period," *Pacific Affairs* 44, 1 (Spring 1971): 39–64. On Cambodia, see Paul Bergue, "L'Habitation Européene au Cambodge," *Revue Indochinoise* 1 (1905): 490–499; and R. Garry, "L'Urbanisation au Cambodge," *Civilisations* 17 (1967): 83–106.

**Malaysia:** Of the studies of individual cities in Southeast Asia, those on Singapore are perhaps the most numerous. C. B. Buckley's *Anecdotal History of Old Times in Singapore* (1902, repr. 1965), is a rather diffuse but detailed historical background. Other historical studies are William R. Roff, "The Malayo-Muslim World of Singapore at the Close of the Nineteenth century," *Journal of Asian Studies* 24 (1964): 75–90, and Png Poh Seng, "The Straits Chinese in Singapore: A Case of Local Identity and Sociocultural Accommodation," *Journal of Southeast Asian History* 10, 1 (1969): 95–114. The first issue of the 1969 *Journal of Southeast Asian History* commemorates the 150th anniversary of the founding of modern Singapore, and it contains many articles of interest. On the integration of immigrant communities to the urban life of Singapore in the nineteenth and twentieth centuries, see Maurice Freedman, "Immigrants and Associations: Chinese in Nineteenth Century Singapore," *Comparative Studies in Society and History* 3 (1960–1961): 25–48, and his *Chinese Family and Marriage in Singapore* (1957). Also of interest is Judith Djamour, *Malay Kinship and Marriage in Singapore* (1959). On Bawean patterns of settlement in Singapore, see J. Vredenbregt, "Bawean Migrations: Some Preliminary Notes," *Bijdragen tot de Taal-, Land- en Volkenkunde* 120 (1964): 109–137; and Mansor C. Haji Fadzal, "My Baweanese People," *Intisari* 2, 4 (n.d.): 11–71. For studies of cities in Malaysia, see J. M. Gullick, *The Story of Kuala Lumpur (1857–1939)* (1983); Kernial Singh Sandhu et al., eds., *Malaka: The Transformations of a Malay Capital, c. 1400–1980* (2 vols., 1983); *Penang Past and Present, 1786–1963,* published by the city council of Georgetown (1966); and Craig Lockard, "The Southeast Asian Town in Historical Perspective: A Social History of Kuching, Malaysia, 1820–1970" (Ph.D. diss., Univ. of Wisconsin, 1973).

**Indonesia:** On urbanization in Indonesia, Lance Castles has written "The Ethnic Profile of Djakarta," *Indonesia* 3 (1967): 153–204; and Edward Bruner has studied the social and cultural results of Toba Batak migration to Medan in his article "Urbanization and Ethnic Identity in North Sumatra," *American Anthropologist* 63 (June 1961): 508–521. Clifford Geertz's *The Social History of an Indonesian Town* (1965) is a study of "Modjokuto," a small town in Java. The volume of essays entitled *The Indonesian Town: Studies in Urban Sociology* (1958) presents the work of a number of Dutch scholars.

**The Philippines:** Philippine urbanization has received much attention. See Robert R. Reed, *Colonial Manila: The Context of Hispanic Urbanism and Process of Morphogenesis* (1978), and his earlier work, *Hispanic Urbanism in the Philippines: A*

*Study of the Impact of Church and State* (1967). Daniel F. Doeppers has written an excellent study, *Manila, 1900–1941: Social Change in a Late Colonial Metropolis* (1984). Norman G. Owen's "Measuring Mortality in the Nineteenth-Century Philippines," is in his *Death and Disease in Southeast Asia: Explorations in Social, Medical and Demographic History* (1986). In a less scholarly vein, see Mauro Garcia and C. O. Resurrecion, *Focus on Old Manila: A Volume Issued to Commemorate the Fourth Centenary of the City of Manila* (1971). Two very different pictorial introductions to Manila are Luning B. Ira and Isagani R. Medina, *Streets of Manila* (1977), and Emmanuel Torres, *Jeepney* (1979).

EDUCATION AND LANGUAGE: For Southeast Asia in general, the only descriptive work for the period dealt with by this part is J. S. Furnivall, *Educational Progress in Southeast Asia* (1944).

**Burma:** The only available study of Burmese education in general is U Kaung, "A Survey of the History of Education in Burma before the British Conquest and After," *Journal of the Burma Research Society* 46 (Dec. 1963): 1–124. In addition, much useful information is available through official reports.

**Siam:** The only general account of education in Thailand in the years before 1940 is M. L. Manich Jumsai, *Compulsory Education in Thailand* (1951). David K. Wyatt's *The Politics of Reform in Thailand* (1969) is also relevant for developments in education, but only up to 1910. For the decades thereafter, see *Education in Thailand: A Century of Experience* (1970) and the Thai Ministry of Education's *A History of Thai Education* (1976).

**Indochina:** Henri Froidevaux, *L'œuvre scolaire de la France dans nos colonies* (1900), is a useful description of a generally torpid endeavor. For colonial Vietnam, John DeFrancis, *Colonialism and Language Policy in Vietnam* (1977), describes the French promotion of romanized Vietnamese, the way in which Vietnamese journalists took it over, and the heritage of "linguistic inferiority" the French bequeathed Vietnam. David G. Marr, *Vietnamese Tradition on Trial 1920–1945* (1981), on the basis of a matchless knowledge of the Vietnamese sources, treats the same issue but goes beyond it to look at the curricula and primers used in colonial Vietnamese schools. Vietnam was part of a larger empire, so the comparative perspective is also important: see Gail Kelly, "The Presentation of Indigenous Society in the Schools of French West Africa and Indochina, 1918–1938," *Comparative Studies in Society and History* 26 (1984): 523–542, and her "Colonial Schools in Vietnam: Policy and Practice," in P. G. Altbach and Gail Kelly, eds., *Education and Colonialism* (1978). See also chapter 3 of A. Woodside, *Community and Revolution in Modern Vietnam* (1976).

For Cambodia, see Humbert Hess, "L'Enseignement au Cambodge," in *Comptes Rendus des Sciences Coloniales* 4 (1924): 335–343; and Jean Delvert, "L'oeuvre française d'enseignement au Cambodge," *France-Asie* 13 (1956): 309–322. On Laos, see Marjorie Emling, "The Education System in Laos During the French Protectorate, 1893–1945" (M.A. thesis, Cornell Univ., 1969).

**Malaya:** Within Malaysia, "Education in Malaya, 1900–1941," is described by H. R. Cheeseman, *Malayan Historical Journal* 2, 1 (1955): 30–47; D. D. Chelliah, *A Short History of the Educational Policy of the Straits Settlements, 1800–1925* (1947), gives some account of the early period as well. Both of these accounts embody a colonial point of view, and J. Stewart Nagle's *Educational Needs of the Straits Settlements and Federated Malay States* (1928) differs little in emphasis. A more recent summary is provided by T. R. Doraisamy, ed., *150 Years of Education in Singapore* (1969); see also Harold E. Wilson, *Social Engineering in Singapore: Educational Policies and Social Change, 1819–1972* (1978). Two studies of the effects of British educational policy in the peninsular states are Rex Stevenson, *Cultivators and Administrators: British Educational Policy Towards the Malays, 1875–1906* (1975), and Philip Loh Fook Seng, *Seeds of Separatism: Educational Policy in Malaya, 1874–1940* (1975). Francis Wong Hoy Kee and Ee Tiang Hong, *Educa-*

*tion in Malaysia* (1971), is a general discussion that moves from the colonial to the postcolonial period, as does Francis Wong Hoy Kee and Paul Chang Min Phang, *The Changing Pattern of Teacher Education in Malaysia* (1975). Eugene Vijeyasingha, *A History of Raffles Institution, 1823–1963* (1963), and N. J. Ryan and Desmond Tate, *Malay College, 1905–1965: Past and Present* (n.d.), give the history of two of the most influential schools in Singapore and Malaya.

**Indonesia:** The Taman Siswa movement, which developed a widespread private school system in Indonesia in the 1920s and after, and which was founded on ideals of a national culture, is studied by Ruth McVey, "Taman Siswa and the Indonesian National Awakening," *Indonesia* 4 (Oct. 1967): 128–149.

**The Philippines:** Education during the Spanish period is the subject of Henry F. Fox, "Primary Education in the Philippines, 1565–1863," *Philippine Studies* 13, 2 (Apr. 1965): 207–231. For a general history, see Encarnacion Alzona, *A History of Education in the Philippines* (1932). Joseph Ralston Hayden's monumental book, *The Philippines: A Study in National Development* (1942), has excellent chapters tracing the development of education and language during the American regime. The annual reports of the American governors-general contain detailed analyses of the school system as it developed after 1900. For a history of the development of Pilipino, see Ernest J. Frei, *The Historical Development of the Philippine National Language* (1959). See also D. E. Foley, "Colonialism and Schooling in the Philippines," in P. G. Altbach and Gail Kelly, eds., *Education in the Colonial Experience* (1984), 69–95. Renato Constantino has argued that American educational policy was, in fact, miseducation, distorting the Filipino's capacity to see reality clearly. Among his other writings, see *The Miseducation of the Filipinos* (1966).

## Chapter 25: The Philippines

A good introduction to this period is the selection of readings edited by Teodoro A. Agoncillo, *Philippine Nationalism, 1872–1970* (1974). The most important introduction to the Philippine-American experience is the volume edited and introduced by Peter W. Stanley, *Reappraising an Empire: New Perspectives on Philippine-American History* (1984). With these serving as an introduction, it is useful to break the period from 1872 to 1941 into five parts.

**1872–1896:** See John N. Schumacher and Nicholas P. Cushner, *Burgos and the Cavite Mutiny* (1969); Josefa Saniel, *Japan and the Philippines, 1868–1898* (1963); John N. Schumacher, *The Propaganda Movement* (1880–1895) (1973); and Maximo N. Kalaw's classic study, *The Development of Philippine Politics, 1872–1920* (1926). Teodoro A. Agoncillo's important if somewhat unsatisfactory *The Revolt of the Masses* (1956) examines the rise of the nationalist movement. The writings of Jose P. Rizal are most successfully translated by Leon Ma. Guerrero as *The Lost Eden* (1961) and *The Subversive* (1962). Guerrero has also written a biography of Rizal, *The First Filipino* (1963). Rizal has been extensively studied; see among others Rafael Palma's *The Pride of the Malay Race* (1949); Eugene A. Hessel, *The Religious Thought of Jose Rizal* (1983); Pedro A. Gagelonia, *Rizal's Life, Works and Writings* (1974); and an anthology of essays by and about Rizal selected by Gabriel F. Fabella, *Understanding Rizal* (1963). Primary source material can be gleaned from the publications of the National Heroes Commission, including the *Minutes of the Katipunan* (1964). Carlos Quirino has written a biography of Emilio Aguinaldo, *The Young Aguinaldo, from Kawit to Biyak-Na-Bato* (1969).

**1896–1901:** Renato Constantino, *The Philippines: A Past Revisited* (1975), offers an important overview of this period. See also Cesar A. Majul's brilliant study, *The Political and Constitutional Ideas of the Philippine Revolution* (1967), and the biography *Apolinario Mabini: Revolutionary* (1964). The Ateneo de Manila publications of the *Trial of Rizal,* edited by Horacio de la Costa (1961), and the *Trial of Andres Bonifacio,* edited by Virginia Palma-Bonifacio (1963), are significant volumes dealing with the executions of these two famous Filipinos. Mabini's writings have been edited by Alfredo S. Veloso in three volumes for the Mabini centennial (1964). Teodoro A. Agoncillo's *Malolos: The Crisis of the Republic* (1960) is the best single detailed study of the era. One of the best introductions to the Iglesia Filipina Independiente or Aglipayanism is a multivolume work by two Jesuits, Pedro S. de Achutegui and Miguel A. Bernad, vols. 1–2 being *Religious Revolution in the Philippines: The Life and Church of Gregorio Aglipay, 1860–1940* (1960), and vol. 3, *The Religious Coup d'Etat, 1898–1901: A Documentary History* (1971). The most important books on the Philippine-American War are John M. Taylor, ed., *The Philippine Insurrection Against the United States: A Compilation of Documents* (5 vols., 1971–1973); John Morgan Gates, *School Books and Krags: The United States Army in the Philippines, 1898–1902* (1973); and Leon Wolff, *Little Brown Brother* (1960). Milagros C. Guerrero's "Luzon at War: Contradictions in Philippine Society" (Ph.D. diss., Univ. of Michigan, 1977) is excellent. See also John N. Schumacher, *Revolutionary Clergy: The Filipino Clergy and the Nationalist Movement, 1850–1903* (1981).

The motives behind American intervention are analyzed in Ernest R. May, *Imperial Democracy* (1961); Julius W. Pratt, *Expansionists of 1898* (1936); and Walter LaFeber, *The New Empire: An Interpretation of American Expansion, 1860–1898* (1963). Robert L. Beisner's *Twelve Against Empire* (1968) helps to shatter longstanding illusions about the anti-imperialists. See in addition Roger J. Bresnahan, *In the Time of Hesitation: American Anti-Imperialists and the Philippine-American War* (1981) and the disappointing *Sitting in Darkness: Americans in the Philippines* (1984), by David H. Bain.

**1901–1913:** Peter W. Stanley, *A Nation in the Making: The Philippines and the United States, 1899–1921* (1974), is the best introduction to the first decades of the American regime. Glenn A. May's *Social Engineering in the Philippines: The Aims, Execution, and Impact of American Colonial Policy, 1900–1913* (1980), is also essential reading. William J. Pomeroy, *An American-Made Tragedy: Neocolonialism and Dictatorship in the Philippines* (1974), is a Marxist condemnation of American intervention. Peter G. Gowing, *Mandate in Moroland: The American Government of Muslim Filipinos, 1899–1920* (1977), is the best book dealing with the American handling of the Muslim areas. Among the best studies analyzing the development of a political consciousness in the islands are Bonifacio S. Salamanca's *The Filipino Reaction to American Rule, 1901–1913* (1984), and Dapen Liang, *The Development of Philippine Political Parties* (1939, rev. ed. 1971). See also Norman G. Owen, ed., *Compadre Colonialism: Studies on the Philippines Under American Rule* (1970), an uneven but fascinating volume on early American colonial activity. The controversy over the friar lands can be followed in William Cameron Forbes, Dean C. Worcester, and F. W. Carpenter, *The Friar Land Inquiry, Philippine Government* (1970); in the Report of the Committee on Insular Affairs, no. 2289, 61st Congress, 3rd session, March 3, 1911; and in "Disposition of the Friar Lands," a speech by Manuel L. Quezon to the United States Congress, May 1, 1912. Romeo V. Cruz, *America's Colonial Desk in the Philippines, 1898–1934* (1974), and Alfred McCoy and Alfredo Roces, *Philippine Cartoons: Political Caricature of the American Era, 1900–1941* (1985), both are very useful for this period.

**1913–1935:** Bernardita Reyes Churchill, *The Philippine Independence Mission to the United States, 1919–1934* (1983), is a good introduction to this period. Louis E. Gleeck, Jr., has written extensively on the Americans in the Philippines. See his *The American Half-Century* (1984); *The Manila American, 1901–1964* (1977); and *Laguna in American Times: Coconuts and Revolutionaries* (1981). Michael P. Onorato has written of the Harrison and Leonard Wood regimes;

see, most productively, his *A Brief Review of American Interest in Philippine Development and Other Essays* (1968). There are a great many polemical tracts by principals, including both Filipinos and Americans. Read, for example, Jorge Bocobo's *General Leonard Wood and the Law* (1923). Bruno Lasker's *Filipino Immigration* (repr. 1969), and the Institute of Asian Studies, *The Filipino Exclusion Movement, 1927–1935* (1967), examine Filipino migration to Hawaii and the United States. Antonio S. Araneta's "The Communist Party of the Philippines and the Comintern, 1919–1930" (Ph.D. diss., Oxford, 1966) is of interest even though the party was miniscule prior to World War II.

**1935–1941:** The most literate and perceptive analysis of the transition from American rule to Commonwealth status can be found in Theodore Friend's *Between Two Empires* (1965). Manuel L. Quezon's autobiography, *The Good Fight* (1946), reveals more about the president than most of the available scholarly works. Sidney Fine, *Frank Murphy: The New Deal Years* (1979), vol. 2, chaps. 1–5, address the Philippine years of Murphy's career. Victor J. Sevilla, ed., *Justices of the Supreme Court of the Philippines: Their Lives and Outstanding Decisions* (3 vols.; vol. 1, 1984) deals with the period 1901–1944. For a Japanese perspective, see Royama Masamichi and Takeuchi Tatsuji, *The Philippine Polity: A Japanese View* (1967).

## Chapter 26: Burma

For Burma in this period, one must rely for the most part on secondary accounts, notably the general history by John F. Cady, *A History of Modern Burma* (1960), supplemented by the works of John L. Christian, *Modern Burma: A Survey of Political and Economic Development* (1942); Donald Eugene Smith, *Religion and Politics in Burma* (1965); and E. Sarkisyanz, *Buddhist Backgrounds of the Burmese Revolution* (1965). John L. Christian's *Burma and the Japanese Invader* (1945) extends his *Modern Burma*. The most recent scholarship includes Albert D. Moscotti, *British Policy and the Nationalist Movement in Burma, 1917–1937* (1974), and articles by Robert H. Taylor, including "Burma" in Haruhiro Fukui, ed., *Political Parties of Asia and the Pacific* (1985), 99–154; "The Evolution of Burmese Political Thought—1900 to 1940s," in the *Seventh International Conference of the Historians of Asia Proceedings* (1977), 795–812; "Party, Class and Power in British Burma," *Journal of Commonwealth and Comparative Politics* 19, 1 (March 1981): 44–62; and "Politics in Late Colonial Burma: The Case of U Saw," *Modern Asian Studies* 10, 2 (1976): 161–194; plus his "The Relationship between Burmese Social Classes and British Indian Policy on the Behavior of the Burmese Political Elite, 1937–1942" (Ph.D. diss., Cornell Univ., 1974).

The best primary sources are Ba U, *My Burma* (1959); Ba Maw, *Breakthrough in Burma: Memoirs of a Revolution, 1939–1946* (1968); and Maung Maung, ed., *Aung San of Burma* (1962). See also Maurice Collis, *Trials in Burma* (1938), and George Orwell's penetrating novel, *Burmese Days* (1934).

## Chapter 27: Indonesia

The general history of early twentieth-century Indonesia is most usefully surveyed in J. D. Legge's *Sukarno: A Political Biography* (1972) and Bernhard Dahm's *A History of Indonesia in the Twentieth Century* (1971).

From the large number of valuable English-language writings on the social change and political economy of the Netherlands Indies in its heyday during the first four decades of the century, a few of the most useful may be mentioned here. The social history of the "Ethical Policy" period is explored in Robert Van Niel, *The Emergence of the Modern Indonesian Elite* (1960), and in W. F. Wertheim and The Siauw Giap, "Social Change in Java, 1900–1930," *Pacific Affairs* 35, 3 (1962): 223–247. Ruth McVey's *The Rise of Indonesian Communism* (1965) is the definitive work on its subject and on the related political developments in the turbulence of the late 1910s and early 1920s. Two valuable studies of prewar Indonesian politics are John Ingleson, *Road to Exile: The Indonesian Nationalist Movement 1927-1934* (1979), and Susan Abeyasekere, *One Hand Clapping: Indonesian Nationalists and the Dutch, 1939-1942* (1976). Heather Sutherland's *The Making of a Bureaucratic Elite: The Colonial Transformation of the Javanese Priyayi* (1979) opens new insights into the history of the large, widespread, and powerful *priyayi* class. Two fine books—Karl J. Pelzer's *Planter and Peasant: Colonial Policy and the Agrarian Struggle in East Sumatra, 1863-1947* (1979), and Ann Laura Stoler's *Capitalism and Confrontation in Sumatra's Plantation Belt, 1870-1979* (1985)—deal in much the same spirit, but in very different ways, with the long history of the violent frontier plantation zone of East Sumatra. Lance Castles's *Religion, Politics and Economic Behavior in Java: The Kudus Cigarette Industry* (1967) is one of the few studies of Muslim Javanese manufacturers in a Chinese-dominated economic environment.

Education, in a great variety of forms, was basic to the social changes of the early twentieth century. For nonreaders of Dutch, Paul W. Van der Veur's *Education and Social Change in Colonial Indonesia* (1969) provides a useful short guide to the Dutch colonial education system. Taufik Abdullah's *Schools and Politics: Kaum Muda in West Sumatra 1927-1933* (1971), along with James Siegel's *The Rope of God* (1969) and Deliar Noer's *The Modernist Muslim Movement in Indonesia, 1900-1942* (1973), deal with the wide-borne energies—all fundamentally educational whatever their specific form—of Reform Islam in these formative decades.

Perhaps not by chance, most of the best biographical works for Indonesian history come from this period. Raden Adjeng Kartini, *Letters of a Javanese Princess* (1964), is a classic reissued with a fine introductory essay by Hildred Geertz. An important later article, "Raden Ajeng Kartini," *Signs* (Spring 1976): 639-661, is by Jean S. Taylor. Soetan Sjahrir, *Out of Exile* (1949), is a collection of letters written in the 1930s by the nationalist, later prime minister, and represents the more Western pole in Indonesian intellectual life of the time. The more "Javanese" pole is represented by three books about the extraordinary figure of Sukarno: Bernard Dahm's *Sukarno and the Struggle for Indonesian Independence* (1969) deals mainly with Sukarno's earlier years and emphasizes the links between his nationalist politics and Javanese political culture, while *Sukarno, an Autobiography as told to Cindy Adams* (1965), gives his own version as he saw it in the early 1960s. J. D. Legge's biography of Sukarno, mentioned above, is the latest of the three and provides the most balanced treatment. *The Golden Bridge: Toward Indonesia Merdeka,* edited, translated, and introduced by Roger Paget, gives the texts of Sukarno's two most famous speeches.

## Chapter 28: Vietnam

The outstanding Western interpreter of Vietnamese nationalism in the colonial period is David G. Marr. Marr's first book, *Vietnamese Anticolonialism 1885-1925* (1971), treats the royalist movement of the 1880s and the first generation of more modern-thinking Vietnamese patriots. Marr's second book, *Vietnamese Tradition on Trial 1920-1945* (1981), is a fascinating and instructive social and cultural history of the Vietnamese intelligentsia (about ten thousand people, in Marr's estimation) in the last decades of French rule. It surveys their views of everything from the rights of women to the nature of science and the Vietnamese past; nobody seriously interested in modern Vietnam should fail to read it. William J. Duiker, *The Rise of Nationalism in Vietnam 1900-1941* (1976), is a clear assessment of the maturing of a town-based nationalist consciousness in Vietnam by 1940 but does not have the richness of coverage of the Marr volumes. Alexander Woodside, *Community and Revolution in Modern Vietnam* (1976), emphasizes the early nationalists' concern with national organization in the face of colonial manipulation. John McAlister and Paul Mus, *The Vietnamese and Their Revolution* (1970), offers the reflections of a philosophically minded French "old Indochina hand" and scholar on Vietnamese politics.

As to more specialized studies, Hoang Ngoc Thanh and Vu Duc Bang contribute useful accounts of the development of modern Vietnamese literature and of the Dong Kinh Free School, respectively, in Walter F. Vella, ed., *Aspects of Vietnamese History* (1973). Phan Boi Chau, in what was intended to be a final testament written in prison in 1914, explains the "barbaric situation" in which he grew up, in C. Jenkins, Tran Khanh Tuyet, and Huynh Sanh Thong, trans., *Reflections from Captivity: Phan Boi Chau's Prison Notes and Ho Chi Minh's Prison Diary* (1978). Megan Cook, *The Constitutionalist Party in Cochinchina: The Years of Decline 1930–1942* (1977), looks at an interesting non-Communist political movement; and Bao Dai, *Le dragon d'Annam* (1980), though concerned with Vietnamese politics from 1945, gives the last emperor's impressions of life in the Hue palaces and his education in France before World War II.

For the Communists, William Duiker, *The Communist Road to Power in Vietnam* (1981), and Huynh Kim Khanh, *Vietnamese Communism 1925–1945* (1982), examine the early Communists' complex and ambiguous connections with the nationalist movement. No fully satisfactory biography of Vietnam's most important Communist leader yet exists; Jean Lacouture, *Ho Chi Minh: A Political Biography* (1968), is shallow but readable; and Bernard B. Fall, ed., *Ho Chi Minh on Revolution, Selected Writings 1920–1966* (1968, repr. 1984), follows Ho's career through his own pronouncements. Ho's 1942–1943 prison diary, less directly informative than Phan Boi Chau's prison notes, can be read in C. Jenkins et al., *Reflections from Captivity*. Nguyen Khac Vien, *Tradition and Revolution in Vietnam* (1974), written by a mandarin's son and privileged medical school student who became an important international spokesman for Vietnamese communism, contains authoritative speculation on the transition Vietnamese intellectuals made from Confucianism to Marxism. Daniel Hémery, *Révolutionnaires vietnamiens et pouvoir colonial en Indochina* (1975), focuses especially upon Vietnamese Trotskyites and their enemies in Saigon in the 1930s, and the colonial labor movement. The Nghe-Tinh Soviet movement of 1930–1931, a popular and controversial topic, is treated in many of the aforementioned works, including the books by Scott and Popkin. For two recent contributions to the debate, see Martin Bernal, "The Nghe-Tinh Soviet Movement, 1930–1931," *Past and Present* 92 (Aug. 1981): 148–168; and, above all, the learned essay of Hy Van Luong, "Agrarian Unrest from an Anthropological Perspective: The Case of Vietnam," *Comparative Politics* 17, 2 (Jan. 1985): 153–174. Truong Chinh and Vo Nguyen Giap, *The Peasant Question 1937–1938,* trans. Christine White (1974), is an important analysis of the problem by two rising party leaders.

## Chapter 29: Thailand

The general outline of the period is given in David K. Wyatt, *Thailand: A Short History* (1984); B. J. Terwiel, *A History of Modern Thailand, 1767–1942* (1983); and Prince Chula Chakrabongse, *Lords of Life: The Paternal Monarchy of Bangkok, 1782–1932* (1962). Of contemporary general accounts, W. A. Graham, *Siam* (2 vols.; 2nd ed., 1924), is encyclopedic; Virginia Thompson, *Thailand: The New Siam* (1941, repr. 1967), and Kenneth P. Landon, *Siam in Transition: A Brief Survey of Cultural Trends in the Five Years since the Revolution of 1932* (1939, repr. 1968), have an immediacy grounded in the excitement of the late 1930s. Important documents of the period are collected in Chatthip Nartsupha and Suthy Prasartset, *The Political Economy of Siam, 1910–1932* (1981), and Thak Chaloemtiarana, *Thai Politics: Extracts and Documents 1932–1957* (1978). A sensitive general account is William J. Siffin, *The Thai Bureaucracy* (1966). One good door into the cultural history of the period is provided by Wibha Senanan, *The Genesis of the Novel in Thailand* (1975).

The reign of King Vajiravudh (1910-1925) is most fully treated in Walter F. Vella, *Chaiyo! King Vajiravudh and the Development of Thai Nationalism* (1978). The account is by no means exhaustive: see Stephen L. W. Greene, "Thai Government and Administration in the Reign of Rama VI (1910-1925)" (Ph.D. diss., Univ. of London, 1971); the last portion of Tej Bunnag, *The Provincial Administration of Siam 1892-1915* (1977); and Peter Brian Oblas, "Siam's Efforts to Revise the Unequal Treaty System in the Sixth Reign (1910-1925)" (Ph.D. diss., Univ. of Michigan, 1974).

The succeeding reign of King Prajadhipok (1925-1935) has been definitively treated by Benjamin A. Batson, *The End of the Absolute Monarchy in Siam* (1984).

On the "Revolution" of 1932 and the early years of military dominance, see Thawatt Mokarapong, *History of the Thai Revolution, A Study in Political Behavior* (1972); Nicholas Tarling, "King Prajadhipok and the Apple Cart: British Attitudes Towards the 1932 Revolution," *Journal of the Siam Society* 64, 2 ( July 1976): 1-38; M. Sivaram, *The New Siam in the Making: A Survey of the Political Transition in Siam, 1932-1936* (1936; repr. 1981); Virginia Thompson, *Thailand: The New Siam* (1941); E. Thadeus Flood, "Japan's Relations With Thailand, 1928-1941" (Ph.D. diss., Univ. of Washington, 1967); and Pierre Fistié, *L'évolution de la Thaïlande contemporaine* (1967), and *Sous-développement et utopie au Siam, le programme des réformes présentée en 1933 par Pridi Phanomyong* (1969). On the 1940-1941 war with French Indochina, see M. Sivaram, *Mekong Clash and Far East Crisis* (1941), and E. Thadeus Flood, "The 1940 Franco-Thai Border Dispute and Phibun Songkhram's Commitment to Japan," *Journal of Southeast Asian History* 10, 2 (1969): 304-325.

## Chapter 30: Malaya

The principal study of nationalism in Malaya before World War II is William R. Roff, *The Origins of Malay Nationalism* (1967), but reference should also be made to T. H. Silcock and Ungku Abdul Aziz, "Malayan Nationalism," in W. L. Holland, ed., *Asian Nationalism and the West* (1953), and Raden Soenarno, "Malay Nationalism, 1900-1945," *Journal of Southeast Asian History* 1, 1 (1960): 1-28. Usha Mahajani's *The Role of Indian Minorities in Burma and Malaya* (1960), and Tan Cheng Lock's *Malayan Problems from a Chinese Point of View* (1947), deal to some extent with prewar politics in Malaya.

## Chapter 31: Laos and Cambodia

For Laos in this period, the most relevant works are Peter Kemp, *Alms for Oblivion* (1961); Pierre Gentil, *Remous sur le Mekong* (1950); and Katay Don Sasorith, *Le Laos: son évolution politique* (1953). Recent works include "3349" (pseud.), *Iron Man of Laos: Prince Phetsarath Ratanavongsa,* trans. John Murdoch (1978); C. J. Christie, "Marxism and the History of Nationalist Movements in Laos," *Journal of Southeast Asian Studies* 10, 1 (March 1979): 146-158; Geoffrey Gunn, "The Origins of Nationalism and Communism in Laos, 1930-1954" (Ph.D. diss., Monash Univ., 1984); and MacAlister Brown and Joseph J. Zasloff, *Apprentice Revolutionaries: The Communist Movement in Laos, 1930-1985* (1986).

Cambodian nationalism has not yet received a full-scale study. Martin Herz's *Short History of Cambodia* (1958), although otherwise full of errors, is accurate and perceptive on the 1940s. See also Ben Kiernan, *How Pol Pot Came to Power* (1985), chaps. 1-3; V. M. Reddi, *A History of the Cambodian Independence Movement* (1970); and David P. Chandler, *A History of Cambodia* (1983), chaps. 8-9. Elizabeth Becker's *When the War Was Over* (1986) also is useful.

## PART FIVE: SOUTHEAST ASIAN NATIONS IN A NEW WORLD ORDER

### Chapter 32: War, Independence, and Political Transition

Several journalists provide views of the region as World War II approached, notably John Gunther, *Inside Asia* (1939), and Mona Gardner, *The Menacing Sun* (1939); the latter is particularly evocative. On Japanese war planning, see *The Fateful Choice: Japan's Advance Into Southeast Asia, 1939–1941,* ed. James W. Morley (1980), which translates important prewar Japanese planning documents.

Serious study of the wartime experience of Southeast Asians has come relatively recently. Samples of recent scholarship appear in several collections of articles: Josef Silverstein, ed., *Southeast Asia in World War II* (1966); Alfred W. McCoy, ed., *Southeast Asia Under Japanese Occupation* (1979); and William H. Newell, ed., *Japan in Asia 1942–1945* (1981). Good overviews of the period are to be found in Harry J. Benda, "The Japanese Interregnum," in *Imperial Japan and Asia: A Reassessment,* ed. Grant K. Goodman (1967), 65–79, and F. C. Jones, Hugh Borton, and B. R. Pearn, *The Far East 1942–1946* (1955).

The military course of the war might first be approached through the official military histories. For the British, who took major responsibility for most of the region, the standard treatment is S. Woodburn Kirby, *The War Against Japan* (5 vols., 1957–1969), and its natural sequel, Vice Admiral the Earl Mountbatten, *Report to the Combined Chiefs of Staff by the Supreme Allied Commander, South-East Asia 1943–1945* (1951) and *Post-Surrender Tasks: Section E of the Report to the Combined Chiefs of Staff* . . . (1969). Lord Mountbatten's report is importantly supplemented by F. S. V. Donnison, *British Military Administration in the Far East, 1943–45* (1956), and Rajendra Singh, *Official History of the Indian Armed Forces in the Second World War, 1939–45,* vol. 7, *Post-War Occupation Forces: Japan and South-East Asia* (1958). On the American side, the China–Burma–India theater is treated in Charles F. Romanus and Riley Sunderland, *The United States Army in World War II: History of the China–Burma–India Theater* (2 vols., 1953–1956), while naval operations in the Pacific are covered in Samuel Eliot Morison, *History of United States Naval Operations in World War II,* vols. 13 and 15 (1959, 1960). The military reconquest of the Philippines is treated in Robert Ross Smith, *The United States Army in World War II: The War in the Pacific, Triumph in the Philippines* (1963).

Materials dealing with single countries in the wartime and postwar period are offered in the bibliographies for Chapters 33 to 39, while thematic material is organized by subject in the bibliography for Chapter 40. Here we note only a few books of general interest dealing with the postwar period. Histories of the region since 1945 tend to be either long on detail and short on analysis, or vice versa. John F. Cady, *The History of Post-War Southeast Asia: Independence Problems* (1975), and Jan Pluvier, *South-East Asia from Colonialism to Independence* (1974), exemplify the former, while Fred R. von der Mehden, *South-East Asia 1930–1970: The Legacy of Colonialism and Nationalism* (1974), represents the latter.

### Chapter 33: Vietnam

Philippe Devillers, *Histoire du Viet Nam de 1940 à 1952* (1952), written when the outcome of the French war with the Viet Minh still seemed in doubt, is still probably the best detailed history of the last years of French rule. See also Paul Isoart, ed., *L'indochine française 1940–1945* (1982). In English, John T. McAlister, Jr., *Vietnam: The Origins of Revolution* (1969), treats the events after 1945 in some detail. General older works which may still be consulted are Ellen J. Hammer, *The Struggle for Indochina 1940–1955* (1955), and Donald Lancaster, *The Emancipation of French Indochina* (1961). R. A. M. Irving, *The First Indochina War* (1975), is more recent, as is Peter M. Dunn, *The First Vietnam War* (1984), with a particular interest in the British role in Vietnam in 1945. Volume 1 of Allan W. Cameron, ed., *Vietnam Crisis: A Documentary History* (1971), covers the period from 1940 to 1956 and contains the views of the last French proconsuls. On the August Revolution of 1945 and its prelude, see William Duiker, *The Communist Road to Power in Vietnam;* Huynh Kim Khanh, *Vietnamese Communism 1925-1945;* Alexander Woodside, *Community and Revolution in Modern Vietnam;* and, for a suggestive new perspective, Vu Ngu Chieu, "The Other Side of the 1945 Vietnamese Revolution," *Journal of Asian Studies* 45 (1986): 293-328. Archimedes Patti, *Why Vietnam? Prelude to America's Albatross* (1980), gives us the recollections of a sympathetic U.S. military eyewitness to the Viet Minh seizure of power. Vo Nguyen Giap, *Unforgettable Months and Years,* trans. Mai Van Elliott (1975), is on the other hand an account of Vietnamese politics from August 1945 to March 1946 as seen by a top Communist. King Chen, *Vietnam and China 1938-1954* (1969), is an early effort to reconstruct the obscure relationships Vietnamese revolutionaries had with various important Chinese leaders. For the fighting itself, see Jules Roy, *The Battle of Dienbienphu* (1984), and Bernard Fall, *Street Without Joy, Indochina at War 1946-1954* (1961), a famous military journalist's picture. Robert F. Randle, *Geneva 1954: The Settlement of the Indochinese War* (1969), describes the results of the peace negotiations.

The second Indochina war, and the U.S. intervention in Vietnam, have produced an enormous number of books and articles, only a few of which can be listed here. Stanley Karnow's *Vietnam: A History* (1983) is a general, relatively distanced account by a veteran journalist, prepared in conjunction with a 1980s television series. More scholarly histories of the war include James P. Harrison, *The Endless War: Fifty Years of Struggle in Vietnam* (1982), and William S. Turley, *The Second Indochina War: A Short Political and Military History, 1954-1975* (1986). Frances Fitzgerald's classic *Fire in the Lake: The Vietnamese and the Americans in Vietnam* (1972) is a brilliantly written if impressionistically high-flying wartime antiwar analysis. George McT. Kahin, *Intervention: How America Became Involved in Vietnam* (1986), is a meticulously researched analysis of the political side of U.S. intervention, examining the U.S. effort to 1966 to shape a government in Vietnam that would cooperate with U.S. ends. Gabriel Kolko, *Anatomy of a War* (1985), interests itself in the ultimate U.S. failure to create a successful non-Communist government in South Vietnam.

As against Fitzgerald, Kahin, and Kolko, Guenter Lewy, *America in Vietnam* (1978), contends that U.S. intervention was "not without moral justication" but was weakened by "anticolonialist inhibitions"; Kevin Buckley in turn attacks Lewy's "revisionism" in *The New York Review of Books,* Dec. 7, 1978, 19-24. R. B. Smith, *An International History of the Vietnam War* (2 vols., 1983-1985), seeks to place the war in a broader context than that created merely by a study of American-Vietnamese relations; the difficulty with this laudable ambition is that the archives of such other powers as China and the U.S.S.R. are still inaccessible. R. M. Pfeffer, ed., *No More Vietnams? The War and the Future of American Foreign Policy* (1968), is a still-valuable sample of the wartime debate about Vietnam among U.S. policymakers and their academic critics. Wallace J. Thies, *When Governments Collide: Coercion and Diplomacy in the Vietnam Conflict, 1964-1968* (1980), examines the effects of U.S. policymakers' ignorance on their policies.

Documentation of U.S.-Vietnamese relations throughout this period may be found in a number of sources. *The Pentagon Papers: The Defence Department History of United States Decisionmaking on Vietnam, the Senator Gravel Edition* (5 vols., 1971), is a huge anthology of documents with analysis, compiled inside the Pentagon, which was released in sensational circumstances during the war itself; for one important review of it, see G. Kahin, "The Pentagon Papers: A Critical Evaluation," *American Political Science Review* 69 (June 1975): 675-684. Gareth Porter, ed., *Vietnam: The Definitive Documentation of Human Decisions* (2 vols., 1979), is, unfortunately, far from "definitive," being U.S.-centered and giving too little coverage to Vietnamese, especially non-Communist Vietnamese, materials; it is useful all the same. Porter, *Vietnam: A History in Documents* (1981), is an abridgement of these volumes. On efforts to end the war, there are G. Porter, *A Peace Denied: The United States, Vietnam, and the Paris Agreement* (1975), written by an antiwar critic; Ramesh Thakur, *Peacekeeping in Vietnam: Canada, India, Poland, and the International Commission* (1984); and, from the viewpoint of the Nixon government's top foreign policy adviser, Henry Kissinger's long but evasive memoirs, *White House Years* (1979) and *Years of Upheaval* (1982). For critical guidance with Kissinger's memoirs, see, especially, S. Hoffman's articles in *The New York Review of Books,* "How to Read Henry Kissinger," Dec. 6, 1979, 14–29, and "The Return of Henry Kissinger," April 29, 1982, 14–20. Van Tien Dung, *Our Great Spring Victory: An Account of the Liberation of South Vietnam,* trans. John Spragens, Jr. (1977), is the 1975 Communist offensive commander's self-congratulatory description of how the war did end.

We still know far too little about the Vietnamese side of this war. Robert Shaplen, *The Lost Revolution* (1966), is still worth reading as an introduction to the Diem period; so too is Robert Scigliano, *South Vietnam: Nation Under Stress* (1963), as an analysis of the Diem government. Allan E. Goodman, *Politics in War: The Bases of Political Community in South Vietnam* (1973), takes a hopeful wartime look at the south's attempts at holding elections in the 1960s and at the work of non-Communist politicians. Milton Osborne, *Strategic Hamlets in South Vietnam* (1965) compares "counterinsurgency" schemes in Vietnam and Malaysia. C. Stuart Callison, *Land to the Tiller in the Mekong Delta: Land Reform in Four Villages of South Vietnam* (1982), describes southern efforts at land reform. Douglas Pike, *The Viet Cong* (1965), gives a hostile but detailed description of the organizational features of the National Liberation Front. Robert L. Sansom, *The Economics of Insurgency in the Mekong Delta of Vietnam* (1970), by an economist, concludes, against Pike, that although "organization" played a part in Viet Cong successes, it could not have gained them all their support by itself. Jeffrey Race, *War Comes to Long An: Revolutionary Conflict in a Vietnamese Province* (1972), is a brilliant account of why the Viet Cong were successful—at least until the late 1960s—in one Mekong delta province. For central Vietnam, see James W. Trullinger, Jr., *Village at War: An Account of Revolution in Vietnam* (1982). David Hunt, "Village Culture and the Vietnamese Revolution," *Past and Present* (Feb. 1982): 131–157, looks at the National Liberation Front's incomplete attack upon peasants' traditional values; the topic is vital but this article barely begins to touch it. Gerald C. Hickey's *Fire in the Forest,* previously cited, is indispensable to a study of the war in the highlands.

The political and economic life of the Communist state centered in Hanoi is introduced to the reader by William Duiker's two books, *The Communist Road to Power in Vietnam* and *Vietnam: Nation in Revolution,* and by chapter 7 of A. Woodside, *Community and Revolution in Modern Vietnam.* William S. Turley, ed., *Vietnamese Communism in Comparative Perspective* (1980), is a particularly useful collection of nine articles, including two suggestive if inconclusive essays by Georges Boudarel and David Elliott on the attractions of Maoist "ideocracy" versus those of the "administrative state" in Vietnamese communism. G. Boudarel et al., *La bureaucratie au Vietnam* (1983), is a disillusioned and more miscellaneous collection of essays, some of which try to account historically for the repressive nature of the Hanoi dictatorship. Pierre Rousset, "The Peculiarities of Vietnamese Communism," in Tariq Ali, ed., *The Stalinist Legacy* (1984), looks at the riddle of the "Stalinist" behavior of the Vietnamese party; see also P. Rousset, *Communisme et nationalisme vietnamien* (1978). William S. Turley has a useful essay about the "people's army" in J. Zasloff and MacAlister Brown, eds., *Communism in Indochina: New Perspectives* (1975). Thai Quang Trung, *Collective Leadership and Factionalism: An Essay on Ho Chi Minh's Legacy* (1985), briefly looks at the development of factions within the Vietnamese party.

G. Nguyen Tien Hung, *Economic Development of Socialist Vietnam, 1955–1980* (1977), offers a detailed but grim introduction to Hanoi's economic planning and its results to about 1976. Edwin E. Moise, *Land Reform in China and North Vietnam* (1983), is now the most reliable and intelligent study of the north's violent and controversial land reform campaign in the 1950s. A. Woodside, "Decolonization and Agricultural Reform in Northern Vietnam," *Asian Survey* 10 (Aug. 1970): 705–724, looks at some of the ways the wartime farm cooperatives worked, or were supposed to work. François Houtart and Geneviève Lemercinier, *Hai Van: Life in a Vietnamese Commune* (1984), is a pedantic but important study of life in a largely Catholic village 120 kilometers east of Hanoi, as of 1979, on the eve of some economic liberalization. Some of the most important recent studies of the Vietnamese Communist economy are those of Christine White, "Recent Debates in Vietnamese Development Policy," in Gordon White, R. Murray, and C. White, eds., *Revolutionary Socialist Development in the Third World* (1983), and C. White, "Agricultural Planning, Pricing Policy, and Cooperatives in Vietnam," *World Development* 13 (1985): 97–114.

William J. Duiker, *Vietnam Since the Fall of Saigon* (1985), is a reasonable account of Vietnamese foreign and domestic policy since 1975. Nguyen Van Canh, with Earle Cooper, *Vietnam under Communism 1975–1982* (1983), by a knowledgable anti-Communist refugee, discusses its subject with great hostility; Kathleen Gough, *Ten Times More Beautiful: The Rebuilding of Vietnam* (1978), is on the other hand an admiring account by a distinguished leftist anthropologist who is not a Vietnam specialist. For the war between China and Vietnam and its background, the leading work so far is the collection of essays in David W. P. Elliott, ed., *The Third Indochina Conflict* (1981), which includes an enlightening essay by Charles Benoit on the refugees of this period. See also A. Woodside, "Nationalism and Poverty in the Breakdown of Sino-Vietnamese Relations," *Pacific Affairs* 11 (1979): 381–409; and Eugene K. Lawson, *The Sino-Vietnamese Conflict* (1984). On the refugees' adaptation to the West, a good early book in what will presumably be a flood of them is Elliot L. Tepper, ed., *Southeast Asian Exodus: From Tradition to Resettlement* (1980). Of refugee reminiscences, the most significant so far is Truong Nhu Tang, with D. Chanoff and Doan Van Toai, *A Vietcong Memoir* (1985), a remarkable revelation of the disillusionment of a patriotic southerner who had helped organize the Viet Cong and served as justice minister in its provisional government. Nguyen Ngoc Ngan, with E. E. Richey, *The Will of Heaven* (1982), gives a bleak but interesting account of the Communists' takeover of the south, as seen through the eyes of a schoolteacher and former South Vietnamese officer. There is also Doan Van Toai, *Le goulag vietnamien* (1979). *The Vietnam Forum,* published at Yale University, is a source of refugee writing.

## Chapter 34: Cambodia and Laos

**Cambodia:** For a discussion of the closing years of French control in Cambodia, see David P. Chandler, *A History of Cambodia,* chap. 9, and also "The Kingdom of Kampuchea: Japanese Sponsored Independence in Cambodia in World War II," *Journal of Southeast Asian Studies* 17, 1 (1986): 80–93. There are several good studies of postwar Cambodian politics. The most valuable is Philippe Preschez, *Essai sur la democratie au Cambodge* (1961), which can be supplemented by Roger Smith's "Cambodia," in George McT. Kahin, *Governments and Politics of Southeast Asia* (2nd ed., 1964). See also Roger Smith's astute study, *Cambodian Foreign Policy* (1965); Milton Osborne, *Power and Politics in Cambodia* (1973); and R. Prud'homme, *L'economie du Cambodge* (1968). Ben Kiernan has traced the history of Cambodian radicalism in his masterly *How Pol Pot Came to Power* (1985). The best approach to the Sihanouk phenomenon is probably his own memoirs, now published in several volumes in French. His polemical study, *My War with the CIA* (1973), is also of interest, and so is Charles Meyer, *Derrier la sourire Khmer* (1971).

Students of events in Cambodia since 1970 should consult Ben Kiernan and Chanthou Boua, eds., *Peasants and Politics in Cambodia* (1982), a valuable collection of documents, and François Ponchaud, *Cambodia Year Zero* (1978). For a journalistic overview, see Elizabeth Becker's *When the War Was Over* (1986). Michael Vickery's *Cambodia 1975–1982* (1983) is contentious and scholarly; and American policies toward Cambodia are scathingly analyzed in William Shawcross, *Sideshow: Nixon, Kissinger and the Destruction of Cambodia* (1979). For the Democratic Kampuchean era, see David P. Chandler and Ben Kiernan, eds., *Revolution and Its Aftermath in Kampuchea: Eight Essays* (1983), and David P. Chandler, Ben Kiernan, and Chanthou Boua, eds. and trans., *Pol Pot Plans the Future: Confidential Leadership Documents from Democratic Kampuchea, 1976–1977* (1987). There are several harrowing accounts by survivors of the regime. Among the best are Pin Yathai, *L'utopie meurtrière* (1980); Laurence Picq, *Au dela du ciel* (1983); and Someth May, *Cambodian Witness* (1986). For a readable overview, drawing on secondary sources, see Craig Etcheson, *The Rise and Demise of Democratic Kampuchea* (1983). The Cambodian war with Vietnam, and its aftermath, are brilliantly analyzed in Nayan Chanda, *Brother Enemy: The War After the War* (1986), while William Shawcross, *The Quality of Mercy* (1984), examines the aftermath of the Vietnamese invasion. The only scholarly study of the People's Republic of Kampuchea so far is Michael Vickery's helpful *Kampuchea: Politics and Society* (1986).

**Laos:** Material on Laos before independence can be found in Peter Kemp, *Alms for Oblivion* (1961); Pierre Gentil, *Remous sur le Mekong* (1950); and Katay Don Sasorith, *Le Laos: son evolution politique* (1953). On events during 1945, see Henry Allard and Jean Deuve, *Indochine 1945: Témoinages sur une résistance méconnu, la lutte contre les japonais au Laos* (1984). For developments in postwar Laos, see Jean Deuve's invaluable narrative, *Le royaume du Laos, 1949–1965* (1984), which has a helpful documentary appendix; Marek Thee, *Notes of a Witness: Laos and the Second Indo-China War* (1973); and C. J. Christie, "Marxism and the History of the Nationalist Movements in Laos," *Journal of Southeast Asian Studies* 10 (1979): 146–158. Two memoirs of the postwar period, translated by John B. Murdoch, make good reading: *Lao Issara: The Memoirs of Oun Sananikone* (1975); and *Iron Man of Laos: Prince Phetsarath Ratanavongsa* (1978). Hugh Toye's *Laos: Buffer State or Battleground* (1968) and Arthur Dommen's *Conflict in Laos: The Politics of Neutralization* (rev. ed., 1971) are still valuable, as is Nina Adams and Alfred McCoy, eds., *Laos: War and Revolution* (1970). Charles A. Stevenson, *The End of Nowhere* (1972), is a bitter, heartfelt account that should be read alongside Fred Branfman, comp., *Voices from the Plain of Jars* (1972). Paul F. Langer and Joseph Zasloff's *North Vietnam and the Pathet Lao: Parties in the Struggle for Laos* (1970) is also useful. The most recent analysis of contemporary Lao politics is MacAlister Brown and Joseph J. Zasloff, *Apprentice Revolutionaries: The Communist Movement in Laos, 1930–1985* (1986). Other important studies of postrevolutionary Laos include Martin Stuart Fox, ed., *Contemporary Laos: Studies in the Politics and Society of the Lao Peoples' Democratic Republic* (1982); Arthur J. Dommen, *Laos: Keystone of Indochina* (1985); and Grant Evans and Kelvin Rowley, *Red Brotherhood of War* (1984). The Moscow-published *Laos* (1985) is filled with excellent photographs of the 1975–1985 period.

## Chapter 35: Thailand

General treatments of Thailand's recent history are few, and none is completely satisfactory. D. K. Wyatt, *Thailand: A Short History* (1984), includes an abbreviated narrative in a narrow analytical scheme. Charles F. Keyes, *Thailand: Buddhist Kingdom as Modern Nation-State* (1987), is very stimulating, particularly with respect to current trends and developments. John L. S. Girling, *Thailand: Society and Politics* (1981), provides a comprehensive analysis but little narrative; while Nigel Brailey, *Thailand and the Fall of Singapore: A Frustrated Asian Revolution* (1986), is based only on Western sources. The thick collection of documents edited by Thak Chaloemtiarana, *Thai Politics: Extracts and Documents 1932–1957* (1978), goes some of the way to providing the reader with a sense of immediacy. A useful anthology is Clark D. Neher, ed., *Modern Thai Politics: From Village to Nation* (rev. ed., 1979). Wolf Donner, *The Five Faces of Thailand: An Economic Geography* (1978), is a very useful reference.

The wartime period has received some much-needed treatment in recent years. See particularly Charnvit Kasetsiri, "The First Phibun Government and its Involvement in World War II," *Journal of the Siam Society* 62, 2 (July 1974): 25–88; Thamsook Numnonda, "Pibulsongkram's Thai Nation-Building Programme during the Japanese Military Presence, 1941–1945," *Journal of Southeast Asian Studies* 9, 2 (Sept. 1978): 234–247, and *Thailand and the Japanese Presence, 1941–1945* (1977); Benjamin A. Batson, "The Fall of the Phibun Government, 1944," *Journal of the Siam Society* 62, 2 (July 1974): 89–120; and John B. Haseman, *The Thai Resistance Movement during the Second World War* (1978). Useful firsthand accounts are provided in the memoirs of foreign minister Direk Jayanama, *Siam and World War II,* trans. Jane Godfrey Keyes (1978); Andrew Gilchrist, *Bangkok Top Secret* (1970); Peter Kemp, *Alms for Oblivion* (1961); and Nicol Smith and Blake Clark, *Into Siam, Underground Kingdom* (1946). On the diplomatic crisis at the end of the war, see Nicholas Tarling, "Atonement before Absolution: British Policy towards Thailand during World War II," *Journal of the Siam Society* 66, 1 (Jan. 1978): 22–65; James V. Martin, Jr., "Thai-American Relations in World War II," *Journal of Asian Studies* 22, 4 (1963): 451–467; and Herbert A. Fine, "The Liquidation of World War II in Thailand," *Pacific Historical Review* 34, 1 (1965): 65–82.

On political developments in the postwar period, a useful beginning point is Thak Chaloemtiarana's *Thailand: The Politics of Despotic Paternalism* (1979), which though primarily concerned with Sarit Thanarat has much to say about his predecessors. Charles F. Keyes, *Isan: Regionalism in Northeastern Thailand* (1967), is an important introduction to Thailand's most important regional problem. Rayne Kruger, *The Devil's Discus* (1964), is the only full discussion on the death of King Ananda but is not the last word on the subject. Pierre Fistié, *L'évolution de la Thaïlande contemporaine* (1967), which has a good deal of interesting information on the rule of Phibun. Thai voices are heard in the translations of memoirs and recollections in Jayanta Kumar Ray, *Portraits of Thai Politics* (1972), and the somewhat myopic memoirs of Pridi Phanomyong (Pridi Banomyong), *Ma vie mouvementée et mes 21 ans d'exil en Chine populaire* (1974).

On the Sarit-Thanom era, from 1957 to 1973, the incisive monograph by Thak Chaloemtiarana, already cited, is an essential beginning point. Several very stimulating essays are included in *Change and Persistence in Thai Society: Essays in Honor of Lauriston Sharp,* ed. G. William Skinner and A. Thomas Kirsch (1975); and an especially important critical essay is Benedict Anderson, "Studies of the Thai State: The State of Thai Studies," in Eliezer Ayal, ed., *The Study of Thailand* (1979), 193–247. On domestic politics, administration, and the bureaucratic elite, see Fred W. Riggs, *Thailand: The Modernization of a Bureaucratic Polity* (1966); William J. Siffin, *The Thai Bureaucracy: Institutional Change and Development* (1966); T. H. Silcock, ed., *Thailand: Social and Economic Studies in Development* (1967); David F. Haas, *Interaction in the Thai Bureaucracy: Structure, Culture and Social Exchange* (1979); and Likhit Dhiravegin, *Political Attitudes of the Bureaucratic Elite and Modernization in Thailand* (1973) and *The Bureaucratic Elite of Thailand* (1978). Important domestic minorities are dealt with in excellent fash-

548 *Bibliography*

ion by G. William Skinner, *Chinese Society in Thailand: An Analytical History* (1957) and *Leadership and Power in the Chinese Community of Thailand* (1958); Boonsanong Punyodyana, *Chinese-Thai Differential Assimilation in Bangkok: An Exploratory Study* (1971); and not so powerfully by Peter A. Poole, *The Vietnamese in Thailand* (1970), and Nantawan Haemindra,"The Problem of the Thai-Muslims in the Four Southern Provinces of Thailand," *Journal of Southeast Asian Studies* 7 (1976): 197–225, and 8 (1977): 85–105.

Internal conflict and insurgency are treated in Donald E. Weatherbee, *The United Front in Thailand: A Documentary Analysis* (1970); Thomas Lobe, *United States National Security Policy and Aid to the Thailand Police* (1977); Jeffrey Race, "The War in Northern Thailand," *Modern Asian Studies* 8, 1 (1974): 85–112; George K. Tanham, *Trial in Thailand* (1974); and M. Ladd Thomas, *Political Violence in the Muslim Provinces of Southern Thailand* (1975). On relations with the United States, see Donald E. Nuechterlein, *Thailand and the Struggle for Southeast Asia* (1965); David A. Wilson, *The United States and the Future of Thailand* (1970); and J. Alexander Caldwell, *American Economic Aid to Thailand* (1974).

On the critical 1973–1976 period, its background and aftermath, see David Morell and Chai-anan Samudvanij, *Thailand: Reform, Reaction and Revolution* (1981); Andrew Turton, Jonathan Fast, and Malcolm Caldwell, eds., *Thailand: Roots of Conflict* (1978); E. Thadeus Flood, "The Thai Left Wing in Historical Context," *Bulletin of Concerned Asian Scholars* (Apr.–Jun 1975): 56–67; Saneh Chammarik, "Thai Politics and the October Revolution," *Journal of Social Science Review* (Bangkok) 1, 1 (1976): 1–41; Ben Anderson, "Withdrawal Symptoms: Social and Cultural Aspects of the October 6 Coup," *Bulletin of Concerned Asian Scholars* 9, 3 (1977): 13–30. David W. P. Elliott, *Thailand: The Origins of Military Rule* (1978), is useful. On foreign policy, see Ganganath Jha, *Foreign Policy of Thailand* (1979), and Sarasin Viraphol, *Directions in Thai Foreign Policy* (1976).

The role of Buddhism in recent Thai public life is explored by Charles F. Keyes, "Buddhism and National Integration in Thailand," *Journal of Asian Studies* 30, 3 (1971): 551–567, and "Political Crisis and Militant Buddhism in Contemporary Thailand," in *Religion and Legitimation of Power in Thailand, Burma and Laos,* ed. Bardwell Smith (1978); and Somboon Suksamran, *Political Buddhism in Southeast Asia* (1976). A broader view is taken by Frank Reynolds, "Civic Religion and National Community in Thailand," *Journal of Asian Studies* 36 (Feb. 1977): 267–282; while S. J. Tambiah, *The Buddhist Saints of the Forest and the Cult of Amulets* (1984), goes below the surface commonly presented to the West. Recent Buddhist thought is the subject of Donald K. Swearer, *Buddhism in Transition* (1970).

On economic change, see James C. Ingram, *Economic Change in Thailand, 1850–1970* (1971); T. H. Silcock, *The Economic Development of Thai Agriculture* (1970); Prateep Sondysuwan, ed., *Finance, Trade and Economic Development in Thailand* (1975); Paul B. Trescott, *Thailand's Monetary Experience: The Economics of Stability* (1971), which is unusually sensitive and readable; and Sein Lin and Bruce Esposito, "Agrarian Reform in Thailand: Problems and Prospects," *Pacific Affairs* 49, 3 (1976): 425–442. Peasants' concerns are considered in Toru Yano, "Land Tenure in Thailand," *Asian Survey* 8, 10 (1968): 853–863; and government's response to them in Herbert J. Rubin, *The Dynamics of Development in Rural Thailand* (1974). Recent critical, and indigenous, scholarship is well represented in Vichitvong na Pombhejara, ed., *Readings in Thailand's Political Economy* (1978). Puey Ungphakorn, *Glancing Back, Looking Forward* (1977), by the former governor of the Bank of Thailand and rector of Thammasat University, is important.

There could hardly be a better glimpse into Thai rural life and its changes over the past generation than Khamsing Srinawk's enthralling *The Politician and*

*Other Stories* (1973). A general overview of contemporary Thailand is given in the official *Thailand in the 80s* (1984), which provides useful data and fine photographs.

## Chapter 36: Burma

The largest body of accessible literature on Burma describes politics and society from the onset of the Second World War. Other than memoirs by participants, the bulk of these studies was written by foreigners who lived or studied in the country during the 1950s. The flavor of the wartime period was described from a variety of contemporary viewpoints, internal and external. See John L. Christian, *Burma and the Japanese Invader* (1945); Ba Maw, *Breakthrough in Burma: Memoirs of a Revolution, 1939–1946* (1969); Nu, *Burma Under the Japanese* (1954); Maung Maung, ed., *Aung San of Burma* (1962); and Thein Pe Myint, "Wartime Traveller," translated in Robert H. Taylor, *Marxism and Resistance in Burma, 1942–1945* (1984).

Contrasting analytical views of the period are found in Dorothy H. Guyot, "The Burma Independence Army: A Political Movement in Military Garb," in Josef Silverstein, ed., *Southeast Asia in World War II* (1966); Ba Shin, *The Roots of the Revolution* (1962); and Robert H. Taylor, "Burma in the Anti-Fascist War," in Alfred W. McCoy, ed., *Southeast Asia Under Japanese Occupation* (1979). Also see Dorothy H. Guyot's "The Political Impact of the Japanese Occupation of Burma" (Ph.D. diss., Yale Univ., 1966).

Studies by foreign observers of the initial years of independence include Frank N. Trager, *Burma: From Kingdom to Republic* (1966); John F. Cady, *A History of Modern Burma* (1958); Hugh Tinker, *The Union of Burma* (4th ed., 1968); Lucian W. Pye, *Politics, Personality, and Nation Building: Burma's Search for Identity* (1962); Frank N. Trager, *Toward a Welfare State in Burma* (1959); Richard A. Butwell, *U Nu of Burma* (1963); Maung Maung, *Burma and General Ne Win* (1969); and Maung Maung, *Burma's Constitution* (2nd ed., 1961). Nu, *U Nu—Saturday's Son* (1975), provides the most accessible but not always obvious discussion of the politics of the 1950s by a key actor, the former prime minister.

There have been few studies of Burma's politics since the 1962 coup. The most complete are Josef Silverstein, *Burma: Military Rule and the Politics of Stagnation* (1977), and David I. Steinberg, *Burma's Road toward Development: Growth and Ideology Under Military Rule* (1981). One set of interpretations of the meaning of the period are given in F. K. Lehman, ed., *Military Rule in Burma Since 1962* (1981). The ideology of the ruling party is set forth in Burma Socialist Programme Party, *The System of Correlation of Man and His Environment* (1962, 1963), which also includes "The Burmese Way to Socialism" and the party constitution.

The Burmese Communist movement after independence is most clearly analyzed in the work of John Badgley; see his "The Communist Parties of Burma," in R. A. Scalapino, ed., *The Communist Revolution in Asia* (2nd ed., 1969), and "Burmese Communist Schisms," in J. W. Lewis, ed., *Peasant Rebellion and Communist Revolution in Asia* (1974). Charles B. Smith, Jr., *The Burmese Communist Party in the 1980s* (1984), documents more recent directions in Burmese Communist thought. Local government is discussed in Badgley's *Politics Among Burmans* (1974), a rare study of local opinion, and in Melford Spiro, "Factionalism and Politics in Village Burma," in Marc J. Swartz, ed., *Local Level Politics: Social and Cultural Perspectives* (1968); and Manning Nash, "Party Building in Upper Burma," *Asian Survey* 11, 4 (April 1963): 197–202.

The question of national unity as related to ethnicity, cultural pluralism, and separatism has been one of the most vexing for Burma's postwar political leaders. The essays in Peter Kunstadter, ed., *Southeast Asian Tribes, Minorities, and Nations* (1967), provide a good overview and analysis of the relevant ethnography. Contrasting interpretations of the political implications of this data are provided in Josef Silverstein, *Burmese Politics: The Dilemma of National Unity* (1980), and Robert H. Taylor, "Perceptions of Ethnicity in the Politics of Burma," *Southeast Asian Journal of Social Science* 10, 1 (1982): 7–22.

The economic development of Burma since independence is reviewed in the Steinberg volume referred to above, the Burma chapter in Frank H. Golay, Ralph Anspach, M. Ruth Pfanner, and Eliezer B. Ayal, *Underdevelopment and Economic Nationalism in Southeast Asia* (1969), and, for the first decade, in Louis J. Walinsky, *Economic Development in Burma, 1951–1960* (1962). The fate of the Indian minority after independence is discussed at the conclusion of N. R. Chakravarti, *The Indian Minority in Burma* (1971), and Moshe Yegar, *The Muslims of Burma* (1972).

## Chapter 37: Malaysia, Singapore, and Brunei

The Japanese conquest of Malaya and Singapore between December 1941 and February 1942 has been the subject of much description and reminiscence, but we refer here only to three firsthand and authoritative accounts: A. E. Perceval, *The War in Malaya* (1949); H. Gordon Bennett, *Why Singapore Fell* (1944); and Masanobu Tsuji, *Singapore: The Japanese Version* (1960). There are also numerous accounts of the Japanese occupation of Malaya by those who experienced it: F. Spencer Chapman's *The Jungle Is Neutral* (1949) is particularly interesting for its account of the formation and activities of Chinese Communist-organized (MCP) resistance to the Japanese, and Chin Kee Onn's *Malaya Upside Down* (1946) conveys something of life at that time for the civilian. Relatively little scholarly work has been done on the occupation period, but two articles by Yoji Akashi should be cited: "Japanese Military Administration in Malaya: Its Formation and Evolution in Reference to the Sultans, the Islamic Religion, and the Moslem Malays," *Asian Studies* (Manila) 7, 1 (1969): 81–110; and "Japanese Policy Towards the Malayan Chinese," *Journal of Southeast Asian Studies* 1, 2 (1970): 61–89. Cheah Boon Kheng, *Red Star over Malaya: Resistance and Social Conflict During and After the Japanese Occupation* (1983), is an important contribution to studies of social change originating in this period.

The best introduction to postwar Malayan politics in the 1980s is R. S. Milne and Diane K. Mauzy, *Politics and Government in Malaysia* (2nd rev. ed., 1986); but see also Gordon P. Means, *Malaysian Politics* (2nd ed., 1976). Stanley Bedlington's *Malaysia and Singapore: The Building of New States* (1978) is a succinct but useful survey. For a Marxist view, see Mohamed Amin and Malcolm Caldwell, eds., *Malaya: The Making of a Neo-Colony* (1977). On constitutional questions, see M. Suffian b. Hashim, *An Introduction to the Constitution of Malaysia* (2nd ed., 1976), and the same author's coedited volume of essays by various hands, *The Constitution of Malaysia: Its Development, 1957–1977* (1978).

The introduction and abandonment of the Malayan Union scheme is discussed in James de Vere Allen, *The Malayan Union* (1967); and in somewhat greater detail in Mohamed Noordin Sopiee's *From Malayan Union to Singapore Separation: Political Unification in the Malayan Region, 1945–65* (1974). Michael R. Stenson's *Industrial Conflict in Malaya: Prelude to the Communist Revolt in 1948* (1970) focuses on labor relations during the early postwar period; and Cheah Boon Kheng examines MCP organization in *The Masked Comrades: A Study of the Communist United Front in Malaya, 1945–48* (1979). The fullest account of the Communist insurgency in Malaya known as the "Emergency" is given in Anthony Short, *The Communist Insurrection in Malaya, 1948–1960* (1975); but see also Richard Clutterbuck, *Riot and Revolution in Singapore and Malaya, 1945–1963* (1973; rev. repr. issued as *Conflict and Violence in Singapore and Malaysia, 1945–1983,* 1985); and Gene Z. Hanrahan, *The Communist Struggle in Malaya* (1954).

Lucian Pye, *Guerrilla Communism in Malaya* (1954), is an interesting attempt to understand the nature of Chinese participation in the struggle.

A number of studies have been made of the processes and problems of rural Chinese "resettlement" during the Emergency, notably J. B. Perry Robinson, *Transformation in Malaya* (1955); Kernial Singh Sandhu, "The Saga of the 'Squatter' in Malaya," *Journal of Southeast Asian History* 5, 1 (March 1964): 143–177; and Han Suyin's novel, . . . *And the Rain My Drink* (1956). A comparison between fighting the Emergency in Malaya and the American war in Vietnam, by a British participant in the former, is Robert Thompson's *Defeating Communist Insurgency: The Lessons of Malaya and Vietnam* (1966).

Three works bearing directly on Malay politics in the early post-1945 period are A. J. Stockwell, *British Policy and Malay Politics during the Malayan Union Experiment, 1942–48* (1979); Firdaus Haji Abdullah, *Radical Malay Politics: Its Origins and Early Development* (1985); and John Funston, *Malay Politics in Malaya: A Study of UMNO and PAS* (1980). A lively Malay political memoir of this period is Ahmad Boestamam, *Carving the Path to the Summit* (1979). Politics within the Chinese community is discussed in Margaret Clark Roff, "The MCA, 1948–65," *Journal of Southeast Asian History* 4, 2 (1965): 40–53; and Wang Gungwu's "Chinese Politics in Malaysia," *China Quarterly* 43 (1970): 1–30, gives a more general perspective. See also Loh Kok Wah, *The Politics of Chinese Unity in Malaysia* (1983), which has a greater emphasis on the later period, as does the MCA's own study, *Malayan Chinese: Towards National Unity* (1982).

There have been many discussions of ethnicity and politics in Malaysia, among the most notable of which are, in alphabetical order, M. Brennan, "Class, Politics and Race in Modern Malaysia," *Journal of Contemporary Malaysia* 12, 2 (1982): 188–215; H. M. Dahlan, ed., *The Nascent Malaysian Society: Developments, Trends, and Problems* (1976); Cynthia Enloe, *Multi-Ethnic Politics: The Case of Malaysia* (1970); David S. Gibbons, "National Integration and Cultural Diversity: The Case of Malaysia," in S. S. Hueh, ed., *Development in Southeast Asia: Issues and Dilemmas* (1972), 115–143; Ismail Kassim, *Race, Politics and Modernization: A Study of the Malaysian Electoral Process* (1979); Judith Nagata, *Malaysian Mosaic: Perspectives from a Poly-Ethnic Society* (1979); and Nagata's edited volume, "Pluralism in Malaysia: Myth and Reality; A Symposium on Singapore and Malaysia," *Contributions to Asian Studies* 7 (1975): 1–138; Alvin Rabushka, *Race and Politics in Urban Malaya* (1973); and Michael Stenson, *Class, Race and Colonialism in West Malaysia: The Indian Case* (1980).

Karl von Vorys, *Democracy Without Consensus: Communalism and Political Stability in Malaysia* (1975), is an excellent study of the political events leading up to and encompassing the Kuala Lumpur riots of 1969 and their aftermath. May 13 itself resulted in a considerable literature, of which the following may be noted: Tunku Abdul Rahman, *May 13: Before and After* (1969); Lee Kam Hing, ed., *The May Tragedy in Malaysia* (1969); National Operations Council, *The May 13 Tragedy: A Report* (1969); Goh Cheng Teik, *The May Thirteenth Incident and Democracy in Malaysia* (1971); Felix Gagliano, *Communal Violence in Malaysia 1969: The Political Aftermath* (1970); John Slimming, *Malaysia: Death of a Democracy* (1969); and Mahathir b. Mohamad, *The Malay Dilemma* (1970). The last, by a future prime minister of Malaysia, was banned for several years after publication.

Malaysia's successive parliamentary elections have been documented and discussed in K. J. Ratnam and R. S. Milne, *The Malayan Parliamentary Election of 1964* (1967); R. K. Vasil, *The Malaysian General Election of 1969* (1972); Chandrasekaran Pillay, *The 1974 General Elections in Malaysia* (1974); Harold Crouch et al., eds., *Malaysian Politics and the 1978 Election* (1980); and Harold Crouch, *Malaysia's 1982 General Election* (1982).

For East Malaysia, Margaret Clark Roff's *The Politics of Belonging: Political*

*Change in Sabah and Sarawak* (1974) analyzes the growth of political consciousness during the early years of Malaysia, a subject also dealt with in James P. Ongkili, *Modernization in East Malaysia, 1960–1970* (1972). R. H. W. Reece documents the end of an era in his *The Name of Brooke: The End of White Raja Rule in Sarawak* (1982); and see also Sanib Said, *Malay Politics in Sarawak, 1946–1966* (1985). Later political change in Sarawak is dealt with by Michael B. Leigh, *The Rising Moon: Political Change in Sarawak* (1974), and Peter Searle, *Politics in Sarawak 1970–1976: The Iban Perspective* (1983).

The early years of postwar political activity in Singapore are described in Yeo Kim Wah, *Political Development in Singapore, 1945–1955* (1973), and in Chan Heng Chee's *A Sensation of Independence: A Political Biography of David Marshall* (1984). Chan Heng Chee, *The Dynamics of One Party Dominance: The PAP at the Grassroots* (1976), is the definitive work on the People's Action Party; but see also the earlier Pang Cheng Lian, *Singapore's People's Action Party: Its History, Organization and Leadership* (1971), and Thomas J. Bellows, *The People's Action Party of Singapore: Emergence of a Dominant Party System* (1970). A hagiographic account of Lee Kuan Yew may be found in Alex Josey's *Lee Kuan Yew* (1968), and a scathing account of governance in the city state in T. J. S. George, *Lee Kuan Yew's Singapore* (1973). Carolyn Choo has discussed Singapore after Lee Kuan Yew in *Singapore: The PAP and the Problem of Political Succession* (1985). Riaz Hassan, ed., *Singapore: Society in Transition* (1976), is an excellent collection of essays on all aspects of Singapore society.

Little of consequence has been published on Brunei in the post-World War II period, but Ranjit Singh, *Brunei 1839–1983: The Problems of Political Survival* (1984), is a straightforward account of the state's modern history.

On economics, the most important works include J. J. Puthucheary, *Ownership and Control of the Malaysian Economy* (1960), which examines the structure of ownership; E. H. Fisk and H. Osman-Rani, eds., *The Political Economy of Malaysia* (1982), an excellent collection of essays on political and economic matters; Donald Snodgrass, *Inequality and Economic Development in Malaysia* (1980); and J. C. Jackson and M. Rudner, eds., *Issues in Malaysian Development* (1979), and David Lim, ed., *Readings on Malaysian Economic Development* (1975).

There is a strong vein of left-wing, radically reinterpretive material on the Malaysian economy, well represented in a number of articles in the *Journal of Contemporary Asia* between 1979 and 1981 and in Shamsul A.B., "The Politics of Poverty Eradication: The Implementation of Development Projects in a Malaysian District," *Pacific Affairs* 56 (1983): 455–476; and Tan Loong-hoe, "The State and the Distribution of Wealth within the Malay Society of Peninsular Malaysia," *Southeast Asian Affairs* (1981): 217–232.

The standard published work on the demography of peninsular Malaya remains T. E. Smith, *Population Growth in Malaya: An Analysis of Recent Trends* (1952), but attention should also be drawn to J. C. Caldwell, "The Demographic Background," in T. H. Silcock and E. K. Fisk, eds., *The Political Economy of Independent Malaya* (1963). On the immigrant populations, see R. N. Jackson, *Immigrant Labour and the Development of Malaya, 1796–1920* (1961). Manjit Singh Sidhu and Gavin W. Jones, eds., *Population Dynamics in a Plural Society: Peninsular Malaysia* (1981), is a collection of essays on a wide range of demographic issues. Gavin W. Jones and Lim Lin Lean, "Scenarios for Future Population Growth in Malaysia," *Kajian Malaysia* (Penang) 3, 2 (1985): 1–24, looks at evolving demographic patterns in the light of government policies. On a related issue of importance, see Lim Lin Lean et al., *Continuing Fertility Transitions in a Plural Society: Ethnic Trends and Differentials in Peninsular Malaysia* (1985). For Singapore, see Saw Swee-hock, *Singapore Population in Transition* (1970).

Some of the problems facing the Malay peasant and his land are discussed in T. B. Wilson, *The Economics of Padi Production in North Malaya, Part I: Land Ten-*

*ure, Rents, Land Use and Fragmentation* (1959); much amplified for the 1980s by James C. Scott, *Weapons of the Weak* (1986); and see also S. Husin Ali, *Poverty and Landlessness in Kelantan, Malaysia* (1983). General studies of the Malay rice economy include J. T. Purcal, *Rice Economy: A Case Study of Four Villages in West Malaysia* (1971); Masuo Kuchiba et al., *Three Malay Villages: A Sociology of Padi Growers in West Malaysia* (1979); and Akimi Fujimoto, *Income Sharing among Malay Peasants: A Study of Land Tenure and Rice Production* (1983). On government land development schemes, see C. MacAndrews, *Mobility and Modernization: The Federal Land Development Authority and its Role in Modernizing the Rural Malays* (1977), and two earlier articles, Robert Ho, "Land Settlement Projects in Malaya: An Assessment of the Role of the Federal Land Development Authority," *Journal of Tropical Geography* 12 (1965): 1–15, and R. Vikkramatileke, "State Aided Rural Land Colonisation in Malaya: An Appraisal of the F.L.D.A.," *Annals of the Association of American Geographers* 55 (1965): 377–403.

## Chapter 38: Indonesia

Two fine articles provide a good introduction to the Japanese conquest and rule of Indonesia: Benedict Anderson's "Japan: 'The Light of Asia,'" in Josef Silverstein, ed., *Southeast Asia in World War II* (1966); and Anthony Reid, "Indonesia: From Briefcase to Samurai Sword," in Alfred W. McCoy, ed., *Southeast Asia Under Japanese Occupation* (1980). Other important works in the large literature are Harry J. Benda's pioneering work, *The Crescent and the Rising Sun: Indonesian Islam under the Japanese Occupation, 1942–1945* (1959); Benda, James K. Irikura, and Koishi Kishi, eds., *Japanese Military Administration in Indonesia: Selected Documents* (1965); and Anthony Reid and Oki Akira, eds., *The Japanese Experience in Indonesia: Selected Memoirs of 1942–1945* (1985).

Two books in English cover the Indonesian Revolution over its whole span. One is George McT. Kahin's *Nationalism and Revolution in Indonesia* (1952), much of it researched in Indonesia during the latter part of the revolution itself. The other is Anthony J. S. Reid's *The Indonesian National Revolution, 1945–50* (1974). Two other works concentrate on the violent formative phase of the revolution in late 1945 and early 1946: Benedict Anderson's *Java in a Time of Revolution: Occupation and Resistance, 1944–1946* (1972); and John R. W. Smail, *Bandung in the Early Revolution, 1945–46: A Study in the Social History of the Indonesian Revolution* (1964). The striking variety of forms taken by the revolution in different areas across the archipelago is illustrated in *Regional Dynamics of the Indonesian Revolution* (1985), a set of regional cases, three in Java and Sumatra and one each in Sulawesi and Ambon, edited by Audrey R. Kahin. Alastair M. Taylor's *Indonesian Independence and the United Nations* (1960) covers the unusually important role played by the United Nations in the Indonesian case, while Robert J. McMahon's *Colonialism and the Cold War: The United States and the Struggle for Indonesian Independence* (1981) covers the similarly important role of the United States in the Indonesian Revolution. Idrus' mordant short novel, *Surabaya*, translated in *Indonesia* 5 (April 1968): 1–28, about the revolutionary battle in November 1945, is a masterpiece.

For the period between 1950 and 1965, two remarkably well-informed political narratives—Herbert Feith's *The Decline of Constitutional Democracy in Indonesia* (1962) and Daniel Lev's *The Transition to Guided Democracy: Indonesian Politics, 1957–59* (1966)—carry the story most of the way. Feith's "Dynamics of Guided Democracy," in Ruth McVey, ed., *Indonesia* (1963) and J. A. C. Mackie, *Problems of the Indonesian Inflation* (1967), continue the line toward Armageddon in 1965. *Indonesian Political Thinking, 1945–1965,* edited by Feith and Lance Castles, surveys the great variety of Indonesian schools of thought, with examples drawn from writings and speeches over the period. A similar publication— Benedict Anderson and Audrey Kahin, eds., *Interpreting Indonesian Politics: Thir-*

*teen Contributions to the Debate* (1982)—overlaps the Feith-Castles volume and includes writings published as late as 1981. Ruth McVey's "The Post-Revolutionary Transformation of the Indonesian Army," *Indonesia* 11 (April 1971): 131–176, and *Indonesia* 13 (April 1972): 147–181, marvelously illuminates not only the history of the spontaneously created army itself but also the general politics of Indonesia as well. Barbara S. Harvey's *Permesta, Half a Rebellion* (1977) is an engaging study of one of the regional army rebellions of the late 1950s. Probably the best of Rex Mortimer's books on this period is *Indonesian Communism Under Sukarno: Ideology and Politics, 1959–1965* (1974).

Perhaps the most useful way to approach the "New Order" in Indonesia (1966 onward) is to follow a series of five important writings which together suggest that Suharto's regime may best be understood as a revival and continuation of the old bureaucratic Netherlands state. The works, in chronological order, are Harry J. Benda, "The Pattern of Reforms in the Closing Years of Dutch Rule in Indonesia," *Journal of Asian Studies* 25, 4 (1966): 589–605; Ruth T. McVey, "The Beamtenstaat in Indonesia" (1977), published in Anderson and A. Kahin, eds., *Interpreting Indonesian Politics*, 84–91; Heather Sutherland, *The Making of a Bureaucratic Elite: The Colonial Transformation of the Javanese Priyayi* (1979); Benedict R. O'G. Anderson, "Old State, New Society: Indonesia's New Order in Comparative Perspective," *Journal of Asian Studies* 42, 2 (1983): 477–496; and Daniel S. Lev, "Colonial Law and the Genesis of the Indonesian State," *Indonesia* 40 (Oct. 1985): 57–74.

Other important works on the New Order include Benedict R. Anderson and Ruth T. McVey, *A Preliminary Analysis of the October 1, 1965 Coup in Indonesia* (1971); Harold Crouch, *The Army and Politics in Indonesia* (1978); Donald K. Emmerson, *Indonesia's Elite: Political Culture and Cultural Politics* (1976); and Richard Robison, "Culture, Politics and Economy in the Political History of the New Order," *Indonesia* 31 (April 1981): 1–29.

A few examples may suggest the variety and vigor of contemporary arts in Indonesia. Pending translations of the most recent novels of Indonesia's finest writer, Pramoedya Ananta Toer, Keith Foulcher's "*Bumi Manusia* and *Anak Semua Bangsa:* Pramoedya Ananta Toer Enters the 1980's," *Indonesia* 32 (Oct. 1981): 1–15, provides a useful discussion of two of these works, written during Pramoedya's fifteen-year exile in a remote penal colony in eastern Indonesia. William H. Frederick introduces the musical form sometimes called "Islamic Rock" in "Rhoda Irama and the Dangdut Style: Aspects of Contemporary Indonesian Popular Culture," *Indonesia* 34 (Oct. 1982): 103–131. Judith Becker's *Traditional Music in Modern Java: Gamelan in a Changing Society* (1980) shows changes in the quintessential art form of Java. Stephanie Morgan and Laurie Jo Sears, eds., *Aesthetic Tradition and Cultural Transition in Java and Bali*, shows such changes in a variety of the arts.

The two most useful and convenient works on rural conditions in Indonesia —especially Java, of course—are Benjamin White's "Agricultural Involution and Its Critics: Twenty Years After," *Bulletin of Concerned Asian Scholars* 15, 2 (1983): 18–31, and Gary E. Hanson, ed., *Agricultural and Rural Development in Indonesia* (1981).

Research dealing with the accelerating changes affecting peasants since independence in 1949 includes Gillian Hart's comprehensive and compelling summary of what has happened to Javan peasants in recent decades, *Power, Labor and Livelihood: Processes of Change in Rural Java* (1986), and the articles by Ann Stoler, "Rice Harvesting in Kali Loro: A Study of Class and Labor Relations in Rural Java," *American Ethnologist* 4 (1977): 678–698; Franz Husken, "Landlords, Sharecroppers and Agricultural Laborers: Changing Labour Relations in Rural Java," *Journal of Contemporary Asia* 9, 2 (1979): 140–151; Masri Singarimbun, "Sriharjo Revisited," *Bulletin of Indonesian Economic Studies* 12, 2

(July 1976): 117–125; and the monograph by Rex Mortimer, *The Indonesian Communist Party and Land Reform* (1972). An early bibliography surveying the literature is M. A. Jaspan, *Social Stratification and Social Mobility in Indonesia* (1959).

The October 1984 issue of *Indonesia,* devoted to the theme of religion and politics in Indonesia, includes four articles on Islam. An admirable short description of Javanese Islam in recent times may be found in Part 2 of Clifford Geertz, *The Religion of Java* (1960). The classical pair of studies on Indonesian Islam deal with Aceh (North Sumatra): C. Snouck Hurgronje, *The Achehnese* (2 vols., 1906), covering the late nineteenth century, and James Siegel's grand *The Rope of God* (1969), which deals with Reform Islam, the most powerful force in Acehnese society in the twentieth century. Two works by Howard Federspiel survey two of the most important twentieth-century Muslim movements: "The Muhammadijah: A Study of an Orthodox Islamic Movement in Indonesia," *Indonesia* 10 (Oct. 1970): 57–80, and *Persatuan Islam: Islamic Reform in 20th Century Indonesia* (1970). *Adat, Islam, and Christianity in a Batak Homeland* (1981), by Susan Rodgers Siregar, introduces the variety of social-religious options in another part of Sumatra just north of Minangkabau. C. van Dijk's *Rebellion Under the Banner of Islam: The Darul Islam in Indonesia* (1981) surveys an important challenge to the essentially secular Indonesian state in various parts of the country in the 1940s and 1950s.

On demography, Geoffrey McNicoll and Masri Singarimbun, *Fertility Decline in Indonesia: Analysis and Interpretation* (1987), is important.

## Chapter 39: The Philippines

**Wartime:** The war years in the Philippines are shrouded in controversy. See, for example, David J. Steinberg's *Philippine Collaboration in World War II* (1967), and Teodoro A. Agoncillo's *The Fateful Years* (2 vols., 1965). Mauro Garcia has published a valuable collection of documents on the *Japanese Occupation of the Philippines* (1965), and many of the participants in the war including Jorge Vargas, Jose P. Laurel, and Claro M. Recto have published memoirs. Alfred W. McCoy has an important essay in *Southeast Asia under Japanese Occupation: Transition and Transformation* (1980) and a major work on the subject in progress. Teodoro A. Agoncillo, *The Burden of Proof: The Vargas-Laurel Collaboration Case, with Jorge B. Vargas' Sugamo Diary* (1984), offers a revisionist's defense of Laurel and Vargas. Military historians have written extensively on all of the campaigns, and spy buffs are urged to read Carlos Quirino's *Chick Parsons: America's Master Spy in the Philippines* (1984). See also Carol M. Petillo, *Douglas MacArthur: The Philippine Years* (1981).

**The Old Order:** The best introduction to the early postwar political era is Ronald K. Edgerton, "The Politics of Reconstruction in the Philippines, 1945–1948" (Ph.D. diss., Univ. of Michigan, 1975). Vicente A. Pacis has written *President Sergio Osmeña: A Fully Documented Biography* (1971), but this great Filipino still awaits a proper biography. See also Jose V. Abueva, *Ramon Magsaysay: A Political Biography* (1971), and Marcial P. Lichauco, *Roxas: The Story of a Great Filipino and of the Political Era in Which he Lived* (1952), which is flawed as a work of scholarship. Francis L. Starner, *Magsaysay and the Philippine Peasantry: The Agrarian Impact on Philippine Politics, 1953–1956* (1961), is useful. See also Emerenciana Y. Arcellana, *The Social and Political Thought of Claro M. Recto* (1981); Carlos Quirino, *Amang: The Life and Times of Eulogio Rodriguez, Sr.* (1983); the many books of essays by Nick Joaquin, for example, *Reportage on Politics* (1981); and Carolina G. Hernandez,"The Extent of Civilian Control of the Military in the Philippines, 1946–1976" (Ph.D. diss., State University of New York at Buffalo, 1979). The best works on the Hukbalahap are Benedict J. Kerkvliet, *The Huk Rebellion: A Study of Peasant Revolt in the Philippines* (1977), and Eduardo Lachica, *Huk: Philippine Agrarian Society in Revolt* (1971). Luis Taruc, the leader of the Huk movement, wrote a number of books, the most important being *Born of the People* (1953).

**The Marcos Era:** To understand Ferdinand Marcos it is essential but not sufficient to read from his own voluminous publications. See, for example, *Toward a New Partnership: The Filipino Ideology* (1983); *Progress and Martial Law* (1981); *In Search of Alternatives: The Third World in an Age of Crisis* (1980); and "Encounter with Destiny: Termination of Martial Law," speech, January 17, 1981 (1981). Not to be outdone, Imelda Marcos also had published material prepared for her delivery. See, for example, *A Humanist Approach to Development and Other Selected Speeches* (1981) and *Paths to Development* (1981). There was also a cottage industry of hagiography; for example, Jose M. Crisol, *Valor: World War II Saga of Ferdinand Marcos* (1983). Another aspect of the same industry were books explaining the constitution, edicts, and laws of martial law. See, for example, Jose Aruego, *The New Philippine Constitution Explained: Including the Constitutional Amendments* (1981), and *The Philippine Government in Action and the Philippine Constitution* (1982). Juan Ponce Enrile, *Toward New Horizons* (1974), and Arturo M. Tolentino, *The Philippines and the Law of the Sea: A Collection of Articles, Statements and Speeches* (1982), offer insights into two key Marcos supporters. There is a fascinating literature from those who were in opposition, including Rubin R. Canoy, *The Counterfeit Revolution: Martial Law in the Philippines* (1980); Raul S. Manglapus, *Philippines: The Silenced Democracy* (1976); Primitivo Mijores, *The Conjugal Dictatorship of Ferdinand and Imelda Marcos* (1976); and Stephen Psinakis, *Two Terrorists Meet* (1981). Psinakis, a son-in-law of the Lopez family, described in fascinating detail his and Benigno Aquino's encounters with Imelda Marcos in New York, revealing the interlocking way in which the Philippine elite functioned even during martial law.

There are a great many government documents and reports of official agencies, including hearings before the United States House of Representatives and the United States Senate. For information on the issue of human rights, see *The Report of an Amnesty International Mission to the Republic of the Philippines, November 1981* (1982) and *The Philippines, A Country in Crisis: A Report by the Lawyers Committee for International Human Rights* (1983). Jose Maria Sison, one of the founders of the New People's Army, has published *Prison and Beyond: Selected Poems, 1958–1983* (1984). The Muslim struggle for autonomy and challenge to national unity is examined in T. S. J. George, *Revolt in Mindanao: The Rise of Islam in Philippine Politics* (1980); Lela G. Noble, "The Moro National Liberation Party in the Philippines," *Pacific Affairs* 49, 3 (1976): 405–424; and Samuel K. Tan, *The Filipino Muslim Armed Struggle, 1900–1972* (1977). Among the best analyses written during the Marcos era, see Carl H. Landé, "Philippine Prospects After Martial Law," *Foreign Affairs* 59 (1981): 1147–1168; *Marcos and Martial Law in the Philippines*, ed. David A. Rosenberg (1979); and *The Philippines after Marcos*, ed. R. J. May and Francisco Nemenzo (1985), which was written a year too soon. Gerald H. Hill has written *The Aquino Assassination: The True Story and Analysis of the Assassination of Philippine Senator Benigno S. Aquino, Jr.* (1983), to which Nick Joaquin adds *The Aquinos of Tarlac: An Essay on History as Three Generations* (1983). The first in-depth analyses of the post-Marcos era can be found in Robert Shaplen's "Letters from Manila" published in *The New Yorker* on August 25, 1986, and the following week. Perhaps the most important early post-Marcos book is *Crisis in the Philippines: The Marcos Era and Beyond*, ed. John Bresnan (1986). Read also Eduardo Lachica, "The Philippines: A Critical Transition," *Asian Issues* (1985): 1–16. For a vivid photo essay, see *Bayon Ko: Images of the Philippine Revolt* (1986).

There is an extensive literature dealing with the Philippine-American relationship, including the issues of neocolonialism, the charge of U.S. economic dominance, the role of the military bases, and the intangibles that contribute to "the special relationship." Claude A. Buss, *The United States in the Philippines: Background for Policy* (1977), is a good place to begin, since Buss was a senior officer in the prewar Office of the High Commissioner and has been a shrewd observer of the Philippines for half a century. Jose D. Ingles, *Philippine Foreign Policy* (1982); Eduardo Z. Romualdez, *A Question of Sovereignty: The Military Bases in the Philippine-American Relations, 1944–1979* (1980); and Purificacion C. Quisumbing, *Beijing-Manila Detente, Major Issues: A Study in Chinese-ASEAN Relations* (1983), all deal with specific aspects of Philippine foreign policy. Steven R. Shalom, *The United States and the Philippines* (1981), and Carl A. Grunder and William E. Livezey, *The Philippines and the United States* (1973), address long-term aspects of the relationship. Robert Manning's "The Philippines in Crisis," *Foreign Affairs* 63 (1984–1985): 392–410, and Carl H. Landé and Richard Hooley, "Aquino Takes Charge," *Foreign Affairs* 64 (1986): 1087–1102, are the two best initial assessments of the fall of Marcos and the rise of Corazon Aquino.

Bernardo M. Villegas, *Strategies for Crisis* (1983) and *Readings on Philippine Economic Development* (1981), are a good introduction to the economic dilemma of the Philippines in the 1980s. Waldon F. Bello, *Development Debacle: The World Bank in the Philippines* (1982), and Vicencio R. Jose, ed., *Mortgaging the Future: The World Bank and IMF in the Philippines* (1982), explore the complex world of international finance and national debt. V. Valdepenas and G. Bautista, *The Emergence of the Philippine Economy* (1977), and Gustav Ranis, "Economic Development and Financial Institutions," Yale Economic Growth Center Discussion Paper (1977), offer further information.

Remigio E. Agpalo, *Philippine Interest Groups and Their Role in Modernization and Development* (1977), and Harry T. Oshima, *The Transition to an Industrial Economy in Monsoon Asia* (1984), both explore the consequences of economic development and political interaction in a developing nation. Brian Fegan, *Rent Capitalism in the Philippines* (1981) and *Land Reform and Technical Change in Central Luzon: The Rice Industry Under Martial Law* (1982), explore at the local level the social consequences of economic change. Jeremias J. Montemayor, *The Philippine Agrarian Reform Program* (1976), and Rolf Hanisch, *Land Reform in the Philippines: Decision-Making Processes and Problems of Implementation* (1977), describe the modest initial successes and structural dilemmas of Marcos's land reform efforts. See also Gelia T. Castillo, *Beyond Manila: Philippine Rural Problems in Perspective* (1980); and Ernst Fedder, *Perverse Development* (1983), which discuss issues of rural development. Edmund K. Oasa has explored "The International Rice Research Institute and the Green Revolution. A Case Study on the Politics of Agricultural Research" (Ph.D. diss., Univ. of Hawaii, 1981), on which another perspective is Robert F. Chandler, *An Adventure in Applied Science: A History of the International Rice Research Institute* (1982). John F. Doherty has taken a critical look at *The Philippine Urban Poor* (1985).

A good introduction to contemporary literature is *Philippine Contemporary Literature in English and Pilipino*, ed. Asuncion David-Maramba (1978). Among the many novelists and short story writers are Leoncio P. Deriada, *The Road to Mawab and Other Stories* (1984), and Francisco Sionil José, *Platinum: Ten Filipinos' Stories* (1983).

## Chapter 40: The Transformation of Southeast Asia

GENERAL: The initial political science literature on the region after independence concentrated on the questions of communism and nationalism, often seeing the two as antithetical, whereas in reality they were often co-equal and equally indigenous to the region. The most reliable study of the external links of the region's Communist movements through the early 1960s is Charles B. McLane, *Soviet Strategies in Southeast Asia* (1966). The essays in Frank N. Trager, ed., *Marxism in Southeast Asia* (1959), now have a somewhat dated flavor but indicate the issues of their day. One of the first attempts to assess the impact of nationalism in the region was Rupert Emerson, *From Empire to Nation: The Rise to Self-Assertion of Asian and African Peoples* (1960), which remains an insightful study. Clifford Geertz, ed., *Old Societies and New States: The Quest for Modernity in Asia and Africa* (1963), contains early essays from the now questionable modernization theses of an earlier generation of scholarship. George McT. Kahin, *Governments and Politics of Southeast Asia* (2nd ed., 1964), remains, though dated, the most valuable empirically based single volume on the initial postcolonial situations in the region. Roger M. Smith, ed., *Southeast Asia: Documents of Political Development and Change* (1974), contains a large number of vital primary documents of use to beginning students. The most ambitious attempt by a single author to encapsulate postindependence political history in one volume is John F. Cady, *The History of Post-war Southeast Asia: Independence Problems* (1975).

Articles on individual countries in the annual January and February issues of *Asian Survey,* and in the annual *Southeast Asian Affairs* published by the Institute of Southeast Asian Studies in Singapore, are useful for keeping up-to-date on recent developments.

The sections below follow roughly the sequence of themes taken up in Chapter 40. Material on most topics is discussed in greater detail in the bibliographies to the country chapters of Part Five (Chapters 33–39).

INTERNATIONAL RELATIONS: General works on the centripetal as well as the centrifugal forces at work in Southeast Asia since the war are Russell H. Fifield, *The Diplomacy of Southeast Asia, 1945–1958* (1959) and *Americans in Southeast Asia: The Roots of Commitment* (1973); Evelyn Colbert, *Southeast Asia in International Politics 1941–1956* (1977); and Milton E. Osborne, *Region of Revolt: Focus on Southeast Asia* (1971). There is also much useful information in the reportage of Robert Shaplen, *Time Out of Hand: Revolution and Reaction in Southeast Asia* (1969), and Dennis Bloodworth, *An Eye for the Dragon: Southeast Asia Observed, 1954–1970* (1970). An unusual theme is treated in Alfred W. McCoy, *The Politics of Heroin in Southeast Asia* (1972).

The Bandung Conference is treated in George McT. Kahin, *The Asian-African Conference, Bandung, 1955* (1955), while an analysis of the Geneva Conference of 1954, with emphasis on the legal viewpoint, is Robert T. Randle, *Geneva 1954: The Settlement of the Indochinese War* (1969). The most detailed work on the Indonesian-Malaysian conflict is J. A. C. Mackie, *Konfrontasi: The Indonesia-Malaysia Dispute, 1963–1966* (1974); but see also Jan M. Pluvier, *Confrontations: A Study in Indonesian Politics* (1965). Other works on the international relations of island Southeast Asia include Nancy McHenry Fletcher, *The Separation of Singapore from Malaysia* (1969); Michael Leifer, *The Philippine Claim to Sabah* (1968); Chandran Jeshurun, *Malaysian Defence Policy: A Study in Parliamentary Attitudes, 1963–1973* (1980); and Michael Liefer, "Decolonization and International Status: The Experience of Brunei," *International Affairs* 54 (1978): 240–252.

The rise and demise of the Southeast Asia Treaty Organization is treated in Leszek Buszynski, *SEATO: The Failure of an Alliance Strategy* (1983), on which see also S. Chawla, M. Gurtov, and A. Marsot, *Southeast Asia Under the New Balance of Power* (1974). Its nonmilitary successor, in a sense, is the Association of Southeast Asian Nations, on which see *ASEAN: A Bibliography* (1985) for an extensive coverage of the literature. On regional relations in the 1980s, see Donald F. Weatherbee, ed., *Southeast Asia Divided: The ASEAN-Indochina Crisis* (1985), which includes important documents.

ECONOMIC TRANSFORMATIONS: A good earlier analysis of external control and influence in Southeast Asian economies is in Frank Golay et al., eds., *Underdevelopment and Economic Nationalism in Southeast Asia* (1969). More recent general works include *Diversity and Development in Southeast Asia: The Coming Decade,* ed.

Guy J. Pauker, Frank H. Golay, and Cynthia H. Enloe (1977); John Wong, *ASEAN Economies in Perspective: A Comparative Study of Indonesia, Malaysia, the Philippines, Singapore and Thailand* (1979); and Hans Christoph Rieger, *ASEAN Cooperation and Intra-ASEAN Trade* (1986). A great deal of interesting work dealing with the region as a whole has come out of the Singapore University Press, including, for example, in its seminar series volumes on *Japan as an Economic Power and Its Implications for Southeast Asia* (1974) and on *Multinational Corporations and Their Implications for Southeast Asia* (1973). A very different situation is that in socialist Vietnam: see, for example, Tan Teng Lang, *Economic Debates in Vietnam* (1986), for a consideration of Vietnamese options for economic development. Works on the economies of individual countries of the region are included in the bibliographies of Chapters 33–39.

THE CONTEXT OF POLITICS: The political sociology of the region is little developed, but Hans-Dieter Evers, "Group Conflict and Class Formation," in Evers, ed., *Modernization in Southeast Asia* (1973), and Carl Landé, "Networks and Groups in Southeast Asia: Some Observations on the Group Theory of Politics," *American Political Science Review* 68 (1973): 103–127, are pioneering efforts in this regard. Political parties are surveyed in Haruhiro Fukui, ed., *Political Parties of Asia and the Pacific* (1985).

DEMOGRAPHY: Population growth has been extremely important among the socioeconomic factors that have conditioned the political environment and economic development of Southeast Asian countries since World War II. The demographic situation is treated in such works as Wilfredo F. Arce and Gabriel C. Alvarez, *Population Change in Southeast Asia* (1983), and Gavin W. Jones, *Demographic Transition in Asia* (1984). Two anthologies, separated in time by a decade, suggest the dimensions of the problems involved: J. Kantner and L. McCaffrey, eds., *Population and Development in Southeast Asia* (1975); and Philip M. Hauser, Daniel B. Suits, and Naohiro Ogawa, eds., *Urbanization and Migration in ASEAN Development* (1985).

EDUCATION: The development of mass education to suit newly independent societies in the region since World War II has been studied primarily on a country-by-country basis. One broader survey, Francis Wong Hoy Kee's *Comparative Studies in Southeast Asian Education* (1973), is rather dry and descriptive but provides a good introduction to the central issues, while a more specialized issue is the concern of Rolf Vente and Chow Kit Boey, eds., *Education and Training for Industrial Development in Singapore and Other ASEAN Countries* (1984). Joseph B. Tamney, ed., *Youth in Southeast Asia: Edited Proceedings of the Seminar . . .* (1972), treats young people in a broader context.

**Thailand:** The most useful survey would appear to be Keith Watson, *Educational Development in Thailand* (1982).

**Vietnam:** For the attempted educational revolution in Vietnam, see Alexander Woodside, "The Triumphs and Failures of Mass Education in Vietnam," *Pacific Affairs* 56, 3 (Fall 1983): 401–427.

**Malaysia:** Two background studies on education are Ho Seng Ong, *Education for Unity in Malaya* (1952), an interesting but idiosyncratic study by a prominent Malaysian teacher, and Frederic Mason, *The Schools of Malaya* (1959), a brief, factual study. Margaret Clark Roff, "The Politics of Language in Malaya," *Asian Survey* 7 (1967): 316–329, discusses some of the political implications of education policies in the decade after independence. The only monographic study of education in Malaysia in the postwar period is Francis Wong Hoy Kee and Ee Tiang Hong, *Education in Malaysia* (1971). For Singapore, H. E. Wilson, *Social Engineering in Singapore: Educational Policies and Social Change, 1819–1972* (1978), though substantially historical, is also useful for the contemporary period.

**Indonesia:** A useful survey of the literature is R. Murray Thomas, Sutan

Zanti Arbi, and Soedijarto, eds., *Indonesian Education, An Annotated Bibliography,* vol. 1 (1973). C. E. Beeby, *Assessment of Indonesian Education: A Guide in Planning* (1979), examines primary and secondary schools. See Murray Thomas, "Effects of Indonesian Population Growth on Educational Development, 1940–1969," *Asian Survey* 9, 7 (1969).

**The Philippines:** The most useful survey attempting to chart the nature of change not only in education but in all other aspects of Philippine life is John J. Carroll's *Changing Patterns of Social Structure in the Philippines 1896–1963* (1969). This compendium includes an excellent bibliography. See also the articles contained in the two volumes published by the Institute of Philippine Culture, *Modernization: Its Impact in the Philippines* (1967–1969).

Modern education has been promoted both for the sake of economic and social change and to hasten political development. In many cases, students have worked to effect political change. A few important cases are discussed by Philip G. Altbach, "Student Movements in Historical Perspective: The Asian Case," *Journal of Southeast Asian Studies* 1 (1970): 74–84; Suchit Bunbongkarn, "Higher Education and Political Development in Thailand" (Ph.D. diss., Fletcher School of Law and Diplomacy, 1969); Ross Prizzia and Narong Sinsawadi, *Thailand: Student Activism and Political Change* (1974); and Robert O. Tilman, "Education and Political Development in Malaya," in Tilman, ed., *Man, State, and Society in Contemporary Southeast Asia* (1969).

Rural Society: James C. Scott, *The Moral Economy of the Peasant: Rebellion and Subsistence in Southeast Asia* (1976), was an important benchmark in the application of social and economic theory to the study of peasant political behavior in Southeast Asia. Scott has followed up this study with a more detailed analysis of peasant political and economic behavior in one Malaysian village in the recent period in his important *Weapons of the Weak* (1986). Samuel Popkin, *The Rational Peasant* (1979), in part an attempt to rebut Scott, starts from different premises about the nature of peasant behavior. *Everyday Forms of Peasant Resistance in Southeast Asia,* ed. James C. Scott and Benedict Kerkvliet (1986), sets rural political behavior in a broader context. The essays in Andrew Turton and Shigeharu Tanabe, eds., *History and Peasant Consciousness in South East Asia* (1984), seek to extrapolate peasant political concepts from a materialist perspective.

Another body of politically important literature attempts to explain the changing context of political behavior in Southeast Asian societies during the past hundred or more years. Much of this literature examines how changing patterns of state-formation and demands on the population have changed popular means of protest and identity with the rulers. Among the best of these essays are Michael Adas, "From Avoidance to Confrontation: Peasant Protest in Precolonial Southeast Asia," *Comparative Studies in Society and History* 23 (1981): 217–247 (which can also be read as an alternative to Scott and Popkin), and Ruth McVey, "Local Voices, Central Power," in McVey, ed., *Southeast Asian Transformations* (1978).

Bureaucracy: For the problems and transformations of the postwar bureaucracy, see James Guyot, "Bureaucratic Transformation in Burma," in Ralph Braibanti, ed., *Asian Bureaucratic Systems Emergent from the British Imperial Tradition* (1966); William J. Siffin, *The Thai Bureaucracy* (1966); Fred J. Riggs, *Thailand: The Modernization of a Bureaucratic Polity* (1966); and Claude-Gilles Gour, *Institutions constitutionelles et politiques du Cambodge* (1965). An interesting glimpse at a very different tradition is Thai Quang Trung, *Collective Leadership and Factionalism: An Essay on Ho-Chi-Minh's Legacy* (1985).

On Malaysia, S. W. Jones, *Public Administration in Malaya* (1953), is historical in treatment and useful for later comparison, as is Robert Heussler, *Completing a Stewardship: The Malayan Civil Service 1942–1957* (1983). Robert O. Tilman, *Bureaucratic Transition in Malaya* (1964), is a study of the process of "Malayanization" of the public services. Gayl Ness, *Bureaucracy and Rural Development in Malaysia* (1967), and M. J. Esman, *Administration and Development in Malaysia* (1972), deal with the macro level of development administration; while Peter J. Wilson, *A Malay Village and Malaysia: Social Values and Rural Development* (1967), and J. H. Beaglehole, *The District: A Study of Decentralization in West Malaysia* (1976), examine various aspects of the micro level. Mavis Puthucheary, *The Politics of Administration: The Malaysian Experience* (1978), is an outstanding study of the relationships between bureaucrats and politicians.

Also pertinent to the problems and transformations of bureaucracy in Indonesia are Selosoemardjan, *Social Changes in Jogjakarta* (1962); Leslie Palmier, *Social Status and Power in Java* (1960); and Everett Hawkins, "Job Inflation in Indonesia," *Asian Survey* 6, 5 (May 1966).

Among many outstanding works published by the Institute of Public Administration in the Philippines, José C. Abueva's *Focus on the Barrio; the Story Behind the Birth of the Philippine Community Development Program Under President Ramon Magsaysay* (1959) is perhaps the best for this subject.

On "corruption," see W. F. Wertheim, "Sociological Aspects of Corruption in Southeast Asia," in his *East-West Parallels* (1964); Syed Hussein Alatas, *The Sociology of Corruption: The Nature, Function, Causes and Prevention of Corruption* (1968); and Jon S. T. Quah, "Bureaucratic Corruption in the ASEAN Countries: A Comparative Analysis of their Anti-Corruption Strategies," *Journal of Southeast Asian Studies* 13 (1982): 153–177.

Contemporary Southeast Asian law has been little studied, and mostly for the Islamic states. See Daniel S. Lev, *Islamic Courts in Indonesia: A Study in the Political Bases of Legal Institutions* (1972), and M. B. Hooker, *Islamic Law in Southeast Asia* (1984).

On the assumption of political roles by soldiers, see "Military Elites in Southeast Asia," ed. James F. Guyot and Ann Ruth Willner, in a special issue of the *Journal of Comparative Administration* (Nov. 1970). John J. Johnson, ed., *The Role of the Military in Underdeveloped Countries* (1962), includes chapters on Indonesia, Burma, and Thailand. Zakaria Ahmad and Harold Crouch, eds., *Military-Civilian Relations in South-East Asia* (1985), is a more recent general treatment. On Indonesia, see Harold A. Crouch, *The Army and Politics in Indonesia* (1978). Views of the Thai Army include David Elliott, *Thailand: The Origins of Military Rule* (1978); and Thomas A. Marks, "October 1976 and the Role of the Military in Thai Politics," *Modern Asian Studies* 14 (1980): 603–644, and "Professionalism in the Royal Thai Army," *Naval Institute Proceedings* 99 (1973): 46–53.

Few groups better demonstrate the major changes that have taken place in Southeast Asian societies than women, who have both assumed national political roles and been thrust into modern economic functions. Penny Van Esterick, ed., *Women of Southeast Asia* (1982), offers a good introduction to the subject. Mi Mi Khaing, *The World of Burmese Women* (1985), can be sharply contrasted with Arlene Eisen, *Women and Revolution in Vietnam* (1984), and Gavin W. Jones, ed., *Women in the Urban and Industrial Workforce, Southeast Asia and East Asia* (1984). Lenore Manderson, *Women, Politics and Change: The Kaum Ibu UMNO Malaysia, 1945–1972* (1980), examines the role of women in Malay politics during the early independence period. Evelyn Hong, ed., *Malaysian Women: Problems and Issues* (1983), is a collection of essays exploring the position of women in Malaysia today, several dealing with women factory workers. Ong Ai-hwa's *Women and Industry: Malay Peasants in Coastal Selangor 1975–80* (1987) is a study of Malay peasant women drawn into the electronics labor force in one of the country's free-trade zones.

The articles in B. Herring, ed., *Indonesian Women: Past and Present* (1977) are both historical and contemporary. Research on Javan peasant women and the family is a fairly new field. Hildred Geertz's early work, *The Javanese Family* (1961), is still useful, although it has been criticized recently. So is Celia Mather's "Industrialization in the Tangerang Regency of West Java: Women Workers and the Islamic Patriarchy," *Bulletin of Concerned Asian Scholars* 15, 2 (1983): 2–17.

Work on women in the Philippines includes Herminia M. Ancheta, *Filipino Women in National Building: A Compilation of Brief Biographies* (1984), and *Women in the Philippines: A Country Report,* by the National Commission on the Role of Filipina Women (1980). See also Maria C. Velez, ed., *Images of the Filipina: A Bibliography* (1975).

RELIGION: An introduction to the general subject of modern religion in Southeast Asia is Fred R. von der Mehden, *Religion and Nationalism in Southeast Asia* (1963).

**Buddhism:** Much of the material cited in the bibliographies for Chapters 5 and 35 are also relevant for more recent periods, including Robert Lester, *Theravada Buddhism in Southeast Asia* (1973); and Donald K. Swearer, *Buddhism and Society in Southeast Asia* (1981). Note especially the bibliographies in Charles F. Keyes, *Thailand: Buddhist Kingdom as Modern Nation State* (1986), and Melford Spiro, *Buddhism and Society: A Great Tradition and its Burmese Vicissitudes* (1972).

For changes in religion in Cambodia, see Thierry de Beaucé, "Le Cambodge: Bouddhisme et Developpement," *Esprit* 35, 363 (Sept. 1967): 265–279; and on Laos, Martin Stuart-Fox and Rod Bucknell, "Politicization of the Buddhist Sangha in Laos," *Journal of Southeast Asian Studies* 13 (1982): 60–80.

**Islam:** Religious belief and social and political behavior associated with it have been of considerable consequence in Islamic Southeast Asia since World War II. For a useful collection of essays on the region as a whole, see Ahmad Ibrahim et al., eds., *Readings on Islam in Southeast Asia* (1985). For Indonesia, Harry J. Benda, *The Crescent and the Rising Sun: Indonesian Islam under the Japanese Occupation* (1958), is an important account of this formative period, and C. A. O. van Nieuwenhuijze, *Aspects of Islam in Post-Colonial Indonesia* (1958), contains five thoughtful essays on the transition years from 1942 to 1949. B. J. Boland, *The Struggle of Islam in Modern Indonesia* (1971), is a careful study of Islamic issues as they manifested themselves in political life during the first quarter century of independence. The rise to prominence toward the end of this period of the state ideology Panca Sila, and the issues it posed for Muslims and others, are not well represented in the literature in English; but see the excellent collection of documents and discussion in Marcel Boneff et al., eds., *Pantjasila, trente années de debats politiques en Indonesie* (1980). Muhammad Kamal Hassan's *Muslim Intellectual Responses to "New Order" Modernization in Indonesia* (1982) is an outstanding study of the intellectual history of this period. Two general articles of interest on Islam and the state in Indonesia should be noted: Ruth T. McVey, "Faith as the Outsider: Islam in Indonesian Politics," in James P. Piscatori, ed., *Islam in the Political Process* (1983), 199–225, and McVey's "Islam Explained," a review article in *Pacific Affairs* 54 (1981): 260–287. For more culturally interpretive studies of Islam and social behavior in Java, see Mitsuo Nakamura, *The Crescent Arises over the Banyan Tree: A Study of the Muhammadiyah Movement in a Central Javanese Town* (1983); and Robert W. Hefner, "The Political Economy of Islamic Conversion in Modern East Java," in William R. Roff, ed., *Islam and the Politics of Meaning: Comparative Studies of Muslim Discourse* (1987).

Much less scholarly attention has been paid to Islam and public life in Malaysia. Clive S. Kessler's *Islam and Politics in a Malay State: Kelantan, 1838–1969* (1978) is an important study of the reflexive relationships between ideology and politics; see also two of Kessler's articles, "Islam, Society and Political Behaviour: Some Comparative Implications of the Malay Case," *The British Journal of Sociology* 22 (1972): 33–50, and "Islam: Resurgence and Resistance in

Southeast Asia," *Southeast Asian Chronicle* 75 (1980): 1–11. Judith Nagata, *The Reflowering of Malaysian Islam: Modern Religious Radicals and their Roots* (1984), has useful discussions of several of the major *dakwah* groups, but has been criticized on perspective and historical accuracy.

For Thailand, Surin Pitsuwan's *Islam and Malay Nationalism: A Case Study of the Malay-Muslims of Southern Thailand* (1985) is a historical study with a strong contemporary focus. For the Philippines, both Samuel K. Tan, *The Filipino Muslim Armed Struggle, 1900–1972* (1977), and T. J. S. George, *Revolt in Mindanao: The Rise of Islam in Philippine Politics* (1980), are stronger on political event than on Islamic interpretation.

**Christianity:** The role of Christianity in contemporary Southeast Asia is examined in Gerald H. Anderson, ed., *Christ and Crisis in Southeast Asia* (1969).

Among the more interesting analyses of modern religion in the Philippines are Jaime Bulatao and Vitaliano Gorospe, *Split-Level Christianity* (1966); Marcelino Foronda, "The Canonization of Rizal," *Journal of History* (Philippines) 8 (1960): 1–48; and Richard L. Deats, comp., *The Filipino in the Seventies: An Ecumenical Perspective* (1973). See also Miguel A. Bernad, *Tradition and Discontinuity: Essays on Philippine History and Culture* (1983), and Renato Constantino, *Insight and Foresight* (1977), since these are two of the most intelligent if different observers of the contemporary Philippine scene. Jaime T. Licauco, *The Magicians of God: The Amazing Stories of Philippine Faith Healers* (1981), provides an interesting contrast to *John Paul II, The Pope to the Filipino People: The Complete Speeches of John Paul* (1981). On Indonesia, see Paul B. Pedersen, *Batak Blood and Protestant Soul: The Development of National Batak Churches in North Sumatra* (1970).

**Folk Religion:** Three fine works show the powerful influence of animism in contemporary Indonesia. Shelley Errington's "Embodied *Sumange'* in Luwu," *Journal of Asian Studies* 42 (1983): 545–570, shows how pervasive animist conceptions are in the way Muslim Bugis of South Sulawesi order their world. Part I of Clifford Geertz's *The Religion of Java* (1960), and Koentjaraningrat's "Javanese Magic, Sorcery and Numerology," *Masyarakat Indonesia* 1 (1979): 37–52, provide guidance in the immense domain of Javanese animism. Paul Stange's "The Logic of Rasa in Java," *Indonesia* 38 (1984): 113–134, is a readily accessible introduction to the flourishing mysticism of the twentieth-century Javanese *kebatinan* movements.

URBAN TRENDS: (NOTE: For other works on this topic, see bibliography for Chapter 24.) The best general study on this subject remains T. G. McGee, *The Southeast Asian City* (1967). Some of the best developed work has been done in the Philippines. Aprodicio A. Laquian has studied the problems of the city of Manila in his book *The City in Nation Building: Politics and Administration in Metropolitan Manila* (1966). His later *Slums Are for People* (1969) is a detailed analysis of Manila's urban problem and a developmental project in its Tondo section. See also Mary R. Hollnsteiner, "The Urbanization of Metropolitan Manila," in *Modernization: Its Impact in the Philippines,* vol. 4 (1969), 147–174; Richard L. Stone, *Philippine Urbanization: The Politics of Public and Private Property in Greater Manila* (1973); Emmanuel Torres, *Jeepney* (1979); Jose V. Abueva, Sylvia H. Guenno, and Elsa P. Jurado, *Metro Manila Today and Tomorrow* (1972); and Daniel F. Doeppers, *Manila 1900–1941: Social Change in a Late Colonial Metropolis* (1984).

Urbanization in Malaysia has been the subject of a growing literature. Lim Heng Kow, *The Evolution of the Urban System in Malaya* (1978), is a general treatment by a geographer. T. G. McGee has made a number of important contributions, notably *Proletarianization, Industrialization, and Urbanization in Asia: A Case Study of Malaysia* (1982); "Malay Migration to Kuala Lumpur City: Individual Adaptation to the City," in B. M. Du Toit and H. I. Safa, eds., *Migration and Urbanization* (1975); and "The Cultural Role of Cities: A Case Study of

Kuala Lumpur," *Journal of Tropical Geography* 17 (1963): 178–196. Manjit Singh Sidhu's study, *Kuala Lumpur and Its Population* (1978), may be supplemented by Yip Yat Hoong and Low Kwai Sim, *Urbanization and Economic Development with Special Reference to Kuala Lumpur* (1985), and Ishak Shari, "Squatters: The Urban Poor in Kuala Lumpur," in B. A. Mokhzani and Khoo Siew Mun, eds., *Some Case Studies of Poverty in Malaysia* (1977), 109–125. Other useful articles that may be mentioned are Kok Lim Lian, "Levels, Trends and Patterns of Urbanisation in Peninsular Malaysia, 1957–1980," *Ilmu Masyarakat* (Kuala Lumpur) 9 (1985): 16–39, and Peter Rimmer and G. C. H. Cho, "Urbanization of the Malays since Independence: Evidence from West Malaysia, 1957–1970," *Journal of Southeast Asian Studies* 12 (1981): 349–363.

Bangkok's growth is treated by Larry Sternstein, "The Growth of the Population of the World's Preeminent 'Primate City': Bangkok at its Bicentenary," *Journal of Southeast Asian Studies* 15 (1984): 43–68.

On political changes in a major Southeast Asian city during a revolution, see William S. Turley, "Urban Transformation in South Vietnam," *Pacific Affairs* 49 (1976): 607–624.

CULTURE: Benedict Anderson, "The Languages of Indonesian Politics," *Indonesia* 1 (1966): 99–116, merits careful study. James Peacock, *Rites of Modernization: Symbols and Social Aspects of Indonesian Proletarian Drama* (1969), is helpful for understanding changes in Indonesia. Lance Castles, "Notes on the Islamic School at Gontor," *Indonesia* 1 (1966): 30–45, provides a fine contemporary picture of a *pondok,* with indications of its economic and political implications.

The inaugural issue of *International Popular Culture* (1979) is focused on Philippine pop culture, including comics, rock film, and other manifestations.

An excellent introduction to the contemporary literature of the region is *Essays on Literature and Society in Southeast Asia: Political and Sociological Perspectives,* ed. Tham Seong Chee (1981), which covers all the countries of the region except Laos. Philip N. Jenner, *Southeast Asian Literatures in Translation: A Preliminary Bibliography* (1973), is a useful guide to materials in English, though it is too out-of-date to include such titles as Patricia M. Milne, *Selected Short Stories of Thein Pe Myint* (1973). On the Philippines, see Silverio Baltasar, *Philippine Literature Past and Present* (1981); Resil B. Mojares, *Origins and Rise of the Filipino Novel: A Generic Study of the Novel Until 1940* (1983); and the extensive literary criticism of E. San Juan, Jr. On the transformation of traditional theater, see James R. Brandon, *Theatre in Southeast Asia* (1967). The press is the main concern of John A. Lent, ed., *The Asian Newspapers' Reluctant Revolution* (1971), and John A. Lent, *Asian Mass Communications: A Comprehensive Bibliography* (1975).

NATIONAL INTEGRATION: Much of the current literature tends to focus on minorities and problems of national integration, fueled as it is by conflict and crisis. See, for example, John T. McAlister, Jr., *Southeast Asia: The Politics of National Integration* (1973). A good collection of articles dealing with historical as well as contemporary aspects of "minority problems" is Victor T. King and W. D. Wilder, eds., "Southeast Asia and the Concept of Ethnicity," special issue of the *Southeast Asian Journal of Social Science* 10, 1 (1982). The Chinese minorities of the region, once considered to be a major divisive force, received little attention in the 1970s and 1980s; but see *The Chinese in Southeast Asia* (4 vols., 1983–1987), by various editors. See also Wang Gungwu, *Community and Nation: Essays on Southeast Asia and the Chinese* (1981).

On the expression of division in violence, see Lim Joo-Jock and Vani S., ed., *Armed Separatism in Southeast Asia* (1984); Lim Joo-Jock and Vani S., ed., *Armed Communist Movements in Southeast Asia* (1985); and Chandran Jeshurun, ed., *Governments and Rebellions in Southeast Asia* (1985).

# INDEX

For terms referring to major countries and peoples of Southeast Asia—e.g., Malaysia, Indonesia, Filipino, British Burma—it seems of little value to list every place where they are mentioned in the text. Under these terms in the index are listed only references pertaining to the formation or dissolution of the political unit per se or to the term itself. General information on these peoples and places will be found under the appropriate subject headings—e.g., administration, international relations, language, nationalism, trade.

# NOTES ON THE AUTHORS

**David P. Chandler** holds degrees from Harvard College, Yale University, and the University of Michigan. From 1958 to 1966 he was a U.S. Foreign Service Officer and served two years in Phnom Penh. Since 1972, he has taught at Monash University in Australia, and since 1978 he has served as research director of its Center of Southeast Asian Studies. His books include *The Land and People of Cambodia* (1972), *Cambodia Before the French: Politics in a Tributary Kingdom, 1794–1848* (1974), and *A History of Cambodia* (1983). He co-edited (with Ben Kiernan) *Revolution and its Aftermath in Kampuchea: Eight Essays* (1983) and *Pol Pot Plans the Future: Confidential Leadership Documents from Democratic Kampuchea* (1987).

**William R. Roff** received an M.A. degree from the Victoria University of Wellington in New Zealand and the Ph.D. from the Australian National University. Since 1969 he has been professor of history at Columbia University, having previously taught in Australia and at the University of Malaya. His publications include *The Origins of Malay Nationalism* (1967), *Kelantan: Religion, Society and Politics in a Malay State* (1974), and *Islam and the Politics of Meaning: Comparative Studies of Muslim Discourse* (1987).

**John R. W. Smail,** professor of history at the University of Wisconsin-Madison, received the Ph.D. in Southeast Asian history from Cornell University in 1964. His research interests are in Indonesia and the general history of Southeast Asia. He is the author of *Bandung in the Early Revolution, 1945–1946*. Along with courses in Southeast Asian history he teaches in the Wisconsin Comparative World History Program.

**David Joel Steinberg** was educated at Phillips Academy, Malvern College, England, and Harvard College. He won Fulbright, Woodrow Wilson, and National Defense Education Act fellowships while earning an M.A. and Ph.D. from Harvard University. He spent ten years teaching Southeast Asian history at the University of Michigan, rising to the rank of full professor. For over a decade he has been in university administration, since 1985 as president of Long Island University. He has consulted for the Ford Foundation, the United Nations, and the United States Government, serving as a member of the international observer team to the 1986 Philippine elections. Among his writings are *Philippine Collaboration in World War II* (1967) and *The Philippines: A Singular and a Plural Place* (1982).

**Robert H. Taylor** received a B.A. from Ohio University, an M.A. from Antioch College, and a Ph.D. from Cornell University. He has taught in the Washington, D.C., public schools, at Wilberforce University, and at the University of Sydney, and at present as a lecturer in politics at the School of Oriental and

African Studies, University of London, where he teaches Southeast Asian politics and international relations. His publications include *Marxism and Resistance in Burma, 1941–1945; Thein Pe Myint's "Wartime Traveler"* (1984), *The State in Burma* (1987), and articles on modern Burma's politics and economics. He co-edited *Context, Meaning and Power in Southeast Asia* (1986) and *ASEAN-EC Economic and Political Relations* (1986).

**Alexander Woodside** received a B.A. in modern history from the University of Toronto in 1960 and a Ph.D. in history and Far Eastern languages from Harvard University in 1968. He began the study of modern Vietnamese at Cornell in 1964–1965. In 1965–1967 he conducted research for his dissertation on early nineteenth-century Vietnam in Saigon, Paris, Hong Kong, and Tokyo. He taught history at Harvard University between 1968 and 1975, serving at the first Young Professor of Sino-Vietnamese studies at that university. Since 1975 he has taught Southeast Asian and Chinese history at the University of British Columbia in Canada. He is the author of *Vietnam and the Chinese Model* (1971) and *Community and Revolution in Modern Vietnam* (1976), and co-editor, with David K. Wyatt, of *Moral Order and the Question of Change; Essays on Southeast Asian Thought* (1982).

**David K. Wyatt** studied philosophy at Harvard College and Southeast Asian history at Cornell University. He taught at the School of Oriental and African Studies, University of London, and at the University of Michigan before returning to Cornell in 1969, where he has served as director of the Southeast Asia Program and chairman of the Department of History, and where he is now professor of Southeast Asian history. He has traveled extensively in Thailand and Laos. His publications include several translations of Thai chronicles, as well as *The Politics of Reform in Thailand* (1969), and *Thailand: A Short History* (1984).